INTRODUCTION TO SUBSURFACE IMAGING

Describing and evaluating the basic principles and methods of subsurface sensing and imaging, clear and comprehensive treatment links theory to a wide range of real-world applications in medicine, biology, security and geophysical/environmental exploration. It integrates the different sensing techniques (acoustic, electric, electromagnetic, optical, X-ray, or particle beams) by unifying the underlying physical and mathematical similarities, and computational and algorithmic methods. Time-domain, spectral, and multisensor methods are also covered, whilst all the necessary mathematical, statistical, and linear systems tools are given in useful appendices to make the book self-contained. Featuring a logical blend of theory and applications, a wealth of color illustrations, homework problems, and numerous case studies, this is suitable for use as both a course text and as a professional reference.

BAHAA SALEH is the Dean of the College of Optics and Photonics at the University of Central Florida. Prior to this he was Chair of the Department of Electrical and Computer Engineering at Boston University and Deputy Director of the NSF Gordon Center for Subsurface Sensing and Imaging Systems. He authored *Photoelectron Statistics* (1978) and co-authored *Fundamentals of Photonics* (2007, 2nd edition), and he is Fellow of IEEE, OSA, SPIE, and the Guggenheim Foundation. He has received numerous awards, including the 1999 OSA Esther Hoffman Beller Award for outstanding contributions to optical science and engineering education, the 2006 Kuwait Prize for his contributions to optical science, and the 2008 Distinguished Service Award of OSA.

On rare occasions, one encounters a book that defines a field. Such is the character of *Introduction to Subsurface Imaging* by Bahaa Saleh (Editor and Principal Author). The book is authoritative, comprehensive, beautifully illustrated, and clearly written. It will remain the definitive work on this subject for years to come.

Joseph W. Goodman, Stanford University

This comprehensive multi-disciplinary text bears the authoritative stamp of its principal author and editor, Bahaa Saleh. He has taken different applications of subsurface imaging, from searching for landmines to breast cancer detection, and presented them in a unified way. This is essential reading for researchers in all branches of optical imaging.

Chris Dainty, National University of Ireland, Galway

Introduction to Subsurface Imaging takes a unique application-oriented approach to image science. The result is a powerful survey including physical phenomena ranging from millimeter waves to x-rays and state of the art image analysis estimation algorithms. The quality, quantity and clarity of the graphics and images presented, of central importance to an imaging text, is particularly noteworthy.

David Brady, Duke University

INTRODUCTION TO SUBSURFACE IMAGING

BAHAA SALEH

University of Central Florida

Shaftesbury Road, Cambridge CB2 8EA, United Kingdom

One Liberty Plaza, 20th Floor, New York, NY 10006, USA

477 Williamstown Road, Port Melbourne, VIC 3207, Australia

314–321, 3rd Floor, Plot 3, Splendor Forum, Jasola District Centre, New Delhi – 110025, India

103 Penang Road, #05–06/07, Visioncrest Commercial, Singapore 238467

Cambridge University Press is part of Cambridge University Press & Assessment,
a department of the University of Cambridge.

We share the University's mission to contribute to society through the pursuit of
education, learning and research at the highest international levels of excellence.

www.cambridge.org
Information on this title: www.cambridge.org/9781107000810

First published 2011
Reprinted 2019

A catalogue record for this publication is available from the British Library

ISBN   978-1-107-00081-0   Hardback

Additional resources for this publication at www.cambridge.org/9781107000810

Contents

Authors and Contributors

Preface	Bahaa Saleh[1,6] and Michael Silevitch[2]
Chapter 1	Bahaa Saleh[1,6]
Chapter 2	Bahaa Saleh[1,6]
Chapter 3	Bahaa Saleh[1,6]
Chapter 4	Bahaa Saleh,[1,6] with contributions by Eric Miller[5]
Chapter 5	Eric Miller,[5] Clem Karl,[1] and Bahaa Saleh[1,6]
Chapter 6	Miguel Vélez-Reyes,[4] James Goodman,[4] and Bahaa Saleh[1,6]
Chapter 7	Badri Roysam,[3] with contributions by Bahaa Saleh[1,6]
Chapter 8	Carey Rappaport,[2] with contributions by Jose Martinez[2] and Bahaa Saleh[1,6]
Chapter 9	Steve McKnight,[2] with contributions by Bahaa Saleh[1,6]
Appendix A	Bahaa Saleh[1,6]
Appendix B	Eric Miller,[5] with contributions by Bahaa Saleh[1,6] and David Castañón[1]
Appendix C	Bahaa Saleh[1,6]
Appendix D	Bahaa Saleh,[1,6] Badri Roysam,[3] and Carey Rappaport[2]

---

[1] Boston University
[2] Northeastern University
[3] Rensselaer Polytechnic Institute
[4] University of Puerto Rico at Mayagüez
[5] Tufts University
[6] University of Central Florida

Preface

In many sensing and imaging problems, the object is covered by some medium that conceals or obscures its relevant features. The object may emit some wave, field, or stream of particles that penetrate the medium and may be observed by a detector. Alternatively, a wave, field, or stream of particles may be used as a probe that travels through the medium and is modified by the object before it travels back through the medium on its way to the detector. The challenge is to extract information about the subsurface target in the presence of the obscuring medium.

Subsurface imaging (SSI) problems arise in a wide range of areas: geophysical exploration or environmental remediation under the earth or the ocean, medical examination and diagnosis inside the body, basic studies of the biological processes inside the cell, and security inspections for explosives or contraband concealed in luggage. While these problems involve many sensing modalities (mechanical, acoustic, electric, magnetic, electromagnetic, optical, X-ray, electrons, or other particles), they all seek to infer internal structure from complex and distorted signals received outside the obscuring volume. They often employ similar physical and mathematical models and use similar computational and algorithmic methods.

This textbook introduces the field of subsurface imaging, its principles, methods, and applications, using a unifying framework that strives to integrate the diverse topics, which are often presented separately in different science and engineering textbooks or in various venues of the research literature. A unifying multidisciplinary approach is critical to exploiting the commonalities that exist among these disparate subsurface imaging problems. A *diverse problems, similar solutions* strategy should help in changing the present compartmentalized approach to such problems and stimulate cross-disciplinary dialog.

Breadth and depth. One of the most challenging aspects of writing a textbook on an interdisciplinary subject dealing with a rich variety of topics, such as SSI, is to strike the right balance between breadth and depth. We have endeavored to maintain a reasonable depth of exposition of the basics and an adequate level of the mathematical treatment, along with a sufficiently broad coverage of many state-of-the-art technologies. Our goal is to help in the education of a new generation of students with an awareness of the commonalities that often underlie diverse technologies, as well as situations requiring a multidisciplinary approach.

Emphasis. For a textbook of a necessarily limited length, it is essential to limit the scope by judicious selection of areas of emphasis. Here, we emphasize *fields and waves*, including electromagnetic waves at various regions of the spectrum and acoustic waves, as the SSI probes, rather than particles such as electrons and positrons, which are also used in SSI. We adopt a *linear systems* approach to describe wave propagation through the medium and interaction with the target, and use linearizing approximations to model image formation. Likewise, in solving inversion problems, the emphasis is on use of linear methods and matrix techniques.

Readership. This textbook is suitable for a course on SSI serving seniors or first-year graduate students in electrical, mechanical, or biomedical engineering; or physics, geoscience, or computer science. To make it self-contained for the various audiences, a number of appendices cover prerequisite mathematical and engineering topics. Our ultimate aim is to help prepare students for further graduate study or employment in government and industry in areas of sensing and imaging in the broad domain of environmental, medical, biological, industrial, and defense applications.

Examples and problems. A number of examples are distributed throughout the text and a set of problems are provided at the end of each chapter. Problems are numbered in accordance with the chapter sections to which they apply.

Book website. A website (http://www.cambridge.org/saleh) provides image data for use in the problem sets, a Solutions Manual with solutions to selected problems accessible only to registered instructors, as well as PowerPoint slides for the use of instructors.

This textbook was written under the auspices of the **The Bernard M. Gordon Center for Subsurface Sensing and Imaging Systems** (Gordon-CenSSIS). A multi-university National Science Foundation Engineering Research Center (NSF-ERC), Gordon-CenSSIS was founded in 2000 with a mission to develop new technologies for the detection of hidden objects — and to use those technologies to meet real-world subsurface challenges in areas such as noninvasive breast cancer detection and underground pollution assessment. The Center's multidisciplinary approach combines expertise in wave physics (electromagnetics, photonics, and ultrasonics), multisensor fusion, image processing, and tomographic reconstruction and visualization. In order to achieve its mission the Center has undertaken an effort to blend this expertise into the creation of the common building blocks needed for a unifying approach to attack the diverse problems associated with subsurface detection and imaging.

Over the years a number of undergraduate and graduate level courses in SSI were developed and taught at the four core university partners of Gordon-CenSSIS (Northeastern University, Boston University, Rensselaer Polytechnic Institute, and the University of Puerto Rico at Mayagüez). The textbook represents the distillation of the material from these Center-affiliated courses into one common framework. As indicated above, it is hoped that this framework will form the basis of a systematic discipline focused on the methodology of *finding hidden things*. As with any discipline, it is anticipated that its framework will evolve and mature through the contributions of those students, researchers, and practitioners who grapple with the material and make it their own. This maturation and growth of the field of SSI sparked by the SSI textbook will hopefully become a lasting legacy of Gordon-CenSSIS and the many colleagues who contributed to its development.

Acknowledgements

The authors are grateful to members of the Gordon-CenSSIS leadership who helped with the initial planning of this textbook and provided guidance during the course of its development: Center Director Michael Silevitch;[2] Thrust Leaders David Castañón,[1] David Kaeli,[2] Stephen W. McKnight,[2] Carey M. Rappaport,[2] Ronald Roy,[1] Badri Roysam,[3] and Miguel Vélez-Reyes;[4] former Board Director and Dean of Engineering Al Soyster;[2] Lester A. Gerhardt;[3] Horst Wittmann;[2] and members of the Scientific Advisory Board and the Industrial Advisory Board.

We are most appreciative of the technical contributions made by several colleagues: Ronald Roy,[1] Robin Cleveland,[1] Kai E. Thomenius,[9] Birsen Yazici,[3] Charles DiMarzio,[2] Todd Murray,[1,10] Shawn Hunt,[4] and Richard H. Moore.[7]

Special thanks are also extended to other colleagues who graciously provided comments or technical assistance: Ayman Abouraddy,[1,6] Paul Barbone,[1] Irving Bigio,[1] Dana Brooks,[2] Matt Dickman,[2] Aristide Dogariu,[6] David Isaacson,[3] Janusz Konrad,[1] Vidya Manian,[4] Edwin Marengo,[2] Ann Morgenthaler,[2] Jonathan Newell,[3] Homer Pien,[7] Samuel Rosario-Torres,[4] Michael Ruane,[1] Hanumant Singh,[8] Charles Stewart,[3] Malvin Teich,[1] and Karl Weiss.[2]

We are indebted to many students and former students and postdoctoral associates who have posed excellent questions that helped us during the preparation of the manuscript. In particular, we mention Asad Abu-Tarif, Ali Can, Carlo Dal Mutto, Hari Iyer, Kumel Kagalwala, Amit Mukherjee, Birant Orten, Eladio Rodriguez-Diaz, Mohammed Saleh, Ivana Stojanovic, and Charlene Tsai.

Administrative assistance provided by the Gordon-CenSSIS staff and other support personnel is also much appreciated: John Beaty,[2] Deanna Beirne,[2] Kristin Hicks,[2] Brian Loughlin,[2] Mariah Nobrega,[2] Anne Magrath,[2] Wayne Rennie,[1] and Denise Whiteside.[6]

We are grateful to the National Science Foundation (NSF) for the financial support provided for the Gordon Center for Subsurface Sensing and Imaging Systems. Many of the NSF site visitors have also made valuable comments on various drafts of this textbook.

---

[1] Boston University
[2] Northeastern University
[3] Rensselaer Polytechnic Institute
[4] University of Puerto Rico at Mayagüez
[5] Tufts University
[6] University of Central Florida
[7] Massachusetts General Hospital
[8] Woods Hole Oceanographic Institution
[9] General Electric
[10] University of Colorado at Boulder

Permissions to reproduce or adapt images and diagrams were generously granted by the following authors and publishers: Fig. 1.1-1a, IBM; Fig. 1.1-1b, Saumitra R. Mehrotra, Gerhard Klimeck, and Wikipedia; Fig. 1.1-1c, Richard Wheeler and Wikipedia; Fig. 1.1-1d, NIH; Fig. 1.1-1e, Dartmouth College Electron Microscope Facility and Wikipedia; Fig. 1.1-1f, Barticus Ksheka and Wikipedia; Fig. 1.1-1g, MB and Wikipedia; Fig. 1.1-1h, Marine Geoscience Data System (MGDS); Fig. 1.1-1i, NASA; Fig. 1.1-1j, NASA; Fig. 1.1-2, Jeremy Kemp and Wikipedia; Fig. 1.5-1, SPIE; Fig. 2.2-3, Kebes and Wikipedia; Fig. 2.2-4, NASA and Wikipedia; VACIS image on page 41, US Department of Homeland Security and Wikipedia; X-ray image on page 59, US Transportation Security Administration; Fig. 2.4-1a, Nevit Dilmen and Wikipedia; Fig. 2.4-1b, Bleiglass and Wikipedia; Fig. 2.4-1d, Kai Thomenius; Fig. 2.4-1e, Douglas Cowan; Fig. 3.2-6, Alberto Diaspro, Paolo Bianchini, Giuseppe Vicidomini, Mario Faretta, Paola Ramoino, Cesare Usai, and Wikimedia; image on page 119, US Transportation Security Administration and Wikimedia; Fig. 3.2-14 and Fig. 3.2-15, Jeremy Kemp and Wikipedia; Fig. 3.2-23 and Fig. 3.2-24, OSA; Fig. 4.1-14, Mikael Häggström and Wikipedia; Fig. 4.2-6(*b*), Tapatio and Wikipedia; Fig. 4.2-8, Wikipedia; Fig. 4.4-7, Kasuga Huang and Wikimedia; Fig. 4.4-8, Keith Johnson; Fig. 4.5-7, David Isaacson and Jonathan Newell; image on page 236, NASA; Fig. 6.1-4 and Fig. 6.3-1, Elsevier; image on page 253, Ian Duke and Wikipedia; Fig. 6.4-5, NASA; Fig. 6.4-8 and Fig. 6.4-9, SPIE; Fig. 7.1-8, Asad Abu Tarif; Fig. 7.1-10 and Fig. 7.3-1, Hanu Singh; Fig. 7.5-1, Paul Carson; Fig. 7.5-2, Asad Abu Tarif; Fig. 9.3-1, Richard H. Moore; Fig. 9.3-2 and Fig. 9.3-3, Qianqian Fang and David Boas.

Outline and Roadmap

An overview (Chapter 1) defining the subsurface imaging (SSI) problem and highlighting its principal challenges is followed by eight chapters and four appendices divided into four parts:

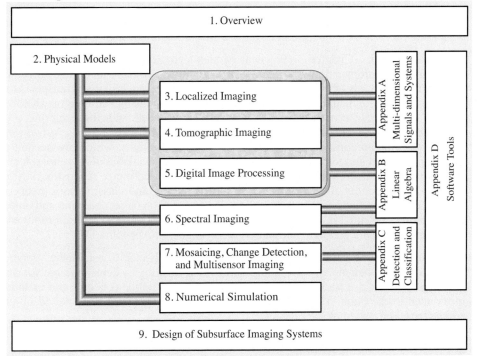

I. Centerpiece. The *centerpiece* of the book is Chapters 3–5.

- Chapter 3 covers localized (point-by-point) imaging, including conventional lens-based imaging, scanning system, time-of-flight ranging (as in radar, sonar, and lidar), and interferometric imaging (as in optical reflectometry).
- Chapter 4 covers tomographic imaging, i.e., probing by use of multiple intersecting rays, beams, or waves, as in X-ray computed tomography (CT), diffraction tomography, diffuse optical tomography (DOT), and electrical impedance tomography (EIT). Whenever applicable, analytical methods of inversion are presented.
- Chapter 5. The description of imaging systems in terms of continuous functions related by integral transforms is here replaced by a discrete description based on sampling and matrix relations. Reconstruction and inversion based on matrix methods are covered and the role of noise is assessed.

II. Extensions. The basic ideas covered in the *centerpiece* are extended and generalized in Chapters 6–8.

- Chapter 6 (Spectral Imaging) generalizes localized and tomographic imaging to include measurements with probes at multiple wavelengths. These can be very effective in the discrimination between different types of targets based on their spectral signatures. It also generalizes the inversion methods of Chapter 5 and poses new inverse problems associated with multispectral imaging.

- Chapter 7 extends subsurface imaging to measurements with multiple sensors. Methods for the registration of measurements of different segments of an object, or the same segment seen by multiple sensors, are important tools in modern SSI. Image-understanding applications, such as target detection and object classification, are found in this chapter and also in Chapter 6.
- Chapter 8 is an overview of methods of numerical simulation, which are necessary for dealing with real-world SSI problems for which analytical solutions and approximations are not applicable. These techniques are used to test forward models and to implement numerical solutions. Readers with that interest will benefit from this overview.

Instructors may select one or more of these topics in addition to the core material, depending on their own backgrounds and the special nature of their programs.

III. Background. Chapter 2 (Physical Models) provides background material on waves and their propagation and interaction with various media, including processes such as reflection, absorption, elastic and inelastic scattering, radiative transport, and diffusion. These are the most common processes used in sensing and imaging. Knowledge of all of these processes is not necessary to proceed with the centerpiece of the book, and the material in this *background* chapter may be used as *just-in-time* references. Mathematical backgrounds of signals and systems, which are needed to describe localized and tomographic imaging systems are available in Appendix A and tools from linear algebra that are necessary for matrix-based image reconstruction are available in Appendix B. A brief overview of detection and classification theory is provided in Appendix C as a background for the material on target detection and object classification presented in Chapters 6 and 7. Short outlines of some relevant toolboxes for image processing and field simulation are available in Appendix D.

IV. Guidelines and case studies. The final piece, Chapter 9, establishes general guidelines for systematically designing subsurface imaging systems suitable for any new application. Case studies of real examples demonstrate the concepts and methods introduced in the book. This chapter, or at least Sec. 9.1, should be included in any course based on this book.

An Introductory Course
This book can be used by readers with different needs and backgrounds. It provides instructors an opportunity to select topics relevant to their areas of emphasis. The following depicts an example of material that can be used for a single-semester course:

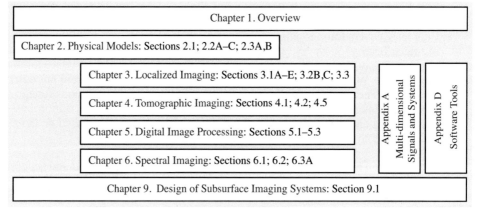

Table of Imaging Technologies

Probing Technology		Physical Model	Imaging Configuration	Inversion
Acoustic				
	SONAR	Sec. 2.1C	Sec. 3.2C	Sec. 3.3
	UDT	Sec. 2.1A	Sec. 4.3B	Sec. 5.3D
Electromagnetic				
	RADAR	Sec. 2.1B	Sec. 3.2C	Sec. 3.3
	GPR	Sec. 2.1B	Sec. 4.2B	Sec. 4.2B
	MRI	Sec. 2.3C	Sec. 4.4D	Sec. 4.4D
	EIT	Sec. 2.1B	Sec. 4.5B	Sec. 4.5B
Optical				
	LSCM	Sec. 2.1A	Sec. 3.2B	Sec. 3.3B
	OCT	Sec. 2.1A	Sec. 3.2D	Sec. 3.3
	DOT	Sec. 2.2D	Sec. 4.5A	Sec. 5.4D
	ODT	Sec. 2.1A	Sec. 4.3B	Sections 5.1C, 5.3D, 5.4D
X-ray & γ-ray				
	CT	Sec. 2.2A	Sec. 4.1C	Sections 4.1B, 5.1C, 5.3D, 5.4D
	SPECT	Sec. 2.2A	Sec. 4.1D	Sec. 4.1B
	PET	Sec. 4.1D	Sec. 4.1D	Sec. 4.1B
Acoustic/Optical				
	PAT	Sec. 4.2C	Sec. 4.2C	Sec. 4.2C

Acronyms

SONAR	Sound navigation and ranging
UDT	Ultrasonic diffraction tomography
RADAR	Radio detection and ranging
GPR	Ground penetrating radar
MRI	Magnetic resonance imaging
EIT	Electrical impedance tomography
LSCM	Laser scanning confocal microscopy
OCT	Optical coherence tomography
DOT	Diffuse optical tomography
ODT	Optical diffraction tomography
CT	Computed tomography
SPECT	Single-photon emission computed tomography
PET	Positron emission tomography
PAT	Photoacoustic tomography

1

Overview

1.1 Subsurface Imaging: Scope and Applications

Imaging is the measurement of the spatial distribution of some physical property of an object by use of an instrument such as a camera, an optical or ultrasonic scanner, a microscope, a telescope, a radar system, or an X-ray machine. The spatial scale of the object may range from subnanometer to light years, as illustrated by the pictorial examples in Fig. 1.1-1. Numerous medical, biological, geophysical, oceanographic, atmospheric, and industrial applications exist, and each field has its tools, methods, and nomenclature. However, despite the wealth of applications and the breadth of spatial scales, a number of basic principles and methodologies are common among all imaging systems. This book highlights these principles, with an ultimate goal of introducing a unified framework for these broad applications.

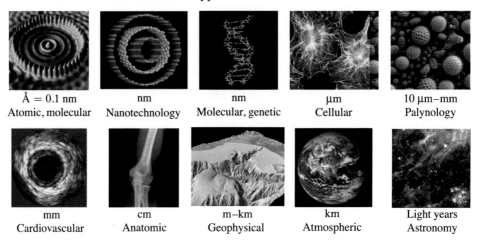

Å = 0.1 nm	nm	nm	μm	10 μm–mm
Atomic, molecular	Nanotechnology	Molecular, genetic	Cellular	Palynology
mm	cm	m–km	km	Light years
Cardiovascular	Anatomic	Geophysical	Atmospheric	Astronomy

Figure 1.1-1   Imaging applications at various spatial scales.

Subsurface imaging (SSI) is the imaging of an object buried below the surface of a medium, such as soil, water, atmosphere, or tissue. The imaging process is mediated by some *field*, *wave*, or stream of *particles* that probe the medium, and is modified by the object before it is detected by a sensor, as illustrated in Fig. 1.1-2. A significant impediment is that the surface and the medium, and any clutter therein, also modify the probe (and possibly prevent it from reaching the object or the sensor). The imaging system must separate contributions made by the object from those made by the surface and volumetric clutter.

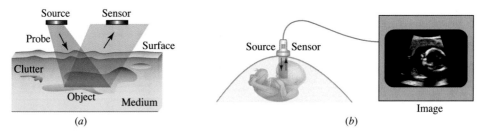

Figure 1.1-2   (*a*) SSI. (*b*) Ultrasonic imaging of a fetus as an example of SSI.

Imaging Probes.   The imaging process is mediated by some *field*, *wave*, or stream of *particles*, which we generically call the *probe*[1] or the probing wave. The probe "reads" the object and communicates the information to the sensor.

> Examples of probes:
> - An *electrostatic field* can be used to monitor the spatial distribution of the electric conductivity of an object. A *magnetic field* can be used to probe the presence of metal.
> - *Electromagnetic waves* at various bands of the spectrum (low-frequency, radiowave, microwave, millimeter waves, terahertz, optical, X-rays, γ-rays) travel in the form of *waves* (which may be approximated by rays when the wavelength is short). They are commonly used for imaging a variety of objects. Likewise, *mechanical* and *acoustic waves* (e.g., seismic and ultrasonic) have widespread imaging applications.
> - Beams of accelerated *particles* may also be used for imaging. For example, an electron beam is used in the scanning electron microscope (SEM), and nuclear particles are used in medical imaging.

This text emphasizes imaging by means of electromagnetic and acoustic fields and waves, but other probes are also discussed.

Imaging Configurations.   Imaging systems can take several configurations. A self-luminous object generates its own signal (field, wave, or particles), which may be observed and used to construct the image without the need for an external probe, as illustrated in Fig. 1.1-3(*a*). Examples of this type of *passive* imaging are a star emitting electromagnetic radiation intercepted by a telescope in an observatory, a hot object sensed by a thermal imaging camera, or a biological organ injected with radioactive isotopes such as those used in nuclear medicine. Alternatively, in *active* imaging the image is formed by use of an external probe (field, wave, or particles) that interacts with the object. Such a probe may be transmitted through or reflected from the object, as illustrated in Fig. 1.1-3(*b*) and (*c*), respectively. In some applications, the probe excites *contrast agents* injected into the object, which emit radiation that is detected by the sensor. Examples include fluorescent dyes that emit visible light and bubbles that enhance the scattering of ultrasonic probes.

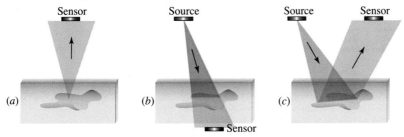

Figure 1.1-3   Imaging modalities. (*a*) Self-luminous object, which requires no probe. (*b*) Probe beam transmitted through the object. (*c*) Probe beam reflected or scattered from the object.

Imaged Physical Property.   In this book, the physical property that is measured by the imaging system is called the **alpha** property, and is denoted by the symbol α. In most cases, α is a scalar function of position $\mathbf{r} = (x, y, z)$, i.e., is a three-dimensional (3D) distribution (a map). The actual physical nature of α depends on the probe used. Examples of physical parameters that are sensed by various probes are listed in Fig. 1.1-4.

---

[1] In medical imaging the term "probe" often refers to a contrast agent, a substance injected into the object to enhance contrast (see Sec. 2.4).

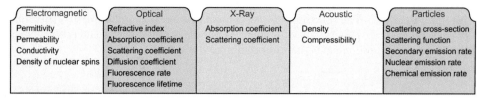

Figure 1.1-4   Examples of the physical property α for various probes. See also Table 9.1-1.

The sensed property α depends on the physical process involved in the interaction of the probe with the object, as described in some detail in Chapter 2.

Examples of interaction processes characterized by the sensed property α:

- Reflection or refraction at boundaries within the object
- Absorption
- Scattering from objects of various shapes
- Diffusion through random and turbid media
- Fluorescence (delayed re-emission at a different wavelength following absorption of electromagnetic radiation)
- Interaction of electric and magnetic fields with bound or free charges in insulating or conducting materials.
- Magnetic resonance (scattering of radiowaves from the spins associated with hydrogen atom nuclei subjected to a magnetic field)
- Thermal emittance (of a self-luminous source emitting infrared radiation).

Mapping Other Underlying Object Properties.   The purpose of subsurface imaging may be the mapping of structural, mechanical, chemical, environmental, biological, physiological, or other functional properties that are not directly sensed by the probe. Such parameters, which are of interest to the user, are generically referred to in this book as the **beta** parameters β, and may be scalar or vector functions of position **r** and time t.

Examples of user property β:

- Density, pressure, temperature
- Young's modulus of elasticity, bulk modulus and fluid elasticity, viscosity
- Humidity, moisture content, porosity, pH number, thermal resistivity
- Molecular or ion concentration, chemical composition
- Crystallographic atomic structure
- Biological and physiological properties such as blood flow, tissue oxygenation, hemoglobin concentration, metabolic rates, and membrane integrity; in medical imaging, the term **functional imaging**, as opposed to **structural imaging**, is used for such measurements
- Concentration of extrinsic markers such as dyes, chemical tags, chromophores and fluorphores, and fluorescence protein markers
- Gene expression, cellular differentiation, morphogenesis.

Ideally, the sensed spatial distribution α is proportional to the functional distribution β, and sometimes α is itself β. However, the two distributions may be related by some mathematical relation (e.g., time delay, time average over some duration, spatial average over some local neighborhood, or a nonlinear operation such as saturation). This is represented by the system illustrated in Fig 1.1-5.

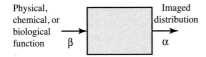

Figure 1.1-5 Relation between the sensed physical distribution α and an underlying distribution β that is useful to the user.

Image-Understanding Applications.   In certain applications, obtaining the full spatial distribution of α or β may not be necessary. The user may only be interested in estimating some property of the object, such as:

- *Shape*, *size*, or *location* of the center of some target
- *Number* of targets of certain type
- *Average value* of a property such as humidity, oxygenation, or temperature
- Statistical measures of a random distribution, such as average *contrast*, *graininess*, or *orientation* and *anisotropy* of the scene texture.

In other applications, the user may be interested in detecting the presence or absence of a particular material (such as underground oil, water, minerals, or pollution plumes; explosives in luggage; or cardiovascular plaque), a hidden target (such as landmine, weapon, wreck site, or archaeological artifact), or some feature or anomaly in the object (such as a crack or cavity). In any of these applications, the goal is to reach a binary decision on the presence or absence of something. Detailed examples of **detection** problems are provided in Chapter 9.

One may also be interested in classifying objects based on features exhibited in the sensed distribution α or the underlying distribution β. For example, an underwater imaging system may aim at classifying various regions into classes such as deep water, sand, reef crest, mangrove, or sea grass. Detailed examples of **classification** problems are provided in Chapter 6. In any case, it is essential that the imaging system be designed with the ultimate goal of the application in mind.

1.2   Challenges of Subsurface Imaging

A. Limited Resolution

A principal challenge in imaging is *localization*, which is the ability of the imaging instrument to extract information on an effect or a property at a single point without being "contaminated" by similar effects at other neighboring points. An instrument with this capability can measure the entire spatial distribution of the property by means of point-by-point scanning. Perfect localization is, of course, an idealization. Real imaging instruments using waves, fields, or particles can localize within a spot of finite dimensions, rather than a point. The size of that spot determines the spatial **resolution** of the instrument, i.e., the dimension of the finest spatial detail that can be discerned by the instrument.

Localization

Localization in 2D Imaging.   For a two-dimensional (2D) object, such as a planar surface, a probe beam can be focused to intersect the object plane at a tiny spot centered at the point of interest. The full spatial distribution of the object is constructed by point-by-point scanning, as depicted in Fig. 1.2-1(a). The resolution is determined by the dimensions of the probe spot. Alternatively, a sensor collecting only from a tiny spot in the plane of a uniformly illuminated object may be used in a scanning mode, as shown in Fig. 1.2-1(b). A parallelized version of this configuration, which does not require scanning, uses a set of sensor rays directed through a pinhole, as illustrated schematically in Fig. 1.2-1(c). This configuration is implemented in optical imaging by use of a lens, as shown in Fig. 1.2-1(d). The **lens** has the remarkable capability of collecting light emitted from each point in the object plane *in any direction* and directing it to a single conjugate point in the image plane. The object and image planes are located at distances from the lens satisfying the imaging equation ($1/d_1 + 1/d_2 = 1/f$, where f is the focal length). The sensor, e.g., a CCD camera, detects emissions from all points of the object simultaneously, but each element of the CCD corresponds to a single conjugate point (or, in reality, a tiny spot) on the object, so that no scanning is required.

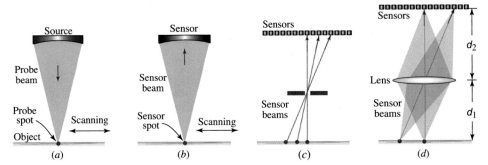

Figure 1.2-1 Configurations for imaging a 2D object. (*a*) Scanning by use of a focused probe beam intersecting the object plane at a single point (spot). The sensor collects from *all* points of the object uniformly. (*b*) Scanning a uniformly illuminated object, or a self-luminous object, by use of a sensor collecting from only a single point (spot) of the object. (*c*) Parallel scanning of a uniformly illuminated object using a pinhole camera (a *camera obscura*). (*d*) A single-lens imaging system.

Resolution.   The resolution of an imaging system is the dimension of the finest spatial detail in the object that can be discerned in the acquired image. This length equals the width of the scanned spot (the small circle in Fig. 1.2-1). If an object with a single bright *point*, in an otherwise dark field, is imaged with such a scanning spot, the result will be an image with a single bright *spot*, so that the point is seen as a spot. Two bright points in the object separated by

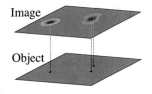

a distance smaller than the width of scanned spot cannot by easily resolved since their image is two overlapping spots. Since it is not possible to focus a wave to a spot of size much smaller than the wavelength, the resolution is most often (but not always) limited by the wavelength. The shorter the wavelength, the better the resolution. For example, X-rays form images with better resolution than infrared light, while microwaves or radiowaves have worse resolution under otherwise equal conditions.

Localization in 3D Imaging.   Since imaging is a noncontact process mediated by waves, fields, or particles, which must travel through other points of the 3D object on their way to and from a selected internal point, localization can be very challenging. As it travels through the object, a focused probe beam illuminates a region shaped like an apex-to-apex double-cone with the apexes at the focus, as depicted in Fig. 1.2-2(*a*). We call this illuminated volume the **probe spot**. Likewise, as shown in Fig. 1.2-2(*b*), a sensor cannot be sensitive to only a single isolated point inside the 3D object; it rather responds to points within an extended volume, which we call the **sensor spot**, e.g., having the same double-cone shape if a focusing element is used. In the pinhole camera, shown in Fig. 1.2-2(*c*), the sensor spot is approximately a straight line passing through the pinhole. In the single-lens imaging system shown in Fig. 1.2-2(*d*), the sensor spot has the double-cone shape, or a tilted version thereof. The image of a 3D object recorded by such a system contains a "perfect" replica of the slice of the object passing through the focus (i.e., satisfying the imaging equation), contaminated by blurred images of all of the out-of-focus planes.

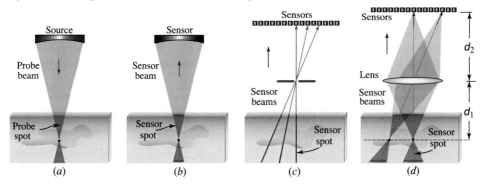

(a) (b) (c) (d)

Figure 1.2-2 Four inadequate configurations for imaging a 3D object. (a) Scanning using a focused probe beam. The sensor collects from all points uniformly. (b) Scanning a uniformly illuminated (or self-luminous) object by use of a focused sensor beam. (c) Imaging by use of rays passing through a pinhole. Each sensor beam (ray) is defined by a single sensor and the pinhole. (d) An ideal single-lens image-forming system. In all cases, each sensor is responsive to an extended region (volume or line) in the object, instead of a single point.

Multiple Scattering

Another principal challenge in 3D imaging is that the probe wave, on its way to a selected point inside the object, may change its direction as a result of scattering from scatterers at intervening points within the object or in neighboring clutter. Scattering from clutter creates background noise that contaminates the measurement. Also, on its way to the sensor, the wave modified by one point within the object may be modified again by other scatterers in the object before it reaches the sensor. This type of multiple scattering, which causes cross-interaction among points of a thick object, thwarts localization and diminishes resolution. Multiple scattering does not occur in the 2D imaging of a thin planar object since the probe wave accesses each point of the object directly, and the modified wave reaches the sensor without encountering other points.

Multiple scattering makes the imaging equation generally **nonlinear**, i.e., the sensed wave is not a weighted superposition of contributions from various points in the object. Nonlinear processes are difficult to model and analyze. Consider, for example, the imaging of two scatterers in a homogeneous medium, as illustrated in Fig. 1.2-3. An incoming probe wave may be scattered from each of the scatterers independently, as illustrated in Fig. 1.2-3(a). For this type of scattering, the principle of superposition applies, and the field sensed by the sensor is simply the weighted sum of contributions from each of the scatterers, i.e., the imaging is **linear**.

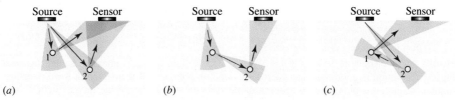

(a) (b) (c)

Figure 1.2-3 Scattering of a probe wave from two scatterers. (a) Direct scattering. (b) Double scattering from scatterer 1 followed by scatterer 2. (c) Double scattering from scatterer 2 followed by scatterer 1.

In the double scattering scenarios shown in Fig. 1.2-3(*b*) and (*c*), the wave scattered from the first scatterer may be scattered again from the second, or vice versa. In a triple scattering process, one of the scatterers is visited twice. For a larger number of scatterers, the possibilities for multiple scattering are endless and the complexity of the problem can be enormous. It is fortunate, however, that in many applications of SSI, the scattering is sufficiently weak so that the contribution of double scattering is small, and contributions of multiple scattering are even smaller. Approximations, such as the *Born approximation*, which is described in Chapter 2, exploit the weakness of the scattering effect to develop linearized models of imaging. This book is primarily concerned with this linearized regime.

B. Limited Penetration and Weak Contrast

Penetration Depth.   Subsurface imaging is often hindered by a medium that absorbs or scatters the incoming probe wave, preventing it from reaching the target. Likewise, emission from a self-luminous object may be absorbed or scattered by the medium and never reaches the sensor. A necessary condition for successful subsurface imaging is that the wave reaching the sensor must retain sufficient power so that it is detectable with sufficient accuracy. As described in Chapter 2, the penetration depth (the distance at which the power of the probe is reduced by a certain factor) depends on the properties of the medium and the nature of the wave, including its wavelength. For example, a medium may be totally opaque to light, but penetrable by sound or X-rays. Subsurface imaging may not at all be possible for objects that are deeply buried below or behind a sufficiently thick layer of a highly absorbing medium.

Tradeoff between Penetration and Resolution.   Waves of higher frequencies (shorter wavelengths) can be configured in narrower beams and focused into tighter spots. However, high-frequency waves often encounter greater attenuation in the medium and, therefore, have shorter penetration depth. The tradeoff between depth penetration and angular or transverse localization is exemplified in **ground-penetrating radar (GPR)**, which is based on measurement of the echo signal at locations along parallel lines (see Fig. 1.2-4). This technique is used in geophysical applications, including detection of buried objects or boundaries in a variety of media, including soil, rock, pavements, fresh water, and ice. When transverse localization is difficult because the wavelength is long, imaging may be accomplished with "fat" overlapping beams, in which case tomographic reconstruction is necessary, as described in Sec. 1.3B and later in Sec. 4.2B.

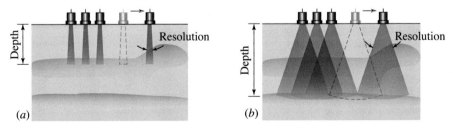

Figure 1.2-4   Tradeoff between penetration and resolution. (*a*) GPR imaging at high frequency; angular resolution is good, but the penetration depth is poor. (*b*) GPR imaging at lower frequency; angular resolution is poor, but the penetration depth is greater. Tomographic reconstruction may be necessary.

Contrast. In many applications the selected probing wave translates large variations of the β property, which the user desires to know, into small variations of the observed α property. The result is an image of weak contrast, which may not be adequate to recognize the target features or distinguish it from the surrounding background noise. For example, when a biological cell is viewed under the conventional optical microscope, which measures optical absorption, various morphological structures are hardly visible since their optical absorption is practically the same. However, viewing the cell under the phase-contrast microscope, which measures the refractive index, can reveal morphological features. One must therefore use the imaging modality that is most sensitive to the object property of interest. Another approach is to change the object itself by injecting an extrinsic substance to which the probing wave is more sensitive. Known as **contrast agents**, such substances attach themselves selectively to various elements of the object, as illustrated pictorially in Fig. 1.2-5. An example is the use of optically absorbing stains and dyes, which are distributed selectively within biological cells, to view internal morphological structures.

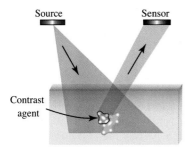

Figure 1.2-5 Imaging an object with injected contrast agents that are attached selectively to certain targets.

Noise and Clutter. Noise arises from random fluctuations within the detector or from extraneous waves that reach the detector independent of the target. As illustrated in Fig. 1.2-6, such waves may be created by scattering from clutter or random inhomogeneities in the medium, or from rough surfaces and boundaries that must be crossed by the incoming and/or the outgoing waves. In the presence of high noise, meaningful variations of the sensed property of the object must have greater contrast in order to be distinguished from the background random fluctuations. Known clutter may be avoided by use of carefully selected directions of view (or multiple views) bypassing clutter centers, as well as advanced detection algorithms.

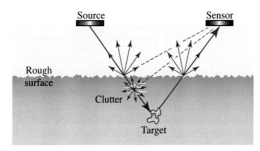

Figure 1.2-6 Scattering from a rough surface or from clutter or random inhomogeneities in the medium can reach the sensor and constitute background noise contaminating the signal received from the probed target.

1.3   Localized and Tomographic Imaging

There are two distinct approaches for addressing the localization challenge of 3D imaging:

- **Localized Imaging.** In this approach, the probe and sensor spots are configured such that their intersection, which we call the **scanned spot**, is a single point (or tiny volume). This ensures that, for each measurement, the sensor is responsive to approximately a single point in the object. The full 3D distribution is, of course, constructed by scanning over all points of the object. We will refer to this configuration simply as localized imaging.

- **Tomographic Imaging.** In this approach, physical localization is replaced with computational localization. The scanned spot is an extended region, so that a single measurement by the instrument is responsive to the sum of contributions from many points of the object within that spot. The measurement is repeated from multiple views such that these spots intersect, enabling each point of the object to contribute to multiple measurements. Taken together, these measurements are used to compute the individual contributions of all points. This form of **computational imaging** will be referred to in this book as **tomographic imaging**, **multiview tomography**, or simply **tomography**.

Localized and tomographic imaging are described in some detail in Chapter 3 and Chapter 4, respectively. The following are short previews.

A.   Localized Imaging

Spatial Localization.   A number of configurations can be used to ensure that the scanned spot (the intersection of the probe and the sensor spots) is a single point (or a tiny volume). In the configuration shown in Fig. 1.3-1(a), the two conical spots associated with focused beams intersect at a single point (i.e., the apexes of the cones coincide). This is the basis of **confocal imaging**, which is used in **laser scanning fluorescence confocal microscopy**, as will be described in Chapter 3 (Sec. 3.2B). In the example depicted in Fig. 1.3-1(b), the probe beam illuminates a single planar slice of the 3D object so that the probe spot is a sheet. The scattered waves generated at points of that slice are observed by normal 2D imaging using a lens, for example, so that the sensor spot is a double-cone region intersecting the sheet at a point. The process is repeated slice by slice. This configuration is adopted in the **slit-lamp ophthalmoscope**, which is used to examine different planes of the human eye (the lens, vitreous humor, retina, and optic nerve).

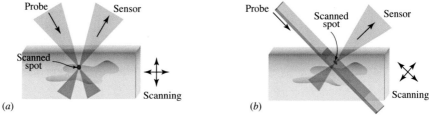

Figure 1.3-1   (a) In confocal imaging, the probe and sensor spots are co-focused onto the same point. (b) The probe beam illuminates a 2D slice of the 3D object and each slice is viewed by the sensor.

Time-of-Flight Localization.   Another type of localization is based on the use of a pulsed narrow probe beam and a time-sensitive sensor. The pulse travels through the object and is reflected from interior boundaries, creating echos that are detected by the sensor. A time trace of the received signal reveals the times of arrival and the strengths of the echos. An echo arriving after a roundtrip time t originates from a reflector at a depth $d = vt/2$, where v is the pulse propagation velocity, assumed to be constant and known. The process is repeated by moving the probe beam to a different position and determining the depths of reflectors at each position. This principle is used in radar, sonar, and lidar imaging, as described in Sec. 3.2C. If the probe beam has some angular spread, as illustrated in Fig. 1.3-2(b), then the probe spot has the shape of the beam, while the sensor spot corresponding to a time of arrival t is a spherical surface of radius $d = vt/2$, identifying a specific range. The dimensions of the scanned spot, which is the intersection of these two spots, determine the resolution.

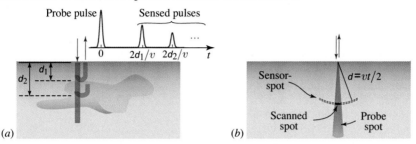

(a)   (b)

Figure 1.3-2   (a) Range localization by measurement of the time of flight of echos of a pulsed probe. (b) For a beam of finite angular width the scanned spot is a spherical cap.

B. Tomographic Imaging

In multiview tomography, each view is an observation of the object with a scanned spot (the intersection of the probe and the sensor spots) that extends over a large region. The object distribution is computed from multiple measurements with overlapping scanned spots. The following are some of the principal configurations.

Ray Tomography.   The simplest example of multiview tomography is ray tomography, which is the basis of X-ray **computed tomography** (**CT**). Here, each probe is a ray and the sensor is assumed to have no angular sensitivity, so that the scanned spot is the probe ray itself. The intensity of each ray diminishes by an amount dependent on the total absorption it encounters along its path, so that each sensor measures the sum of the absorption coefficients at all points of the ray. The medium is probed by a large number of intersecting rays, so that each point in the object is probed by many rays. A sufficient

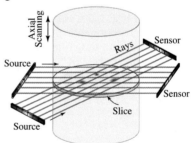

Figure 1.3-3   Imaging by axial slicing and ray tomography within each slice.

number of measurements are made so that the unknown values of the absorption at all points of the object can be computed. In X-ray CT, the object is usually divided into parallel slices orthogonal to the axial direction, as illustrated in Fig. 1.3-3. Each slice is probed by a set of parallel rays in the plane of the slice. The object is rotated or, equivalently, the sources and sensors are rotated, in order to scan the slice in multiple directions. The process is repeated for each slice. This is why the technique is also called **computed axial tomography** (**CAT**). Ray tomography is the subject of Sec. 4.1.

Range Tomography.   In a time-of-flight imaging configuration, such as that in Fig. 1.3-2(b), the sensor spot is a spherical surface of radius equal to the range, which is determined by the time of flight of the probe pulse. If the probe beam is not localized in the angular direction, then the scanned spot is an extended region in the form of a spherical cap with angular width equal to that of the divergent probe beam. If the probe/sensor module moves to a new location, as illustrated in Fig. 1.3-4, then a new set of scanned spots, in the form of spherical caps centered about a new location, provides a new view of the same object. With a sufficient number of views, the spatial distribution of a complex object may be computed. This configuration of tomographic imaging, called range tomography, is described in Sec. 4.2.

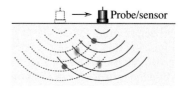

Figure 1.3-4   Range tomography.

Wave Tomography.   At wavelengths not much shorter than the spatial scale of the details of the object, the ray model is inadequate and the probe must be treated as a wave that spreads as it travels and is modified by the spatially varying properties of the object (wave propagation in various media is described in Chapter 2). For example, a wave traveling through a medium with a few small inhomogeneous spots is scattered as shown in Fig. 1.3-5. By probing in multiple directions (views) and measuring the scattered fields in each case, the distribution of the scatterers may be computed. This imaging modality, which is applicable to optical waves, radiowaves, and ultrasonic waves, is also called **diffraction tomography** and is described in Sec. 4.3.

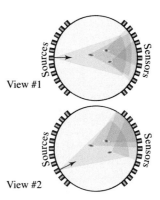

Figure 1.3-5   Imaging of three scatterers by use of probe waves from multiple directions. Two views are shown.

Examples of other configurations for the placement of sources and detectors are shown in Fig. 1.3-6 for a number of applications. In all of these configurations, computational techniques are used to figure out the spatial distribution of the object that is consistent with the collected data and the known physical laws, which the probe wave or field must obey in the medium. These multiview imaging configurations and their applications are described in Chapter 4.

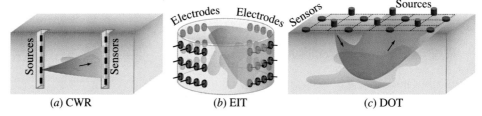

Figure 1.3-6   Examples of tomographic imaging. (*a*) **Cross-well radar (CWR)**: transmitting antennas placed in underground holes generate radiowaves that are detected by antennas at other holes. The permittivity and conductivity of the medium are mapped tomographically for geophysical applications. (*b*) In **electrical impedance tomography (EIT)**, the conductivity and permittivity of the object are inferred from electrical measurements on the outer surface. A small alternating current is injected through each conducting electrode and the resulting electrical potential is measured at all other electrodes. (*c*) In **diffuse optical tomography (DOT)**, modulated light is emitted from each of a set of light-emitting diodes into a turbid or diffusive medium and the light is detected by a set of detectors. As a result of strong scattering, light diffuses in all directions, much like heat, and reaches detectors on the same surface. A spatial map of the inhomogeneous optical properties of the medium is computed.

1.4 Mathematics of Subsurface Imaging

Quantitative SSI is based on a mathematical description of the propagation of the probing wave (or incident field), their interaction with the object, and the generation of the sensed wave (or field), as well as the processes of measurement and data acquisition. Various branches of mathematics are used, including partial differential equations, linear integral transformations, and matrix algebra.

A. Field Equations: Partial Differential Equations

As illustrated in Fig. 1.4-1, the process of SSI is mediated by a wave/field $\mathbf{U}$, which is initiated by the probe and modified by the object as it propagates through the medium and ultimately reaches the sensor. As the wave/field interacts with the object it is altered in a way sensitive to a position-dependent physical property $\alpha = \alpha(x, y, z)$. The value of $\mathbf{U} = \mathbf{U}(x, y, z)$ generated at the source is denoted $\mathbf{U}_\mathrm{p}$ and that measured by the sensor is denoted $\mathbf{U}_\mathrm{s}$.

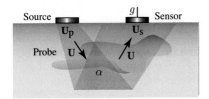

Figure 1.4-1   The SSI model.

Field Equation(s).   The wave/field $\mathbf{U} = \mathbf{U}(x, y, z)$ obeys equations dictated by the physics of propagation in the medium, which we write in the generic form

$$\mathcal{O}\{\mathbf{U}, \alpha\} = 0, \qquad (1.4\text{-}1)$$

Field Equation

called the **field equation**. Here, $\mathcal{O}$ is a mathematical operator representing the physical law that governs propagation in a medium characterized by the property α. The field equation has boundary conditions set by the known incident probe field $\mathbf{U}_\mathrm{p}$ and the field $\mathbf{U}_\mathrm{s}$ measured by the sensors (see Fig. 1.4-1). The goal of imaging is to estimate α, given the boundary conditions $\mathbf{U}_\mathrm{p}$ and $\mathbf{U}_\mathrm{s}$, i.e., to solve (1.4-1).

An important example is a scalar wave of angular frequency ω propagating in an inhomogeneous medium with velocity $v = v(x, y, z)$. Here, $\mathbf{U}$ is a scalar function of position $U = U(x, y, z)$ that obeys a partial differential equation known as the Helmholtz equation

$$\left[\frac{\partial^2}{\partial x^2} + \frac{\partial^2}{\partial y^2} + \frac{\partial^2}{\partial z^2} + \alpha^2 \right] U = 0. \qquad (1.4\text{-}2)$$

Here, $\alpha = \omega/v$. Imaging involves solving (1.4-2) for U and $\alpha = \alpha(x, y, z)$, given the boundary values U_p and U_s.

This and other differential equations governing electromagnetic and acoustic fields are described in Chapter 2. In most applications, the field equation is a *linear* partial differential equation in $\mathbf{U}$, as for (1.4-2), but it can be *nonlinear* if the intensity of the probe is sufficiently high so that it alters the properties of the medium as it probes it.

B. Imaging Equations: Linear Integral Relations

Imaging Equation.   It is useful to somehow convert (1.4-1) into an explicit relation expressing the measured field U_s in terms of the unknown object distribution α. We call such a relation the *imaging equation*. This equation is readily available in simple imaging configurations. For example, when a 2D object is imaged by a lens, as in Fig. 1.2-1, α is confined to a plane that is mapped point by point to the sensed field U_s. Another example is ray tomography, Fig. 1.3-3, for which the reading of each sensor is a sum of contributions from α along the ray path. However, in a general configuration, such as that in Fig. 1.4-1, finding the imaging equation is not easy; and if it can be found, it would generally be nonlinear, even if the field equation is linear in U. For example, in the Helmholtz equation (1.4-2), the coefficient v appears in a nonlinear term proportional to U/v^2.

Linearized Imaging Equation.   As mentioned earlier, certain approximations aiming at addressing the linearization challenge allow us to linearize the imaging equation and express U_s as a linear transformation of α. This means that U_s at each sensor is a weighted superposition of α at all positions within the object. In this case, the sensor measurement g, which is usually proportional to U_s, is also linearly related to α. Thus, the measurement g may be regarded as the output of a linear system whose input is α. To use the terminology of linear systems, we will use the symbol f, instead of α, to denote the object distribution and write the imaging equation as a linear relation:

$$g = \mathcal{L}(f), \tag{1.4-3}$$

Linearized Imaging Equation

where $\mathcal{L}$ represents the linear system. In this equation, f and g may represent 3D, 2D, or 1D functions, depending on the configuration. For example, when a 3D object is imaged by a localized imaging system, $g(x, y, z)$ is a linear transformation of $f(x, y, z)$, expressed, e.g., in the form of a 3D convolution

$$g(x, y, z) = h(x, y, z) \otimes f(x, y, z), \tag{1.4-4}$$

Convolution

where $h(x, y, z)$ is a 3D function, called the point spread function. Methods of signals and systems, including the operation of multidimensional convolution, are summarized in Appendix A, and applied to 2D and 3D localized imaging in Chapter 3.

Another example of the generic linear operation in (1.4-3) is the process of projection of a 2D function $f(x, y)$ in the direction of the y axis. The result is the linear relation

$$g(x) = \int_{-\infty}^{\infty} f(x, y)\, dy, \tag{1.4-5}$$

Projection

which describes one view in ray tomography (with rays traveling along the y direction). This, and other linear transformations describing measurements in multiview tomography are presented in Chapter 4.

C. Digital Imaging Equations: Matrix Algebra

Discretization. Since the object and image distributions represent physical quantities, they are described by continuous functions, $f(x, y, z)$ and $g(x, y, z)$, related by linear integral transformations derived from physical laws. In reality, however, an image is detected by a finite number of sensors that record discrete data. The object distribution $f(x, y, z)$ may also be discretized and represented by an array of numbers representing, e.g., a spatially sampled version of the continuous distribution at points of a 3D periodic lattice, where each unit cell (e.g., a cube) is called a **voxel** (much like the discretization of a 2D continuous image as a set of **pixels**). The result is a 3D array $f(n_x, n_y, n_z)$, where n_x, n_y, and n_z are integers ranging from 1 to N_x, N_y, and N_z, respectively. The total number of voxels in the array is therefore $N = N_x N_y N_z$. The 3D distribution of an anatomic organ may, for example, contain $512 \times 512 \times 512$ voxels. Likewise, the set of measurements may be cast as an array $g(m_x, m_y, m_z)$, representing a 3D image with $M = M_x M_y M_z$ samples, or a set of M_z views, each of which is a 2D image with $M_x M_y$ pixels.

Imaging Matrix. The linear imaging equation (1.4-3) may also be discretized and written as a set of linear algebraic equations relating the measurement to the object samples. These equations may further be expressed as a single matrix equation. This is accomplished by stacking columns of the 3D array $f(n_x, n_y, n_z)$ into a single column matrix (a vector) **f** with elements f_n, where $n = 1, 2, \cdots, N$. The data collected by the sensor(s) are also arranged in the form of a column vector $\mathbf{g} = (g_1, g_2, \cdots, g_M)$ of dimension M. With this discrete representation, the linear imaging equation (1.4-3) becomes a matrix equation

$$\mathbf{g} = \mathbf{Hf}, \tag{1.4-6}$$

Matrix Imaging Equation

where **H** is an $M \times N$ matrix related to the operator $\mathcal{L}$. The discrete and matrix representations of the linear imaging equation are described in Chapter 5; and Appendix B covers some basic aspects of matrix algebra.

Discrete Field Equation. Instead of discretizing a linearized imaging equation (1.4-3) that was derived from the field equation (1.4-1) by use of some approximation, it is sometimes necessary or useful to begin with the field equation itself and convert it to a discrete form. The result of this process is a set of algebraic equations relating elements of the discrete field $U(n_x, n_y, n_z)$ to those of the discrete object distribution $\alpha(n_x, n_y, n_z)$. Solving these algebraic equations numerically, the field U_s at the sensors may be computed if the object distribution $\alpha(n_x, n_y, n_z)$ is known everywhere. This so-called **forward model** is equivalent to the imaging equation. It is not necessarily linear. The use of such computational simulation techniques to construct the forward model is described in Chapter 8.

D. Inversion

Another principal challenge in subsurface imaging is the solution of the inverse problem – reconstruction of the object distribution from the measured data. This problem would not arise for a perfectly localized imaging system since the measured image $g(x, y, z)$ would be proportional to the unknown object distribution $f(x, y, z)$. However, because of factors such as the finite resolution of the imaging process, the sampling error caused by the limited number of sensors, and the measurement noise, this is never the case.

For a high-resolution localized imaging system using a large number of accurate sensors, the measured image $g(x, y, z)$ can be very close to the true object $f(x, y, z)$ so that inversion is a matter of correction of these effects. However, for tomographic imaging, none of the measured views resembles the true object, and computation is an inherent component of the imaging process. Reconstruction in the presence of sampling error, limited number of views, model uncertainty, and measurement noise is not easy, as will be amply demonstrated in this text.

Under linearized conditions, the system is described by the linear imaging equation $g = \mathcal{L}(f)$. Inversion means the computation of f from the measurement g, assuming that the operation $\mathcal{L}(.)$ is known. In a few special cases, described in Chapter 3 and Chapter 4, an inverse operation $\mathcal{L}^{-1}$ is known analytically, so that under ideal conditions the inversion is straightforward.

In most cases, however, no analytical solution exists. The imaging problem is then discretized and formulated as a matrix equation $\mathbf{g} = \mathbf{Hf}$. Since the matrix $\mathbf{H}$ is quite large and is not a square matrix because the number of observations is often smaller than the number of unknowns, inversion is not always easy. Further, the solution may not exist, and if it does, it may not be unique. More importantly, the solution may not be stable, i.e., small changes in the data (resulting from noise) may yield overly large changes in the resulting solution. When these effects occur, the problem is said to be **ill-posed**. These issues are addressed in Chapter 5. A brief background of relevant concepts from linear algebra is provided in Appendix B.

1.5   Dynamic, Multispectral, Multisensor, and Multiwave Imaging

As mentioned earlier, in 3D imaging the sensed property is represented by a position-dependent function $\alpha = \alpha(\mathbf{r})$, where $\mathbf{r} = (x, y, z)$. Imaging scenarios of even higher dimensions are also of interest:

- **Dynamic imaging** systems deal with objects that are time varying so that $\alpha = \alpha(\mathbf{r}, t)$ is a function of space and time, and the imaging system is four-dimensional (4D). The time dependence may be i) independent of the probe, e.g., when imaging moving, pulsating, or fluctuating targets, or ii) initiated by the probe, e.g., molecular change or chemical reaction lasting for some time ater the application of an optical or electromagnetic pulse.
- **Spectral imaging** systems observe a wavelength-dependent property represented by the 4D function $\alpha = \alpha(\mathbf{r}, \lambda)$, which is a function of the wavelength λ. The human visual system observes color objects that are position, time, and wavelength dependent; this is a five-dimensional system.
- **Multisensor imaging** instruments combine the images acquired independently by different imaging modalities, such as X-rays, radiowaves, and ultrasonic waves, to perform tasks such as the mapping of an underlying physical or biological property to which all sensors are sensitive, or the detection/classification of a target. Human and animal sensory systems combine visual (optical) and auditory (acoustic) data to achieve tasks such as target location and identification.
- **Multiwave imaging** systems use multiple waves, e.g., electromagnetic and acoustic, that interact inside the medium, e.g., one wave generating or modulating another in such a way that the information is acquired better, or new information is delivered.

Dynamic Imaging. If the object varies slowly relative to the response time of the image acquisition system, which is determined by factors such as the width of the probe pulse and the response time of the sensor, then capturing a 4D dynamic image $\alpha(\mathbf{r}, t)$ may be accomplished by simply measuring a sequence of independent static 3D images $\alpha(\mathbf{r}, t_1), \alpha(\mathbf{r}, t_2), \cdots$ and forming a video image. However, if the object changes rapidly during the course of probing, then its time dynamics will be blurred, or washed out. For example, when depth information is acquired by measuring the time-of-flight of a pulsed probe of too long a duration, then the measured time profiles will be averaged over that duration, and spatial localization may also be confounded by temporal variation of the object. Imaging of fast phenomena requires faster probe pulses and complex configurations for separating variation in space and time. While spatio-temporal imaging of fast phenomena, such as chemical reactions and molecular dynamics, is an important application, these advanced technologies are beyond the scope of this text. There are, however, some special types of dynamics that can be addressed without difficulty. For example, if the target is a rigid body moving with a constant velocity, then the reflected wave encounters a Doppler shift, i.e., its frequency is shifted by an amount proportional to the velocity of the reflecting object. Thus, the echo of a pulsed probe carries information on both the range of the target and its velocity. This is the basis of Doppler radar imaging.

Multispectral Imaging. Since the sensed property $\alpha(\mathbf{r})$ represents the response of the medium to the incoming probe wave, it is generally frequency dependent. This is because it is governed by the process of interaction with atoms and molecules of the medium, a process that has a finite response time or involves resonance phenomena with unique spectral characteristics. We therefore write $\alpha = \alpha(\mathbf{r}, \omega)$, where ω is the angular frequency. For example, a reflecting surface may have an optical reflectance whose frequency (or wavelength) dependence defines its color. In certain applications it is useful to use, as probes, a set of waves/fields of different frequencies/wavelengths that measure alpha parameters $\alpha_1, \alpha_2, \ldots, \alpha_N$ of the object. The combined measurements may be used to determine an underlying beta property β, or several such properties $\beta_1, \beta_2, \ldots, \beta_M$. For example, a measurement of the distribution of optical absorption or fluorescence $\alpha(\mathbf{r})$ at N wavelengths may be used to determine the concentrations $\beta_1(\mathbf{r}), \beta_2(\mathbf{r}), \ldots, \beta_M(\mathbf{r})$ of M different materials, molecules, or species of known spectral absorption or fluorescence profiles. This is particularly easy if these profiles do not overlap, so that they may be measured independently. If these profiles do overlap, then some algebraic operations may be used to estimate the concentrations. This is known as the **unmixing** problem. As an example, Fig. 1.5-1 illustrates the process of identification of various cellular structures revealed by observing fluorescence at different wavelengths. Multispectral imaging is the subject of Chapter 6.

Multisensor Imaging. In multisensor (or multimodality) imaging, probes of different physical nature are used to measure different properties $\alpha_1, \alpha_2, \cdots$. These independent measurements may be used together to better reveal a single underlying property β, or to make a better decision on the existence of some anomaly. For example, optical and ultrasonic probes may be used independently to measure the optical and ultrasonic properties of a biological tissue, and the measurements may be used for cancer detection. One modality may offer an image with good resolution but weak contrast, while the other exhibits good contrast albeit with poor resolution. Multisensor imagers may also be used to extract different information about the object; e.g., one modality acquiring morphological information, while the other capturing functional information such as metabolic rates. Future airport screening systems are expected to be multimodal, including backscattered X-ray imaging and/or millimeter wave imaging, integrated with chemical and trace-explosives spectroscopic detection systems. Multisensor imaging is covered in Chapter 7.

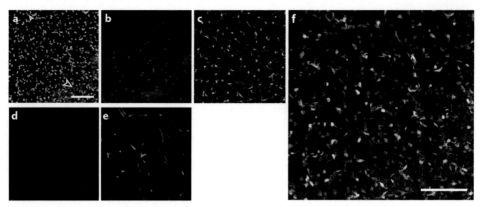

Figure 1.5-1   A five-channel multispectral image of a section of a rat hippocampus (an area buried deep in the forebrain) imaged by use of five labels, each with different spectral distribution. After unmixing, separate channels representing distinct cellular structures are obtained: (*a*) CyQuant-labeled cell nuclei (cyan), (*b*) NeuroTrace-labeled Nissl substance (purple), (*c*) Iba1-labeled microglia (yellow), (*d*) GFAP-labeled astrocytes (red), and (*e*) EBA-labeled blood vessels (green). The composite image in panel (*f*) illustrates a rich data set describing the position and morphology of the various nuclei and cell types and vasculature. The scale bar is 50 μm and the imaged section of this 3D object is 100 μm in depth. The 2D images shown are maximum intensity projections, i.e., at each (x, y) position, the maximum intensity at all depths z is shown. Adapted from (C. S. Bjornsson, G. Lin, Y. Al-Kofahi, A. Narayanaswamy, K. L. Smith, W. Shain, B. Roysam, Associative image analysis: a method for automated quantification of 3D multi-parameter images of brain tissue, *Journal of Neuroscience Methods*, Vol. 170(1), pp. 165–178, 2008).

Multiwave Imaging.   In multiwave imaging, waves of different physical nature are designed to interact within the medium and generate a single image with superior characteristics. Such interaction may also enable the acquisition of new physical information about the object that is not obtainable by any of the waves individually. While *multisensor imaging* benefits from the post-processing of images obtained *independently* by two modalities, each possibly lacking in some aspect (e.g., resolution *or* contrast), a *multiwave* imaging system generates a single image designed to combine the best of each (e.g., both contrast *and* resolution).

In the following two examples of dual-wave imaging, optical and ultrasonic waves play different roles as they are used simultaneously for imaging through a scattering medium such as biological tissue. The following properties of light and ultrasound are exploited:

(a) optical absorption images are typically of high contrast, but the localization of light in tissue is poor (because of scattering) so that the spatial resolution is not adequate;

(b) ultrasonic images in tissue lack contrast, but the spatial resolution is high (because ultrasound is less sensitive to scattering);

(c) light travels much faster than sound so that a pulse of light can illuminate all points of an object almost simultaneously.

■ **Photoacoustic Tomography (PAT).**   In this dual-wave system the optical absorption coefficient $\alpha(\mathbf{r})$ is measured by use of an *optical* wave that generates an *ultrasonic* wave, which is detected by the sensor. The optical wave is a short pulse that illuminates the object uniformly and is absorbed at a rate proportional to $\alpha(\mathbf{r})$. The absorbed light heats up the medium and, by virtue of the thermoacoustic effect, generates at each position an ultrasonic pulse with intensity proportional to $\alpha(\mathbf{r})$. These pulses travel through the medium to a bank of ultrasonic detectors that measure their times of arrival and determine their range (distance to each detector). These data are sufficient to compute the strength and locations of the ultrasonic sources (by use of range tomography, a geometrical method described in Sec. 4.2) and therefore estimate $\alpha(\mathbf{r})$.   Although the light rays do not travel in straight lines in the scattering medium, since light is fast all points within the object are excited almost simultaneously. Because sound is not strongly scattered, the time of arrival of each ultrasonic pulse is proportional to its distance, so that localization based on geometry is possible. This dual-wave approach, therefore, offers good spatial resolution combined with high contrast. PAT is described in more detail in Sec. 4.2C.

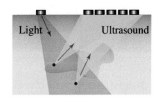

- **Acousto-Optic Tomography.**   In this dual-wave scanning system the optical absorption coefficient of a scattering medium is measured by use of combined optical and ultrasonic probe beams focused onto the same point. Since the optical beam cannot be focused to a sufficiently small spot because of scattering in the medium, it cannot by itself produce a high-resolution image – although it can produce a high-contrast image. This limitation is mitigated by means of the ultrasonic beam, which can be focused to a much smaller spot because ultrasonic scattering is less significant. The ultrasonic beam modulates the unabsorbed optical beam by altering its frequency (a process similar to the Doppler shift) only within the tiny focal spot of the ultrasound, which lies within the larger focal spot of the light. By use of an appropriate filter, only the frequency-shifted light is sensed; this is the light that originates from the small focal spot of the ultrasound. The scanned image will, therefore, enjoy the high resolution of ultrasound (sub-millimeter) *and* the high contrast associated with measurement of the optical absorption coefficient.

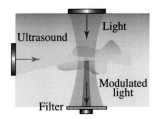

Other dual-wave configurations exploit the large difference between the speeds of two waves by using the fast wave to record a "movie" of the slow wave. For example a fast ultrasonic wave can be used to track the propagation of a much slower elastic shear wave.

Polarization-Sensitive Imaging.   A transverse wave, such as an electromagnetic wave, oscillates in either (or both) of two orthogonal directions, denoted 1 and 2, in the plane normal to the direction of propagation. If the probe wave is polarized in one direction, the sensed wave will generally have components in both directions. The medium parameter α in this case has four values α_{11}, α_{12}, α_{21}, and α_{22}, which determine the polarization components 1 and 2 of the sensed wave for probe waves polarized in the directions 1 or 2. Measurement of the two polarization components reveals useful information on the direction-sensitive properties of anisotropic media, such as crystals or fibrous material, or distinguish between scattering from a rough surface and a subsurface target as illustrated in Fig. 1.5-2. The technique may also be used to map the concentration of certain organic and biological materials that exhibit polarization rotation. Polarization-sensitive imaging may be regarded as a special example of dual-wave imaging (here, the two waves are coupled via the anisotropic medium).

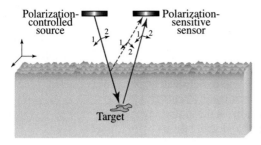

Polarization-controlled source

Polarization-sensitive sensor

Target

Figure 1.5-2 Polarization measurement can distinguish between scattering from a rough surface and a subsurface target.

Registration and Mosaicing.   When multiple probes are used to image the same object, the geometrical configurations of the imaging systems must be accurately aligned so that various measurements meant to refer to the same point are not inadvertently displaced. Accurate registration of multispectral or multisensor images is essential to the precise fusion of the collected data and to meaningful inferences based on the underlying common property β. Registration is also essential for imaging large objects by means of a series of measurements collated to form one large image, a mosaic. It is also a tool for detection of changes in the object. Registration, mosaicing, change detection, and multisensor imaging are covered in Chapter 7.

Review Exercise

Describe the difference between each of the following:
  (a) *alpha* and *beta* properties of the medium;
  (b) structural imaging and functional imaging;
  (c) resolution and contrast;
  (e) localized and tomographic imaging;
  (f) spatial localization and time-of-flight localization;
  (g) field equation and imaging equation;
  (h) linear and nonlinear imaging;
  (i) forward model and inversion;
  (j) ray tomography and wave tomography;
  (k) spectral imaging and dynamic imaging;
  (l) multisensor imaging and multiwave imaging.

Physical Models

Electromagnetic waves (including radio, optical, and X-rays) and acoustic waves are used widely as probes for subsurface imaging. This chapter provides a brief description of the principal properties of these waves and their interaction with matter via processes such as absorption, reflection, refraction, and scattering. These processes modify a probe wave so that the sensed wave carries information on the properties of the medium, its boundaries, and the object buried within.

2.1   Waves: Electromagnetic and Acoustic

A. Waves

A wave is a physical property that exhibits oscillatory variation in both time and space corresponding to propagation with some velocity. Mechanical waves, such as sound, propagate in a medium, while electromagnetic waves, such as radiowaves and light, may also propagate in vacuum. A wave transfers energy as it travels from one location to another. It changes direction at planar boundaries between different media, leading to reflection and refraction, and it acquires curvature at curved boundaries so that it may be focused or defocused. A wave is scattered into many directions when it falls onto a small object or inhomogeneity, and is diffracted as it travels through narrow apertures. Since waves are sensitive to the spatial distribution of the medium through which they propagate (and to objects located within), they are suitable for use as probes in subsurface imaging systems (Fig. 2.1-1).

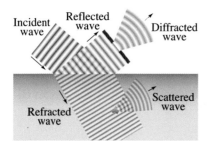

Figure 2.1-1   A probe wave is reflected and refracted at a planar surface. The reflected wave is diffracted from an aperture. The refracted wave is scattered from a target.

Wave Equation

A wave is described mathematically by a function of position $\mathbf{r} = (x, y, z)$ and time t, denoted $u(\mathbf{r}, t)$ and known as the **wavefunction**. The physical meaning of this function depends on the nature of the wave (mechanical, electromagnetic, etc.). In a linear homogeneous medium, the wavefunction $u(\mathbf{r}, t)$ satisfies a partial differential equation called the **wave equation**,

$$\nabla^2 u - \frac{1}{v^2} \frac{\partial^2 u}{\partial t^2} = 0,$$

(2.1-1)
Wave Equation

where v is the wave velocity, which is characteristic of the medium, and ∇^2 is the Laplacian operator, which is $\nabla^2 = \partial^2/\partial x^2 + \partial^2/\partial y^2 + \partial^2/\partial z^2$ in Cartesian coordinates. This equation permits oscillatory solutions that are harmonic functions of time and space, but pulsed waves are also permitted. Because the wave equation is linear, the **principle of superposition** applies, i.e., if $u_1(\mathbf{r}, t)$ and $u_2(\mathbf{r}, t)$ represent possible waves, then $u(\mathbf{r}, t) = u_1(\mathbf{r}, t) + u_2(\mathbf{r}, t)$ also represents a possible wave.

A measure of the intensity of the wave is the mean-square value of the wavefunction $I(\mathbf{r}, t) = \langle u^2(\mathbf{r}, t) \rangle$, where the operation $\langle \cdot \rangle$ denotes averaging over over a time interval much longer than the time of a cycle of the oscillating wave. A definition of the intensity and the power in terms of actual physical quantities will be specified for electromagnetic and acoustic waves in Sec. 2.1B and Sec. 2.1C, respectively.

Harmonic Waves

A harmonic wave has a wavefunction with harmonic time dependence,

$$u(\mathbf{r}, t) = a(\mathbf{r}) \cos[\omega t + \varphi(\mathbf{r})], \tag{2.1-2}$$

where

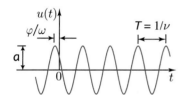

$a(\mathbf{r}) =$ amplitude

$\varphi(\mathbf{r}) =$ phase

$\nu =$ frequency (cycles/s or Hz)

$\omega = 2\pi\nu =$ angular frequency (radians/s)

$T = 1/\nu = 2\pi/\omega =$ period (s).

The wavefunction is a harmonic function of time with frequency ν at all positions, and the amplitude and the phase are generally position dependent.

It is convenient to represent the real wavefunction $u(\mathbf{r}, t)$ in (2.1-2) in terms of a **complex wavefunction**

$$U(\mathbf{r}, t) = U(\mathbf{r}) \exp(j\omega t), \tag{2.1-3}$$

where the time-independent factor $U(\mathbf{r}) = a(\mathbf{r}) \exp[j\varphi(\mathbf{r})]$ is referred to as the **complex amplitude**. The wavefunction $u(\mathbf{r}, t)$ is therefore related to the complex amplitude by

$$u(\mathbf{r}, t) = \text{Re}\{U(\mathbf{r}) \exp(j\omega t)\} = \tfrac{1}{2}[U(\mathbf{r}) \exp(j\omega t) + U^*(\mathbf{r}) \exp(-j\omega t)], \tag{2.1-4}$$

where the symbol $*$ signifies complex conjugation. At a given position $\mathbf{r}$, the complex amplitude $U(\mathbf{r})$ is a complex variable [depicted in Fig. 2.1-2(a)] whose magnitude $|U(\mathbf{r})| = a(\mathbf{r})$ is the amplitude of the wave and whose argument $\arg\{U(\mathbf{r})\} = \varphi(\mathbf{r})$ is the phase. The complex wavefunction $U(\mathbf{r}, t)$ is represented graphically in Fig. 2.1-2(b) by a phasor that rotates with angular velocity ω (radians/s). Its initial value at $t = 0$ is the complex amplitude $U(\mathbf{r})$.

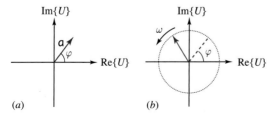

Figure 2.1-2   Representations of a harmonic wave at a fixed position $\mathbf{r}$: (a) the complex amplitude $U = a \exp(j\varphi)$ is a fixed phasor; (b) the complex wavefunction $U(t) = U \exp(j\omega t)$ is a phasor rotating with angular velocity ω radians/s.

Since the mean-square value $\langle u^2(\mathbf{r}, t) \rangle = \langle a^2 \cos^2(\omega t + \phi) \rangle = \langle \tfrac{1}{2} a^2 [1 + \cos[2(\omega t + \phi)]] \rangle = \tfrac{1}{2} a^2 = \tfrac{1}{2} |U(\mathbf{r})|^2$, the squared absolute value $|U(\mathbf{r})|^2$ is a measure of the wave **intensity** [W/m^2]. The power P [W] flowing into an area normal to the direction of propagation of the wave is the integrated intensity over that area.

The **wavefronts** are the surfaces of equal phase, $\varphi(\mathbf{r}) = $ constant. The constants are often taken to be multiples of 2π so that $\varphi(\mathbf{r}) = 2\pi q$, where q is an integer. The wavefront normal at position $\mathbf{r}$ is parallel to the gradient vector $\nabla\varphi(\mathbf{r})$ (a vector that has components $\partial\varphi/\partial x$, $\partial\varphi/\partial y$, and $\partial\varphi/\partial z$ in a Cartesian coordinate system). It represents the direction at which the rate of change of the phase is maximum.

Helmholtz Equation

Substituting $U(\mathbf{r}, t) = U(\mathbf{r}) \exp(\mathrm{j}\omega t)$ into the wave equation (2.1-1) and equating the terms that are proportional to $\exp(\mathrm{j}\omega t)$ we obtain another differential equation describing the spatial dependence of for the complex amplitude $U(\mathbf{r})$, called the **Helmholtz equation**:

$$\nabla^2 U + k^2 U = 0,$$

(2.1-5)
Helmholtz Equation

where

$$k = \frac{\omega}{v}$$

(2.1-6)
Wavenumber

is referred to as the **wavenumber**. Different solutions of this equation are obtained from different boundary conditions.

Plane Waves

The simplest solution of the Helmholtz equation in a homogeneous medium is the plane wave,

$$U(\mathbf{r}) = U_0 \exp\left(-\mathrm{j}kz\right),$$

(2.1-7)
Plane Wave

where k is the wavenumber and U_0 is a complex constant. Since the phase of the wave is $\arg\{U(\mathbf{r})\} = \arg\{U_0\} - kz$, the surfaces of constant phase (wavefronts) obey $kz = 2\pi q + \arg\{U_0\}$ with q integer. This is the equation describing parallel planes (hence the name "plane wave") perpendicular to the direction of propagation, the z axis. Consecutive planes are separated by a distance $\lambda = 2\pi/k$, so that

$$\lambda = \frac{v}{\nu},$$

(2.1-8)
Wavelength

where λ is called the **wavelength**. Since $|U(\mathbf{r})|^2 = |U_0|^2$, the plane wave has a constant intensity everywhere in space.

The corresponding wavefunction obtained from (2.1-4) is

$$u(\mathbf{r}, t) = |U_0| \cos\left[\omega t - kz + \arg\{U_0\}\right] = |U_0| \cos\left[\omega(t - z/v) + \arg\{U_0\}\right].$$

(2.1-9)

The wavefunction is therefore periodic in time with period $1/\nu$, and periodic in space with period $2\pi/k$, which is equal to the wavelength λ (see Fig. 2.1-3). Since the phase of the complex wavefunction, $\arg\{U(\mathbf{r}, t)\} = \omega(t - z/v) + \arg\{U_0\}$, varies with time and position as a function of the variable $t - z/v$ (see Fig. 2.1-3), v is called the **phase velocity** of the wave.

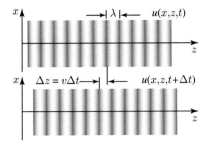

Figure 2.1-3 A plane wave traveling in the z direction is a periodic function of z with spatial period λ. It travels a distance Δz in time $\Delta t = \Delta z/v$. At any fixed z, it is a periodic function of t with temporal period $1/\nu$.

Plane Wave in Arbitrary Direction.   The wavefunction

$$U(\mathbf{r}) = U_0 \exp(-\mathrm{j}\mathbf{k} \cdot \mathbf{r})$$
$$= U_0 \exp\left[-\mathrm{j}(k_x x + k_y y + k_z z)\right] \quad (2.1\text{-}10)$$

describes a plane wave with complex amplitude U_0 traveling in the direction of the vector $\mathbf{k} = (k_x, k_y, k_z)$, called the **wavevector**. Substituting (2.1-10) into the Helmholtz equation (2.1-5) yields the relation $k_x^2 + k_y^2 + k_z^2 = k^2$, so that the magnitude of the wavevector $\mathbf{k}$ is the wavenumber k. Since the phase of the wave is $\arg\{U(\mathbf{r})\} = \arg\{U_0\} - \mathbf{k} \cdot \mathbf{r}$, the surfaces of constant phase (wavefronts) obey $\mathbf{k} \cdot \mathbf{r} = k_x x + k_y y + k_z z = 2\pi q + \arg\{U_0\}$ with q integer. This is the equation describing parallel planes perpendicular to the wavevector $\mathbf{k}$. Consecutive planes are separated by the wavelength $\lambda = 2\pi/k$.

Superposition of Plane Waves.   A wave $U(x, y, z)$ may be described as a sum of plane waves:

$$U(x, y, z) \approx \iint\limits_{-\infty}^{\infty} F(k_x, k_y)\, \mathrm{e}^{-\mathrm{j}(k_x x + k_y y + k_z z)}\, \mathrm{d}k_x \mathrm{d}k_y, \quad k_z = \sqrt{k^2 - k_x^2 - k_y^2}. \quad (2.1\text{-}11)$$

The plane-wave component with the wavevector $\mathbf{k} = (k_x, k_y, k_z)$ has a complex amplitude $F(k_x, k_y)$. By appropriate selection of the function $F(k_x, k_y)$, arbitrary waves can be synthesized. Note, however, that components for which $k_x^2 + k_y^2 > k^2$ will decay exponentially with z since they will have an imaginary k_z. Such plane-wave components are known as **evanescent waves**. Equation (2.1-11) permits us to compute $U(x, y, z)$ at any z if we know $U(x, y, 0)$. This can be seen by substituting $z = 0$ in (2.1-11) to obtain

$$U(x, y, 0) \approx \iint\limits_{-\infty}^{\infty} F(k_x, k_y)\, \mathrm{e}^{-\mathrm{j}(k_x x + k_y y)}\, \mathrm{d}k_x\, \mathrm{d}k_y. \quad (2.1\text{-}12)$$

The right-hand side of (2.1-12) is proportional to the two-dimensional (2D) inverse Fourier transform (see Appendix A) of the 2D function $F(k_x, k_y)$. If the 2D function $U(x, y, 0)$ is known, its Fourier transform can be calculated, and $F(k_x, k_y)$ can be used in (2.1-11) to determine $U(x, y, z)$. This Fourier approach is useful in understanding wave propagation and in solving inverse problems, as will be shown in subsequent chapters of this book.

Spherical Waves

Another simple solution of the Helmholtz equation (in spherical coordinates) is the spherical wave

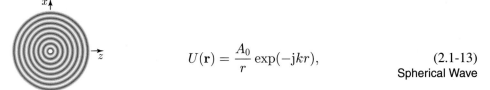

$$U(\mathbf{r}) = \frac{A_0}{r} \exp(-jkr), \qquad (2.1\text{-}13)$$

Spherical Wave

where r is the distance from the origin, $k = \omega/c$ is the wavenumber, and A_0 is a constant. Since $|U(\mathbf{r})|^2 = |A_0|^2/r^2$, the intensity of the wave is inversely proportional to the square of the distance. Taking $\arg\{A_0\} = 0$ for simplicity, the wavefronts are the surfaces $kr = 2\pi q$ or $r = q\lambda$, where q is an integer. These are concentric spheres separated by a radial distance $\lambda = 2\pi/k$ that advance radially at the phase velocity v.

Superposition of Spherical Waves.   A wave $U(\mathbf{r})$ may be described as a superposition of spherical waves originating from a set of points $\mathbf{r}'$ within some volume or area:

$$U(\mathbf{r}) = \int s(\mathbf{r}') \frac{e^{-jk|\mathbf{r}-\mathbf{r}'|}}{4\pi\,|\mathbf{r}-\mathbf{r}'|} \, d\mathbf{r}'. \qquad (2.1\text{-}14)$$

Here, the complex amplitude of the spherical wave originating from the point $\mathbf{r}'$ is proportional to $s(\mathbf{r}')$. This type of wave decomposition is useful in studying wave diffraction and scattering, as will be shown in subsequent sections of this book.

Gaussian Beams

The Gaussian beam is a wave confined about an axis and undergoing minimal divergence. It is an approximate solution to the Helmholtz equation, valid for small divergence angles. The optical waves generated by most lasers are Gaussian beams.

A Gaussian beam propagating along the z direction has a complex amplitude

$$U(\mathbf{r}) = U_0 \frac{W_0}{W(z)} \exp\left[-\frac{\rho^2}{W^2(z)}\right] \exp\left[-jkz - jk\frac{\rho^2}{2R(z)} + j\zeta(z)\right], \qquad (2.1\text{-}15)$$

where $\rho = \sqrt{x^2 + y^2}$ is the radial distance,

$$W(z) = W_0 \sqrt{1 + \left(\frac{z}{z_0}\right)^2}, \quad R(z) = z\left[1 + \left(\frac{z_0}{z}\right)^2\right], \quad \zeta(z) = \tan^{-1}\frac{z}{z_0}, \qquad (2.1\text{-}16)$$

and the parameters W_0 and z_0, which define the **beam waist** and **depth of focus**, respectively, are related by

$$z_0 = \pi\frac{W_0^2}{\lambda}. \qquad (2.1\text{-}17)$$

At any z, the intensity $I(\rho, z) \propto |U(\rho, z)|^2$ so that

$$I(\rho, z) = I_0 [W_0/W(z)]^2 \exp[-2\rho^2/W^2(z)] \qquad (2.1\text{-}18)$$

is a Gaussian function of the radial distance ρ. It has its peak value $I_0 = I(0,0)$ at the beam center ($\rho = z = 0$) and decreases as ρ increases or the magnitude $|z|$ increases. The total power carried by the beam is $P = \frac{1}{2}\pi W_0^2 I_0$. The beam width $W(z)$ increases with z in accordance with (2.1-16). In the plane $z = 0$, the beam has a minimum radius W_0, and the beam achieves its best focus and maximum intensity I_0 at the beam center. In either direction, the beam gradually grows "out of focus." The axial distance within which the beam width is no greater than $\sqrt{2}W_0$ is therefore equal to the depth of focus $2z_0$. Away from the center, in the far zone ($z \gg z_0$), $W(z) \approx W_0 z/z_0$, i.e., increases linearly with z. The angle $\theta_0 = W_0/z_0$, therefore, represents the **angular width** or the beam divergence (see Fig. 2.1-4), and in view of (2.1-17),

$$\theta_0 = \frac{2}{\pi}\frac{\lambda}{2W_0} \qquad (2.1\text{-}19)$$
$$\text{Angular Width}$$

so that the angular width is of the order of the ratio of the wavelength to the beam diameter $2W_0$. The minimum diameter and the depth of focus of a focused Gaussian beam are related to the angular width θ_0 by

$$2W_0 = \frac{2}{\pi}\frac{\lambda}{\theta_0}, \qquad 2z_0 = 2\pi\frac{\lambda}{\theta_0^2}. \qquad (2.1\text{-}20)$$
$$\text{Width and Depth of Focus}$$

These parameters are important when the beam is used for imaging, since they determine the transverse and axial resolution, respectively. Both parameters are proportional to the wavelength and both can be reduced by use of a large angular width.

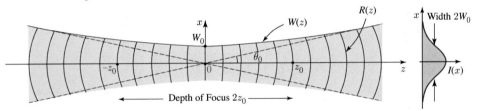

Figure 2.1-4   The distribution of a Gaussian beam in the z plane is a Gaussian function with width $W(z)$ that increases away from the plane of focus ($z = 0$). The beam is characterized by the waist radius W_0, the angle of divergence θ_0, and the depth of focus $2z_0$. The radius of curvature $R(z)$ of the wavefronts has its minimum value (maximum curvature) in the plane $z = z_0$.

The phase of the wave in (2.1-15) is composed of three terms. The first, kz, is the phase of a plane wave. The second represents wavefront bending with a radius of curvature $R(z)$, which is dependent on z. At $z = 0$, $R(z)$ is infinite, so that the wavefronts are planar, i.e., they have no curvature. The radius decreases to a minimum value of $2z_0$ at $z = z_0$, where the wavefront has the greatest curvature. The radius of curvature subsequently increases as z increases further until $R(z) \approx z$ for $z \gg z_0$. The wavefronts are then approximately the same as those of a spherical wave. The pattern of the wavefronts is identical for negative z, except for a change in sign. The third term in (2.1-15), $\zeta(z)$, represents a phase retardation independent of ρ.

▶ Problem 2.1-1

Damped Waves

A wave traveling through an absorptive or scattering medium is attenuated and its amplitude and intensity decay exponentially, as illustrated in Fig. 2.1-5. This phenomenon is mathematically modeled by use of the notion of a complex propagation constant

$$k = \beta - j\alpha/2, \tag{2.1-21}$$

where α and β are real numbers. A plane wave described by the complex amplitude $U(z) = U_0 \exp(-jkz)$ becomes

$$U(z) = U_0 \exp(-\alpha z/2) \exp(-j\beta z). \tag{2.1-22}$$

Since the constant β in (2.1-22) determines the phase of the wave, it determines the phase velocity of the attenuated wave via the relation $v = \omega/\beta$. The corresponding wavelength (see Fig. 2.1-5) is therefore $\lambda = 2\pi/\beta = v/\nu$.

Since the intensity is proportional to $|U|^2$ it decays exponentially,

$$I(z) = I(0) \exp(-\alpha z), \tag{2.1-23}$$

as shown in Fig. 2.1-5. The rate α is known as the **attenuation coefficient** (also called the **extinction coefficient**). The intensity $I(z)$ drops to $1/e = 0.37$ of its initial value I_0 at a distance α^{-1} called the **penetration depth**. It drops to half its initial value at a distance $\ln 2/\alpha = 0.693/\alpha$, called the **half-value thickness**. In certain applications, the symbol μ is commonly used, in place of α, to denote the attenuation coefficient.

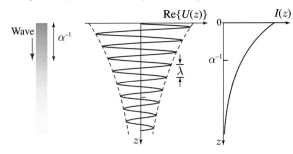

Figure 2.1-5 Decay of the amplitude $U(z)$ and the intensity $I(z)$ of a damped wave in a medium with attenuation coefficient α.

Upon transmission through a layer of thickness d, the transmittance $\mathcal{T} = I(d)/I(0)$ (ratio of the transmitted intensity to the incident intensity) is given by

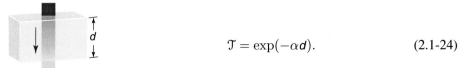

$$\mathcal{T} = \exp(-\alpha d). \tag{2.1-24}$$

The product $\alpha d = -\ln \mathcal{T}$ is called the **absorbance**.

Wave Generation

The wavefunction $U(\mathbf{r})$ created by a distributed source $s(\mathbf{r}')$ obeys the Helmholtz equation:

$$\left(\nabla^2 + k^2\right) U(\mathbf{r}) = -s(\mathbf{r}). \tag{2.1-25}$$

For a source extending over a finite volume V, the solution of (2.1-25) is given by the integral

$$U(\mathbf{r}) = \int_V s(\mathbf{r}') \frac{e^{-jk|\mathbf{r}-\mathbf{r}'|}}{4\pi|\mathbf{r}-\mathbf{r}'|} \, d\mathbf{r}', \tag{2.1-26}$$

which is recognized as a superposition of spherical waves, as in (2.1-14), with the wave centered at the source point $\mathbf{r}'$ having an amplitude proportional to the source function $s(\mathbf{r}')$.

Equivalence Theorem.   One of the most important principles in wave propagation theory, the equivalence theorem involves replacing an actual three-dimensional (3D) source by an equivalent source on a closed surrounding surface, so that the two sources produce the same field at points outside the surface. Consider a source extending over a volume V and assume that S is a closed surface that encloses the source, as shown in Fig. 2.1-6(a). An equivalent surface source s_{eq} on S generates the same field as the original volume source at all points outside S. This may be expressed generically in terms of spherical waves emitted by each point on the surface or in the volume:

$$U(\mathbf{r}) = \int_V s(\mathbf{r}') \frac{e^{-jk|\mathbf{r}-\mathbf{r}'|}}{4\pi|\mathbf{r}-\mathbf{r}'|}\, d\mathbf{r}' = \int_S s_{eq}(\mathbf{r}'') \frac{e^{-jk|\mathbf{r}-\mathbf{r}''|}}{4\pi|\mathbf{r}-\mathbf{r}''|}\, d\mathbf{r}'', \qquad (2.1\text{-}27)$$

i.e., the equivalent source $s_{eq}(\mathbf{r}'')$ on S and the actual source $s(\mathbf{r}')$ in V radiate the same field $U(\mathbf{r})$ at all points $\mathbf{r}$ outside S. The equivalence theorem is developed further in Sec. 8.3. For electromagnetic problems, which involve electric and magnetic fields, two different kinds of equivalent sources are used: electric and magnetic.

Huygens' principle, which was developed in the context of optics, is an example of the equivalence theorem. Here, the surface S coincides with a wavefront, as illustrated in Fig. 2.1-6(b). Each point $\mathbf{r}''$ on the wavefront S of the wave radiated by $s(\mathbf{r}')$ can be considered as a new source of a spherical wave with an amplitude $s_{eq}(\mathbf{r}'') \propto U(\mathbf{r}'')$, so that $s_{eq}(\mathbf{r}'')$ and $s(\mathbf{r}')$ generate the same wavefunction $U(\mathbf{r})$ at points $\mathbf{r}$ outside the surface S.

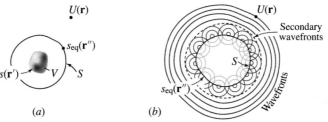

(*a*)   (*b*)

Figure 2.1-6   (*a*) An actual source $s(\mathbf{r}')$ and an equivalent source $s_{eq}(\mathbf{r}'')$ generate the same field $U(\mathbf{r})$. (*b*) Huygens' principle: points on a wavefront S generate spherical secondary waves that add up to generate the wavefunction $U(\mathbf{r})$.

Wave Diffraction

When a wave is transmitted through an aperture in a screen and travels some distance in free space, its wavefront is modified and its intensity distribution deviates slightly or substantially from the aperture shadow, depending on the distance, the dimensions of the aperture, and the wavelength. It is difficult to determine exactly the manner in which the screen modifies the incident wave, but the propagation in free space beyond the aperture is always governed by the Helmholtz equation.

Diffraction Equation.   The simplest theory of diffraction is based on the *assumption* that the incident wave is transmitted without change at points within the aperture, but is reduced to zero at points on the back side of the opaque part of the screen (see Fig. 2.1-7). If $U_0(\mathbf{r}')$ and $s(\mathbf{r}')$ are the complex amplitudes of the wave at points $\mathbf{r}'$ immediately to the left and right of the screen, respectively, then in accordance with this assumption, $s(\mathbf{r}') = U_0(\mathbf{r}')p(\mathbf{r}')$, where the function $p(\mathbf{r}')$, called the aperture function, equals unity at points inside the aperture and zero outside the aperture. In accordance with the Helmholtz equation, the diffracted wave at a position $\mathbf{r}$ in the observation plane is given by

$$U(\mathbf{r}) = \int_A s(\mathbf{r}') \frac{e^{-jk|\mathbf{r}-\mathbf{r}'|}}{4\pi|\mathbf{r}-\mathbf{r}'|}\, d\mathbf{r}', \qquad s(\mathbf{r}') = U_0(\mathbf{r}')p(\mathbf{r}'), \qquad (2.1\text{-}28)$$

where A is the aperture plane. This expression means that the diffracted wave $U(\mathbf{r})$ is a superposition of spherical waves generated by a continuum of sources within the aperture. The amplitude of the spherical wave generated at the position $\mathbf{r}'$ is simply that of the incoming wave $U_0(\mathbf{r}')$ within the aperture, in accordance with the Huygens principle. For example, if the aperture plane is at $z = 0$ and the observation plane is at z, and $s(\mathbf{r}')$ is a function $s(x', y')$, then the double integral in (2.1-28) may, in principle, be evaluated to obtain the wavefunction $U(x, y, z)$ in the observation plane.

Fresnel Diffraction.   At a sufficiently large distance z, such that $x, y \ll z$, the distance $|\mathbf{r} - \mathbf{r}'|$ between a source point $\mathbf{r}'$ and an observation point $\mathbf{r}$ in the integrand of (2.1-28) may be approximated in the denominator by $|\mathbf{r} - \mathbf{r}'| \approx z$ and in the exponent by

$$|\mathbf{r} - \mathbf{r}'| = \sqrt{(x - x')^2 + (y - y')^2 + z^2} \approx z + \frac{1}{2z}[(x - x')^2 + (y - y')^2]. \quad (2.1\text{-}29)$$

Under this approximation, known as the Fresnel approximation, the integral in (2.1-28) may be evaluated analytically and the result is known as Fresnel diffraction.

Fraunhofer Diffraction.   At an even longer distance d, the term $(x'^2 + y'^2)/z^2$ in the expansion of the squares in (2.1-29) has negligible effect on the result of the integral in (2.1-28), so that the magnitude of the diffracted field is

$$|U(x, y, z)| \approx \frac{1}{4\pi z} \left| \iint\limits_{-\infty}^{\infty} s(x', y') \exp\left[j\frac{k}{z}(xx' + yy') \right] \, dx' \, dy' \right|. \quad (2.1\text{-}30)$$

This approximation is known as the Fraunhofer approximation and the result is known as Fraunhofer diffraction. The right-hand side of (2.1-30) is recognized as the magnitude of the two-dimensional Fourier transform $S(k_x, k_y)$ of the source function $s(x, y)$ evaluated at the spatial frequencies $k_x = kx/z$ and $k_y = ky/z$. (For a review of properties of 1D and 2D Fourier transforms see Appendix A).

For example, if the aperture is a circle of diameter D illuminated by a plane wave of intensity $I_0 = |U_0|^2$, then $I(x, y, z) = |U(x, y, z)|^2$ is a function of $\rho = \sqrt{x^2 + y^2}$, known as the the the Airy pattern and shown in Fig. 2.1-7,

$$I(\rho, z) = I_m \left| \frac{2J_1(\pi\rho/\rho_a)}{\pi\rho/\rho_a} \right|^2, \quad I_m = \left(\frac{\pi}{4} \frac{D}{\rho_a} \right)^2 I_0, \quad \rho_a = \frac{\lambda z}{D}, \quad (2.1\text{-}31)$$

where J_1 is the Bessel function. The first zero of this pattern occurs at a radius $W = 1.22\rho_a$ so that $W = 1.22\lambda z/D$. It follows that the angle of divergence of the diffracted wave $\theta_0 \approx W/z$ is

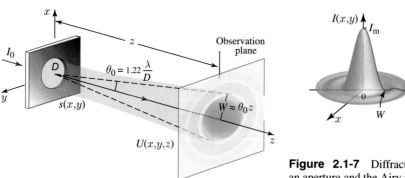

Figure 2.1-7   Diffraction through an aperture and the Airy pattern.

$$\theta_0 = 1.22\frac{\lambda}{D}.$$

(2.1-32)
Angular Width

Compare this to the divergence angle of a Gaussian beam, $\theta_0 = (2/\pi)\lambda/D$, where $D = 2W_0$. In general, the divergence angle is proportional to the ratio of the wavelength and the diameter of the beam waist or the aperture diameter. Note, however, that these expressions are valid only for small angles.

B. Electromagnetic Waves

An electromagnetic wave is described by two *vector* fields that are functions of position and time: the **electric field** $\mathcal{E}(\mathbf{r}, t)$ and the **magnetic field** $\mathcal{H}(\mathbf{r}, t)$. Therefore, six scalar functions of position and time are generally required to completely describe the electromagnetic wave. These six functions are related, since they must satisfy the celebrated set of coupled partial differential equations known as Maxwell's equations. In free space, Maxwell's equations are

$$\nabla \times \mathcal{H} = \epsilon_0 \frac{\partial \mathcal{E}}{\partial t} \tag{2.1-33}$$

$$\nabla \times \mathcal{E} = -\mu_0 \frac{\partial \mathcal{H}}{\partial t} \tag{2.1-34}$$

$$\nabla \cdot \epsilon_0 \mathcal{E} = 0 \tag{2.1-35}$$

$$\nabla \cdot \mu_0 \mathcal{H} = 0, \tag{2.1-36}$$

where the constants $\epsilon_0 \approx (1/36\pi) \times 10^{-9}$ F/m and $\mu_0 = 4\pi \times 10^{-7}$ H/m [MKS units] are, respectively, the free-space **electric permittivity** and the **magnetic permeability**. A necessary condition for $\mathcal{E}$ and $\mathcal{H}$ to satisfy Maxwell's equations is that each of their components satisfies the wave equation,[1] (2.1-1), with velocity $v = c$, where

$$c = \frac{1}{\sqrt{\epsilon_0 \mu_0}} \approx 3 \times 10^8 \text{ m/s} \tag{2.1-37}$$

is the speed of light in free space.

As illustrated in Fig. 2.1-8, the range of frequencies of electromagnetic waves extends from a few hertz to 10^{21} Hz, and beyond. It includes radiowaves, microwaves, optical waves, X-rays, and γ-rays.   Millimeter waves (MMW) and terrahertz (THz) waves are nestled between microwaves and optical waves. The optical band includes infrared (IR), visible, and ultraviolet (UV) waves. Soft X-rays overlap the range of extreme ultraviolet (EUV) and hard X-rays overlap the range of long-wavelength γ-rays. These many bands and sub-bands offer vast possibilities for subsurface imaging applications.

Wave Propagation in a Dielectric Medium

In a charge-free, lossless, linear, homogeneous, and isotropic dielectric medium, Maxwell's equations apply, but the constants ϵ_0 and μ_0 are replaced, respectively, by

---

[1] The wave equation may be derived from Maxwell's equations by applying the curl operation $\nabla\times$ to (2.1-34), making use of the vector identity $\nabla \times (\nabla \times \mathcal{E}) = \nabla(\nabla \cdot \mathcal{E}) - \nabla^2 \mathcal{E}$, and then using (2.1-33) and (2.1-35) to show that each component of $\mathcal{E}$ satisfies the wave equation. A similar procedure is followed for $\mathcal{H}$.

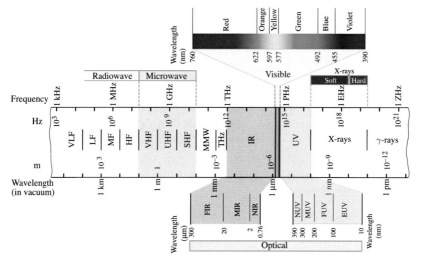

Figure 2.1-8   The electromagnetic spectrum.

the dielectric permittivity ϵ and the magnetic permeability μ, which are characteristics of the medium. Electromagnetic waves travel in such a medium with a speed

$$v = \frac{1}{\sqrt{\epsilon\mu}} = c/n, \qquad (2.1\text{-}38)$$

where the ratio $c/v = n = \sqrt{(\epsilon/\epsilon_0)(\mu/\mu_0)}$ is called the refractive index.

A time-harmonic wave of angular frequency ω travels in such a medium with a wavenumber $k = \omega\sqrt{\epsilon\mu} = \omega/v$. This corresponds to a phase velocity $v = c/n$ and a wavelength $\lambda = v/\nu = c/n\nu$, so that $\lambda = \lambda_0/n$, where $\lambda_0 = c/\nu$ is the wavelength in free space. Thus, for a given angular frequency ω, the wavelength in the medium is reduced relative to that in free space by the factor n. As a consequence, the wavenumber $k = 2\pi/\lambda$ is increased relative to that in free space $(k_0 = 2\pi/\lambda_0)$ by the factor n. As the wave propagates through media of different dielectric properties, its frequency remains the same, but its velocity, wavelength, and wavenumber are altered: $v = c/n$, $\lambda = \lambda_0/n$, and $k = nk_0$. The wavelengths displayed in Fig. 2.1-8 are in free space $(n = 1)$.

Transverse Electromagnetic Plane Waves

For a time-harmonic fields of angular frequency ω, Maxwell's equations take the form:

$$\nabla \times \mathbf{H} = \mathrm{j}\omega\epsilon\mathbf{E} \qquad (2.1\text{-}39)$$

$$\nabla \times \mathbf{E} = -\mathrm{j}\omega\mu\mathbf{H} \qquad (2.1\text{-}40)$$

$$\nabla \cdot \epsilon\mathbf{E} = 0 \qquad (2.1\text{-}41)$$

$$\nabla \cdot \mu\mathbf{H} = 0. \qquad (2.1\text{-}42)$$

The simplest solution of this set of equations is the transverse electromagnetic (TEM) plane wave. The wavefronts are planar, the direction of propagation is the same everywhere, and the electric and magnetic fields are orthogonal to one another and to the direction of propagation. For a wave traveling in the z direction with the electric field in the x direction, the magnetic field must be in the y direction. The complex amplitudes are

$$E_x = E_0 \exp(-\mathrm{j}kz)$$
$$H_y = H_0 \exp(-\mathrm{j}kz), \tag{2.1-43}$$

and the ratio of the electric and magnetic fields equals the characteristic **impedance** of the medium

$$\frac{E_0}{H_0} = \eta = \sqrt{\frac{\mu}{\epsilon}} \quad [\Omega]. \tag{2.1-44}$$

For nonmagnetic media $\mu = \mu_0$, whereupon $\eta = \sqrt{\mu_0/\epsilon}$ may be written in terms of the impedance of free space

$$\eta_0 = \sqrt{\frac{\mu_0}{\epsilon_0}} \approx 120\pi \approx 377\,\Omega \tag{2.1-45}$$

via

$$\eta = \frac{\eta_0}{n}, \tag{2.1-46}$$

where $n = \sqrt{\epsilon/\epsilon_0}$. The **intensity** of the wave is

$$I = \mathrm{Re}\left\{\frac{1}{2}E_0^* H_0\right\} = \frac{|E_0|^2}{2\eta} = \frac{1}{2}\eta\,|H_0|^2 \quad [\mathrm{W/m^2}]. \tag{2.1-47}$$

The **power** (units of watts) flowing into an area A normal to the direction of propagation of the wave is the integrated intensity $P = IA$. The **energy** (units of joules) collected in a time interval T is PT.

▶ Problem 2.1-2

Polarization

The polarization of an electromagnetic wave is determined by the orientation of the electric field. The TEM wave described in (2.1-43) is said to be **linearly polarized** in the x direction. Likewise, a TEM wave linearly polarized in the y direction has its electric field pointing in the y direction. The sum of two such waves with complex amplitudes E_{0x} and E_{0y} is equivalent to a linearly polarized wave at some oblique direction in the x–y plane, only if the phases of E_{0x} and E_{0y} are the same; the angle depends on the ratio of their magnitudes. If the phases of E_{0x} and E_{0y} are different, then the wave is said to be **elliptically polarized** since the tip of the electric field vector generally traces an ellipse as the wave propagates. If the phase difference is $\pi/2$ and the magnitudes are equal, the wave is said to be **circularly polarized** since the tip of the electric field vector traces a circle. Two directions of rotation are possible, depending on which of the components, E_{0x} and E_{0y}, is leading; these correspond to right- and left-circularly polarized waves.

Dipole Waves

The electromagnetic wave radiated in the far-field region by an electric dipole with dipole moment **p** pointing in the z direction has a magnetic field pointing in the azimuthal direction and an orthogonal electric field pointing in the polar direction of a spherical coordinate system. In free space, the fields are

$$H_\phi = k^2 c p \sin\theta \, \frac{\exp(-jkr)}{4\pi r}, \qquad (2.1\text{-}48)$$

$$E_\theta = \eta_0 H_\phi. \qquad (2.1\text{-}49)$$

Since the field strength is proportional to $\sin\theta$, the radiation pattern is donut shaped with a null value in the direction of the dipole. The wavefronts are spherical (like a scalar spherical wave). This wave is radiated by a rod antenna of length much shorter than a wavelength. It also appears in the theory of electromagnetic scattering from a point object (Rayleigh scattering; see Sec. 2.2C).

   A dual electromagnetic wave is that radiated by a magnetic dipole with dipole moment **m** pointing in the z direction. It has an electric field pointing in the azimuthal direction and an orthogonal magnetic field pointing in the polar direction; the strengths of these fields' amplitudes are proportional to $\sin\theta$:

$$E_\phi = \eta_0 k^2 m \sin\theta \, \frac{\exp(-jkr)}{4\pi r}, \qquad (2.1\text{-}50)$$

$$H_\theta = E_\phi / \eta_0. \qquad (2.1\text{-}51)$$

This wave is radiated by a small loop antenna in a plane orthogonal to the z axis, and also appears in the theory of radiation from magnetic spins (see Sec. 2.3C).

Photons

For an accurate description of the interaction of electromagnetic radiation with matter it is necessary to invoke the concept of the **photon** as a particle that carries the electromagnetic energy and travels at the speed of light. Electromagnetic radiation of frequency ν consists of a stream of photons, each carrying an energy $E = h\nu$, where $h = 6.63 \times 10^{-34}$ J s is **Planck's constant**. For example, an infrared photon of wavelength $\lambda = 1$ µm (frequency $= 3 \times 10^{14}$ Hz) has energy $h\nu = 1.99 \times 10^{-19}$ J $= 1.99 \times 10^{-19}/1.6 \times 10^{-19}$ electron-volts (eV)$= 1.24$ eV. An X-ray photon of wavelength 1 nm has a 1000 times greater energy, and a γ-ray photon carries even greater energy. Conversions among photon wavelength, frequency, and energy are shown in Fig. 2.1-9. Because photons of higher frequency carry larger energy, the particle nature of light becomes increasingly important as the frequency increases.

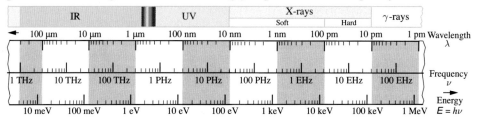

Figure 2.1-9   Photon wavelength λ, frequency ν, and energy E (specified in units of electron-volts).

Electrons

Particles, such as electrons, also exhibit wave behavior, including interference and diffraction, which limits their use for subsurface imaging. The wavelength of a particle is related to its momentum p by the de Broglie relation $\lambda = h/p$, where h is the Planck's constant. The relativistic momentum of a particle with rest mass m_0 and velocity v is $p = m_o v / \sqrt{1 - v^2/c^2}$. An electron accelerated to a kinetic energy E has a velocity $v = \sqrt{2E/m_o}$. Therefore, a 10 kV electron beam used in scanning electron microscope (SEM) has a wavelength $\lambda = 12.3 \times 10^{-12}$ m = 12.3 pm, while the wavelength of a 200 kV beam used in transmission electron microscopy (TEM) is 2.5 pm, which is shorter than the wavelength of X-rays.

C. Acoustic Waves

An acoustic wave is a mechanical wave propagating in a medium. The wavefunction described in Sec. 2.1A represents either the density perturbation $\rho(\mathbf{r}, t)$, the pressure perturbation $p(\mathbf{r}, t)$, or the velocity $\mathbf{u}(\mathbf{r}, t)$ of motion at position $\mathbf{r}$ and time t. Such quantities refer to perturbations from equilibrium conditions. The wave velocity v is the velocity of sound.

In fluids (gases or liquids), acoustic waves are described by the laws of fluid mechanics. If the acoustic wave represents a small perturbation of the medium, the conservation of mass and conservation of momentum equations can be approximated by the linear equations

$$\nabla \cdot \mathbf{u} = -\kappa \frac{\partial p}{\partial t} \tag{2.1-52}$$

$$\nabla p = -\rho_0 \frac{\partial \mathbf{u}}{\partial t}, \tag{2.1-53}$$

where ρ_0 is the quiescent density (i.e., the density in the absence of the sound wave) and κ is the compressibility, which equals the inverse of the bulk modulus (the stiffness). For an ideal gas, κ is inversely proportional to the quiescent pressure.

Speed of Sound.   By applying the div operation $\nabla \cdot$ on (2.1-53) and using (2.1-52), we conclude that the p satisfies the wave equation (2.1-1) with a velocity

$$v = \frac{1}{\sqrt{\rho_0 \kappa}}, \tag{2.1-54}$$

Speed of Sound

the speed of sound in the medium. Since the density perturbation $\rho = (\rho_0 \kappa) p = p/v^2$ is proportional to the pressure perturbation it also satisfies the wave equation. In accordance with (2.1-53), the velocity vector $\mathbf{u}$ must be in the direction of the pressure gradient, i.e., the direction of the velocity perturbation is parallel to the direction of propagation of the wave and the velocity perturbation u also satisfies the wave equation. Therefore, in fluids, acoustic waves are longitudinal (compressional) waves.

Frequency.   The frequency of the acoustic wave extends over the infrasonic, audio, ultrasonic, and hypersonic bands, as defined in Fig. 2.1-10.

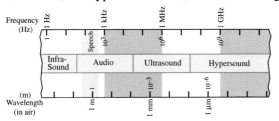

Figure 2.1-10   The acoustic spectrum.

Impedance.   For a harmonic acoustic wave of angular frequency ω the velocity and pressure perturbations obey the Helmholtz equation with wavenumber $k = \omega/v$. For a plane wave traveling in the z direction, the complex wavefunctions of the velocity and pressure perturbation take the form

$$P_0 \exp(-\mathrm{j}kz)\exp(\mathrm{j}\omega t), \qquad U = U_0 \exp(-\mathrm{j}kz)\exp(\mathrm{j}\omega t), \qquad (2.1\text{-}55)$$

where P_0 and U_0 are the corresponding amplitudes. By direct substitution in (2.1-52) and (2.1-53) it follows that the ratio of the pressure and velocity amplitudes P_0/U_0 equals the characteristic impedance of the medium

$$\eta = \sqrt{\frac{\rho_0}{\kappa}} = \rho_0 v. \qquad (2.1\text{-}56)$$
Impedance

Intensity.   The average acoustic intensity is

$$I = \mathrm{Re}\left\{ \frac{1}{2} P_0^* U_0 \right\} = \frac{|P_0|^2}{2\eta} = \frac{1}{2}\eta |U_0|^2 \quad [\mathrm{W/m^2}]. \qquad (2.1\text{-}57)$$
Intensity

Units.   The acoustic pressure amplitude P_0 is usually measured in units of pascal [1 Pa = 1 N/m^2 = 1 kg/(m s^2)] or in bar (1 bar = 1 MPa = 10^6 Pa). The velocity amplitude U_0 is measured in units of m/s. The acoustic impedance η is measured in units of Rayleigh (Rayls) (Pa s/m). The pressure amplitude is also measured in decibel (dB) units. A pressure amplitude P_0 is equivalent to $20\log_{10}(P_0/P_{\mathrm{ref}})$ dB, where P_{ref} is a reference pressure amplitude, which depends on the application. When the pressure amplitude is expressed in dB units, it is important to correctly specify the reference value employed. Standard convention uses $P_{\mathrm{ref}} = 20\ \mu$Pa for airborne sound and 1 μPa for underwater sound, or, more generally, for gases and liquids. It is customary to report the pressure amplitude in a liquid as 80 dB (re 1 μPa), for example.

The acoustic intensity I is measured in units of W/m^2 and expressed in dB units as $10\log_{10}(I/I_{\mathrm{ref}})$ dB, where I_{ref} is a reference intensity. The convention is to employ reference intensities of 1×10^{-12} W/m^2 and 6.7×10^{-19} W/m^2 for gases and liquids, respectively.

As an example, a sound wave of pressure amplitude $P_0 = 1$ kPa (or 180 dB re 1 μPa) in water (impedance 1.48 M Rayls) has a velocity amplitude $U_0 = P_0/\eta = 10^3/(1.48 \times 10^6) = 0.676 \times 10^{-3}$ m/s and intensity $I = P_0 U_0/2 = 338$ W/m^2, or 145 dB (re 10^{-12} W/m^2).

Summary.   A fluidic medium is characterized by its quiescent density ρ_0 and compressibility κ. These two parameters determine the velocity of sound $v = 1/\sqrt{\rho_0 \kappa}$ and the characteristic impedance $\eta = \sqrt{\rho_0/\kappa}$. An acoustic wave is a longitudinal (compressional) wave characterized by its pressure amplitude P_0, velocity amplitude $U_0 = P_0/\eta$, and intensity $|P_0|^2/2\eta$. The speed and the impedance for selected media are listed in Table 2.1-1

Table 2.1-1   Approximate values of the speed of sound v (m/s) and the acoustic impedance in units of M Rayls (10^6 Rayls) for various media. These values depend on the temperature and other physical conditions.

	Air (STP)	Water 22°	Ice	Aluminum (rolled)	Steel (stainless)	Wood (oak)	Granite	Blood	Fat	Bone
Velocity	330	1480	3990	6421	5790	4000	6500	1570	1460	3000
Impedance	4×10^{-4}	1.48	3.66	17.33	49.7	2.9	17.6	1.61	1.38	7.80

▶ Problems 2.1-3–2.1-5

Transverse Acoustic Waves.   Transverse acoustic waves do not exist in fluids and soft tissues, but do exist in solids, which exhibit a restoring force to transverse motions given by the shear modulus. The same wave equation applies and shear waves constitute a key component to understanding sound propagation in solid media. The two general classes of acoustic waves, compressional and transverse, can become coupled at boundaries, where boundary conditions mandate the continuity of pressure and vector velocity across the interface. A compressional wave traveling through a liquid and non-normally incident on a solid surface will launch a shear wave into the solid.

Elastic and Seismic Waves.   An elastic wave is a mechanical wave that propagates in an elastic or viscoelastic material. In addition to compressional waves, the elasticity of solid materials allows for transverse waves, or **shear waves**, for which the mechanical disturbance is orthogonal to the direction of wave propagation. A shear wave is characterized by its shear stress amplitude, transverse velocity amplitude, and intensity. When they occur in the Earth, as a result of an earthquake or man-made disturbance, elastic waves are called **seismic waves**. Compressional and shear waves are also referred to as **P-waves** and **S-waves**, respectively, and their wave velocity are denoted v_p and v_s.

2.2   Wave Interaction I

This section covers some of the basic characteristics of various processes of interaction between a wave and the medium within which it travels. Absorption is a principal process that depletes the power carried by the wave and, therefore, limits the distances it can reach under a surface. Scattering from fine inhomogeneities in the medium also results in the attenuation of the wave and the extinction of its power. The attenuation coefficient of a damped wave is often written as a sum $\alpha = \alpha_a + \alpha_s$, where α_a is the **absorption coefficient** and α_s is the attenuation coefficient attributed to scattering. Reflection at the surface and also at boundaries between macroscopic objects such as layers within the medium is another process that diminishes the probing wave.

Absorption, scattering, and reflection are inherent and unavoidable in subsurface imaging, but they can also prove useful for providing information about the local characteristics of the media and can be used to map their spatial distributions.

A. Absorption

The physical origin of wave absorption depends on the nature of the wave and the medium, which also dictate the spectral dependence of the absorption coefficient.

Absorption of Electromagnetic Waves in Lossy Dielectric Media

When an electromagnetic wave travels through a lossy dielectric medium with electric permittivity ϵ and finite conductivity σ (siemens/m or S/m) the resultant absorption/attenuation is often modeled mathematically by a complex permittivity

$$\epsilon' = \epsilon \left(1 + \frac{\sigma}{j\omega\epsilon}\right) \tag{2.2-1}$$

and an associated complex propagation constant $k = \omega\sqrt{\epsilon'\mu}$ so that

$$k = \beta - j\alpha/2 = \omega\sqrt{\epsilon\mu}\sqrt{1 + \frac{\sigma}{j\omega\epsilon}}. \tag{2.2-2}$$

For a medium with given parameters ϵ, μ, and σ, this relation may be used to determine the attenuation coefficient α and the propagation constant β (from which the phase velocity $v = \omega/\beta$ and the wavelength $\lambda = 2\pi/\beta$ may be determined). It is evident that the attenuation coefficient and the phase velocity are inherently dependent on the angular frequency ω, a property known as **dispersion**.

A critical frequency ω_c at which $\sigma = \omega\epsilon$ governs the nature of propagation in this medium. If $\omega \ll \omega_c$, then $\alpha \approx \sqrt{2\mu\sigma\omega}$, i.e., the absorption coefficient is proportional to $\sqrt{\omega}$. In the opposite limit, $\omega \gg \omega_c$, $\alpha \approx \sigma\sqrt{\mu/\epsilon}$ is frequency independent.

EXAMPLE 2.2-1.   *Attenuation of Electromagnetic Waves in Various Media.* Figure 2.2-1 illustrates the dependence of the attenuation coefficient α for media with various conductivities σ and dielectric constants $\epsilon_r = \epsilon/\epsilon_0$. These graphs are readily computed by use of (2.2-2). For example, the attenuation coefficient of ground at frequencies above 10 MHz is constant at ~ 1 (m^{-1}), i.e., the penetration depth is 1 m. At these frequencies, seawater and copper have higher attenuation (shorter penetration depth). For example, the penetration depth of copper at 10 GHz is only 10 μm. The phase velocity $v = \omega/\beta$ of waves traveling in these media may similarly be determined by use of (2.2-2) (see Problem 2.2-1).

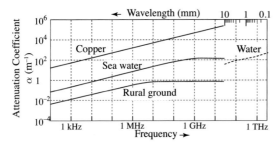

Figure 2.2-1   Attenuation coefficient of radiowaves in copper ($\epsilon_r = 1, \sigma = 5.8 \times 10^7$ S/m), seawater ($\epsilon_r = 80, \sigma = 4$ S/m), and rural ground ($\epsilon_r = 14, \sigma = 10^{-2}$ S/m) computed by use of (2.2-2) (solid curve), and measured values for millimeter and THz waves in water (dashed curve).

In the previous model and example, the dielectric constant and the conductivity were assumed to be frequency independent. In general, this is not the case, and other dielectric models exist. For example, in the Nth order Debye model,

$$\epsilon' = \epsilon_0 \left[\epsilon_r^\infty + \sum_{n=1}^{N} \frac{a_n}{1 + j\omega\tau_n} \right], \tag{2.2-3}$$

where τ_n are relaxation times and ϵ_r^∞ and a_n are constants. In this model, the dielectric constant and the conductivity are frequency dependent.

▶ Problems 2.2-1, 2.2-2

Absorption of Optical Waves

The absorption of light is accompanied by transitions between the atomic or molecular energy levels. It is proportional to the concentration of the absorbing atoms or molecules. Each transition is a resonance phenomenon characterized by strong frequency dependence of the absorption coefficient (and also the phase velocity). Spectra near resonance, therefore, reveal the local chemical environment.

Under certain simplifying assumptions, the propagation coefficient in a resonant medium may be modeled by the relation

$$k = \beta - j\alpha/2 = (\omega/c)\sqrt{1 + \chi}, \qquad \chi = \chi_0 \frac{\omega_0^2}{\omega_0^2 - \omega^2 + j\omega\,\Delta\omega}, \tag{2.2-4}$$

where ω_0 is the resonance angular frequency, and χ_0 and $\Delta\omega$ are parameters representing the absorption strength and the spectral width of the transition, respectively. The absorption coefficient α and the phase velocity $v = \omega/\beta$ (and the corresponding refractive index $n = c/v$) may be readily determined from this relation.

The material often has several such resonant absorptions with different resonance frequencies so that $k = (\omega/c)\sqrt{1 + \chi}$ with

$$\chi = \sum_{\ell} \chi_{\ell} \frac{\omega_{\ell}^2}{\omega_{\ell}^2 - \omega^2 + j\omega\,\Delta\omega_{\ell}}, \tag{2.2-5}$$

where the index $\ell = 1, 2, \cdots$ refers to the ℓth transition. The frequency dependence of the absorption coefficient and the refractive index then have the form illustrated schematically in Fig. 2.2-2.

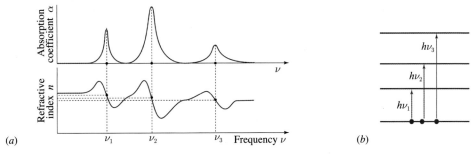

Figure 2.2-2 (*a*) Frequency dependence of the absorption coefficient and the refractive index in a medium exhibiting resonance at frequencies ν_1, ν_2, ν_3 corresponding to atomic transition energies $h\nu_1, h\nu_2, h\nu_3$, where h is Planck's constant. (*b*) Energy-level diagram.

Transparency Windows.   At frequencies away from any of the resonance frequencies, $\alpha \approx 0$, so that the medium is approximately transparent and the refractive index is approximately constant. Glass, for example, exhibits this phenomenon at wavelengths in the visible band. As shown in Fig. 2.2-3, water also has a window of transparency centered about the visible region. As shown in Fig. 2.2-4, biological tissue has a transparent window in a near-infrared band nestled between absorption bands of water in the mid-infrared and hemoglobin in the visible. At wavelengths within this window, light penetrates significantly through the tissue, a phenomena that can be observed by pressing a thumb against a a red laser pointer. The difference between the absorption coefficients of light in oxygenated (HbO_2) and deoxygenated (Hb) hemoglobin is used in finger-clip-on blood oxygenation sensors.

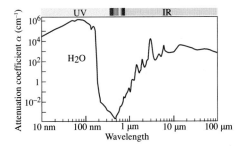

Figure 2.2-3   Absorption of light in water.

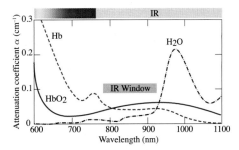

Figure 2.2-4   Absorption in biological tissue results from water and hemoglobin.

Figure 2.2-5 shows the wavelength dependence of the total transmittance of the atmosphere for electromagnetic radiation. Windows of transparency exist for microwaves, midinfrared (in the 2–5 µm band and near 10 µm), and visible waves. Absorption by atmospheric gases blocks other infrared and millimeter waves. UV and shorter wavelengths are blocked by scattering and by the upper atmosphere.

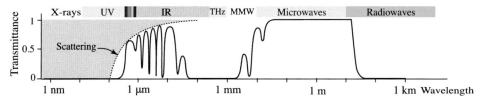

Figure 2.2-5　Schematic of wavelength dependence of opacity (1-transmittance) of the atmosphere.

Beer–Lambert Law.　Since the absorption coefficient α is proportional to the absorbers' concentration c (moles per unit volume), it is often written as $\alpha = c\kappa$, where κ is a proportionality coefficient, called the **molar absorptivity**. The transmittance $\mathcal{T}$ through a distance d, therefore, obeys the relation,

$$\mathcal{T} = \frac{I_1}{I_0} = \exp(-\alpha d) = \exp(-c\kappa d), \qquad (2.2\text{-}6)$$

Beer–Lambert Law

called the Beer–Lambert law.

When two substances with concentrations c_1 and c_2 and known wavelength-dependent molar absorptivities $\kappa_1(\lambda)$ and $\kappa_2(\lambda)$ are present, the overall absorption coefficient is the sum

$$\alpha(\lambda) = c_1\kappa_1(\lambda) + c_2\kappa_2(\lambda). \qquad (2.2\text{-}7)$$

The concentrations c_1 and c_2 may be determined if the absorption coefficient $\alpha(\lambda)$ is measured at two wavelengths, since two linear algebraic equations may be obtained from (2.2-7) and solved for the unknown concentrations. This approach is used, e.g., to determine the concentrations of oxygenated and deoxygenated hemoglobin in blood, a technique known as **oximetry** (see Sec. 6.3A).

Absorption of X-Rays

X-rays generally penetrate objects that are opaque to visible light. The absorption of X-rays depends primarily on the electron density (and thus on the atomic number) and the density of the absorbing atoms. For example, bone is more dense and contains Ca, which has a higher atomic number than the C, O, and N atoms in soft tissue. Consequently, the absorption coefficient of bone is significantly greater than that of soft tissue. In X-ray radiography, a uniform X-ray illumination creates a negative image of the bone distribution within the surrounding tissue. A contrast agent with high X-ray absorption coefficient, such as iodine, is injected into the veins to help create an X-ray image of blood vessels (an angiogram) (contrast agents are described in Sec. 2.4).

In medical applications of X-ray computed axial tomography (CAT or CT), the attenuation coefficient α is often denoted by the symbol μ and normalized to that of distilled water at standard pressure and temperature μ_{H_2O} by use of the Hounsfield scale. In Hounsfield units (HU):

$$\mu_{HU} = \frac{\mu - \mu_{H_2O}}{\mu_{H_2O}} \times 1000. \qquad (2.2\text{-}8)$$

Examples of absorption coefficients in HU units are:

	Air	Fat	Water	Muscle	Bone
μ_{HU}	−1000	−120	0	+40	400–1000

A material with absorption coefficient of 1000 HU, such as compact bone, has an absorption coefficient (cm^{-1}) that is twice that of water. For X-ray photons at 50 keV (see Fig. 2.1-9), the absorption coefficient of water is 0.214 (1/cm).

An example of the spectral dependence of the X-ray absorption coefficient is shown in Fig. 2.2-6. X-ray absorption spectroscopy is widely used to provide information on the local structure and the electronic states in matter.

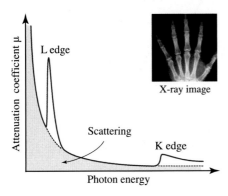

Figure 2.2-6 Typical dependence of the X-ray attenuation coefficient μ on the photon energy $h\nu$. The contribution of scattering to attenuation is marked by the shaded area. An X-ray radiograph of a hand is shown in the inset.

Absorption of γ-Rays

Since γ-ray photons have short wavelengths (below 10 pm) corresponding to high energy (above 100 keV), their penetration depth is quite large (several inches in packed soil or concrete). The absorption of γ-rays can result in atomic ionization via the photoelectric effect, Compton scattering (an inelastic process that generates electrons and γ-ray photons of lower energy), or generation of electron–positron pairs by interaction with atomic nuclei. Owing to their tissue-penetrating property, γ-rays (like X-rays) can be used in imaging (by means of CT scans) and radiation therapy. However, as a form of ionizing radiation, they can cause tissue damage and permanent cellular changes, potentially leading to cancer.

Because of their highly penetrating property, γ-rays are also used in imaging large container cargo, as illustrated by the side picture obtained by a mobile Vehicle and Cargo Inspection System (VACIS) developed by the SAIC corporation.

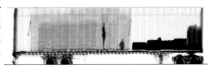

Absorption of Acoustic Waves

Ultrasonic waves are absorbed in various media, with the absorbed energy usually converted into heat. The absorption coefficient α increases with the frequency. A phenomenological dependence of the form $\alpha \propto \omega^a$ is often observed with $a = 1$ to 2 (see Table 2.2-1). As an example, for soft tissues at 1 MHz, α corresponds to 1 dB/cm (i.e., traveling a distance 10 cm through the soft tissue results in a 10 dB attenuation or reduction of intensity by a factor of 10). The attenuation increases with frequency as $\alpha \propto \omega^a$, where $a = 1.1$–1.2.

Table 2.2-1   Half-value thickness $\ln 2/\alpha$ at two frequencies, and the parameter a in the relation $\alpha \propto \omega^a$

	2 MHz	5 MHz	a
Air	0.6 mm	0.1 mm	1.96
Water	340 cm	54 cm	2
Blood	8.5 cm	3 cm	1.14
Bone	1 mm	0.4 mm	1
Liver	1.5 cm	0.5 cm	1.3

More complex frequency dependence of the absorption coefficient is associated with relaxation processes. These result in components of k of the form

$$k = \beta - j\frac{\alpha}{2} = \frac{\omega}{v_0} - j\frac{\alpha_0}{2} - \sum_\ell \frac{\omega}{v_\ell} \frac{j\omega\tau_\ell}{1 + j\omega\tau_\ell}, \tag{2.2-9}$$

where τ_ℓ is the relaxation time of the ℓth relaxation process, and v_0, α_0, and v_ℓ are constants. The corresponding attenuation coefficient is therefore

$$\alpha = \alpha_0 + \sum_\ell \alpha_\ell \frac{\omega^2 \tau_\ell^2}{1 + \omega^2 \tau_\ell^2}, \tag{2.2-10}$$

where $\alpha_\ell = (v_\ell \tau_\ell)^{-1}$. The contribution of each of the terms of (2.2-10) to the attenuation coefficient varies as ω^2 for $\omega \ll 1/\tau$ but approaches a constant for $\omega \gg 1/\tau$, where τ is the relevant relaxation time. The overall frequency dependence of α is illustrated in Fig. 2.2-7.

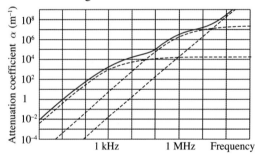

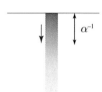

Figure 2.2-7   Frequency dependence of the ultrasonic absorption coefficient due to relaxation phenomena.

▶ Problem 2.2-3

Dispersion

As evident from the discussion in the previous section, waves travel in most media with frequency-dependent (or wavelength-dependent) attenuation coefficient $\alpha(\omega)$. Also, the propagation constant $\beta(\omega)$ is often not a linear function of frequency so that the wave velocity $v = \beta/(\omega/c)$ is also frequency dependent. Such media are said to be **dispersive**. When a pulsed wave travels in a dispersive medium its shape can be altered since each of its constituent frequency components undergoes different attenuation, and travels with a different velocity so that it encounters a different time delay. As the pulse propagates deeper into the medium, it is broadened, distorted, and its zero-crossings are shifted. This effect, called **dispersion**, or temporal dispersion, can be described mathematically by use of methods of linear systems (see Appendix A). When a pulsed wave is used to measure the distance to a reflective object embedded in a dispersive medium by estimating the roundtrip travel time, dispersion can limit the resolution of the measurement because of the increased uncertainty in signal timing.

B. Reflection and Refraction

Waves are reflected at the boundaries between different media. The amount of reflection depends on the mismatch between the impedances. A plane wave traveling in a direction normal to a planar boundary between two different media generates a reflected plane wave and a transmitted plane wave, both traveling normal to the boundary. If the impedances of the first and second media are η_1 and η_2, then the amplitude reflectance r (ratio of the amplitude of the reflected wave to that of the incident wave) is

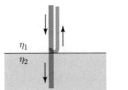

$$r = \frac{\eta_2 - \eta_1}{\eta_2 + \eta_1}. \qquad (2.2\text{-}11)$$
Amplitude Reflectance

The reflectance (ratio of the intensity of the reflected wave to that of the incident wave) is therefore $\mathcal{R} = |r|^2$. The reflection is almost total ($\mathcal{R} \approx 1$) if one medium has a much smaller, or a much larger, impedance than the other. The transmittance (ratio of the intensity of the transmitted wave to that of the incident wave) is $\mathcal{T} = 1 - \mathcal{R}$.

Reflection of Electromagnetic Waves

For lossless dielectric media, $\eta = \sqrt{\mu_0/\epsilon} = \eta_0/\sqrt{\epsilon_r}$, where $\eta_0 = 377\ \Omega$. Therefore, the amplitude reflectance of a normally-incident radiowave or a microwave at the boundary between two lossless dielectric media with dielectric constants ϵ_{r1} and ϵ_{r2} is

$$r = \frac{\sqrt{\epsilon_{r1}} - \sqrt{\epsilon_{r2}}}{\sqrt{\epsilon_{r1}} + \sqrt{\epsilon_{r2}}}. \qquad (2.2\text{-}12)$$

For example, the reflectance at the boundary of air ($\epsilon_r = 1$ and dry soil with $\epsilon_r = 3$) is $\mathcal{R} = |r|^2 = 0.072$ so that approximately 93% of the power is transmitted through the soil.

For lossy dielectrics or metals, the permittivity $\epsilon' = \epsilon(1 + \sigma/j\omega\epsilon)$ is complex and the impedance $\eta = \sqrt{\mu_0/\epsilon'}$ is also complex. In this case, the reflectance is inherently frequency dependent. Figure 2.2-8 shows the frequency dependence of the reflectance of a wave incident from air onto three materials: copper, seawater, and ground. The reflection from copper is almost total ($\mathcal{R} \approx 1$), since the high conductivity of copper corresponds to a very small impedance.

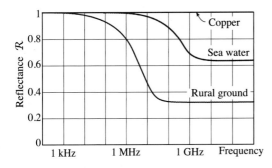

Figure 2.2-8   Reflectance at the boundary between air and each of three materials: copper ($\epsilon_r = 1, \sigma = 5.8 \times 10^7$), seawater ($\epsilon_r = 80, \sigma = 4$), and rural ground ($\epsilon_r = 14, \sigma = 10 \times 10^{-2}$).

▶ Problem 2.2-4

Reflection of Optical Waves

In optics, the impedance $\eta = \eta_0/n$ is described in terms of the refractive index n. Equation (2.2-11) then takes the equivalent form:

$$r = \frac{n_1 - n_2}{n_1 + n_2}. \tag{2.2-13}$$

As an example, at $\lambda = 600$ nm, the reflectance of an optical wave at the boundary of air ($n = 1$) and water ($n = 1.333$) is $\mathcal{R} = |r|^2 = 0.02$, or 2%.

Reflection of Acoustic Waves

The amplitude reflectance of an acoustic wave at the boundary of various materials may be determined by use of (2.2-11). Using the values of the acoustic impedance listed in Table 2.1-1, Table 2.2-2 lists some values of amplitude reflectance at boundaries between various materials.

Table 2.2-2   Amplitude reflectance r at boundaries between various materials

Air–water	Water–air	Air–steel	Water–steel	Air–soft tissue	Bone–muscle
1	−1	1	0.942	0.99	0.41

Because the reflection at the boundary between air and water or tissue is very high, ultrasonic transducers used in medical imaging are butted against the body and an impedance-matching gel is often used to minimize the reflection.

Reflection and Refraction of Oblique Waves

A plane wave crossing a planar boundary between two media at some angle undergoes a combination of reflection and refraction, as illustrated in Fig. 2.2-9(a). Since the wavefronts of these waves must be matched at the boundary (i.e., $\mathbf{k} \cdot \mathbf{r}$ must be the same), the components of the wavevectors in the plane of the boundary must be equal. This requires that $k_1 \sin \theta_1 = k_2 \sin \theta_2 = k_3 \sin \theta_3$, where the subscripts 1, 2, and 3 represent the incident, refracted (transmitted), and reflected waves, respectively. Since the incident and reflected waves lie in the same medium, $k_1 = k_3$ so that $\theta_3 = \theta_1$, i.e., the angle of reflection is always equal to the angle of incidence. Since $k_1 = \omega/v_1$ and $k_2 = \omega/v_2$, where v_1 and v_2 are the phase velocities in the two media, the angles of refraction and incidence are related by

$$\frac{\sin \theta_2}{\sin \theta_1} = \frac{v_2}{v_1}, \tag{2.2-14}$$
Snell's Law

a relation known as Snell's law. For optical waves, $v_1 = c/n_1$ and $v_2 = c/n_2$, where n_1 and n_2 are the refractive index of the media. In this case, (2.2-14) becomes

$$n_1 \sin \theta_1 = n_2 \sin \theta_2. \tag{2.2-15}$$

For incidence into a denser medium ($n_2 > n_1$), $\theta_2 < \theta_1$. For an acoustic wave incident into a denser medium ($v_2 > v_1$), so that $\theta_2 > \theta_1$.

The reflectance and transmittance at an oblique angle depend on the nature of the wave, whether it is longitudinal (e.g., an acoustic compressional wave) or transverse (e.g., electromagnetic or shear elastic wave), and on the polarization in the transverse case, whether it is perpendicular (transverse electric (TE)) or parallel (transverse magnetic (TM)) to the plane of incidence [see Fig. 2.2-9(b)]. The reflection and transmission coefficients, which are respectively the ratios of the reflected and transmitted

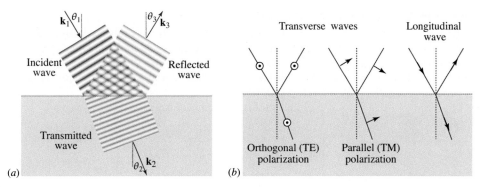

Figure 2.2-9 (a) Reflection and refraction. (b) Directions of the incident, reflected, and transmitted fields for a transverse wave with perpendicular (TE) and parallel (TM) polarization, and for a longitudinal wave (e.g., a compressional acoustic wave or a seismic P-wave).

field amplitudes to the incident field amplitude, are related to the angles of incidence and refraction and to the impedance of the media (assumed to be homogeneous and isotropic) by the following equations:

$$r = \frac{\eta_2 \sec\theta_2 - \eta_1 \sec\theta_1}{\eta_2 \sec\theta_2 + \eta_1 \sec\theta_1}, \quad t = 1 + r,$$

(2.2-16)
Electromagnetic Wave (TE) and Longitudinal Wave

$$r = \frac{\eta_2 \cos\theta_2 - \eta_1 \cos\theta_1}{\eta_2 \cos\theta_2 + \eta_1 \cos\theta_1}, \quad t = (1 + r)\frac{\cos\theta_1}{\cos\theta_2}.$$

(2.2-17)
Electromagnetic Wave (TM)

The relations (2.2-16) and (2.2-17), together with the relation $\sin\theta_2 = (v_2/v_1)\sin\theta_1$, can be readily used to determine the reflectance $\mathcal{R} = |r|^2$ and transmittance $\mathcal{T} = |t|^2$ as functions of the angle of incidence θ_1 for media with given impedance η and velocity v. Since the characteristic impedance η is generally complex (e.g., for lossy media), the reflection and transmission coefficients are generally complex. When η_1 and η_2 are real, total reflection and total transmission may occur at certain angles:

- **Total reflection.** For all waves, if $v_1 < v_2$, the reflection is total, i.e., $\mathcal{R} = 1$, for all incidence angles $\theta_1 \geq \theta_c$, where $\theta_c = \sin^{-1}(v_1/v_2)$ is the critical angle.
- **Total transmission.** For electromagnetic waves of parallel polarization and for longitudinal acoustic waves, the transmittance $\mathcal{T} = 1$ and the reflectance $\mathcal{R} = 0$ at a special incidence angle $\theta_B = \tan^{-1}(\eta_1/\eta_2)$, called the Brewster angle.

Reflection at boundaries involving anisotropic media may result in partial conversion of an electromagnetic wave from one polarization to another. Likewise, reflection of an elastic wave at a boundary with a solid medium can result in conversion between a compressional and a shear wave. This occurs, for example, when a seismic wave reflects at boundaries between different layers of earth. In this case, there are four reflection coefficients for the P-waves and S-waves: $\mathcal{R}_{PP}, \mathcal{R}_{PS}, \mathcal{R}_{SP}, \mathcal{R}_{SS}$. These obey equations known as the **Zoeppritz equations**.

▶ Problems 2.2-5–2.2-7

Multilayer Transmission and Reflection

The transmission and reflection of a plane wave through the multiple boundaries of a layered medium may be determined by tracing reflections and transmissions at the boundaries, and including the effect of propagation through the media in-between. For a single layer of width d with two boundaries, the amplitude transmittance and reflectance are given by the **Airy's formulas:**

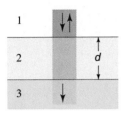

$$t_{13} = \frac{t_{12} t_{23} \exp(-j\varphi)}{1 - r_{21} r_{23} \exp(-j2\varphi)}, \qquad (2.2\text{-}18)$$

$$r_{13} = r_{12} + \frac{t_{12} t_{21} r_{23} \exp(-j2\varphi)}{1 - r_{21} r_{23} \exp(-j2\varphi)}, \qquad (2.2\text{-}19)$$
Airy's Formulas

where t_{12} and r_{12} are the amplitude transmittance and reflectance at the first boundary, and t_{23} and r_{23} are the amplitude transmittance and reflectance at the second boundary, and $\varphi = kd$ is the phase shift encountered by the wave as it travels through the width d of the layer in-between.

Anti-Reflection Impedance-Matching Layers

The reflection at the boundary between two media may be eliminated, or reduced, by use of a layer of a third medium with an intermediate impedance. By use of the Airy formulas, it can be shown that if the width of the layer equals a quarter of the wavelength in the layer, so that $\phi = \pi/2$, then the overall reflectance vanishes if

$$\eta_2 = \sqrt{\eta_1 \eta_3}, \qquad (2.2\text{-}20)$$

where η_1 and η_3 are the impedances of the original media and η_2 is the impedance of the anti-reflection layer.

For optical waves, thin films are used as anti-reflection coatings to minimize the reflection at the boundary between air and glass. Likewise, the transmission of ultrasonic waves from air into a denser medium, such as the human body in medical applications or metal in nondestructive testing applications, is enhanced by use of a layer of a third medium with impedance satisfying (2.2-20).

▶ Problem 2.2-8

Nonplanar Refractive Surfaces

Nonplanar boundaries may be used to modify the wavefront of a wave, since they introduce different refractions at different positions. A spherical boundary is often used to convert a plane wave into a spherical wave, i.e., focus the plane wave. One or more spherical boundaries convert a spherical wave emitted from a point to another spherical wave centered at a distant point. These are the principal properties of the lens. Lenses are used for focusing and imaging. Figure 2.2-10 illustrates the construction of an optical and an acoustic lens (e.g., using a sapphire rod with an embedded niobium titanate spherical material).

The laws of reflection and refraction are applicable to planar boundaries that extend over distances much greater than the wavelength. If the boundaries change rapidly over distances comparable to a wavelength, these laws are not applicable and the problem must be treated as a scattering problem. For example, the dimensions of a radiowave or microwave parabolic mirror (dish), which focus the wave by reflection, must be much larger than a wavelength.

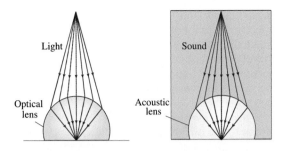

Figure 2.2-10 Optical and acoustic lenses.

C. Scattering

Wave scattering from fine or coarse inhomogeneities, or from vibrating molecules or suspended or moving particles in the medium, is important in subsurface imaging since it can be a valuable source of information on the signature and properties of the scatterers. Scattering may also result in attenuating or diverting the waves involved in the imaging process. There are numerous types of scattering, which may be classified into the following general categories:

- **Elastic and inelastic scattering.** In elastic scattering, the frequency of the scattered wave is the same as that of the incident wave – there is no exchange of energy with the medium, only the direction is changed. An example is the scattering from fine or coarse inhomogeneities or rigid bodies, as in Rayleigh and Mie scattering, which are described in this section. Inelastic scattering involves change of frequency and exchange of energy with molecules or moving particles. An example is luminescence, fluorescence, and Raman scattering, which are described in Sec. 2.3A.
- **Linear and nonlinear scattering.** In linear scattering, the amplitude of the scattered wave is proportional to that of the incident wave and the principle of superposition applies. In nonlinear scattering, the amplitudes of the scattered and incident waves are nonlinearly related. Examples include harmonic generation and stimulated scattering processes, which are described in Sec. 2.3B.

Rayleigh Scattering

Rayleigh scattering is a form of elastic scattering engendered by variations in the medium caused, for example, by the presence of particles whose sizes are much smaller than the wavelength or by random inhomogeneities at a scale finer than a wavelength.

Scattering of a Scalar Wave from a Point Object.   If a scalar plane wave of complex amplitude U_0 traveling in a homogeneous medium encounters a small object with properties different from the surrounding medium, then a spherical wave centered about the object is generated (Fig. 2.2-11). The dimensions of the object must be much smaller than the wavelength so that the object may be regarded as a point.

It will be shown in the next subsection that for an object located at the origin ($\mathbf{r} = \mathbf{0}$), the complex amplitude of the scattered spherical wave is

$$U_{\mathrm{s}}(\mathbf{r}) = S \frac{e^{-\mathrm{j}kr}}{4\pi r}, \tag{2.2-21}$$

where

$$S = (k_{\mathrm{s}}^2 - k^2)VU_0 = \omega^2(v_{\mathrm{s}}^{-2} - v^{-2})VU_0. \tag{2.2-22}$$

Here, V is the volume of the scattering object, k and k_s are the wavenumbers in the background and the object media, respectively, and v and v_s are the associated phase velocities. Thus, the amplitude of the scattered wave S is proportional to the amplitude of the incident wave U_0, the volume V, and the square of the frequency ω. The intensity of the scattered wave is therefore proportional to ω^4, so that waves of short wavelength undergo substantially greater scattering than long wavelengths. Rayleigh scattering is responsible for the blue color of the sky.

The amplitude of the scattered wave is also proportional to $(k_s^2 - k^2)$. Therefore, for an electromagnetic wave, it is proportional to the difference of the dielectric constants of the background and object $(\epsilon_{rs} - \epsilon_r)$. For an optical wave, it is proportional to the difference of the squared refractive indexes $(n_s^2 - n^2)$. For an ultrasonic wave, it is proportional to the difference of the density-compressibility product $(\rho_s \kappa_s - \rho \kappa)$.

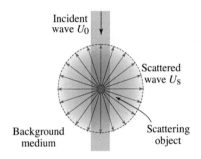

Incident wave U_0

Scattered wave U_S

Background medium

Scattering object

Figure 2.2-11   A scalar plane wave incident on a scattering point object creates a spherical scattered wave.

The intensity of the scattered wave,

$$I_s = |U_s|^2 = \left(k_s^2 - k^2\right)^2 \frac{V^2}{(4\pi r)^2} I_0, \tag{2.2-23}$$

is inversely proportional to the radial distance r but is independent of the direction so that the total scattered power $P_s = I_s 4\pi r^2$. Using the relations $k = \omega/v = 2\pi/\lambda$, $k_s = \omega/v_s$, where λ is the wavelength in the background medium, the scattered power and intensity may be related to the incident intensity by:

$$P_s = \sigma_s I_0, \qquad I_s = \frac{\sigma_s}{4\pi r^2} I_0, \tag{2.2-24}$$

where

$$\sigma_s = \left(\frac{v^2 - v_s^2}{v_s^2}\right)^2 \left(\frac{2\pi}{\lambda}\right)^4 \frac{V^2}{4\pi}, \tag{2.2-25}$$

called the **scattering cross-section**, may be regarded as the area of an aperture that intercepts the incident wave and collects an amount of power equal to the actual scattered power.

If the scattering object is a sphere of radius a, then $V = 4\pi a^3/3$ and

$$\sigma_s = \left(\pi a^2\right) \frac{64}{9}\pi^4 \left(\frac{v^2 - v_s^2}{v_s^2}\right)^2 \left(\frac{a}{\lambda}\right)^4, \tag{2.2-26}$$

i.e., is equal to the product of the physical area of the scatterer πa^2, which intercept the incident intensity, and a small dimensionless factor proportional to $(a/\lambda)^4$. For example, if $a/\lambda = 0.1$ and $(v^2 - v_s^2)/v_s^2 = 0.1$, then this factor equals $\approx 7 \times 10^{-4}$, or 0.07%. The power P_s is reradiated isotropically and the remaining power in the incident wave is diminished by this small amount. As we will subsequently see, if the number of scatterers is large, the overall effect can result in significant attenuation of the incident wave.

Scattering of a Transverse Electromagnetic Wave from a Point Object. While the scattering of a scalar wave from a small object is isotropic, the scattering of a transverse wave, such as an electromagnetic wave, has a nonuniform directional pattern. An incident plane wave oscillating along the direction of the unit vector $\hat{\mathbf{e}}$ (see Fig. 2.2-12) creates a source S given by (2.2-22) oscillating in the same direction $\hat{\mathbf{e}}$. The scattered wave generated by this source in the direction of the vector $\mathbf{k}$ is generated by the orthogonal component of the source, $S \sin \theta$, where θ is the angle between $\hat{\mathbf{e}}$ and $\mathbf{k}$, so that the amplitude of the scattered wave is given by (2.2-21) with S replaced by $S \sin \theta$. The intensity in (2.2-23) must therefore be multiplied by $\sin^2 \theta$. Consequently, no scattering occurs in the direction parallel to $\hat{\mathbf{e}}$ since no transverse wave can be created by such a source. Scattering is maximum when $\theta = 90°$, i.e., the direction of the scattered wave is orthogonal to $\hat{\mathbf{e}}$. The angular distribution of the scattered wave, therefore, has the donut-shaped pattern illustrated in Fig. 2.2-12. The total scattered power, which equals the integrated intensity, is two-thirds of the total scattered power in the isotropic (scalar) case. This may be shown by noting that the integral of an isotropic function and that of the function $\sin \theta$ over the surface of a sphere differ by a factor of 2/3:

$$\int_0^{2\pi} \int_0^{\pi} I_s\, r^2 \sin \theta\, d\theta\, d\varphi = 4\pi r^2 I_s, \qquad \int_0^{2\pi} \int_0^{\pi} I_s \sin^2 \theta\; r^2 \sin \theta\, d\theta\, d\varphi = \tfrac{8}{3}\pi r^2 I_s.$$

The scattering cross-section given by (2.2-25) must therefore be modified to

$$\sigma_s = \left(\frac{v^2 - v_s^2}{v_s^2}\right)^2 \left(\frac{2\pi}{\lambda}\right)^4 \frac{V^2}{6\pi}, \tag{2.2-27}$$

and

$$P_s = \sigma_s I_0, \qquad I_s = \frac{\sigma_s}{4\pi r^2} \sin^2 \theta\, I_0. \tag{2.2-28}$$

For a spherical scatterer (2.2-26) is modified to

$$\sigma_s = \left(\pi a^2\right) \tfrac{128}{27} \pi^4 \left(\frac{v^2 - v_s^2}{v_s^2}\right)^2 \left(\frac{a}{\lambda}\right)^4. \tag{2.2-29}$$

▶ Problem 2.2-9

Mie Scattering

Scattering from Large Objects. It is not easy to determine the scattering from an object extending over dimensions comparable to, or greater than, a wavelength. In the scalar case, the problem may be regarded as a wave traveling in an inhomogeneous medium and obeying the Helmholtz equation with a spatially varying wavenumber

$$\left[\nabla^2 + k^2(\mathbf{r})\right] U = 0. \tag{2.2-30}$$

Inside the scattering volume, $k(\mathbf{r}) = k_s(\mathbf{r}) = \omega/v_s(\mathbf{r})$, i.e., the scattering medium is allowed to be nonuniform. In the background medium, which is assumed to be

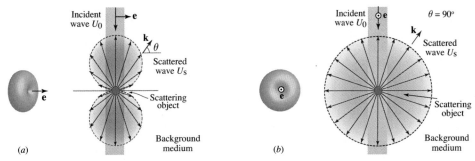

Figure 2.2-12 A transverse electromagnetic plane wave polarized in the direction of the unit vector ê scattered from a point object creates a scattered electric-dipole wave with a donut pattern. (*a*) Plane of polarization. (*b*) Orthogonal plane.

homogeneous, $k(\mathbf{r}) = k = \omega/v$ is uniform. By writing $k^2(\mathbf{r}) = k^2 + [k^2(\mathbf{r}) - k^2]$, (2.2-30) may be rewritten in the form of a Helmholtz equation with a source:

$$\left(\nabla^2 + k^2\right) U = -s, \tag{2.2-31}$$

where

$$s(\mathbf{r}) = [k_s^2(\mathbf{r}) - k^2]U(\mathbf{r}). \tag{2.2-32}$$

The solution of (2.2-31) is

$$U(\mathbf{r}) = \int_V s(\mathbf{r}')\frac{e^{-jk|\mathbf{r}-\mathbf{r}'|}}{4\pi\,|\mathbf{r} - \mathbf{r}'|}\,\mathrm{d}\mathbf{r}', \tag{2.2-33}$$

i.e., the scattered wave $U(\mathbf{r})$ is a superposition of spherical waves generated by a continuum of sources with amplitude $s(\mathbf{r}')$ at position $\mathbf{r}'$ within the volume of the scattering object. Unfortunately, the integral in (2.2-33) cannot be readily used to determine $U(\mathbf{r})$ since, in accordance with (2.2-32), the source $s(\mathbf{r}')$ is dependent on the scattered wave $U(\mathbf{r})$ itself, which is unknown.

The Born Approximation. If the scattering is weak, then it is safe to assume that the incident wave U_0 is unaffected by the process of scattering so that the total wavefunction U in the expression for the scattering source in (2.2-32) is approximately equal to the incident wavefunction U_0, i.e,

$$s(\mathbf{r}) \approx [k_s^2(\mathbf{r}) - k^2]U_0(\mathbf{r}). \tag{2.2-34}$$

This expression may be used in (2.2-33) to determine an approximation for the scattered wavefunction. This commonly used approximation is known as the Born approximation. Implicit in the assumption of weak scattering is the fact that the wave scattered from one point in the object is not subsequently scattered from another point, i.e., multiple scattering is a negligible second-order effect.

In the limiting case for which the volume V of the scattering object is much smaller than a wavelength, the source distribution in (2.2-34) may be expressed mathematically in terms of a delta function, i.e., $s(\mathbf{r}) \approx (k_s^2 - k^2)U_0 V \delta(\mathbf{r})$. When substituted in the integral in (2.2-33), the expressions in (2.2-21) and (2.2-22) are reproduced.

For objects of dimensions not much smaller than the wavelength, the integral in (2.2-33) must be evaluated to obtain the scattering pattern, which is sensitive to the size and shape of the scattering object. This type of scattering, illustrated in Fig. 2.2-13, is called **Mie scattering**. It is responsible for the white glare around light sources in the presence of mist and fog.

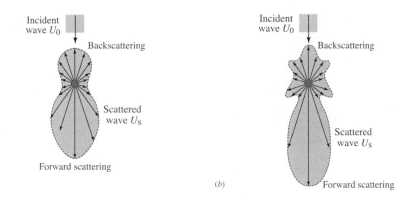

Figure 2.2-13   Mie scattering.

Dynamic Scattering

Doppler Shift.   If a wave of frequency ν and velocity v is reflected or scattered from an object moving with a velocity v_o in a direction at an angle θ, as shown in Fig. 2.2-14, then the frequency of the reflected wave ν_r is shifted by an amount $\Delta\nu_D = \nu_r - \nu$ given by

$$\nu_r - \nu = 2\frac{v_o \cos\theta}{v}\nu, \tag{2.2-35}$$

called the **Doppler shift**. This phenomenon is used to measure the velocity of moving targets.

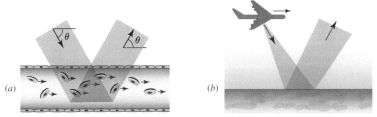

Figure 2.2-14   Doppler shift upon (a) scattering from a uniformly moving target and (b) scattering of a wave generated by a moving source.

Applications include: **Doppler radar**, which is used for weather measurements and air traffic control; **Doppler sonar**, which is used for marine and oceanic observations; **laser Doppler velocimetry**, which is used for measurement of the speed of fluids, e.g., blood flow. Likewise, when a wave of frequency ν is emitted from a source moving with a velocity v_s and is reflected from a stationary target at an angle θ, then the frequency of the reflected wave ν_r is shifted by an amount $\Delta\nu_D = 2(v_s \cos\theta/v)\nu$. This effect is used to measure the angle of a target in relation to the moving source.

Dynamic Scattering.   Rayleigh scattering from particles undergoing random thermal (Brownian) motion in a fluid (see Fig. 2.2-15) is accompanied by multiple Doppler shifts proportional to the components of the random particle velocities along the direction of the incident wave. The scattered wave will therefore have a finite spectral width corresponding to the multiple spectral shifts. While the incident wave is monochromatic and coherent (for example, an optical wave generated by a laser), the scattered wave is random (incoherent) and its intensity undergoes random fluctuations. By measuring these fluctuations, the spectral distribution may be determined and the velocity distribution estimated. Although Rayleigh scattering from a fixed particle is

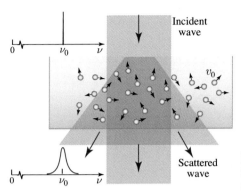

Figure 2.2-15 Rayleigh scattering from particles in Brownian motion is accompanied by spectral broadening.

a form of *elastic* scattering, the scattering from randomly moving particles involves spectral shifts and is technically *inelastic*. However, since these shifts are very small (because the particle velocities are significantly smaller than the speed of light), this type of scattering is known as **quasi-elastic light scattering**.

Dynamic light scattering may be used to measure the diffusion coefficient of the particles. Knowing the viscosity of the medium, the particle size can be calculated. Particle size distributions may also be estimated from the exact spectral distribution of the scattered light.

D. Diffusion

Multiple scattering occurs when waves propagate through media with a high density of scatterers, such as suspended particles, fine dust, or small-scale random irregularities or inhomogeneities. Such conditions exist in the atmosphere, biological tissue, and turbid media such as cloudy water. Since the wave changes direction as it bounces from one scatterer to the next, as shown in Fig. 2.2-16(a), the medium appears translucent and cannot be seen through clearly. For example, as illustrated in Fig. 2.2-16(b), light transmission through a sheet of ground glass is characterized by partial opacity as well as loss of resolution.

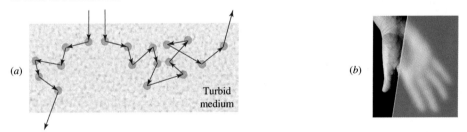

Figure 2.2-16 (a) Multiple scattering in a highly scattering or turbid medium. (b) Imaging through ground glass.

In such media, it is not practical to describe wave propagation in terms of the wave equation or to follow a wave as it bounces randomly from one scatterer to another before it leaves the medium. However, since the phase of the wave is randomized under these conditions, coherence is lost and interference effects are washed out, so that a description in terms of radiometric quantities is more appropriate. These include:

- Irradiance [W/m^2] = power crossing a unit area
- Radiance [W/(m^{2}sr)] = power per unit area in a cone of unit solid angle.

Wave propagation is then described in terms of radiation transport (or radiative transfer). We first consider the transmission and reflection of radiation in such media using idealized simple models before we turn into more complex descriptions.

Reflection and Transmission in a Scattering Medium

Attenuation Caused by Scattering.   Propagation through a medium with a high concentration of scatterers is accompanied by attenuation. The irradiance I (W/m^2) transported along the z axis in a medium with an average of N small scatterers per unit volume, each with a scattering cross-section σ_s, is attenuated exponentially with an attenuation coefficient

$$\mu_s = N\sigma_s. \qquad (2.2\text{-}36)$$

This may be shown by considering a cylinder with cross-sectional area A and incremental length dz along the direction of the incident radiation, the z axis. The cylinder has $NAdz$ scatterers, each scattering a small amount of power $\sigma_s I$. Therefore, the total change is

$$\Delta IA = -\sigma_s(NA\Delta z)I. \qquad (2.2\text{-}37)$$

It follows that $\Delta I = -\sigma_s NI\Delta z$ so that

$$\frac{dI}{dz} = -\mu_s I, \qquad (2.2\text{-}38)$$

where $\mu_s = N\sigma_s$ is called the **scattering coefficient**. The solution of this equation is $I(z) = I(0)\exp(-\mu_s z)$ so that $I(z)$ decays exponentially with an attenuation coefficient equal to the scattering coefficient μ_s [cm^{-1}]. The inverse μ_s^{-1} (cm) represents the **mean free path**, i.e., the average distance between two consecutive scattering events.

Radiation traveling in media exhibiting combined scattering and absorption is attenuated with an attenuation coefficient equal to the sum of the two coefficients:

$$\mu = \mu_a + \mu_s. \qquad (2.2\text{-}39)$$

where μ_a is the absorption coefficient (previously denoted as α_a). Clearly, the wavelength dependence of these two coefficients is different since they are based on different physical effects.

Reflection Caused by Scattering.   When radiation travels through a scattering medium, backscattering at different points along the path adds up. After traveling a distance z in the forward direction, an initial irradiance I_0 drops to $I = I_0 \exp(-\mu z)$. The contribution to the backscattered wave generated between z and $z+dz$ is therefore $\mu_s I dz = \mu_s I_0 \exp(-\mu z)dz$. Upon traveling another distance z in the backward direction, the intensity of this contribution drops by another factor $\exp(-\mu z)$, becoming $\mu_s I_0 \exp(-2\mu z)dz$. Therefore, for a layer of thickness d, the accumulated backscattered intensity is the integral

$$I_s = \int_0^d \mu_s I_0 \exp(-2\mu z)\, dz = I_0 \frac{\mu_s}{2\mu}\left[1 - \exp(-2\mu d)\right].$$

In the presence of a bottom reflector with reflectance $\mathcal{R}_b$, the intensity $I_0 \exp(-\mu d)$ that arrives at the bottom is multiplied by $\mathcal{R}_b$ and attenuated once more on its way back, generating an intensity $I_1 = I_0 \mathcal{R}_b \exp(-2\mu d)$. The sum of the backscattered and reflected intensities $I_s + I_1$ divided by the initial intensity I_0 provides the overall reflectance of the layer:

$$\mathcal{R} = \frac{1}{2} \frac{\mu_s}{\mu} [1 - \exp(-2\mu d)] + \mathcal{R}_b \exp(-2\mu d). \tag{2.2-40}$$

This is called the diffuse reflectance of the layer. For a thick layer of the medium, such that $\mu d \gg 1$, $\exp(-2\mu d) \ll 1$ and $\mathcal{R} \approx \mu_s/2\mu = \mu_s/2(\mu_s + \mu_a)$. The ratio

$$\mathcal{A} = \frac{\mu_s}{\mu_s + \mu_a} \tag{2.2-41}$$

is called the **albedo** of the medium. It determines the diffuse reflectance of the thick medium and is proportional to the fraction of the extinction coefficient attributed to scattering.

The transmittance of the layer $\mathcal{T} = I_t/I_0$ may similarly be determined by the integral

$$\mathcal{T} = \int_0^d \exp(-\mu z)\mu_s \exp[-\mu(d - z)]\, dz = \mu_s d \exp(-\mu d). \tag{2.2-42}$$

For a sufficiently thick medium ($\mu d \gg 1$), $\mathcal{T} \approx 0$, so that all radiation is either absorbed or reflected.

The Kubelka–Munk Model.   In the previous model of propagation in a scattering medium, backscattering of the incoming radiation was included, but backscattering of the backscattered radiation was not. The Kubelka–Munk model includes this effect by expressing the changes of the intensity of the downward and upward radiation, I_d and I_u, in the form of coupled differential equations

$$\frac{dI_d}{dz} = -\mu I_d + \mu_s I_u \tag{2.2-43}$$

$$-\frac{dI_u}{dz} = -\mu I_u + \mu_s I_d, \tag{2.2-44}$$

where $\mu = \mu_s + \mu_a$. The first terms in the right-hand sides of these equations represent attenuation. The second term in the right-hand side of (2.2-43) represents backscattering of the upward radiation, which feeds the downward radiation. Likewise, the second term in the right-hand side of (2.2-44) represents backscattering of the downward radiation, which feeds the upward radiation. For a layer extending between $z = 0$ and $z = d$, if $\mathcal{R}_b = I_u(d)/I_d(d)$ is the reflectance of the bottom boundary, then the solution of (2.2-43) and (2.2-44) under this boundary condition leads to the following expression for the overall diffuse reflectance $\mathcal{R} = I_u(0)/I_d(0)$,

$$\mathcal{R} = \frac{(\mathcal{A} - \mathcal{R}_b)\tanh\left(\mu d\sqrt{1 - \mathcal{A}^2}\right) + \mathcal{R}_b\sqrt{1 - \mathcal{A}^2}}{(1 - \mathcal{A}\mathcal{R}_b)\tanh\left(\mu d\sqrt{1 - \mathcal{A}^2}\right) + \sqrt{1 - \mathcal{A}^2}}, \tag{2.2-45}$$

If $\mu_s \ll \mu_a$, i.e., scattering is much weaker than absorption, then $\mathcal{A} \ll 1$, and (2.2-45) reproduces (2.2-40).

Equation (2.2-45) for the reflectance is useful in acquiring information on the absorption and scattering coefficients, the depth, and the bottom reflectance. Applications include underwater and skin imaging (see Sec. 6.4). For example, if $\mathcal{R}_b = 0$, i.e., the bottom boundary is nonreflective (*black*) and if $d \to \infty$, i.e., the layer is sufficiently thick so that $\tanh(\mu d\sqrt{1 - A^2}) \to 1$, then (2.2-45) simplifies to

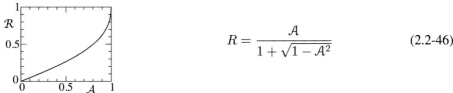

$$R = \frac{A}{1 + \sqrt{1 - A^2}} \qquad (2.2\text{-}46)$$

so that R is completely determined by the albedo A. This equation may be inverted to yield $A = 2R/(1 + R^2)$, so that the ratio μ_s/μ may be readily estimated by measurement of the reflectance R.

Effect of Reflectance at the Boundary.   If a turbid medium is illuminated from an adjacent medium of different impedance, then the overall reflectance may be obtained by tracing the transmitted and reflected radiation. If $\mathcal{T}_{12}$, $\mathcal{T}_{21}$, $\mathcal{R}_{12}$, and $\mathcal{R}_{21}$ are the transmittance and reflectance of the boundary in the directions shown, and if $\mathcal{R}_2$ is the diffuse reflectance of the turbid medium, as given by (2.2-40) or (2.2-45), then the overall reflectance of the boundary and the turbid layer underneath is

$$\mathcal{R} = \mathcal{R}_{12} + \mathcal{T}_{12}\mathcal{T}_{21}\mathcal{R}_2 \frac{1}{1 - \mathcal{R}_{21}\mathcal{R}_2}. \qquad (2.2\text{-}47)$$

The first term $\mathcal{R}_{12}$ represents direct reflectance from the boundary. The term $\mathcal{T}_{12}\mathcal{T}_{21}\mathcal{R}_2$ represents reflectance of the turbid medium, including double transmission through the boundary. The ratio $1/(1 - \mathcal{R}_{21}\mathcal{R}_2) = 1 + (\mathcal{R}_{21}\mathcal{R}_2) + (\mathcal{R}_{21}\mathcal{R}_2)^2 + \cdots$ contains terms representing single, double, and multiple internal reflections within the turbid medium. This expression is similar to the Airy's formula (2.2-19), which is applicable to the reflection of a coherent wave from a two-layer medium.

Effect of Scattering Anisotropy.   The previous expressions for the reflectance of a scattering medium do not account for the anisotropic radiation pattern of the scattering process, which can be significant for large scatterers (as in Mie scattering). One measure of the degree of scattering anistropy is the mean cosine $g = \langle \cos\theta \rangle$, called the **scattering anisotropy coefficient**. For isotropic scattering, the angular distribution $p(\theta)$ is uniform so that $g = 0$. For distributions for which forward scattering is much stronger than side or backscattering, g can be near unity. One way to describe an *anisotropic* process with a scattering coefficient μ_s and an anisotropy coefficient g is in terms of an equivalent *isotropic* scattering process with a smaller scattering coefficient

$$\mu_s' = (1 - g)\mu_s, \qquad (2.2\text{-}48)$$

called the **reduced scattering coefficient**. The macroscopic average behavior of the two processes is equivalent. For example, if $g = 0.9$, $\mu_s' = 0.1\mu_s$, so that the mean free path $1/\mu_s' = 10 \times 1/\mu_s$, i.e., 10 anisotropic scattering events are approximated by a single isotropic scattering event. With this equivalence, expressions for the reflectance and transmittance through the scattering medium that were derived under the assumption of isotropy may be readily used. For example, the reflectance in (2.2-40) is proportional to the **reduced or transport albedo**

$$A' = \frac{\mu_s'}{\mu_s' + \mu_a}. \qquad (2.2\text{-}49)$$

Multiflux Model.   One limitation of the Kubelka–Munk model is that it only considers two directions, i.e., accounts for only forward and backward scattering. This model works surprisingly well to characterize the reflection of paint, skin, and other layered media. Multiflux models use a finite set of directions representing some tessellation of the unit sphere and express the energy fluxes in terms of coupled differential equations. Such models are more useful in describing propagation in heterogeneous three-dimensional tissues. This subject is beyond the scope of this textbook.

Monte Carlo Models.   Monte Carlo models consider light to travel in straight lines between scattering or absorption events, and use random number generators to simulate the change of direction that occurs at each scattering event in accordance with the scattering function $p(\theta)$. The result is a set of different trajectories that are averaged to determine the reflectance and transmittance of the medium. For accurate simulation, in principle, knowledge of the scattering phase function is required. In practice, for reflectance or transmittance measurements, multiple scattering averages over the phase functions and only the scattering coefficient and anisotropy are required. Monte Carlo models are useful, provided that the medium can be considered infinite and homogeneous in the two transverse directions. A Monte Carlo computer program is available for media composed of multiple layers.[2] It can be used in other cases, but becomes computationally costly with increasing medium complexity.

▶ Problem 2.2-10

Diffusion Model

It is helpful to visualize the energy transport process in terms of a large collection of *particles* transporting energy, and such particles are conveniently called *photons*, although this is not a quantum phenomenon. Photons migrate through the medium in Brownian motion along random trajectories, as illustrated in Fig. 2.2-16(a). The average photon flux density φ (particles per second per unit area, also called the *fluence*) obeys radiative transfer equations. When the scattering is sufficiently strong so that scattering is effectively isotropic (independent of direction), these equations may be approximated by a partial differential equation – the heat equation (also called the diffusion equation):

$$\frac{1}{v}\frac{\partial \varphi}{\partial t} = D\,\nabla^2 \varphi, \qquad (2.2\text{-}50)$$

where v is the velocity of light in the medium and D is a constant called the **diffusion coefficient**[3] (units of [m]). The diffusion coefficient is related to the reduced scattering coefficient $\mu'_s = (1-g)\mu_s$ by $D = 1/3\mu'_s$. An initially nonuniform spatial distribution of φ gradually becomes uniform as time passes, much like heat. Given appropriate boundary conditions, this equation may be solved analytically or numerically.

Photon-Density Waves.   The imaging of objects embedded in turbid media may be facilitated by modulating the optical intensity sinuosoidally at an angular frequency Ω, which is necessarily much smaller than the angular frequency of light ω. In this case, φ varies as $\Phi \exp(\mathrm{j}\Omega t)$, so that (2.2-50) gives

$$\left(\nabla^2 - \mathrm{j}\frac{\Omega}{vD}\right)\Phi = 0. \qquad (2.2\text{-}51)$$

---

[2]L. Wang, S. L. Jacques, and L. Zheng, MCML – Monte Carlo modeling of light transport in multi-layered tissues, *Computer Methods and Programs in Biomedicine*, Vol. 47, pp. 131–146, 1995.

[3]When this equation describes heat conduction, φ is the temperature and vD is the thermal diffusivity.

This equation is mathematically identical to the Helmholtz equation $(\nabla^2 + k^2)\Phi = 0$, with

$$k^2 = -j\frac{\Omega}{vD} = -j\frac{3\Omega}{v}\mu_s'. \tag{2.2-52}$$

It follows that φ propagates like a wave, called the photon-density wave, with a complex wavenumber

$$k = \beta_e - j\alpha_e = \sqrt{-j3\Omega\mu_s'/v}.$$

This wave is therefore a damped wave with attenuation coefficient α_e and propagation constant β_e given by

$$\alpha_e = \beta_e = \sqrt{\frac{3\Omega}{2v}\mu_s'}. \tag{2.2-53}$$

Since the propagation wavelength $\lambda_e = 2\pi/\beta_e = 2\pi/\alpha_e$, the penetration depth $1/\alpha_e = \lambda_e/2\pi$, i.e., is smaller than the propagation wavelength, so that the wave is very highly damped. Since the penetration depth is dependent on the modulation frequency Ω different frequencies can be used to reach different depths. Also, since the phase velocity $v_e = \Omega/\beta_e = \sqrt{2v\Omega/3\mu_s'}$ is strongly dependent on Ω, strong dispersion, which causes the temporal spreading of pulses, is inherent in this type of wave. Otherwise, the photon-density wave reflects, refracts, and diffracts just like an ordinary wave. The generation of a photon-density spherical wave by means of point source is illustrated in Fig. 2.2-17.

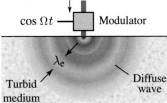

$\cos\Omega t$ — Modulator

Turbid medium

λ_e

Diffuse wave

Figure 2.2-17   A light source whose intensity is modulated at an angular frequency Ω creates in a turbid medium a damped photon-density spherical wave of wavelength λ_e and penetration depth $\alpha_e = 2\pi/\lambda_e$.

Diffuse Waves in Lossy Media.   If the turbid medium is also absorptive, then the diffusion equation becomes

$$\frac{1}{v}\frac{\partial\varphi}{\partial t} = D\nabla^2\varphi - \mu_a\varphi, \tag{2.2-54}$$

where $D^{-1} = 3(\mu_s' + \mu_a)$. This corresponds to a Helmholtz equation

$$(\nabla^2 + k^2)\phi = 0, \qquad k^2 = -(j\Omega/v + \mu_a)/D = -3(\mu_s' + \mu_a)(\mu_a + j\Omega/v). \tag{2.2-55}$$

The attenuation coefficient α_e and the propagation constant β_e of the photon-density wave may then be determined from the relation

$$\beta_e - j\alpha_e = \sqrt{-3(\mu_s' + \mu_a)(\mu_a + j\Omega/v)}, \tag{2.2-56}$$

and are dependent on both of the medium parameters μ_s' and μ_a, as well as the modulation frequency Ω. In the special case, $\Omega = 0$, i.e., the incoming light is steady instead of modulated, $\beta_e = 0$, i.e., the photon density is simply a decaying function (not propagating) with an attenuation coefficient $\alpha_e = \sqrt{3\mu_a(\mu_s' + \mu_a)}$, which is commonly denoted in the literature by the symbol μ_{eff}.

▶ Problems 2.2-11, 2.2-12

2.3   Wave Interaction II

A. Inelastic Scattering

Rayleigh and Mie scattering entail no change in the wavelength, i.e., the scattered photon has the same wavelength (and energy) as the incident photon. Such energy-conserving interaction is known as **elastic scattering**. Luminescence, fluorescence, and Raman scattering are examples of inelastic scattering for which the wavelength is altered by the scattering process. These processes are useful in subsurface imaging, since they reveal the spectral signature of the atoms and molecules that cause the scattering.

Photoluminescence and Fluorescence

Photoluminescence involves the resonant absorption of a photon via a transition between the ground state and a real excited state; the subsequent relaxation of the excited state back to the ground state results in the emission of a luminescence photon, as illustrated in Fig. 2.3-1. The emitted photon has a longer wavelength (smaller energy) than the incident photon. Nonradiative downward transitions can be part of the process, as indicated by the dashed line in Fig. 2.3-1. An example is the glow emitted by some materials after exposure to ultraviolet light. The term **radioluminescence** is used when the photons are in the X-ray or γ-ray region.

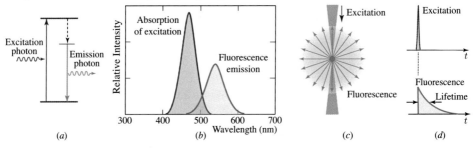

Figure 2.3-1   Photoluminescence/fluorescence. (*a*) Energy-level diagram showing transitions for absorption and emission. (*b*) Spectra of absorption and emission. (*c*) Spatial distributions of excitation and emission. (*d*) Temporal distributions of emission following an excitation pulse.

Fluorescence is a special case of photoluminescence satisfying certain transition conditions. Fluorescence lifetimes are usually relatively short (often 0.1 to 20 ns), so that the luminescence photon is promptly emitted following excitation (this is in contrast to *phosphorescence*, which is characterized by transitions with much longer lifetimes, i.e., substantial delay between excitation and emission). Fluorescent materials (e.g., dyes) have specific excitation and emission spectra and fluoresce only when the excitation is applied. In **fluorescence microscopy**, the spatial distribution of fluorescence can be used to map the concentration of the fluorescing molecules (fluorochromes), which may be made to attach to specific molecules to be imaged. Fluorescent proteins have become the contrast marker of choice in biological imaging (see Sec. 2.4). Further, since the fluorescence lifetime is characteristic of the molecules and their chemical environment, **fluorescence lifetime imaging** is used to map this environment (e.g., pH, ion concentration, or oxygen saturation in cellular imaging).

Raman Scattering

Raman scattering is an inelastic optical scattering process involving the interaction of light with vibrational, rotational, or other low-frequency modes of the material, including nuclear vibrations of chemical bonds. Following the interaction with a mode of resonance frequency ν_R (energy $h\nu_R$), an incident probe photon of frequency ν_P

emerges either at a lower frequency $\nu_S = \nu_P - \nu_R$ (Stokes scattering) or at a higher frequency $\nu_A = \nu_P + \nu_R$ (anti-Stokes scattering), as displayed in Fig. 2.3-2(a) and (b), respectively. The alteration of photon frequency and energy is brought about by an exchange of energy with the mode so that energy is conserved at the photon level. In **Stokes scattering**, the photon imparts energy to the material system, whereas the reverse occurs in **anti-Stokes scattering**. The shift in energy gives information about the energy of the various modes. For example, the energy distribution of the vibrational modes of the molecule provides a fingerprint of the chemical bonds, which uniquely identifies the molecule. Raman spectroscopy is therefore used for chemical sensing.

In contrast to fluorescence, the Raman effect is not a resonant effect, i.e., it can take place for incident light of any frequency. The excited state is regarded as a "virtual" state. For the fluorescence process (see Fig. 2.3-1), the incident light is completely absorbed and the system is transferred to a real excited state from which it can go to various lower states only after a certain resonance lifetime. Rayleigh scattering (see Sec. 2.2C) is similar to Raman scattering in the sense that the incident photon can have any frequency, but in Rayleigh scattering no frequency shift is encountered since the process is elastic.

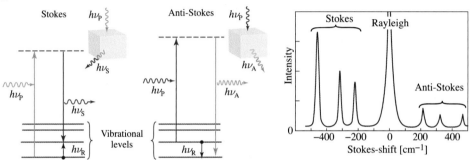

Figure 2.3-2   Energy transitions and Raman spectrum with three Stokes and three anti-Stokes lines. Frequency shifts measured from the frequency of the excitation laser are in units of wavenumber [cm^{-1}], where 100 cm^{-1} is equivalent to 3 THz.

The spectrum of light scattered from a material (gas, liquid, or solid) generally contains a Rayleigh-scattered component, at the incident frequency, together with red-shifted and blue-shifted sidebands corresponding to inelastically scattered Stokes and anti-Stokes components, respectively. Although the sideband power is typically weak for nonresonant interactions, lying about 10^{-7} below that of the incident light, Raman scattering is useful for characterizing materials. In crystalline materials, the vibrational spectrum is generally discrete and the Raman lines are narrow. Glasses, in contrast, have broad vibrational spectra that in turn give rise to broad Raman spectra.

X-Ray, γ-Ray, and Electron Scattering

Scattering of high-energy photons and electrons from matter takes many forms. In **Compton scattering**, medium-energy X-ray and γ-ray photons undergo inelastic scattering off electrons in matter resulting in scattered photons at reduced energy (longer wavelength) and changed direction (the electrons recoil and are ejected from their atoms). Compton scattering is material dependent (the materials with lower atomic number scatter more strongly than the those of higher numbers). **X-ray backscattering** is used for subsurface imaging applications, including advanced luggage and whole body scanners, which detect objects not detectable by regular X-ray scanners.

X-ray image of luggage. (After US Transportation Security Administration).

In certain materials, such as the alkali halides sodium iodide (NaI) and cesium iodide (CsI), X-ray photons are converted into visible photons, a process known as **scintillation**. When combined with an optical detector, X-ray scintillators may be used as X-ray detectors. High-energy photons bombarding an atomic nucleus may cause **electron–positron pair production**. As described in Sec. 4.1D, this process is used in **positron emission tomography (PET)**. An electron beam focused on matter may emits low-energy secondary electrons, light (a process known as **cathodoluminescence**) or X-rays. These emissions are used in various types of **electron microscopy**.

B. Nonlinear Scattering

Nonlinear Media.   In linear media, parameters such as the dielectric permittivity, the compressibility, the refractive index, and the absorption and scattering coefficients are characteristics of the medium that are independent of the amplitude or intensity of the wave. The following are fundamental consequences of linearity: (i) The principle of superposition is applicable. (ii) The speed of wave propagation is independent of the wave intensity. (iii) Two waves traveling in the same region do not interact. (iv) The frequency of the wave is not altered by passage through the medium. Linearity often fails when the wave is sufficiently intense since the properties of the medium become dependent on the wave amplitude. The medium is then said to be nonlinear and the following phenomena are exhibited: (i) The speed of the wave may depend on the wave's own intensity. (ii) Two waves traveling in the same region may interact and exchange energy, so that the principle of superposition is not applicable. (iii) The frequency of the wave may be altered as it travels through the medium.

In acoustics, nonlinear effects are exhibited in media such as tissue at levels of intensity readily generated by focused pulsed ultrasonic beams. Microbubbles, used as ultrasonic contrast agents for tissue imaging, exhibit nonlinear effects that can be used for ultrasonic imaging. In optics, the nonlinear behavior of certain crystals is readily observed by use of pulsed and focused laser beams.

Harmonic Generation

In a linear medium, the amplitude of the scattering source s is proportional to that of the incident wave u so that the scattered wave has the same frequency as the incident wave. This is not the case in a nonlinear medium and this results in a number of interesting phenomena.

Second-Harmonic Generation (SHG).   Certain media exhibit second-order nonlinearity of the form $s \propto u^2$. In such media, a wave of frequency $\nu = \omega/2\pi$ may generate a scattered wave of frequency 2ν since u^2 contains a term proportional to $(e^{j\omega t})^2 = e^{j2\omega t}$. This process is called second-harmonic generation. For optical waves, the process may be regarded as a combination of two photons, each of frequency ν and energy $h\nu$ to generate a photon of frequency 2ν and energy $2h\nu$. Similarly, two waves of frequencies ν_1 and ν_2 may interact and generate a third wave of frequency

$$\nu_1 + \nu_2 = \nu_3. \tag{2.3-1}$$

This process is called **sum frequency generation (SFG)**. Conservation of momentum requires that the wavevectors be related $(\mathbf{k}_1 + \mathbf{k}_2 = \mathbf{k}_3)$ so that the directions of the three waves are related.

Third-Harmonic Generation (THG).   Likewise, in third-order nonlinear media, $s \propto u^3$ so that a wave of frequency ν may generate a scattered wave of frequency 3ν in a process of third-harmonic generation. Four waves with frequencies related by

$$\nu_1 + \nu_2 = \nu_3 + \nu_4 \tag{2.3-2}$$

can be coupled within the medium in a process called four-wave mixing. Conditions of conservation of momentum dictate a fixed relation between the directions of the four waves.

Multiphoton Luminescence and Fluorescence

Two photons of the same energy may "cooperate" to raise the system to a higher energy level, where it undergoes photoluminescence or fluorescence, as shown schematically in Fig. 2.3-3. For example, a pair of photons, each with energy $h\nu_1$, arriving together at a molecule may be absorbed, a process known as **two-photon absorption**. The molecule subsequently emits a single photon with energy $h\nu_2 < 2\,h\nu_1$, and the process is called two-photon fluorescence. Since the probability of observing two independent photons arriving simultaneously at the same point is the square of the probability of observing a single such photon, the two-photon absorption rate is proportional to the square of the incident intensity I^2. This is an example of *nonlinear absorption*.

Two-photon fluorescence is the basis of an imaging technique known as **two-photon microscopy** (see Sec. 3.2B). A fluorescent molecule (**fluorophore**), linked to specific locations in a specimen, absorbs a pair of photons that arrive in its vicinity, and then emits a single fluorescence photon, which is detected.

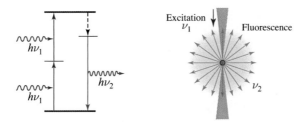

Figure 2.3-3   Two-photon fluorescence. Nonradiative relaxation is marked by the dashed line.

Multiphoton fluorescence is also useful in microscopy. Here, the rate of m-photon absorption is proportional to I^m, where $m = 1, 2, \ldots$ and the energy of the fluorescent photon is $h\nu_2 < mh\nu_1$.

▶ Problem 2.3-1

Stimulated Raman Scattering (SRS)

Two optical waves at the pump frequency ν_P and the Stokes frequency ν_S may interact with a vibrational mode of resonance frequency $\nu_R = \nu_P - \nu_S$ via *stimulated* Raman scattering, as shown in Fig. 2.3-4. Assuming that the vibrational mode is initially unexcited, then a Stokes photon of energy $h\nu_S$ may stimulate a process by which a pump photon scatters from the vibrational mode and generates an additional Stokes photon *in the same direction*, thereby amplifying the Stokes light *coherently*. The surplus energy of the pump photon is transferred to the vibrational mode. Known as SRS, this process bears some similarity to the process of stimulated emission, which underlies lasers (except that the latter is a resonant process, i.e., two optical waves with any frequencies such that $\nu_P - \nu_S = \nu_R$ would work). Like Raman scattering, SRS is useful as a spectroscopic and chemical sensing tool, since it can reveal the underlying vibrational characteristics of the material. However, it requires signicant power and thus imposes stringent limits on the material.

Coherent Anti-Stokes Raman Spectroscopy (CARS)

The sensitivity of Raman spectroscopy can be enhanced by making use of two probe waves interacting with the vibrational mode of the material under investigation, as

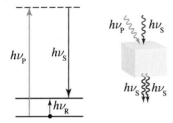

Figure 2.3-4 Stimulated Raman scattering (SRS).

shown in Fig. 2.3-5. The first probe excites the mode via a stimulated Raman process and creates a Stokes wave. The second probe interacts with the excited mode via an anti-Stokes process, bringing the mode to its ground state and generating an anti-Stokes wave, which is measured. As a result of the two processes, no net energy is deposited to the vibrational mode. However, the extended medium acts as a third-order nonlinear medium that coherently mixes the four waves and ultimately generates a strong anti-Stokes wave. If the frequencies of the two pump waves and the Stokes and anti-Stokes waves are ν_{P1}, ν_{P2}, ν_S, and ν_A, respectively, and ν_R is the frequency of the vibrational mode, then

$$\nu_S = \nu_{P1} - \nu_R \qquad \text{Stokes process}$$

$$\nu_A = \nu_{P2} + \nu_R \qquad \text{Anti-Stokes process}$$

$$\nu_S + \nu_A = \nu_{P1} + \nu_{P2}, \qquad 4-\text{wave mixing condition}$$

which is the condition of four-wave mixing in a third-order nonlinear material [see (2.3-2)].

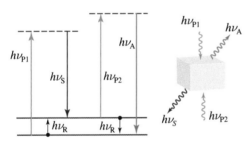

Figure 2.3-5 Coherent anti-Stokes Raman spectroscopy (CARS).

The process, called **coherent anti-Stokes Raman scattering (CARS)**, is used for identifying chemical samples with excellent chemical sensitivity and selectivity. It is also used for chemically mapping biological cells and tissues.

In comparison with conventional Raman spectroscopy, CARS produces a much stronger signal (typically greater by several orders of magnitude). This may be attributed to the stimulated (as opposed to spontaneous) nature of the molecular excitation, and the coherent addition of the anti-Stokes waves generated by the different molecules.

While the emitted wave in Raman spectroscopy is red-shifted, CARS emission is blue-shifted relative to the incident probe beams. This is preferred when dealing with samples that fluoresce, since the red-shifted fluorescence does not overlap with the CARS emission. Additionally, because of the nature of four-wave mixing, the anti-Stokes wave may be emitted in a separate direction from the pump beams, thus facilitating the detection process.

C. Nuclear Magnetic Resonance

The interaction of a radiowave with the magnetic spins of protons in the nuclei of atoms, such as hydrogen, is an electromagnetic scattering effect that has been success-fully exploited in **magnetic resonance imaging (MRI)**.

When the magnetic dipole associated with a nuclear spin is subjected to a steady magnetic field $\mathbf{B}_0$, a magnetic torque is created forcing the spin vector to rotate about the direction of $\mathbf{B}_0$ at a frequency ω_0 proportional to B_0. A radiowave $\mathbf{B}_1$ of frequency $\omega = \omega_0$ can drive this resonant system to emit a scattered radiowave at the same frequency, as illustrated in Fig. 2.3-6(a). The strength of the emission (the scattering cross-section) is proportional to the local density of spins (atoms). This effect is called **nuclear magnetic resonance (NMR)**. The relation between the resonance frequency (called the Larmor frequency) and the steady magnetic field is $\omega_0 = \gamma B_0$, where $\gamma = 2.675 \times 10^8$ s^{-1}T^{-1} is a constant known as the gyromagnetic ratio. For $B_0 = 1$ T = 10000 Gauss), the resonance frequency is $\nu_0 = \omega_0/2\pi \approx 42.6$ MHz. Modern MRI machines operate with magnetic fields of a few tesla.[4]

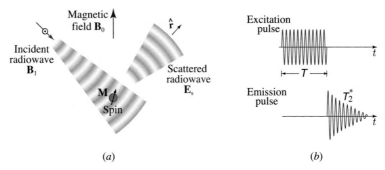

(a)   (b)

Figure 2.3-6   (a) Scattering of a radiowave from nuclear magnetic spins subjected to a steady magnetic field. (b) An incident radiowave pulse of duration T at the resonance frequency drives the spin system to emit a scattered pulse at the same frequency.

Physical Model of NMR.   The principal physics of NMR is captured by the **Bloch equation**, which describes the dynamics of the magnetization vector $\mathbf{M}$ (the sum of the magnetic dipole moments associated with the spins in a unit volume):

$$\frac{d\mathbf{M}}{dt} = -\gamma \mathbf{B} \times \mathbf{M}, \tag{2.3-3}$$

where $\mathbf{B} = \mathbf{B}_0 + \mathbf{B}_1$ is the total magnetic field. These fields control the magnetization vector $\mathbf{M}$ via (2.3-3). The solution of the Bloch equation (2.3-3) is a vector $\mathbf{M}$ that rotates about the direction of the vector $\mathbf{B}$ at an angular velocity γB without changing its magnitude M, as illustrated schematically in the drawing next to (2.3-3). In the absence of the radiowave, $\mathbf{B} = \mathbf{B}_0$ is constant so that $\mathbf{M}$ rotates about a fixed direction at an angular velocity $\omega_0 = \gamma B_0$. In the presence of the radiowave $\mathbf{B}_1$, the direction of $\mathbf{B}$ is itself time varying so that $\mathbf{M}$ rotates about a moving axis, much like the precession of a top.

---

[4]The Earth's magnetic field is about 0.5 Gauss = 5×10^{-5} T.

Radiation.   In accordance with electromagnetic theory, a magnetic dipole $\mathbf{M}$ at position $\mathbf{r} = \mathbf{0}$ pointing in the z direction and oscillating at frequency ω emits into free space an electromagnetic field in the azimuthal direction

$$E_\phi = \eta_0 k^2 M \sin\theta \frac{\exp(-jkr)}{4\pi r} \qquad (2.3\text{-}4)$$

at a distance r in the far zone (i.e., at distances much longer than the wavelength), where $k = \omega/c$. The total emitted field is the sum of the fields emitted by the oscillating magnetization vectors at all locations within the scattering object.

Excitation.   To maximize the scattering cross-section, the oscillating component of $\mathbf{M}$ must be maximum. This is accomplished by use of a radiowave pulse of a specific magnitude and duration in a direction orthogonal to the steady magnetic field (see Fig. 2.3-6). Before the application of the pulse, the spins are aligned along the axis of rotation (the direction of $\mathbf{B}_0$, which is taken to be the z axis); the oscillating component of $\mathbf{M}$ is therefore zero. The application of a radiowave pulse of magnitude $\mathbf{B}_1$ in the x direction causes the magnetization vector $\mathbf{M}$ to rotate about the x axis with an angular velocity $\omega_1 = \gamma B_1$ (while also rotating about the z axis with angular velocity $\omega_0 = \gamma B_0$). If the pulse duration T is such that $\omega_1 T = \pi/2$, then at the end of the pulse, $\mathbf{M}$ is rotated by $90°$, i.e., ends up lying in the x–y plane. After the radiowave pulse is removed, $\mathbf{M}$ rotates about the z axis at the resonance frequency ω_0. In this case, the oscillating component of $\mathbf{M}$ is maximum and the greatest emission is obtained. The process is illustrated in Fig 2.3-6(b).

Radiation Decay.   The idealized Bloch equation does not allow for decay of the magnitude of the emitted radiation. In reality, the three components of the magnetization vector M_x, M_y, and M_z do decay with different time constants depending on the medium:

- Interaction of the spins with the surrounding atoms results in loss of their alignment with the steady magnetic field and leads to decay of the axial component M_z with a time constant T_1 representing spin–lattice relaxation.
- The transverse components of $\mathbf{M}$ decay with a time constant T_2 as a result of phase decoherence. This is attributed to thermal effects introducing random variations of the relative phases among the spins that constitute the magnetization vector, thereby diminishing its magnitude.
- Inhomogeneities of the medium result in slight variations in the value of the local steady magnetic field. This results in slight variations in the associated resonance frequencies and the spin angular velocities, thereby diminishing the transverse components of $\mathbf{M}$. This effect has a time constant T_2^*, which is included in T_2.

In brain MRI, T_1 and T_2 are of the order of 0.5–1 s and 50–100 ms, respectively, and T_2^* is of the order of 40 ms for $B_0 = 1.5$ T.

Decay phenomena are captured in a revised Bloch equation:

$$\frac{d\mathbf{M}}{dt} = -\gamma \mathbf{B} \times \mathbf{M} - \frac{M_x \hat{\mathbf{x}} + M_y \hat{\mathbf{y}}}{T_2} + \frac{(M_0 - M_z)\hat{\mathbf{z}}}{T_1}, \qquad (2.3\text{-}5)$$

where M_0 is a constant.

Resurrected Radiation: Spin Echo.   If T_2^* is the shortest of all time constants, i.e., is the dominant cause of the decay of the emitted field, then the misalignment of the

spins may be reversed, thereby reviving the emission in the form of a pulse, called
spin echo. This may be accomplished by applying a second excitation pulse of twice
the area (i.e., a π pulse for which $\omega_1 T = \gamma B_1 T = \pi$). As illustrated in Fig. 2.3-
7, following the arrival of the first $\pi/2$ pulse, the spins rotate in the x-y plane with
an angular velocity ω_0. As a result of inhomogeneities in the medium, some spins
are slightly slower, while others are slightly faster. This results in an increasing spin
misalignment and concomitant decay of the transverse component of the magnetization
vector. The application of a π pulse causes a rotation of all spins by an angle of 180°
about the x axis. This brings back the spins to the x-y plane in reversed order, placing
the slow spins ahead of the fast ones. Upon further free rotation within the x–y plane,
the fast spins catch up with the slow ones, creating a temporary full alignment that lasts
for a short duration during which an echo pulse is emitted.

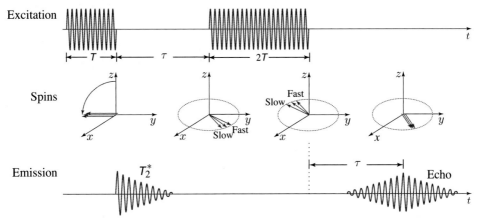

Figure 2.3-7   An incident radiowave pulse of duration T at the resonance frequency drives the spin
system to emit a scattered wave at the same frequency. The emitted wave decays rapidly as a result of
increasing misalignments between fast and slow spins. A second incident radiowave pulse of duration
$2T$ reverses the spins, placing the slow ahead of the fast. When they realign, an echo pulse is emitted.

The observation of the amplitudes and widths of the initial emitted pulse and the
spin echo pulse provide valuable information on the density of spins as well as other
medium properties, which enables **functional magnetic resonance imaging** (FMRI).

D. Fields and Waves in Inhomogeneous Media

Physical models for fields and waves in media with position-dependent properties is a
central problem in subsurface imaging, since the ultimate goal is to estimate the spatial
distribution of these properties by applying probes and measuring the resultant field. As
mentioned in Chapter 1, the unknown distributions are position-dependent parameters
in the partial differential equation(s) obeyed by the fields, and the incident probe and
the measurements are boundary conditions. This section provides examples of these
equations for various probes and media.

In general, wave propagation in a medium with gradually varying properties may be
described by a wave equation with position-dependent propagation velocity $v(\mathbf{r})$ and
attenuation coefficient $\alpha(\mathbf{r})$. This holds only when these parameters change slowly so
that they are approximately constant within a distance of the order of a wavelength.
The Helmholtz equation then becomes

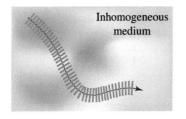

Inhomogeneous
medium

$$\nabla^2 U + k^2(\mathbf{r})U = 0, \qquad (2.3\text{-}6)$$

where $k(\mathbf{r}) = \omega/v(\mathbf{r}) - j\alpha(\mathbf{r})/2$ is a spatially varying complex wavenumber. Waves traveling in such a medium are refracted gradually at planes orthogonal to the gradient vectors of the medium properties.

If the spatial scale of the changes in the medium properties is smaller than a wavelength, then (2.3-6) is not applicable, and the basic physical laws that are used to derive the Helmholtz equation in the homogeneous case must be revised to include the spatial dependence of all parameters. This, of course, depends on the physical nature of the wave, as described subsequently.

Electromagnetic Waves in Lossless Inhomogeneous Media. The propagation of a harmonic electromagnetic wave in a lossless nonmagnetic medium with a spatially varying dielectric permittivity $\epsilon = \epsilon(\mathbf{r})$ is described by Maxwell's equations:

$$\nabla \times \mathbf{H} = j\omega\epsilon\mathbf{E} \qquad (2.3\text{-}7)$$

$$\nabla \times \mathbf{E} = -j\omega\mu_0\mathbf{H} \qquad (2.3\text{-}8)$$

$$\nabla \cdot \epsilon\mathbf{E} = 0 \qquad (2.3\text{-}9)$$

$$\nabla \cdot \mathbf{H} = 0. \qquad (2.3\text{-}10)$$

Equations (2.3-7) and (2.3-8) may be combined into a generalized Helmholtz equation for the electric field:

$$\frac{\epsilon_0}{\epsilon} \nabla \times (\nabla \times \mathbf{E}) = \frac{\omega^2}{c^2}\mathbf{E}, \qquad (2.3\text{-}11)$$

where $c = 1/\sqrt{\mu_0\epsilon_0}$ is the free-space speed of light. The magnetic field satisfies a different equation:

$$\nabla \times \left(\frac{\epsilon_0}{\epsilon} \nabla \times \mathbf{H}\right) = \frac{\omega^2}{c^2}\mathbf{H}. \qquad (2.3\text{-}12)$$

Equation (2.3-11) may also be written in the form

$$\nabla^2\mathbf{E} + \nabla\left(\frac{1}{\epsilon} \nabla\epsilon \cdot \mathbf{E}\right) + k^2\mathbf{E} = 0, \qquad (2.3\text{-}13)$$
Generalized Helmholtz Equation

where $k = k(\mathbf{r}) = \sqrt{\epsilon(\mathbf{r})/\epsilon_0}\,\omega/c = \omega/v(\mathbf{r})$ is a spatially varying wavenumber and $v(\mathbf{r})$ is a spatially varying velocity.

The validity of (2.3-13) can be demonstrated by employing the following procedure. Use the identity $\nabla \times (\nabla \times \mathbf{E}) = \nabla(\nabla \cdot \mathbf{E}) - \nabla^2\mathbf{E}$, valid for a rectilinear coordinate system. Invoke (2.1-42) and the identity $\nabla \cdot \epsilon \mathbf{E} = \epsilon \nabla \cdot \mathbf{E} + \nabla \epsilon \cdot \mathbf{E}$, which provides $\nabla \cdot \mathbf{E} = -(1/\epsilon)\nabla \epsilon \cdot \mathbf{E}$. Finally, substitute in (2.3-11) to obtain (2.3-13).

For a medium with slowly varying dielectric constant, i.e., when $\epsilon(\mathbf{r})$ varies sufficiently slowly, the second term on the left-hand side of (2.3-13) is negligible in comparison with the first, so that (2.3-6) is reproduced. Equation (2.3-6) is also applicable in the special case when $\nabla \epsilon \cdot \mathbf{E} = 0$, i.e., $\nabla \epsilon$ is orthogonal to $\mathbf{E}$. This occurs if ϵ varies along a single direction orthogonal to the direction of the field $\mathbf{E}$.

Electromagnetic Waves in Lossy Inhomogeneous Media.   A lossy dielectric inhomogeneous medium is described by position-dependent conductivity $\sigma = \sigma(\mathbf{r})$ and electric permittivity $\epsilon = \epsilon(\mathbf{r})$. These may be combined into a complex permittivity $\epsilon' = \epsilon + \sigma/j\omega$, as in (2.2-1). Since Maxwell's equations (2.3-7)–(2.3-10) apply with ϵ replaced by ϵ', the generalized Helmholtz equations also apply with this substitution.

Electrostatic Fields in Lossy Inhomogeneous Media.   In the limit $\omega = 0$, the relation $\nabla \cdot \epsilon'\mathbf{E} = 0$, which is a generalized version of (2.3-9), yields

$$\nabla \cdot \sigma \mathbf{E} = 0. \tag{2.3-14}$$

This equation is also a direct consequence of the continuity equation $\nabla \cdot \mathbf{J} = 0$ for the electric current density $\mathbf{J}$ and the linear relation $\mathbf{J} = \sigma \mathbf{E}$, which underlies Ohm's law. If the electric field is written in terms of an electrostatic potential V as $\mathbf{E} = -\nabla V$, (2.3-14) becomes the Laplace equation for an inhomogeneous medium:

$$\boxed{\nabla \cdot \sigma \nabla V = 0.} \tag{2.3-15}$$
Generalized Laplace Equation

This equation (2.3-15) is the basis of **electrical resistance tomography**, a subsurface imaging technique based on electrical measurements of voltages and currents on the surface of a volume to infer the conductivity distribution $\sigma = \sigma(\mathbf{r})$ inside the volume (see Sec.4.5B).

Diffuse Waves in Inhomogeneous Turbid Media.   For a lossy turbid medium in which the scattering coefficient, the absorption coefficient, and the diffusion coefficient are position-dependent functions $\mu_s' = \mu_s'(\mathbf{r})$, $\mu_a = \mu_a(\mathbf{r})$, and $D = D(\mathbf{r})$, respectively, the diffusion equation (2.2-55) takes the form

$$\boxed{\left(\frac{1}{D}\nabla.D\nabla + k^2\right)\Phi = 0,} \tag{2.3-16}$$

where $D^{-1} = 3(\mu_s' + \mu_a)$ and

$$k^2 = -(j\Omega/v + \mu_a)/D = -3(\mu_s' + \mu_a)(j\Omega/v + \mu_a). \tag{2.3-17}$$

Equation (2.3-16) is the basis of **diffuse optical tomography**, a subsurface imaging technique based on measurement of the intensity of light (modulated at some frequency Ω propagating in a turbid medium to infer the scattering coefficient $\mu_s'(\mathbf{r})$ and the absorption coefficient $\mu_a(\mathbf{r})$ (see Sec. 4.5A).

Acoustic Waves in Inhomogeneous Media.   For an inhomogeneous medium, the linearized laws of fluid mechanics (conservation of mass, conservation of momentum, and equation of state) are:

$$\rho_0 \nabla \cdot \mathbf{u} + \mathbf{u} \cdot \nabla \rho_0 = -\frac{\partial \rho}{\partial t} \tag{2.3-18}$$

$$\nabla p - \frac{\rho}{\rho_0} \nabla p_0 = \rho_0 \frac{\partial \mathbf{u}}{\partial t} \tag{2.3-19}$$

$$\frac{\partial p}{\partial t} + \mathbf{u} \cdot \nabla p_0 = c_0^2 \left(\frac{\partial \rho}{\partial t} + \mathbf{u} \cdot \nabla \rho_0 \right), \tag{2.3-20}$$

where both ρ_0 and v can be position dependent.

Appropriate combination of these terms results in the generalized wave equation

$$\frac{1}{\rho_0} \nabla \cdot (\rho_0 \nabla p) - \frac{1}{v^2} \frac{\partial^2 p}{\partial t^2} = 0. \tag{2.3-21}$$

For a harmonic wave of angular frequency ω, this yields the generalized Helmholtz equation

$$\boxed{\left(\frac{1}{\rho_0} \nabla \cdot \rho_0 \nabla + k^2 \right) P = 0,}$$

(2.3-22)
Generalized Helmholtz Equation

where $k = \omega/v$, $v = 1/\sqrt{\rho_0 \kappa}$, ρ_0, and κ are the position-dependent parameters of the inhomogeneous medium.

2.4   Contrast Agents

In many subsurface imaging applications, the observed property α of the target of interest is not sufficiently different from that of the surrounding medium α_b, so that the contrast $(\alpha - \alpha_b)/\alpha_b$ is much too low. This occurs, for example, when substances with low concentration are to be imaged, or when attempting to discriminate between substances with similar observable quantities. In some applications it is possible to introduce one or more extrinsic substances, known as **contrast agents**, that can artificially enhance the contrast, thereby allowing us to image objects that are ordinarily unobservable. From an imaging standpoint, contrast agents have a physical property of their own α_c that is much greater than α or α_b. If the contrast agents can be injected into the target, but not into the surrounding medium, then the distinction between the target and the background is enhanced, since the new contrast will be $(\alpha_c + \alpha - \alpha_b)/\alpha_b \approx \alpha_c/\alpha_b$.

An example is the X-ray imaging of a blood vessel. A contrast agent, such as iodine, may be injected into the blood stream, but not into the surrounding soft tissue. Since iodine is a strong X-ray absorber, contrast between the blood vessel and the tissue will be greatly enhanced, and an X-ray image will show the contours of the vessel much better. Another example is the imaging of two substances with similar observable properties α_1 and α_2. If a contrast agent attaches to both substances nonpreferentially, then no contrast enhancement is achieved. However, if the contrast agent can be attached to one substances but not the other, then contrast is enhanced and the selected substance can be imaged. As we will see in this section, certain molecular contrast agents can indeed attach exclusively to certain molecules, thus enabling **molecular imaging**.

Confining a contrast agent to a selected target may only be partial. Suppose that $\beta(\mathbf{r})$ is the spatial distribution of the density or concentration of some material, and $\alpha(\mathbf{r}) \propto \beta(\mathbf{r})$ is some observed property, such as the absorption coefficient. If the injected contrast agent distributes itself everywhere with a concentration $\beta_c(\mathbf{r})$ proportional to that of the host substance $\beta(\mathbf{r})$, and if the observed property $\alpha_c(\mathbf{r}) \propto \beta_c(\mathbf{r})$, then there will be no enhancement in contrast since $\alpha_c(\mathbf{r}) \propto \alpha(\mathbf{r})$. However, if the contrast agent distributes itself preferentially, e.g., is directed more to areas of low or high concentration, or to areas of certain morphologies in the host material, then contrast enhancement in the mapping of $\beta(\mathbf{r})$ may be possible.

A. Nontargeted and Targeted Contrast Agents

Selective targeting is essential to contrast enhancement. Nevertheless, since the selectivity/specificity of the targeting process varies, contrast agents are often divided into *nontargeted* and *targeted* categories, as described by the following examples. Targeted agents bind with high selectivity, so that they can be used to image selected substances or conditions, or even molecules. The following are examples of applications of nontargeted and targeted contrast agents (see Fig. 2.4-1).

Nontargeted Contrast Agents

- **Radiocontrast Agents for X-Ray Imaging.** Inspection of the digestive tract by X-ray radiography is commonly assisted by administering substances, known as radiocontrast agents (e.g., barium sulfate), that absorb X-rays strongly compared with soft tissues. Iodine-based radiocontrast agents are also commonly injected into the blood stream to enhance X-ray contrast for blood vessels and blood pool areas. The imaging process that reveals blood vessels by use of a contrast agent is commonly called **angiography**.
- **Fluorescein for Retinal Angiography.** Fluorescein is a fluorescent substance that can be injected into the blood stream to help reveal the blood vessels and blood flow patterns in optical images of the patients eye.
- **Microbubbles for Ultrasonic Imaging.** Gas-filled microbubbles serve as excellent contrast agents for ultrasonic imaging of soft tissue because they exhibit a monopole resonance response (at a frequency scaling inversely with the bubble size), which leads to a dramatic elevation in the backscatter cross-section of both individual bubbles and bubbly assemblages. Microbubbles are used in a variety of imaging scenarios involving blood flow and/or perfusion, such as the imaging of vascular flow anomalies, heart valve function, and perfusion into the myocardium of the heart.
- **Stains and dyes** are used to highlight structures in tissues for viewing by an optical microscope. Stains are necessary to view cells and organelles within individual cells. They are also used to help visualize the morphology of materials such as the lamellar structures of semicrystalline polymers. Fluorescence dyes are used routinely in optical microscopy (see Sec. 3.2B and Example 6.3-1 in Chapter 6).
- **Nanoparticles.** Gold nanoparticles can be used as X-ray contrast agents for angiography and kidney imaging. Metallic nanoparticles also have potential applications in ultrasonic imaging and MRI. These particles can be fabricated with peak optical resonance at selected wavelengths, from near-UV to mid-IR, so that they can serve to alter the scattering and absorption properties of light at these wavelengths.
- **Quantum Dots**. These are nanoscale ($\approx$20 nm) crystals of various materials (e.g., cadmium selenide and zinc sulfide) that exhibit broad absorption spectra and very

narrow emission spectra with highly controllable peak wavelengths. They are also very long lived compared with organic fluorophores.

Targeted Contrast Agents

- **Radioactive Isotopes.** Fluorodeoxyglucose (FDG) is a radioactive analogue of glucose in which the fluorine atom is replaced by the radioactive isotope ^{18}F. This substance accumulates in any area that is intensively taking up glucose to support a metabolic activity (e.g., active tumors). FDG reveals itself in PET (see Sec. 4.1D) due to its radioactivity.
- **Molecular contrast agents** are even more specific in their targeting, attaching themselves to specific biochemicals of interest. Nanoparticles and quantum dots can also serve as molecular-specific contrast agents. The remainder of this section is devoted to molecular contrast agents and their applications.

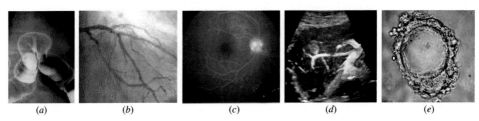

(a)   (b)   (c)   (d)   (e)

Figure 2.4-1   Examples of contrast-enhanced images using various contrast agents. (*a*) Gastrointestinal X-ray image (showing colonic herniation) using barium as a contrast agent. (After Wikipidia.) (*b*) Coronary angiography using a radio-opaque contrast agent. (After Wikipidia.) (*c*) Fluorescein retinal angiography. (*d*) Bubble ultrasonic image of the liver with the hepatic vasculature highlighted by injected microbubbles; a brightish oval shaped object just to the left of the image center is a hemangioma (benign tumor). (After Siemens.) (*e*) Stained muscle stem cell (after Cowan Laboratory Gallery, Children's Hospital, Boston).

B. Molecular Contrast Agents

Attaching a molecular contrast agent to a molecule of interest is commonly known as **labeling** or **tagging**. The problem of imaging specific substances by tagging is commonly referred to as **molecular imaging**.[5] A **molecular image** is a spatial map (2D or 3D) of the distribution of a selected molecular species. Ideally, the image is bright wherever the molecule of interest is present, and dark elsewhere. A good molecular contrast agent is chemically specific (i.e., attaches exclusively to specific molecules), spectrally characteristic (i.e., has a unique spectral signature), strongly fluorescent (so that it provides high contrast with the background), and stoichiometric (i.e., it is possible to quantify the concentration/amount of the molecule of interest from the observed contrast). Whenever a contrast agent is used in a living system, it is also desirable that it does not alter the distribution or activity of the substance being imaged.

Targeting Mechanism.   Figure 2.4-2 provides a *lock and key* analogy to illustrate the molecular targeting mechanism. One part of the molecular contrast agent (the *key*) selectively matches a characteristic part of the molecule of interest (the *lock*). The *key* part is chosen to match the molecule of interest. In biochemistry, the lock portion of the molecule of interest is usually called the **receptor**, and the key portion of the contrast

---

[5]This term is distinct from *single-molecule imaging*, which is the process of mapping the spatial distribution of a single molecule by use of special extremely high resolution techniques (see Sec. 3.2B).

agent is called the **ligand**. If the lock and key are chosen well, the molecular contrast agent will bind selectively to the molecule of interest, while ignoring other molecules in the neighborhood. The part of the receptor that helps in the binding is called the **binding site**. The strength of binding is termed the **binding affinity**. The binding does not have to be permanent, but should certainly last long enough to permit imaging. It is helpful if the binding of the contrast agent does not perturb the behavior of the molecule of interest. One commonly used method for producing organic molecules with specific ligands is to leverage the immune systems of animals. In this context, the molecules of interest are called **antigens**. When a molecule of interest is introduced into an animal, its immune system generates a matching defensive molecule known as an **antibody**. Antibodies can be harvested and used to build molecular contrast agents.

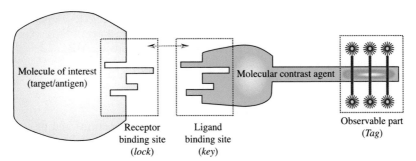

Figure 2.4-2   Molecular contrast agent targeting a molecule of interest: analogy to a "lock" and "key".

Tags.   Another part of the contrast agent is an observable entity, called the **tag**. This may be composed of molecular entities that are capable of providing contrast via some physical property that can be monitored by the selected imaging modality (e.g., ultrasound, optical, X-ray, MRI, PET). Molecular contrast agents are currently available for most major imaging modalities, and many new contrast agents are being developed.[6] Often, the tag contains multiple observable units (e.g., six such units are shown in Fig. 2.4-2) to provide a stronger signal, allowing highly sensitive (amplified) detection of rare molecules of interest. Several methods are in use for producing tags. For example, fluorescent tags may be attached to antibodies, a technique called **immunofluorescence**. A large number of organic as well as inorganic compounds are used as tags. One revolutionary advance has been the development of **fluorescent proteins**. A gene of interest is modified by adding a short segment that produces a naturally fluorescent protein. Once this genetic modification is made, the animal/plant produces a fluorescently tagged version of its natural protein. Using fluorescent protein labeling, biological processes of interest in living systems can be imaged with negligible perturbation of the organism, providing a much greater level of insight to biologists. The following are some examples of tags:

- Phosphatidylserine (PS) is a molecule of interest for studying programmed cell death (apoptosis). The protein named Annexin-V is a ligand that binds selectively to PS.
- Nanoparticles of cross-linked iron oxide (CLIO) have been developed for MRI imaging because the accumulation of CLIO nanoparticles in cells causes a reduction in signal intensity with T2-weighted MRI spin-echo pulse sequences.

---

[6]See the database MICAD (Molecular Imaging & Contrast Agent), http://micad.nih.gov, a freely accessible database for scientific information on molecular imaging and contrast agents for biomedical applications, maintained by the National Library of Medicine.

- The fluorescent tag named Cy5.5 is effective in the near-IR band (700–900 nm). This band avoids the background fluorescence interference of natural biomolecules, providing a high contrast between target and background tissues.

Multiplexed Tags.   Multiplexing is the use of multiple contrast agents to highlight multiple molecules of interest simultaneously. This technique is particularly useful when one is interested in the interrelationships between the molecules of interest. For example, the presence of two different tags at a point in the specimen (a.k.a. **co-localization**) can provide information that neither tag can provide by itself. More generally, **associations** among multiple molecules are highly informative about structural and/or functional relationships among entities in the tissue.

Multimodal Tags.   Some molecular contrast agents have been developed specifically for use in multimodal imaging. As an example, the contrast agent "Annexin V–cross-linked iron oxide–Cy5.5" is used for multimodal imaging using MRI and near-infrared imaging. Annexin V has also been tagged with radioactive fluorine (^{18}F) for imaging using PET.

Molecular Imaging of Biomarkers

Molecular imaging enables the visualization of cellular functions and molecular processes in living organisms *in vivo* (i.e., in a living organism) by monitoring fine changes in special molecules that interact chemically with and reveal information on their surroundings. This process is markedly different from conventional imaging techniques that rely on the measurement of macroscopic quantities such as density or elasticity.

Biomarkers.   In biomedical applications, one is usually interested in molecules that are informative about specific conditions or biological processes such as metabolism, cell death, and vessel proliferation (angiogenesis). Such molecules are known as **molecular markers** or **biomarkers**. From a medical standpoint, biomarkers are valuable because they are capable of monitoring changes at the cellular level that occur well before any gross anatomic changes (clinical symptoms) become apparent. This capability is particularly valuable in early cancer diagnosis and treatment. For example, a suitable biomarker can reveal the effect of chemotherapy in a matter of days, while gross anatomical changes to a lesion may take more than a month to become detectable. The importance of molecular imaging in biomedicine is now widely recognized. It has the potential to alter the manner in which medicine is practiced in several ways: helping detect life-threatening diseases well before symptoms appear, ensuring that therapeutic drugs reach desired locations, helping match life-saving drugs to the genetic make-up of the patient, and helping direct therapeutic intervention to specific locations of interest.

Imaging Biomarkers.   Detecting a biomarker in a living system without a contrast agent is usually impossible. Living beings are composed of tens of thousands of species of molecules. There are more than 10000 proteins in a mammalian cell, many of which are present in very small quantities. Since proteins are built out of a common set of molecular building blocks (amino acids), it is difficult to image a specific protein of interest from others based on their constituent atoms. Indeed, a cell appears practically transparent under a brightfield microscope. However, each protein has a characteristic three-dimensional shape (conformation). This property can be exploited to develop contrast agents capable of highlighting any chosen protein with incredible specificity. Indeed, fluorescent, chromogenic (a.k.a. **stains**), and bio-luminescent contrast agents are an irreplaceable tool in the modern biological laboratory.

2.5   Sources and Detectors

Sources and detectors are essential components of imaging systems. The following are principal technologies used at various electromagnetic and acoustic spectral bands:

	Ultrasonic	Radiowave	Microwave	Optical	X-rays	γ-rays
SOURCES	Piezoelectric transducer	Antenna		LED Laser	X-ray tube Synchrotron	Isotopes
DETECTORS				PMT Photodiode CCD	Film Phosphor Scintillator	Geiger

This section provides a brief overview of some of these sources and detectors and an outline of their principal spatial, spectral, temporal, and polarization characteristics that are pertinent to their use in subsurface imaging.

A.   General Characteristics of Sources and Detectors

Sources

Power.   The total deliverable power (watts) is one of the key parameters that characterize the source. The source power must be sufficiently high so that, upon interaction with the object, the power received by the detector is greater than the noise level. However, it is important not to subject the object to a level of power density (or field strength) exceeding its threshold for damage, breakdown, or toxicity.

Directional Pattern.   An important characteristic of the source is the directional pattern. It depicts the angular distribution of the radiation, i.e., the relative strength of the radiated field in the **far zone**, typically displayed as a function of the angles θ and ϕ in a spherical coordinate system, but sometimes plotted as a function of the transverse coordinates x and y, as in the case of laser beams. The **angular width** of the pattern is an important parameter that characterizes narrow beams such as those used in scanning systems. For sources used in the **near zone** (or generating waves focused sharply onto a focal point), full characterization of the 3D spatial distribution $U_p(x, y, z)$ is usually necessary.

Spectral and Temporal Distributions.   Harmonic radiowaves and ultrasonic waves can be easily generated by use of sinusoidal (single-frequency) electric excitation. These are often tunable (i.e., the frequency can be varied) within a spectral range dictated by the structure of the antenna or transducer. However, electromagnetic waves at optical frequencies and higher do have finite spectral width, which can be very small for special single-mode lasers. Harmonic waves are, of course, continuous waves (CW), but can also be operated in a pulsed mode. A pulsed wave has a spectrum of finite width centered about a central frequency [see Fig. 2.5-1(*b*)]. Certain sources generate incoherent emissions, which have random waveforms with a broad average spectral distribution, as shown in Fig. 2.5-1(*c*).

Polarization.   The polarization of the electromagnetic wave can be important in determining its interaction with the medium in processes such as refraction and scattering, and is that basis of polarization-sensitive imaging. Certain sources generate linearly polarized radiation with controllable plane of polarization, but others produce randomly polarized radiation.

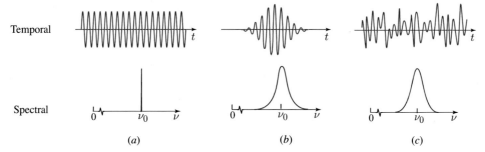

Temporal

Spectral

(a)   (b)   (c)

Figure 2.5-1   Temporal and spectral profiles. (*a*) Harmonic wave. (*b*) Pulsed wave. (*c*) Incoherent wave.

Detectors

Responsivity.   A detector measures the wave amplitude (e.g., in units of V/m or Pa), the intensity (W/cm^2), or the power (W) by generating a proportional electrical signal, e.g., an electric current (A) or electric pulses producing clicks in a counter at a proportional rate. The conversion ratio determines the responsivity of the detector.

Noise.   The reading of any detector is always contaminated by noise, which results from inherent fluctuations in the measured signal, or random uncertainties in the measuring apparatus. One measure of the quality of detection is the **signal-to-noise ratio (SNR)**, which is the ratio of the signal power to the noise power. The smaller the noise power, the larger the SNR. The sensitivity of the detector is often defined as the minimum detectable signal (amplitude or power) for a given SNR.

Spectral Response.   The detector's responsivity is a function of the wavelength that extends over a finite spectral range within which the detector is usable. When a detector is used to measure a pulsed wave, the spectral width of the pulse must fall within the spectral band of the detector, i.e., the detector must be sufficiently fast to follow the pulse profile.

Directional Pattern.   The angular dependence of the responsivity of a detector is also one of the principal characteristics. Some transducers operate as either transmitters or receivers (or as transceivers, serving both functions concurrently). Examples are radiowave antennas and ultrasonic piezoelectric transducers. These devices obey a reciprocity property by which the directional pattern is the same for transmission and reception. Highly directive detectors can reject undesired background radiation, which typically extends over a large angle, and therefore favor the desired signal, which is typically confined to a small angle.

B. Radiowave Transmitters and Receivers

The principal component of radiowave transmitters and receivers is the antenna. It is a reciprocal device that converts a radio-frequency electric current into an electromagnetic radiowave, or vice versa. Physically, the antenna is an arrangement of conductors in some geometrical configuration (rod or set of parallel rods, loop, horn, parabolic dish, strip, etc.), as illustrated in Fig. 2.5-2, connected to an electric circuit. In the transmitter mode, an electronic oscillator generates a sinusoidal voltage at the desired frequency, which is amplified or modulated on its way to the antenna. In the receiver mode, the electromagnetic field induces an electric current into the antenna, which creates a voltage that is amplified and demodulated to extract the incoming information.

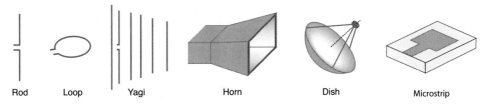

| Rod | Loop | Yagi | Horn | Dish | Microstrip |

Figure 2.5-2   Antennas.

Radiation Pattern.   An antenna is characterized by a **radiation pattern** that depicts the relative strength of the radiated field (in the transmitting mode) or the response (in the receiving mode) as a function of direction. The directionality of an antenna is measured by the antenna **directive gain**, $G_D(\theta, \phi)$, defined as the ratio of the intensity in the direction (θ, ϕ) and the average intensity for all directions at the same distance. The antenna **directivity** is the maximum value of the directive gain.

For a simple vertical rod of length much smaller than a wavelength, the antenna acts as an electric dipole that emits a field proportional to $\sin \theta$ (where θ is measured from the rod or loop axis). The radiation pattern, therefore, has the donut shape shown in Fig. 2.5-3(a). It has its maximum value for horizontal directions $(\theta = \pi/2)$ and is omnidirectional (uniform) in the azimuthal direction ϕ. It has a null along the axis of the antenna $(\theta = 0$ or $\pi)$, so that the antenna does not radiate or receive along the direction of the rod. The directivity of the short dipole antenna is 3/2. Rod antennas of length not much smaller than a wavelength are also omnidirectional (in ϕ) , as expected from symmetry, and have a null along the axis, but the dependence on θ is different.

Antennas with preferred direction(s) in the horizontal plane may be constructed by using additional conducting rods of certain lengths and spacings, constituting an antenna array as in the Yagi antenna (Fig. 2.5-2). Elements of an antenna array may be coupled to a common source or load, and phased to produce a specific directional pattern.

A parabolic dish antenna with a source located at the focus [Fig. 2.5-3(b)] can produce highly directional, beam-like radiation with directivity $(\pi D/\lambda)^2$ if the wavelength λ is much shorter than the diameter of the dish D [recall from (2.1-32) that the angle subtended by the beam is $1.22\lambda/D$].

(a)   (b)

Figure 2.5-3   Directional patterns of (a) dipole and (b) dish antennas.

Antenna Effective Area.   Because of reciprocity, the directional pattern in the receiving mode equals the radiative pattern in the transmitting mode. The **receiver effective area**, also called the effective aperture or the antenna cross-section, is

$$\sigma_e(\theta, \phi) = \frac{\lambda^2}{4\pi} G_D(\theta, \phi).$$ (2.5-1)

The power collected by the antenna when it receives radiation of intensity I (W/m^2) from the (θ, ϕ) direction equals $I\sigma_e$ (assuming that the antenna is connected to a matched impedance).

Spectral Characteristics.   An antenna of a specific length and geometry is tuned to a specific frequency, the resonance frequency, and is effective for a band of frequencies centered about that frequency. Some antennas are designed to function at multiple resonant frequencies, and others are effective over broad bands. The **bandwidth** depends on factors such as the thickness of the wires, the tapering of components (e.g., in a horn antenna), and the use of multiple elements tuned to multiple bands.

Polarization of an antenna radiation is the orientation of the electric field (E-plane) of the radiowave with respect to the Earth's surface. For example, a vertical dipole antenna radiates an omnidirectional field with vertical polarization. If mounted horizontally, it radiates horizontal polarization (but not ominidirectionally).

C. Optical Sources and Detectors

Optical Sources

The principal light sources used in subsurface imaging are the laser and the light-emitting diode (LED).

Lasers.   The laser is an optical oscillator comprising an optical amplifier and optical feedback. Amplification is based on the process of light amplification by stimulated emission of radiation, in which a photon stimulates an excited atom or molecule to emit an additional photon, and the process is repeated. Atoms or molecules are raised to an excited state by use of a pump, e.g., an ordinary light source, or electric current excitation in a semiconductor laser. Feedback is provided by two parallel mirrors creating a resonator. The laser can emit light in a set of possible modes, each with a unique spatial distribution (directional pattern). The simplest and most common mode is the Gaussian beam (see Sec. 2.1A) since it combines energy confinement about the beam axis with minimum divergence in the far zone. The following is a list of lasers that are commonly used in various imaging applications, along with representative values of their main characteristics:

- **Argon-ion lasers** operate at a wavelength of 515 nm and can deliver 10 W of CW power and pulses of 100 ps duration at 100 MHz repetition rates.
- **Ti:Sapphire lasers** operate in the 780–950 nm wavelength range and can deliver 5 W of CW power and pulses of 10 fs duration at a repetition rate of 80 MHz. It can be frequency doubled to deliver milliwatts of power at 390–475 nm wavelengths.
- **Neodymium:YAG lasers** operate at 1064 nm and can deliver 50 W of CW power and pulses of 7 ps duration.
- **Fiber lasers**: ytterbium-doped silica-glass fiber lasers operate at 1075 nm and can deliver 1.5 kW of CW power. Erbium-doped silica-glass fiber lasers operate at 1550 nm with up to 100 W of CW power and pulses of duration 200 fs. These lasers are not tunable, but their small size offers a design advantage.
- **CO_2 lasers** operate at 10.6 μm and can deliver 500 W of CW power and pulses of 20 ns duration.

Light-Emitting Diodes (LEDs).   The LED is a semiconductor device (p–n junction, or diode) in which light is spontaneously emitted following radiative transitions from the conduction band into the valence band. Each such transition is a process of recombination of an electron and a hole accompanied by the emission of a photon. Electrons are excited into the conduction band by injection of electrons and holes in a forward biased a p–n junction. LEDs can have wavelengths ranging from 375 to 1625 nm and powers ranging from milliwatts to a few watts, depending on the semiconductor material or compounds used.

Laser diodes.   Laser diodes (LD) are LEDs with feedback (introduced by polishing the surfaces of the semiconductor to make mirrors) and with greater injected electric current. Like LEDs, the wavelengths of LDs can be anything from 375 to 1625 nm, depending on the semiconductor material, and the powers can be as high as 10 W. Laser diodes can be pulsed with pulse duration as short as 50 ps, a repetition rate up to 80 MHz, and an average power of up to a few mW (lower power for shorter pulses). Unfortunately, the beam quality is not very good and it can be difficult to use them for diffraction-limited imaging.

Comparison.   The directional pattern of the laser is much narrower than that of the LED, and the spectral distribution is much narrower, as illustrated in Fig. 2.5-4. An LED has a spectral width greater than 10 THz, while a single-mode laser may have a much narrower spectral width of 1 MHz, i.e., is almost monochromatic. The spectral width $\Delta\nu$ defines the coherence time $\tau_c = 1/\Delta\nu$ and the coherence length $\ell_c = c\tau_c$, so that a laser has a much longer coherence time and much greater coherence length than an LED. Within the coherence length, the light behaves as a coherent wave obeying the laws of propagation that are described in Sec. 2.1. However, for optical systems involving path length differences greater than the coherence length, the light behaves incoherently, so that the principle of superposition applies to intensities instead of amplitudes.

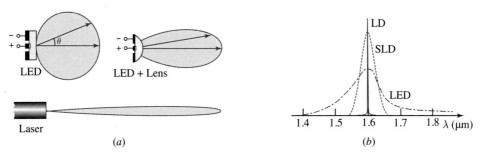

Figure 2.5-4   (*a*) Directional patterns of LEDs and lasers. (*b*) Spectral distributions of light emitted by an LED, a superluminescent light-emitting diode (SLD), and a laser diode (LD) made of the same semiconductor.

Optical Detectors

The principal optical detectors used in optical sensing and imaging are the photomultiplier tube (PMT), the photodiode, the array detector, and the charge-coupled device (CCD), illustrated in Fig. 2.5-5.

Photomultiplier Tubes (PMTs).   The PMT is a light detector with high sensitivity and ultra-fast response. A typical PMT consists of a vacuum tube with a photoemissive cathode (photocathode) that coverts an incoming photon into a free electron, which is accelerated by the applied voltage and directed to a set of electrodes (dynodes) serving as amplifying stages. Upon impact with the first dynode, the electron produces additional electrons by a process of secondary emission. These are directed to the next dynode to produce more secondary electrons. All electrons are eventually collected by the anode to produce a measurable electric current pulse corresponding to more than 10^6 electrons. The PMT may therefore be used as a photon counter.

An imaging device that makes similar use of secondary emission is the **microchannel plate**. It consists of an array of millions of capillaries whose interior walls behave as continuous dynodes, multiplying the photocurrent generated at each position [Fig. 2.5-5(*b*)]. Microchannel plates are used to measure faint images, and the electric signals generated may be displayed as an amplified image. This combination is called an **image intensifier**.

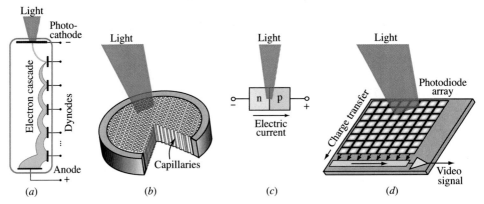

Figure 2.5-5   Optical detectors. (*a*) PMT. (*b*) Microchannel plate used for image intensifiers. (*c*) Photodiode. (*d*) CCD.

Photodiodes.   A photodiode is a reverse-biased semiconductor p–n junction [Fig. 2.5-5(*c*)]. An absorbed photon results in the excitation of an electron into the conduction band and the creation of a hole in the valence band. In the presence of the electric field in the junction, electrons and holes move and create an electric current in the external circuit proportional to the incident photon flux. The **avalanche photodiode (APD)** is a photodiode in which the applied voltage is sufficiently high so that the moving electrons and holes create additional electrons and holes by a process of impact ionization. As a result, the electric current generated is greater and the device has a higher sensitivity.

CMOS Array Detectors and Charge Coupled Devices (CCDs).   An array of photodiodes may be used as an image sensor. Modern sensors, such as those used in digital cameras, employ *complementary metal oxide–semiconductor* (CMOS) active-pixel technology. The photoelectric current generated at each photodiode is converted to a voltage, which is read out, by the chip circuitry. The result is a video signal providing a sampled and digitized version of the image. An alternative technology, with similar image quality, is the analog CCD. Here, the photoelectric charge generated by the detectors is transferred sequentially, one pixel at a time, to generate an analog video signal representing the image [Fig. 2.5-5(*d*)].

Spectral Characteristics.   The wavelength dependence of the photodetector responsivity (A/W) is dictated mainly by the absorption spectra of the photodetection material (the material of the photocathode in a PMT or the semiconductor used in photodiodes). A large menu of materials exists. For example, silicon photodetectors can be used in the 500–1100 nm band, germanium photodetectors extend from 900 to 1600 nm, and germanium doped with various materials can be used to detect waves at longer wavelengths (up to 200 μm in the far IR).

D. X-Ray and γ-Ray Sources and Detectors

Sources.   X-rays are commonly generated by collision of an electron beam with a metal target, principally tungsten, as illustrated in Fig. 2.5-6(*a*). Molybdenum is used to generate soft X-rays, which are used in mammography. The kinetic energy released from the decelerating electrons is converted into broad band X-rays (a process called **Bremsstrahlung**). Gamma rays are generated by transitions within atomic nuclei.

Detectors.   X-ray detectors rely on conversion of X-ray photons to visible photons, which are detected by optical detectors. A common conversion mechanism is **fluorescence** or **phosphorescence**. A fluorescent screen is placed in contact with the emulsion of a photographic plate or film in a cassette, as illustrated in Fig. 2.5-6(*b*). When X-ray photons strike the screen, the visible light emitted exposes the film. Another conversion mechanism is **scintillation**. Scintillating material such as sodium iodide (NaI) converts X-ray photons to visible photons, which are detected by an adjacent photodetector, such as a photomultiplier. These detectors are called **scintillators**, or scintillation counters. Yet another increasingly common detection method, **digital radiography**, is based on **photostimulable luminescence** (PSL). Electrons excited by the X-ray photons in a phosphor material are *trapped* in *color centers* in the crystal lattice, and remain so until released by a laser beam scanning the plate, whereupon photons are emitted and detected by a photodetector.

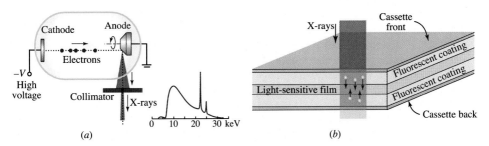

Figure 2.5-6   (*a*) Generation of X-rays in a rotating anode X-ray tube and a typical X-ray spectrum. (*b*) Detection of X-rays by use of a fluorescent screen and photographic film.

Geiger counters detect X-rays and γ-rays by a process of ionization of gas atoms in a vacuum tube. A high voltage is applied between a cylindrical cathode and a wire anode in a tube containing the gas. As an X-ray or γ-ray photon enters the tube, it ionizes the gas and forms an electron and an ion. As these charged particles accelerate, they cause further ionization by collision with the gas atoms, and an avalanche process is initiated. The outcome is a measurable pulse of electric current in the external circuit corresponding to a count. The device, therefore, serves as a photon counter, much like the optical APD, which counts optical photons. The photon counting rate in both devices is proportional to the intensity of the radiation.

E. Acoustic Sources and Detectors

An acoustic transducer converts an electrical signal into an acoustic wave with proportional amplitude, or vice versa. Most ultrasonic transducers are based on the **piezo-**

electric effect (alternative methods include magnetostriction and capacitive actuation). Piezoelectricity is the ability of some materials (notably crystals and certain ceramics) to generate an electric charge (and thereby induce a voltage across the material) in response to applied mechanical stress. This property may be used to detect sound [Fig. 2.5-7(a)]. The converse effect also exists, namely, the production of stress and/or strain when an electric field is applied – a property used to generate sound [Fig. 2.5-7(b)]. Since the response time of piezoelectric devices is short, they can operate as excellent ultrasonic transducers (receivers, transmitters, and transcievers). A typical radiation/reception power pattern is shown in Fig. 2.5-7 (c).

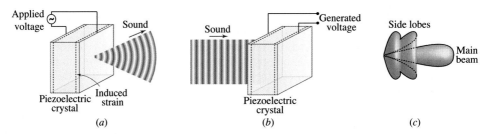

Figure 2.5-7 Piezoelectric ultrasonic transducer used as: (a) source and (b) detector. (c) Directional pattern.

F. Phased-Array Sources and Detectors

The directional patterns of sources and detectors may be altered by use of components, such as mirrors and lenses, that alter the wavefront by introducing position-dependent delays (phase shifts). Alternatively, arrays of sources (or detectors) may be combined to generate a single beam whose directional pattern may be controlled by variable phase shifts built into the elements of the array.

The wavefront of a plane wave traveling in the z direction may be altered by introducing a phase shift $\phi(x, y)$ that depends on the transverse coordinates. For example, a linear phase shift $\phi(x, y) \propto x$ converts a plane wave $\exp(-\mathrm{j}kz)$, which travels along the z axis, into an oblique plane wave $\exp[-\mathrm{j}(k_x x + k_z z)]$. This is readily accomplished in optics by use of a thin prism whose width increases linearly with x, as illustrated in Fig. 2.5-8(a).

Likewise, a quadratic phase shift $\phi(x, y) \propto (x^2 + y^2)$ converts the planar wavefronts into parabolic wavefronts. This wavefront curvature redirects the wave so that it converges to a single point (focus), or curves it backward so that it appears to be coming from a single point. In optics, such a quadratic phase is introduced by use of a lens (convex or concave) whose thickness varies quadratically with the transverse coordinates [Fig. 2.5-9(a)].

For radiowaves and acoustic waves, the position-dependent phase may be introduced electronically at the source. For example, Fig.2.5-8(b) depicts an array of rod antennas placed at equal distances in the transverse direction x and fed by electric currents with equal phase shifts $\Delta\phi$ between successive elements. The phase of the radiating sources, therefore, increases linearly with x, albeit in a discrete fashion, as illustrated in Fig. 2.5-8(d). By analogy with the optical prism, the radiation will favor a specific angle that can be controlled by changing the phase difference $\Delta\phi$. The same concept can be applied to ultrasonic transducers, as shown in Fig. 2.5-8(c). The system is called a phased-array source and is used for scanning in radar and sonar imaging. The discretization error will introduce beam divergence with an angular width inversely proportional to the number of elements.

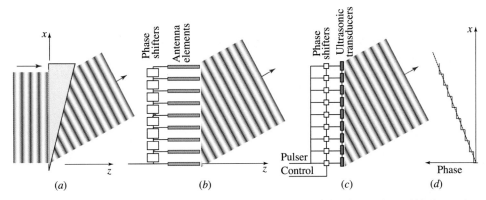

Figure 2.5-8   (*a*) A prism deflects an incident plane wave by introducing a phase shift that varies linearly with *x*. (*b*) Phased-array antenna. (*c*) Phased-array ultrasonic transducer. (*d*) Continuous linear phase introduced by the prism (straight line) and discrete linear phase introduced by the phased-array system (ragged line).

Phased arrays may also be programmed to generate focused waves. An array of ultrasonic transducers, for example, may be driven with quadratically varying phase, as illustrated in Fig. 2.5-9. The system is used to generate focused ultrasound.

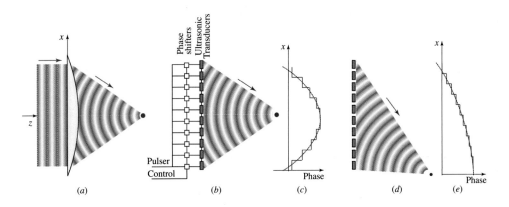

Figure 2.5-9   (*a*) A lens focuses an incident plane wave by introducing a phase shift that varies quadratically with *x*. (*b*) Phased-array ultrasonic transducer used to generate a focused ultrasonic wave. (*c*) Continuous quadratic phase introduced by the lens and discrete quadratic phase introduced by the phased-array system. (*d*) Same as in (*b*) but with a different profile of the delay, generates a wave focused at a shifted position.

Further Reading

Acoustics

A. Leger and M. Deschamps, *Ultrasonic Wave Propagation in Non Homogeneous Media*, Springer, 2009.

T. D. Rossing and N. H Fletcher, *Principles of Vibration and Sound*, 2nd ed., Springer, 2004.

L. E. Kinsler, A. R. Frey, A. B. Coppens, and J. V. Sanders, *Fundamentals of Acoustics*, 4th ed., Wiley, 2000.

D. T. Blackstock, *Fundamentals of Physical Acoustics*, Wiley, 2000.

J. A. Zagzebski, *Essentials of Ultrasound Physics*, Mosby, 1996.

A. D. Pierce, *Acoustics: An Introduction to Its Physical Principles and Applications*, McGraw-Hill, 1989.

P. M. Morse and K. U. Ingard, *Theoretical Acoustics*, Princeton University Press, 1987.

Electromagnetics

W. H. Hayt, Jr. and J. A. Buck, *Engineering Electromagnetics*, 7th ed., McGraw-Hill, 2006.

M. N. O. Sadiku, *Elements of Electromagnetics*, 4th ed., Oxford University Press, 2006.

J. A. Kong, *Electromagnetic Wave Theory*, 2nd ed., Wiley, 1990; EMW Publishing, 2005.

Z.-P. Liang and P. C. Lauterbur, *Principles of Magnetic Resonance Imaging: A Signal Processing Perspective*, IEEE Press, 1999.

W. C. Chew, *Waves and Field in Inhomogeneous Media*, IEEE, 1999.

J. D. Jackson, *Classical Electrodynamics*, 3rd ed., Wiley, 1998.

Optics

B. E. A. Saleh and M. C. Teich, *Fundamentals of Photonics*, 2nd ed., Wiley, 2007.

F. L. Pedrotti, L. M. Pedrotti, and L. S. Pedrotti, *Introduction to Optics*, 3rd ed., Prentice Hall, 2006.

M. Born and E. Wolf, *Principles of Optics*, 7th ed., Cambridge University Press, 2002.

E. Hecht, *Optics*, Addison–Wesley, 4th ed., 2002.

J. C. Stover, *Optical Scattering: Measurement and Analysis*, 2nd ed., SPIE, 1995.

Diffuse Light and Tissue Optics

F. Martelli, S. Del Bianco, A. Ismaelli, and G. Zaccanti, *Light Propagation through Biological Tissue and Other Diffusive Media: Theory, Solutions, and Software*, SPIE, 2009.

L. V. Wang and H.-I. Wu, *Biomedical Optics*, Wiley, 2007.

V. Tuchin, *Tissue Optics: Light Scattering Methods and Instruments for Medical Diagnosis*, 2nd ed., SPIE, 2007.

R. Splinter and B. A. Hooper, *An Introduction to Biomedical Optics*, Taylor & Francis, 2006.

A. Dunn and R. Richards-Kortum, Three-dimensional computation of light scattering from cells, *IEEE Journal on Selected Topics in Quantum Electronics*, Vol. 2, pp. 898–905, 1996.

A. Yodh and B. Chance, Spectroscopy and imaging with diffusing light, *Physics Today*, Vol. 48, pp. 34–40, 1995.

R. C. Haskell, L. O. Svaasand, T. T. Tsay, T. C. Feng, M. S. McAdams, and B. J. Tromberg, Boundary conditions for the diffusion equation in radiative transfer, *Journal of the Optical Society America A*, Vol. 11, pp. 2727–2741, 1994.

T. J. Farrell, M. S. Patterson, and B. Wilson, A diffusion theory model of spatially resolved, steady-state diffuse reflectance for the noninvasive determination of tissue optical properties *in vivo*, *Medical Physics*, Vol. 19, pp. 879–888, 1992.

Sensors

T. Williams, *Thermal Imaging Cameras: Characteristics and Performance*, CRC, 2009.

J. Fraden, *Handbook of Modern Sensors: Physics, Designs, and Applications*, 3rd ed., AIP, 2004.

Physics of Medical Imaging

P. Suetens, *Fundamentals of Medical Imaging*, 2nd ed., Cambridge University Press, 2009.

J. R. Bushberg, J. A. Seibert, E. M. Leidholdt, Jr., and J. M. Boone, *The Essential Physics of Medical Imaging*, 2nd ed., Lippincott Williams & Wilkins, 2002.

Problems

2.1-1 **Optical and Ultrasonic Beams.** Determine and compare the angular width θ_0 and the depth of focus $2z_0$ of optical and ultrasonic Gaussian beams of equal waist radius, $W_0 = 1$ mm. The optical beam has wavelength of 1 μm and is traveling in air. The ultrasonic wave has frequency of 10 MHz and is traveling in a medium for which the velocity of sound is $v = 1000$ m/s. If the power of the beams is 1 mW, what is the peak intensity at a distance $z = z_0$ and at $z = 2z_0$?

2.1-2 **Amplitude of an Electromagnetic Wave.** Determine the electric field amplitude [V/m] and the magnetic field amplitude [A/m] of an electromagnetic plane wave of intensity 1 mW/cm² in free space and in a nonmagnetic medium with $\epsilon = 2\epsilon_0$.

2.1-3 **Amplitude of an Acoustic Wave.** Determine the pressure amplitude [Pa] and the velocity amplitude (m/s) of an acoustic wave or intensity 10 mW/cm² in air and in water.

2.1-4 **Spherical Acoustic Wave.** A sphere of 10 cm nominal radius pulsates at 100 Hz and radiates a spherical wave into air. If the intensity is 50 mW/m² at a distance of 1 m from the center of the sphere, determine the acoustic power radiated, the surface velocity of the sphere, and the pressure amplitude and velocity amplitude of the wave at distance of 50 cm from the center of the sphere.

2.1-5 **Acoustic Beam.** A circular piston-type sonar transducer of 0.5 m radius is mounted in an "infinite" baffle and radiates 5 kW of acoustic power in water at 10 kHz. Determine the width of the beam at a distance at which the intensity is down by 10 dB, assumed to be in the far zone. What is the axial pressure level in dB re 1 μbar (1 bar = 10^6 Pa) at a distance of 10 m from the face of the transducer?

2.2-1 **Velocity of an Electromagnetic Wave in a Lossy Medium.** Use (2.2-2) and the relation $v = \omega/\beta$ to plot the refractive index $n = c/v$ as a function of frequency for the three materials in Example 2.2-1.

2.2-2 **Impedance of an Electromagnetic Wave in a Lossy Medium.** For lossy dielectrics or metals, the permittivity $\epsilon' = \epsilon(1 + \sigma/j\omega\epsilon)$ is complex and the impedance $\eta = \sqrt{\epsilon_0/\epsilon'}$ is also complex. For seawater with $\epsilon_r = 80$ and $\sigma = 4$, plot the magnitude of the impedance as a function of frequency in the 1 kHz to 10 GHz range.

2.2-3 **Attenuation of an Acoustic Wave in Water.** The attenuation coefficient of an ultrasonic wave in water at 1 MHz corresponds to a half-value thickness of 3.4 m. What is the maximum depth at which a target can be detected using a probe wave producing an intensity of 100 mW/cm² if the detector's sensitivity is 1 mW/cm²? Assume that the transducer is immersed in water so that reflection is not present. Determine the maximum depth for subsurface imaging if the frequency is increased to 2 MHz.

2.2-4 **Reflection and Attenuation of an Electromagnetic Wave.** A 1 MHz electromagnetic wave is used to probe a 1 m deep estuary with mixed fresh and seawater. Determine the percentage of power reflected at the water surface and the percentage of power that is reflected from the bottom ground after transmission through water and propagation back into air. The water is a mixture of seawater and fresh water with $\sigma = 0.01$ S/m and $\epsilon_r = 80$, and the bottom ground has $\sigma = 0.01$ S/m and $\epsilon_r = 14$. Neglect scattering and assume that the water and ground surfaces are perfectly flat. What is the delay time between the first and second echos received in air (resulting from direct reflection at the water surface and reflection at bottom surface)?

2.2-5 **Reflection and Transmission of an Acoustic Wave at Fluid–Fluid Interface.** When an acoustic plane wave is reflected from a fluid–fluid interface it is observed that at normal incidence the pressure amplitude of the reflected wave is half that of the incident wave. As the angle of incidence is increased, the amplitude of the reflected wave first decreases to zero and then increases until at 30° the reflected wave is as strong as the incident wave. Find the density and sound speed in the second medium if the first medium is water.

2.2-6 **Oblique Transmission of an Acoustic Wave at Air–Water Boundary.** A plane acoustic wave of frequency 500 Hz and pressure level 80 dB (re 20 μPa) in air is incident on the calm surface of a lake at an angle θ_1 from normal incidence.

(a) What are the pressure and velocity amplitudes of the incident wave?

(b) What is the maximum value of θ_1 that will still permit propagation into the water?

(c) For $\theta_1 = 10°$, what is the intensity of the sound wave (re 10^{-12} W/m²) in the water?

(d) How do the answers of (a), (b), and (c) change if the frequency is doubled?

2.2-7   **Total Transmission of an Electromagnetic Wave at Air–Water Boundary.** A plane electromagnetic wave is to be used for underwater imaging. What should be the polarization and the angle of incidence necessary for total transmission at the air–water boundary? Assume that the wavelength is $\lambda = 600$ nm, the absorption coefficient is negligible (see Fig. 2.2-4), and the refractive indexes of air and water are $n = 1$ and 1.333, respectively.

2.2-8   **Impedance-Matching Layer for Enhancement of Transmission.** You want to maximize the transmission of a plane sound wave from water into aluminum at normal incidence using an impedance-matching layer. What must be the optimum characteristic impedance of this layer? If the frequency of the wave is 20 kHz, what must be the density of the material and the speed of sound in it. The velocity and impedance of water and aluminum are listed in Table 2.1-1.

2.2-9   **Extinction by Scattering.** If the Rayleigh scattering cross-section of a single small spherical particle is $\sigma_s = 10^{-10}$ m^2 for light of 800 nm wavelength, determine the total power scattered from the particle when the incident intensity is 1 W/m^2. What is the intensity of the scattered light in the backward direction at a distance of 1 m? Is this polarization dependent? If light travels through a medium with $N = 10^9$ such particles per cubic meter, determine the extinction coefficient of light traveling through the medium. What is the extinction coefficient if the wavelength is changed to 400 nm?

2.2-10   **Transmission through Fog.** Consider a large patch of fog sufficiently thick that, seen from the air, it is not possible to see the ground. Suppose that the optical properties of this fog bank are: $\mu_s = 10^{-6}$ m^{-1}, $g = 0.8$, and $\mu_a = 7 \times 10^{-4}$ m^{-1}.

(a) Compute the diffuse reflectance $\mathcal{R}$.

(b) Now suppose that embedded in the fog bank is a denser fog layer of height $d = 100$ m, having the same properties, except that $\mu_s = 10^{-5}$ m^{-1}, beginning at a depth d_1 and ending at a depth $d_1 + d$. Determine the reflectance and plot it as a function of d_1.

2.2-11   **Diffuse Optical Wave.** The intensity of light from a laser is modulated sinusoidally at a frequency $f = 100$ MHz and focused onto a point at the boundary between air and a diffusive nonabsorptive medium for which the photon density obeys the diffusion equation. If the reduced scattering coefficient $\mu_s' = 10$ cm^{-1} and the velocity $v = c/n$ with $n = 1.38$, determine the principal properties of the photon-density wave: attenuation coefficient, penetration depth, propagation constant, velocity, and wavelength. Sketch the dependence of the penetration depth on the modulation frequency f. Repeat this problem if the diffusive medium has an attenuation coefficient $\mu_a = 0.1$ cm^{-1}.

2.2-12   **Pulsed Diffuse Optical Wave.** The intensity of light from a laser is modulated to create a very short pulse (an impulse) that is focused onto a point at the boundary between air and a diffusive nonabsorptive medium for which the photon density obeys the diffusion equation. Show that the time-varying photon density

$$\varphi(\mathbf{r}, t) = \frac{v}{(4\pi Dvt)^{3/2}} \exp\left(-\frac{r^2}{4Dvt}\right)$$

is a solution to the diffusion equation (2.2-50), where r is the distance from the illumination point, D is the diffusion coefficient, and v is the velocity of light in the medium. Plot $\varphi(\mathbf{r}, t)$ as a function of time t at several distances r, and also as a function of r at a set of fixed times t. Describe the physical significance of these plots.

2.3-1   **Gaussian Beam in Multiphoton Fluorescence.** The rate of m-photon absorption is proportional to I^m, where I is the optical intensity. If a Gaussian beam of intensity $I(\rho, z)$, width W_0, and depth of focus $2z_0$ (see (2.1-15)) is used, plot the rate of fluorescence as a function of ρ at $z = 0$ and as a function of z at $\rho = 0$, for $m = 1, 2, 3$, to demonstrate that the fluorescence is more confined to the beam center for larger m.

Localized Imaging

There are two principal configurations for imaging a three-dimensional (3D) object:
- **Localized imaging**, which is described in this chapter.
- **Tomographic imaging**, which is described in Chapter 4.

There are two configurations for localized probing of a 3D object:
- **Axial sectioning**, i.e., dividing the object into a set of axial lines parallel to the z axis in the depth direction, as shown in Fig. 3.0-1(a), and imaging each of these axial lines as a one-dimensional (1D) object – a function of z. Each 1D image is called an **A-scan**. A set of A-scans may be used to form a planar 2D image, e.g., in the x–z plane, called a **B-scan**, as shown in Fig. 3.0-1(b). A set of parallel B-scans may be used to form the entire 3D image.
- **Lateral sectioning**, i.e., dividing the object into lateral (transverse) planar slices, as shown in Fig. 3.0-1(c), and imaging each of these slices as a two-dimensional (2D) object, i.e., a function of x and y. Each 2D image is called a **C-scan** and the 3D image takes the form of a stack, called the z-**stack**.

In any of these configurations, the resolution of scanning and sectioning in the lateral and axial directions is dictated by the ability to localize the probe beam and/or the sensor beam, which is limited principally by the wavelength; the shorter the wavelength, the easier it is to localize.

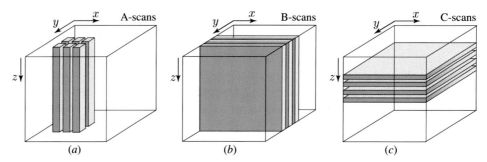

Figure 3.0-1   Scanning a 3D object. (a) Axial sectioning with A-scans. (b) Axial sectioning with B-scans. (c) Lateral sectioning with C-scans forming a z-stack.

This chapter begins in Sec. 3.1 with an introduction to localized imaging of 2D objects (or 2D lateral slices of a 3D object), including mathematical and physical models. Section 3.2 extends this description to 3D localized imaging by use of a set of parallel 2D lateral slices (C-scans) or a set of 1D axial lines (A-scans), with a special emphasis on methods of axial localization, including spatial, temporal, and interferometric methods. The quality of the measured image is limited by many factors, principally the finite resolution of the imaging system, which is associated with image blur. Section 3.3 is a brief introduction to image restoration, i.e., processes for the full or partial recovery of the true object distribution from the measured image, given information on the physical and mathematical model of the degradation process(es).

3.1 Two-Dimensional Imaging

We consider in this section the localized imaging of a 2D object, such as a planar surface, or a lateral slice of a 3D object. As described in Chapter 1, 2D localized imaging may be readily implemented by one of two systems:

(i) A **scanning** system employing a focused probe beam and/or a sensor beam that reads points of the image sequentially.

(ii) A **gazing** system that reads points of the image simultaneously by employing configurations such as shadow imaging or image formation by means of a lens.

In either of these two modalities, the image is acquired in a localized fashion, i.e., each point of the image corresponds ideally to a single point of the object. In reality, since the size of the scanning spot is finite and the gazing image formation system is imperfect, a single point on the image gathers contributions from many points within a small patch in the object. The size of this patch, which is of the order of a wavelength, determines the **resolution** of the imaging system, i.e., the ability of the system to discern neighboring points or lines. Mathematical models describing the relation between the image and the object distributions, and the associated resolution of the imaging system, will be described subsequently in this section.

A. Gazing, Scanning, and Near-Field Imaging

Gazing Systems

In a gazing configuration, points of the object are simultaneously mapped to the image plane such that each point of the object ideally has a distinct corresponding point in the image. This is readily obtained in shadow imaging, an example of which is the X-ray imaging system shown in Fig. 3.1-1(a). In optical imaging, a lens may be used, as depicted in Fig. 3.1-1(b). The object and image planes are located at specific distances d_1 and d_2 from the lens satisfying the imaging equation ($1/d_1 + 1/d_2 = 1/f$, where f is the lens focal length). The sensor (e.g., a photographic film or a CCD detector) measures emissions from all points of the object simultaneously and without the need for scanning.

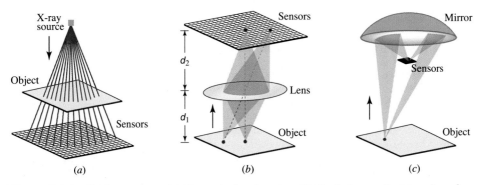

Figure 3.1-1   Gazing systems. (a) X-ray shadow imaging. (b) Single-lens optical imaging of an object illuminated uniformly, as in photography or microscopy, or a self-luminous object, as in passive thermal (infrared) imaging. (c) Imaging a self-luminous object by use of a spherical reflector (mirror) as in telescopy or passive THz imaging.

Scanning Systems

In a scanning system, the probe beam is focused onto a single point (ideally) in the plane of the object. The full 2D spatial distribution of the object is constructed by use of point-by-point raster scanning, as illustrated in Fig. 3.1-2.

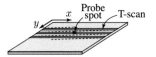

Figure 3.1-2   Raster scanning of a 2D object or a lateral slice of a 3D object. Each line is called a T-scan and the full slice is called a C-scan, as also shown in Fig. 3.0-1.

Focusing of the probe beam may be readily accomplished by use of a mirror or a lens. This is most common in optical imaging systems [Fig. 3.1-3(*a*)], but acoustic lenses are also used to focus acoustic beams. These may be implemented by use of spherical boundaries between materials of different acoustic impedance [Fig. 3.1-3(*b*)]. Electron beams may be focused by magnetic fields [Fig. 3.1-3(*c*)]. Phased-array electromagnetic and acoustic sources may also be used to produce focused probe beams (see Sec. 2.5F).

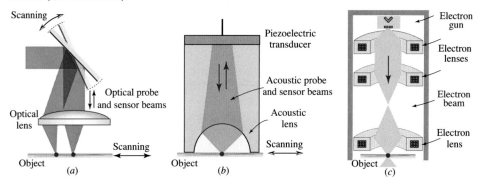

Figure 3.1-3   (*a*) Optical scanning. (*b*) Acoustic scanning. (*c*) Electron-beam scanning.

The scanning process may be implemented by moving the object or the probe beam. This may be accomplished mechanically by moving a stage on which the object is placed or by moving the probe beam using a rotating mirror. Electronic rotation of electromagnetic or acoustic beams is also often implemented via phased arrays (see Sec. 2.5F).

B. Mathematical Models of Image Formation

We begin with general mathematical models of image formation. Models applicable to specific physical systems commonly used for imaging will be described subsequently.

A 2D imaging system maps a 2D distribution $f(x, y)$, called the *object*, into a 2D distribution $g(x, y)$ measured by the detector, called the *image*. Ideally, $g(x, y) \propto f(x, y)$, i.e., the spatial distributions are identical except for a scaling factor, representing brightness adjustment. However, as a result of a number of degradations, the image $g(x, y)$ is never exactly proportional to the true object $f(x, y)$. It is useful to model their relationship by a mathematical operation derived from the physics of the imaging process, and to be able to invert this operation in order to recover $f(x, y)$ from the measured $g(x, y)$.

We regard $f(x, y)$ and $g(x, y)$ as the input and output of a system characterized by some mathematical model and look for the inverse system. The following subsections list some of the basic models for 2D imaging systems.

1. Geometric Transformations

A geometric transformation of an image yields a copy of the image in a different coordinate system. A change of the coordinate system from $\mathbf{r} = (x, y)$ to $\mathbf{r}' = (x', y')$ reassigns the value of the input image at the point $\mathbf{r} = (x, y)$ to the output image at the new point $\mathbf{r}' = (x', y')$. The geometric transformation is defined by a function $\mathbf{r}' = T(\mathbf{r})$, which relates the new coordinates $\mathbf{r}' = (x', y')$ to the old coordinates $\mathbf{r} = (x, y)$. The input–output relation for such a system is

$$g(\mathbf{r}') = f(\mathbf{r}), \quad \mathbf{r}' = T(\mathbf{r}). \tag{3.1-1}$$
Geometric Transformation

The following is a list of some of the basic geometric transformations.

Translation.   The simplest geometric transformation is just a translation of the image in coordinate space, $\mathbf{r}' = \mathbf{r} + \mathbf{r}_0$, where $\mathbf{r}_0 = (x_0, y_0)$. Such a transformation may be encountered as a result of a shift of the position of the camera or the object.

$$g(x + x_0, y + y_0) = f(x, y), \tag{3.1-2}$$
Translation

Scaling.   A magnified (expanded) or minified (contracted) image is proportional to a geometrically scaled version of the object distribution, i.e., $\mathbf{r}' = s\mathbf{r}_0$, so that

$$g(sx, sy) = f(x, y), \tag{3.1-3}$$
Scaling

where s is a scaling factor representing magnification (for $s > 1$) or minification (for $s < 1$). In such a system, the value $f(x, y)$ at the point with coordinates (x, y) in the object plane is assigned to a point with coordinates (sx, sy) in the image plane. Magnification/minification is not actually a degradation, since it is inherently expected in imaging systems such as microscopes and telescopes, and since it can be easily reversed by minification/magnification of the appropriate amount.

■ MATLAB function g=imresize(f,s) implements scaling with scale factor s.

Rotation.   Image rotation occurs naturally as a result of rotation of the sensor or the object. Rotation by an angle θ is described by the matrix relation

$$\begin{bmatrix} x' \\ y' \end{bmatrix} = \begin{bmatrix} \cos\theta & -\sin\theta \\ \sin\theta & \cos\theta \end{bmatrix} \begin{bmatrix} x \\ y \end{bmatrix}, \tag{3.1-4}$$

which may be written in the matrix form $\mathbf{r}' = \mathbf{R}(\theta)\mathbf{r}$, where $\mathbf{R}(\theta)$ is the rotation matrix. It follows that

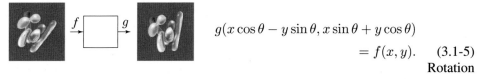

$$g(x \cos \theta - y \sin \theta, x \sin \theta + y \cos \theta)$$
$$= f(x, y). \qquad (3.1\text{-}5)$$

Rotation

Combinations of rotation and translations are known as **Euclidean transformations**.

■ MATLAB function g=imrotate(f,θ) implements rotation of f by θ degrees in a counterclockwise direction around the center point of f.

Similarity Transformations.   Combinations of rotation, translation, and scaling are known as similarity transformations. These shape-preserving transformations are often encountered in the imaging of rigid bodies and are described by the matrix operation

$$\mathbf{r}' = s\mathbf{R}(\theta)\mathbf{r} + \mathbf{r}_0, \qquad (3.1\text{-}6)$$

Similarity

where $\mathbf{R}(\theta)$ is the rotation matrix, s is the scaling factor, and $\mathbf{r}_0$ is the translation vector. The special case $s = 1$ describes the Euclidean transformation and the special case $s = 1, \theta = 0$ reduces to the translation operation.

Affine Transformations.   The general linear transformation

$$\mathbf{r}' = \mathbf{A}\mathbf{r} + \mathbf{r}_0, \qquad (3.1\text{-}7)$$

Affinity

where $\mathbf{A}$ is an arbitrary 2×2 matrix and $\mathbf{r}_0$ is an arbitrary translation vector, is called an affine transformation. It extends the similarity transformation by adding the ability to scale nonuniformly, skew, and shear (e.g., transforming a rectangle into a parallelogram). Equation (3.1-7) is often expressed in the homogeneous matrix form

$$\begin{bmatrix} \mathbf{r}' \\ 1 \end{bmatrix} = \begin{bmatrix} \mathbf{A} & \mathbf{r}_0 \\ \mathbf{0} & 1 \end{bmatrix} \begin{bmatrix} \mathbf{r} \\ 1 \end{bmatrix}, \qquad (3.1\text{-}8)$$

where the right-hand side is a 3×3 matrix applied on a vector with three elements $(x, y, 1)$.

■ MATLAB function g=imtransform(f,tform) implements an affine geometric transformation with matrix $\mathbf{A}$ and displacement vector $\mathbf{r}_0 = (x_0, y_0)$ defined by the function: tform = maketform([A_{11} A_{12} x_0; A_{21} A_{22} y_0; 0 0 1]).

Quadratic Transformations.   Nonlinear classes of geometric transformations are necessary to describe the imaging of rigid but nonflat objects, accounting for effects such as the curvature of the surface of the object (e.g., the Earth surface in remote sensing and the surface of the retina in retinal imaging). An example is the quadratic transformation

$$\begin{bmatrix} \mathbf{r}' \\ 1 \end{bmatrix} = \begin{bmatrix} \mathbf{B} & \mathbf{A} & \mathbf{r}_0 \\ \mathbf{0} & \mathbf{0} & 1 \end{bmatrix} \mathbf{X}(\mathbf{r}) \qquad (3.1\text{-}9)$$

where $\mathbf{B}$ is an arbitrary 2×3 matrix, $\mathbf{A}$ is an arbitrary 2×2 matrix, $\mathbf{X}(\mathbf{r})$ is a vector with elements $(x^2, xy, y^2, x, y, 1)$, and $\mathbf{r}_0$ is a translation vector with elements (x_0, y_0). This transformation is characterized by 12 parameters that may be adjusted to model particular geometric distortions.

▶ Problem 3.1-1

2. Contrast Modification and Nonuniform Modulation

Contrast Modification. Ideally, the sensor has a linear response, i.e., generates a signal proportional to the physical quantity it is supposed to measure. Practically, the sensor has a finite **dynamic range**, which limits the range of values that can be measured. This range is limited at the strong-signal end by saturation, and at the weak-signal end by random noise or uncertainty in the apparatus. The sensor response is therefore generally nonlinear. One commonly used model is a power-law relation, which is linear in a log–log scale:

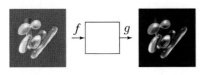

$$g(x, y) = [f(x, y)]^{\gamma}, \qquad (3.1\text{-}10)$$

Contrast Modification

where the exponent γ (the slope in a log–log scale) is called the contrast index. Within this range $(\Delta g/g) = \gamma(\Delta f/f)$, so that if $\gamma > 1$, the sensor amplifies **image contrast** $\Delta f/f$, i.e., the image appears to have higher contrast and a greater dynamic range. The opposite occurs if $\gamma < 1$. Such effects must be accounted for to correctly model an imaging systems.

Nonuniform Modulation. As a result of nonuniform illumination or nonuniform detection (spatial dependence of the sensor responsivity), an image $f(x, y)$ may be modulated by a nonuniform factor $\eta(x, y)$ so that

$$g(x, y) = \eta(x, y)f(x, y). \qquad (3.1\text{-}11)$$

Modulation introduced by the detector may be easily corrected if the modulation function is measured during the calibration process. However, modulation introduced by the illumination is usually dependent on environmental conditions, which are not easily controlled or reproduced.

▶ Problem 3.1-2

3. Linear Blur

A more serious image degradation involves spatial spread, which may result from imperfect focusing, wave diffraction, aberrations in the imaging systems, or motion during the imaging process. As a result of spread from one point into the neighboring points, the value of the object at each point contributes not to just one corresponding point of the image, but to a small patch – a blur spot – surrounding that point. If the imaging system is linear, then the overall image distribution is the sum of the overlapping blur spots that are created by all of the object points. In such systems, the relation between the image $g(x, y)$ and the object $f(x, y)$ may be described mathematically by use of linear systems theory, generalized to two dimensions, as described in Appendix A. The object and image are regarded as input and output to the linear system, so that

$$g(x, y) = \iint\limits_{-\infty}^{\infty} h(x, y; x', y')f(x', y') \, dx' \, dy', \qquad (3.1\text{-}12)$$

where $h(x, y; x', y')$ is a weighting function of (x, y) that represents the blur spot generated by a fixed point at (x', y').

Point Spread Function.   If the system is also shift invariant, i.e., the blur distribution, measured from the originating point is the same regardless of the location of that point, then $g(x, y)$ is related to $f(x, y)$ by the 2D convolution

$$g(x, y) = \int\!\!\int_{-\infty}^{\infty} h(x - x', y - y') f(x', y') \, \mathrm{d}x' \, \mathrm{d}y'$$

$$= h(x, y) \otimes f(x, y), \qquad\qquad (3.1\text{-}13)$$

Linear Blur

where $h(x, y)$ is the **impulse response function** (see Appendix A). This function is, of course, the distribution of the blur spot associated with the spatial spread. This is why it is also called the **point spread function (PSF)**. The linear shift-invariant system is characterized completely by its PSF.

■ MATLAB function g=conv2 (h, f) implements a discrete version of the 2D convolution in (3.1-13) (see Appendix A).

Receptive Function.   The process of linear spatial spread may also be visualized from a different perspective. We fix our attention to a point in the image plane and determine the spatial distribution of contributions it received from points of the object. It turns out that the point $(0, 0)$ in the image plane receives contributions from a patch in the object plane with distribution $\eta(x, y) = h(-x, -y)$, called the **receptive function** (see Appendix A).

Transfer Function.   It is also customary to describe linear shift-invariant imaging systems in the Fourier domain. The convolution relation (3.1-13) in the spatial domain is equivalent to multiplication in the Fourier domain:

$$G(k_x, k_y) = H(k_x, k_y) F(k_x, k_y), \qquad\qquad (3.1\text{-}14)$$

where $G(k_x, k_y)$, $H(k_x, k_y)$, and $F(k_x, k_y)$ are the 2D Fourier transforms of $g(x, y)$, $h(x, y)$, and $f(x, y)$, respectively. The function $H(k_x, k_y)$, called the system's **transfer function**, characterizes the system completely. A harmonic input function at the spatial frequencies $k_x/2\pi$ and $k_y/2\pi$ cycles/mm, or lines/mm, produces a harmonic output function of the same spatial frequencies but with complex amplitude multiplied by the factor $H(k_x, k_y)$, so that the transfer function represents how each spatial frequency component is treated by the system.

Resolution.   One measure of the quality of an imaging system is its ability to image fine spatial details. This is determined by the highest spatial frequency that can be transmitted from the object to the image. A quantitative measure is the width of the transfer function $H(k_x, k_y)$, i.e., the system's **bandwidth**. Another measure is the resolution of the system, i.e., the closest distance between two points (or two parallel lines) in the object that can be discerned in the image. This measure is set by the width of the blur spot, i.e., the PSF $h(x, y)$. Since the width of the PSF is inversely proportional to the width of the transfer function (because one function is the Fourier transform of the other), these two measures are equivalent. Figure 3.1-4 illustrates this principle.

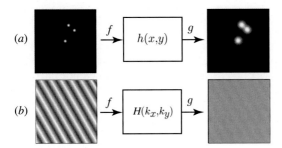

(a)

(b)

Figure 3.1-4 (a) When two points in the object are closer than the width of the PSF, their images overlap and appear like a single point, so that they cannot be resolved. (b) An object in the form of a spatial harmonic function of spatial frequency greater than the system's bandwidth is washed out and appears to be approximately uniform.

▶ Problems 3.1-3–3.1-5

In the following sections, the PSF and the corresponding transfer function, along with their widths, will be determined for basic gazing and scanning optical systems under coherent and incoherent illumination.

C. Coherent Imaging Systems

A wave described by a deterministic wavefunction $u(\mathbf{r}, t)$, such as a harmonic spherical or dipole wave, is said to be coherent. An imaging system using such a wave is described by the linear transformation (3.1-12) or the convolution (3.1-13), where the functions $f(x, y)$ and $g(x, y)$ represent the wave's complex amplitude $U(x, y)$ in the object and image planes, respectively. The relation between these amplitude distributions is linear, since the principle of superposition is applicable to the wave amplitude.

Diffraction-Limited Coherent Imaging

Under coherent illumination, the PSF of an imaging system using an ideal lens in perfect focus is determined by the size and shape of the lens aperture in relation to the wavelength λ. The geometry of the aperture is characterized by a function $p(x, y) = 1$, for points (x, y) within the aperture, and zero, otherwise, called the **pupil function**. For such a **diffraction-limited** system, the PSF is

$$h(x, y) \propto P\left(\frac{2\pi}{\lambda d_2} x, \frac{2\pi}{\lambda d_2} y\right), \tag{3.1-15}$$

where $P(k_x, k_y)$ is the Fourier transform of the pupil function $p(x, y)$, and d_2 is the distance between the lens and imaging plane (see Fig. 3.1-5).
For example, if the aperture is circular with diameter D, then

$$h(x, y) \propto \frac{2J_1(\pi\rho/\rho_a)}{\pi\rho/\rho_a}, \qquad \rho = \sqrt{x^2 + y^2}, \quad \rho_a = \lambda d_2/D, \tag{3.1-16}$$

where $J_1(.)$ is the Bessel function. The PSF $h(x, y)$ is a circularly symmetric function illustrated in Fig. 3.1-5. This function drops to zero at a radius $\rho_s = 1.22\rho_a$, or

$$\rho_s = 1.22\lambda\frac{d_2}{D}, \tag{3.1-17}$$

and oscillates slightly before it vanishes. The radius ρ_s is therefore a measure of the size of the blur spot. If the system is focused at ∞, then $d_1 = \infty$, $d_2 = f$, the focal length, and

$$\rho_s = 1.22\lambda F_\#, \tag{3.1-18}$$

where $F_\# = f/D$ is a characteristic parameter of the lens, called the F-number. A lens of smaller $F_\#$ (larger apertures) has a narrower PSF and, therefore, provides better image quality. This assumes, of course, that the larger lens does not introduce geometrical aberrations due to imperfections in its shape. Another characteristic figure of the lens is the numerical aperture $\mathrm{NA} = \sin\theta$, where θ is the angle subtended by the lens radius at the focal point. The width of the PSF may generally be written as

$$\boxed{\rho_s = 0.61\frac{\lambda}{\mathrm{NA}}.} \tag{3.1-19}$$
Radius of PSF

When $\theta \ll 1$, $\mathrm{NA} \approx D/2f = F_\#/2$, so that (3.1-18) is recovered.

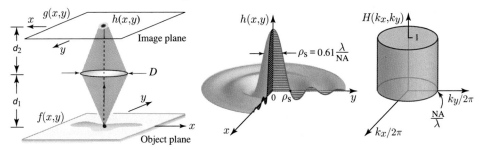

Figure 3.1-5   The PSF $h(x,y)$ and the corresponding transfer function $H(k_x, k_y)$ of a diffraction-limited coherent imaging system with a circular aperture. The PSF has a width $\rho_s = 0.61\lambda/\mathrm{NA}$ directly proportional to the wavelength λ and inversely proportional to the numerical aperture NA and the transfer function has width $0.61/\rho_s = \mathrm{NA}/\lambda$. The system is a low-pass spatial filter with cutoff spatial frequency NA/λ (lines/mm), which is simply $1/\lambda$ in the limit $\mathrm{NA} = 1$.

▶ Problem 3.1-6

Effect of Defocusing and Lens Aberration
Defocused Systems.   If a system with pupil function $p(x,y)$ is not focused, then

$$h(x,y) \propto P_1\left(\frac{2\pi}{\lambda d_2}x, \frac{2\pi}{\lambda d_2}y\right), \tag{3.1-20}$$

where $P_1(k_x, k_y)$ is the Fourier transform of the generalized pupil function $p_1(x,y) = p(x,y)\exp\left[-j\pi(x^2 + y^2)/\lambda d_e\right]$ and $1/d_e = 1/d_1 + 1/d_2 - 1/f$ is the focusing error (in units of inverse distance). Thus the defocusing error is equivalent to a phase factor that modulates the pupil function. This phase factor, which is a quadratic function of x and y proportional to the focusing error, results in broadening of the blur spot beyond its diffraction-limited size and deterioration of the spatial resolution.

Lens Aberration.   Lens aberration is also modeled as another phase factor modulating the pupil function. Its dependence on x and y is often expressed in a Taylor series expansion, with each term representing some type of aberration. For example, the terms proportional to $(x^2 + y^2)^2$ and $(x^2 + y^2)x$ are called *longitudinal spherical aberration* and *coma*, respectively. Lens aberration results in additional image blur and reduction of the resolution.

D. Incoherent Imaging Systems: Microscopy

In an incoherent imaging system the image and object distributions are related by the linear relations (A.2-13) or (3.1-13), where the functions $f(x, y)$ and $g(x, y)$ represent the wave intensity $I(x, y) \propto |U(x, y)|^2$ in the object and image planes, respectively. Here, the principle of superposition applies to the intensities instead of the amplitudes.

Coherent versus Incoherent Imaging

It will be shown below that if $h_c(x, y)$ is the PSF of a shift-invariant system under *coherent* illumination, then

$$h_{in}(x, y) \propto |h_c(x, y)|^2 \qquad\qquad (3.1\text{-}21)$$

Coherent vs Incoherent PSF

is the PSF of the same system under *incoherent* illumination. Here, the vector $\mathbf{r}$ is used to denote a point (x, y) in the plane.

☐ **Proof.** To simplify the notations for this proof we use the vector $\mathbf{r}$ to denote a point (x, y) in the plane. We begin with the linear relation (3.1-13) between the input and output complex amplitudes $U_1(\mathbf{r})$ and $U_2(\mathbf{r})$, which are random functions:

$$U_2(\mathbf{r}) = h_c(\mathbf{r}) \otimes U_1(\mathbf{r}) = \int h_c(\mathbf{r} - \mathbf{r}')U_1(\mathbf{r}')\, d\mathbf{r}'. \qquad (3.1\text{-}22)$$

The measured intensity in the image plane is $I_2(\mathbf{r}) = \langle|U_2(\mathbf{r})|^2\rangle$, where $\langle\cdot\rangle$ represents the operation of averaging. Therefore, by direct substitution from (3.1-22) in $I_2(\mathbf{r}) = \langle U_2^*(\mathbf{r})U_2(\mathbf{r})\rangle$, we see that $I_2(\mathbf{r})$ equals a fourfold integral with the function $\langle U_1^*(\mathbf{r}')U_1(\mathbf{r}'')\rangle$ in the integrand. This is the correlation of the random function $U_1(\mathbf{r})$ at the points $\mathbf{r}'$ and $\mathbf{r}''$ of the object plane. For an incoherent wave, $\langle U_1^*(\mathbf{r}')U_1(\mathbf{r}'')\rangle \propto I_1(\mathbf{r}')\delta(\mathbf{r}' - \mathbf{r}'')$, i.e., the correlation vanishes for any pair of separate points. These delta functions reduce the fourfold integral to the double integral [over $\mathbf{r} = (x, y)$]

$$I_2(\mathbf{r}) \propto \int |h_c(\mathbf{r} - \mathbf{r}')|^2 I_1(\mathbf{r}')\, d\mathbf{r}' = |h_c(\mathbf{r})|^2 \otimes I_1(\mathbf{r}), \qquad (3.1\text{-}23)$$

so that the PSF of the incoherent system $h_{in}(\mathbf{r})$ is proportional to $|h_c(\mathbf{r})|^2$.   ■

Diffraction-Limited Incoherent Imaging

As an example, under incoherent illumination, the diffraction-limited imaging system described in Sec. 3.1C has a PSF

$$h(x, y) \propto \left|\frac{2J_1(\pi\rho/\rho_a)}{\pi\rho/\rho_a}\right|^2, \qquad \rho = \sqrt{x^2 + y^2}, \qquad \rho_a = \lambda d_2/D, \qquad (3.1\text{-}24)$$

illustrated in Fig. 3.1-6. This circularly symmetric function has a radius (to the first zero) $\rho_s = 1.22\rho_a = 0.61\lambda/\text{NA}$, where NA is the numerical aperture of the lens. As illustrated in Fig. 3.1-6(c) two points separated by a distance ρ_s cannot be easily discerned from their image since the PSFs overlap significantly. This is why

$$\rho_s = 0.61\frac{\lambda}{\text{NA}} \qquad\qquad (3.1\text{-}25)$$

Resolution

is a good measure of the **resolution** of the system. For state-of-the-art microscope objectives of $\text{NA} = 1.5$ operated at $\lambda = 500$ nm, $\rho_s \approx 203$ nm.

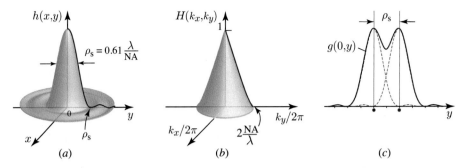

Figure 3.1-6   An incoherent diffraction-limited imaging system with a circular aperture. (*a*) PSF $h(x,y)$ and (*b*) its corresponding transfer function $H(k_x, k_y)$ (called the optical transfer function). (*c*) Cross-section $g(0, y)$ of the image of two points of equal intensity separated by a distance $\rho_s = 0.61\lambda/\text{NA}$. The highest spatial frequency imaged by the system is $1.22/\rho_s = 2\text{NA}/\lambda$ (lines/mm).

▶ Problems 3.1-7, 3.1-8

Effect of Defocusing and Lens Aberration

As another example, the PSF for a defocused imaging system is

$$h_{\text{in}}(x, y) \propto \left| P_1\left(\frac{2\pi}{\lambda d_2}x, \frac{2\pi}{\lambda d_2}y \right) \right|^2, \tag{3.1-26}$$

where $P_1(k_x, k_y)$ is the Fourier transform of the generalized pupil function, which depends on the focusing error. This general expression describes diffraction and defocusing effects, as well as lens aberration, since these effects are included in the generalized pupil function. At a sufficiently large focusing error, the ray defocusing effect dominates and $h_{\text{in}}(x, y)$ in (3.1-26) approaches a distribution equal to a shadow of the aperture. For example, for a circular aperture, $h_{\text{in}}(x, y)$ becomes a circ function of diameter given by (3.1-27).

Defocused System in the Geometrical Optics Limit.   If diffraction is ignored, then the PSF $h(x, y)$ can be determined by treating the wave as a collection of rays. For example, for a defocused single-lens optical imaging system, $h(x, y)$ is a shadow of the lens aperture. For a circular aperture of diameter D, $h(x, y)$ is a circular spot of diameter

$$D_s = D \frac{d_2}{d_e}, \tag{3.1-27}$$

where $1/d_e = |1/d_1 + 1/d_2 - 1/f|$ is the focusing error (units of m^{-1}) and f is the lens focal length. This may be readily shown by use of the relations $D_s/D = (d_2 - d_{20})/d_{20}$ and the condition for imaging $1/d_{10} + 1/d_2 = 1/f$, as illustrated in Fig. 3.1-7. Equation (3.1-27) is also applicable when the object is closer to the lens, so that $1/d_1 + 1/d_2 - 1/f < 0$.

The diameter D_s of the blur spot is an inverse measure of resolving power and the image quality. A small value of D_s means that the system is capable of resolving fine details. Since D_s is proportional to the aperture diameter D, the image quality may be improved by use of a small aperture. A small aperture corresponds to a reduced sensitivity of the system to focusing errors, so that it corresponds to an increased "depth of focus."

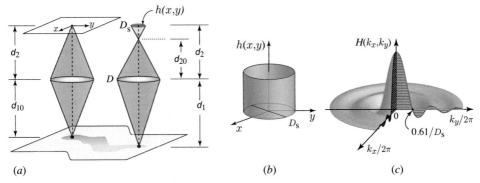

Figure 3.1-7 (*a*) Rays in focused (right) and defocused (left) imaging systems. (*b*) The PSF of the defocused system is a cylinder of diameter D_s. (*c*) Transfer function of defocused system.

▶ Problem 3.1-9

Microscopy

A conventional optical microscope uses one or more lenses to produce a highly magnified image of a uniformly illuminated object (sample). The image may be viewed through a lens (called the eye-piece) or detected directly using a CCD camera connected to a computer and displayed on a monitor. The illumination may be reflected from or transmitted through the sample so that the image provides the distribution of the sample reflectance or transmittance. In standard **bright-field microscopy**, the sample is illuminated from below and the transmitted light is observed from above. If the sample is highly transparent, it is often useful to block the directly transmitted light so that only the light scattered by the sample is observed. This approach, called **dark-field microscopy**, serves to enhance the contrast of biological samples.

The magnification and resolution of an optical microscope are determined primarily by the objective lens (the lens collecting the light from the object). The magnification, which typically ranges from 5× to 100×, is governed by the focal length. The resolution is determined by the numerical aperture NA in accordance with (3.1-25) for diffraction-limited imaging. For high-magnification high-resolution applications, an oil-immersion objective is used (the air gap between the lens and the sample is filled with oil with matching refractive index to enhance the numerical aperture) to enhance the numerical aperture and thereby the resolution.

Microscopy with uniform illumination is called **wide-field microscopy**. A microscope may also construct the image by use of a probe beam scanning the sample, as described in Sec. 3.1E. Other types of microscopy described in this chapter include fluorescence scanning microscopy (Sec. 3.1E), various types of phase-sensitive microscopy (Sec. 3.1H), and 3D microscopy (Sec. 3.2B).

E. Scanning Systems: Fluorescence Scanning Microscopy

In a scanning system, the probe wave is focused such that it intersects the object plane at, ideally, a single point. Likewise, the sensor is ideally sensitive to the same single point. Under these ideal conditions, as the object is scanned, a perfect image of the object's spatial distribution is constructed. In reality, the probe distribution $p(x, y)$, called the *probe spot*, and the detector receptive function $\eta(x, y)$, called the *sensor spot*, are spots of finite size so that the measured image is a distorted version of the true object distribution. Since $p(x, y)$ is the value of the probe at the point (x, y) and $\eta(x, y)$ is the signal recorded by the detector if the object distribution is a single point of unit amplitude located at the position (x, y), the PSF of the scanning system is simply the product

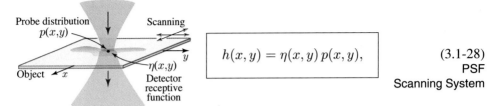

Probe distribution $p(x,y)$

Scanning

y

$\eta(x,y)$

Object x

Detector receptive function

$$h(x, y) = \eta(x, y)\, p(x, y),$$

(3.1-28)
PSF
Scanning System

The narrower of these two distributions sets the resolution of the overall scanning system. Clearly, the system is shift invariant, since the probe and sensor beams are not altered as the object is scanned.

As an example, consider an optical scanning system, such as a scanning microscope, for which the probe beam is generated by imaging a point source S onto the object plane, as illustrated in Fig. 3.1-8. The sensing system collects light from this point and directs it to a point detector D using another imaging system. The object is moved in the x–y plane in a scanning pattern and the signal generated by the detector is recorded. If the probe and the detection imaging systems are ideal, then the PSF of the scanning system is a delta function and the resolution is perfect. In reality, the probe and sensor systems have PSFs $h_{\mathrm{p}}(x, y)$ and $h_{\mathrm{d}}(x, y)$, respectively, so that $p(x, y) = h_{\mathrm{p}}(x, y)$ and $\eta_{\mathrm{d}}(x, y) = h_{\mathrm{d}}(-x, -y)$ is the receptive function of the sensing system (see Sec. A.2B in Appendix A). The PSF of the overall scanning system is then the product

$$h(x, y) = \eta_{\mathrm{d}}(x, y)\, h_{\mathrm{p}}(x, y).$$

(3.1-29)

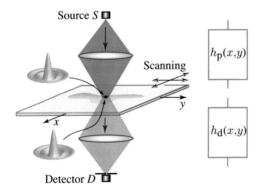

Source S ◻

$h_{\mathrm{p}}(x,y)$

Scanning

y

$h_{\mathrm{d}}(x,y)$

x

Detector D ◻

Figure 3.1-8 An optical scanning system. The probe and detection systems have PSFs $h_{\mathrm{p}}(x, y)$ and $h_{\mathrm{d}}(x, y)$, respectively. For a point source and a point detector, and diffraction-limited lenses, these functions have the distribution shown in Fig. 3.1-6(a) with width $0.61\lambda/\mathrm{NA}$, where NA is the lens numerical aperture.

Effect of Finite Size of Source and Detector on the Scanner's PSF.   If the source has a distribution $S(x, y)$ that extends over a finite size, then the focused probe has a distribution

$$p(x, y) = h_{\mathrm{p}}(x, y) \otimes S(x, y).$$

(3.1-30)

Likewise, if the detector extends over a finite area and has a responsivity $D(x, y)$, then the receptive function of the sensing system is

$$\eta(x, y) = D(-x, -y) \otimes h_{\mathrm{d}}(-x, -y).$$

(3.1-31)

The impulse response function of the overall scanning system is the product

$$h(x, y) = \underbrace{[D(-x, -y) \otimes h_{\mathrm{d}}(-x, -y)]}_{\text{sensor spot } \eta(x,y)} \underbrace{[h_{\mathrm{p}}(x, y) \otimes S(x, y)]}_{\text{probe spot } p(x,y)}. \quad (3.1\text{-}32)$$

The resolution of the scanning system, which is determined by the width of the impulse response function, is therefore governed by the size of the source and the quality of the probe focusing system, as well as the size of the detector and the quality of the sensor collection system.

Coherent Scanners.   For a coherent scanner, the distribution $p(x, y)$ in (3.1-28) is that of the probe *field*, and the impulse response functions in (3.1-29) relate input and output *fields*. The object distribution $f(x, y)$ measured by the scanner is then the spatial distribution of the object transmission coefficient $\mathrm{t}(x, y)$.

Incoherent Scanners.   For an incoherent scanner, the distribution $p(x, y)$ in (3.1-28) is that of the probe *intensity*, and the impulse response functions in (3.1-29) relate input and output *intensities*. The object distribution $f(x, y)$ measured by the scanner is, in this case, the spatial distribution of the object transmittance $\mathcal{T}(x, y) = |\mathrm{t}(x, y)|^2$, or the object reflectance if the scanner is operated in the reflection mode.

Fluorescent Scanning Microcopy.   The fluorescent scanning microscope has become an important tool in the modern life science laboratory. As illustrated in Fig. 3.1-9, it is a scanning microscope in which photons of the focused probe beam are absorbed by fluorescent molecules (fluorophores) in the sample at a rate proportional to the probe intensity (see Sec. 2.3A). This results in fluorescence and emission of incoherent radiation at a different wavelength, which is collected by the objective lens and directed to the detector. This is an incoherent scanner that measures the rate of fluorescence, which is proportional to the density of the fluorescent molecules. The PSF of such a system is determined by (3.1-28), and (3.1-30)–(3.1-31). Dyes, such as fluorescein or rhodamine, may be injected into the specimen to serve as contrast agents, and fluorescent proteins may be selectively attached to specific molecules for molecular and cellular imaging (see Sec. 2.4). The image shows the structure that was labeled with great specificity.

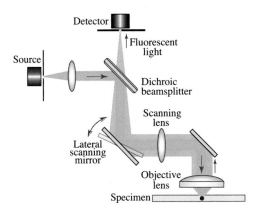

Figure 3.1-9 Fluorescence scanning microscope. An illumination (excitation) beam generated by the source is focused onto the specimen. Fluorescent light, emitted at a different wavelength, is collected by the detector. The excitation light that might be reflected from the specimen is prevented from reaching the detector by use of the dichroic beamsplitter (which separates different wavelengths in different directions).

F. Imaging with Resolution Exceeding the Diffraction Limit

A diffraction-limited imaging system with a numerical aperture NA is simply a low-pass spatial filter with cutoff spatial frequency NA/λ (lines/mm), as illustrated in Fig. 3.1-5. If the highest spatial frequency of the object is smaller than this cutoff frequency, as illustrated in Fig. 3.1-10(a), then the image is a perfect replica of the object. However, if the object has spatial frequencies greater than NA/λ, corresponding to spatial details smaller than λ/NA, as illustrated in Fig. 3.1-10(b), then these high frequencies are suppressed and the image is a blurred version of the object. The resolution of the imaging system is therefore of the order of λ/NA. Can the suppressed high spatial frequencies be recovered? While mathematical techniques can be used to recover some of the lost high spatial frequencies (based on prior information about the spatial distribution of the object), the result is highly sensitive to noise. However, the optical system itself may be altered to permit these high spatial frequencies to be transmitted to the detector, as described next.

Imaging with Structured Illumination

If the object is illuminated with a sinusoidal spatial distribution $\exp[-j(q_x x + q_y y)]$, then the object distribution $f(x, y)$ becomes $f(x, y)\exp[-j(q_x x + q_y y)]$. If $F(k_x, k_y)$ is the Fourier transform of $f(x, y)$, then in accordance with the frequency translation property of the Fourier transform (see Appendix A, page 389), the Fourier transform of the modulated distribution is the translated distribution $F(k_x - q_x, k_y - q_y)$, as shown in Fig. 3.1-10(c). This translation process lowers some of the high spatial frequencies below the cutoff frequency NA/λ of the imaging system, so that they can be transmitted to the detector. Repeating this process with illuminations of different spatial frequencies (q_x, q_y), spatial frequencies above NA/λ, but below $2NA/\lambda$, can be transmitted to the image plane. The resolution can therefore be enhanced by a maximum factor of 2. The measured data for each illumination spatial frequency (q_x, q_y) must be processed using computational techniques [collate the segments of the Fourier transforms of the images that are measured at each frequency (q_x, q_y) to construct the overall Fourier transform $F(k_x, k_y)$ of the object, and compute its inverse Fourier transform to recover the object distribution $f(x, y)$]. Structured illumination may also be applied to incoherent imaging systems, which are described by a triangular transfer function with cutoff spatial frequency $2NA/\lambda$, as shown in Fig. 3.1-6.

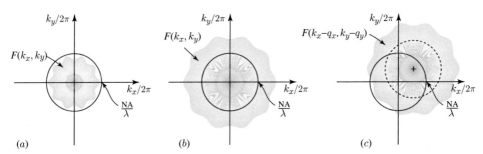

Figure 3.1-10   A diffraction-limited imaging system is equivalent to a low-pass spatial filter — a circular window of radius equal to the cutoff spatial frequency NA/λ. (a) An object $f(x, y)$ whose highest spatial frequency is smaller than NA/λ, i.e., whose Fourier transform $F(k_x, k_y)$ lies within a circle of radius NA/λ, is imaged perfectly. (b) The image of an object with spatial frequencies greater than NA/λ is blurred, since spatial frequencies higher than NA/λ (outside the red circle) are suppressed. (c) Sinusoidal illumination displaces the Fourier transform, brining high spatial frequencies within the circular window of the low-pass filter.

Near-Field Imaging

The diffraction limit may be circumvented if a source, or aperture, of sub-wavelength dimensions is allowed to be placed within a sub-wavelength distance from the plane of the object.

A wave *can* be localized to a spot with dimensions much smaller than a wavelength *within a single plane*. The difficulty is that the wave spreads rapidly at a short distance away from that plane, whereupon the spot diverges and acquires a size exceeding the wavelength. At yet greater distances, the wave ultimately becomes a spherical wave. Hence, the diffraction limit can be circumvented if the object is brought to the very vicinity of the sub-wavelength spot, where it is illuminated before the beam waist grows.

This may be implemented in a scanning configuration by passing the illumination beam through an aperture of diameter much smaller than a wavelength, as depicted in Fig. 3.1-11. The object is placed at a sub-wavelength distance from the aperture (usually less than half the diameter of the aperture) so that the beam illuminates a sub-wavelength-size area of the object. Upon transmission through the object, a spherical wave is formed whose amplitude is proportional to the object transmittance at the location of the spot illumination. The resolution of this imaging system is therefore of the order of the aperture size, which is much smaller than the wavelength. An image is constructed by raster-scanning the illuminated aperture across the object and recording the optical response via a conventional far-field imaging system. The technique is known as **near-field imaging**.

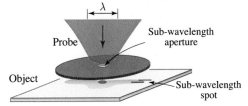

Figure 3.1-11   A scanning imaging system using a sub-wavelength aperture placed at a sub-wavelength distance from the object.

Scanning Near-Field Optical Microscopy (SNOM).   SNOM is typically implemented by sending the illumination light through an optical fiber with an aluminum-coated tapered tip, as illustrated in Fig. 3.1-12. The light is guided through the fiber by total internal reflection. As the diameter of the fiber decreases, the light is guided by reflection from the metallic surface, which acts like a conical mirror. Aperture diameters and spatial resolutions of the order of tens of nanometers are achieved in SNOM with visible light. Since the tip of the fiber scans the object at a distance of only a few nanometers, an elaborate feedback system must be employed to maintain the distance for a specimen of arbitrary topography. Applications of SNOM include non-destructive characterization of inorganic, organic, composite, and biological materials and nanostructures.

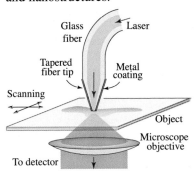

Figure 3.1-12   An optical fiber with a tapered metal-coated tip for near-field imaging.

G. Single-Molecule Imaging: STORM and PALM

Two-Point Resolution Versus One-Point Localization. As mentioned earlier in this chapter, the resolution of an imaging system is generally determined by the width ρ_s of its PSF. Two points at a distance closer than ρ_s cannot be easily resolved [see Fig. 3.1-13(a)] in the presence of noise. For a diffraction-limited microscope, $\rho_s = 0.61\lambda/\text{NA}$, which cannot be significantly smaller than a wavelength (e.g., with a state-of-the-art lens of numerical aperture $\text{NA} = 1.5$, $\rho_s \approx \lambda/2.5 = 200$ nm for $\lambda = 500$ nm). Can a *single* small target (e.g., a bright point of dimensions much smaller than ρ_s in a dark background) be localized with precision much better than ρ_s? For example, can a single fluorescent molecule of size 2 nm be localized with an accuracy of a few nanometers when imaged by a diffraction-limited microscope operated at wavelengths of the order of a few hundred nanometers? The answer is yes! The resolution length ρ_s does indeed limit the separation necessary for *two points* to be resolved [Fig. 3.1-13(a)], but it does not limit in the same way the ability to localize the position of a *single point* [Fig. 3.1-13(b)]. The image of a single point is simply the PSF of the imaging system centered at that point. The PSF of a diffraction-limited system is a symmetric function whose peak lies at its center. Evidently, the location of the peak (or the center) can be estimated with precision much smaller than the width ρ_s of the PSF; the actual value depends on the signal-to-noise ratio of the measurement. The estimation is often done by fitting to the known PSF distribution (or to a Gaussian function). A single point can therefore be localized with an accuracy that is a small fraction of ρ_s, and this process may be called **super-localization**.

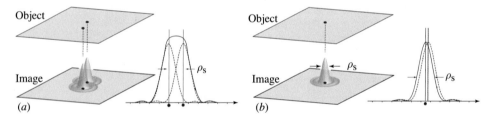

Figure 3.1-13 (a) Two-point resolution. Two points closer than a resolution length ρ_s cannot be resolved since their PSFs add up to form a function with very close peaks (almost a single peak), instead of a double-peaked distribution. (b) One-point localization. The location of a single point can be determined from the location of the center of its image with precision much better than ρ_s.

Single-Molecule Fluorescence Microscopy.   Based on the previous argument, a single molecule with an attached fluorescent label, such as a fluorescent protein, can be localized by measuring its image (the PSF) and determining its center. This type of single-molecule fluorescence microscopy has a precision significantly better than a wavelength (e.g., a few nanometers for a wavelength of a few hundred nanometers). The key premise for this type of microscopy is that the object is a single point. Clearly, it also works if the object is a collection of points separated by distances greater than ρ_s, so that the acquired image is a collection of nonoverlapping PSFs whose centers can be estimated independently, as illustrated in Fig. 3.1-14. In this case, the object distribution is restored by simply replacing each PSF with a single point precisely placed at its center.

Stochastic Optical Reconstruction Microscopy (STORM).   Single-molecule imaging also applies to an object with a large collection of molecules, each emitting flashes of light at random times, at a sufficiently low rate such that no two or more emissions

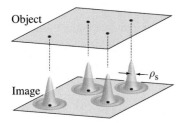

Object

Image

$\leftarrow\!\rho_{\mathrm{s}}$

Figure 3.1-14 The locations of many points with nonoverlapping PSFs can be determined with precision much better than the width ρ_{s} of the PSF.

occur within the area of the PSF within a detection time interval. The detector must therefore be sufficiently fast to capture the spatial distribution of the image of each individual emission (the PSF) before new emissions occur within the PSF area. Because of the random nature of the emissions, this concept of stochastic sampling of molecular emissions is known as stochastic optical reconstruction microscopy (STORM).

Photoactivated Localization Microscopy (PALM). The stochastic measurement that is the basis of STORM may be implemented by use of a control mechanism of photoactivation by which photoactivatable (or photoswitchable) fluorescence molecules are turned on and off at will; the technique is known as photoactivated localization microscopy (PALM) or fluorescence photoactivated localization microscopy (FPALM). Flashes of illumination at a special wavelength(s) turn on (activate) fluorescence from labels attached to the molecules in fixed cells. When an illumination flash is applied, a few single molecules are turned on and their image is recorded. The result is a set of nonoverlapping PSFs. Those fluorescent labels are then turned off, by means of photobleaching, before the process is repeated to image a new set of fluorescing molecules. Many thousands of PSF positions are ultimately determined, from which the overall distribution is reconstructed. Spatial details of dimensions much smaller than the width of the PSF can therefore be obtained. This is why such a technique is often said to offer sub-diffraction or sub-wavelength resolution. PALM and STORM have been recently applied to intracellular imaging.

3D Single-Molecule Imaging. If a single molecule is imaged by one of the 3D imaging techniques described in Sec. 3.2, the result would be a 3D PSF centered at the position of the molecule. This position may be localized with a precision better than the dimensions of the PSF in the transverse and axial directions. The same principle of PALM and STORM may therefore be generalized to map 3D distributions of fluorescing molecules.

H. Imaging of Phase Objects: PCM and DIC Microscopy

A phase object is an object that modifies the phase of an incoming wave without altering its magnitude. It multiplies the complex wavefunction of the wave by a unimodular factor $t(x, y) = \exp[\mathrm{j}\phi(x, y)]$, which represents the information contained in the object. As an example, when probed by an optical wave, a living cell acts approximately as a pure phase object. Seeing it under the optical microscope usually requires the use of stains, fluorescent markers, or other contrast agents (see Sec. 2.4) that are mapped by their intensity distribution. This usually requires that the cells themselves be fixed, or killed.

Since an incoherent wave is sensitive to the intensity transmittance (or reflectance) of the object, it cannot be directly used to image a phase object. Further, when a coherent wave is used for this purpose, the phase of the transmitted or reflected wave must be measured. This does not pose any special difficulty for acoustic waves or electromagnetic waves at radiowave and microwave frequencies, but direct measurement of the phase at optical, X-ray, or electron-beam frequencies is not easy.

There are two methods of imaging a phase object that generates a wave with complex wavefunction of uniform intensity, $U_o(x, y) = \exp[j\varphi(x, y)]$:

- **Phase Imaging by Coherent Filtering.** The wave $U_o(x, y)$ is filtered with an appropriate filter of impulse response function $h(x, y)$ so that the intensity is

$$I(x, y) \propto |h(x, y) \otimes U_o(x, y)|^2.$$

- **Interferometric, Homodyne, or Holographic Phase Imaging.** The wave $U_o(x, y)$ is mixed with a reference wave $U_r(x, y)$ so that the intensity is

$$I(x, y) \propto |U_o(x, y) + U_r(x, y)|^2.$$

Implementations of these two methods are discussed next.

Low-Pass Filter: Defocused Phase Imaging

The intensity of a perfect image of a phase object $U_o(x, y) = \exp[j\varphi(x, y)]$ is uniform, i.e., carries no information on the phase $\varphi(x, y)$. However, if the object is filtered with a low-pass filter, e.g., by use of a defocused imaging system, then the intensity carries some information on $\varphi(x)$. This is demonstrated by the example in Fig. 3.1-15 for a 1D phase object $U_o(x, y) = \exp[j\varphi(x)]$. A perfect image of this object has a uniform intensity. If filtered by an imaging system with rectangular impulse response function $h(x)$, the resultant intensity becomes sensitive to changes of the phase distribution. At locations where the phase is constant, the intensity is constant at its maximum value. Where the phase changes, destructive interference leads to a drop in intensity. A phase change of π leads to a dip in the intensity profile reaching zero (a dark spot) at the center.

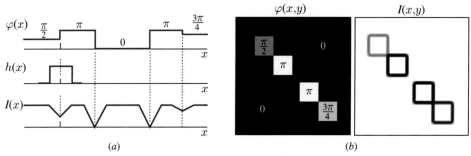

$$(a) \qquad\qquad\qquad\qquad (b)$$

Figure 3.1-15   (a) Imaging of a 1D phase object $\varphi(x)$ with a coherent filter of impulse response function $h(x)$ yields an intensity distribution $I(x) = |h(x) \otimes \exp[j\varphi(x)]|^2$. (b) Imaging of a 2D phase object $\varphi(x, y)$ (128×128 pixels) with a filter $h(x, y)$ in the form of a square function (5×5 pixels).

Differential Filter: Differential Interference Contrast (DIC) Microscopy

A filter with impulse response function $h(x, y) = [\delta(x + \Delta x) - \delta(x)]\delta(y)$ is equivalent to subtracting the wave $U_o(x, y)$ from a displaced version of itself $U_o(x + \Delta x, y)$. The intensity of the difference is therefore $I(x, y) = |U_o(x + \Delta x, y) - U_o(x, y)|^2$. In the limit $\Delta x \to 0$, $I(x, y) \propto |\partial U_o(x, y)/\partial x|^2$. If $U_o(x, y) = \exp[j\varphi(x, y)]$, then

$$\frac{\partial U_o(x, y)}{\partial x} = j \exp[j\varphi(x, y)]\frac{\partial \varphi(x, y)}{\partial x}$$

so that

$$I(x, y) \propto \left|\frac{\partial \varphi(x, y)}{\partial x}\right|^2.$$

The observed image is therefore proportional to the squared magnitude of the derivative of the phase distribution, so that the difference in optical density (refractive index) will be detected as a difference in relief (intensity). An example is illustrated in Fig. 3.1-16.

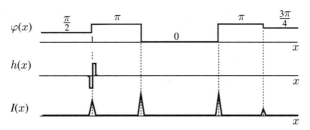

Figure 3.1-16 Imaging of a phase object of phase distribution $\varphi(x)$ with a coherent differential filter $h(x)$ yields an intensity distribution $I(x) \propto |\partial\varphi(x,y)/\partial x|^2$.

Differential imaging is implemented in microscopy by use of a beam splitter and a beam combiner to create two displaced images with π phase, as illustrated schematically in Fig. 3.1-17(a). These are implemented by use of polarizing prisms, which separate the two images as two orthogonal polarizations. This technique is known as differential interference contrast (DIC) microscopy, or Nomarski microscopy.

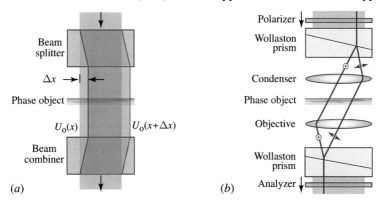

Figure 3.1-17 Differential interference contrast (DIC) microscopy. (a) Basic principle. (b) Implementation using polarizers, polarizing beam splitters, and lenses.

Phase Filter: Phase Contrast Microscopy

A weak phase object with phase $\varphi(x,y) = \bar{\varphi} + \Delta\varphi(x,y)$, where $\bar{\varphi}$ is the average of $\varphi(x,y)$ and $|\Delta\varphi(x,y)| \ll 1$, generates a wavefunction

$$U_o(x,y) = \exp[j\varphi(x,y)] = \exp[j\bar{\varphi} + j\Delta\varphi(x,y)] = \exp(j\bar{\varphi})\exp[j\Delta\varphi(x,y)]$$
$$\approx \exp(j\bar{\varphi})[1 + j\Delta\varphi(x,y)] \propto 1 + j\Delta\varphi(x,y).$$

This phase object may be altered to provide an intensity image by introducing a phase shift of $\pi/2$ into the constant component, leaving the variable component unchanged, i.e.,

$$U_o(x,y) = 1 + j\Delta\varphi(x,y)$$
$$\Rightarrow U(x,y) = j + j\Delta\varphi(x,y),$$

so that the intensity is proportional to $|1 + \Delta\varphi(x,y)|^2 \approx 1 + 2\Delta\varphi(x,y)$, which is linearly related to the phase image. A phase difference is therefore detected as an intensity contrast. The operation is equivalent to an imaging system with transfer function

$$H(k_x, k_y) \propto 1 + j\delta(k_x)\delta(k_y),$$

which introduces a phase factor j into only the components of zero spatial frequency.

Such a filter is implemented optically by placing a small glass plate of quarter-wavelength thickness into the back focal plane of the imaging lens (which displays the Fourier transform of the object distribution), as illustrated in Fig. 3.1-18. This technique, which was introduced into the optical microscope by Fritz Zernike, is known as **phase contrast microscopy**. The same principle is used in radio engineering to convert frequency modulation (FM) into amplitude modulation (AM). In FM, the phase of the radio signal carries the information in the form of a function of time $\phi(t)$. The introduction of a $\pi/2$ phase shift between the temporally modulated component and the carrier converts FM into AM.

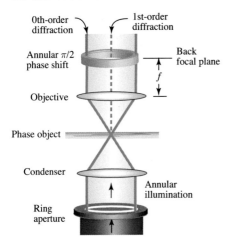

Figure 3.1-18   The phase contrast microscope. The object is illuminated at an angle by means of an annular (ring) aperture, and a phase shift of $\pi/2$ is introduced into the zeroth-order diffraction.

Interferometric Phase Imaging

Another approach for measuring the phase of a wave U_o is to mix it with a reference wave U_r derived from the same source. The intensity of the sum of the two waves is measured using a square-law detector, as illustrated schematically in Fig. 3.1-19(a), yielding

$$I \propto |U_o + U_r|^2 = (U_o + U_r)^*(U_o + U_r) = |U_o|^2 + |U_r|^2 + U_o^*U_r + U_oU_r^*,$$

so that

$$I = I_r + I_o + 2\sqrt{I_r I_o}\cos(\varphi_o - \varphi_r),\qquad(3.1\text{-}33)$$

where $I_o \propto |U_o|^2$ and $I_r \propto |U_r|^2$ are the intensities of the individual waves, and φ_o and φ_r are their phases. The signal recorded by the detector may therefore be expressed in terms of the ratio of the two intensities and the phase difference,

$$R = I_o/I_r,\quad \varphi = \varphi_o - \varphi_r,$$

in the form

$$i(\varphi) \propto 1 + R + 2\sqrt{R}\cos\varphi. \tag{3.1-34}$$
Interferogram

The interferogram $i(\varphi)$ is, therefore, a sinusoidal function of the phase difference φ. As shown in Fig. 3.1-19(a), peak values occur when φ is zero or an integer multiple of 2π, and minimum values occur when φ is an odd multiple of π. The interferogram therefore contains information on both the phase and the intensity of the measured wave U_o relative to the reference wave U_r. The visibility of the interferogram, defined as the ratio of the amplitude of the sinusoidal component to the average value, $V = 2\sqrt{R}/(1 + R)$, has a maximum value of unity when $R = 1$. In this case, $i(\varphi) \propto 1 + \cos\varphi$. If the phase object has a spatial distribution $\varphi_o(x, y)$ and if the interferometer is balanced, i.e., $R = 1$ and $\varphi = \varphi_o(x, y)$, then the detector measures an image

$$i(x, y) \propto 1 + \cos\varphi_o(x, y), \tag{3.1-35}$$

which may be used to estimate the phase phase function $\varphi_o(x, y)$. Since a specific value of i may result from multiple values of φ_o, separated by 2π, an ambiguity arises in this estimation problem. The technique is therefore useful only when measuring phase changes smaller than 2π.

The interferogram is measured by an interferometer, which is an instrument that splits a coherent wave into two components and subsequently recombines them at a detector. One component is transmitted through the object and becomes the object wave U_o, while the other serves as the reference wave U_o. An example is the Mach–Zehnder interferometer depicted in Fig. 3.1-19(b).

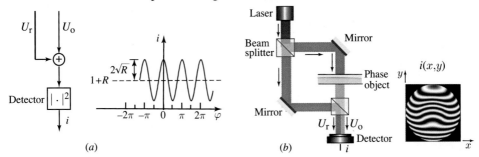

Figure 3.1-19 (a) Phase measurement by mixing with a reference wave before detection. The measured intensity is a sinusoidal function of the phase difference φ. (b) A Mach–Zehnder interferometer with the phase object $\varphi_o(x, y)$ in one arm. The measured interferogram $i(x, y)$ is used to estimate the phase function $\varphi_o(x, y)$.

The filter $H(k_x, k_y) \propto 1 + j\delta(k_x)\delta(k_y)$, which is the basis of phase contrast microscopy, may also be interpreted as an interferometer. The first term produces the object wave $U_o(x, y)$. The second term, which produces a uniform wave proportional to the spatial average of $U_o(x, y)$, provides a uniform reference wave. The detected superposition is therefore an interferogram from which the magnitude and phase of the object can be computed. The $\pi/2$ phase factor j in this case is of no significance. This filter may be implemented by use of a diffraction grating, which make "copies" of $U_o(x, y)$. The first diffraction order is filtered with a pinhole in the Fourier plane to create the reference wave, and the second generates the object wave itself. Higher orders are removed with an aperture in the Fourier plane. This approach is the basis of **diffraction phase microscopy**.[1]

---

[1] G. Popescu, T. Ikeda, R. R. Dasari, and M. S. Feld, Diffraction phase microscopy for quantifying cell structure and dynamics, *Optics Letters*, Vol. 31, pp. 775–777, 2006.

3.2 Three-Dimensional Imaging

Localized imaging of a 3D object requires localization in both the axial direction and the lateral (or transverse) plane. Localization in a lateral plane may be accomplished by 2D scanning with a highly focused beam or by gazing with a high-quality lens, as was described in Sec. 3.1. Localization in the axial (depth) direction, i.e., lateral sectioning, may be achieved by use of one of the following methods:

(a) **Spatial Localization.** A gazing imaging system with a short depth of focus selects a single slice of the 3D object in the plane of focus; the neighboring out-of-focus slices make only weak and blurred contributions. Likewise, a scanning system using a probe beam and a sensor beam that are highly focused onto the same point is responsive principally to that point, with other neighboring points contributing only slightly.

(b) **Temporal Localization.** The time of flight of a narrow pulse can be a good marker of the range or depth, which may be used for localization along the axial direction.

(c) **Interferometric Localization.** A slice of a 3D object may be selected by mixing the reflected wave with a reference wave; the resultant interference pattern is sensitive to the difference between the distances traveled by the reference and probe beams and can by used to determine the range.

These three methods of localization will be described in turn in this section, but first we digress a bit to cover an important issue in 3D imaging—the nonlinear nature of the imaging process.

A. Linearization

As mentioned in Chapter 1, the principal difficulty in the imaging of a 3D object is that the probe wave, on its way to a point within the object, is modified by the intervening points. Also, on its way to the sensor, the wave modified by one point may be modified again by other points of the object. This complex effect does not occur in the 2D imaging of a thin planar object since the probe wave accesses each point of the object directly, and the modified wave reaches the sensor without encountering other points of the object. Multiple interaction with points of a thick object makes the imaging equation generally nonlinear, i.e., the amplitude of the sensed wave is not a weighted superposition of the object distribution $\alpha(\mathbf{r})$ at various positions. To demonstrate the effect of multiple interactions between points of a thick object we consider some simple examples.

Example 1. Multiple Absorbing Layers.   The transmittance of a homogeneous layer with absorption coefficient α_1 and thickness d_1 is $\mathcal{T} = \exp(-\alpha_1 d_1)$. If another layer of absorption coefficient α_2 and thickness d_2 is butted against the first layer, the overall transmittance is $\mathcal{T} = \exp(-\alpha_2 d_2)\exp(-\alpha_1 d_1) = \exp\{-[\alpha_1 d_1 + \alpha_2 d_2]\}$. It is evident in this case that the light is weakened by transmission through the first layer before it enters the second layer and gets weakened again. Since this effect is compounded, the relation between the measurement $\mathcal{T}$ and the object parameters α_1 and α_2 is not linear. The same principle applies to more than one layer, or a continuum of layers with position-dependent absorption coefficient $\alpha(z)$, in which case $\mathcal{T} = \exp[-\int \alpha(z)\,dz.]$ Fortunately, this nonlinear relation between $\mathcal{T}$ and $\alpha(z)$ can be linearized by use of a mathematical operation defining a new variable $g = -\ln(\mathcal{T})$ so that $g = \int \alpha(z)\,dz$. By virtue of the property that the logarithmic transformation converts multiplication into addition, the new variable g is now linearly related to $\alpha(z)$.

Example 2. Two Reflectors.   Consider now the reflection of a plane wave from the two boundaries of a homogeneous slab embedded in a homogeneous medium. In this example, the imaged property α is the reflection coefficient, which is zero everywhere except at the boundaries where it takes the values r_1 and r_2. As described in Sec. 2.2B, the incoming probe wave undergoes a set of multiple reflections and transmissions from the two boundaries so that the total reflected wave is an infinite sum of reflected waves with diminishing amplitudes. In this simple example, a mathematical expression for the amplitude of the overall reflection coefficient of the slab in terms of the reflection coefficients r_1 and r_2 of the two boundaries can be derived from the Airy formulas (2.2-19),

$$r = r_1 + \frac{(1 - r_1^2)r_2 \, e^{-j2\varphi}}{1 + r_1 r_2 \, e^{-j2\varphi}}, \qquad (3.2\text{-}1)$$

where $\varphi = kd$ is the phase shift encountered by the wave as it travels through the width d of the slab. This equation is obtained from (2.2-19) by substituting $t_{12} = 1 + r_{12}$ and $r_{12} = -r_{21} = r_1$ for the first boundary, and similarly for the second boundary. It is evident from (3.2-1) that the amplitude of the reflected wave, which equals r times that of the incident wave, is *not* a weighted superposition of r_1 and r_2. A special case demonstrating this type of nonlinear behavior is that if $r_1 = 1$, then $r = 1$ regardless of the value of r_2. This is to be expected, since in this case the first boundary reflects the probe wave fully, preventing it from reaching the second boundary.

In the other limit of weak reflection, i.e., r_1 and r_2 are small, (3.2-1) can be linearized. This is accomplished by applying the approximation $(1 + \Delta)^{-1} \approx (1 - \Delta)$ to the denominator of the second term of (3.2-1) and neglecting all quadratic terms in r_1 and r_2 to obtain

$$r \approx r_1 + e^{-j2\varphi} \, r_2. \qquad (3.2\text{-}2)$$

In this approximation r is approximately a linear superposition of r_1 and r_2 so that the reflected wave is the sum of reflection from the first boundary plus reflection from the second boundary delayed by a phase 2φ. Reflections of reflections have been ignored, and the weakening of the incident wave as it crosses the first boundary is also ignored. This is the essence of the linearizing approximation as applied to the reflection problem. This approximation is also valid when the characteristic impedance of the slab is not significantly different from that of the surrounding medium, i.e., when the contrast between the object and the medium is small.

Example 3. Multiple Reflectors.   The reflection coefficient of a multilayered medium with N boundaries can be determined by successive application of the Airy formula. The result is obviously a complicated function of the reflection coefficients $r_1, r_2, \cdots, r_N$ of the boundaries. However, in the linearized approximation, (3.2-2) may be generalized to provide the linear superposition

$$r \approx r_1 + e^{-j2\varphi_2} \, r_2 + e^{-j2\varphi_3} \, r_3 + \cdots + e^{-j2\varphi_N} \, r_N, \qquad (3.2\text{-}3)$$

where φ_m is the phase encountered by the wave as it travels from the front boundary to the mth boundary.

Example 4. Homogeneous Medium with Scatterers.   The same principle applies to the imaging of a finite number of scatterers in a homogeneous medium. In the linearized approximation, the incoming probe wave is scattered from each of the scatterers independently, as illustrated in Fig. 3.2-1(a). Scattering of the scattered waves, as shown in Fig. 3.2-1(b) and (c), is neglected. Also, changes of the probe wave that result from scattering are insignificant.

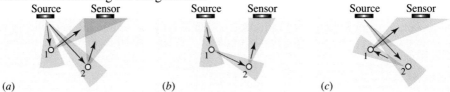

(a)   (b)   (c)

Figure 3.2-1   Scattering of a probe wave from two scatterers. (a) Direct scattering. (b) Double scattering from scatterer 1 followed by scatterer 2. (c) Double scattering from scatterer 2 followed by scatterer 1.

For N scatterers located at positions $\mathbf{r}_1, \mathbf{r}_2, \cdots, \mathbf{r}_N$, the amplitude of the sensed wave in the linearized scattering approximation is a linear superposition of contributions from each of the scatterers,

$$U(\mathbf{r}) \approx \sum_{m=1}^{N} s_m(\mathbf{r}_m) \phi_m(\mathbf{r} - \mathbf{r}_m), \tag{3.2-4}$$

where $s_m(\mathbf{r}) = \sqrt{4\pi\sigma_{sm}}\, U_\mathrm{p}(\mathbf{r})$, $U_\mathrm{p}(\mathbf{r})$ is the amplitude of the probe wave at the position $\mathbf{r}$, and σ_{sm} is the scattering cross-section and $\phi_m(\mathbf{r})$ is the scattering pattern of the mth scatterer, normalized such that the radiated power is unity (see Sec. 2.2C). Again, the linear imaging equation (3.2-4) is not applicable in the presence of the kind of double scattering illustrated in Fig. 3.2-1(b)–(c).

Linearized Imaging of a Nonhomogeneous Medium

A formal theory of scattering from a nonhomogeneous object was developed in Sec. 2.2C under the Born approximation. This theory leads to the linearized imaging equation

$$U(\mathbf{r}) \approx \int s(\mathbf{r}') \frac{e^{-jk|\mathbf{r}-\mathbf{r}'|}}{4\pi |\mathbf{r} - \mathbf{r}'|} \, d\mathbf{r}', \tag{3.2-5}$$

$$s(\mathbf{r}) = [k_\mathrm{s}^2(\mathbf{r}) - k^2] U_\mathrm{p}(\mathbf{r}), \tag{3.2-6}$$

where $U_\mathrm{p}(\mathbf{r})$ is the probe wave, $k_\mathrm{s}(\mathbf{r}) = \omega/v_s(\mathbf{r})$, $v_s(\mathbf{r})$ is the local wave velocity in the nonhomogeneous medium, $k = \omega/v$, and v is the velocity of the wave in the background medium. Note that (3.2-5) is similar to (3.2-4), where here the scattering pattern $\phi(\mathbf{r})$ emitted by each point of the continuous scattering medium is simply a spherical wave $(1/4\pi r) \exp(-jkr)$.

The function to be imaged in this case is $[k_\mathrm{s}^2(\mathbf{r}) - k^2]$, which is determined by the position-dependent properties of the medium. Since the contrast is not large, $[k_\mathrm{s}^2(\mathbf{r}) - k^2] = [k_\mathrm{s}(\mathbf{r}) - k][k_\mathrm{s}(\mathbf{r}) + k] \approx 2k[k_\mathrm{s}(\mathbf{r}) - k]$, which is proportional to the deviation of the refractive index, or the inverse velocity, from the background value. The linearized imaging approximation simplifies the imaging equation and makes it possible to solve the inverse problem for 3D objects, i.e., reconstruct the object distribution from the sensed wave, as will be described in Chapter 5. This approximation, which is used extensively throughout this text, is applicable to localized imaging, as described in this chapter, and also to distributed imaging, which will be introduced in Chapter 4.

B. Spatial Localization: Confocal Microscopy, Multiphoton Fluorescent Microscopy

Lateral Gazing and Axial Scanning

An imaging system using a lens, as shown in Fig. 3.2-2(a), is designed to form a sharp image of a single preferred plane (the plane satisfying the imaging equation $1/d_1 + 1/d_2 = 1/f$). When viewing a 3D object under uniform illumination, the sensor collects a sharp image of the preferred plane along with defocused images from all the other planes. The farther the plane from the preferred plane, the more blurred is its image. Since the details of a severely blurred image are washed out, the sharp image is the most visible while all other images form an unsharp background, so that the system is highly selective to the preferred plane. This provides axial localization. If the object is scanned in the axial direction, an image of the entire 3D object is obtained as a set of 2D slices – a z-stack. Axial resolution is enhanced by use of an imaging system with a short depth of focus (by use of a lens with a large numerical aperture).

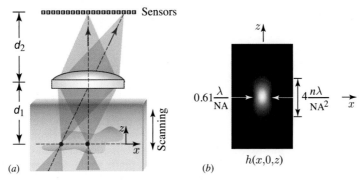

Figure 3.2-2 (a) 3D imaging system using combined 2D gazing and axial scanning. (b) Cross-section of the PSF $h(x, y, z)$ in the $y = 0$ plane shown as a brightness image. The transverse and axial resolutions are $0.61\lambda/\mathrm{NA}$ and $4n\lambda/\mathrm{NA}^2$, respectively.

Mathematical Model. In the linearized imaging approximation, the imaging process obeys the principle of superposition so that the mapping between the scanned 3D distribution $g(x, y, z)$ and the actual 3D object $f(x, y, z)$ is a linear relation. If the system is assumed to be shift invariant in the axial and lateral directions, then this relation is described by a 3D convolution:

$$g(x, y, z) = h(x, y, z) \otimes f(x, y, z)$$

$$= \iiint\limits_{-\infty}^{\infty} h(x - x', y - y', z - z') f(x', y', z')\, \mathrm{d}x'\, \mathrm{d}y'\, \mathrm{d}z', \quad (3.2\text{-}7)$$

where $h(x, y, z)$ is the PSF of the 3D imaging system. As in the 2D case, the functions $f(x, y, z)$ and $g(x, y, z)$ represent the amplitude or the intensity of the wave, depending on whether the emitted light (or the illumination from the incoming probe wave) is coherent or incoherent, respectively.

3D PSF. The PSF $h(x, y, 0)$ in the focused plane is of course the 2D PSF described in Sec. 3.1 and shown in Fig. 3.1-5 and Fig. 3.1-6 in the diffraction-limited perfectly focused case. Its width is $0.61\lambda/\mathrm{NA}$, where NA is the lens numerical aperture. The distribution of $h(x, y, z)$ in the axial direction is governed by the effect of defocusing. The width of $h(0, 0, z)$, which is the depth of focus of the imaging system, is $4n\lambda/\mathrm{NA}^2$, i.e., is inversely proportional to NA^2. A brightness image of the function $h(x, 0, z)$ is illustrated schematically in Fig. 3.2-2(b). The full 3D function $h(x, y, z)$ has the basic shape of two cones with common apex. This can be readily seen in Fig. 3.2-2(a) by examining the pattern of light that feeds a single point in the output sensor plane. This pattern is the receptive function $\eta(x, y, z)$, which is an inverted version of $h(x, y, z)$, i.e., $h(x, y, z) = \eta(-x, -y, -z)$, as described in Appendix A.

Confocal Scanning

Combined lateral and axial localization may be achieved in a point-by-point scanning configuration. The probe is a beam focused onto the scanned point, and the sensing system detects emission from that point onto a point detector. Emission from any other point in the illuminated region arrives in the detection plane as a blurred patch, which mostly misses the point detector. Since the probe beam and the sensor beam are focused onto the same point this configuration is called **confocal scanning**.

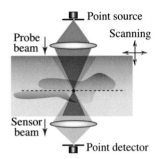

Laser Scanning Confocal Microscopy (LSCM).   In LSCM, which is an embodiment of confocal scanning illustrated in Fig. 3.2-3, the probe is a laser beam focused onto the scanned point in the specimen by use of a lens with high numerical aperture and short depth of focus. The light emitted from this point by backscattering or fluorescence is imaged by the same lens and directed to a detector placed behind a pinhole at a location satisfying the imaging equation, so that most emission from the point passes through the pinhole as in Fig. 3.2-3(a). Emission from another point closer to the lens or farther from the lens is imaged in the detection plane in the form of a blurred patch and most of it misses the pinhole, as shown in Fig. 3.2-3(b) and (c). Thus the system is endowed with a more precise axial slicing capability. A 3D image is ultimately formed by moving the point at the coincident foci of the probe and sensor beams to different locations within the object. This is accomplished by either moving the object itself in the lateral and axial directions, or by means of a rotating mirror and a translated lens in the optical system.

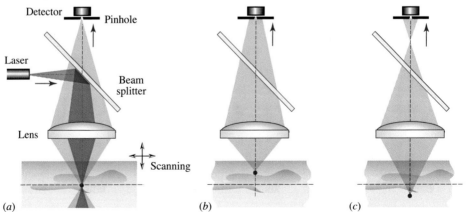

Figure 3.2-3   (a) LSCM. Scattered light from a point in the plane of focus is imaged onto the pinhole. (b) Light from a point above the plane of focus creates a blur spot much wider than the pinhole. (c) Light from a point below the plane of focus creates a blur spot much wider than the pinhole.

PSF of the Confocal Scanning System.   The PSF of a confocal scanning system may be determined by generalizing the approach used for 2D scanning systems in Sec. 3.1E. If $p(x, y, z)$ is the distribution of the probe intensity and $\eta(x, y, z)$ is the signal recorded by the detector for a single point emitting at the point (x, y, z), then the PSF of the scanning system is the product

$$h(x, y, z) = \eta(x, y, z)\, p(x, y, z). \tag{3.2-8}$$

PSF, LSCM

These functions are measured in a coordinate system centered at the scanned point. If a point source is used, then $p(x, y, z)$ equals the PSF of the probe focusing system $h_{\mathrm{p}}(x, y, z)$ under incoherent illumination. Likewise, if the detector is a point detector (or the pinhole is of negligible width), then $\eta(x, y, z) = h_{\mathrm{d}}(-x, -y, -z)$, where $h_{\mathrm{d}}(x, y, z)$ is the PSF of the detection system for incoherent light (such as fluorescent light). These two systems are the same in the LSCM configuration in Fig. 3.2-3. The functions $p(x, y, z)$ and $\eta(x, y, z)$ and their narrower product $h(x, y, z)$ are sketched in Fig. 3.2-4. Evidently, the improvement in resolution accrues from the double focusing effect enabled by the confocal geometry.

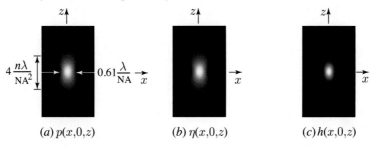

(a) $p(x,0,z)$ (b) $\eta(x,0,z)$ (c) $h(x,0,z)$

Figure 3.2-4   Confocal scanning microscopy. (a) Probe intensity $p(x, y, z)$ generated by the point source. (b) Receptive function of the point detector $\eta(x, y, z)$ is identical to (a). (c) PSF $h(x, y, z) = p(x, y, z)\eta(x, y, z)$ is a narrower function whose dimensions determine the axial and lateral resolution of the system. All functions are centered about the scanned point. The brightness images show only the dependence on x and z; these functions are circularly symmetric about the z axis.

If the source and detector extend over finite areas, then the distributions in Fig. 3.2-4 will be broader. The finite areas of the source and the detector therefore play a crucial role. Mathematically, the new distributions are determined by the convolutions:

$$p(x, y, z) = h_{\mathrm{p}}(x, y, z) \otimes [S(x, y)\delta(z)], \quad \eta(x, y, z) = h_{\mathrm{d}}(-x, -y, -z) \otimes [D(x, y)\delta(z)],$$

where $S(x, y)$ and $D(x, y)$ are the source distribution and the detector responsivity, respectively.

Two-Photon Fluorescence LSCM

As described in Sec. 2.3A, two-photon fluorescence is a process involving two-photon absorption followed by fluorescence. For each pair of absorbed excitation photons, a single fluorescent photon is emitted with an energy less than twice the energy of a single probe photon. Therefore, if the excitation is of wavelength λ, the fluorescence will have a wavelength longer than $\lambda/2$. The fluorescence rate is proportional to the absorption rate, which is proportional to the square of the intensity distribution of the excitation beam and to the density of the absorbing molecules. The imaging system scans the object and maps the spatial distribution of this density.

Resolution.   If $p(x, y, z)$ is the spatial distribution of the excitation (the probe beam), then the rate of fluorescence is proportional to $p^2(x, y, z)$. If $\eta(x, y, z)$ is the distribution of the sensing beam, then the PSF of the overall imaging system is the product

$$h(x, y, z) \propto \eta(x, y, z)\, p^2(x, y, z). \qquad (3.2\text{-}9)$$

PSF, 2-Photon LSCM

The difference between (3.2-9) and (3.2-8) is that $p(x, y, z)$ is squared. Since the function $p^2(x, y, z)$ is narrower than $p(x, y, z)$, both the axial and the lateral resolutions of two-photon fluorescence LSCM are better than those of conventional (single-photon) fluorescence LSCM. For example, for a Gaussian beam (see Sec. 2.1A) the width of the lateral distribution $\exp(-2x^2/W^2)$ is a factor of $\sqrt{2}$ smaller than that of $\exp(-x^2/W^2)$. Likewise, the width of the axial distribution $[1 + z^2/z_0^2]^{-2}$ is a factor of 1.55 smaller than that of $[1 + z^2/z_0^2]^{-1}$, as illustrated in Fig. 3.2-5. The lateral and axial widths of the PSF are therefore significantly reduced by use of the two-photon process. An example of an actual image is shown in Fig. 3.2-6.

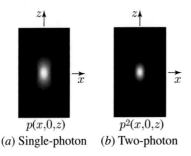

$p(x,0,z)$ $p^2(x,0,z)$

(*a*) Single-photon   (*b*) Two-photon

Figure 3.2-5   Distribution of the excitation functions $p(x, 0, z)$ and $p^2(x, 0, z)$ for (*a*) single-photon and (*b*) two-photon fluorescence.

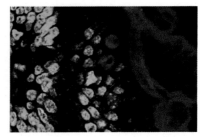

Figure 3.2-6   Image of a 16 μm cryostat section of mouse intestine stained with a combination of fluorescent stains, obtained by two-photon laser scanning confocal fluorescence microscopy. (After Alberto Diaspro *et al.*, via Wikimedia.)

Another advantage of two-photon fluorescence is that the photons of the probe wave have twice the wavelength (one half of the energy) of photons that could generate fluorescence in a process of single-photon fluorescence from the same material. For example, if the wavelength of the probe photons in single-photon fluorescence is in the visible range, the wavelength of the photons used in two-photon fluorescence would be in the infrared. This can be an advantage for media for which the penetration depth is greater at longer wavelength. In such media, the penetration depth of photons with the required energy to cause single-photon fluorescence may be too short, while photons with twice the wavelength can travel deeper and still cause fluorescence by a two-photon process.

Since the cross-section for two-photon fluorescence is much smaller than that for single-photon fluorescence, the intensity of the laser must be much greater, and ultrashort pulsed lasers (e.g., Ti–sapphire lasers) are often necessary. In certain applications, the effect of optical damage or photo-toxicity must be considered. Multiphoton fluorescence microscopy has also been developed and does offer an even greater enhancement of resolution, but requires greater light intensities.

The resolution enhancements offered by the combined use of the confocal configuration and the multi-photon excitation have transformed the optical microscope into a truly 3D imaging system with wide applications in a variety of fields.

Stimulated Emission Depletion (STED) Fluorescence Scanning Microscopy

Stimulated emission depletion (STED) is a method for improving the resolution of fluorescence LSCM by reducing the spot size of the excitation process. The idea is to use two pulsed collinear probe beams with different wavelengths and different spatial distributions, both centered about the scanned point – an excitation beam and a de-excitation beam, as illustrated in Fig. 3.2-7:

- The excitation beam is a focused laser beam with a diffraction-limited spatial distribution of spot radius $\rho_s = 0.61\lambda/\text{NA}$, as in (3.1-24), and a wavelength tuned to the absorption wavelength of the fluorophores.
- The de-excitation beam has a donut-shaped spatial distribution and a longer wavelength tuned to the fluorescence transition.

These beams are applied as a sequence of two short pulses, one immediately following the other, leading to the following processes:

(a) The pulse of the excitation beam excites (activates) all the fluorophores within the diffraction-limited spot area. These fluorophores begin to fluoresce and emit at the longer emission wavelength.
(b) The immediate application of the de-excitation beam pulse serves to rapidly de-activate the excited fluorophores at points of the body of the donut by means of a process of stimulated emission, thereby depleting the excited state and preventing the fluorophores from further emission.
(c) Since the fluorophores in the center of the donut have not been de-excited (de-activated), they continue to emit (fluoresce) and their emitted photons are col-lected by the detector and used for imaging.

If the intensity of the de-excitation donut beam is sufficiently high, most excited fluo-rophores are depleted and only those in a small area around the center of the beam are able to emit. The size of the emission spot is therefore reduced to a small fraction of the diffraction-limited PSF, so that the scanning system has resolution as small as tens of nanometers.

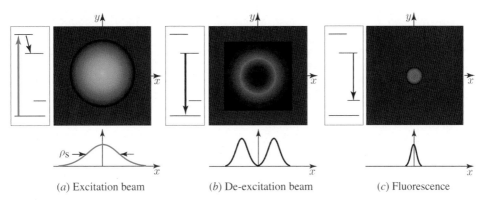

(a) Excitation beam   (b) De-excitation beam   (c) Fluorescence

Figure 3.2-7   STED LSCM. (a) Short-wavelength beam focused to a spot of radius ρ_s excites the fluorophors. (b) Long-wavelength beam with a donut spatial distribution de-excites the fluorphores by a process of STED. (c) Since fluorophores within the donut hole have not been de-excited, they emit fluorescence at the longer wavelength. The radius of this spot is much smaller than ρ_s. This compressed spot is the effective PSF of the scanning system. Energy-level diagrams show the corresponding atomic/molecular transition in each case.

C. Temporal Localization: Radar, Sonar, and Lidar

Axial localization may be realized by measuring the time(s) of arrival of the echo(es) of a pulsed wave reflected from the target or from boundaries between layers therein. As illustrated in Fig. 3.2-8, the times of arrival of the echoes, $\tau_1, \tau_2, \tau_3, \ldots$, are related to the distances between the reflecting boundaries $d_1, d_2, d_3, \ldots$ by

$$\tau_1 = 2d_1/v_1, \quad \tau_2 - \tau_1 = 2d_2/v_2, \quad \tau_3 - \tau_2 = 2d_3/v_3, \quad \cdots, \tag{3.2-10}$$

where $v_1, v_2, v_3, \ldots$, are the velocities in the successive layers. If these velocities are known, then the distances (ranges) of these boundaries may be readily determined from the echo arrival times.

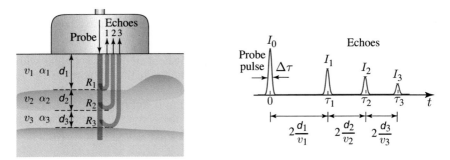

Figure 3.2-8   Localization by measurement of return times of echoes.

The intensities of the echo pulses provide information on the reflectances at the boundaries, which are proportional to the square of the impedance differences between successive layers. In the absence of extinction, i.e., if the media do not absorb or scatter, these intensities $I_1, I_2, I_3, \ldots$ are related to the intensity of the original pulse I_0 by

$$I_1 = R_1 I_0, \quad I_2 = R_2 T_1^2 I_0, \quad I_3 = R_3 T_2^2 T_1^2 I_0, \quad \cdots, \tag{3.2-11}$$

where R_m and T_m are the reflectance and transmittance at the mth boundary ($m = 1, 2, \cdots$), respectively, and $T_m = 1 - R_m$. It has been implicitly assumed here that reflections of the reflected waves do not contribute significantly. These equations can be readily solved for the reflectance of the boundaries. If the reflection is weak, then $T_m \approx 1$ and the intensity of the mth echo $I_m \approx R_m I_0$ is simply proportional to the reflectance R_m. This approximation is equivalent to the linearized approximation described in Sec. 3.2A.

In the presence of wave extinction,

$$I_1 \approx \exp(-2\alpha_1 d_1) R_1 I_0,$$
$$I_2 \approx \exp[-2(\alpha_1 d_1 + \alpha_2 d_2)] R_2 I_0, \tag{3.2-12}$$
$$I_3 \approx \exp[-2(\alpha_1 d_1 + \alpha_2 d_2 + \alpha_3 d_3)] R_3 I_0,$$

$$\cdots,$$

where $\alpha_1, \alpha_2, \alpha_3, \ldots$ are the attenuation coefficients of the interstitial layers. If the attenuation coefficients are known, and with the distances $d_1, d_2, d_3, \ldots$ calculated by use of (3.2-10), the normalized intensities

$$i_1 = (I_1/I_0) \exp[2(\alpha_1 d_1)] \approx R_1,$$

$$i_2 = (I_2/I_0) \exp[2(\alpha_1 d_1 + \alpha_2 d_2)] \approx R_2, \qquad (3.2\text{-}13)$$

$$i_3 = (I_3/I_0) \exp[2(\alpha_1 d_1 + \alpha_2 d_2 + \alpha_3 d_3)] \approx R_3,$$

$$\ldots,$$

can be used to calculate the reflection coefficients $R_1, R_2, R_3, \ldots$ Approximating the attenuation coefficients by one average value α, and the velocities by one average value v, (3.2-13) may be written in the simpler form

$$i_m = (I_m/I_0) \exp(2\alpha v \tau_m) \approx R_m, \qquad m = 1, 2, 3, \ldots \qquad (3.2\text{-}14)$$

The normalization of intensities defined by (3.2-14) is known as the **time-gain compensation (TGC)**.

Axial Resolution.   The resolution of the echo-based imaging system is determined by the pulse width τ_p, since two pulses arriving within this time may not be readily resolved. This corresponds to a resolution distance $d_p = v\tau_p$ in a medium for which the velocity of the probe wave is v. Typical pulse widths and resolution distances depend on the nature of the probe wave, as illustrated by the following examples (Fig. 3.2-9).

- **Radar pulses** at frequencies in the range 300 MHz–300 GHz. Pulses of durations $\tau_p = 1$ μs–10 ps occupy distances $d_p = 300$ m–3 mm in free space.

- **Optical pulses** at wavelength 0.3–10 μm. Pulses of duration 1 ns, 1 ps, and 1 fs in free space have spatial spreads $d_p = 30$ cm, 0.3 mm, and 0.3 μm, respectively.

- **Ultrasonic pulses** at frequencies in the 2–10 MHz band. Pulses may be as short as a few microseconds, or even nanoseconds. In a medium with sound velocity of 1 km/s, pulses of duration 1 μs and 1 ns have spatial spread $d_p = 1$ mm and 1 μm, respectively.

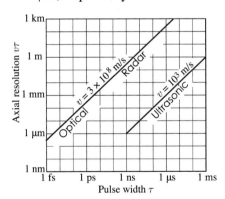

Figure 3.2-9   Axial resolution versus pulse width for an electromagnetic wave in free space and an ultrasonic wave in a medium with sound velocity 1 km/s.

Mathematical Model.   If the reflectors are distributed, instead of localized, i.e., the reflectance is a function $f(z)$ of the range z, then the echo signal would also be a distributed function $p_0(t)$ related to the pulse distribution $p(t)$ by the convolution,

$$p_0(t) = p(t) \otimes f(vt) = \int_{-\infty}^{\infty} p(t - t') f(vt') \, dt'. \qquad (3.2\text{-}15)$$

In the special case when the object is composed of a set of localized reflectors, i.e., $f(z) = \sum_m f_m \delta(z - z_m)$, the convolution in (3.2-15) gives $p_0(t) = \sum_m f_m p(t - \tau_m)$, where $\tau_m = z_m/v$, corresponding to a time profile similar to that in Fig. 3.2-8.

Equation (3.2-15) may also be written in terms of the z variable, which equals vt as

$$g(z) = h(z) \otimes f(z), \quad h(z) = p(z/v),$$

(3.2-16)
Pulsed Axial Imaging

where $g(z) = p_0(z/v)$ is a scaled version of the received signal and the PSF $h(z) = p(z/v)$ is a scaled version of the probe pulse profile $p(t)$.

The distortion resulting from the finite width of the probe pulse $p(t)$ is therefore modeled as a linear system with PSF $h(z) = p(z/v)$, so that the width of $h(z)$ is $d_p = v\tau_p$. This is the size of the blur spot in the axial direction, i.e., the axial resolution, as mentioned earlier. As illustrated in Fig. 3.2-10, each echo is a pulse of width d_p and height proportional to the strength of the reflection. Reflections from neighboring boundaries overlap and may not be discernible if they are closer than the axial resolution.

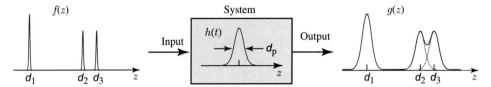

Figure 3.2-10   Effect of the finite width of the probe pulse on the received signal, which is a sum of delayed echos.

Radiowave Imaging: Radar

Radar systems use short pulses of electromagnetic radiation in the form of narrow beams. They operate in the 300 MHz–300 GHz band, corresponding to wavelengths in the 1 m to 1 mm range. Radial localization is implemented by transmitting a short (nanosecond) pulse and measuring the time of arrival of the signal reflected from the target, as illustrated in Fig. 3.2-11. The pulse reflected from a target at a range r is delayed by time $2c/r$. If the pulse width is τ_p, then the range resolution is $c\tau_p$.

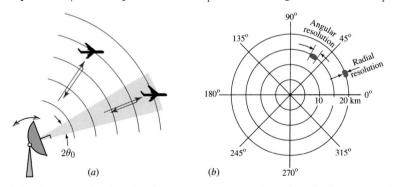

(a)   (b)

Figure 3.2-11   (a) Radar imaging by measurement of the echo of electromagnetic pulses transmitted in narrow beams. (b) Chart showing radial and angular location of detected targets.

The radar antenna transmits a sequence of pulses in each direction, i.e., it repeats the measurement several times. To avoid any ambiguity, the echo generated by one transmitted pulse must be received before the following pulse is transmitted. The pulse repetition rate determines the "unambigous range." Angular localization is implemented by use of a narrow beam generated by highly directive rotating antennas. The angular resolution equals the beam angular width. For example, at 30 GHz ($\lambda = 1$ cm) an

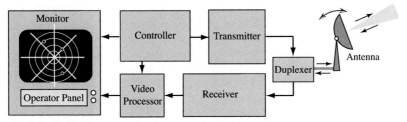

Figure 3.2-12   Radar imaging system. The transmitter generates and directs timed pulse sequences to the antenna. Echo pulses received by the antenna are directed by the duplexer to the receiver, which amplifies the data and sends a digital signal to the video processor for display of target locations.

antenna of diameter $D = 1$ m has an angular width $\theta_0 \approx \lambda/D = 10^{-2}$ rad ($\approx 0.6°$). A block diagram of a radar system is depicted in Fig. 3.2-12.

The maximum detectable range of the radar system is set by equating the received power to the background noise level. As described in Sec. 2.5B, the received power P_r is related to the transmitted power P_t by the radar equation

$$P_r = \frac{1}{(4\pi)^3} \frac{\lambda^2 \sigma}{r^4} G_t^2 P_t, \tag{3.2-17}$$

where r is the range, σ is the scattering cross-section of the target, and G_t is the antenna directive gain.

Radar systems are used to measure the position and velocity (by measuring the Doppler shift), and in some advanced systems the shape of objects. For example, commercial airliners are equipped with radar devices that warn of obstacles and give accurate altitude readings. Ground-based radar is used routinely for guiding and landing aircraft. Radar is also used for marine navigation and to map geographical areas. Meteorologists use radar for weather forecasting and to monitor precipitation and severe weather conditions. Radar is also used to study the planets and the solar ionosphere as well as other moving particles in outer space. Various radar tracking and surveillance systems are used for defense and scientific studies.

Ground-Penetrating Radar (GPR).   Radar may be used for subsurface geophysical applications, including detection of buried objects, such as mines or tunnels, or boundaries in a variety of media, including soil, rock, pavements, fresh water, and ice. Instead of scanning the direction of the probe beam by rotating the antenna, the radar echo signal is measured at multiple locations along parallel lines. The difficulty is that transverse localization is often not adequate, since at the short wavelengths (high frequencies) necessary to generate narrow beams, the attenuation is often too high so that the penetration depth is limited (see Fig. 1.2-4). For example, penetration depths of many meters are possible in dry sandy soil, limestone, granite, and concrete, but are limited to a few centimeters in moist soil. In the absence of transverse localization, the technique is only useful for target detection (see, e.g., Sec. 9.2), but not for spatial mapping (imaging). However, as described in Sec. 4.2B, 2D and 3D imaging may be accomplished with "fat" overlapping beams by use of tomographic methods to reconstruct the object distribution.

Millimeter-Wave Radar.   Millimeter-wave radar imagers are used for noninvasive airport security screening. Since clothing and other organic materials are translucent in the millimeter-wave band, the system can be used as a whole-body imager. The probe wave is transmitted from two antennas illuminating the front and back simultaneously as they rotate around the body.

The wave reflected back from the body, or objects on the body, is used to construct 3D front and back images, as shown by the side figure (after US Transportation Security Administration). At wavelengths of a few millimeters it is possible to produce a small beam with antennas of small size, which are suitable for portable or handheld use (suitable, e.g., for search of abandoned bags). Using only a ten-inch antenna it is possible to generate a beam spot size of a few inches at a ten-foot standoff distance. Millimeter-wave radar technology uses FM probe waves instead of conventional pulsed waves, as described next.

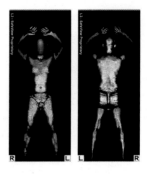

FM Continuous Wave (FMCW) Radar.   Instead of using a periodically pulsed wave to acquire range information, it is possible to use a continuous wave (CW) with periodic FM for the same purpose. As shown in Fig. 3.2-13(a), in pulsed radar the pulse train of the received wave is compared with that of the transmitted wave, and the time delay τ, which is proportional to the range, is measured. For FMCW radar, the difference between the frequencies of the received and the transmitted waves at any time can be used to determine the time delay and hence the range.

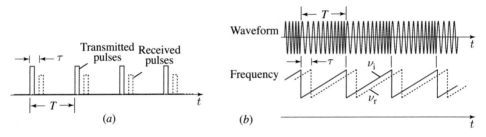

Figure 3.2-13   (a) Pulsed radar. (b) FMCW radar.

Assume, for example, that the frequency is modulated by a triangular (saw-tooth) periodic train, as shown in Fig. 3.2-13(b), so that the instantaneous frequency $\nu_i = \nu_0 + \Delta\nu t/T$ increases linearly from a minimum of ν_0 at the beginning of the frequency sweep to a maximum of $\nu_0 + \Delta\nu$ at the end of the sweep. This occurs during the sweep period T. Although the CW wave has a constant amplitude, its time-varying frequency has the time reference necessary for measuring time delay. If the received wave is delayed by time τ, then its instantaneous frequency is $\nu_r = \nu_0 + \Delta\nu(t-\tau)/T$. The frequency difference $\nu_i - \nu_r = (\tau/T)\Delta\nu$ is therefore proportional to the time delay τ, which is proportional to the range. Note that if the target is moving, then the Doppler shift may be misconstrued as time delay. To avoid this problem, $\Delta\nu$ must be significantly greater than any expected Doppler shift.

As an example, an active millimeter-wave radar system may be operated at 94 GHz with a sweep frequency $\Delta\nu = 2$ GHz and a sweep period $T = 10$ μs. A target at a 1 m distance corresponds to a roundtrip time delay of 7 ns and a frequency difference of 2 GHz × 7 ns / 10 μs = 1.4 MHz. Range resolution of a few inches is possible (the actual value is limited by noise). At 94 GHz ($\lambda \approx 3$ mm), beams with a few degrees of spread can be easily generated and used in a scanning mode.

Unlike a conventional pulsed radar system, which uses large magnetrons to generate the necessary high peak-power short pulses, FMCW radar uses solid-state technology at significantly lower constant power.

Ultrasonic Imaging: Sonar and Medical Diagnostic Ultrasound

Acoustic systems generate images based on the structure of "echo returns" due to variability associated with interfaces and structure. Image contrast derives from the extent to which mechanical properties (density and compressibility) vary from point to point. Sound propagation is very sensitive to small changes in mechanical properties; contrast as small as 0.1% can be easily resolved. An illustrative example employing biomedical imaging is given in Fig. 3.2-14.

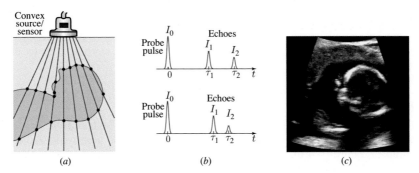

Figure 3.2-14   (*a*) Ultrasonic imaging by measurement of the time delays of echoes generated by reflections of an ultrasonic pulse from boundaries between different media. (*b*) For each beam direction, the echo scan traces points of the boundaries and forms an A-scan. (*c*) The image is constructed from multiple A-scans in the form of a B-scan displayed as a brightness image (after Wikipedia).

SONAR.   Acoustic imaging systems employ frequencies that depend on the scales of the propagation environment and the structures they are intended to resolve. Conventional underwater acoustic imaging systems employ a technique called **SONAR** (sound navigation and ranging) to detect the presence of objects based on reflections from variability within the medium associated with interfaces and microstructure. The frequency used depends on the target range and the length scales one wishes to resolve. Low-frequency active (LFA) SONAR is used to detect submarines in deep water at kilometer ranges and employs frequencies in the order of 1 kHz. In a medium possessing a sound speed on the order of 1.5 km/s, this corresponds to a wavelength of 1.5 m, which establishes the minimum scales that can be resolved by sensing echo returns. Intermediate-frequency SONARs operate in the 50 kHz range (wavelength of order 3 cm) and are used to find fish, as well as by torpedoes to both home in on and determine its range to target (for fusing the charge).

Medical diagnostic ultrasonic imaging systems are designed to image millimeter-scale structures in the human body. They operate in the 210 MHz band using short (1.5 cycle) pulses of width in the 150 to 750 ns range. In a medium for which the sound velocity is 1.5 km/s, this corresponds to wavelengths from 0.75 to 0.15 mm, and axial resolution ranging from 1 mm to 200 nm. Angular localization is implemented by use of a rotating narrow beam generated by a phased-array transducer (see Sec. 2.5F). The angular resolution is determined by the beam angular width. For example, for a transducer with dimension $D = 1$ mm the angular width at wavelength $\lambda = 0.1$ mm is $\theta_0 \approx \lambda/D = 10^{-1}$ rad. A block diagram of an ultrasonic imaging system is shown in Fig. 3.2-15.

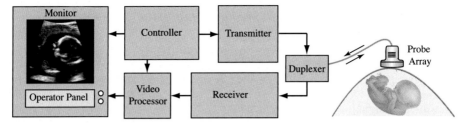

Figure 3.2-15   Ultrasonic imaging system. The transmitter generates timed pulse sequences and a beam-forming signal that controls the probe array. Echo data are directed by the duplexer to the receiver. The receiver has an RF preamplifier and a demodulator. It extracts pulse times and heights, generates the TGC, converts the polar scan into pixels on a rectilinear grid, and sends a digital signal to the video processor. The operator panel has controls for setting the scan angle, the focal location, and other options.

Optical Imaging: Lidar

Optical pulses may also be used for time-resolved ranging. The technique is sometimes referred to as light detection and ranging (**LIDAR**), and the acronym LADAR (laser detection and ranging) is used in military applications. Three factors can limit the range resolution of this technique:

- **Pulse Width.** As depicted in Fig. 3.2-9, for optical pulses of duration 1 ns, 1 ps, and 1 fs, the range resolution in free space is 30 cm, 0.3 mm, and 0.3 µm, respectively. Sub-millimeter range resolution therefore requires the use of sub-picosecond optical pulses, and finer resolution is obtained only by use of femtosecond pulses.

- **Detector Speed.** The ability of the detector to resolve the exact time of arrival of the reflected pulse is limited by its response time. For example, if the detector's response time is 10 ps, it cannot resolve the time of arrival of the reflected pulse(s) with resolution better than 3 mm. In this case, there is no benefit in using probe pulses shorter than 10 ps. However, slow detectors can be used to resolve short pulses by use of interferometric configurations, as will be described in the next section.

- **Medium Dispersion.** In dispersive media, the velocity is frequency dependent, so that different Fourier components of an optical pulse travel at different velocities and the pulse is broadened at a rate inversely proportional to the original pulse width. This effect can be significant for ultrashort pulses traveling deep into a dispersive medium.

Time-Resolved Imaging in Diffusive Media.   Time-resolved axial scanning is not appropriate in a diffusive medium since the probe waves change direction at random as a result of scattering. A pulsed probe wave traveling through such a medium crosses a thick object over an extended window of time, as illustrated schematically in Fig. 3.2-16. For optical probes, we may think in terms of a large number of photons traveling through the object. A *lucky* portion of the photons arrive directly without encountering any scatterers. These so-called *ballistic* photons arrive first. Another portion of photons travel with minor changes of direction and are called *snake* photons. They take a little longer time to arrive. Other photons undergo multiple redirections, including complete reversals, and arrive late. These are called the *diffusive* photons (see Sec. 2.2D). Evidently, the ballistic photons form a sharp image of an object buried in the diffusive medium. The diffusive photons change their transverse location, at random, after they have crossed the buried object, so that the shadow image they form is highly blurred. If the ballistic photons are separated from the snake and diffusive photons by using a fast shutter or time gate, the sharp image may be recovered. Since light travels at a speed of a few tenths of a millimeter per picosecond in human tissue, the shutter must operate at speeds of the order of picoseconds in order to discern the ballistic photons from the diffusive photons. Such switches are available using photonics technology. This method permits imaging under human tissue at depths of a few millimeters.

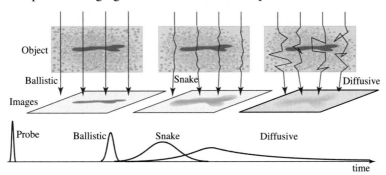

Figure 3.2-16 Transmission of optical rays through a diffusive medium.

▶ Problems 3.2-1, 3.2-2

Reflection Seismology

The principle of depth determination by measurement of the time it takes for a reflected pulse to arrive at the sensor is also used in seismic imaging. A seismic pulse is generated by a controlled source, such as a dynamite explosion or an air gun, and reflections from features in the Earth's subsurface are observed with on-land geophones and/or in-water hydrophones, which convert the temporal profile of the received seismic pressure into an electrical signal, called a **seismogram**. Each peak in the seismogram represents a reflection event whose time corresponds to a specific distance from the source to the sensor via a reflector, and whose strength depends on the change of seismic impedance at the reflection boundary. Reflection seismology is used to map geologic structures, such as rock formation, and predict subsurface oil, gas, or water reservoirs.

The seismic data can be collected by means of a transmitter and a receiver attached at a fixed distance and moving together, as illustrated in Fig. 3.2-17. For a layered medium, and if only reflections at the boundaries are considered, i.e., scattering from the boundaries and any clutter are ignored, then the seismogram recorded at each position of the transmitter–receiver assembly will show peaks corresponding to reflection from the boundaries at points immediately below the midpoint between the transmitter and receiver. If L is the transmitter–receiver distance, then a depth z corresponds to a time delay

$$\tau = 2\frac{\sqrt{z^2 + (L/2)^2}}{v}, \tag{3.2-18}$$

where v is the velocity (an average of 6 km/s). The depth z corresponding to an echo pulse arriving after a roundtrip time τ may be readily computed from (3.2-18). The record of echos at each distance x may be readily used to determine the depth profile of the underground layers.

Reflection seismology is more complex than this simple model. One complication is that there are two types of seismic waves, P-waves and S-waves, with different velocities and angle-dependent reflectance. Additionally, one wave type may be converted into the other at an oblique boundary, in accordance with the Zoeppritz equations (see Sec. 2.2B).

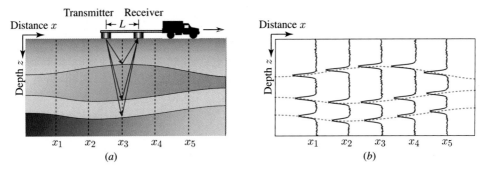

Figure 3.2-17   (*a*) Reflection seismology from underground layers. (*b*) Seismogram recorded at uniformly distributed positions of the transmitter–receiver assembly.

Also, unlike ultrasonic waves or the high-frequency electromagnetic waves used in radar, because of their long wavelength, seismic waves undergo scattering in addition to reflection and cannot be adequately localized. A tomographic approach is necessary for accurate imaging. For each of an array of sources, seismograms are recorded by an array of sensors (seismometers) distributed at widely separated locations and tomographic data processing using the techniques described in Chapter 4 is necessary.

D. Interferometric Localization: Optical Reflectometry

Interferometric Localization: (i) Coherent Harmonic Wave

A harmonic (monochromatic) plane wave of angular frequency ω and wavelength λ undergoes a phase shift $\varphi = \omega\tau_o = 2\pi d_o/\lambda$ when it is delayed by a time $\tau_o = d_o/v$ as it travels a distance d_o. By measuring the phase of the wave, the time delay and the distance traveled may, in principle, be estimated. As described in Sec. 3.1H, the phase of a wave may be measured by mixing it with a reference wave in an interferometer. For example, in the Michelson interferometer shown in Fig. 3.2-18, light from a laser source is split into two beams of equal intensities, one of which is used as the probe wave and the other as a reference. The probe wave is reflected from the object and the reference wave is reflected from a mirror. These reflected waves are directed by the beam splitter to the detector, where the intensity of their superposition is measured.

Let the $U(t - \tau_{\mathrm{m}})$ and $rU(t - \tau_o)$ be the wave functions of the reference and the object waves at the detector, where τ_{m} and τ_o are the associated delay times, r is the complex amplitude reflectance of the object, and $U(t) = A_0 \exp(j\omega t)$. The total intensity measured by the detector is

$$|U(t-\tau_{\mathrm{m}})+rU(t-\tau_o)|^2 = |U(t-\tau_{\mathrm{m}})|^2+|r|^2|U(t-\tau_o)|^2+2\,\mathrm{Re}\{U^*(t-\tau_{\mathrm{m}})rU(t-\tau_o)\}$$

$$= I_0 + |r|^2 I_0 + 2I_0\,\mathrm{Re}\{r\exp[j\omega_0(\tau_{\mathrm{m}} - \tau_o)]\},$$

where $I_0 = |A_0|^2$. If $r = |r|\exp(j\varphi_r)$, then the signal recorded by the detector is

$$i(\tau_{\mathrm{m}}) \;\propto\; 1 + |r|^2 + 2|r|\cos[\omega(\tau_{\mathrm{m}} - \tau_o) + \varphi_r]. \qquad (3.2\text{-}19)$$

Interferogram

This periodic function of the delay time difference $\tau = \tau_{\mathrm{m}} - \tau_o$ is called an interferogram. Since the interferogram is recorded by moving the mirror, it is often expressed in terms of the distances $d_r = c\tau_{\mathrm{m}}$, $d_o = c\tau_o$, and the difference $d = d_r - d_o = c\tau$.

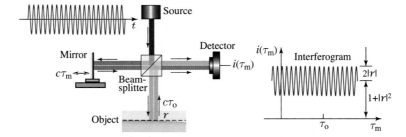

Figure 3.2-18   Interferogram generated by a harmonic wave in a Michelson interferometer.

The fringes of the interferogram have a visibility (ratio of the amplitude of the sinusoidal component to the background) equal to $2|\mathsf{r}|/(1+|\mathsf{r}|^2)$. This may be used to determine the reflectance $\mathcal{R} = |\mathsf{r}|^2$ of the object. If r is known to be real, i.e., $\varphi_\mathsf{r} = 0$, then the depth of the object d_o may be estimated by noting that the interferogram has a maximum value when $\tau = 0$, i.e., when $\tau_o = \tau_\mathrm{m}$ or $d_o = d_\mathsf{r}$. However, since there are many maxima separated by the period $2\pi/\omega$, which corresponds to a distance $c(2\pi/\omega) = \lambda$, there is an ambiguity in the estimation of the depth equal to an integer multiple of the wavelength. This poses a principal difficulty, known as the phase wrap problem.

Measurement of Depth Topography.   When the range (depth or elevation) of the surface of the object is position dependent, i.e., $d_o = d_o(x, y)$, the measured intensity at a fixed position of the mirror (fixed d_r) is an image determined from (3.2-19) by substituting $\tau = d/c$ and $\omega = 2\pi c/\lambda$,

$$i(x, y) \propto 1 + |\mathsf{r}|^2 + 2|\mathsf{r}| \cos \left[2\pi \frac{d_\mathsf{r} - d_o(x, y)}{\lambda} + \varphi_\mathsf{r} \right], \qquad (3.2\text{-}20)$$

as illustrated in Fig. 3.2-19. This image, which is a spatial interferogram, carries information on the topography of the surface. This type of interferometric topography or profilometry is useful when measuring changes of dimensions smaller than a wavelength. However, when measuring greater depth variation, the ambiguity resulting from the phase wrapping effect, i.e., the inability to distinguish phase shifts different by multiples of 2π, can make the measurement difficult to interpret.

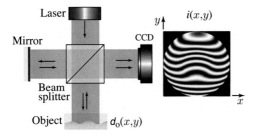

Figure   3.2-19 Interferogram $I(x, y)$ recorded by a CCD camera in a Michelson interferometer used to image the topography of a surface of depth $d_o(x, y)$.

Can the Interferogram Be Used for Axial Imaging?   While the interferogram in (3.2-19) provides some information on the reflectance and the distance $d_o = c\tau_o$ to a single reflector, it cannot be used to simultaneously locate multiple reflectors at different depths within an object, i.e., it cannot be used for axial imaging (estimation of the reflectance r as a function of the depth z). Suppose, for example, that the object has two reflectors with amplitude reflectance r_1 and r_2 at depths d_1 and d_2, corresponding to time delays τ_1 and τ_2. In this case, the interferogram

$$i(\tau_{\mathrm{m}}) \propto 1 + \mathcal{R}_{\mathrm{b}} + 2|r_1| \cos\left[\omega(\tau_{\mathrm{m}} - \tau_1) + \varphi_1\right] + 2|r_2| \cos\left[\omega(\tau_{\mathrm{m}} - \tau_2) + \varphi_2\right],$$

(3.2-21)

has two sinusoidal terms of the same angular frequency ω but different amplitudes and phases ($\mathcal{R}_{\mathrm{b}}$ is a constant background, and φ_1 and φ_2 are the phases associated with r_1 and r_1). Since the sum of the sinusoidal terms is equal to a single sinusoidal function of τ_{m} with frequency ω and an amplitude and a phase related to the amplitudes and phases of the two components, it is not possible to uniquely separate the two amplitudes and two phases (four unknowns and two equations) to provide estimates for the reflectance and depths of the two reflectors. We will see next that a pulsed or an incoherent wave (instead of a harmonic wave) may be used for axial localization. We will also show in Sec. 4.4B that if the frequency ω of the harmonic wave is swept while the detected signal i in (3.2-21) is measured, the result may be used to compute the locations and reflectance of multiple reflectors; but since this technique is tomographic in nature (i.e., the measurement at each frequency contains information on all reflectors), it is presented in Chapter 4, instead of here.

Interferometric Localization: (ii) Coherent Pulsed Wave

As mentioned earlier, optical pulses may be used for time-resolved axial imaging; the shorter the pulse width, the greater the spatial resolution. The difficulty is that optical detectors are not sufficiently fast to resolve ultrashort pulses (picoseond and femtosecond pulses), but this difficulty may be overcome by use of an interferometer.

Consider the Michelson interferometer shown in Fig. 3.2-20 and assume that the reference wave and reflected probe wave have wave functions $U(t - \tau_{\mathrm{m}})$ and $rU(t - \tau_{\mathrm{o}})$ at the detector. Here, $U(t) = A(t)\exp(j\omega_0 t)$ represents an optical pulse whose complex envelope $A(t)$ is a function of short duration τ_{p} and central frequency ω_0. The total intensity is proportional to $|U(t - \tau_{\mathrm{m}}) + rU(t - \tau_{\mathrm{o}})|^2$. If the detector is slow in comparison with the pulse width, it simply measures the area under the intensity function. This is the same as the area under the function $|U(t) + rU(t + \tau)|^2$, where $\tau = \tau_{\mathrm{m}} - \tau_{\mathrm{o}}$. Integrating the four terms in the sum

$$|U(t) + U(t + \tau)|^2 = |U(t)|^2 + |r|^2|U(t + \tau)|^2 + rU^*(t)U(t + \tau) + r^*U(t)U^*(t + \tau)$$

leads to the following expression for the measured signal:

$$i(\tau) = (1 + |r|^2)G(0) + 2\,\mathrm{Re}\,\{rG(\tau)\} = G(0)\left[1 + |r|^2 + \mathrm{Re}\,\{rg(\tau)\}\right], \quad (3.2-22)$$

where

$$G(\tau) = \int_{-\infty}^{\infty} U^*(t)U(t + \tau)\,\mathrm{d}t \qquad (3.2-23)$$

is the autocorrelation function of the pulse envelope, $G(0)$ is the area under the pulse intensity, and $g(\tau) = G(\tau)/G(0)$.

Substituting $U(t) = A(t)\exp(j\omega_0 t)$ in (3.2-23), we obtain $G(\tau) = G_A(\tau)\exp(j\omega_0\tau)$, where $G_A(\tau)$ is the envelope autocorrelation function of $A(t)$. Since $|G(\tau)| = |G_A(\tau)|$ it follows that $g(\tau) = |g(\tau)|\exp(j\omega_0\tau + \varphi_A)$, where $\varphi_A = \arg\{G_A(\tau)\}$. With $\tau = \tau_{\mathrm{m}} - \tau_{\mathrm{o}}$, we express the interferogram in (3.2-22) in terms of the mirror delay time τ_{m} as

$$i(\tau_{\mathrm{m}}) \propto 1 + |r|^2 + 2|r||g(\tau_{\mathrm{m}} - \tau_{\mathrm{o}})| \cos[\omega_0(\tau_{\mathrm{m}} - \tau_{\mathrm{o}}) + \varphi],$$

(3.2-24)

Pulsed-Wave
Interferogram

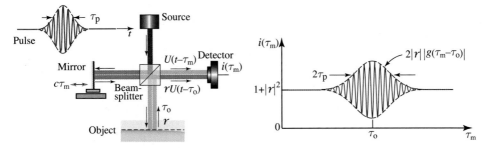

Figure 3.2-20   Interferogram generated by a pulsed probe wave is centered at a time delay $\tau = \tau_0$ and extends over an interval equal to twice the pulse width.

where $\varphi = \varphi_A + \arg\{r\}$. This is a sinusoidal interferogram with fringes at a frequency ω_0 and visibility (ratio of the amplitude of the sinusoidal component to the background component) proportional to $|g(\tau)|$, the magnitude of the normalized pulse autocorrelation function. The maximum visibility of the fringe pattern is $2|r|/(1 + |r|^2)$, which may be used to estimate the reflectance $\mathcal{R} = |r|^2$. The fringes extend over the width of the autocorrelation function, which is twice the pulse width τ_p, and diminish at greater magnitudes of τ. Pulsed-wave interferometry can therefore provide absolute measurement of the range without encountering the phase wrapping ambiguity that arises in interferometry with a coherent, monochromatic, CW source.

Interferometric Localization: (iii) Low-Coherence Wave

A partially coherent wave with short coherence time, generated by a CW source of large spectral width such as a lamp or an LED, can also be used for interferometric range measurement. The resultant interferograms are similar to those generated in pulsed-wave interferometry. Here, the fringes extend over a time interval equal to the source's coherence time, which is inversely proportional to the spectral width, so that broadband sources with short coherence time can provide high-resolution range information. Before this concept is developed, we digress briefly for a description of the principal statistical characteristics of partially coherent light.

(i) Temporal Characteristics. A partially coherent wave is represented by a random wavefunction $U(t)$ characterized by the autocorrelation function,

$$G(\tau) = \langle U^*(t)U(t+\tau)\rangle, \tag{3.2-25}$$

Coherence Function

which is the average of the product of $U^*(t)U(t+\tau)$ as a function of the time delay τ. In the parlance of optical coherence theory, this function is known as the **coherence function**. For $\tau = 0$, $G(0) = \langle |U(t)|^2 \rangle$ so that $G(0)$ equals the average intensity I. A measure of the degree of coherence is the normalized coherence function, $g(\tau) = G(\tau)/G(0)$, called the **complex degree of coherence**. Its absolute value cannot exceed unity, i.e., $0 \le |g(\tau)| \le 1$. The width of $|g(\tau)|$, denoted τ_c, serves as a measure of the memory time of the random fluctuations and is known as the **coherence time**. For $\tau \gg \tau_c$ the fluctuations of $U(t)$ and $U(t+\tau)$ are completely uncorrelated. The coherence time τ_c corresponds to a distance $\ell_c = c\tau_c$, known as the **coherence length**. The wave is effectively coherent if ℓ_c is much greater than all optical path-length differences encountered.

(ii) Spectral Characteristics. The **power spectral density** $S(\omega)$ of the random function $U(t)$ is the Fourier transform of the autocorrelation function $G(\tau)$. The function $S(\omega)$ is usually confined to a narrow band centered about a central frequency ω_0 and its width is the **spectral width** $\Delta\omega = 2\pi\Delta\nu$, which is also specified as a wavelength range $\Delta\lambda = (\lambda^2/c)\Delta\nu$. Because of the Fourier-transform relation between $S(\omega)$ and $G(\tau)$, their widths are inversely related. A light source of broad spectrum has a short coherence time, and vice versa. For Gaussian spectra $\tau_c = 0.44/\Delta\nu = 0.44(\lambda^2/c\Delta\lambda)$. For example, for an LED, the coherence length $\ell_c = 10\text{--}30$ µm, corresponding to coherence time $\tau_c = 33\text{--}100$ fs. For a He–Ne laser, $\ell_c = 10$ cm–300 m, corresponding to $\tau_c = 0.33$ ns–1 µs.

Low-Coherence Optical Reflectometry.   If a partially coherent wave $U(t)$ with intensity $I_0 = \langle |U(t)|^2 \rangle$, coherence function $G(\tau) = \langle U^*(t)U(t+\tau) \rangle$, and complex degree of coherence $g(\tau) = G(\tau)/G(0)$ is used for optical reflectometry in the Michelson interferometer configuration shown in Fig. 3.2-21, then the measured signal is proportional to the averaged the total intensity $i \propto \langle |U(t-\tau_m) + rU(t-\tau_o)|^2 \rangle$, where τ_m and τ_o are the delay times encountered by the reference and object beams, respectively, and r is the amplitude reflectance of the object. Since the wave $U(t)$ is stationary (i.e., its statistical properties are the same at any time), $i \propto \langle |U(t) + rU(t+\tau)|^2 \rangle$, where $\tau = \tau_m - \tau_o$. Therefore,

$$i \propto \langle |U(t)|^2 + |r|^2\, |U(t+\tau)|^2 + r\, U^*(t)U(t+\tau) + r^*\, U(t)U^*(t+\tau) \rangle$$
$$= I_0(1 + |r|^2 + 2\,\mathrm{Re}\,\{r\,G(\tau)\} = 2I_0\left[1 + \mathrm{Re}\,\{r\,g(\tau)\}\right].$$

If $U(t) = A(t)\exp(j\omega_0\tau)$, where $A(t)$ is the envelope and ω_0 is the central frequency, then $G(\tau) = G_A(\tau)\exp(j\omega_0\tau)$, where $G_A(\tau)$ is the autocorrelation function of the envelope $A(t)$, then the signal measured by the detector may be expressed in terms of the mirror delay time τ_m by substituting $\tau = \tau_m - \tau_o$:

$$i(\tau_m) \propto 1 + |r|^2 + |r||g(\tau_m - \tau_o)|\cos\left[\omega_0(\tau_m - \tau_o) + \varphi\right], \qquad (3.2\text{-}26)$$

(3.2-26)
Low-Coherence
Interferogram

where $\varphi = \arg\{G_A(\tau_m - \tau_o)\} + \arg\{r\}$. The interferogram exhibits fringes of frequency ω_0 extending over a narrow range of τ centered at τ_o, which is proportional to the object range. The maximum visibility of the fringe pattern is $2|r|/(1 + |r|^2)$, which may be used to estimate the reflection coefficient of the object. The visibility is also proportional to the normalized coherence function $|g(\tau)|$, so that it diminishes as $|\tau|$ exceeds the coherence time τ_c. The width of the interference pattern is therfore equal to the coherence time τ_c. This means that the interference occurs (i.e., the sinusoidal pattern is visible) only when the optical path difference is smaller than the coherence length ℓ_c so that the range resolution is governed by the coherence length.

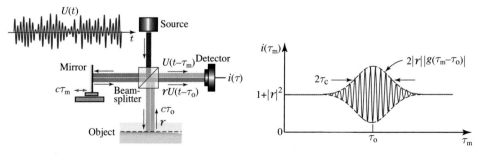

Figure 3.2-21   The interferogram generated by a partially coherent wave extends over a time delay of the order of the coherence time.

Optical Coherence "Tomography" (OCT)

Optical reflectometry may be used for 3D imaging by employing a combination of scanning in the lateral direction by means of a localized beam, and interferometric localization in the axial direction by use of either a short optical pulse, as in Fig. 3.2-20, or a partially coherent continuous wave of short coherence time (broad spectrum), as in Fig. 3.2-21. This technique, which is commonly called optical coherence tomography (OCT), is suitable for profiling the topography of a multilayered medium by measuring the reflectance and the depth of each of the layer boundaries for each of the transverse locations, as illustrated in Fig. 3.2-22. Note that OCT is a *localized* imaging method in which the 3D image is reconstructed point by point in both the transverse and axial directions; it is *not* a tomographic technique! The term "tomography" is actually a misnomer.

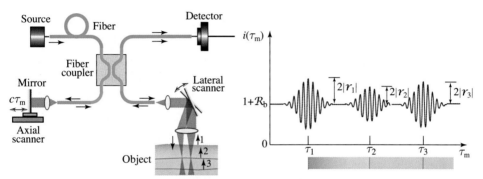

Figure 3.2-22 Fiber-optic implementation of optical coherence tomography. A source emits a short optical pulse or a partially coherent CW with a short coherence time (broad spectrum) into an optical fiber. Serving as a beamsplitter, a fiber coupler splits the incoming light into two components. One is reflected from the movable mirror and directed to the detector after a time delay τ proportional to the pathlength. The other component is directed to the object whereupon it undergoes reflections from the various boundaries. These reflections are directed to the detector, undergoing time delays $\tau_1, \tau_2, \ldots$, proportional to the depths of the boundaries. The detector measures the average intensity of the superposed waves as a function of τ, which is controlled by the mirror. Reflections from these boundaries result in an interferogram with sets of interference fringes centered at $\tau = \tau_1, \tau = \tau_2, \ldots$, i.e., corresponding to mirror positions with pathlengths matching the locations of the object boundaries. The amplitudes of these sets of fringes are proportional to the amplitude reflectance of the layers $r_1, r_2, \ldots$, and the background term $\mathcal{R}_b$ represents the intensity of the wave reflected from the object (including interference between neighboring reflectors). The object is scanned in the transverse directions, using rotating mirrors, and a new interferogram is generated at each transverse location to complete the 3D imaging process.

Resolution.   The axial resolution of an OCT system using a pulsed source is determined by the pulse width. For example, a $\tau_p = 10$ fs pulse in a medium of refractive index n has a resolution of $(c/n)\tau_p = 2.3$ μm. The axial resolution of an OCT system using a partially coherent source is determined by the coherence length in the medium $\ell_c = (c/n)\tau_c$ so that

$$\text{Resolution} = 0.44\frac{\lambda^2}{n\,\Delta\lambda}\,. \tag{3.2-27}$$

Superluminescent light emitting diodes (SLD), which are commonly used in OCT, have a broad spectral width and a short coherent time. For example, a source with $\Delta\lambda = 100$ nm at $\lambda = 800$ nm in a medium of refractive index $n = 1.3$ has a resolution of approximately 2 μm. This is superior to ultrasonic imaging, which has resolution of tens of micrometers. Lateral resolution is determined by the wavelength and the numerical aperture of the focused optical beam.

Spectral-Domain Optical Coherence Tomography.   Instead of measuring the intensity as a function of the time delay τ introduced by the moving mirror in the reference arm of the interferometer, the mirror may be held fixed and the intensity measured as a function the angular frequency ω. The source may be either a harmonic wave whose frequency is varied (swept-frequency OCT), or a broadband source combined with a frequency-selection mechanism (a spectrometer) at the detection side of the interferometer. This type of spectral-domain optical reflectometry is called spectral-domain OCT. Here, the interferogram $I(\omega)$ contains the desired information on the reflectance and depth of various reflectors, but the contributions of the reflectors are not directly delineated in the interferogram, as is the case in the time-domain interferogram $I(\tau)$ in Fig. 3.2-22. Some computation (an inverse Fourier transform) is necessary to perform this separation, as will described in Sec. 4.4B. Therefore, in contrast with time-domain OCT, spectral-domain OCT is a truly tomographic system.

Applications.   OCT has proven to be an effective noncontact noninvasive low-power optical imaging technique in clinical medicine, particularly the imaging of transparent tissue such as the retinal nerve fiber layer (RNGL), subcutaneous blood vessels, vascular walls and placques. Clinical applications of retinal imaging include visualization and analysis of retinal histology and disorders such as diabetic retinopathy, macular degeneration, contour changes in the optical disk, branch retinal vein occlusion, macular edema and degeneration, glaucoma damage. The fiber-based design, illustrated in Fig. 3.2-22, allows integration with small catheters/endoscopes. A polarization version of OCT images tissues with collagen or elastin fibers: muscle, tendons, and normal and thermally damaged soft tissues. Other biological applications include imaging of human skin and human cochlea, and imaging of small animals. Other engineering applications include industrial nondestructive testing as well as art conservation, restoration, and forensics. OCT imaging can be performed at or near real time. The apparatus is compact, portable, noncontact, and can be combined with laser spectroscopy and Doppler imaging for flow imaging.

EXAMPLE 3.2-1.   *Application of OCT to Retinal Imaging.* Cross-sectional images (B-scans) are now routinely used to construct 3D images of various parts of the human retina under normal and diseased conditions. Fig. 3.2-23 shows a cross-sectional image of the macula (a spot near the center of the retina around 5 mm in diameter and having near its center the fovea, which is responsible for central vision).

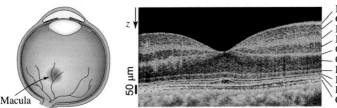

Figure 3.2-23   Cross-sectional image (B-scan) of the human macula. Various layers are shown, with layers with the highest reflectance appearing red and those with minimum reflectance appearing blue or black. (After M. Wojtkowski, V. J. Srinivasan, T. H. Ko, J. G. Fujimoto, A. Kowalczyk, J. S. Duker, Ultrahigh-resolution, high-speed, Fourier domain optical coherence tomography and methods for dispersion compensation, *Optics Express*, Vol. 12, p. 2404, 2004).

EXAMPLE 3.2-2.   *Application of OCT to visualize underdrawings in old paintings.* Underdawings in old paintings can be visualized beneath the overlying paint and varnish by exploiting the fact that different paints have significantly different infrared absorption properties. Good results are obtained by use of high-resolution IR photography. 3D-OCT is also capable of analyzing all of the layers in the painting and generally provide a more comprehensive and detailed characterization of historical artwork, as in the example depicted in Fig. 3.2-24.

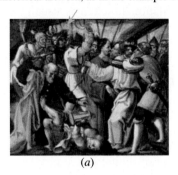
(*a*)
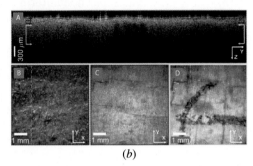
(*b*)

Figure 3.2-24   (*a*)The Renaissance painting "Arrest of Christ" (circa 1520) was examined by OCT and found to have underdrawings in the area marked by the green square and arrow. (*b*) Panel A is a cross-sectional image (B-scan). Colored arrows indicate the locations of three layers: varnish (red), paint (blue), and underdrawing (green) layers. The C-scans of each of these layers were axially summed to form the voxel projection *en face* images shown in panels B, C, and D. The dashed line indicates the location of the B-scan in Panel A. The image in Panel D shows the underdrawing, which is not visible in the painting. After (D. C. Adler, J. Stenger, I. Gorczynska, H. Lie, T. Hensick, R. Spronk, S. Wolohojian, N. Khandekar, J. Y. Jiang, S. Barry, A. E. Cable, R. Huber, and J. G. Fujimoto, Comparison of three-dimensional optical coherence tomography and high resolution photography for art conservation studies, *Optics Express*, Vol. 15, p. 15972, 2007.)

▶ Problems 3.2-3, 3.2-4

3.3   Image Restoration

Image restoration is the reconstruction of an object distribution $f(\mathbf{r})$ from the measured image $g(\mathbf{r})$, assuming a known mathematical model for the imaging system. Models describing various image formation systems were described in Sec. 3.1B. We distinguish here two classes: systems involving no spatial spread (i.e., point-to-point transformations) and others with PSFs of finite spatial extent.

A. Systems with No Spatial Spread

The inversion of systems described by point-to-point transformations is, in principle, straightforward. For example, a geometric transformation defined by the operation $\mathbf{r}' = \mathbf{T}(\mathbf{r})$ (e.g., magnification or rotation) can be easily reversed by applying the inverse operation $\mathbf{T}^{-1}$ (e.g., minification or counter-rotation, respectively). However, in situations when an image has different segments, each of which is suffering from a slightly different geometric transformation, then restoration requires bringing the different segments into alignment, a process known as **registration** (see Chapter 7).

Restoration of an object that has undergone contrast modification, e.g., $g = f^{\gamma}$, can also be readily implemented by use of an inverse modification $g^{1/\gamma}$ at every point of the image. In the presence of error or noise, contrast modification can result in error amplification and must therefore be judiciously applied.

Restoration of the degradation introduced by nonuniform modulation, which is often caused by nonuniform illumination or spatially varying sensor responsivity, may also be readily reversed if precisely known. One approach is to convert the multiplication in the relation $g(\mathbf{r}) = m(\mathbf{r})f(\mathbf{r})$ into an addition by taking the logarithm $\log g(\mathbf{r}) = \log m(\mathbf{r}) + \log f(\mathbf{r})$. Since the nonuniform modulation function is usually slowly varying, it can be filtered out by using of an appropriate spatial filter. This type of operation is known as a **homomorphic filter**.

B. Linear Systems with Spatial Blur: Deblurring

If the imaging system involves spatial spread, e.g., one described by a linear filter with PSF h, then the inversion process, called **deblurring** or **deconvolution**, is more subtle and may be highly sensitive to small noise in the measurement, or uncertainty of the model. Some principles of image restoration (inversion) are addressed briefly in this section, and are revisited in Chapter 5 in the context of digital image processing, for which the object and/or the image are represented by discrete systems.

Convolution Model.   If the imaging system is linear and shift invariant, the imaging equation is the convolution

$$g(\mathbf{r}) = h(\mathbf{r}) \otimes f(\mathbf{r}), \tag{3.3-1}$$

where $f(\mathbf{r})$ and $g(\mathbf{r})$ are the object and image distributions, respectively, and $h(\mathbf{r})$ is a known PSF. The inverse process is then called **deconvolution**. Inversion of shift-variant systems is described in Chapter 5. The convolution model is applicable to many imaging systems:

- For a 1D system (A-scan), such as axial imaging by radar, sonar, or interferometric reflectometry (e.g., OCT), $\mathbf{r} = z$, so that (3.3-1) is a 1D convolution $g(z) = h(z) \otimes f(z)$.
- For a 2D system (C-scan), such as the imaging of a planar object or a slice of a 3D object obtained by use of a lens or a scanning system, $\mathbf{r} = (x, y)$, so that (3.3-1) is a 2D convolution.
- For a 3D system, as in the combined lateral and axial imaging of a 3D object using confocal microscopy, $\mathbf{r} = (x, y, z)$ and (3.3-1) is a 3D convolution.

Inversion (Deconvolution).   Image restoration involves the inversion of the convolution equation (3.3-1) to compute $f(\mathbf{r})$, given $g(\mathbf{r})$ and $h(\mathbf{r})$. This may appear to be a straightforward problem, since convolution is equivalent to multiplication in the Fourier domain (see Appendix A), i.e.,

$$G(\mathbf{k}) = H(\mathbf{k})F(\mathbf{k}), \tag{3.3-2}$$

where $F(\mathbf{k})$, $G(\mathbf{k})$, and $H(\mathbf{k})$ are the Fourier transforms of $f(\mathbf{r})$, $g(\mathbf{r})$ and $h(\mathbf{r})$, respectively. Here, the spatial frequency $\mathbf{k}$ represents a 1D variable k_z, 2D variables (k_x, k_y), or 3D variables (k_x, k_y, k_z), depending on the problem at hand. Equation (3.3-2) may be readily inverted by applying an inverse filter $H_r(\mathbf{k}) = H^{-1}(\mathbf{k})$ to the measured image. The result is

$$F(\mathbf{k}) = H^{-1}(\mathbf{k})G(\mathbf{k}). \tag{3.3-3}$$

Ill-Posedness.   As described in Sec. 3.1C and Sec. 3.1D, the transfer function $H(\mathbf{k})$ of a typical imaging system is a low-pass filter that vanishes at sufficiently high spatial frequencies, but may drop to zero and exhibit side lobes with decreasing amplitudes as the frequency increases. An example of the filter $H(\mathbf{k})$ and its inverse $H_{\mathrm{r}}(\mathbf{k})$ are shown in Fig. 3.3-1(a) and (b). The inverse filter has a very large magnitude at very high frequencies and also near the zeros of $H(\mathbf{k})$, with infinite values at the zeros. Consequently, inverse filters can amplify noise and are very sensitive to measurement errors. This is why the image inversion problem is often said to be **ill-posed**. This subject is discussed again in Sec. 5.2 in the context of digital image processing and discrete inverse problems.

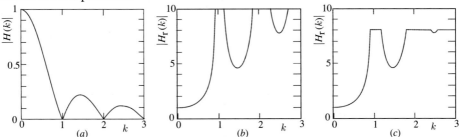

Figure 3.3-1   Magnitude of the transfer function of (a) the imaging system, (b) inverse filter, (c) truncated inverse filter.

Inversion in the Presence of Noise.   The inversion system must account for the noise and uncertainties that contaminate the measurement. In the presence of additive noise, the imaging equation takes the form

$$g(\mathbf{r}) = h(\mathbf{r}) \otimes f(\mathbf{r}) + w(\mathbf{r}), \tag{3.3-4}$$

where $w(\mathbf{r})$ is a random function representing the noise. The inversion process aims at finding an estimate of the object $\hat{f}(\mathbf{r})$ that is as close as possible to the true object $f(\mathbf{r})$. In the Fourier domain, (3.3-4) gives

$$G(\mathbf{k}) = H(\mathbf{k})F(\mathbf{k}) + W(\mathbf{k}), \tag{3.3-5}$$

where $W(\mathbf{k})$ is the Fourier transforms of $w(\mathbf{r})$.

If the estimate $\hat{f}(\mathbf{r})$ is simply the measured image $g(\mathbf{r})$ filtered through the inverse filter $H_{\mathrm{r}}(\mathbf{k}) = H^{-1}(\mathbf{k})$, then the estimate $\hat{f}(\mathbf{r})$ has a Fourier transform

$$\hat{F}(\mathbf{k}) = H_{\mathrm{r}}(\mathbf{k})G(\mathbf{k}) = F(\mathbf{k}) + H^{-1}(\mathbf{k})W(\mathbf{k}). \tag{3.3-6}$$

Therefore, in the absence of noise, $\hat{F}(\mathbf{k}) = F(\mathbf{k})$ so that $\hat{f}(\mathbf{r}) = f(\mathbf{r})$ is a perfect estimate. However, the noise $W(\mathbf{k})$ will by amplified by the factor $H^{-1}(\mathbf{k})$, which can be very large at frequencies for which $H(\mathbf{k})$ is very small, leading to unacceptable reconstructions, even for the smallest amount of noise.

Truncation and Regularization.   One approach to addressing the problem of noise amplification by the inverse filter is to truncate its dynamic range by clamping its magnitude at some maximum value, as illustrated in Fig. 3.3-1(c). Another is to replace the inverse filter with a filter of transfer function

$$H_{\mathrm{r}}(\mathbf{k}) = \frac{H^*(\mathbf{k})}{|H(\mathbf{k})|^2 + a^2}, \tag{3.3-7}$$

where a is a real constant selected to prevent division by zero. When $|H(\mathbf{k})| \gg a$, $H_I(\mathbf{k})$ becomes an inverse filter $1/H(\mathbf{k})$, but for $|H(\mathbf{k})| \ll a$, $H_I(\mathbf{k}) \approx H^*(\mathbf{k})/a^2$, which is a small number that vanishes at sufficiently high frequencies. This type of regularization is discussed again in Sec. 5.4 in the context of discrete inverse problems.

Wiener Filter.   The Wiener filter is a linear filter that minimizes the mean-square error between the estimated image and the true image. It assumes some statistical knowledge of the noise function $w(x, y)$ and the class of images $f(x, y)$ to be restored. The result of this optimization turns out to take the form in (3.3-7) with the a spatial-frequency-dependent parameter $a^2 = S_n(\mathbf{k})/S_f(\mathbf{k})$, where $S_n(\mathbf{k})$ and $S_f(\mathbf{k})$ are average spectral distributions of the noise power and image power, respectively. When the $\mathbf{k}$ dependence of $S_n(\mathbf{k})$ and $S_f(\mathbf{k})$ is not known, a good choice of the parameter a^2 is the inverse of the signal-to-noise ratio SNR, so that

$$H_r(\mathbf{k}) = \frac{H^*(\mathbf{k})}{|H(\mathbf{k})|^2 + 1/\text{SNR}}. \qquad (3.3\text{-}8)$$

Signal-to-Noise Ratio (SNR).   The SNR is defined as the ratio of the mean-square value of the image to the variance of the noise, i.e., the ratio of the spatial average of $[f(\mathbf{r}) \otimes h(\mathbf{r})]^2$ to the noise variance σ_w^2. It is often expressed in units of decibel $[10 \log_{10}(\text{ratio})]$.

EXAMPLE 3.3-1.   *Wiener Filter Restoration of a Blurred Image.* This example is a demonstration of image blurring and deblurring applied to a 2D image $f(x, y)$ of a biological cell, sampled as a 160×160 pixel array.

(a) The image $f(x, y)$, shown in Fig. 3.3-2(a), is blurred by a diffraction-limited system of PSF $h(x, y)$ given by (3.1-24), with a radius $\rho_s = 10$ pixels. The blurred image $f(x, y)$ is computed by use of the MATLAB function g=imfilter(f,h,'symmetric'), which uses symmetric boundary conditions in order to reduce the edge effect. The result is displayed in Fig. 3.3-2(b).

(b) Noise $w(x, y)$ of root-mean-square value σ_w is generated by use of the MATLAB function w=sigma*randn(size(g)) and added to the image $g(x, y)$.

(c) The image is restored by use of the MATLAB Wiener deconvolution function fr=deconvwnr(g+w,h,1/SNR). In this example, σ_w was adjusted such that SNR = 24 dB. The resultant image $\hat{f}(x, y) = f_r(x, y)$ is displayed in Fig. 3.3-2(c).

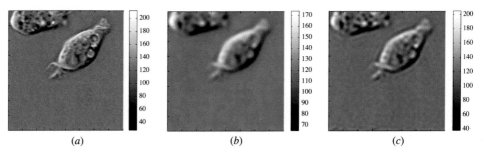

(a)   (b)   (c)

Figure 3.3-2   Example of image restoration using a Wiener filter. (a) Original image f. (b) Blurred image g. (c) Restored image $\hat{f}$.

▶ Problems 3.3-1, 3.3-2

Further Reading

Image Processing

R. C. Gonzalez, R. E. Woods, and S. L. Eddins, *Digital Image Processing Using MATLAB*, 2nd ed., Gatesmark, 2009.

J. C. Russ and J. C. Russ, *Introduction to Image Processing and Analysis*, 2nd ed., CRC, 2008.

R. C. Gonzalez and R. E. Woods, *Digital Image Processing*, 3rd ed., Addison-Wesley, 2007.

Optical Imaging

T. Yoshizawa (ed.), *Handbook of Optical Metrology*, CRC, 2009.

B. Javidi, F. Okano, and J-Y Son (eds.), *Three-dimensional Imaging, Visualization, and Display*, Springer, 2008.

B. E. A. Saleh and M. C. Teich, *Fundamentals of Photonics*, 2nd ed., Wiley, 2007, Chaps. 4 and 11.

O. K. Ersoy, *Diffraction, Fourier Optics, and Imaging*, Wiley, 2007.

J. W. Goodman, *Introduction to Fourier Optics*, 3rd ed., Roberts, 2005.

H. Barrett and K. Myers, *Foundations of Image Science*, Wiley, 2003.

C. S. Williams and O. A. Becklund, *Introduction to the Optical Transfer Function*, Wiley, 1989; SPIE, 2002.

M. Gu, *Advanced Optical Imaging Theory*, Springer, 1999.

Microscopy

A. Diaspro (ed.), *Nanoscopy and Multidimensional Optical Fluorescence Microscopy*, CRC, 2010.

A. H. Zewail and J. M. Thomas, *4D Electron Microscopy: Imaging in Space and Time*, Imperial College Press, 2009.

W. E. Moerner, New directions in single-molecule imaging and analysis, *Proceedings of the National Academy of Science*, Vol. 104, pp.12596–12602, 2007.

R. C. Willis, Portraits of life, one molecule at a time, *Analytical Chemistry*, Vol. 79, pp. 1785–1788, 2007.

G. Cox, *Optical Imaging Techniques in Cell Biology*, CRC, 2007.

J. B. Pawley (ed.), *Handbook of Biological Confocal Microscopy*, 3rd ed., Springer Science & Business Media, 2006.

B. R. Masters, *Confocal Microscopy and Multiphoton Excitation Microscopy, The Genesis of Live Cell Imaging*, SPIE, 2006.

W. R. Zipfel, R. M. Williams, and W. W. Webb, Nonlinear magic: multiphoton microscopy in the biosciences, *Nature Biotechnology*, Vol. 21, pp. 1369–1377, 2003.

M. Dyba and S. W. Hell, Focal spots of size $\lambda/23$ open up far-field fluorescence microscopy at 33 nm axial resolution, *Physical Review Letters*, Vol. 88, p. 163901, 2002.

D. B. Murphy, *Fundamentals of Light Microscopy and Electronic Imaging*, Wiley–Liss, 2001.

E. J. Sánchez, L. Novotny, and X. S. Xie, Near-field fluorescence microscopy based on two-photon excitation with metal tips, *Physical Review Letters*, Vol. 82, pp. 4014–4017, 1999.

S. Bradbury and B. Bracegirdle, *Introduction to Light Microscopy*, Springer, BIOS, 1998.

Ultrasonic Imaging

T. Szabo, *Diagnostic Ultrasound Imaging: Inside Out*, Academic, 2004.

H. Medwin and C. S. Clay, *Fundamentals of Acoustical Oceanography*, Academic, 1998.

L. M. Brekhovskikh, Y. P. Lysanov, L. M. Brekhovskikh, and Y. Lysanov, *Fundamentals of Ocean Acoustics*, 3rd ed., Springer-Verlag Telos, 2003.

R. J. Urick, *Principles of Underwater Sound*, reprint edition, Peninsula Pub, 1996.

L. C. Lynnworth, *Ultrasonic Measurements for Process Control: Theory, Techniques, Applications*, Academic Press, 1989.

L. W. Schmerr, Jr., *Fundamentals of Ultrasonic Nondestructive Evaluation: A Modeling Approach*, Plenum, 1998.

A. D. Waite, *Sonar for Practising Engineers*, 3rd ed., Wiley, 2001.

M. Fink, W. A. Kuperman, J.-P. Montagner, and A. Tourin (eds.), *Imaging of Complex Media with Acoustic and Seismic Waves*, Springer, 2002.

C.B. Scruby and L.E. Drain, *Laser Ultrasonics: Techniques and Applications*, Adam Hilger, 1990.

Radar and Lidar

R. Richmond and S. Cain, *Direct Detection LADAR Systems*, SPIE, 2010.

J. S. Lee and E. Pottier, *Polarimetric Radar Imaging: From Basics to Applications*, CRC, 2009.

M. A. Richards, *Fundamentals of Radar Signal Processing*, McGraw-Hill, 2005.

I. V. Komarov, S. M. Smolskiy, and D. K. Barton, *Fundamentals of Short-Range FM Radar*, Artech, 2003.

M. I. Skolnik, *Introduction to Radar Systems*, 3rd ed., McGraw-Hill, 2002

R. J. Sullivan, *Microwave Radar: Imaging and Advanced Processing*, Artech, 2000.

W.-M. Boerner and H. Uberall, *Radar Target Imaging*, Springer, 1994.

Medical and Biological Imaging

R. Frostig (ed.), *In Vivo Optical Imaging of Brain Function*, 2nd ed., CRC, 2009.

J. L. Prince and J. Links, *Medical Imaging Signals and Systems*, Prentice Hall, 2005

G. Cox (ed.), *Optical Imaging Techniques in Cell Biology*, CRC, 2006.

A. Webb, *Intro to Biomedical Imaging*, IEEE Press–Wiley, 2003.

W. R. Hendee and E. R. Ritenour, *Medical Imaging Physics*, 4th ed., Wiley–Liss, 2002.

Z.-H. Cho, J. P. Jones, and M. Singh, *Foundations of Medical Imaging*, Wiley, 1993.

R. A. Robb (ed.), *Three-Dimensional Biomedical Imaging*, Vols. I and II, CRC, 1985.

A. Macovski, *Medical Imaging Systems*, Prentice-Hall, 1983.

Optical Coherence Tomography

W. Drexler and J. G. Fujimoto (eds.), *Optical Coherence Tomography: Technology and Applications*, Springer, 2008.

M. E. Brezinski, *Optical Coherence Tomography: Principles and Applications*, Academic, 2006.

W. Drexler (ed.), *Optical Coherence Tomography and Coherence Techniques*, Vol. 2, *Progress in Biomedical Optics and Imaging*, SPIE, 2005.

W. Drexler (ed.), *Optical Coherence Tomography and Coherence Techniques*, Vol. 1, *Progress in Biomedical Optics and Imaging*, SPIE, 2003.

B. E. Bouma and G. J. Tearney (eds.), *Handbook of Optical Coherence Tomography*, Marcel Dekker, 2002.

Problems

3.1-1 **Geometric Transformations.** Use the MATLAB image `cell.tif`, which may be loaded to the MATLAB workspace by use of the MATLAB function `f=imread('cell.tif')`, to demonstrate the operations of scaling by a factor of 2, rotation by an angle $\theta = 90°$, and affine transformation with matrix $\mathbf{A}$ of elements $[A_{11} \ A_{12} \ A_{21} \ A_{22}] = [3 \ 1 \ 1 \ 2]$ and no displacement.

3.1-2 **Contrast Modification.** Use the MATLAB image `cell.tif`, which may be loaded to the MATLAB workspace by use of the MATLAB function `f=imread('cell.tif')`, to demonstrate the effect of contrast modification via the transformation $g = f^\gamma$ with $\gamma = 0.2$ and $\gamma = 4$. Compare the resultant images.

3.1-3 **Linear Blur of Self-Portrait.** Load a self-portrait to the MATLAB workspace, and convert it to a gray-scale image f of dimension 200×200 (See Sec. D.1 of Appendix D). Filter this image with a filter of uniform PSF h of value 1/25 for the 5×5 central pixels and zero otherwise. This is called the boxcar filter. Use the MATLAB function `g=conv2(h,f)`. Print the original image f and the blurred image $g = f \otimes h$. Repeat for a boxcar filter of dimensions 10×10 and compare your results.

3.1-4   **Adding Noise to an Image.** Consider the blurred image $g = f \otimes h$ of the self-portrait f that
was generated in Problem 3.1-3. Compute the mean-squared value of g. Use the MATLAB
function imnoise(g,'gaussian',m,v) to add Gaussian white noise with mean $m =$
zero and variance v such that the signal-to-noise ratio SNR = 10 dB. Display the original
image, the blurred image, and the noisy blurred image.

3.1-5   **2D Fourier Transform.** Generate the following 128×128 images and compute their 2D
Fourier transforms using the MATLAB function fft2. Display the original function and the
magnitude of the Fourier transform by use of the MATLAB function imshow:

(a) Centered square function of dimensions 20×20, with other pixels set at a value 0.

(b) The MATLAB image cell.tif, which may be loaded to the MATLAB workspace by
use of the MATLAB function f=imread('cell.tif').

3.1-6   **Imaging System with a Square Aperture.** Derive an expression for the PSF and the transfer
function of a diffraction-limited coherent imaging system using a lens with a square aperture
of width D. Derive an expression for the width of the blur spot similar to (3.1-17).

3.1-7   **Edge Response of Various Imaging Systems.** A diffraction-limited infrared imaging system
using a lens with a square pupil function of dimension $D = 1$ cm and focal length $f = 2$ cm
images a far object ($d_1 = \infty$) with spatial distribution in the form of an edge $f(x, y) =$
0 for $x < 0$, and $f(x, y) = 1$ for $x > 0$. The illumination is uniform and the wavelength
$\lambda = 1$ μm. Plot the spatial distribution of the image as a function of x, indicating all pertinent
dimensions in each of the following cases:

(a) The illumination is incoherent and the system is defocused at $d_2 = 1.99$ cm. Ignore
diffraction.

(b) The illumination is coherent and the system is focused ($d_2 = 2$ cm).

(c) The illumination is incoherent and the system is focused ($d_2 = 2$ cm).

3.1-8   **Motion Blur.** An ideal camera moves in the x direction with constant velocity v during exposure. If the exposure time is T, derive an expression for the PSF and the transfer function of
the imaging system. Demonstrate the effect of such motion on the image used in Problem 3.1-
3, assuming that $vT = 10$ pixels.

3.1-9   **Imaging of a Nonplanar Surface.** A camera is used to image a uniformly illuminated
nonplanar object made of four planes, much like the steps of a staircase. Each step is covered
with two white strips in a black background, as illustrated in Fig. P3.1-9. The camera uses a
perfect lens of focal length $f = 50$ mm and a square aperture of width $D = 20$ mm, and is
focused on step #2, which lies at a distance $d_1 = 1$ m from the lens. Neighboring steps are
separated by a distance $d_r = 20$ cm (the riser) and the width of a step is $L = 5$ cm. The width
of each strip is 5 mm and their center-to-center separation is $L_1 = 7.5$ mm. Determine the 2D
image captured by the camera and plot a profile of the image across the strips. Assume that
light is treated as rays, i.e., ignore its wave nature. If the wave nature is taken into account,
do you expect the results to significantly change if $\lambda = 0.5$ μm?

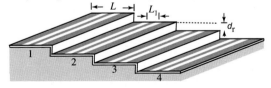

Figure   P3.1-9   Staircase-like
nonplanar object.

3.2-1   **Axial and Transverse Resolution of Various Systems.** Determine the axial and transverse
resolution of the following systems:

(a) An ultrasonic imaging system using 2 μs pulses at a frequency of 5 MHz in a medium
with sound velocity of 1.5 km/s. The transducer diameter is 3 mm and the beam is
focused on a target is at a distance of 6 cm.

(b) A radar imaging system using 10 ns pulses of frequency 3 GHz if the antennna diameter
is 1 m and the target distance is 10 km.

(c) A laser scanning microscope operating at a wavelength of 800 nm using a lens of numerical aperture NA = 0.5. The medium has a refractive index $n = 1.3$.

3.2-2   **Ultrasonic A-Scan.** A 15 MHz unfocused baffled piston source is embedded in a medium of density $\rho_1 = 998$ kg/m^3 and speed of sound $v_1 = 1481$ m/s, through which sound attenuation is negligible. The transducer is driven in pulse–echo mode and the transmitted ultrasonic pulse encounters a 5 mm layer of material of density $\rho_2 = 3400$ kg/m^3 and unknown speed of sound v_2. The received signal is displayed on an oscilloscope and it is found that (i) the time delay between the two signals corresponding to each of the interfaces is 2.2 μs and (ii) the amplitude of the signal corresponding to the second interface is 2% of that corresponding to the first interface.

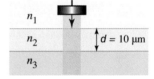

(a) Determine the attenuation coefficient of medium 2 in Np/cm.

(b) Describe how your solution would be affected if the transducer was replaced by a point source/receiver driven in pulse–echo mode.

3.2-3   **Axial and Transverse Resolution of Various Systems.** Repeat Problem 3.2-1 for an optical coherence tomography imaging system with an 800 nm wavelength and spectral width of 100 nm. The medium has a refractive index $n = 1.3$.

3.2-4   **Optical Coherence Tomography.** Sketch the OCT interferogram obtained from reflections at two boundaries between media with refractive indexes $n_1 = 1.3$, $n_2 = 1.35$, and $n_3 = 1.4$. The width of the intermediate layer is 10 μm. The light source is of low coherence with a 1 μm central wavelength and a coherence length $\ell_c = 4$ μm in free space.

3.3-1   **Deconvolution of an Ultrasonic A-Scan.** An ultrasonic A-scan of a three-layer (two-boundaries) medium was obtained by use of a pulsed ultrasonic source. The times of arrival of echos from the surface and the two boundaries are 5, 8, and 11 μs, respectively. The amplitudes of these echos are 1, 0.8, and 0.8, respectively (in arbitrary units). If the probe pulse is a Gaussian function $\exp(-t^2/2\tau_p^2)$ with $\tau_p = 1$ μs, plot the received signal as a function of time. Add noise such that the resultant SNR = 30 dB. Use a Wiener filter for deconvolution and plot the resultant signal. Examine the effect of noise by running the program several times.

3.3-2   **Deconvolution using a Wiener Filter.** Consider the self-portrait that was generated in Problem 3.1-3. Filter this image with a boxcar filter of dimensions 7×7 and add noise such that SNR = 5 dB. Now, restore the image using a Wiener filter (see Example 3.3-1).

Tomographic Imaging

In **localized imaging**, each measurement is sensitive to a single point, or a small patch, within the object, so that the object distribution may be constructed by taking measurements at a set of points filling the object space, as illustrated in Fig. 4.0-1(*a*). As mentioned in Sec. 3.1B, this patch, called the scanned spot, is the intersection of the probe spot and the sensor spot. In **tomographic imaging**, by contrast, the scanned spot is an extended region of some shape, so that each measurement receives contributions from many points distributed within that spot. Each measurement is then not, by itself, sufficient to discern the individual contributions of the many points within its scanned spot. Nevertheless, by using multiple measurements with overlapping or crossing scanned spots, a set of measurements can be sufficient to figure out the overall object distribution by use of computational methods.

For example, in **ray tomography**, the scanned spot is a straight line (a ray) and each measurement provides the sum of the values of the object distribution along points of that line. Measurements by use of a set of parallel lines oriented in different directions, as illustrated in Fig. 4.0-1(*b*), can be sufficient to compute the object distribution. Another example is **range tomography**. Here, for a two-dimensional (2D) object, the scanned spot is a circle perimeter – the locus of points at the same distance (range) from a fixed point. Each measurement represents the sum of values of the object function at all points on the circle perimeter. Measurements using sets of concentric circles centered at multiple points, as illustrated in Fig. 4.0-1(*c*), provide sufficient data to compute the object distribution. Other scanned spots, which are not necessarily limited to lines or curves and are not necessarily uniform functions, may also be used, as we will see later in this chapter.

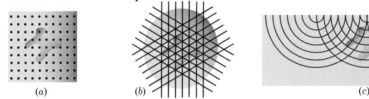

(*a*)   (*b*)   (*c*)

Figure 4.0-1 Scanned spots for (*a*) localized imaging, (*b*) ray tomography, and (*c*) range tomography.

Tomographic imaging (also called multiview tomography, or simply tomography) may also be described in terms of a set of probes observing the object from multiple *views*. Each view *v* produces a *sub-image*. For example, each set of parallel rays in ray tomography is a *view* and each view is identified by its direction. In range tomography, each view is a set of concentric circles identified by its center.

As in localized imaging, the mathematical basis for tomographic imaging is linear system theory. This is predicated on the assumption that the imaging process is linear for each of the views. This may be based on an approximation such as the Born approximation. The measured sub-image $g^{(v)}(\mathbf{r})$ for the *v*th view is then related to the object distribution $f(\mathbf{r}')$ by the linear transformation

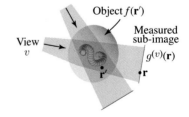

$$g^{(v)}(\mathbf{r}) = \int h^{(v)}(\mathbf{r};\mathbf{r}')f(\mathbf{r}')\,\mathrm{d}\mathbf{r}',$$

(4.0-1)
Tomographic Imaging

where $\mathbf{r}$ is a point in the measured sub-image and $\mathbf{r}'$ is a point in the object. Equation (4.0-1) simply states that the measured vth sub-image at position $\mathbf{r}$ is a weighted super-position of the object distribution $f(\mathbf{r}')$ for each view, where the $h^{(v)}(\mathbf{r};\mathbf{r}')$ represents the weights for the vth view. When plotted as a function of $\mathbf{r}$ for a fixed $\mathbf{r}'$, $h^{(v)}(\mathbf{r};\mathbf{r}')$ yields the point spread function of the imaging system for the vth view. When plotted as a function of $\mathbf{r}'$ for a fixed $\mathbf{r}$, $h^{(v)}(\mathbf{r};\mathbf{r}')$ becomes the receptive function of the imaging system for the vth view. The distinction between these two related functions is described in Appendix A (see Fig. A.2-4).

For a special class of tomographic systems, the receptive function $h^{(v)}(\mathbf{r};\mathbf{r}')$ for each point $\mathbf{r}$ of the image is zero everywhere except at points on a line or a curve. In ray tomography, each measurement at a fixed position $\mathbf{r}$ is simply the sum of values of the object function $f(\mathbf{r}')$ along a line [Fig. 4.0-1(b)]. In range tomography, the sum is taken along the perimeter of a circle [Fig. 4.0-1(c)].

Dimensionality. Note that the dimensions of the object function $f(\mathbf{r}')$ and the measured sub-images $g^{(v)}(\mathbf{r})$ are different. When imaging a three-dimensional (3D) object, the position variable $\mathbf{r}' = (x', y', z')$ is 3D and the position variable $\mathbf{r}$ for the measured sub-image in each view can be two-dimensional (2D), i.e., $\mathbf{r} = (x, y)$. When a 2D object is imaged tomographically (e.g., for computed axial tomography (CT) where the object is a planar 2D slice of a 3D object), $\mathbf{r}' = (x', y')$ is 2D, while each measured sub-image is a function of a one-dimensional (1D) position variable, called a *projection* and often denoted by the symbol s, instead of r'.

Fourier Transform Methods in Tomography. For a class of tomographic systems, described in this chapter, multidimensional Fourier transform techniques can simplify the multiview imaging equations considerably, as they do for conventional linear shift-invariant systems. When the object is 2D and the sub-images are 1D, it turns out that the 1D Fourier transform of each sub-image is simply a slice of the 2D Fourier transform of the object. Likewise, for a 3D object and 2D sub-images, the 2D Fourier transform of each sub-image is a slice of the 3D Fourier transform of the object, (planar or spherical slice, depending on the application). In the Fourier domain, therefore, the tomographic imaging equation (4.0-1) is equivalent to a slicing or sampling operation. Measurements at different views provide a set of slices that are sufficient for a complete construction of the Fourier transform of the object, and hence the object itself. This is the underlying mathematical principle of many tomographic methods.

This chapter introduces several methods of tomographic imaging. The simplest are **ray tomography** and **range tomography**. These are described in Sec. 4.1 and Sec. 4.2, respectively. In **wave tomography**, also called **diffraction tomography**, the probes are extended planar or spherical waves illuminating the object from different angles. The waves are scattered from the object in accordance with the theory presented in Sec. 2.2C. The problem is cast as a tomographic system with a receptive function in the form of a spherical wave. Diffraction is then cast as slicing in the Fourier domain, as in ray tomography, albeit with circular instead of linear slices. This more advanced topic is covered in Sec. 4.3. Section 4.4D introduces **frequency-encoded tomography**, which is the basis of magnetic resonance imaging (MRI). Here, imaging is based on encoding the object with a set of position-dependent resonance frequency patterns. The temporal profile of the total emission for each pattern can be used to estimate a slice of the Fourier transform of the object distribution. Reconstruction is then performed by use of techniques similar to those of ray tomography.

The principal challenge in tomography is the inverse problem: reconstruction of the object from the multiview images. In this chapter, we first develop analytic recon-struction techniques resulting in inversion formulas based on continuous functions and an infinite number of views. These formulas are then discretized for implementation based on a finite number of views and discretized object and images. Another approach, presented in Chapter 5, is based on discretizing the forward imaging equations up front and solving the inverse equation as an algebraic reconstruction problem. The discrete representation of images, the limitations related to the finiteness of the number of views, and the associated computational issues are addressed in Chapter 5.

4.1   Ray Tomography

Ray tomography is a technique for probing the absorption coefficient of an object by use of multiple rays (for example, X-rays). Each ray is assumed to travel through the object without changing its direction. The intensity of the ray at the exit depends on the total absorption along the ray path. If $\alpha(\mathbf{r})$ is the absorption coefficient at position $\mathbf{r}$, then the ray transmittance

$$\mathcal{T} = \exp\left[-\int_{\text{ray}} \alpha(\mathbf{r}) \, d\ell\right],$$

where the line integral is along the path of the ray. It follows that

$$-\ln(\mathcal{T}) = \int_{\text{ray}} \alpha(\mathbf{r}) \, d\ell.$$

This integral is called the *sum ray* or the *projection*. Projections along multiple rays in multiple directions are measured and the distribution of the absorption coefficient $\alpha(\mathbf{r})$ is to be estimated. A principal application of ray tomography, X-ray computed tomography (CT), will be described in Sec. 4.1C.

Ray Transmission as a Projection

In the spirit of our systems approach, we think of the absorption function $\alpha(\mathbf{r})$ as the input to a linear system and denote it $f(\mathbf{r})$. For a given ray, the output of the system is the measurement $-\ln(\mathcal{T})$, which we denote g_{ray}, so that $g_{\text{ray}} = \int_{\text{ray}} f(\mathbf{r}) \, d\ell$. For parallel rays pointing in the direction v, called the v rays, we obtain a distribution $g^{(v)}(\mathbf{s})$, where $\mathbf{s}$ is the coordinate of a ray in the sensor plane. Therefore,

$$g^{(v)}(\mathbf{s}) = \int h^{(v)}(\mathbf{s}, \mathbf{r}) f(\mathbf{r}) \, d\mathbf{r}, \qquad (4.1\text{-}1)$$

Projection Equation

where $h^{(v)}(\mathbf{s}, \mathbf{r})$ is a line delta function of $\mathbf{r}$ that vanishes everywhere except along the path of the ray, which is marked by the direction v and the position $\mathbf{s}$. The right-hand side of (4.1-1) is called a **projection** along the v direction. Equation (4.1-1) is a special form of the generic relation (4.0-1), called the projection equation. The impulse response function $h^{(v)}(\mathbf{r}; \mathbf{r}')$ in ray tomography is a delta function, which is the mathematical equivalent of a ray. The objective of ray tomography is to determine the object $f(\mathbf{r})$ from the set of projections $g^{(v)}(\mathbf{s})$ associated with the set of directions v, i.e., invert the projection equation (4.1-1).

Projection Equation for 2D Objects

The description of ray transmission as a projection is now applied to a 2D geometry. The 2D object $f(x, y)$, which may be a slice of a 3D object in the case of X-ray CT, as illustrated in Fig. 4.1-1, is measured by use of parallel rays pointing along different directions within the plane. For each direction, a 1D projection is recorded.

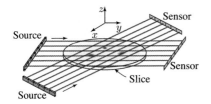

Figure 4.1-1 Physical configuration for 2D ray tomography.

Projection along the x direction.   In the simple special case of rays pointing along the x axis, a ray located at $y = s$ is described by the delta function $\delta(y - s)$ so that (4.1-1) takes the simple form

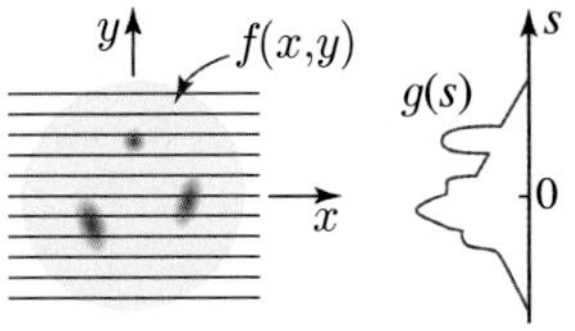

$$g(s) = \iint_{-\infty}^{\infty} \delta(y - s) f(x, y) \, dx \, dy = \int_{-\infty}^{\infty} f(x, s) \, dx.$$

Similarly, for projection along the y direction, $g(s) = \int_{-\infty}^{\infty} f(s, y) \, dy$.

Projection along an arbitrary direction.   In the general case of rays at an angle θ with the y axis, the projection is denoted by the function $g_\theta(s)$, where the angles θ represent the views v. As illustrated in Fig. 4.1-2(a), a ray at an angle θ that is displaced by a distance s from the origin follows a line described by the equation $x' = s$, or $x \cos \theta + y \sin \theta = s$. We may think of this ray as a 2D distribution defined by the delta function $\delta(x \cos \theta + y \sin \theta - s)$. Therefore,

$$g_\theta(s) = \iint_{-\infty}^{\infty} \delta(x \cos \theta + y \sin \theta - s) f(x, y) \, dx \, dy. \qquad (4.1\text{-}2)$$

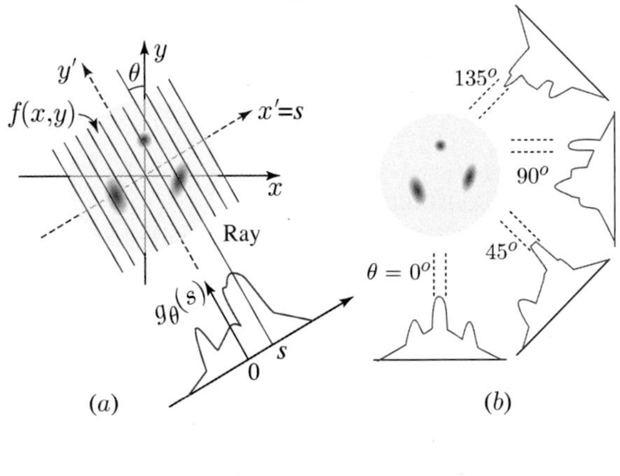

Figure 4.1-2 (a) Projection of the 2D distribution $f(x, y)$ along a direction making an angle θ with the y axis produces a 1D function $g_\theta(s)$ of the distance s from the origin. (b) Projections at four angles: $\theta = 0°, 45°, 90°, 135°$.

As an example, for $\theta = 0$, the ray lies on the line $x = s$, and $g_0(s) = \int f(s, y)\mathrm{d}y$ is the projection of $f(x, y)$ along the y axis. Similarly, for $\theta = \pi/2$, the ray lies on the line $y = s$, and $g_{\pi/2}(s) = \int f(x, s)\mathrm{d}x$ is the projection of $f(x, y)$ along the x axis.

The projection equation (4.1-2) may be written as a single integral by using a coordinate system (s, u) aligned with the ray. The $(x, y) \rightarrow (s, u)$ coordinate rotation

$$s = x \cos\theta + y \sin\theta \qquad\qquad x = s \cos\theta - u \sin\theta$$

$$u = -x \sin\theta + y \cos\theta \qquad\qquad y = s \sin\theta + u \cos\theta$$

can be used to express (4.1-2) as

$$g_\theta(s) = \int_{-\infty}^{\infty} f(s \cos\theta - u \sin\theta,\ s \sin\theta + u \cos\theta)\, \mathrm{d}u\,.$$

(4.1-3)
Projection
Equation

The objective of ray tomography is to invert this equation, i.e., to determine the object $f(x, y)$ from the projections $g_\theta(s)$ at all angles θ.

A. Radon Transform and Projection–Slice Theorem

Radon Transform

Definition.   We may regard the projections $g_\theta(s)$ in (4.1-3), for *all* angles θ from 0 to 180°, as a 2D function $g(s, \theta)$ related to the object 2D distribution $f(x, y)$ by the transformation

$$g(s, \theta) = \int_{-\infty}^{\infty} f(s \cos\theta - u \sin\theta,\ s \sin\theta + u \cos\theta)\, \mathrm{d}u\,.$$

(4.1-4)
Radon
Transform

This mapping from the object function $f(x, y)$ to the projections function $g(s, \theta)$ is known as the **Radon transform** and is denoted symbolically as an operator $\mathcal{R}$ so that:

$$\xrightarrow{\ f\ } \boxed{\ \mathcal{R}\ } \xrightarrow{\ g\ } \qquad\qquad g = \mathcal{R}f. \qquad\qquad (4.1\text{-}5)$$

■ MATLAB equation g=radon(f) performs a discretized form of the Radon transform defined in (4.1-4), where f and g are matrices representing discretized versions of $f(x, y)$ and $g(x, y)$, respectively.

Properties of the Radon Transform.   Some of the principal properties of the Radon transform are:

- The Radon transform is linear, i.e., $\mathcal{R}(a_1 f_1 + a_2 f_2) = a_1 \mathcal{R}f_1 + a_2 \mathcal{R}f_2$, where f_1 and f_2 are functions and a_1 and a_2 are constants.
- The Radon transform is rotationally invariant, i.e., if $g = \mathcal{R}f$ and f_ϕ equals f rotated by an angle ϕ, then the Radon transform $g_\phi = \mathcal{R}f_\phi$ of f_ϕ equals g rotated by the same angle ϕ.
- The Radon transform has an inverse, i.e., f may be computed from g. This property will be shown subsequently.

Radon Transform of an Isolated Point (the Sinogram). For a function $f(x, y)$ with a single bright point at the location (x_0, y_0) in a dark background, i.e.,

$$f(x, y) = \delta(x - x_0)\delta(y - y_0),$$

we see from Fig. 4.1-3(a) that each projection is a function that is zero everywhere except at a single point at some location s, which is dependent on θ. By substitution in (4.1-4), it can be shown[1] that

$$g(s, \theta) = \delta(x_0 \cos\theta + y_0 \sin\theta - s).$$

This is a function that is zero everywhere except on a curve satisfying the relation $s = x_0 \cos\theta + y_0 \sin\theta$, which is a sinusoidal function of θ, known as the **sinogram**. It has an amplitude $\sqrt{x_0^2 + y_0^2}$ and values $s = x_0$ at $\theta = 0$, $s = y_0$ at $\theta = 90°$, and $s = -x_0$ at $\theta = 180°$, as illustrated in Fig. 4.1-3(a).

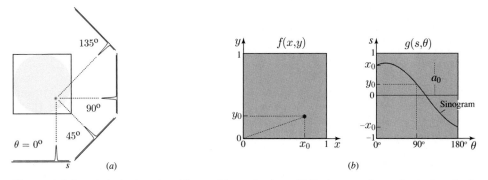

Figure 4.1-3 (a) A single-point object and its projections. (b) Radon transform of a single point is a sinusoidal curve (a sinogram).

Radon Transform of Several Isolated Points. Since the Radon transform is linear, the Radon transform of a distribution composed of several isolated points is the sum of sinusoidal curves, as shown in Fig. 4.1-4.

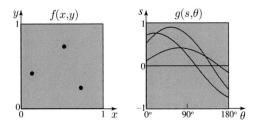

Figure 4.1-4 Radon transform of three points is three sinusoidal curves.

An arbitrary distribution composed of a continuum of points has a Radon transform comprising a superposition of sinusoidal curves, as demonstrated in the following example.

---

[1] This may be shown by use of a limiting argument, since the product of two delta functions is not well defined.

EXAMPLE 4.1-1.   *Radon Transform of a Phantom.* Figure 4.1-5 shows brightness images of a phantom $f(x, y)$ and its Radon transform $g(s, \theta)$ computed by use of the MATLAB function `g=radon(f)`. This phantom of a uniform rectangle and a graded ellipse, hereafter referred to as the rectangle–ellipse phantom, is used subsequently in this chapter and also in Chapters 5 and 8 to test various applications. The phantom is available as a MATLAB file *f_ellipse_sq.mat* in the book website.

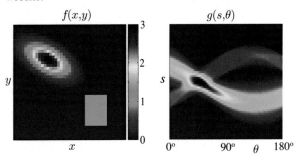

Figure 4.1-5   Images (in false color) representing a phantom $f(x, y)$ and its Radon transform $g(s, \theta)$. These functions are represented in MATLAB by matrices of size 41×41.

▶ Problem 4.1-1

Projection–Slice Theorem

The relation between the projections $g_\theta(s)$ and the object function $f(x, y)$ takes a simpler form in the Fourier domain (see Appendix A for a summary of the 1D and 2D Fourier transform). If $F(k_x, k_y)$ is the 2D Fourier transform of $f(x, y)$ and $G_\theta(k_s)$ is the 1D Fourier transform of the projection $g_\theta(s)$ with respect to s at a fixed θ, then it will be shown that

$$G_\theta(k_s) = F(k_s \cos \theta, k_s \sin \theta).$$

(4.1-6)
Projection–Slice Theorem

Since $F(k_s \cos \theta, k_s \sin \theta)$ is a slice of $F(k_x, k_y)$ at the points $k_x = k_s \cos \theta$ and $k_y = k_s \sin \theta$, i.e., along a line passing through the origin at an angle θ, the 1D Fourier transform of the projection is simply equal to a slice of the 2D Fourier transform of the object function at the angle θ, as illustrated in Fig. 4.1-6. This relation is known as the **projection–slice (P–S) theorem**.

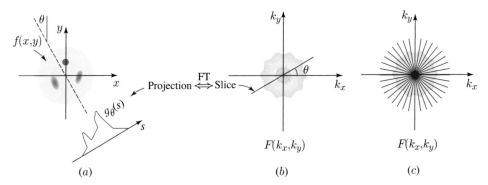

Figure 4.1-6   (a) A function $f(x, y)$ and its projection $g_\theta(s)$. (b) The 1D Fourier transform of a projection $G_\theta(k_s)$ equals a slice of the 2D Fourier transform $F(k_x, k_y)$. (c) Multiple radial slices used to reconstruct $F(k_x, k_y)$ from multiple projections.

□   **Proof of the P–S Theorem.** The P–S theorem may be easily proved in the special case of projection along the y axis ($\theta = 0$). In this case,

$$g_0(x) = \int_{-\infty}^{\infty} f(x,y)\, \mathrm{d}y. \tag{4.1-7}$$

The 2D Fourier transform of $f(x,y)$ [see (A.2-2)] evaluated at $k_y = 0$ is

$$F(k_x, 0) = \iint_{-\infty}^{\infty} f(x,y)\, \mathrm{e}^{\mathrm{j}k_x x}\, \mathrm{d}x\, \mathrm{d}y = \int_{-\infty}^{\infty} \mathrm{e}^{\mathrm{j}k_x x} \int_{-\infty}^{\infty} f(x,y)\, \mathrm{d}y\, \mathrm{d}x \tag{4.1-8}$$

Substituting from (4.1-7) into (4.1-8), we obtain

$$F(k_x, 0) = \int_{-\infty}^{\infty} g_0(x)\, \mathrm{e}^{\mathrm{j}k_x x}\, \mathrm{d}x = G_0(k_x). \tag{4.1-9}$$

This proves the P–S theorem for the special case $\theta = 0$. Since rotation of a function $f(x,y)$ by an angle θ rotates its Fourier transform by the same angle, the P–S theorem must apply for all angles. ■

▶ Problems 4.1-2, 4.1-3

Inversion by Use of the Projection–Slice Theorem

The P–S theorem suggests a method of reconstructing the distribution $f(x,y)$ from its projections. The Fourier transform of each projection provides a slice of the 2D Fourier transform of $F(k_x, k_y)$. If projections at all angles are measured, slices covering the entire (k_x, k_y) plane may be determined, as illustrated in Fig. 4.1-6(c). A 2D inverse Fourier transform of $F(k_x, k_y)$ reproduces $f(x,y)$. Since in real systems the number of projections is finite, the slices lie on a polar grid and must be interpolated into a rectangular grid before the inverse Fourier transform is computed using numerical techniques. Clearly, the accuracy of interpolation is poor at high spatial frequencies. A more accurate reconstruction of a function from its projection is provided by the method of filtered backprojection discussed in the next section.

B. Inversion by Filtered Backprojection

Backprojection

Backprojection is the redistribution of each sum ray uniformly at all points of the ray. Each point receives values from all the backprojected rays passing through it, at all angles, as illustrated in Fig. 4.1-7(b). This is equivalent to summing all the projections passing through the point. When a projection $g_\theta(s)$ is backprojected, it creates the distribution

$$f_{\mathrm{b}}(x,y) = \int_0^{\pi} \int_{-\infty}^{\infty} g_\theta(s)\delta(x\cos\theta + y\sin\theta - s)\, \mathrm{d}s\, \mathrm{d}\theta \tag{4.1-10}$$

or

$$f_{\mathrm{b}}(x,y) = \int_0^{\pi} g_\theta(x\cos\theta + y\sin\theta)\, \mathrm{d}\theta. \tag{4.1-11}$$

Backprojection

The backprojection operation is represented symbolically by an operator $\mathcal{B}$ so that (4.1-11) is written in the compact symbolic form

$$f_b = \mathcal{B}g. \tag{4.1-12}$$

Clearly, backprojection is a linear operation, i.e., the backprojection of a sum is the sum of the backprojections.

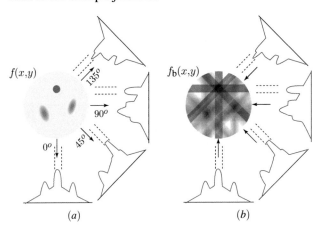

(a)   (b)

Figure 4.1-7 (*a*) Four projections of an object function $f(x, y)$. (*b*) Reconstruction of the object by four backprojections.

Backprojection Theorem. The backprojections of the projections do not reproduce the object function. Instead, they produce a filtered version of the object function. It can be shown that if $g = \mathcal{R}f$ and $f_b = \mathcal{B}g = \mathcal{B}\mathcal{R}f$, then

$$f_b(x, y) = f(x, y) \otimes h_e(x, y), \qquad h_e(x, y) = 1/\sqrt{x^2 + y^2} = 1/\rho. \tag{4.1-13}$$

This means that the backprojected image equals the original image filtered by a 2D filter whose impulse response function is a circularly symmetric inverse-law function $1/\rho$, illustrated in Fig. 4.1-8(*a*). In the system relating f_b to f, each point of f generates a decaying function $1/\rho$ centered about the point. This blur filter has a transfer function $H_e(k_x, k_y) = 2\pi/\sqrt{k_x^2 + k_y^2} = 2\pi/k_\rho$, which is an identical circularly symmetric inverse-law function, representing a low-pass filter, as illustrated in Fig. 4.1-8(*b*). The suppression of the high spatial frequencies may be attributed to "thinning" of the radial slices as the spatial frequency increases. In the Fourier domain, the convolution relation in (4.1-13) is equivalent to a multiplication:

$$F_b(k_x, k_y) = F(k_x, k_y)H_e(k_x, k_y), \qquad H_e(k_x, k_y) = 2\pi/\sqrt{k_x^2 + k_y^2} = 2\pi/k_\rho. \tag{4.1-14}$$

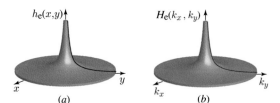

(a)   (b)

Figure 4.1-8 2D filter that relates the backprojected image f_b to the original object f. (*a*) Impulse response function. (*b*) Transfer function.

☐ **Proof of Backprojection Theorem.** To prove (4.1-14), we use the definition of the backprojection in (4.1-11) and write the projection g_θ in terms of its 1D Fourier transform G_θ so that

$$f_b(x,y) = \frac{1}{2\pi} \int_0^\pi \left[\int_{-\infty}^\infty G_\theta(k_\rho) e^{jk_\rho(x\cos\theta + y\sin\theta)} \, dk_\rho \right] d\theta. \tag{4.1-15}$$

We next write $f(x,y)$ in terms of its 2D Fourier transform expressed in a polar coordinate system:

$$f(x,y) = \frac{1}{2\pi} \int_0^\pi \int_0^\infty F(k_\rho\cos\theta, k_\rho\sin\theta) e^{jk_\rho(x\cos\theta + y\sin\theta)} k_\rho \, dk_\rho \, d\theta.$$

$$= \frac{1}{2\pi} \int_0^\pi \int_{-\infty}^\infty G_\theta(k_\rho) e^{jk_\rho(x\cos\theta + y\sin\theta)} |k_\rho| \, dk_\rho \, d\theta. \tag{4.1-16}$$

where we have used the P–S theorem (4.1-6). Finally, by comparing (4.1-15) and (4.1-16) we conclude that the only difference between the Fourier transforms of $f(x,y)$ and $f_b(x,y)$ is the factor $1/|k_\rho|$, as claimed by the backprojection theorem, so that (4.1-14) follows.   ∎

Filtered Backprojection

Since the relation between the backprojected image f_b and the original object f is represented by a 2D low-pass filter H_e, the application of an inverse filter $H_i = 1/H_e$ on the backprojected image should reproduce the original image. The operation of backprojection followed by filtering with an inverse filter of transfer function $H_i(k_x, k_y) = \sqrt{k_x^2 + k_y^2} = k_\rho$, as shown in Fig. 4.1-9(a), is called filtered backprojection. Ideally, it leads to an image $\hat{f}(x,y) = f(x,y)$. If this filtering operation is denoted by the symbol $\mathcal{H}_i$, then the steps leading to this perfect reconstruction are denoted symbolically as

$$\hat{f} = \mathcal{H}f_b = \mathcal{H}_i\mathcal{B}g = \mathcal{H}_i\mathcal{B}\mathcal{R}f = f.$$

It follows that $\mathcal{H}_i\mathcal{B}\mathcal{R}$ must be the identity operation, so that the inverse Radon transform

$$\mathcal{R}^{-1} = \mathcal{H}_i\mathcal{B}, \tag{4.1-17}$$

i.e., it is implemented by backprojection followed by 2D filtering with the inverse filter H_i.

$H_i(k_x, k_y)$ $\qquad\qquad\qquad$ $H_i(k)$

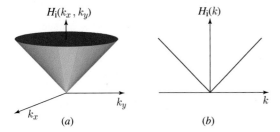

(a) $\qquad\qquad\qquad$ (b)

Figure 4.1-9 Filters for filtered backprojection. (a) Transfer function of the 2D inverse filter H_i. (b) Transfer function of the 1D filter H_i.

Backprojected Filtered Projections.   The operations of backprojection followed by filtering in (4.1-17) may be reversed. Each of the 1D projections that constitute the Radon transform $g(s, \theta)$ is filtered with a 1D filter of transfer function $H_i(k) = |k|$ (a ramp filter), as illustrated in Fig. 4.1-9(b), before the backprojection operation is implemented. In view of the P–S theorem, this change of order of filtering and backprojection should have no effect on the result. The process may be denoted operationally by $\hat{f} = \mathcal{B}\mathcal{H}_i g = \mathcal{B}\mathcal{H}_i \mathcal{R} f = f$, so that the inverse Radon transform is also given by

$$\mathcal{R}^{-1} = \mathcal{B}\mathcal{H}_i. \tag{4.1-18}$$

Note that the filter $\mathcal{H}_i$ in (4.1-17) is a 2D filter applied to the 2D backprojected image f_b, while the filter $\mathcal{H}_i$ in (4.1-18) is a 1D filter applied to each of the 1D projections individually (see Fig. 4.1-10). Since it is easier to implement 1D filters, most implementations of the inverse Radon transform are based on (4.1-18), i.e., do 1D filtering of the projections before backprojection.

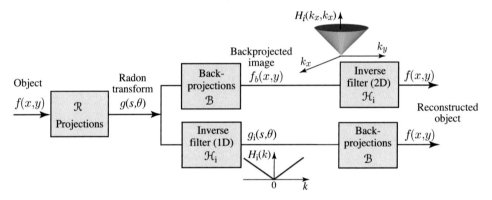

Figure 4.1-10   Two methods for inversion of the Radon transform by filtered backprojection.

■ MATLAB equation f = iradon(g) performs the inverse Radon transform via a discretized version of filtered backprojection.

One advantage of the filtered backprojection method is that it can be applied even if a full set of projections at all angles is not available. Clearly, the quality of reconstruction deteriorates if the number of projections is small or the projections are limited to a finite angular aperture, as illustrated in Example 4.1-2. Also, the inverse filter associated with filtered backprojection amplifies noise (see Sec. 3.3). This effect is demonstrated in Example 4.1-3.

EXAMPLE 4.1-2.   *Effect of Finite Number of Projections and Limited Aperture on Ray Tomography.* We examine the quality of ray tomographic reconstruction using filtered backprojection for the rectangle–ellipse phantom used in Example 4.1-1. We consider four configurations:

(a) A full aperture covering the 0°–179° angular range with 180 projections
(b) A full aperture covering the 0°–179° angular range with only 20 projections
(c) A limited aperture covering the 0°–90° angular range with 180 projections
(d) A limited aperture covering the 45°–135° angular range with 20 projections.

The original phantom and the reconstructed image in these four configurations are illustrated in Fig. 4.1-11. We see that when we sample densely in angle over the full 180°, filtered backprojection provides an accurate reconstruction of both the rectangular block and the smooth ellipse. As the amount of data available to the algorithm is reduced, we see "streaking" artifacts even in the case where data are collected over the full 180°. For the two 90° aperture cases, not only are the streaks evident, but the shapes of both structures are distorted.

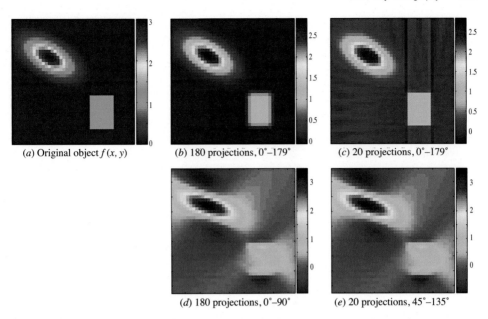

(*a*) Original object $f(x, y)$ (*b*) 180 projections, 0°–179°   (*c*) 20 projections, 0°–179°

(*d*) 180 projections, 0°–90°   (*e*) 20 projections, 45°–135°

Figure 4.1-11 Reconstructions by filtered backprojection in a noise-free environment.

EXAMPLE 4.1-3. *Effect of Noise on Ray Tomography.* If the calculations described in Example 4.1-2 are repeated in the presence of a small amount of noise added to the data, the reconstruction results are shown in Fig. 4.1-12. The degradation resulting from noise is apparent.

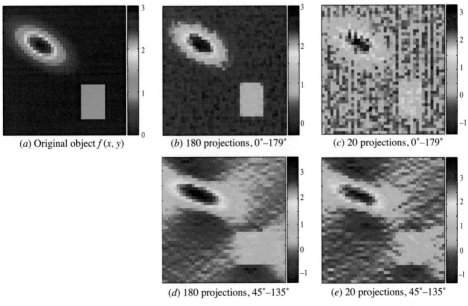

(*a*) Original object $f(x, y)$ (*b*) 180 projections, 0°–179°   (*c*) 20 projections, 0°–179°

(*d*) 180 projections, 45°–135°   (*e*) 20 projections, 45°–135°

Figure 4.1-12 Reconstructions by filtered backprojection in the presence of added noise such that the signal-to-noise ratio SNR = 30 dB.

The effect of noise may be reduced by use of a truncated or windowed filter, instead of the straight inverse filter $H_i(k) = |k|$. A popular windowed filter is the Shepp–Logan filter:

$$H_i(k) = |k/k_m| \operatorname{sinc}(k/k_m) \operatorname{rect}(k/k_m), \qquad (4.1\text{-}19)$$

where k_m is a regularization parameter representing the spatial bandwidth of the inverse filter (see Sec. 3.3B).

▶ Problems 4.1-4 – 4.1-7

C. Computed Axial Tomography (CT)

A common implementation of ray tomography is X-ray computed axial tomography (CAT), also known simply as computed tomography (CT). In the CT configuration, illustrated in Fig. 4.1-13(a), a 3D object is divided into slices orthogonal to the axial direction (the z axis) and each slice is imaged independently by use of parallel rays within its plane. The direction of the rays is changed, e.g., by rotating the sources and sensors, and the set of 1D projections is recorded. Alternatively, the rays may be fan shaped, as in the CT scanner shown in Fig. 4.1-13(b). Once the 3D distribution of the object is computed, it can be visualized in a variety of configurations, for example by displaying slices along any other axis.

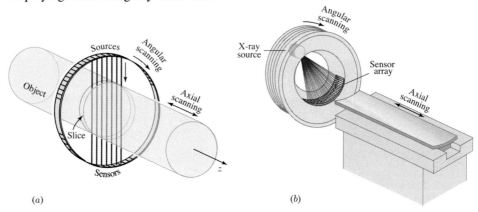

(a)   (b)

Figure 4.1-13 CAT is a combination of axial slicing, which is a form of localized probing, and 2D ray tomography in the transverse plane. (a) Parallel rays emitted by an array of X-ray sources are transmitted through each slice of the object and detected by array detectors. (b) Fan-shaped rays used in a medical CT scanner.

Medical imaging applications of X-ray CT include cranial, chest, cardiac, abdominal and pelvic imaging. An example of X-ray CT images of the brain is shown in Fig. 4.1-14. CT scanners are also used for nondestructive testing of materials and for the study of biological and paleontological specimens.

Digital Breast Tomosynthesis.   In conventional mammography, two low-dose X-ray images of each breast are usually taken: a top-to-bottom projection and a side-to-side projection. Breast cancer lesions, which are denser than the surrounding healthy fibroglandular breast tissue, appear as irregular white areas. These two 2D projections, however, may not show lesions obstructed by dense healthy fibroglandular tissue in the

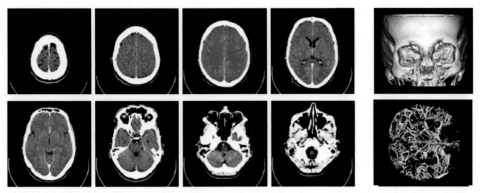

Figure 4.1-14 Eight slices of a cranial X-ray CT scan (from top to the base of the skull). An intravenous contrast medium was used. Top right: a volume rendering shows the high-density bones. Bottom right: the bone is removed using an image processing segmentation tool to show the previously concealed vessels. (Public domain images, courtesy of Mikäel Haggström, Radiology, Uppsala University Hospital; wikipedia.org/wiki/X-ray_computed_tomography.)

projection directions. Digital breast tomosynthesis (DBT), or simply tomosynthesis, is a new technique of X-ray 3D imaging of the breast based on ray tomography.

DBT uses multiple low-dose X-ray projections of each breast from many angles, typically 11 different angles covering a span of $40°$, as shown in Fig. 4.1-15. The breast is positioned as in a conventional mammogram (but only a little pressure is applied) and the images are taken with an X-ray tube moving in an arc around the breast. The projections are processed using ray tomography techniques, such as filtered backprojection, and a 3D image of the breast is computed. The image is usually displayed in the form of a series of slices, or rotated in space for more careful examination, or viewed in 3D to bring structures into relief. It is believed that this new breast imaging technique will make breast cancers easier to detect (see Sec.9.3).

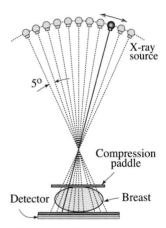

Figure 4.1-15 Tomosynthesis.

D. Emission Tomography (SPECT and PET)

In emission tomography there are no probe rays that are transmitted through the object in selected directions, as is the case of absorption tomography (e.g., X-ray CT). Here, photons are emitted from within the object spontaneously and in random directions. A mechanism must therefore be devised for selecting parallel rays in each of a set of directions so that the projections necessary for ray tomography are obtained. This is usually accomplished by use of a bank of detectors, each equipped with a collimator that selects one direction and rejects all others. Various approaches for solving the angular selection problem have led to different technologies of emission tomography, as we now show.

Single-Photon Emission Computed Tomography (SPECT)

Single-photon emission computed tomography (SPECT) is a nuclear medicine imaging technique based on detection of gamma-ray photons emitted from radionuclides (radio isotopes) injected into the body. The apparatus measures the 3D distribution $f(\mathbf{r})$ of the rate of emission, which is proportional to the density distribution of the injected radionuclides. Since emissions are in all directions, some mechanism of selecting parallel rays in each direction is necessary. This is accomplished by use of a gamma-ray collimator attached to the gamma-ray detector (see Sec. 2.5D). Implemented by means of a thick sheet of lead with parallel holes, the collimator ensures that only rays emitted from the body in a direction parallel to the axes of the holes are detected. This ensures that each image is indeed a projection of the 3D object onto a 2D plane. The camera is rotated around the patient, typically every $3°$–$6°$, and normally covers a full $360°$. The system is illustrated schematically in Fig. 4.1-16. The time taken to obtain each projection is typically 15–20 s, so that the total scan time is in the range of 15–20 min. Reconstruction of the 3D object from the 2D projections is implemented by use of techniques of ray tomography, such as filtered backprojection.

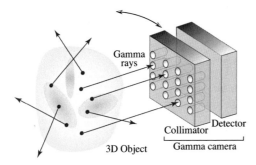

Figure 4.1-16 Single-photon emission computed tomography (SPECT).

Attenuated Ray Tomography. In emission tomography, some of the emitted photons may be absorbed in the medium before they arrive at the detector. Since photons travel different distances to the detector and since the attenuation is generally nonuniform, this effect can distort the SPECT measurement. If $\alpha(x, y)$ is the attenuation coefficient at position (x, y), then the ray tomography equation (4.1-2) must be modified to

$$g_\theta(s) = \int\!\!\!\int_{-\infty}^{\infty} \delta(x \cos\theta + y \sin\theta - s) f(x, y) w_\theta(x, y) \, \mathrm{d}x \, \mathrm{d}y, \qquad (4.1\text{-}20)$$

where

$$w_\theta(x, y) = \exp\left[-\int_0^{\infty} \alpha(x + u' \sin\theta, y - u' \cos\theta) \, \mathrm{d}u'\right] \qquad (4.1\text{-}21)$$

is a weighting function representing the attenuation encountered between the point (x, y) and the detector, along the direction designated by the angle θ.

This may be shown by following the radiation emitted from the position (x, y) as it travels along the ray to the detector. After it travels a distance u' it reaches a point of coordinates (x', y'), where $x' = x + u' \sin \theta$ and $y' = y - u' \cos \theta$. Between u' and $u' + \Delta u'$, the radiation is attenuated by a factor $\alpha(x', y') \Delta u'$ so that, upon reaching the detector, the intensity drops by the factor $w(x, y) = \exp\left[-\int \alpha(x', y')\, du'\right]$. The lower limit of the integral is $u' = 0$. The upper limit equals the distance from the point (x, y) to the detector; but since the attenuation function $\alpha(x', y')$ is zero outside the object, this limit may be conveniently replaced by ∞. Upon substitution for x' and y', (4.1-21) follows.

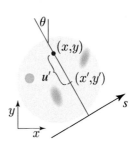

Modern scanners estimate the attenuation by use of an integrated X-ray CT scanner, which can also provide additional anatomical information. With the function $w_\theta(x, y)$ known, the modified ray tomography equation (4.1-20) may then be inverted for the unknown γ-ray emission distribution $f(x, y)$. Although mathematical techniques exist of estimating both $f(x, y)$ and $\alpha(x, y)$ from SPECT measurements, they are beyond the scope of this book.[2]

Positron Emission Tomography (PET)

Positron emission tomography (PET) is another nuclear medicine technique of 3D imaging of functional processes in the body. Here, ray collimation relies on a special physical process of positron–electron annihilation and generation of gamma-ray photons that are always emitted in pairs traveling in exactly opposite directions. The simultaneous detection of two photons therefore identifies a line on which the emitter lies.

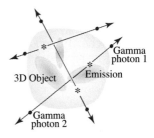

Photon-Pair Process. The body is injected with a positron-emitting short-lived radioactive tracer isotope, which is chemically incorporated in metabolically active molecules. After traveling up to a few millimeters the emitted positron annihilates with an electron, producing a pair of gamma-ray photons moving in exactly opposite directions. These are detected by gamma-ray detectors (see Sec. 2.5D). The rate of the detected gamma-ray photon pairs is proportional to the rate of positron emission, which is proportional to the density of the injected isotopes incorporated in metabolically active molecules. PET therefore measures the distribution of metabolic activity. This is the object function $f(\mathbf{r})$ to be computed from the scanner data.

The scanner is made of a large number of sensors distributed uniformly on a circular ring, as illustrated in Fig. 4.1-17. Each pair of sensors observes *coincidence events*, i.e., the simultaneous detection of photons in a pair of sensors. This is proportional to the rate of positron emission from any of the points on the line connecting the two sensors, i.e., to the integral of $f(\mathbf{r})$ along this line, called the **line of response (LOR)**. Each LOR is marked by its angle θ and position s, and readings from parallel LORs at an angle θ provide the projection $g_\theta(s)$ defined in conventional ray tomography. If the data are collected for a sufficient number of angles, then conventional techniques,

[2] See, e.g., S. Bellini, M. Pacentini, C. Cafforio, and F. Rocca, Compensation of tissue absorbtion in emission tomography, *IEEE Transactions on Acoust. Speech & Signal Proc.*, Vol. 27, pp. 213–218, 1979.

such as filtered backprojection, may be used to recover the object distribution $f(\mathbf{r})$. In principle, time-of-flight information may be used to determine the exact location of emission along the LOR by measuring the difference between the times of arrival of the two photons, and in this case the need for tomography would be obviated. However, for this to be possible, the response time of the detectors must be sufficiently short in order to acquire such information with acceptable spatial resolution (remember that the speed of light in the medium is less than 0.3 mm per picosecond).

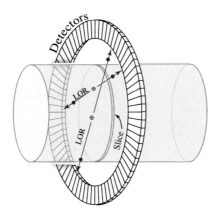

Figure 4.1-17   Schematic of the PET scanner.

Extraneous Effects.   In practice, a number of extraneous effects must be accounted for before processing the PET data through the usual filtered backprojections.

- Attenuation correction compensates for the different attenuation encountered by photons traveling different distances along the LORs. Contemporary scanners estimate attenuation by use of an integrated X-ray CT scanner.
- Noise in the PET system is inherently more severe than in the CT system. Since the number of photon coincidences in a typical PET scanner is of the order of millions (as compared to a few billion photon counts in a CT scanner), random fluctuations are significantly greater. Reconstructions based on filtered backprojection therefore tend to have artifacts across the image. Other reconstruction techniques designed to deal with the effect of noise are preferred, but tend to require greater computer resources.

Other effects include photon scattering, background random coincidences, detector dead time (the inability of a detector to respond during a short period following the detection of a photon), and the detector's angular sensitivity.

3D Scanners.   Early PET scanners used a single ring of detectors, as illustrated in Fig. 4.1-17, and operated in a configuration of 2D tomography combined with axial scanning. More modern scanners now include multiple rings, forming a cylinder of detectors. Full 3D tomography is obtained by detecting photon coincidences at detectors within the same ring as well as detectors in different rings, i.e., use photon pairs traveling in all directions, instead of only those traveling in a transverse plane. By collecting more coincidences, the level of noise is reduced. However, 3D PET scanners are more sensitive to photon scattering, since they allow the interaction between different transverse planes.

4.2 Range Tomography

As described in Sec. 3.2C, radar, sonar, and lidar imaging systems use a localized configuration for which range localization is accomplished by measurement of the time of flight of a reflected or backscattered pulsed wave, while angular localization is obtained by use of a narrow probe beam. If angular localization is not possible or not adequate, then tomographic techniques may be adopted.

A. Configurations and Reconstruction

Location of a Single Scatterer by Triangulation. Consider, for example, an imaging system with wide-angle probe and sensor beams, and assume for simplicity that the source and sensor are collocated. The time of arrival $\tau = 2R/v$ of a short pulse reflected or backscattered from a single scatterer provides information on the range R, but no directional information. However, by repeating the measurement with sources/sensors located at two other positions, as illustrated in Fig. 4.2-1, the scatterer may be located by triangulation (using the three measured ranges and the coordinates of the three devices to compute the coordinates of the scatterer). The same approach may be used to determine the location of an earthquake from seismic measurements of the arrival times of P- and S-waves at a number of dispersed surface locations.

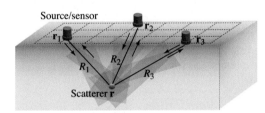

Figure 4.2-1   Locating a single burried scatterer at a position vector $\mathbf{r} = (x, y, z)$ by measuring the ranges $R_1 = |\mathbf{r}_1 - \mathbf{r}|$, $R_2 = |\mathbf{r}_2 - \mathbf{r}|$, and $R_3 = |\mathbf{r}_3 - \mathbf{r}|$ from three positions $\mathbf{r}_1$, $\mathbf{r}_2$, and $\mathbf{r}_3$ of the source/sensor on the surface. Three equations are solved to determine the three unknown coordinates (x, y, z).

This simple approach is not adequate if the object contains multiple scatterers at unknown positions. In this case, more measurements are necessary, as illustrated in Fig. 4.2-2. The range information provided by a sufficiently large number of measurements taken at different locations (constituting multiple views) can be used to determine the positions of the scatterers. This necessitates a tomographic approach – a process called **range tomography**.

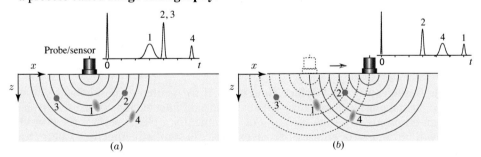

Figure 4.2-2   Range tomography by use of pulsed wide-angle probe/sensor beams and time-of-flight measurement. (*a*) Received echos at one source/sensor location. (*b*) Received echos at a second source/sensor location.

Monostatic Configuration.   Consider first a configuration for which the source and sensor are collocated, or a single device is used to perform both functions. This monostatic configuration is implemented by use of a single antenna or ultrasonic transducer transmitting and receiving simultaneously. If a pulse is transmitted from one position

$\mathbf{r}_\mathrm{s}$ at time $t = 0$, then the echo received at time $t = 2R/v$ comes from all scatterers located on the surface of a semi-sphere of radius R centered at the sensor, where $2R = vt$, as shown in Fig. 4.2-2(a). The received signal is therefore the integral of contributions from all scatterers at positions $\mathbf{r}$ on this surface, i.e., points for which

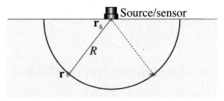

$$2|\mathbf{r}_\mathrm{s} - \mathbf{r}| = vt.$$

This is analogous to a "projection" in ray tomography, except here the projection path is the surface of a semi-sphere instead of a straight line. As t increases, projections along concentric spheres with increasing radius are measured. To complete the tomographic paradigm, the same measurement must be repeated with other sources/sensors at different locations (or by moving a single source/sensor to a new location) to take other view of the object, as illustrated in Fig. 4.2-2(b). The new measurements generate

projections along new sets of concentric spheres. Since these sets intersect, independent information is provided for each point. If measurements are made at a sufficient number of different positions, then it is possible to compute the locations and the strengths of all scatterers, i.e., determine the object distribution, much the same as in ray tomography. If the source/sensor is at a sufficiently long distance from the scatterers, then the concentric spheres may be approximated by parallel planes and the process becomes similar to that of ray tomography.

Bistatic Configuration.   Range tomography may also be applied in the bistatic configuration, for which the source and sensor are separated. The projection surface in this case is an ellipsoid with the source and sensor at the two foci, defined by the equation

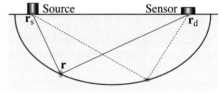

$$|\mathbf{r} - \mathbf{r}_\mathrm{s}| + |\mathbf{r} - \mathbf{r}_\mathrm{d}| = vt,$$

where $\mathbf{r}_\mathrm{s}$, $\mathbf{r}_\mathrm{d}$, and $\mathbf{r}$ are the positions of the source, the sensor, and the scatterer respectively, v is the velocity in the medium, and t is the pulse time of flight.

Range Tomography for Surface Imaging.   If the scatterers are known to lie on a surface, then the projection paths will be the lines of intersections of the semi-spheres (or semi-ellipsoids) with the surface. For example, for a planar surface the projection paths will be circles (or ellipses). As an example, in **synthetic aperture radar (SAR)** the ground reflectance is imaged by use of a moving monostatic side-looking antenna located in the air, as illustrated in Fig. 4.2-3. At each location of the antenna, a pulsed electromagnetic beam illuminates a spot of finite area (determined by the antenna aperture) and the times of arrival and amplitudes of the pulses received as a result of scattering from the surface are recorded. Each time delay marks a range, corresponding to points on an arc. Each location of the antenna therefore provides projections of the ground reflectance on a set of concentric arcs. If the surface is not planar, then the projections are intersections of spheres with the ground topography.

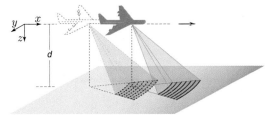

Figure 4.2-3 Synthetic aperture radar (SAR) as an example of range tomography. The projection paths are sets of concentric arcs

Reconstruction by Backprojection. One approach for reconstructing the object distribution from the set of projections along the projection paths (surfaces of semi-spheres in the monostatic case, half ellipsoids in the bistatic case, or concentric circles in the SAR configuration) is backprojection. Much like in ray tomography, for each position of the source and sensor, the signal measured at delay time t is distributed uniformly among all points of the projection path (e.g., a semi-sphere of radius $R = vt/2$ centered at the source/sensor in the monostatic case). A point that contains a scatterer will align with the peak of the received signal for all positions of the source and sensor, and will therefore have a strong peak in the backprojection. Note that in ray tomography, both projections and backprojections involve real signals representing intensity. In range tomography with electromagnetic, acoustic, or seismic waves, the measured signals represent complex amplitudes so that contributions from various backprojections exhibit interference. Reconstruction by backprojection is known in the seismic imaging literature as **Kirchhoff migration**. Other more sophisticated inversion methods account for factors such as the wave nature of the probe, the finite width of the probe pulse, and the wave polarization (or the existence of P- and S-waves in seismic applications).

EXAMPLE 4.2-1. *Monostatic Range Tomography for Two-Point Scatterers.* In this example of 2D range tomography, there are two point scatterers buried at coordinates $(x, z) = (0, -30)$ and $(60, -40)$ (units of cm) in a medium for which the wave velocity $v = c/3$ (e.g., soil with dielectric constant $9\epsilon_0$). A monostatic antenna is moved along the x axis (in the ground surface), from $x = -100$ cm to $x = +100$ cm. The probe pulse is a Gaussian function of time $p(t) = \exp(-t^2/\tau^2)$ of width parameter $\tau = 0.2$ ns. At the position of a scatterer, the incident probe field is approximated as $(1/r) \exp[-(t - r/v)^2/\tau^2]$, where r is the distance from the antenna to the scatterer and $v = c/3$ is the propagation velocity in the soil. The scattered field is proportional to the scattering cross-section σ and the returned signal radiates as if it originates from a point source at the position of the scatterer. Thus, the returned field is $(\sigma/r^2) \exp[-(t - 2r/v)^2/\tau^2]$. The observed signal $u(x, t)$, which is the sum of the contributions of the two scatterers, is presented in Fig. 4.2-4(a) as a function of the antenna position x and time t. Note the two intersecting hyperbolic contours characteristic of range tomography. To reconstruct an image of the subsurface in the plane of GPR

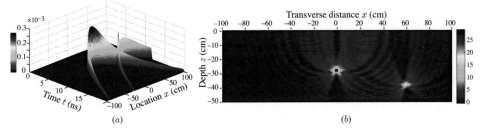

(a)   (b)

Figure 4.2-4 GPR using wide-angle antenna and range tomography for two point scatterers at locations $(x, z) = (0, -30)$ and $(60, -40)$ under a surface. (a) Received signal as a function of the antenna location x and the time t. (b) Magnitude of the superposition of the waves backprojected from all antennas as a function of x and z.

motion, the signal $u(x, t)$ is backprojected (or backpropagated) from each receiver to every point on the x–z plane after introducing a time delay equal to twice the travel time v/r from that point to the receiver. The reconstruction is obtained by adding all the backprojected waves. The result is shown in Fig. 4.2-4(b). Clearly, the strongest intensity levels correspond to the actual positions of the scatterers.

▶ Problems 4.2-1– 4.2-3

Reconstruction by Time Reversal. Consider a configuration in which a pulsed probe wave illuminates an object with scatterers and the scattered wave is sensed by an array of sensors, as illustrated in Fig. 4.2-5(a). The temporal profiles of the detected signals carry information on the locations of the scatterers and the propagation delays within the medium. If each signal is time reversed and used to generate a new pulsed wave with proportional amplitude, as illustrated in Fig. 4.2-5(b), then the superposition of these waves will form a composite wave identical to the original scattered wave but traveling backward in space, retracing the same path back to the scatterers. Time reversal may be accomplished by recording each signal and subsequently playing it backward so that the components that arrive first are sent last, and vice versa. Instead of physically generating the backward propagating wave, this may be accomplished only computationally. Locations where the generated virtual wave converges will identify the locations of the scatterers as in backprojection.

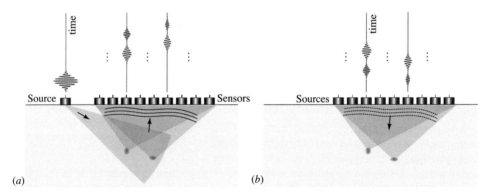

(a)   (b)

Figure 4.2-5   (a) Measurement of the scattered wave by an array of sensors. (b) Generation of an identical, but backward propagating, wave by use of sources driven by time-reversed signals.

Reconstruction by time reversal is, in principle, possible since the wave equation in a non-homogeneous and non-abosorbing medium is time-reversal invariant (because it contains only second-order time derivatives). This implies that for every solution $u(\mathbf{r}, t)$ representing a wave traveling from a source to some surface, there exists, in principle, a solution $u(\mathbf{r}, -t)$ that retraces the same path within the medium from the surface back to the original source, as if time went backwards. If $u(\mathbf{r}_d, t)$ is the field at the surface (the plane of the sensors), then the time-reversed field $u(\mathbf{r}_d, T - t)$, generated after a delay time T, will converge back toward the scatterers. Ideally, the wave amplitude $u(\mathbf{r}_d, t)$ must be measured at all points $\mathbf{r}_d$ on a closed surface and the sensors must be sufficiently fast to follow the most rapid temporal variation in the received wave. Since sensor arrays have finite size and response time, this places certain limitations on the implementation of time-reversed reconstruction. Also, since details of scatterers smaller than the wavelength will generate evanescent waves that do not propagate to the sensors, these details cannot be recovered. Nevertheless, time-reversal methods have been used in a number of applications, including acoustic imaging[3], ground penetrating radar,[4] and geophysical imaging.[5]

Simplified Theory of Range Tomography. Assume that a source located at the position $\mathbf{r}_s$ generates a pulsed beam of amplitude $a(\mathbf{r}-\mathbf{r}_s)p(t-|\mathbf{r}_s-\mathbf{r}|/v)$ at the position $\mathbf{r}$ in the medium, where $a(\mathbf{r})$ is the beam spatial pattern, $p(t)$ is the pulse profile, and $|\mathbf{r}_s - \mathbf{r}|/v$ is the propagation time delay. A scatterer of isotropic cross-section $f(\mathbf{r})$ at $\mathbf{r}$ generates a spherical wave centered at $\mathbf{r}$ with a proportional amplitude. Therefore, the amplitude at a sensor located at $\mathbf{r}_d$ is proportional to the product

$$a(\mathbf{r}-\mathbf{r}_s)p[t - \tau(\mathbf{r}_s, \mathbf{r}_d; \mathbf{r})]\frac{f(\mathbf{r})}{|\mathbf{r}_d - \mathbf{r}|},$$

where

$$\tau(\mathbf{r}_s, \mathbf{r}_d; \mathbf{r}) = \frac{|\mathbf{r} - \mathbf{r}_s|}{v} + \frac{|\mathbf{r}_d - \mathbf{r}|}{v} \tag{4.2-1}$$

is the total time of travel from the source to the sensor via the scatterer. The signal measured by the sensor is the sum of contributions of all scatterers,

$$g^{(\mathbf{r}_s, \mathbf{r}_d)}(t) = \int h^{(\mathbf{r}_s, \mathbf{r}_d)}(t; \mathbf{r}) f(\mathbf{r}) \, d\mathbf{r}, \tag{4.2-2}$$

where

$$h^{(\mathbf{r}_s, \mathbf{r}_d)}(t; \mathbf{r}) = \frac{a(\mathbf{r} - \mathbf{r}_s)}{|\mathbf{r}_d - \mathbf{r}|} p[t - \tau(\mathbf{r}_s, \mathbf{r}_d; \mathbf{r})]. \tag{4.2-3}$$

Equation (4.2-2) describes the measured temporal profile for the source and sensor positions $(\mathbf{r}_s, \mathbf{r}_d)$ as a linear transformation of the object distribution $f(\mathbf{r})$. It has the generic form of the tomographic imaging equation (4.0-1), where the source and sensor locations represent the view (v). The inverse problem in this case amounts to estimating $f(\mathbf{r})$ given the measured signals $g^{(\mathbf{r}_s, \mathbf{r}_d)}(t)$ at various locations $\mathbf{r}_s$ and $\mathbf{r}_d$.

If the pulse is very short, then the measured signal at time t is the integral of $f(\mathbf{r})$ over all points for which $t = \tau(\mathbf{r}_s, \mathbf{r}_d; \mathbf{r})$. These points lie on an ellipsoid with foci at $\mathbf{r}_s$ and $\mathbf{r}_d$, as described earlier. Clearly, a probe pulse of finite width, or a pulse that has been broadened because of dispersion during propagation through the medium, would limit the range resolution of each measurement, and will consequently limit the overall spatial resolution of the reconstructed object.

As an example, for the SAR monostatic configuration in Fig. 4.2-3, $\mathbf{r}_s = \mathbf{r}_d = (x_s, 0, 0)$ and $\mathbf{r} = (x, y, d)$, so that the temporal profile of the measurement at any antenna position x_s is a linear transformation of the scattering function $f(x, y)$. If the aircraft is sufficiently high so that $|x - x_s| \ll d$ and $|y| \ll d$, and assuming that the antenna is omnidirectional, (4.2-2) and (4.2-3) yield the approximate relation

$$g^{(x_s)}(t) \propto \iint p\left[t - \tau_o - \tau_o \frac{(x_s - x)^2 + y^2}{2d^2}\right] f(x, y) \, dx dy, \tag{4.2-4}$$

---

[3]M. Fink, Time reversed acoustics, *Physics Today*, Vol. 50, pp. 34–39, March 1997.

[4]F. Foroozan and A. Asif, Time reversal ground penetrating radar: range estimation with Cramér-Rao lower bounds, *IEEE Transactions on Geoscience and Remote Sensing*, Vol. 48, pp. 3698–3708, 2010.

[5]C. S. Larmat, R. A. Guyer, and P. A. Johnson, Time-reversal methods in geophysics, *Physics Today*, Vol. 63, pp. 31–35, August 2010.

where $\tau_o = 2d/v$. Although the antenna pattern is broad (i.e., its aperture is small), the scanned amplitude $g^{(x_s)}(t)$ as a function of t and x_s may be used to invert (4.2-4) to obtain $f(x, y)$ with a spatial resolution equal to that of an antenna with a larger (synthetic) aperture.

Note that in this simplified model multiple scattering was neglected and the velocity of propagation through the medium was assumed to be constant. If the variation of velocity in a nonhomogeneous medium is not significant, then an average velocity may be used. Also, the waves were assumed to be scalar; for electromagnetic or elastic waves the vector nature of the wave must be accounted for.

B. Ground-Penetrating Radar (GPR)

GPR senses objects buried in soil by sending out very short pulses of microwave from an antenna located at the surface and observing the times of arrival and the relative amplitudes of the received echos using the same (monostatic) or another (bistatic) antenna, also at the surface (Fig. 4.2-6). The antenna(s) are moved to a different location and the measurement is repeated using the range tomography configuration illustrated in Fig. 4.2-2. Radar echoes are formed by scattering from the object if it has a dielectric constant different from that of the background. Unlike the radar scanning system described in Sec. 3.2C, which uses beams of small angle, the beams used in GPR are necessarily wide angled so that echos arrive from multiple directions. The depth range of GPR is limited by the penetration depth, which depends on the type of soil and the frequency, and the power used.

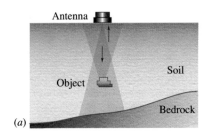

Figure 4.2-6   (a) GPR. (b) GPR survey of an archaeological site. The wheel trailing behind the transmitter/receiver antennas is an odometer that controls data collection (after Wikipedia).

Reconstruction is accomplished by use of backprojection, time-reversal, or other techniques. Ideally, if the probe pulse were infinitely short, the GPR transverse observation line sufficiently long, the ground surface perfectly flat (or with precisely known height), and the scatterers are infinitesimally small, their position could be determined precisely. Multiple scatterers could be imaged, as long as the interaction between scatterers is small.

Earth science applications of GPR include the study of bedrock, soils, and groundwater. Engineering applications include locating and testing of buried structures, tunnels, landfills, and contaminant plumes. GPR is also used in archaeology and the detection of mines (see Sec. 9.2).

C. Photoacoustic Tomography (PAT)

As mentioned briefly in Sec. 1.5, photoacoustic tomography (PAT) is a dual-wave technique for 3D imaging of optical absorption in biological tissue by making use of the photoacoustic effect (emission of ultrasound caused by absorption of light). As illustrated schematically in Fig. 4.2-7, at each position where the light is absorbed, a sound pulse is generated. Since light is much faster than sound, the ultrasonic pulses generated at the various locations are practically synchronized in time. By use of multiple ultrasonic sensors that measure the time of arrival of the sound pulses, range tomography may be used to compute the location and the strength of the sound sources, and hence the distribution of optical absorption.

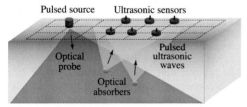

Figure 4.2-7 Photoacoustic tomography (PAT).

The reasoning behind the choice of an optical–ultrasonic dual-wave system for tissue imaging, instead of purely optical or purely ultrasonic imaging, is as follows:

- Since light is strongly scattered within the tissue, it travels along random paths so that time-of-flight range measurement is not feasible (unless some complex gating mechanism is used as described in Sec. 3.2C). Optical imaging by other localized means, such as confocal scanning, is limited to small depths (not exceeding the optical transport mean free path). By contrast, ultrasonic scattering in tissue is weaker by two to three orders of magnitude, so that ultrasonic imaging by means of time-of-flight measurements, and also by conventional ultrasonic scanning, offers better spatial resolution.
- The contrast of ultrasonic imaging is relatively weak. Conversely, optical absorption has a much greater contrast and may also reveal physiological functions if measured at multiple wavelengths, thereby offering possibilities for functional imaging.
- Since PAT is based on the measurement of optical absorption by means of an acoustic localization mechanism, it combines the advantages of both modalities – the high-contrast-associated optical absorption together with the high spatial resolution afforded by ultrasounic imaging. The depth limitation of optical imaging in diffusive media is not a barrier in PAT since the optical probe serves only to simultaneously excite sound at all locations of optical absorbers and need not be localized.

Applications. Perhaps the most promising application area for PAT is in the detection and diagnosis of tumors buried deep within tissue. Tumor tissue can be distinguished from healthy tissue due to the fact that tumor growth is accompanied by a large number of blood vessels. The resulting increase in blood volume leads to high local absorption of incident light and a photoacoustic response that exceeds that of the background tissue. In this case, an enhanced photoacoustic response indicates the presence of a tumor, while the arrival time and shape of the photoacoustic signal are used to infer both the location and size of the tumor. There are a number of photoacoustic systems that have been designed specifically for the detection of breast cancer. The experimental configuration is illustrated in Fig. 4.2-8. In all of these systems, a pulsed laser source, typically delivered though an optical fiber or fiber bundle, is used to irradiate the breast and an array of transducers is used to detect the photoacoustic response. Multiple wavelength photoacoustic generation can also be employed in order to obtain functional information about the tumor, such as blood oxygenation level, which can provide insight into the tumor state (benign or malignant). PAT-based breast cancer detection and diagnosis is still in its infancy, but promising results obtained thus far indicate that this technology is well suited for this application and may supplement (or perhaps someday replace) conventional mammography. PAT also has potential for the detection of other types of tissue abnormalities, such as prostate cancer or brain lesions.

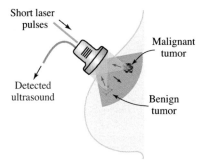

Figure 4.2-8 Breast cancer detection using PAT. Optical energy from laser pulses is absorbed and emitted acoustically. An array of highly sensitive transducers detect acoustic waves emitted by tumors, which are characterized by increased blood concentration. Malignant tumors are characterized by decreased oxygenation, while benign growth has normal oxygenation. The detected image maps blood volume and oxygentation.

In addition to deep-tissue studies, PAT has been applied to small-animal imaging. The motivation for this work stems from the fact that small-animal models are used in many studies across the biological sciences, and noninvasive techniques to determine structural and functional information are required. PAT has been used, for example, to image the vasculature of an intact rat brain, through the skull, as shown in Fig. 4.2-9. Panel (a) shows the basic schematic of the experiment, where a single transducer is rotated around the mouse while the photoacoustic signals are collected at multiple angles. This data is then used to construct the image shown in panel (b). PAT has also been used to visualize the blood flow changes in the rat brain resulting from external stimuli of the whiskers. A high-resolution version of PAT, referred to as functional photoacoustic microscopy, has been developed in which a tightly focused ultrasonic transducer with a broad bandwidth is used to detect the photoacoustic response generated at two different optical wavelengths. Using this approach, functional images of individual blood vessels have been demonstrated, along with high-resolution images of the near-surface vasculature.

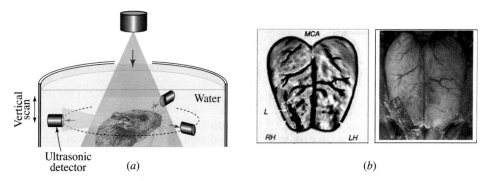

(a)   (b)

Figure 4.2-9   (a) Schematic of a photoacoustic imaging system of a rat brain. (b) Acquired photoacoustic image shows the distribution of optical absorption in the rat brain (black = minimum, white = maximum). A lesion L is detected. A subsequent open-skull photo is also shown (after Wikipedia.) See G. Ku, X. Wang, X. Xie, G. Stoica, and L. V. Wang, Imaging of tumor angiogenesis in rat brains in vivo by photoacoustic tomography, *Applied Optics*, Vol. 44, pp. 770–775, 2005.

PAT is potentially suitable for a variety of application areas in which optical contrast or property information is required, but where pure optical imaging techniques are not suitable due to, for example, optical scattering. Additional applications range from imaging skin lesions to the detection of early stage cancers in the digestive system.

4.3 Wave Tomography

Wave tomography, also called **diffraction tomography**, is a method for imaging an object by use of a set of probe waves (plane waves, spherical waves, or beams of finite width) illuminating the object from different directions, and measurement of the complex amplitude (magnitude and phase) of the scattered wave in each case at points in a planar area, as illustrated in Fig. 4.3-1. A full-wave theory is used and the ray approximation is not invoked so that the wavelength does not have to be short.

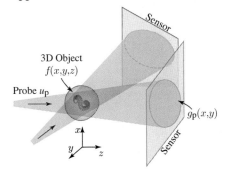

Figure 4.3-1 Wave tomography.

For a nonabsorbing medium, under linearizing approximations such as the Born approximation (see Sec. 2.2C), the imaging equation (4.0-1) is applicable and may be written in the special form,

$$g_p(\mathbf{r}) = \int h(\mathbf{r}; \mathbf{r}') u_p(\mathbf{r}') f(\mathbf{r}') \, d\mathbf{r}'. \qquad (4.3\text{-}1)$$

Imaging Equation

Here, each view uses a probe wave $u_p(\mathbf{r})$, which may be a plane wave $\exp(-j\mathbf{k}_p\mathbf{r})$ traveling along the direction of a wavevector $\mathbf{k}_p$, a spherical wave $|\mathbf{r} - \mathbf{r}_p|^{-1} \exp(-jk|\mathbf{r} - \mathbf{r}_p|)$ originating from a position $\mathbf{r}_p$, or a beam pointing in a direction marked by the index p, which identifies the view. The function $f(\mathbf{r}')$ represents the object distribution and is related to the refractive index $n(\mathbf{r})$ by the relation

$$f(\mathbf{r}) = [k_s^2(\mathbf{r}) - k^2] = \frac{\omega^2}{c^2}[n_s^2(\mathbf{r}) - n^2],$$

where ω is the angular frequency and $n_s(\mathbf{r})$ and n are the refractive indexes of the object and the background media, respectively, in accordance with (2.2-34). The function $g_p(\mathbf{r})$ in (4.3-1) is the measured wave amplitude for the pth view. The kernel $h(\mathbf{r}; \mathbf{r}')$ is the impulse response function (PSF or Green's function) for propagation in the homogeneous background medium. This is simply a spherical wave centered at the position $\mathbf{r}'$, i.e.,

$$h(\mathbf{r}; \mathbf{r}') = \frac{e^{-jk|\mathbf{r}-\mathbf{r}'|}}{4\pi\,|\mathbf{r} - \mathbf{r}'|}. \qquad (4.3\text{-}2)$$

The inversion problem is therefore the estimation $f(\mathbf{r}')$ given the measurements $g_p(\mathbf{r})$ and the probe waves $u_p(\mathbf{r}')$.

A. Fourier Theory of Wave Tomography

To prepare for solving the diffraction tomography inversion problem, we first consider the inversion of the generic relation

$$g(\mathbf{r}) = \int s(\mathbf{r}') \frac{e^{-jk|\mathbf{r}-\mathbf{r}'|}}{4\pi\,|\mathbf{r} - \mathbf{r}'|} \, d\mathbf{r}', \qquad (4.3\text{-}3)$$

which represents the radiation of a field $g(\mathbf{r})$ by a 3D source $s(\mathbf{r})$, where $k = n\omega/c$ is the wavenumber. This relation is obtained from (4.3-1) with $s(\mathbf{r}) = u_\mathrm{p}(\mathbf{r})f(\mathbf{r})$, $g(\mathbf{r}) = g_\mathrm{p}(\mathbf{r})$, and $h(\mathbf{r}; \mathbf{r}')$ given by (4.3-2).

Special Case: Radiation from a Planar Object. For a planar object with distribution $s(x, y)$ located in the plane $z = 0$ and radiating a wave with amplitude $g(x, y)$ in the observation plane $z = d$, (4.3-3) may be expressed in the Fourier domain (the **k** space) as a spatial filtering operation

$$G(k_x, k_y) = H(k_x, k_y)\, S(k_x, k_y), \tag{4.3-4}$$

where $G(k_x, k_y)$ and $S(k_x, k_y)$ are the 2D Fourier transforms of $g(x, y)$ and $s(x, y)$, respectively, and

$$H(k_x, k_y) = \frac{\exp(-\mathrm{j}k_z d)}{2\mathrm{j}k_z}, \quad k_z = \sqrt{k^2 - k_x^2 - k_y^2}, \tag{4.3-5}$$

is the spatial transfer function, the Fourier transform of the impulse response function $(1/4\pi r)\exp(-\mathrm{j}kr)$, where $r = \sqrt{x^2 + y^2 + d^2}$ [see (A.2-8) and (A.2-9)]. Radiation is therefore regarded as a spatial filter, but a physical interpretation is illustrated in Fig. 4.3-2. The component of the Fourier decomposition of the source function $s(x, y)$ with spatial frequencies (k_x, k_y), which has an amplitude $S(k_x, k_y)$, generates a plane wave of wavevector $\mathbf{k} = (k_x, k_y, k_z)$ that creates in the observation plane a 2D harmonic function of spatial frequencies (k_x, k_y) and amplitude $G(k_x, k_y)$ proportional to $S(k_x, k_y)$. The factor $\exp(-\mathrm{j}k_z d)$ is a result of propagation a distance d in the z direction, and $k_x^2 + k_y^2 + k_z^2 = k^2$. The plane wave may be focused by a lens as a single spot in the back focal plane. Each spot corresponds to a unique spatial frequency so that the distribution is proportional to the Fourier transform $S(k_x, k_y)$ of $s(x, y)$.

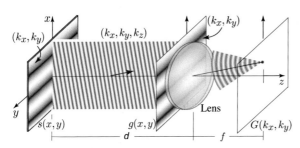

Figure 4.3-2 Each spatial harmonic component of the planar source $s(x, y)$ is radiated as a plane wave, creating a 2D spatial harmonic function in any parallel plane. The plane wave may be focused by a lens as a single spot in the lens back focal plane, where the Fourier transform of $s(x, y)$ may be measured.

If the radiated wave amplitude $g(x, y)$ is measured (magnitude and phase), then the inversion problem – determining the source function $s(x, y)$ – may be solved by use of an inverse filter (see Sec. 3.3). Note, however, that for spatial frequencies for which the point (k_x, k_y) lies outside a circle of radius k in the **k** plane (i.e., $\sqrt{k_x^2 + k_y^2} > k = 2\pi/\lambda$), corresponding to source details finer than a wavelength, the factor k_z in the exponent of (4.3-5) becomes imaginary, leading to exponential attenuation. These components correspond to severely attenuated waves (called evanescent waves) that do not reach the observation plane, and cannot be recovered.

Since it is difficult to measure the phase of $g(x, y)$, one approach is to measure the magnitude $|G(k_x, k_y)|$ of its Fourier transform (by placing a detector in the lens back focal plane) from which $|S(k_x, k_y)|$ may be determined [by use of (4.3-4)], and also measure the magnitude $|s(x, y)|$ (by using a detector in the lens imaging plane). Knowledge of $|s(x, y)|$ and $|S(k_x, k_y)|$ are sufficient to determine the complex source function $s(x, y)$.

Radiation from a 3D Object: The Radiation–Slice Theorem.   Radiation from a 3D source may also be described in terms of plane waves, each associated with a Fourier component of the source distribution. The harmonic component of the source function $s(x, y, z)$ with spatial frequencies (k_x, k_y, k_z) and amplitude equal to the 3D Fourier transform $S(k_x, k_y, k_z)$ can generate a plane wave of wavevector $\mathbf{k} = (k_x, k_y, k_z)$ that travels to the observation plane and create a 2D harmonic function of spatial frequencies (k_x, k_y) and amplitude $G(k_x, k_y)$ proportional to $S(k_x, k_y, k_z)$. Here, however, only the components with spatial frequencies (k_x, k_y, k_z) that satisfy the condition $k_x^2 + k_y^2 + k_z^2 = k^2$ can radiate. In the Fourier domain, these components lie on the surface of a sphere of radius $k = \omega/v = 2\pi/\lambda$, called the **Ewald sphere**. The radiation equation (4.3-3) may therefore be written in the Fourier domain as

$$G(k_x, k_y) = H(k_x, k_y) \, S(k_x, k_y, k_z), \quad k_z = \sqrt{k^2 - k_x^2 - k_y^2}. \qquad (4.3\text{-}6)$$

Radiation–Slice
Theorem

Here, $G(k_x, k_y)$ is the 2D Fourier transform for the radiated field $g(x, y)$ in the observation plane $(z = d)$ and $H(k_x, k_y)$ is the same transfer function in (4.3-5). This relation, which we call the **radiation–slice theorem**, means that the 2D Fourier transform of the measured field $g(x, y)$ is proportional to a slice of the 3D Fourier transform of the source function $s(x, y, z)$ at points on the Ewald sphere, as illustrated schematically in Fig. 4.3-3.

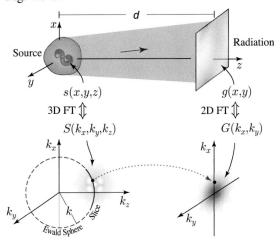

Figure 4.3-3 Radiation–slice theorem. A 3D source $s(x, y, z)$ radiates a wave with amplitude $g(x, y)$ in the $z = d$ plane. The 2D Fourier transform $G(k_x, k_y)$ of $g(x, y)$, which may be observed in the back focal plane of a lens, is proportional to values of the 3D Fourier transform $S(k_x, k_y, k_z)$ of the source at points on a spherical slice of radius $k = \omega/v = 2\pi/\lambda$.

Diffraction–Slice Theorem

In a scattering configuration, such as that in Fig. 4.3-4, the source $s(\mathbf{r}) = u_\mathrm{p}(\mathbf{r}) f(\mathbf{r})$, where $\mathbf{r} = (x, y, z)$. If the probe wave $u_\mathrm{p}(\mathbf{r})$ is a plane wave with wavevector $\mathbf{k}_\mathrm{p}$, then $s(\mathbf{r}) = \exp(-j\mathbf{k}_\mathrm{p} \cdot \mathbf{r}) f(\mathbf{r})$ so that, in accordance with the frequency translation property of the Fourier transform, $S(\mathbf{k}) = S(k_x, k_y, k_z)$ is a shifted version of the Fourier transform $F(\mathbf{q}) = F(q_x, q_y, q_z)$ of the object function $f(\mathbf{r}) = f(x, y, z)$, i.e.,

$$S(\mathbf{k}) = F(\mathbf{k} - \mathbf{k}_\mathrm{p}).$$

Thus, the spatial frequency component $\mathbf{q} = \mathbf{k} - \mathbf{k}_\mathrm{p}$ of the object can convert the probe plane wave into a scattered plane wave with wavevector $\mathbf{k} = \mathbf{k}_\mathrm{s}$, where

$$\mathbf{k_s} = \mathbf{k_p} + \mathbf{q}.$$

This can only occur if the magnitude of the vector $\mathbf{k_s} = \mathbf{k_p} + \mathbf{q}$ equals the wavenumber $k = 2\pi/\lambda$, i.e., if $\mathbf{q}$ lies on an Ewald sphere displaced by the wavevector $\mathbf{k_p}$.

As an example, if the vector $\mathbf{k_p} = (0, 0, k)$ points in the z direction, then $S(k_x, k_y, k_z) = F(k_x, k_y, k_z - k)$ and (4.3-6) becomes

$$G(k_x, k_y) = H(k_x, k_y) \, F\left(k_x, k_y, k_z - k\right), \quad k_z = \sqrt{k^2 - k_x^2 - k_y^2}. \qquad (4.3\text{-}7)$$

Diffraction–Slice Theorem

This relation implies that the 2D Fourier transform of the scattered field is a slice of the 3D Fourier transform of the object distribution $F(k_x, k_y, k_z)$ of the form of a spherical surface, as illustrated in Fig. 4.3-4. We call this property the diffraction–slice theorem, but it is also known in the literature as the **Fourier diffraction theorem**.

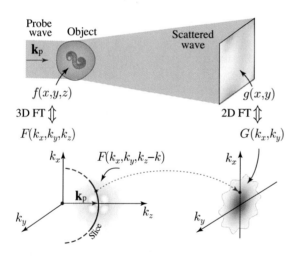

Figure 4.3-4 A plane wave of wavevector $\mathbf{k_p} = (0, 0, k)$ is scattered from an object $f(x, y, z)$ and the scattered wave amplitude $g(x, y)$ is measured. The Fourier transform of $g(x, y)$ is a spherical slice of the 3D Fourier transform of the object function $F(k_x, k_y, k_z - k)$. The sphere is centered at the origin and its radius is k.

For a probe wave traveling in an arbitrary direction $\mathbf{k_p}$ and observed in an orthogonal plane, the measured 2D field yields another spherical slice of $F(k_x, k_y, k_z)$, as shown in the right figure. Multiple probes pointing in different directions therefore correspond to multiple spherical slices all passing through the same point, forming a 3D petal structure lying within a spherical region of radius $2k$, called the **limiting Ewald sphere**, as illustrated in Fig. 4.3-5.

Inversion. If the diffracted fields g_p are measured (magnitude and phase) with multiple probe waves pointing in all $\mathbf{k_p}$ directions, then we may use the diffraction–slice theorem to reconstruct $F(k_x, k_y, k_z)$, from which the 3D object distribution $f(x, y, z)$ may be determined by use of a 3D inverse Fourier transform. This assumes that $F(k_x, k_y, k_z)$ lies entirely within the limiting Ewald sphere. If the scattered waves are measured with probe waves within a finite angle, then there will be some missing slices. The missing data may be estimated by combined use of prior information on $f(x, y, z)$ and incomplete data on $F(k_x, k_y, k_z)$. An iterative algorithm going back and forth between the position and spatial-frequency domains may be used to obtain the distribution $f(x, y, z)$ that satisfies the prior constraints on $f(x, y, z)$ and is consistent with the measured slices of $F(k_x, k_y, k_z)$.

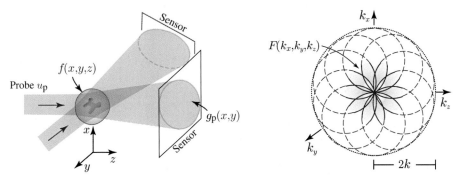

Figure 4.3-5 The 2D Fourier transform of the scattered field for each probe wave is a spherical slice of the object 3D Fourier transform $F(k_x, k_y, k_z)$. This petal-like slicing structure samples the function $F(k_x, k_y, k_z)$ at points within a sphere of radius $2k$.

Comparison with Ray Tomography. The diffraction–slice theorem of wave tomography is similar to the P–S theorem of ray tomography (Sec. 4.1A), as Fig. 4.3-6 illustrates. In wave tomography, as ω increases, the radius of the spherical slice increases and it may be approximated by a planar surface normal to the wavevector $\mathbf{k}_p$ in the limit of very high frequency (e.g., X-rays). In this limit, the plane wave acts as a collection of parallel rays, and the diffraction–slice theorem yields the P–S theorem. The similarity between wave tomography and ray tomography suggests that the inversion techniques developed for ray tomography can be applied to wave tomography. In fact, a technique similar to filtered backprojection in ray tomography has been developed for wave tomography, as will be described subsequently.

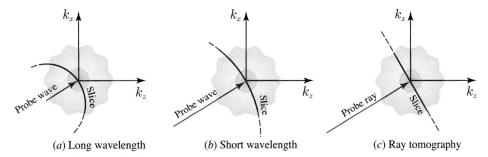

Figure 4.3-6 (*a*) Diffraction slice in wave tomography. (*b*) Diffraction slice in wave tomography at a higher frequency (shorter wavelength). (*c*) Projection slice in ray tomography. In the limit of very high frequency (very short wavelength, as in X-ray tomography), the spherical slice becomes approximately planar so that wave tomography approaches ray tomography.

Diffraction from a Periodic Structure. Crystallography.

As an example of the use of the diffraction–slice theorem, consider elastic scattering from a 3D object with a periodic structure $f(x, y, z)$. Using a Fourier series expansion, $f(x, y, z)$ may be written as a sum of harmonic functions, with the fundamental harmonic component having spatial frequencies $(q_x, q_y, q_z) = (2\pi/\Lambda_x, 2\pi/\Lambda_y, 2\pi/\Lambda_z)$, where Λ_x, Λ_y, and Λ_z are the periods in the x, y, and z directions. The component represented by the vector $\mathbf{q} = (q_x, q_y, q_z)$ corresponds to harmonic variation in the direction of $\mathbf{q}$ with spatial frequency q and period Λ such that $q = 2\pi/\Lambda$, as illustrated in Fig. 4.3-7. When illuminated by a plane wave of wavevector $\mathbf{k}_p$ and wavenumber $k = 2\pi/\lambda$ this Fourier component scatters the probe wave creating another plane wave of wavevector $\mathbf{k}_s = \mathbf{k}_p + \mathbf{q}$. This can occur only if the magnitude of the sum vector $\mathbf{k}_s$ also equals the wavenumber $k = 2\pi/\lambda$, i.e., $\mathbf{q}$ lies on the Ewald sphere. We can think of the process as reflection at an angle θ from the planes of object variation, as shown in Fig. 4.3-7. Using simple geometry, it can be shown that condition $|\mathbf{k}_p + \mathbf{q}| = k$ is met if θ satisfies the relation

$$\sin\theta = \frac{q}{2k} = \frac{\lambda}{2\Lambda}. \tag{4.3-8}$$

The angle θ given by (4.3-8) is called the **Bragg angle** and the process is called **Bragg diffraction**. Other harmonic components of the periodic structures have different periods and orientations, along with their corresponding Bragg angles. Therefore, by illuminating the periodic structure from multiple views and measuring the diffraction patterns in each observation plane, the Fourier transform $F(q_x, q_y, q_z)$ may be constructed by use of (4.3-7), from which the object distribution $f(x, y, z)$ can be calculated.

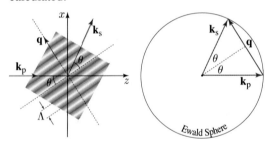

Figure 4.3-7 Scattering of a probe wave of wavevector $\mathbf{k}_p$ and wavenumber $k = 2\pi/\lambda$ from an object with harmonic distribution represented by a vector $\mathbf{q}$ of magnitude $q = 2\pi/\Lambda$ and period Λ. The scattered wave has a wavevector $\mathbf{k}_s$ and wavenumber k. This is allowed if, and only if, the angle θ equals the Bragg angle.

In order to image a periodic structure of period Λ using this method, the wavelength λ must be smaller than 2Λ, so that the Bragg condition in (4.3-8) can be met. For imaging atomic and molecular crystalline structures, X-rays and electron beams have sufficiently short wavelengths for this purpose. The techniques, known as **X-ray diffraction** and **electron diffraction**, are used in **crystallography** to obtain a 3D image of the density of electrons and reconstruct the arrangement of atoms in crystals and other atomic structures.

Wave Tomography for Objects with Cylindrical Symmetry

An object with cylindrical symmetry may be imaged by use of a set of cylindrical probe waves and measurement of the scattered waves as illustrated in Fig. 4.3-9. Here, the object function $f(\mathbf{r}) = f(x, y)$ is 2D, and each of the measured images $g_p(\mathbf{r})$ is a 1D function, which we denote $g_\theta(s)$, where the probe identifier p is now the angle θ of the probe wavevector $\mathbf{k}_p$. This terminology is identical to that of ray tomography (Sec. 4.1). The impulse response function $h(\mathbf{r}; \mathbf{r}')$ in this 2D case is

$$h(\mathbf{r}; \mathbf{r}') = \frac{1}{4j} H_0^{(1)}(k|\mathbf{r} - \mathbf{r}'|), \tag{4.3-9}$$

where $H_0^{(1)}(k\rho)$ is the Hankel function of the first kind and order zero.[6] This is a complex function (see Fig. 4.3-8) similar to the function $\exp(-jkr)/r$, which is applicable to the 3D case. In the 2D case, $\rho = \sqrt{x^2 + y^2}$, and in the 3D case, $r = \sqrt{x^2 + y^2 + z^2}$. The real and imaginary parts of both functions oscillate at a spatial frequency equal to $2\pi/k = \lambda$ and have a linear phase dependence.

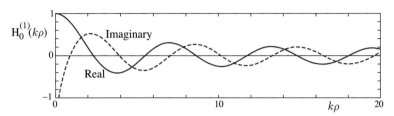

Figure 4.3-8   The real and imaginary parts of the Hankel function of the first kind and order zero.

For a probe plane wave traveling along the y direction, i.e., $\mathbf{k}_p = (0, k)$, the diffraction–slice theorem in (4.3-7) takes the form

$$G(k_x) = H(k_x)\, F\,(k_x, k_y - k)\,, \quad k_y = \sqrt{k^2 - k_x^2}, \tag{4.3-10}$$

Diffraction–Slice Theorem

where

$$H(k_x) = \frac{1}{2j} \frac{\exp(-jk_y d)}{k_y}, \quad k_y = \sqrt{k^2 - k_x^2}. \tag{4.3-11}$$

The measurement provides the values of $F(k_x, k_y)$ at points on the Ewald circle (a circle of radius $k = \omega/v$ and center at $(0, -k)$). A similar relation applies for a probe wave at an arbitrary angle θ, as shown schematically in Fig. 4.3-9.

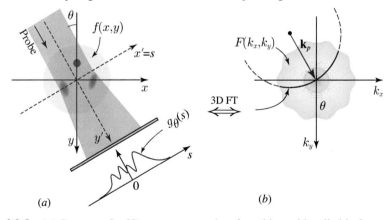

(a)   (b)

Figure 4.3-9   (a) Geometry for 2D wave tomography of an object with cylindrical symmetry. (b) The 1D Fourier transform of the diffracted wave is a slice of the 2D Fourier transform of the object.

---

[6]The Hankel function $H_0^{(1)}(x)$ can be computed by use of the MATLAB function `besselh(0,1,x)`.

Inversion by Filtered Backpropagation. The diffraction–slice theorem (4.3-10) and its generalization to an arbitrary angle θ may be used to derive an explicit formula relating the object function $f(x, y)$ to the measured field $g_\theta(s)$ for probe waves at all angles θ, so that a continuum of slices spans the Fourier transform function $F(k_x, k_y)$ as depicted in Fig. 4.3-9. This formula is derived by writing $f(x, y)$ in terms of its own Fourier transform $F(k_x, k_y)$, changing to polar coordinates, $(k_x, k_y) \rightarrow (k_\rho, \theta)$, and using the diffraction–slice theorem to express the result in terms of $G_\theta(k_\rho)$, which is the Fourier transform of the measurement $g_\theta(s)$. The result of this lengthy derivation is a formula for the reconstructed object:

$$f(x, y) = \int_{-\pi}^{\pi} d\theta \int_{-k}^{k} dk_\rho \, h_r(x, y; k_\rho, \theta) \, G_\theta(k_\rho), \qquad (4.3\text{-}12)$$

where

$$h_r(x, y; k_\rho, \theta) = \frac{k}{8\pi^2} |k_\rho| \, \exp\left\{-j[\gamma d - k_\rho x' - (\gamma - k)y']\right\}, \quad \gamma = \sqrt{k^2 - k_\rho^2},$$
$$(4.3\text{-}13)$$

$k = n\omega/c$, and $x' = x \sin\theta - y \cos\theta$ and $y' = x \cos\theta + y \sin\theta$ are the coordinates (x, y) rotated by an angle θ.

This inversion process, called **filtered backpropagation**, is similar to filtered back-projection in ray tomography. Here, the diffracted field $g_\theta(s)$ is measured for each angle θ and is filtered by a 1D filter before it is backprojected to generate the object distribution. The 1D filter h_r includes the function $|k_\rho|$, as in ray tomography, but spatial frequencies greater than $k = n\omega/c$ are truncated and cannot be recovered. A phase factor is also included in the 1D filter, as indicated by (4.3-13).

B. Ultrasonic and Optical Diffraction Tomography (UDT and ODT)

As mentioned earlier, diffraction tomography is useful in measuring the spatial distribution of the refractive index (or the wave velocity) of a nonabosrbing medium under conditions for which the Born approximation is valid. The wave can be acoustic or electromagnetic (radiowave, microwave, or optical). The technique has been tested for applications in ultrasonic imaging, optical microscopy for cellular imaging, as well as for acoustic and electromagnetic geophysical applications.

Several factors influence the selection of the wavelength λ of the probe wave. Within the spectral range for which the object is transparent, the choice of the wavelength is typically driven by two competing factors. As in localized imaging systems, in limited-view diffraction tomography the shorter the wavelength, the greater the ability to resolve finer spatial details (see Sec. 3.1C). However, waves with shorter wavelength typically suffer greater attenuation and cannot penetrate deeper into the medium (see Sec. 2.2A). There are also many practical, hardware-dependent considerations and tradeoffs that may limit the choice of probing wavelength. Additionally, there is much to be gained by use of multiple wavelengths, as described in Chapter 6.

A principal requirement of diffraction tomography is that both the magnitude and phase of the scattered field g must be measured. While this does not pose a problem in ultrasonic diffraction tomography (UDT), it is a major difficulty in optical diffraction tomography (ODT). In ODT, such measurement may be accomplished interferometrically by use of holography, i.e., by mixing diffracted wave with a reference wave and recording the magnitude of the sum. Alternatively, the magnitudes of scattered wave g and its Fourier transform G may be measured simultaneously. The missing phase of g may then be determined by means of iterative numerical methods. The Fourier transform G may generated optically by use of the Fourier transform property of the lens. Algorithms for phase retrieval have been developed for optical, X-ray, and electron imaging.

4.4 Spectral Tomography

In spectral tomography, an object with spatial distribution $f(\mathbf{r})$ is *viewed* with waves of different frequencies ω and the measurements $g_\omega(\mathbf{r})$ are used for reconstruction. In this section, we introduce important examples of spectral tomography and their applications.

A. Fourier-Transform Tomography

In the field of imaging by use of propagating waves, a measurement g is sometimes related to an unknown 1D distribution $f(z)$ by an integral

$$g = \int f(z) \exp\left(-j\frac{\omega}{v}z\right) dz,$$

where ω is the angular frequency and v is the velocity of propagation. This is encountered, for example, when a wave traveling along the z direction is reflected from an object with reflectors distributed along the z axis. Clearly, the single measurement g is insufficient to reconstruct the source distribution $f(z)$. However, by taking other "views" of the object $f(z)$ with different frequencies ω, a tomographic reconstruction from the multiple measurements $g(\omega)$ can yield the unknown distribution $f(z)$.

It is convenient to express the relation between the measurement $g(\omega)$ and the object distribution $f(z)$ in terms of the wavenumber $k = \omega/v$ as

$$g(k) = \int f(z) \exp(-jkz)\, dz. \tag{4.4-1}$$

Since this is recognized as the 1D Fourier transform of $f(z)$, the reconstruction may be readily computed from $g(k)$ by means of an inverse Fourier transform

$$f(z) = \int g(k) \exp(jkz)\, dk/2\pi. \tag{4.4-2}$$

This type of tomography, which may be called Fourier-transform tomography, is applicable to interferometric axial (depth) imaging, as we will see next.

B. Spectral-Domain Optical Coherence Tomography (OCT)

As described in Sec. 3.2D, optical reflectometry is an interferometric technique based on mixing the probe wave that is reflected from the object with a reference wave, and measuring the intensity of the sum. An interferogram is recorded by varying the time delay τ_r in the reference wave path by means of a movable mirror. However, it was shown that if the source wave is monochromatic with frequency ω, then each of the object's reflecting layers contributes to the interferogram a sinusoidal fringe pattern of frequency ω so that it is not possible to distinguish the contributions of the different reflections. This difficulty is overcome by use of a source wave that is either a pulse of short duration or a continuous wave of low coherence. In either case, the interference fringes resulting from each reflection last for a short duration centered at a time delay corresponding to the location of the reflector. Thus, reflections from layers separated by a short distance can be delineated in the interferogram. This approach is an example of localized axial imaging in which the reflectance as a function of depth is measured point by point. We now introduce a tomographic approach based on Fourier transform tomography.

Swept-Frequency OCT

Axial Imaging by Swept-Frequency Interferometry.   Consider a Michelson interferometer using a monochromatic source of angular frequency ω to probe an object with two reflectors of reflectance r_1 and r_2. Instead of the conventional interferogram, a *spectral interferogram* is recorded by measuring the intensity as a function of ω, with the mirror held fixed (i.e., τ_m is constant). The result is [see (3.2-21)]

$$I(\omega) \propto 1 + \mathcal{R}_b + 2r_1 \cos(\omega\tau_{1m}) + 2r_2 \cos(\omega\tau_{2m}), \qquad (4.4\text{-}3)$$

where $\tau_{1m} = \tau_1 - \tau_m$ and $\tau_{2m} = \tau_2 - \tau_m$, and we have assumed for simplicity that r_1 and r_2 are real. The two reflectors contribute two sinusoidal functions of different periods, $2\pi/|\tau_{1m}|$ and $2\pi/|\tau_{2m}|$ and amplitudes $2r_1$ and $2r_2$. A Fourier analysis of $I(\omega)$ provides the amplitudes and periods of these two Fourier components. The inverse Fourier transform of (4.4-3) is [see Sec. A.1 in Appendix A]

$$i(\tau) \propto (1 + \mathcal{R}_b)\delta(\tau) + r_1\delta(\tau - \tau_{1m}) + r_1\delta(\tau + \tau_{1m}) + r_2\delta(\tau - \tau_{2m}) + r_2\delta(\tau + \tau_{2m}), \qquad (4.4\text{-}4)$$

Therefore, this computational process separates the contributions of the two reflectors, as illustrated in Fig. 4.4-1. Note, however, that there is an ambiguity as to the signs of τ_{1m} and τ_{2rm}. This has to do with the interferometer not being sensitive to which of the two paths is longer. Such ambiguity can be resolved by use of prior information about the object.

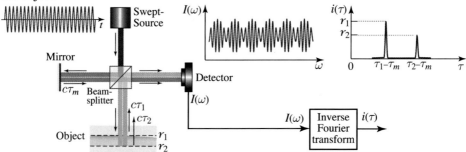

Figure 4.4-1   A spectral interferogram $I(\omega)$ generated by an interferometer using a frequency-swept source. The inverse Fourier transform of $I(\omega)$ is a function $i(\tau)$ containing the reflectance and depth information. This illustration is for two reflectors with amplitude reflectance r_1 and r_2, and depth $d_1 = v\tau_1$ and $d_2 = v\tau_2$.

The analysis in (4.4-3) and (4.4-4) can be readily extended to multiple reflectors. A formulation for continuous reflection described by the complex amplitude reflectance $r(z)$ takes the form

$$I(k) = 1 + \mathcal{R}_b + 2\,\mathrm{Re}\left\{\int r(z)\,e^{jkz}\,dz\right\} = \int [r(z) + r^*(-z)]\,e^{jkz}\,dz. \qquad (4.4\text{-}5)$$

Here, the interferogram was expressed in terms of the variable $k = \omega/c$ instead of ω, and the variable $z = c(\tau - \tau_m)$ instead of τ (i.e., the depth z is measured from the position that matches that of the mirror in the other arm of the interferometer). An inverse Fourier transform of $I(k)$ provides the function $[r(z) + r^*(-z)]$. If the object is known to have no reflections for $z < 0$, then $r(-z) = 0$, for $z > 0$ and the inverse Fourier transfrom of $I(k)$ is simply $r(z)$. The technique is an example of **spectral-domain optical reflectometry** or **Fourier-domain optical reflectometry**. Since it requires a tunable coherent light source whose frequency is swept to generate the spectral interferogram, the technique is also known as **swept-frequency optical reflectometry**.

Low-Coherence Optical Reflectometry: Spectral Domain

An alternative to recording the spectral interferogram $I(\omega)$ by use of a swept-frequency tunable monochromatic source is to use a broadband CW source (i.e. low-coherence source), together with a tunable narrow-band spectral filter that selects one frequency at a time before the detection. The interferogram may also be constructed in one shot by use of a bank of narrowband filters tuned to different frequencies covering the desired spectral range, i.e., a spectrometer. This configuration is illustrated in Fig. 4.4-2.

If $S(\omega)$ is the power spectral density of the source, then the spectral interferogram for an object with two reflectors is the same as (4.4-3), except for the factor $S(\omega)$,

$$I(\omega) \propto S(\omega) \left\{ 1 + \mathcal{R}_{\mathrm{b}} + 2r_1 \cos(\omega\tau_{1m}) + 2r_2 \cos(\omega\tau_{2m}) \right\}, \tag{4.4-6}$$

The inverse Fourier transform of (4.4-6) is (see Sec. A.1 in Appendix A)

$$i(\tau) \propto (1 + \mathcal{R}_{\mathrm{b}})g(\tau) + r_1 g(\tau - \tau_{1m}) + r_1 g(\tau + \tau_{1m}) + r_2 g(\tau - \tau_{2m}) + r_2 g(\tau + \tau_{2m}), \tag{4.4-7}$$

where $g(\tau) = G(\tau)/G(0)$ and $G(\tau)$ is the inverse Fourier transform of $S(\omega)$. The expression in (4.4-7) is identical to that in (4.4-4) except for the delta function $\delta(\tau)$ being replaced by $g(\tau)$, whose width determines the axial resolution of the system.

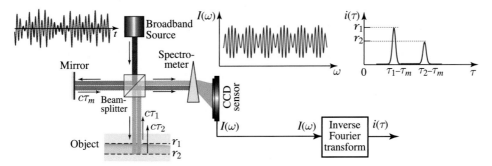

Figure 4.4-2   Spectral-domain interferogram.

▶ Problem 4.3-1

C. Frequency-Encoded Tomography

If all points of a 2D object $f(x, y)$ emit at the same frequency ω, then a measurement of the total emission cannot be used to discern the individual contribution of each point, unless some other mechanism of localization is used. However, if each point of the object is somehow "frequency encoded" to emit at a unique frequency $\omega(x, y)$, then a spectral analysis of the total emission may be used to discern the contributions of different points and reconstruct the object distribution. Suppose, for example, that $\omega(x, y)$ is a linear function of x and y, i.e., $\omega(x, y) = \omega_0 + u_x x + u_y y$, where $u_x = u \cos \theta$ and $u_y = u \sin \theta$ are code parameters. The angle θ is that of the direction of maximum change of the frequency, and u is the maximum rate of change (i.e., the vector $\mathbf{u} = (u_x, u_y)$ is the gradient vector). In this case, the amplitude of the total emitted field at this frequency-encoding angle is

$$g_\theta(t) = \iint f(x, y) \exp[\mathrm{j}\omega(x, y)t]\,\mathrm{d}x\mathrm{d}y = e^{\mathrm{j}\omega_0 t} \iint f(x, y) \exp[-\mathrm{j}(u_x x + u_y y)t]\,\mathrm{d}x\mathrm{d}y. \tag{4.4-8}$$

The 2D image $f(x, y)$ is therefore converted into a 1D temporal function $g_\theta(t)$. This expression is a special case of the general tomographic imaging equation (4.0-1). Here, the object function $f(\mathbf{r})$ is 2D, while the measured "projection" is 1D for each view (i.e., each angle).

Time–Slice Theorem.   Recalling the definition (A.2-1) of the 2D Fourier transform, we see that the temporal profile $g_\theta(t)$ is proportional to the 2D Fourier transform of $f(x, y)$ evaluated at the spatial frequencies $(k_x, k_y) = (u_x t, u_y t) = (ut \cos \theta, ut \sin \theta)$, i.e.,

$$g_\theta(t) = e^{j\omega_0 t} F(ut \cos \theta, ut \sin \theta), \qquad\qquad (4.4\text{-}9)$$

Time–Slice Theorem

so that $g_\theta(t)$ is a radial slice in the Fourier space – a line parallel to passing through the origin at an angle θ, as shown in Fig. 4.4-3. This relation, called the time–slice theorem, is similar to the projection–slice theorem of ray tomography. In fact, the temporal profile $g_\theta(t)$ provides the same information as a projection of the density function $f(x, y)$ along the direction marked by the angle θ.

Inversion.   If the temporal profile $g_\theta(t)$ is measured for all angles θ, then the Fourier transform $F(k_x, k_y)$ may be determined at all values of (k_x, k_y) and an inverse Fourier transform yields an estimate of the object distribution $f(x, y)$. Other techniques of ray tomography may also be used for inversion.

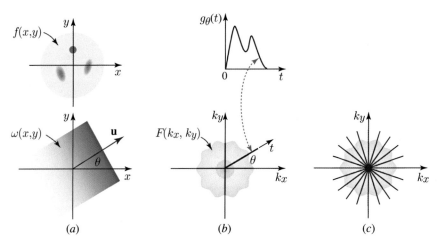

(a)   (b)   (c)

Figure 4.4-3   Frequency-encoded tomography. (a) Emitters of density $f(x, y)$ emit with position-dependent frequency $w(x, y)$ of gradient vector $\mathbf{u}$ pointing at an angle θ. (b) The temporal profile of the total emitted pulse $g_\theta(t)$ equals a slice of the Fourier transform $F(k_x, k_y)$ along a line at angle θ. (c) Slices at multiple angles are radial samples of $F(k_x, k_y)$ that may be used to reconstruct $f(x, y)$.

Generalization to 3D Objects.   The time–slice theorem is also applicable to a 3D distribution $f(x, y, z)$ emitting with position-dependent frequency $w(x, y) = \omega_0 + u_x x + u_y y + u_z z$. The temporal profile of the emitted field $g(t) = e^{j\omega_0 t} F(u_x t, u_y t, u_z t)$, where $F(k_x, k_y, k_z)$ is the 3D Fourier transform of $f(x, y, z)$.

Applications.   Frequency-encoded tomography is used in magnetic-resonance imaging (MRI) to image 2D slices of a 3D object. The frequency encoding is implemented by means of a magnetic field, as described next.

▶ Problem 4.3-2

D. Magnetic Resonance Imaging (MRI)

MRI is based on the process of nuclear magnetic resonance associated with the magnetic spin in the proton of the nucleus of an atom, as described in Sec. 2.3C. A strong steady magnetic field B_0, commonly a few tesla, causes the spins to recess at a resonance frequency ω_0. The recessing spins are interrogated with a pulsed electromagnetic probe wave at the radio frequency ω_f. If $\omega_f = \omega_0$, the spins are excited and they emit a free decaying pulse followed by an echo at the same frequency. The strength of these emissions (the scattering cross-section) is proportional to the local density of atoms, and their time duration provides information on the local molecular environment.

The imaging process is implemented by an ingenious use of the fact that the resonance frequency can be altered by the steady magnetic field. By application of a nonuniform magnetic field, the resultant position-dependent resonance frequency serves as a position marker used for selective excitation of slices of the object. Another nonuniform magnetic field applied during the emission process may be used for frequency-encoded tomographic imaging of the excited slice.

Frequency-Encoded Sectioning

If the external magnetic field applied on a 3D object is a function of position $B_0(x, y, z)$, then the resonance frequency is a proportional function of position $\omega(x, y, z) = \gamma B_0(x, y, z)$, where γ is the gyromagnetic ratio (see Sec. 2.3C). Since the resonance system responds only to excitations at (or very near) its resonance frequency, a probe wave of frequency ω_f excites only points satisfying the resonance condition $\omega_f = \gamma B_0(x, y, z)$. This defines a surface within the 3D object at which the spins respond to the excitation.

For example, if the magnetic field is graded linearly in the z direction, i.e., $B_0(x, y, z) = B_0 + G_z z$, then the resonance frequency is also a linear function

$$\omega(x, y, z) = \omega_0 + u_z z, \tag{4.4-10}$$

where $u_z = \gamma G_z$ is proportional to the gradient of the field. A probe wave of frequency ω_f excites only points on the planar surface defined by the equation $\omega_f = \omega_0 + u_z z$, which defines a slice parallel to the x–y plane at a specific depth z. By varying the frequency ω_f, planar slices at different depths may be selected, as depicted in Fig. 4.4-4.

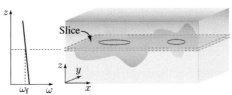

Figure 4.4-4   Excitation of resonant elements within a single planar slice at a prescribed depth by use of a nonuniform magnetic field with a gradient vector in the z direction.

The ability to divide the 3D object into parallel slices in different orientations suggests that full 3D imaging may be accomplished by applying the same techniques of

3D ray tomography. Here, each slice is analogous to an extented ray, and the total emission from a set of parallel slices is a projection. By measuring the projections along all directions, the 3D object distribution may be fully reconstructed by use of a generalization of the Radon transform and its inverse to the 3D case. However, the following alternative approach for imaging each of the sectioned slices by means of frequency-encoded tomography is more commonly used.

Frequency-Encoded Tomography

Once a planar slice of the object is excited, say with a 2D density distribution $f(x, y)$, it is necessary to use some position marker in order to separate the contributions of various positions to the measured total field waveform $g(t)$. This is accomplished by use of another magnetic field that varies linearly with x and y, i.e., $B_0(x, y) = B_0 + G_x x + G_y y$, so that the resonance frequency is also position dependent:

$$w(x, y) = w_0 + u_x x + u_y y, \tag{4.4-11}$$

where $u_x = \gamma G_x$ and $u_y = \gamma G_y$. We can now use the time–slice theorem of frequency-encoded tomography (4.4-9) to write

$$g_\theta(t) = e^{j w_0 t} F(ut \cos \theta, ut \sin \theta), \tag{4.4-12}$$

where $F(k_x, k_y)$ is the 2D Fourier transform of the density $f(x, y)$. By measuring $g_\theta(t)$ for all angles θ, the Fourier transform $F(k_x, k_y)$ may be determined at all values of (k_x, k_y) and an inverse Fourier transform applied to generate the object distribution $f(x, y)$. This process is illustrated in Fig. 4.4-5.

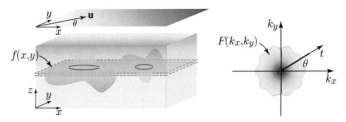

Figure 4.4-5 In the presence of a magnetic field gradient **u** at an angle θ in the x–y plane, the temporal profile of the emission from the distribution $f(x, y)$ is a slice of the Fourier transform $F(k_x, k_y)$.

Combined Frequency-Encoded Sectioning and Tomography

The imaging configuration in MRI is usually based on a combination of frequency-encoded slicing in an axial direction during the excitation process, combined with frequency-encoded tomography in the transverse planes during the emission process. Both processes are controlled by changing the gradients of the steady magnetic field in the axial and transverse directions, in accordance with the following timeline, illustrated in Fig. 4.4-6:

- **Frequency-Encoded Sectioning.** During the excitation process (shaded time intervals), a static magnetic field gradient G_z is applied in the axial direction z. This marks each transverse plane with a unique resonance frequency. For example, the resonance frequency may vary in the range 60 MHz $\pm$ 10 kHz over a distance of 10 cm. The applied radiowave selectively excites a planar transverse slice (parallel to the x–y plane) at some distance $z = z_1$ that has the matching resonance frequency.

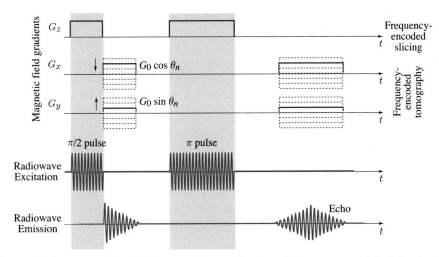

Figure 4.4-6 Protocol for MRI by use of a combination of frequency-encoded slicing in the z direction together with frequency-encoded tomography in the x–y planes.

- **Frequency-Encoded Tomography.** During the emission times (unshaded intervals), the static magnetic field gradient points at an angle θ in the transverse plane. This is accomplished by use of gradient components $G_x = G_0 \cos\theta$ and $G_y = G_0 \sin\theta$. The temporal profile of the pulse emitted from the entire excited slice is observed. This generates a line in the **k**-space (k_x, k_y) at an angle θ.
- The measurement is repeated at a set of uniformly spaced angles θ_n. Once the k-space is adequately filled, an inverse Fourier transform is applied, yielding the density $f(x, y, z_1)$ for the slice $z = z_1$.
- The process is repeated for different slices at distances z_m, $m = 1, 2, \ldots$, to ultimately construct the full 3D density $f(x, y, z)$.

Medical Applications of MRI.   MRI has become an important tool for medical imaging. An MRI machine, such as that shown in Fig. 4.4-7, can image vasculature and blood flow characteristics, for example. It can be used for cancer detection by imaging injected nonradioactive contrast agents that concentrate in abnormal tissue. In **functional MRI**, metabolic processes and physiological changes, such as the difference between oxygen-saturated and desaturated blood, can be detected. Examples of MRI sections of a normal brain are shown in Fig. 4.4-8.

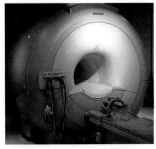

Figure 4.4-7 Philips 3T Achieva clinical MRI scanner (photo after Kasuga Huang, via Wikimedia).

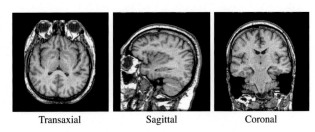

Transaxial   Sagittal   Coronal

Figure 4.4-8 Examples of MRI sections of a normal brain. (After K. A. Johnson and J. A. Becker, *The Whole Brain Atlas*.)

4.5   Generalized Tomography

In each of the methods of tomography described so far in this chapter – ray tomography, range tomography, wave tomography, and spectral tomography – a linear integral transform, called the imaging equation, explicitly relates the measurement in each view to the object distribution. This equation takes a simple form in the Fourier domain, expressing the measurement for each view as a single slice of the object's Fourier transform. Relations such as the projection–slice theorem, the diffraction–slice theorem, and the time–slice theorem can be readily used to solve the inversion problem, i.e., reconstruct the object distribution.

In many tomographic imaging applications, however, no explicit imaging equation is available and the relation between the measurements and the object distribution is expressed implicitly in terms of the field equation – a partial differential equation obeyed by the propagating field, and in which the desired object distribution appears as an unknown spatially varying parameter. As mentioned in Chapter 1, the field equation may be expressed in the generic form

$$\mathcal{O}\{U, \alpha\} = 0, \tag{4.5-1}$$

Field Equation

where $U = U(\mathbf{r})$ represents the wave or field that mediates the imaging, $\alpha = \alpha(\mathbf{r})$ is the position-dependent physical property to be imaged, and $\mathcal{O}$ is a generic mathematical operator representing the partial differential equation (or equations) that U obeys. Actual differential equations governing electromagnetic and acoustic fields are described in Chapter 2. In most applications, the field equation is a *linear* partial differential equation in U, although the relation between the measured U and α is generally *nonlinear*. The most common approach then is to linearize this relation by means of some approximation such as the Born approximation, and obtain an explicit linear relation between the measurement and the object distribution. The inverse problem may then be solved by one of the tomographic methods described in the earlier sections of this chapter, or represented in the form of a matrix operation and inverted by one of the matrix techniques described in Chapter 5. When linearizing approximations are not appropriate, a generalized approach to the inverse problem is necessary.

In generalized tomography, a set of sources and sensors are distributed on the surface, as illustrated in Fig. 4.5-1, and other configurations are also possible (see Fig. 1.3-6). An incident probe field $U_{\mathrm{p}}^{(v)}$ is created by the vth source, and the field $U_{\mathrm{s}}^{(v)}$ is measured at all sensors. This measurement represents the vth "view." The process is repeated for each source to generate other views. In each view, the partial differential equation (4.5-1) must be satisfied under boundary conditions set by the applied probe field and the fields measured by the sensors. The imaging task involves solving this differential equation to determine $\alpha(\mathbf{r})$, given the boundary conditions set by all views. This is an inverse problem that is generally difficult to solve.

Sources ▪
Sensors ◆

Figure 4.5-1   Multiview imaging by use of a set of distributed probes and sensors.

Iterative Solution of the Inverse Problem.   Let us first consider the **forward prob-lem** for which the object distribution $\alpha(\mathbf{r})$ is known. For any applied probe field $U_{\mathrm{p}}^{(v)}$ the linear differential equation $\mathcal{O}\{U, \alpha\} = 0$ may be solved numerically for U, and the fields $U_{\mathrm{s}}^{(v)}$ at the sensors determined. However, since in reality $U_{\mathrm{s}}^{(v)}$ are known but $\alpha(\mathbf{r})$ is unknown, an iterative approach can be used, as illustrated in Fig. 4.5-2. An initial guess of $\alpha(\mathbf{r})$ is used and the fields at the sensors are numerically computed for each of the known applied probes. These fields are compared to the fields $U_{\mathrm{s}}^{(v)}$ that are actually measured, and the average error is determined. An appropriate change in the initial guess of $\alpha(\mathbf{r})$ is calculated such that the error is reduced. The process is repeated iteratively until the error reaches a minimum. The result is a least-error estimate of $\alpha(\mathbf{r})$.

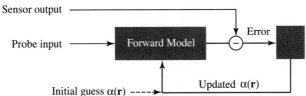

Figure 4.5-2   Iterative approach to inversion using a forward model.

A.   Diffuse Optical Tomography (DOT)

Diffuse optical tomography (DOT) is a technique for imaging biological tissue by use of diffuse light (see Sec. 2.2D). At wavelengths for which the absorption is not significant (in the near infrared), optical waves can travel deeply into the tissue, but the light is strongly scattered from small-scale random inhomogeneities, including cells and subcellular structures, and diffuses in all directions so that it cannot be readily localized within the medium. Nevertheless, diffuse light may be described in terms of the average energy transport represented by the photon-density function $\phi(\mathbf{r})$, which obeys the diffusion equation (2.2-50) with a diffusion coefficient $D = 1/[3(\mu_a + \mu_s')]$, where μ_s' is the reduced scattering coefficient and μ_a is the absorption coefficient of the medium. If the incident light is modulated at an angular frequency Ω, then $\phi(\mathbf{r})$ obeys the Helmholtz equation (2.2-51) and propagates as a highly-damped wave with an effective attenuation coefficient

$$\alpha_e = \mathrm{Re}\{\sqrt{3(\mu_s' + \mu_a)(\mu_a + j\Omega/v)}\} \tag{4.5-2}$$

that depends on the medium parameters μ_s' and μ_a, as well as the modulation frequency Ω [see (2.2-56)]. Measurement of the reflectance of the diffuse optical wave can be used to probe subsurface targets, as illustrated in Fig. 4.5-3.

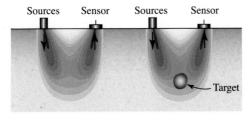

Figure 4.5-3 A photon-density wave launched by a modulated optical source travels into the medium and is scattered back to the surface where it is detected by a sensor. If an absorptive target lies under a source–sensor combination, the detected signal is weaker.

Since the penetration depth depends on the modulation frequency Ω (see Problem 2.2-11), if the measurement of reflectance is repeated at different Ω, then information on μ_s' and μ_a at different depths may be acquired. An alternative approach for depth control is to use structured illumination, as illustrated in Fig. 4.5-4(*b*). Instead of a point source modulated in time, a distributed source modulated in space may be used. A steady illumination source that varies as $\varphi(x,0) = \varphi_0[1 + \cos(qx)]$ creates a photon-density wave $\varphi(x,z) = \varphi(x,0)[\exp(-\mu_a z) + \exp(-\alpha_e z)\cos(qx)]$, which is consistent with the boundary condition at $z = 0$ and satisfies the steady-state diffusion equation $0 = D\nabla^2\varphi - \mu_a\varphi$, if

$$-q^2 + \alpha_e^2 = \mu_a/D = \mu_{\text{eff}}^2, \qquad \mu_{\text{eff}} = \sqrt{3\mu_a(\mu_s' + \mu_a)}.$$

Therefore, the attenuation coefficient of the modulated component

$$\alpha_e = \sqrt{\mu_{\text{eff}}^2 + q^2}, \tag{4.5-3}$$

and hence the penetration depth, can be controlled by varying the spatial modulation frequency q.

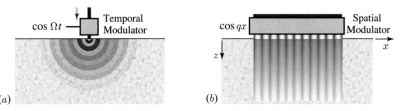

(a) (b)

Figure 4.5-4   Controlling the penetration depth of a diffuse wave by use of (a) temporal modulation, and (b) spatial modulation.

Applications.   The utility of DOT as a diagnostic tool comes from the fact that the parameters of relevance to the light-tissue interaction, μ_s' and μ_a (the *alpha* parameters of this subsurface imaging system) are strongly related to physiologically relevant parameters (*beta* parameters) such as the concentration of oxygenated and deoxenated hemoglobin, lipid, water, and other chromophores within the tissue. Also, since these parameters are dependent on the wavelength of light, μ_s' and μ_a are wavelength dependent (see Fig. 2.2-4). By repeating the measurement at multiple wavelengths in the near-infrared band, this multispectral imaging approach can be used to distinguish between different physiological conditions (see Example 6.3-2). This ability to obtain functional information from diffuse optical data has been found to be useful in a number of applications, most notably breast tumor detection and functional brain imaging. In the case of breast cancer, it is known that tumors tend to consume more oxygen than normal breast tissue, thereby increasing the optical absorption of the tissue in the vicinity of a lesion. Similarly, there is an increase in oxygen uptake in regions of the brain stimulated by a given task.

Mapping.   A full map of the spatial distribution of the medium parameters, $\mu_a(\mathbf{r})$, $\mu_s'(\mathbf{r})$, and $D(\mathbf{r})$, may be obtained by use of the configuration of generalized tomography shown in Fig. 4.5-1. In this case, the generalized Helmholtz equation (2.3-16), which describes a medium with spatially varying parameters, must be used

$$\left(\nabla.D\nabla - j\frac{\Omega}{v} - \mu_a\right)\phi = 0, \tag{4.5-4}$$

Generalized
Helmholtz Equation

where v is the speed of light in the medium and Ω is the modulation angular frequency. This equation must be solved under the boundary conditions set by each of the light sources and the signals generated at each of the detectors. Red or near-infrared light from laser diodes or light-emitting diodes (LEDs) at wavelength in the 650–850 nm band is injected at a number of uniformly distributed points on the skin and the emerging light is detected by photodiodes placed on the skin at other interspersed points. A wide range of source–sensor geometries have been considered. For brain imaging, the sources and detectors are arrayed on a flexible rubber sheet that fits snugly over the head of the subject, as shown in Fig. 4.5-5(a). For breast cancer applications, systems have been constructed in which the sources and detectors are located in a ring surrounding a pendant breast. Alternatively, in a system combining diffuse optical and X-ray mammography, the breast is placed in compression between two plates with the DOT sources and detectors placed on the bottom plate and the top plate, respectively, as shown in Fig. 4.5-5(b) (see also Sec 9.3). In all of these systems, DOT measurements are typically collected at several optical wavelengths and modulation frequencies so that both the spatial and spectral characteristics of the tissue can be determined and used for functional imaging.

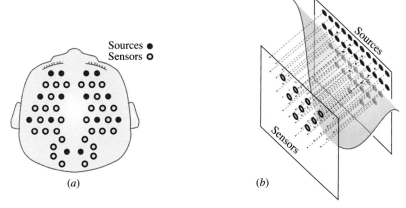

(a)   (b)

Figure 4.5-5 Source and detector configurations for (a) neonatal brain imaging and (b) breast imaging.

Inversion. Solution of the generalized Helmholtz equation under the boundary conditions set by the photon density injected by each source and the corresponding photon densities measured at all sensors can be used to estimate the spatial distributions of $D(\mathbf{r})$ and $\alpha_a(\mathbf{r})$, from which functional parameters can be estimated. As such, the exact inverse problem involves a nonlinear relationship between the observed data and the unknown distributions. Significant advances have recently been made in the development of inversion methods based on approximate linearized models. Analytical methods reminiscent of diffraction tomography were devised for problems in which data were collected on densely sampled, regular grids, a condition not often fulfilled in practice. A rather wide range of numerical methods are based on representing the linearized model in the form of a single matrix operation and using ideas to be discussed in Chapter 5 for the matrix inverse calculation (see Example 5.4-3). This approach has the merit of being applicable to any of the sensor geometries or the nonideal data collection schemes found in fielded instruments.

Though the use of linearized models is convenient, such models are not sufficiently accurate for use in practice. Thus, since the early 2000s the state of the art in DOT inversion has focused on the full, nonlinear problem. Remarkably enough, even here very specialized forms of diffraction tomographic processing methods have been developed again for very regular geometries. Such restrictions can be alleviated in the nonlinear regime by employing numerical iterative methods, which basically require that one solves a sequence of linear problems converging to the *true* solution (see Fig. 4.5-2).

B. Electrical Impedance Tomography (EIT)

Electrical Resistance Tomography (ERT).   ERT is a technique for measuring the spatial distribution of the electric conductivity $\sigma(\mathbf{r})$, which is the inverse of the electric resistivity, by electrical measurements using a set of electrodes distributed on the surface of the object. A known steady electric current generated by a constant current source is injected between a pair of electrodes and the voltage differences at all electrodes are recorded. The process is repeated by injecting the current between other pairs of electrodes and all of the recorded data are used to infer $\sigma(\mathbf{r})$. Various measurement configurations are shown schematically in Fig. 4.5-6. The spatial resolution of this technique depends on the number of data points recorded, i.e., on the number of electrodes used.

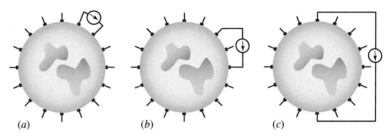

(a)   (b)   (c)

Figure 4.5-6   Various configurations for applying electric currents in ERT and EIT. The current is applied between (a) neighboring electrodes, (b) every other electrode, and (c) diametrically opposite electrodes. In all cases, the voltages are measured between adjacent electrodes.

   In essence, the technique is based on solving the generalized Laplace equation (see Sec. 2.3D),

$$\nabla \cdot \sigma \nabla V = 0, \tag{4.5-5}$$

for the electric potential $V = -\nabla \mathbf{E}$, which is a function of the position $\mathbf{r}$ within the object. The boundary conditions are set by the measured voltages and applied currents at the boundary. Since the electric current density $\mathbf{J} = \sigma \mathbf{E}$, the relation between $\mathbf{J}$ and V is $\mathbf{J} = -\sigma \nabla V$. This relation may be applied at the boundary between the electrode and the medium by considering a pillbox of incremental width $\Delta \ell$ adjacent to the electrode. If the electric current driven *into* the pillbox is i and the area of the electrode is A, then $i/A = \sigma \Delta V / \Delta \ell$, or

$$\sigma A \frac{\Delta V}{\Delta \ell} = i, \tag{4.5-6}$$

which is a statement of Ohm's law (with the resistance of the pillbox equal to $\Delta \ell / \sigma A$). Thus, the boundary condition imposed by the injected current i fixes the value of $\Delta V / \Delta \ell$, or the component of the gradient ∇V in the direction of the normal to the surface at the position of the electrode.

Electrical Impedance Tomography (EIT) is a generalization of ERT aiming at the measurement of both the electric conductivity $\sigma(\mathbf{r})$ and the electric permittivity $\epsilon(\mathbf{r})$, or in general the admittivity $\gamma = \sigma + j\omega\epsilon$ of the object, by use of an alternating electric current source at a low-frequency ω. The frequency dependence of the conductivity and permittivity may also provide valuable information on the object and may be estimated by repeating the measurement at different frequencies ω. In EIT, the pertinent differential equation at points within the volume V of the object is the generalized Laplace equation

$$\nabla \cdot \gamma \nabla V = 0, \qquad \mathbf{r} \in V \tag{4.5-7}$$

The boundary conditions imposed by the injected electric current density at the surface S may be written as

$$\gamma \hat{n} \cdot \nabla V = j, \qquad \mathbf{r} \in S \tag{4.5-8}$$

where j is the component of the injected electric current *density* in the inward direction normal to the surface, and $\hat{n}$ is a unit vector along the outward normal to the surface so that $\hat{n} \cdot \nabla V$ is the rate of change of V along that direction.

Inversion of the ERT/EIT data is a challenging nonlinear inverse problem involving a solution of the generalized Laplace equation (4.5-7) given a finite set of boundary conditions (4.5-8) imposed by the currents injected, as well as the voltages V measured at points on surface of the object. This equation may be linearized and formulated in terms of a matrix relation between the measured voltages and the unknown complex coefficients *gamma* at all positions. Matrix methods can then be used for the inversion. Matrix inversion techniques are described in Chapter 5, which also describes regularization techniques, designed to address ill-posedness, and iterative techniques (Sec. 5.5). The problem may also be solved without linearization by use of the general iterative approach depicted in Fig. 4.5-2. An analytical solution, known as the "D-bar" method has been found that deals with the complex partial derivative operators in this equation using the map of mixed Neumann and Dirichlet boundary conditions. This mathematical approach is beyond the scope of this book.[7]

Applications.   Medical applications of EIT and ERT include monitoring of heart and lung functions (see Fig. 4.5-7), gastric emptying, and location of epileptic foci, as well as detection of skin and breast cancer. Clinical trials of breast imaging for breast cancer detection are being pursued (see Sec. 9.3). Position resolution on the order of 5 mm is expected when a 64×64 electrode array is used. Geophysical and industrial applications include mapping the distribution of oil and water and other conductive fluids in pipelines, finding defects in materials, imaging of the flow of substances in mixing vessels, and monitoring of other industrial processes. EIT can also be used for finding defects inside materials such as tree trunks.

---

[7]D. Isaacson, J. L. Mueller, J. C. Newell and S. Siltanen, Imaging cardiac activity by the D-bar method for electrical impedance tomography, *Physiological Measurement*, Vol. 27, pp. S43–S50, 2006.

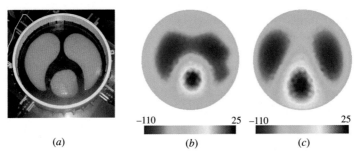

-110   25 -110   25

(a)   (b)   (c)

Figure 4.5-7 (a) A 32-electrode apparatus at Rensselaer Polytechnic Institute, USA, for testing EIT in a 2D circularly symmetric configuration using a phantom of the chest containing "lungs" and "heart" made of agar with varying amounts of added salt. The tank is filled with salt water. (b) Image computed by linearized inversion and (c) by use of the D-bar method.

Further Reading

Ray Tomography

J. Hsieh, *Computed Tomography: Principles, Design, Artifacts, and Recent Advances*, 2nd ed., SPIE, 2009.

S. R. Deans, *The Radon Transform and Some of Its Applications*, Dover, 2007.

W. A. Kalender, *Computed Tomography: Fundamentals, System Technology, Image Quality, Applications*, 2nd ed., Wiley–VCH, 2006.

L. Ehrenpreis, *The Universality of the Radon Transform*, Oxford Science Publications, 2003.

F. Natterer and F. Wubbeling, *Mathematical Methods in Image Reconstruction*, SIAM, 2001.

A. G. Ramm and A. I. Katsevich, *The Radon Transform and Local Tomography*, CRC, 1996.

F. Natterer, *The Mathematics of Computerized Tomography*, Wiley, 1986.

Ground-Penetrating Radar

D. Daniels (ed.), *Ground-Penetrating Radar*, 2nd ed., IEE, UK, 2004.

T. Lo and P. L. Inderwiesen, *Fundamentals of Seismic Tomography, Geophysical Monograph Series*, Society of Exploration Geophysicists, 1994.

Synthetic Aperture Radar

C. E. Yarman, B. Yazici, and M. Cheney, Bistatic synthetic aperture radar imaging with arbitrary trajectories, *IEEE Transacations in Image Processing*, Vol. 17, pp. 84–93, 2008.

B. Yazici, M. Cheney, and C. E. Yarman, Synthetic aperture inversion in the presence of noise and clutter, *Inverse Problems*, Vol. 22, pp. 1705–1729, 2006.

I. Cumming and F. Wong, *Digital Processing of Synthetic Aperture Radar Data: Algorithms and Implementation*, Artech, 2005.

J. C. Curlander and R. N. McDonough, *Synthetic Aperture Radar: Systems and Signal Processing*, Wiley, 1991.

Seismic Imaging

B. L. Biondi, *3D Seismic Imaging*, Society of Exploration Geophysicists, 2006.

C. H. Chapman, *Fundamentals of Seismic Wave Propagation*, Cambridge University Press, 2004.

Photoacoustic Tomography

L. V. Wang (ed.), *Photoacoustic Imaging and Spectroscopy*, CRC, 2009.

S. Y. Emelianov, P.-C. Li, and M. O'Donnell, Photoacoustics for molecular imaging and therapy, *Physics Today*, pp. 34–39, May 2009.

L. V. Wang, Ultrasound-mediated biophotonic imaging, a review of acousto-optical tomography and photo-acoustic tomography, *Disease Markers*, Vol. 19, pp. 123–138, 2003.

M. Xu and L. V. Wang, Photoacoustic imaging in biomedicine, *Review of Scientific Instruments*, Vol. 77, p. 041101, 2006.

Diffraction Tomography

A. C. Kak and M. Slaney, *Principles of Computerized Tomographic Imaging*, SIAM, 2001.

M. Born and E. Wolf, *Principles of Optics*, 7th ed., Cambridge University Press, 1999, Chapter 13.

M. Kaveh, M. Soumekh, and J. Greenleaf, Signal processing for diffraction tomography, *IEEE Transactions on Sonics and Ultrasonics*, Vol. SU-31, pp. 230–239, 1984.

A. J. Devaney, Geophysical diffraction tomography, *IEEE Transactions on Geoscience and Remote Sensing*, Vol. GE-22, pp. 3–13, 1984.

A. J. Devaney, A filtered backpropagation algorithm for diffraction tomography, *Ultrasonic Imaging*, Vol. 4, pp. 336–350, 1982.

Magnetic Resonance Imaging

Z.-P. Liang and P. C. Lauterbur, *Principles of Magnetic Resonance Imaging: A Signal Processing Perspective*, IEEE, 1999.

B. R. Friedman, J. P. Jones, G. Chaves-Munoz, A. P. Salmon, and C. R. B. Merritt, *Principles of MRI*, McGraw-Hill, 1989.

Diffuse Optical Tomography

L. V. Wang and H.-I. Wu, *Biomedical Optics*, Wiley, 2007.

A. P. Gibson, J. C. Hebden, and S. R. Arridge, Recent advances in diffuse optical imaging, *Physics in Medicine and Biology*, Vol. 50, pp. R1–R43, 2005.

D. A. Boas, D. H. Brooks, E. L. Miller, C. A. DiMarzio, M. Kilner, R. J. Gaudette, and Q. Zhang, Imaging the body with diffuse optical tomography, *IEEE Signal Processing*, Vol. 18, pp. 57–75, 2001.

A. G. Yodh and B. Chance, Spectroscopy and imaging with diffusing light, *Physics Today*, Vol. 48, 34–40, 1995.

Electrical Impedance Tomography

D. S. Holder (ed.), *Electrical Impedance Tomography: Methods, History and Applications*, Taylor & Francis, 2004.

M. Hanke and M. Brühl, Recent progress in electrical impedance tomography, *Inverse Problems*, Vol. 19, pp. S65–S90, 2003.

M. Cheney, D. Isaacson, and J. C. Newell, Electrical impedance tomography, *SIAM Review*, Vol. 41, pp. 85–101, 1999.

Problems

4.1-1   **Radon Transform.** Generate the following images and compute their Radon transforms using the MATLAB function `radon`. Display the images and their Radon transforms using `imshow` or `imagesc`.

(a) A 128×128 images with all pixels set at a value 0 except two points, one at (25,25) and another at (50,50) pixels off center.

(b) A 128×128 image of a centered square of size 21×21 in a background set at a value 0.

(c) The Modified Shepp–Logan phantom generated by the MATLAB function
`phantom ('Modified Shepp--Logan', 256)`.

4.1-2   **Demonstration of the P–S Theorem.** Using the Modified Shepp–Logan phantom and its Radon transform that were computed in Problem 4.1-1, demonstrate the P–S theorem. First, determine the projection at the angle $\theta = 0$ from the Radon transform and compute its 1D Fourier transform using the MATLAB function `fft`. Second, compute the 2D Fourier transform of the phantom using the MATLAB function `fft2` and determine the appropriate slice. Compare.

4.1-3   **Radon Transform of a Convolution.** Show that the Radon transform of the 2D convolution of two functions, $f_1 \otimes f_2$ equals the 1D convolution of their Radon transforms, $g_1 \otimes g_2$ for each angle θ. Hint: use the P–S theorem.

4.1-4   **Filtered Backprojection.** The MATLAB function `iradon` is used for the inversion of the Radon transform by means of filtered backprojection. Use this function to compute the inverse Radon transform of the Modified Shepp–Logan phantom, which was computed in Problem 4.1-1. Compare the result with the original phantom. Generate backprojection without filtering by calling `iradon` with "none" Examine the effect of filtering.

4.1-5   **Effect of Number of Projections on Filtered Backprojection.** Generate filtered backprojection reconstructions of the phantom in Problem 4.1-4 for $N = 16, 32, 64$, and 128 angles distributed uniformly in $[0, 180°)$. Based on this experiment and your own visual evaluation, what is the ratio of the number of observations to the number of unknowns (i.e., pixels) that is necessary before filtered backprojection produces reasonable reconstructions?

4.1-6   **Effect of Noise on Filtered Backprojection.** Beginning with the Radon transform of the modified Shepp–Logan phantom used in Problem 4.1-4, add noise such that SNR = 20 dB and 10 dB. Compute the filtered backprojection in each case and compare it with the original image.

4.1-7   **Tomography with Rays of Finite Width.** The Radon transform describes tomography with an ideal ray represented by a delta function $\delta(s)$. If the ray has a distribution of finite width described by the function $u_p(s)$, derive an expression relating the projections $g(s, \theta)$ to the object distribution $f(x, y)$. If a filtered backprojection operation is applied, derive a relation between the recovered distribution $\hat{f}(x, y)$ and the true distribution $f(x, y)$. Suggest a modification of filtered backprojection to account for the ray width.

4.2-1   **Synthetic Aperture Radar.** Simulate the signal $g(t)$ measured by the detector of the monostatic remote-sensing SAR system illustrated in Fig. 4.2-3, assuming that there are only three scatterers on the ground and that the antenna is omnidirectional. Using a coordinate system for which ground is the plane $(z = 0)$, the scatterers are located at points of coordinates $(0, 1, 0)$, $(1, 2, 0)$, and $(-1, 3, 0)$ km, and the sensor path is a straight line pointing along the y direction, beginning at the point $(0, 0, 4)$ and ending at $(0, 4, 6)$. All distances are in units of km. Use the simplified theory of range tomography described in Sec. 4.2B and assume that the scattering cross-sections of the three scatterers are all equal and independent of the directions of the incident or scattered waves. Assume that the probe pulse is a Gaussian function $p(t) = \exp(-t^2/2\tau_p^2)$ of width $\tau_p = 1\mu s$.

4.2-2   **Ground-Penetrating Radar.** Repeat the GPR simulation in Example 4.2-1 when a third scatterer is located at the coordinates $(30, -25)$ cm.

4.2-3   **Ground-Penetrating Radar through Rough Surface.** Repeat the GPR simulation in Example 4.2-1 assuming that the ground surface is rough, with random unspecified height variations of ± 8 cm. Since the height is unknown, the reconstruction process may use the nominal value of the average ground surface height, $z = 0$. This uncertainty will, of course, result in noisy reconstruction. Show that, despite this ambiguity, the strongest intensity levels correspond to the actual positions of the scatterers.

4.3-1   **Spectral-Domain Optical Coherence Tomography.** In spectral domain reflectometry, the spectrum of the superposition of the reflected beam and a reference beam provides a signal with a frequency-dependent component $i(\omega) \propto S(\omega)r\cos(\omega\tau)$, where r is the reflection coefficient, the time delay $\tau = z/v$ is proportional the depth z of the reflector, and $S(\omega)$ is the spectral density of the broadband source. This relation is a simplified version of (4.4-6) under special conditions. Assuming that the reflection coefficient is a distribution $r(z)$, which represents an axial image, the measured signal provides:

$$i(\omega) \propto S(\omega) \int r(z) \cos(\omega z/v) \, dz.$$

Suggest a method of computing the axial distribution $r(z)$ from the measured signal $i(\omega)$. What determines the axial resolution of this imaging system?

4.3-2   **Frequency-Encoded Tomography.** Assume that the Modified Shepp–Logan phantom generated by the MATLAB function `phantom ('Modified Shepp--Logan', 256)` represents the density $f(x, y)$ of particles emitted at a position-dependent frequency. If the frequency varies linearly with x and y, plot the temporal profile of the measured signal $g_u(t)$ in two cases: a) when the magnetic field gradient points in the x direction, and b) when it points in the y direction. Use arbitrary units for the time in your plot.

Digital Image Processing

This chapter addresses two topics: (i) discretization and matrix representation of imaging systems, i.e., digital imaging, and (ii) inversion of the imaging equation, i.e., reconstruction of the unknown object from the measured image for both localized and tomographic imaging systems.

Digital Imaging. In the imaging systems described in Chapters 3 and 4, the object and image distributions are described by continuous functions, $f(\mathbf{r})$ and $g(\mathbf{r})$, related by integral linear transformations. Also, image inversion was realized by means of analytical techniques based on continuous operations such as inverse filtering for shift-invariant systems, as in Sec. 3.3, and inverse Radon transform for tomographic imaging systems based on projections, as in Sec. 4.1. For many imaging systems, explicit analytical methods for inverting the imaging equations do not exist. Also, in reality, an image is detected by a finite number of sensors providing discrete data, which may not contain sufficient information for adequately approximating the transform techniques discussed in Chapters 3 and 4. In ray tomography, for example, when the number of projections is small, the quality of inversion becomes poor, as described in Sec. 4.1B. In these situations, it is useful to also discretize the object function $f(\mathbf{r})$ and represent the imaging equation (the relationship between the finite number of observed measurements and the elements of the discrete object function) by a linear set of algebraic equations. This discretization process converts the continuous imaging model into a digital imaging model relating the array **g** of the observed measurements to the array **f** representing the object. The digital imaging model may also be described by a matrix relation, $\mathbf{g} = \mathbf{Hf}$, where **H** is a matrix representing the imaging system, called the **imaging matrix**. This chapter deals with the discrete and the matrix formulations of the imaging system, as illustrated schematically in Fig. 5.0-1.

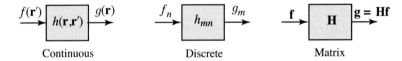

Figure 5.0-1 Models of the imaging system.

Inversion. This chapter also addresses the inversion problem. If an analytical solution of the inverse problem exists in the continuous case, then it may be implemented numerically by direct discretization of the inverse formula. Examples include the formula for inverse filtering and the inverse Radon transform (filtered backprojection). In this chapter, we take a different approach that is applicable to arbitrary linear imaging systems, both single view and multiview. We begin with the discrete or the matrix representation of the forward model, $\mathbf{g} = \mathbf{Hf}$, and develop algorithms for solving the set of algebraic equations relating the measurements **g** to the unknown object **f**, i.e., invert the imaging matrix **H**. There are two primary factors that motivate this approach. First, for many problems, explicit methods for inverting the forward model do not exist. Ray and wave tomography are two very special cases where analytical inversion methods have been developed. For problems involving more complex media, or arbitrary locations of sources and detectors (especially cases where data are not obtained all around the object), explicit inversion methods cannot always be obtained. Moreover, even when they are known, for problems where the locations of sources are restricted, application of methods such as filtered backprojection can result in

190

rather poor reconstructions. Unfortunately, such problems are the rule rather than the exception. For example, in applications ranging from landmine detection to nonde-structive testing, one can only probe the medium of interest from one side. In many geophysical and hydrological applications, the full 3D structure of the subsurface is desired from data that can only be taken from sources and detectors located on the surface and/or in a few boreholes. Likewise, in breast cancer screening using X-ray tomosynthesis (see Sec. 4.1C), the data are not measured over a full 180° aperture as in computed tomography (CT), but only over a span of about 50° (11 projections at an angular spacing of 5°). In general, the inverse problem is particularly difficult when the available sensing geometries are sparse in the space of possible geometries

Noise. Success of any inversion method is often limited by perturbations arising from a wide range of sources such as inaccuracies in the model, uncertainties in the precise locations of sensors, imprecise calibration of the system, or physical fluctuations in the probe or the sensor measurements, to name just a few. Such perturbations are generi-cally called *noise*. As seen in Sec. 3.3 and Sec. 4.1, the presence of even small amounts of noise can distort the reconstruction significantly because the imaging problem is often poorly conditioned. Since a full mathematical description of the various noise sources can be quite complex and would take us far afield of the basic ideas we wish to cover in this chapter, we restrict ourselves here to the most widely used model in which the noise is described by an independent random vector added to the data vector **Hf** in the discrete model.

Linear Algebra Tools. The mathematical tools used in this chapter for reconstruct-ing the object **f** from the noisy data **g**, i.e., inverting the imaging matrix **H**, are based on linear algebra, which is reviewed in Appendix B, as well as simple methods of optimization theory, which are used to minimize the average inversion error.

5.1   Discrete and Matrix Models

As described in Chapter 3, a linear imaging system is described by the imaging equa-tion

$$g(\mathbf{r}) = \int h(\mathbf{r}; \mathbf{r}') f(\mathbf{r}') \, d\mathbf{r}', \qquad (5.1\text{-}1)$$

Imaging Equation
Continuous Form

where $\mathbf{r}$ and $\mathbf{r}'$ are two-dimensional (2D) or three-dimensional (3D) position vectors, depending on the application. This equation relates the observed image g to the object f via the point spread function (PSF) h. For a shift-invariant system, $h(\mathbf{r}; \mathbf{r}')$ is a function of $\mathbf{r} - \mathbf{r}'$, and the right-hand side of (5.1-1) is the operation of convolution.

In the tomographic systems described in Chapter 4, each view is represented by a relation like (5.1-1) so that

$$g^{(v)}(\mathbf{r}) = \int h^{(v)}(\mathbf{r}; \mathbf{r}') f(\mathbf{r}') \, d\mathbf{r}', \qquad (5.1\text{-}2)$$

Multiview Imaging Equation
Continuous Form

where $v = 1, 2, \ldots, V$ is an index labeling the views and V is the number of views. Recall that the variables $\mathbf{r}$ and $\mathbf{r}'$ are position vectors that are either 2D or 3D, depending on the application. In this section, we will first develop discrete and matrix models of the single-view imaging equation (5.1-1) and subsequently generalize these models to the multiview case described by (5.1-2).

A. Single-View Imaging

Discrete Models

A simple discrete version of the continuous imaging equation (5.1-1) may be obtained by replacing the integration with a summation at a set of sufficiently close points:

$$g_{\mathbf{m}} = \sum_{\mathbf{n}} h_{\mathbf{mn}} f_{\mathbf{n}}.$$

(5.1-3)
Imaging Equation
Discrete Form

Here, $g_{\mathbf{m}} = g(\mathbf{r_m})$ is the measured image at the point $\mathbf{r_m}$, $f_{\mathbf{n}}$ is the value of the object function $f(\mathbf{r})$ sampled at $\mathbf{r} = \mathbf{r_n}$, and $h_{\mathbf{mn}} \propto h(\mathbf{r_m}, \mathbf{r_n})$ are coefficients determined by sampling the PSF $h(\mathbf{r}, \mathbf{r'})$. The proportionality constant in the one-dimensional (1D) case is the sampling interval; in the 2D and 3D cases, it is the sampling area and volume, respectively. The indexes $\mathbf{m}$ and $\mathbf{n}$ run over the set of observation points and object sampling points, respectively.

For example, in the 1D case, $\mathbf{n}$ is a single index $n = 1, 2, \ldots$ In the 2D case, a rectilinear sampling grid may be used and $\mathbf{n} = (n_x, n_y)$ is a double index, so that the summation in (5.1-3) is actually a double summation over the integers n_x and n_y. Similarly, in the 3D case, $\mathbf{n} = (n_x, n_y, n_z)$.

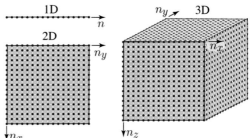

For a 2D shift-invariant system, (5.1-3) may be written as the 2D discrete convolution.

$$g_{m_x, m_y} = \sum_{n_x, n_y} h_{m_x - n_x, m_y - n_y} f_{n_x, n_y}.$$

(5.1-4)

■ MATLAB function g=conv2 (h, f) performs the discrete 2D convolution.

We now present a formal derivation of the discretization process, starting with the continuous imaging equation (5.1-1) and ending with the discrete imaging equation (5.1-3). Since this derivation is not essential to the main material in this chapter, the reader may elect to move directly to the section entitled Matrix Models on page 196.

Discrete Measurements by an Array of Finite-Area Sensors.   In real systems, the measured data are inherently discrete since the image $g(\mathbf{r})$ is measured with a finite number of sensors, such as antennas for electromagnetic systems or ultrasound transducers for acoustic systems, centered about an array of points $\mathbf{r_m}$. If each sensor integrates over a finite area with a distribution function $D(\mathbf{r})$, then the sensor centered at the position $\mathbf{r_m}$ records the signal

$$g_{\mathbf{m}} = \int D(\mathbf{r_m} - \mathbf{r}) g(\mathbf{r}) \, d\mathbf{r}.$$

(5.1-5)

The function $D(\mathbf{r})$ may, e.g., be unity within the sensor area and zero elsewhere, i.e., $D(x, y) = \text{rect}(x/\Delta_g)\,\text{rect}(y/\Delta_g)$, where Δ_g is the pixel size in the detection plane (the $\text{rect}(x)$ function is defined in Table A.1-1 of Appendix A). Substituting from (5.1-1) into (5.1-5), $g_{\mathrm{m}} = \iint D(\mathbf{r_m} - \mathbf{r})h(\mathbf{r};\mathbf{r}')f(\mathbf{r}')\,\mathrm{d}\mathbf{r}\,\mathrm{d}\mathbf{r}'$ so that

$$g_{\mathrm{m}} = \int h_{\mathrm{m}}(\mathbf{r}')f(\mathbf{r}')\,\mathrm{d}\mathbf{r}', \qquad (5.1\text{-}6)$$

where

$$h_{\mathrm{m}}(\mathbf{r}') = \int D(\mathbf{r_m} - \mathbf{r})h(\mathbf{r};\mathbf{r}')\,\mathrm{d}\mathbf{r}. \qquad (5.1\text{-}7)$$

Equation (5.1-6), which relates the discrete measurements g_{m} to the continuous object function $f(\mathbf{r})$, is a first step of the discretization process dictated by the discrete nature of the sensors. It will be followed by a second step of sampling the object function $f(\mathbf{r})$ in order to obtain the fully discrete form (5.1-3).

Discretization of the Object Function: Pixelization and Voxelization. As described in Appendix A, the sampling theorem states that a bandlimited function $f(x)$ may be expressed in terms of its samples $f_n = f(x_n)$ at sampling positions $x_n = n\Delta_{\mathrm{f}}$, where Δ_{f} is a sampling interval selected such that the sampling rate $1/\Delta_{\mathrm{f}}$ is equal to, or greater than, twice the bandwidth. The relation between the continuous function $f(x)$ and its own samples f_n is expressed as

$$f(x) = \sum_n f_n\,\sigma(x - x_n), \qquad (5.1\text{-}8)$$

where $\sigma(x) = \text{sinc}(x/\Delta_{\mathrm{f}})$ is the sampling function, as illustrated in Fig. 5.1-1(a). Other functions $\sigma(x)$, such as the rectangular and triangular functions, are often used for simplicity, as illustrated in Fig. 5.1-1(b) and (c), but (5.1-8) is then only an approximation of the true object function. Delta function sampling, i.e., $\sigma(x) = \delta(x)$, is sometimes used for mathematical simplicity.

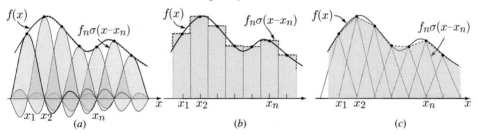

Figure 5.1-1 Representation of a bandlimited function $f(x)$ in terms of its samples f_n using (a) a sinc function $\sigma(x) = \text{sinc}(x/\Delta_{\mathrm{f}})$, which generates an exact representation (if the sampling rate is at twice the bandwidth), (b) a rectangular function $\sigma(x) = \text{rect}(x/\Delta_{\mathrm{f}})$, which generates a piecewise-constant (stair-step) approximation (dashed lines), and (c) a triangular function, $\sigma(x) = \text{rect}(x/\Delta_{\mathrm{f}}) \otimes \text{rect}(x/\Delta_{\mathrm{f}})$, which generates a piecewise-linear approximation (dashed lines).

Coarser discretization, i.e., a larger sampling interval Δ_{f}, leads to greater errors. The kind of error encountered in representing a continuous function $f(x)$ by a piecewise linear approximation, as in Fig. 5.1-1(b), may be estimated by expanding $f(x)$ in a Taylor series expansion $f(x + \Delta_{\mathrm{f}}) = f(x) + \Delta_{\mathrm{f}}\,f' + \frac{1}{2}\Delta_{\mathrm{f}}^2\,f'' + \ldots$, where f' and f'' are the first and second derivatives of f at x. Since the first two terms represent the linear approximation, higher order terms constitute the error. For small Δ_f, the error is approximated by the third term, which is proportional to Δ_f^2. As an example, if $f(x) = \cos(2\pi x/d)$ and $\Delta_f = d/10$, then the error is of the order of $\frac{1}{2}\Delta_f^2(2\pi/d)^2 \approx \pi^2/50$, or about 20%.

The sampling theorem may be generalized to 2D and 3D functions $f(\mathbf{r})$ (see Appendix A) so that

$$f(\mathbf{r}) = \sum_n f_\mathbf{n}\, \sigma(\mathbf{r} - \mathbf{r_n}), \tag{5.1-9}$$

where $\sigma(\mathbf{r})$ is the sampling function.

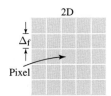

For example, in the 2D case the sampling function $\sigma(x, y)$ may be the product of a rectangular function in x and another in y, defining a sampling square called a **pixel**. In this case, (5.1-9) takes the form

$$f(x, y) = \sum_{n_x} \sum_{n_y} f_{n_x,n_y}\, \sigma(x - x_{n_x}, y - y_{n_y}),$$

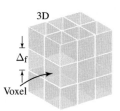

where $\sigma(x, y) = \mathrm{rect}(x/\Delta_f)\,\mathrm{rect}(y/\Delta_f)$ is a box function. This is called the **pixel basis**. Similarly, in the 3D case, the sampling function $\sigma(x, y, z)$ may be the product of three rectangular functions in x, y, and z, defining a sampling cube, called a **voxel**.

Discretization of the Imaging Equation.   With the measurements $g_\mathbf{m}$ expressed in terms of the object continuous function $f(\mathbf{r})$ by (5.1-6), and with the object function $f(\mathbf{r})$ expressed in terms of its own samples $f_\mathbf{n}$ by (5.1-9), we may readily use simple substitution to express $g_\mathbf{m}$ in terms of $f_\mathbf{n}$. The result is the fully discrete imaging equation $g_\mathbf{m} = \sum_\mathbf{n} h_{\mathbf{m,n}} f_\mathbf{n}$ in (5.1-3), with

$$h_{\mathbf{m,n}} = \int h_\mathbf{m}(\mathbf{r})\, \sigma(\mathbf{r} - \mathbf{r_n})\, d\mathbf{r}. \tag{5.1-10}$$

Using (5.1-7), we obtain

$$h_{\mathbf{m,n}} = \iint D(\mathbf{r_m} - \mathbf{r})h(\mathbf{r}; \mathbf{r'})\sigma(\mathbf{r'} - \mathbf{r_n})\, d\mathbf{r}\, d\mathbf{r'}, \tag{5.1-11}$$

which is an expression for the discrete elements $h_{\mathbf{m,n}}$ in terms of the sampling functions $\sigma(\mathbf{r})$, the imaging kernel $h(\mathbf{r}; \mathbf{r'})$, and the measurement function $D(\mathbf{r})$.

If the functions $\sigma(\mathbf{r})$ and $D(\mathbf{r})$ are uniform at points within the pixel or voxel and zero elsewhere, then

$$h_{\mathbf{m,n}} = \int_{\mathbf{r}\,\in\,\text{voxel m}} \int_{\mathbf{r'}\,\in\,\text{voxel n}} h(\mathbf{r}; \mathbf{r'})\, d\mathbf{r}\, d\mathbf{r'}. \tag{5.1-12}$$

If the pixel size is much smaller than the width of the PSF, the integration over the pixels simplifies to sampling, so that

$$h_{\mathbf{m,n}} \propto h(\mathbf{r_m}, \mathbf{r_n}). \tag{5.1-13}$$

Shift-Invariant System.   In the special case when the imaging system is shift invariant, $h(\mathbf{r}; \mathbf{r}') = h(\mathbf{r} - \mathbf{r}')$ and (5.1-11) may be written in the form

$$h_{m,n} = h'(\mathbf{r_m} - \mathbf{r_n}),\tag{5.1-14}$$

where $h'(\mathbf{r})$ is given by the triple convolution

$$h'(\mathbf{r}) = D(\mathbf{r}) \otimes h(\mathbf{r}) \otimes \sigma(\mathbf{r}).\tag{5.1-15}$$

Scanning System.   For a scanning system that uses probe and sensor beams with distributions $p(\mathbf{r})$ and $\eta(\mathbf{r})$, the PSF is

$$h(\mathbf{r}; \mathbf{r}') = \eta(\mathbf{r} - \mathbf{r}')p(\mathbf{r} - \mathbf{r}'),$$

as described in Sec. 3.1E. Since integration over the detector's area is already included in the sensor's receptive function $\eta(\mathbf{r})$, we substitute $D(\mathbf{r}) = \delta(\mathbf{r})$ into (5.1-11) and obtain

$$h_{m,n} = \int \eta(\mathbf{r_m} - \mathbf{r}')p(\mathbf{r_m} - \mathbf{r}')\sigma(\mathbf{r}' - \mathbf{r_n})\, d\mathbf{r}'.\tag{5.1-16}$$

Assuming that we use a pixel basis for representing the object, i.e., we approximate the object distribution f as being constant within each pixel so that the sampling function $\sigma(\mathbf{r})$ is uniform over the pixel or voxel, and zero elsewhere, then

$$h_{m,n} = \int_{\mathbf{r}' \,\in\, \text{voxel } n} \eta(\mathbf{r_m} - \mathbf{r}')p(\mathbf{r_m} - \mathbf{r}')\, d\mathbf{r}',\tag{5.1-17}$$

as illustrated in Fig. 5.1-2 for the 2D and 3D cases.

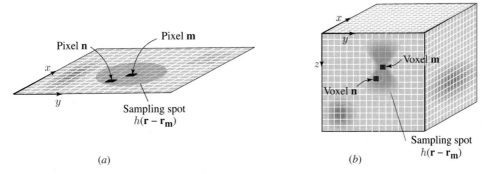

(a)   (b)

Figure 5.1-2   Determination of the discrete PSF of (a) a 2D and (b) a 3D scanning system.

Matrix Models

Lexicographic Ordering.   To write the discrete imaging equation (5.1-3) in a matrix form it is necessary to convert the vector index **n**, which represents multiple scalar indexes [for example, $\mathbf{n} = (n_x, n_y)$ in the 2D case], into a single scalar index n. The conversion method used most often, called *lexicographic* ordering, is illustrated in Fig. 5.1-3. We think of the n_x and n_y indexes as referring to the rows and columns of an array, and we order the elements of this array by *going down* one column at a time. For an $N \times N$ array, $n = 1, 2, \ldots, N^2$. A similar map between n and **n** may be defined in the 3D case for which $\mathbf{n} = (n_x, n_y, n_z)$. We express this lexicographic map in the symbolic form $n = \text{Lex}(\mathbf{n})$. In Exercise 5.1-1, you are asked to provide equations for going back and forth between the lexicographic ordering and the row–column schemes.

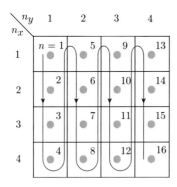

Figure 5.1-3   Lexicographic ordering $n = \text{Lex}(\mathbf{n}) = \text{Lex}(n_x, n_y)$ used to label pixels of a 4 × 4 array. For example, $\text{Lex}(1, 1) = 1$, $\text{Lex}(2, 3) = 10$, and $\text{Lex}(4, 4) = 16$.

▶ Problems 5.1-1

Matrix Imaging Equation.   Using this lexicographic ordering, $g_{\mathbf{m}}$ and $f_{\mathbf{n}}$ in (5.1-3) may be arranged into vectors **f** and **g** with elements f_n and g_m, respectively, where $n = \text{Lex}(\mathbf{n})$ and $m = \text{Lex}(\mathbf{m})$. We may think of

$$H_{m,n} = h_{\mathbf{m},\mathbf{n}} \tag{5.1-18}$$

as the element of a matrix **H** and write (5.1-3) as a matrix-vector equation

$$\mathbf{g} = \mathbf{H}\mathbf{f}, \tag{5.1-19}$$

Imaging Equation
Matrix Form

where **f** is a column matrix whose elements f_n are obtained from $f_{\mathbf{n}}$ by lexicographic ordering, and similarly for **g**.

Summary. The imaging matrix **H** may be determined in two steps. First, we start with the continuous PSF $h(\mathbf{r}, \mathbf{r}')$ and use (5.1-11) or (5.1-12) to determine the discrete PSF $h_{\mathbf{m},\mathbf{n}}$, where $\mathbf{n} = (n_x, n_y)$ and $\mathbf{m} = (m_x, m_y)$. Second, we use (5.1-18) and the lexicographic relations $n = \text{Lex}(\mathbf{n})$ and $m = \text{Lex}(\mathbf{m})$ to determine the elements $H_{m,n}$ of the matrix **H**.

EXAMPLE 5.1-1.   *2D Diffraction-Limited Gazing System.* For the 2D diffraction-limited, incoherent, shift-invariant imaging system with a circular aperture, as described in Sec. 3.1D, the PSF $h(\mathbf{r};\mathbf{r}') = h(\mathbf{r} - \mathbf{r}')$, where

$$h(x,y) \propto \left| \frac{2J_1\left(\pi\sqrt{x^2+y^2}/\rho_a\right)}{\pi\sqrt{x^2+y^2}/\rho_a} \right|^2, \tag{5.1-20}$$

$\rho_a = \lambda/2\mathrm{NA}$, λ is the wavelength, and NA is the numerical aperture. Using square pixels in of size Δ_f and Δ_g in the object and detection planes, respectively, i.e.,

$$\sigma(x,y) = \mathrm{rect}(x/\Delta_f)\,\mathrm{rect}(y/\Delta_f), \quad D(x,y) = \mathrm{rect}(x/\Delta_g)\,\mathrm{rect}(y/\Delta_g),$$

we may substitute these expressions of $h(x,y)$, $\sigma(x,y)$, and $D(x,y)$ into (5.1-15) and use (5.1-14) to compute the discrete PSF $h_{m,n}$ and (5.1-18) to compute the matrix elements $H_{m,n}$. If the sampling grid is sufficiently fine, the functions $\sigma(\mathbf{r})$ and $D(\mathbf{r})$ may be approximated by delta functions so that $h'(\mathbf{r}) \approx h(\mathbf{r})$. In this case,

$$H_{m,n} = \left| \frac{2J_1\left(\pi\sqrt{(x_m-x_n)^2+(y_m-y_n)^2}/\rho_a\right)}{\pi\sqrt{(x_m-x_n)^2+(y_m-y_n)^2}/\rho_a} \right|^2, \tag{5.1-21}$$

where (x_m,y_m) are coordinates of the mth point, which corresponds lexicographically to the pixel (m_x,m_y), i.e., $m = \mathrm{Lex}(m_x,m_y)$, and similarly for (x_n,y_n).

EXAMPLE 5.1-2.   *2D Scanning System.* A scanning system uses probe and sensor beams of Gaussian distributions $p(x,y) = \exp[-2(x^2+y^2)/W_p^2)]$ and $\eta(x,y) = \exp[-2(x^2+y^2)/W_s^2)]$, with widths W_p and W_s, respectively. A rectangular sampling grid is used. From (5.1-17) and (5.1-18), elements of the imaging matrix are given by

$$H_{m,n} = \underset{\mathrm{pixel}\ n}{\iint} \exp\left[-2\frac{(x_m-x)^2+(y_m-y)^2}{W^2}\right]\,dx\,dy, \tag{5.1-22}$$

where W is an effective spot size given by $1/W^2 = 1/W_p^2 + 1/W_s^2$. The integral in (5.1-22) may be evaluated numerically. However, if we use a δ function basis for $f(x,y)$ rather than a pixel basis,

$$H_{m,n} \approx \exp\left[-2\frac{(x_m-x_n)^2+(y_m-y_n)^2}{W^2}\right]. \tag{5.1-23}$$

▶ Problems 5.1-2, 5.1-3

B. Multiview Imaging

For a multiview tomographic system described by the imaging equation (5.1-2), each view may be discretized as was done in the single-view case so that for the vth view

$$g_m^{(v)} = \sum_n h_{m,n}^{(v)}\,f_n, \tag{5.1-24}$$

Multiview Imaging Equation
Discrete Form

where $h_{m,n}^{(v)}$ is obtained from the continuous PSF $h^{(v)}(\mathbf{r};\mathbf{r}')$, the sampling function $\sigma(\mathbf{r})$, and the detector function $D(\mathbf{r})$ by a relation similar to (5.1-11). For point detectors and fine sampling, $h_{m,n}^{(v)} \approx h^{(v)}(\mathbf{r}_m,\mathbf{r}_n)$, i.e., is a sampled version of the PSF of the vth view.

In multiview tomography, a set of probe beams $p^{(v)}(\mathbf{r})$ are used together with sensor beams $\eta(\mathbf{r} - \mathbf{r}_m)$ centered at the measurement points $\mathbf{r}_m$. In this case, as in (5.1-17),

$$h_{m,n}^{(v)} = \int\limits_{r' \in \text{voxel } n} \eta(\mathbf{r_m} - \mathbf{r})p^{(v)}(\mathbf{r})\,d\mathbf{r}. \qquad (5.1\text{-}25)$$

Once $h_{m,n}$ is determined, a lexicographic ordering may be used to write (5.1-24) in the matrix form:

$$\mathbf{g}^{(v)} = \mathbf{H}^{(v)}\mathbf{f}, \qquad (5.1\text{-}26)$$

where $\mathbf{H}^{(v)}$ is a matrix with elements $H_{m,n}^{(v)} = h_{m,n}^{(v)}$. Finally, *stacking* the data from all of the different views $v = 1, 2, \ldots, V$ provides a single matrix equation relating the full set of data to the object distribution:

$$\mathbf{g} = \mathbf{H}\mathbf{f}, \quad \mathbf{g} = \begin{bmatrix} \mathbf{g}^{(1)} \\ \mathbf{g}^{(2)} \\ \vdots \\ \mathbf{g}^{(V)} \end{bmatrix}, \quad \mathbf{H} = \begin{bmatrix} \mathbf{H}^{(1)} \\ \mathbf{H}^{(2)} \\ \vdots \\ \mathbf{H}^{(V)} \end{bmatrix}.$$

$$(5.1\text{-}27)$$
Multiview Imaging Equation
Matrix Form

C. Applications

Ray Tomography

Figure 5.1-4 illustrates the geometry for computation of elements of the imaging matrix **H** for ray tomography (e.g., X-ray CT) in two dimensions. Assuming that we use a pixel basis for representing the object $f(x, y)$, then, as illustrated in Fig. 5.1-4(a), the matrix element:

$H_{m,n}^{(v)}$ = length of intersection of the ray specified by the position and angle parameters (s_m, θ_v) with the area of the nth pixel.

If a ray identified by the indexes (m, v) does not intersect pixel n, the matrix element $H_{m,n}^{(v)} = 0$. The matrix **H** is constructed by stacking the matrices $\mathbf{H}^{(v)}$, as in (5.1-27). Clearly the matrix will be sparse, i.e., most of its elements are zero.

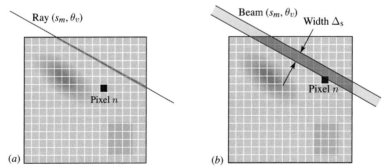

(a)   (b)

Figure 5.1-4   Discrete model of ray tomography: (a) rays of infinitesimal width; (b) beams of finite width.

In practice, a ray is actually a beam of finite width Δ_s, as depicted in Fig. 5.1-4(b) (see also Problem 4.1-7). In this case, the probe beam $p^{(v)}(\mathbf{r})$ and the sensor beam $\eta(\mathbf{r}_m - \mathbf{r})$ in (5.1-25) are a single beam described by a rectangular function of width Δ_s oriented at an angle θ_v and position s_m. The matrix element in this case is:

$$\left| \, H_{m,n}^{(v)} = \text{area of intersection between the beam } (s_m, \theta_v) \text{ and the square pixel } n. \right.$$

▶ Problem 5.1-4

Wave Tomography

In wave tomography, each of a set of sources illuminates the object, and a set of sensors $m = 1, 2, \ldots, M$ detect the scattered signal from each source (view). In this example, we use a 2D geometry and assume point sources located at the positions $\mathbf{r}_v = (x_v, y_v), v = 1, 2, \ldots, V$, and point detectors located at the positions $\mathbf{r}_m = (x_m, y_m), m = 1, 2, \ldots, M$, as illustrated in Fig. 5.1-5. Starting with a pixel representation of the object $f(x, y)$, and assuming a linearized scattering model, we use (5.1-25) with $p^{(v)}(\mathbf{r})$ a spherical wave centered at $\mathbf{r}_v$ and $\eta(\mathbf{r}_m - \mathbf{r})$ a spherical wave centered at $\mathbf{r}_m$, to write

$$H_{m,n}^{(v)} = \underbrace{\iint}_{\text{pixel } n} \underbrace{\frac{e^{-jk\sqrt{(x_m-x)^2+(y_m-y)^2}}}{4\pi\sqrt{(x_m-x)^2+(y_m-y)^2}}}_{\text{scattered wave at } m\text{th sensor}} \underbrace{\frac{e^{-jk\sqrt{(x-x_v)^2+(y-y_v)^2}}}{4\pi\sqrt{(x-x_v)^2+(y-y_v)^2}}}_{v\text{th probe wave}} \, dx \, dy. \tag{5.1-28}$$

One factor in the integrand represents the 2D cylindrical probe wave emitted by the vth source and arriving at a point (x, y) within the nth pixel. The other represents the 2D cylindrical wave scattered by the point (x, y) in the nth pixel, measured at the mth observation point. As before, the overall imaging matrix $\mathbf{H}$ is constructed by stacking the matrices $\mathbf{H}^{(v)}$, as in (5.1-27).

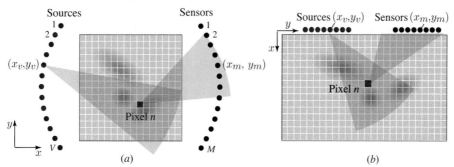

Figure 5.1-5 Wave tomography: (a) transmission configuration; (b) reflection configuration.

Unfortunately, no closed-form expression exists for this double integral, so that numerical methods must be employed. For problems involving large amounts of data or many pixels, numerical evaluation of these integrals is a time-consuming process. Thus, it is not uncommon in practice to employ a δ function basis for $f(x, y)$ rather than a pixel basis. Owing to the sifting property of the delta function, the integral in (5.1-28) goes away and we have

$$H_{m,n}^{(v)} \approx \frac{1}{16\pi^2} \frac{e^{-jk\sqrt{(x_m-x_n)^2+(y_m-y_n)^2}}}{\sqrt{(x_m-x_n)^2+(y_m-y_n)^2}} \frac{e^{-jk\sqrt{(x_n-x_v)^2+(y_n-y_v)^2}}}{\sqrt{(x_n-x_v)^2+(y_n-y_v)^2}}, \tag{5.1-29}$$

where (x_n, y_n) are the coordinates of the center of the nth pixel.

▶ Problems 5.1-5, 5.1-6

5.2   The Inverse Problem

The inverse problem that we consider in this chapter is the recovery of $\mathbf{f}$, the vector of unknowns representing $f(\mathbf{r})$, from the vector of observations $\mathbf{g}$. To distinguish the data-based estimate of $\mathbf{f}$ from the true $\mathbf{f}$, we denote it as $\hat{\mathbf{f}}$.

Noise

In the previous section, where we were concerned largely with obtaining a discrete representation of the forward problem, the data were related to the unknowns through a matrix $\mathbf{H}$. In defining the inverse problems, we modify this relationship a bit to include the effects of noise, which cause $\mathbf{g}$ to be different from the model $\mathbf{Hf}$. There are many options for modeling the noise and incorporating these models into the algorithms for recovering $\mathbf{f}$. We restrict ourselves to the most widely used description in which the perturbations to the data are assumed to be a component added to $\mathbf{Hf}$, i.e.,

$$g = Hf + w,$$

(5.2-1)
Imaging Equation

where $\mathbf{w}$ is a vector of perturbations or *noise*. We further assume that each element of $\mathbf{w}$ is a random variable with zero mean and variance σ_w^2 and that all elements of $\mathbf{w}$ are statistically independent. The signal-to-noise ratio (SNR) in decibels is given by

$$\text{SNR (dB)} = 10 \log_{10} \left[\frac{\|\mathbf{Hf}\|^2}{M\sigma_w^2} \right],$$

(5.2-2)

where $\|\mathbf{Hf})\|^2 = (\mathbf{Hf})^T (\mathbf{Hf})$ is the squared norm of $\mathbf{Hf}$ and M is its length.

Matrix Dimensions and Rank.

The dimensions $M \times N$ of the matrix $\mathbf{H}$ and its rank K play an essential role in the inverse problem (See Appendix B). Several classes of problems can be defined based on the relative values of these numbers, as illustrated in Fig. 5.2-1.

- For a square matrix ($M = N$), we have a number of equations equal to the number of unknowns. The easiest special case is the full-rank matrix, for which $K = N$, i.e., the equations are independent and each equation provides new information on the unknowns, since the matrix is invertible. When the rank is smaller than the dimension, $K < N$, there are fewer independent equations than unknowns.

- For $M > N$, i.e., there are more equations than unknowns, the system is said to be **overdetermined** ($K = N$ in the full-rank case and $K < N$ in the reduced-rank case).

- For $M < N$, i.e., there are fewer equations than unknowns, the system is said to be **underdetermined** ($K = M$ in the full-rank case and $K < M$ in the reduced-rank case).

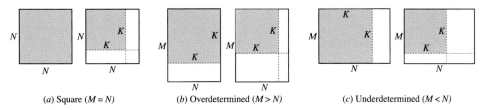

(a) Square (M = N)   (b) Overdetermined (M > N)   (c) Underdetermined (M < N)

Figure 5.2-1 Classification of an $M \times N$ matrix of rank K based on the relative size of M, N, and K. (a) square, $M = N$, (b) overdetermined, $M > N$, (c) underdetermined, $M < N$. Full-rank (K equal to the smaller dimension) and defficient-rank (K smaller than the smaller dimension) cases are shown in each of the three cases.

A. Ill-Posedness

One typically refers to inverse problems for which the information content of the data is limited due to conditions related to the physics of the sensing modality or restrictions on the placement of the sensors as being **ill-posed**. The precise mathematical notion of an ill-posed problem was first formulated in 1902 by the mathematician Jacques Hadamard who was studying the manner in which the solutions to certain partial differential equations were dependent on the boundary data. According to Hadamard, a problem is well posed if three conditions are met:

1. At least one solution *exists*.

2. The solution is *unique*.

3. The solution is *stable* in the sense that its dependence on the boundary data is continuous. Less formally, but perhaps more clearly, the notion of stability implies that small changes in the boundary data should not yield overly large changes in the resulting solution to the underlying problem.

For the inverse problem in (5.2-1), the first two criteria of Hadamard require the existence and uniqueness of a solution **f** for a given set of data **g**. Technically, for the matrix-vector problems of concern to us here, if a solution exists it will always be continuously dependent on **g**. Thus, here the issue of stability will be interpreted a bit less formally in terms of the intuitive idea that the presence of *small* perturbations **w** in the data caused by imperfect sensors should not result in *large* changes to our recovered **f**.

We turn now to the examination of all three of these ideas.

Existence

Linear systems for which there are more rows in **H** than columns ($M > N$), termed **overdetermined** systems, provide classic examples of cases where solutions may not exist. Consider the 3×2 matrix whose range was determined in Example B.2-1 of Appendix B. With noise added, we have

$$\begin{bmatrix} g_1 \\ g_2 \\ g_3 \end{bmatrix} = \begin{bmatrix} 1 & 2 \\ 3 & -4 \\ 4 & 3 \end{bmatrix} \begin{bmatrix} f_1 \\ f_2 \end{bmatrix} + \begin{bmatrix} w_1 \\ w_2 \\ w_3 \end{bmatrix}. \tag{5.2-3}$$

In this case, the inverse problem is to determine the two elements of **f** that give rise to **g**. As described in Example B.2-1, the range of the matrix $R(\mathbf{H})$ is a plane in $\mathbb{R}^3$ generated by vectors that lie in the the linear span of the columns of **H**.

Any vector in $\mathbb{R}^3$ that contains a component along the line perpendicular to this plane, i.e., in $R^{\perp}(\mathbf{H})$ (indicated in Fig. B.2-2 of Appendix B.2-1 by the red line) cannot be exactly produced by any choice of **f**. Because of the presence of noise in the data, in all but the most unlikely of circumstances, **g** will have a component in $R^{\perp}(\mathbf{H})$. Hence a solution to (5.2-3) will not exist. To put it another way, two degrees of freedom as represented by f_1 and f_2 are generally insufficient to provide a representation for the three degrees of freedom in the vector $\mathbf{g}$.

Uniqueness

In contrast to the existence issue, which is most naturally studied in terms of overdetermined linear systems, uniqueness is best understood using the example of an **underdetermined** system where $M < N$. Here one has not just one solution, but an infinite number of them. Moreover, because this abundance of solutions is not impacted by the noise, we simplify the discussion by assuming $\mathbf{w} = \mathbf{0}$. Let us start with a simple example defined by the 2×3 matrix that was examined in Example B.2-1 in Appendix B:

$$\mathbf{H} = \begin{bmatrix} -1.3 & -0.5 & 1.0 \\ -1.0 & 1.0 & 0.0 \end{bmatrix}. \tag{5.2-4}$$

In this case, the range of $\mathbf{H}$ is $\mathbb{R}^2$. Geometrically, the inverse problem here is to use the three degrees of freedom in $\mathbf{f}$ to build vectors in $\mathbb{R}^2$. The extra element of $\mathbf{f}$ implies that in general there will be some flexibility concerning how this is done, as can be easily shown by examples. As was shown in Example B.2-1, $\mathbf{H}$ has a nullspace $N(\mathbf{H})$ spanned by the vector

$$\mathbf{f}_{\text{null}} = \begin{bmatrix} 0.4369 \\ 0.4369 \\ 0.7863 \end{bmatrix}.$$

Thus, any solution to the problem can be written as a linear combination of a vector in $N^{\perp}(\mathbf{H}) = R(\mathbf{H}^{\text{H}})$ plus a component in $N(\mathbf{H})$. By direct calculation, one can verify that $N^{\perp}(\mathbf{H})$ is spanned by the columns of the matrix

$$\mathbf{A} = \begin{bmatrix} -0.5556 & -0.2778 \\ -0.5556 & 0.7222 \\ 0.0000 & 0.0000 \end{bmatrix} \tag{5.2-5}$$

so that we can write any solution to the inverse problem as $\mathbf{f} = \mathbf{A}\mathbf{f}_1 + \alpha\mathbf{f}_{\text{null}}$, where α is an arbitrary real number and $\mathbf{f}_1$ is a vector in $\mathbb{R}^2$. This decomposition should clarify the nonuniqueness inherent in this problem. Because $\mathbf{H}\mathbf{A}$ is just the 2×2 identity matrix and $\mathbf{H}\mathbf{f}_{\text{null}} = \mathbf{0}$, we have that $\mathbf{g} = \mathbf{f}_1$ and can therefore conclude that any solution to the inverse problem may be written as $\hat{\mathbf{f}} = \mathbf{A}\mathbf{g} + \alpha\mathbf{f}_{\text{null}}$. Hence, the choice of α corresponds to the one extra degree of freedom we have in selecting a solution to the problem. Because this choice is arbitrary, there are obviously an infinite number of such solutions.

Stability

To illustrate the more subtle issue of the stability of an inverse problem, we consider a linear system described by a full-rank square matrix $\mathbf{H}$, which is invertible. We solve the inverse problem by use of the inverse matrix $\mathbf{H}^{-1}$, i.e.,

$$\hat{\mathbf{f}} = \mathbf{H}^{-1}\mathbf{g} = \mathbf{f} + \mathbf{H}^{-1}\mathbf{w}. \tag{5.2-6}$$

In the absence of noise, $\hat{\mathbf{f}} = \mathbf{f}$, so that the object $\mathbf{f}$ is perfectly recovered. However, in the presence of noise, $\hat{\mathbf{f}} = \mathbf{f} + \mathbf{H}^{-1}\mathbf{w}$. The noise term $\mathbf{H}^{-1}\mathbf{w}$ in the estimate can be significantly greater than the original noise $\mathbf{w}$ and may lead to instability.

EXAMPLE 5.2-1. *Test of Inversion Stability for Full-Rank Square Matrix.* As an example, we consider a 128×128 square matrix $\mathbf{H}$ with nonzero values only near the diagonal, as shown in Fig. 5.2-2(a). This matrix represents a system for which g_m is a local average of f_n for a narrow band of samples centered about $m = n$. Moreover, the values are more or less constant along the diagonal, so that the averaging kernel does not change appreciably from one n to the next (i.e., the operation is approximately shift invariant). Fig. 5.2-2(b) is a plot of elements of the 64th row of the matrix. This matrix is, strictly speaking, invertible.

We now test the recovery of the object $\mathbf{f}$ shown in Fig. 5.2-3(a) from the image $\mathbf{g}$ by use of the inverse matrix. In the absence of noise, this produces the anticipated results: perfect recovery of $\mathbf{f}$. The addition of noise, however, leads to substantially different reconstruction. Fig. 5.2-3(b) shows the image in the presence of an additive noise vector $\mathbf{w}$ whose elements are zero mean, independent, identically distributed Gaussian random variables with standard deviations equal to 0.04. Reconstruction by use of the inverse matrix yields the estimate $\hat{\mathbf{f}}$ shown in Fig. 5.2-3(c). Evidently, the noise term $\mathbf{H}^{-1}\mathbf{w}$ in (5.2-6) grows in a manner out of proportion to the size of the noise itself. This type of noise amplification is in fact seen across a broad range of problems and is the primary characteristic of the ill-posed nature of these inverse problems.

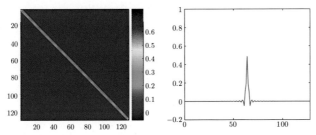

Figure 5.2-2 (a) Brightness map of elements of the $\mathbf{H}$ matrix. (b) Plot of $H(64, n)$, i.e., elements of row 64.

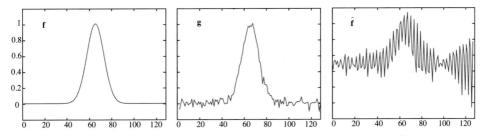

Figure 5.2-3 (a) Object array $\mathbf{f}$. (b) Noisy observation $\mathbf{g}$. (c) Estimated object $\hat{\mathbf{f}}$ determined by applying the inverse matrix $\mathbf{H}^{-1}$ to the observation $\mathbf{g}$.

B. Singular-Value Decomposition

The singular-value decomposition (SVD) of a matrix (see Appendix B) is an expansion that provides useful insight on various aspects of the inverse problem, including existence, uniqueness, and stability. For an $M \times N$ matrix $\mathbf{H}$, the SVD is written as

$$\mathbf{H} = \mathbf{U}\mathbf{\Sigma}\mathbf{V}^{\mathrm{T}} = \sum_{k=1}^{K} \sigma_k \mathbf{u}_k \mathbf{v}_k^{\mathrm{T}}, \qquad (5.2\text{-}7)$$

SVD

where $\mathbf{U} = [\mathbf{u}_1 \ \mathbf{u}_2 \ \dots \mathbf{u}_M]$, $\mathbf{V} = [\mathbf{v}_1 \ \mathbf{v}_2 \ \dots \mathbf{v}_N]$, and $\boldsymbol{\Sigma}$ is an $M \times N$ matrix that is all zeros except along the main diagonal, where $\Sigma_{kk} = \sigma_k \geq 0$, the **singular values**. There are K nonzero singular values. The columns of $\mathbf{U}$, known as the **left singular vectors**, are the eigenvectors of the $M \times M$ square matrix $\mathbf{HH}^{\mathrm{H}}$. The columns of $\mathbf{V}$, known as the **right singular vectors**, are the eigenvectors of the $N \times N$ square matrix $\mathbf{H}^{\mathrm{H}}\mathbf{H}$. The values σ_n^2 are the eigenvalues of either of these square matrices. $\mathbf{U}$ is orthonormal (i.e., $\mathbf{U}^{\mathrm{T}}\mathbf{U} = \mathbf{UU}^{\mathrm{T}} = \mathbf{I}$) and of size $M \times M$. Likewise, $\mathbf{V}$ is orthonormal and of size $N \times N$.

■ MATLAB function $[\mathbf{U}, \boldsymbol{\Sigma}, \mathbf{V}] = \mathtt{svd}(\mathbf{H})$ provides the singular values and singular vectors of the matrix $\mathbf{H}$.

▶ Problem 5.2-1

Inversion of a Full-Rank Square Matrix: Stability

In the special case of an $N \times N$ square matrix $\mathbf{H}$ possessing a full set of N nonzero singular values, $\sigma_1 > \sigma_2 > \cdots > \sigma_N > 0$, i.e., $K = N$, but not necessarily having $\mathbf{U} = \mathbf{V}$. Exploiting the orthonormality of the $N \times N$ matrices $\mathbf{U}$ and $\mathbf{V}$, the inverse of $\mathbf{H} = \mathbf{U}\boldsymbol{\Sigma}\mathbf{V}^{\mathrm{T}}$ is just

$$\mathbf{H}^{-1} = \mathbf{V}\boldsymbol{\Sigma}^{-1}\mathbf{U}^{\mathrm{T}} = \sum_{k=1}^{N} \frac{1}{\sigma_k} \mathbf{v}_k \mathbf{u}_k^{\mathrm{T}},$$

(5.2-8)
Matrix Inverse
Full-Rank

where $\boldsymbol{\Sigma}^{-1} = \mathrm{diag}(\sigma_1^{-1}, \sigma_2^{-1}, \dots, \sigma_N^{-1})$.

The inverse problem may be solved by applying the inverse matrix $\mathbf{H}^{-1}$, represented by the SVD in (5.2-8), on the observation vector $\mathbf{g}$:

$$\hat{\mathbf{f}} = \mathbf{H}^{-1}\mathbf{g} = \mathbf{V}\boldsymbol{\Sigma}^{-1}\mathbf{U}\mathbf{g} = \sum_{k=1}^{N} \frac{1}{\sigma_k}(\mathbf{u}_k^{\mathrm{T}}\mathbf{g})\mathbf{v}_k = \sum_{k=1}^{N} \frac{\gamma_k}{\sigma_k}\mathbf{v}_k,$$

(5.2-9)

where $\mathbf{u}_k$ and $\mathbf{v}_k$ are the kth columns of $\mathbf{U}$ and $\mathbf{V}$, respectively, and $\gamma_k = \mathbf{u}_k^{\mathrm{T}}\mathbf{g}$.

Equation (5.2-9) indicates that the reconstruction $\hat{\mathbf{f}}$ is a superposition of a set of *modes* $\mathbf{v}_k$, each of which is weighted by two scalars: (1) $\mathbf{u}_k^{\mathrm{T}}\mathbf{g}$, the projection of $\mathbf{g}$ onto the basis given by the columns of $\mathbf{U}$, and (2) the inverse of the singular value σ_k. This interpretation implies that the action of the inverse of $\mathbf{H}$ is comprised of two *well-posed* steps between which lies the source of many of the difficulties for linear inverse problems: filtering and multiplication by the inverses of the singular values. The orthonormality of $\mathbf{U}$ and $\mathbf{V}$ implies that there will not be any sensitivity or ill-posedness associated with these operations because they do not amplify (or for that matter attenuate) the "size" (as measured the norm) of the vectors on which they act. The same is most definitely not true of the filtering operation. As indicated by (5.2-9), filtering is performed via multiplication by the diagonal matrix $\boldsymbol{\Sigma}^{-1}$ or, equivalently, scaling each of the γ_k by σ_k^{-1}.

Error. To see the impact of this scaling we substitute $\mathbf{g} = \mathbf{Hf} + \mathbf{w}$ into (5.2-9) to obtain $\hat{\mathbf{f}} = \mathbf{f} + \mathbf{V}\boldsymbol{\Sigma}^{-1}\mathbf{U}^{\mathrm{T}}\mathbf{w}$, so that the reconstruction error is given by

$$\mathbf{e} = \hat{\mathbf{f}} - \mathbf{f} = \mathbf{V}\boldsymbol{\Sigma}^{-1}\mathbf{U}^T\mathbf{w}.$$

To gauge the size of this error we determine the squared norm $\|\mathbf{e}\|_2^2 = \mathbf{e}^T\mathbf{e}$, which may be related to the noise vector $\mathbf{w}$ by $\|\mathbf{e}\|_2^2 = \mathbf{w}^T\boldsymbol{\Sigma}^{-2}\mathbf{w}$. Since $\mathbf{w}$ is random, so is its norm. The following expression for the mean square error $\mathrm{MSE} = E\{\|\mathbf{e}\|_2^2\}$, where $E\{\cdot\}$ is the operation of statistical average (or expectation value), may be determined by using tools from mathematical statistics and the fact that elements of the noise vector $\mathbf{w}$ are statistically independent random variables with zero mean and variance σ_w^2,

$$\mathrm{MSE} = \sigma_w^2 \sum_{k=1}^{N} \frac{1}{\sigma_k^2}. \tag{5.2-10}$$

Therefore, the contribution of each term of the SVD expansion will be proportional to the inverse square of its singular value σ_k. Clearly, even if σ_w is very small, the mean square error will not go to zero since as the singular values σ_k diminish their inverse go to infinity, thereby amplifying the impact of noise.

**EXAMPLE 5.2-2.   *Singular Values Resembling Samples of Transfer Function.*   In this example, the singular vectors of a full-rank square matrix were chosen to behave like sinusoids of increasing frequency. Here we order the singular values not according to their magnitude, but rather according to the frequency of the corresponding singular vector. Since the singular values represent the weight of the SVD modal expansion, we may think of the singular value distribution as analogous to the transfer function of a continuous linear system. The distribution in Fig. 5.2-4(*a*) is akin to a low-pass filter with smallest transfer function around index 85.

As mentioned before, the structure of the singular values will have a rather substantial impact on the stability of reconstruction. As the singular values come closer and closer to zero, the influence of the noise on $\hat{\mathbf{f}}$ grows in a manner out of proportion to the size of the noise itself. More specifically, large-amplitude, high-frequency artifacts become increasingly dominant in the estimates of the object. This type of noise amplification is in fact seen across a broad range of problems, not just this somewhat artificial example, and is the primary characteristic of the ill-posed nature of these inverse problems.

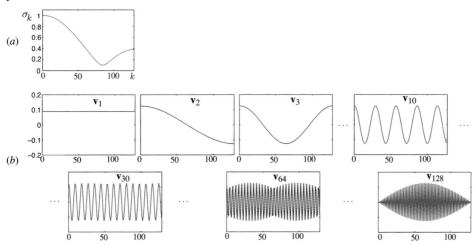

Figure 5.2-4   SVD of the $\mathbf{H}$ matrix in Fig. 5.2-2. (*a*) Singular values σ_k. (*b*) A few of the singular vectors ordered by increasing frequency.

Full-Rank Overdetermined System: Existence

For an overdetermined problem ($M > N$) with $K = N$ nonzero singular values, the singular value matrix Σ takes the form

$$\Sigma = \begin{bmatrix} \Sigma_1 \\ 0 \end{bmatrix} \qquad (5.2\text{-}11)$$

with $\Sigma_1 = \text{diag}\{\sigma_1, \sigma_2, \ldots, \sigma_N\}$ and where for simplicity we assume that all N singular values are nonzero. In terms of the SVD, the imaging equation is $\mathbf{g} = \mathbf{U\Sigma V}^T\mathbf{f} + \mathbf{w}$. Operating on both sides of this equation by $\mathbf{U}^T$, we obtain $\mathbf{U}^T\mathbf{g} = \mathbf{\Sigma V}^T\mathbf{f} + \mathbf{U}^T\mathbf{w}$. Defining $\tilde{\mathbf{f}} = \mathbf{Vf}$, $\tilde{\mathbf{g}} = \mathbf{U}^T\mathbf{g}$ and $\tilde{\mathbf{w}} = \mathbf{U}^T\mathbf{w}$, we have the equivalent problem:

$$\tilde{\mathbf{g}} = \mathbf{\Sigma}\tilde{\mathbf{f}} + \tilde{\mathbf{w}}. \qquad (5.2\text{-}12)$$

For this system, the issue of existence is much clearer. Specifically, by the structure of the matrix Σ, a solution will exist if and only if the last $M - N$ components of the vector $\tilde{\mathbf{g}}$ are exactly zero, a situation not likely to be encountered due to the noise $\tilde{\mathbf{w}}$, which is beyond our control.

Full-Rank Underdetermined System: Uniqueness

For an underdetermined system ($M < N$) with $K = M$ nonzero singular values, the matrix Σ takes the form

$$\Sigma = [\Sigma_1 \quad \mathbf{0}\ ] \qquad (5.2\text{-}13)$$

with $\Sigma_1 = \text{diag}(\sigma_1, \sigma_2, \ldots, \sigma_M)$. In this case, we multiply both sides of the imaging equation by $\mathbf{U}^T$ and define $\tilde{\mathbf{g}} = \mathbf{U}^T\mathbf{g}$, $\tilde{\mathbf{f}} = \mathbf{V}^T\mathbf{f}$, and $\tilde{\mathbf{w}} = \mathbf{V}^T\mathbf{w}$ to obtain (5.2-12). If we take $\tilde{\mathbf{f}}_1$ as the first M elements of $\tilde{\mathbf{f}}$ and $\tilde{\mathbf{f}}_2$ as the remaining $N - M$ components of $\tilde{\mathbf{f}}$, then the noiseless imaging equation takes the form

$$\tilde{\mathbf{g}} = \Sigma_1\tilde{\mathbf{f}}_1 + \mathbf{0}\tilde{\mathbf{f}}_2.$$

In other words, as long as $\tilde{\mathbf{f}}_1 = \Sigma^{-1}\tilde{\mathbf{g}}$, $\tilde{\mathbf{f}}_2$ can be *anything* without impacting the value for $\tilde{\mathbf{g}}$. Hence, the lack of uniqueness in this problem is captured explicitly by the SVD through the identification of $\tilde{\mathbf{f}}_2$ as those degrees freedom whose values have no impact on the $\mathbf{Hf}$ product.

Inversion of a Square Reduced-Rank Matrix: Ill-Posedness

The issue of ill-posedness is quite closely related to those of existence and uniqueness. Keeping with the assumption that $N = M$, let us assume for a moment that, rather than decaying to zero, the singular values were in fact equal to zero for all $k > K$. In this case Σ is of the form

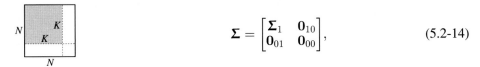

$$\Sigma = \begin{bmatrix} \mathbf{\Sigma}_1 & \mathbf{0}_{10} \\ \mathbf{0}_{01} & \mathbf{0}_{00} \end{bmatrix}, \tag{5.2-14}$$

where $\mathbf{0}_{10}$, $\mathbf{0}_{01}$, $\mathbf{0}_{00}$ are matrices of all zeros and dimensions $K \times (N - K)$, $(N - K) \times K$, and $(N - K) \times (N - K)$, respectively, and $\mathbf{\Sigma}_1 = \mathrm{diag}(\sigma_1, \sigma_2, \ldots, \sigma_k)$. Drawing on the insight provided by (5.2-11) and (5.2-13), we see that (5.2-14) has elements of both nonuniqueness and nonexistence. The bottom block row of zeros implies that in the presence of noise there will generally not be an $\mathbf{f}$ such that $\mathbf{g} = \mathbf{H}\mathbf{f}$. The block of zeros in the upper right block of Σ implies that if we satisfy ourself with ignoring the part of the problem associated with the bottom block of zeros, then the remaining problem is underdetermined, possesses a nullspace, and thus will not have a unique solution.

More generally, one finds that the singular values decay toward zero, but are never exactly equal to zero. In those cases where there is a clear dividing line between "large" and "small" values of σ_k, one could specify an effective K^*, thereby reducing the problem to one where

$$\Sigma = \begin{bmatrix} \mathbf{\Sigma}_1 & \mathbf{0}_{K \times N - K^*} \\ \mathbf{0}_{N - K^* \times K^*} & \mathbf{\Sigma}_{\mathrm{small}} \end{bmatrix}. \tag{5.2-15}$$

Such a system possesses basically the same interpretation as (5.2-14) if one is willing to ignore $\mathbf{\Sigma}_{\mathrm{small}}$. In most cases, however, it is an unfortunate fact that no such clear division exists. Rather, the decay of the singular values is gradual. Such problems do technically admit solutions to the extent that $\hat{\mathbf{f}} = \mathbf{H}^{-1}\mathbf{g}$ exists. However, as we have seen, such solutions will be characterized by noise-induced artifacts caused by the amplification of modes for which σ_k are small, but not easily deemed negligible. Damping out these modes without totally ignoring their contribution is the goal of regularization, to be discussed in Sec. 5.4.

5.3 Pseudo-Inverse

An initial tool used to address the three issues of existence, uniqueness and (to a limited extent) stability is known as the *pseudo-inverse*. It is denoted by the symbol $\mathbf{H}^\dagger$ for the matrix $\mathbf{H}$ and is used to provide the estimate

$$\hat{\mathbf{f}} = \mathbf{H}^\dagger \mathbf{g}. \tag{5.3-1}$$

The pseudo-inverse takes different forms depending on the relations between the dimensions M and N and the rank K of the matrix. In the full-rank case:

Square matrix $(M = N = K)$: $\mathbf{H}^\dagger = \mathbf{H}^{-1}$
Overdetermined case $(M > N = K)$: $\mathbf{H}^\dagger = (\mathbf{H}^T\mathbf{H})^{-1}\mathbf{H}^T$
Underdetermined case $(N > M = K)$: $\mathbf{H}^\dagger = \mathbf{H}^T(\mathbf{H}\mathbf{H}^T)^{-1}$.

In general (arbitrary M, N, K), $\mathbf{H}^\dagger$ is expressed in terms of SVD matrices,

$$\mathbf{H}^\dagger = \mathbf{V}_1 \mathbf{\Sigma}_1^{-1} \mathbf{U}_1^T, \tag{5.3-2}$$

where $\mathbf{\Sigma}_1$ is the $K \times K$ nonzero singular-value submatrix and $\mathbf{U}_1$ and $\mathbf{V}_1$ are the corresponding singular vector submatrices, as defined in Sec. 5.2B and Appendix B. This expression is equivalent to the estimator

$$\hat{\mathbf{f}} = \sum_{k=1}^{K} \frac{1}{\sigma_k} \left(\mathbf{u}_k^{\mathrm{T}} \mathbf{g} \right) \mathbf{v}_k. \tag{5.3-3}$$

Equation (5.3-3) is similar to (5.2-9), except for the limits of the summation. Thus, the pseudo-inverse constructs an estimate $\hat{\mathbf{f}}$ that is quite similar to that which is obtained when $\mathbf{H}$ is invertible, just restricted to the subspaces of $\mathbf{U}$ and $\mathbf{V}$ for which the singular values are nonzero.

■ MATLAB function `pinv(H)` provides the pseudo-inverse of the matrix $\mathbf{H}$.

We now derive the various expressions for pseudo-inverse in each of the different cases separately. Although the results are all remarkably similar, each case highlights different aspects of existence, uniqueness, and stability.

▶ Problem 5.3-1

A. Full-Rank Overdetermined Inverse Problem

As discussed previously in Sec. 5.2A, problems in this class are characterized by an inability to find any $\mathbf{f}$ such that $\mathbf{Hf}$ is equal to the data vector $\mathbf{g}$ because the columns of the $M \times N$ matrix $\mathbf{H}$ with $M > N$ span a subspace of $\mathbb{R}^N$. The pseudo-inverse of $\mathbf{H}$ for this problem is obtained by seeking that $\mathbf{f}$ for which $\mathbf{Hf}$ is as close to $\mathbf{g}$ as is possible. Formally, we have

$$\hat{\mathbf{f}} = \arg \min_{\mathbf{f}} \ \|\mathbf{g} - \mathbf{Hf}\|_2^2. \tag{5.3-4}$$

In Exercise 5.3-2 you are asked to show that the $\hat{\mathbf{f}}$ that solves this minimization problem is

$$\mathbf{H}^{\mathrm{T}} \mathbf{H} \hat{\mathbf{f}} = \mathbf{H}^{\mathrm{T}} \mathbf{g} \quad \rightarrow \quad \hat{\mathbf{f}} = (\mathbf{H}^{\mathrm{T}} \mathbf{H})^{-1} \mathbf{H}^{\mathrm{T}} \mathbf{g}. \tag{5.3-5}$$

The linear system to the left of the arrow in (5.3-5) is known as the *normal equations* and the $\hat{\mathbf{f}}$ solving this system is known as the *linear least-squares* solution to the overdetermined problem. From (5.3-5) it follows that

$$\mathbf{H}^{\dagger} = (\mathbf{H}^{\mathrm{T}} \mathbf{H})^{-1} \mathbf{H}^{\mathrm{T}}. \tag{5.3-6}$$

Pseudo-Inverse
(Overdetermined System)

Note that $\mathbf{H}^{\dagger} \mathbf{H} = \mathbf{I}$.

By substituting the SVD of the matrix $\mathbf{H}$ into the right-hand side of (5.3-6) and recalling that $\mathbf{V} \mathbf{V}^{\mathrm{T}} = \mathbf{V}^{\mathrm{T}} \mathbf{V} = \mathbf{I}$ and $\mathbf{U} \mathbf{U}^{\mathrm{T}} = \mathbf{U}^{\mathrm{T}} \mathbf{U} = \mathbf{I}$, it can be shown that $\mathbf{H}^{\dagger} = \mathbf{V} \mathbf{\Sigma}^{\dagger} \mathbf{U}^{\mathrm{T}}$ and

$$\hat{\mathbf{f}} = \mathbf{V}\boldsymbol{\Sigma}^{\dagger}\mathbf{U}^{\mathrm{T}}\mathbf{g} = \sum_{k=1}^{N}\frac{1}{\sigma_{k}}\left(\mathbf{u}_{k}^{\mathrm{T}}\mathbf{g}\right)\mathbf{v}_{k},$$

(5.3-7)
SVD Reconstruction
(Overdetermined System)

where $\boldsymbol{\Sigma}^{\dagger} = \begin{bmatrix} \boldsymbol{\Sigma}_{1}^{-1} & \mathbf{0} \end{bmatrix}$ and $\boldsymbol{\Sigma}_{1}$ is the diagonal matrix holding the singular values of $\mathbf{H}$.

▶ Problem 5.3-2

B. Full-Rank Underdetermined Inverse Problems

As discussed in Sec. 5.2A, the primary issue in the underdetermined case is the presence of the nullspace for the matrix $\mathbf{H}$ so that many $\mathbf{f}$ vectors exist such that $\mathbf{Hf} = \mathbf{g}$. As in the previous section, the pseudo-inverse is constructed by defining $\hat{\mathbf{f}}$ as the solution to an optimization problem. Here, however, the problem is to select the *smallest* $\mathbf{f}$ that is consistent with the data, i.e.,

$$\hat{\mathbf{f}} = \arg\min_{\mathbf{f}} \|\mathbf{f}\|_{2}^{2}, \quad \text{subject to} \quad \mathbf{Hf} = \mathbf{g}. \tag{5.3-8}$$

The solution to (5.3-8) is called the *minimum-norm* (or just *min-norm*) solution to the underdetermined, full-rank problem $\mathbf{Hf} = \mathbf{g}$.

To solve this optimization problem, we write any $\mathbf{f} \in \mathbb{R}^{N}$ that solves $\mathbf{Hf} = \mathbf{g}$ as the unique sum of two components: $\mathbf{f}_{n} \in \mathrm{N}(\mathbf{H})$ and a second piece $\mathbf{f}_{r} \in \mathrm{N}^{\perp}(\mathbf{H}) = \mathrm{R}(\mathbf{H}^{\mathrm{T}})$. That $\mathbf{f}$ with no component in the nullspace of $\mathbf{H}$ is the solution to (5.3-8). Because the remaining part of the solution $\mathbf{f}_{r}$ lies in the range of $\mathbf{H}^{\mathrm{T}}$, we have $\mathbf{f}_{r} = \mathbf{H}^{\mathrm{T}}\mathbf{x}$ for some vector $\mathbf{x} \in \mathbb{R}^{M}$. Thus, $\mathbf{g} = \mathbf{HH}^{\mathrm{T}}\mathbf{x}$ so that $\mathbf{x} = (\mathbf{HH}^{\mathrm{T}})^{-1}\mathbf{g}$ and finally

$$\hat{\mathbf{f}} = \mathbf{H}^{\mathrm{T}}(\mathbf{HH}^{\mathrm{T}})^{-1}\mathbf{g} \tag{5.3-9}$$

is the solution to (5.3-8). Assuming $\mathbf{H}$ has full row rank, the inverse in (5.3-9) must exist and the solution is unique. Also, from (5.3-9) we see that the pseudo-inverse of $\mathbf{H}$ for the underdetermined full-rank problem is

$$\mathbf{H}^{\dagger} = \mathbf{H}^{\mathrm{T}}(\mathbf{HH}^{\mathrm{T}})^{-1}. \tag{5.3-10}$$

Pseudo-Inverse
(Underdetermined System)

Again, plugging the SVD of $\mathbf{H}$ in (5.3-10) yields the now-familiar formula

$$\hat{\mathbf{f}} = \mathbf{V}\boldsymbol{\Sigma}^{\dagger}\mathbf{U}^{\mathrm{T}}\mathbf{g} = \sum_{k=1}^{M}\frac{1}{\sigma_{k}}\left(\mathbf{u}_{k}^{\mathrm{T}}\mathbf{g}\right)\mathbf{v}_{k}.$$

(5.3-11)
SVD Reconstruction
(Underdetermined System)

Note that the only difference between this version of the pseudo-inverse and the one in (5.3-7) is the range for k in the summation.

▶ Problem 5.3-3

C. Reduced Rank Problems

In the most general case where there are $K < \min(M, N)$ nonzero singular values, Σ is of the form

$$\Sigma = \begin{bmatrix} \Sigma_1 & 0_{10} \\ 0_{01} & 0_{00} \end{bmatrix} \qquad (5.3\text{-}12)$$

with $\Sigma = \mathrm{diag}(\sigma_1, \sigma_2, \ldots, \sigma_K)$ and the sizes of the zero block are dependent on the value of K and whether $M < N$, $M > N$, or $M = N$. The SVD of $\mathbf{H}$ is now written as

$$\mathbf{H} = [\mathbf{U}_1 \ \mathbf{U}_0] \begin{bmatrix} \Sigma_1 & 0_{10} \\ 0_{01} & 0_{00} \end{bmatrix} \begin{bmatrix} \mathbf{V}_1^\mathsf{T} \\ \mathbf{V}_0^\mathsf{T} \end{bmatrix}. \qquad (5.3\text{-}13)$$

Following the discussion on page 207, the bottom block row of Σ indicates that in general $\mathbf{g}$ will not be in the range of $\mathbf{H}$. The upper right block of zeros shows that even if $\mathbf{g}$ were in (or were made to be in) $R(\mathbf{H})$, there would still be a nullspace to the problem so nonuniqueness would be an issue. Because this class of problems is a blend of that seen in the previous two subsections, it should come as no surprise that the pseudo-inverse is derived using elements of both previous cases.

To be more precise, $\hat{\mathbf{f}}$ here is obtained as the min-norm solution to the linear problem where the data $\mathbf{g}$ is projected into the range of $\mathbf{H}$. Formally, we have

$$\hat{\mathbf{f}} = \arg\min_{\mathbf{f}} \ \|\mathbf{f}\|_2^2 \quad \text{subject to} \quad \mathbf{Hf} = P_{R(\mathbf{H})}\mathbf{g}. \qquad (5.3\text{-}14)$$

Using the methods from Sec. 5.3B and Sec. 5.3C, the unique solution to (5.3-14) is $\hat{\mathbf{f}} = \mathbf{H}^\dagger \mathbf{g}$ with

$$\mathbf{H}^\dagger = \mathbf{V}_1 \Sigma_1^{-1} \mathbf{U}_1^\mathsf{T}, \qquad (5.3\text{-}15)$$

Pseudo-Inverse
(Reduced Rank)

or equivalently

$$\hat{\mathbf{f}} = \mathbf{V}\Sigma^\dagger \mathbf{U}^\mathsf{T}\mathbf{g} = \sum_{k=1}^{K} \frac{1}{\sigma_k} \left(\mathbf{u}_k^\mathsf{T}\mathbf{g}\right) \mathbf{v}_k, \qquad (5.3\text{-}16)$$

SVD Reconstruction
(Reduced Rank)

just as before.

The preceding results may be shown by noting that $P_{R(\mathbf{H})} = \mathbf{U}_1\mathbf{U}_1^\mathsf{T}$ and that the solution of (5.3-14) must be of the form $\mathbf{V}_1\mathbf{x}$, where $\mathbf{x}$ satisfies

$$\mathbf{H}\mathbf{V}_1\mathbf{x} = \mathbf{U}_1\mathbf{U}_1^\mathsf{T}\mathbf{g},$$

from which we obtain $\mathbf{x} = \Sigma_1^{-1}\mathbf{U}_1^\mathsf{T}\mathbf{g}$, which yields (5.3-15).

D. Examples and Applications

To illustrate the performance of the pseudo-inverse and motivate the need for additional work in stabilizing the solution to the linear inverse problem, we consider here two examples.

EXAMPLE 5.3-1.   *Limited-View Ray Tomography.*   We reconsider here the ray tomography example discussed in Example 4.1-2. Specifically, we seek to find better reconstructions of the phantom object shown in Fig. 4.1-11 from a limited amount of ray tomographic data (Fig. 5.3-1). The region of interest is taken to be a square whose sides are all 1 m in length. The data are acquired over an aperture extending from $45°$ to $135°$ where we collect 20 projections, each of which is sampled 50 times. Following the discussion in Sec. 5.1C, we use a pixel basis for representing $f(\mathbf{r})$ with 41 pixels in each direction so that we have a total of $41^2 = 1681$ unknowns to be recovered. Because of the geometry of the problem, not all samples of all projections intersect the grid of pixels. Eliminating these from the data set reduces the number of data points from 1000 to 876. Thus we have an underdetermined problem.

Before examining the pseudo-inverse results, some insight can be gained from exploring the structure of the SVD for this problem. In Fig. 5.3-2, the singular values are plotted on a logarithmic scale. Here we notice first that there are in fact 876 nonzero singular values. Thus, numerically at least, the matrix is full rank and we can use the pseudo-inverse of Sec. 5.3B to compute the reconstruction. This, though, will cause problems, because while there are no singular values that are exactly zero, there are 16 that are less than 10^{-16} in magnitude. Referring to the discussion surrounding (5.2-9), we expect that these singular values will greatly amplify the noise in the data. Specifically, the $\mathbf{v}_k$ *modes* associated with small singular values will dominate the solution.

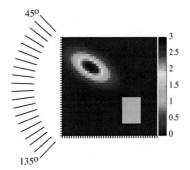

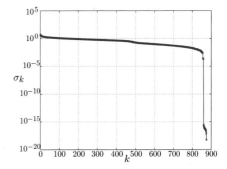

Figure 5.3-1   Original 41×41 pixel object imaged via 20 projections between $45°$ to $135°$.

Figure 5.3-2   Singular values of the $\mathbf{H}$ matrix for the ray tomography example.

To better understand the structure of the $\mathbf{v}_k$, we plot a few in Fig. 5.3-3. To interpret these images, recall from Sec. 5.1A that the vector $\mathbf{f}$ represents a *stacked-up* (lexicographically converted) version of the pixels or samples in the image we are seeking to recover. Thus, by *unstacking* $\mathbf{f}$ we can build an array that takes the form of an image, providing an image of the object. Now, according to (5.2-9), our estimate of $\mathbf{f}$ is obtained as a linear combination of $\mathbf{v}_k$. In Fig. 5.3-3, we show specifically the unstacked $\mathbf{v}_k$ images associated with singular values $k = 1, 10, 300,$ and 870. As was the case with the 1D example in Sec. 5.2A, as the index of the singular value increases, the structure of the associated singular vector grows increasingly oscillatory. Indeed, for index $k = 870$ (whose singular value is in the really small range), $\mathbf{v}_k$ looks essentially random. Thus, adding a substantial factor of this component to the reconstruction will severely degrade the quality of the reconstruction because the large factor $1/\sigma_{870}$ will amplify the noise in the data.

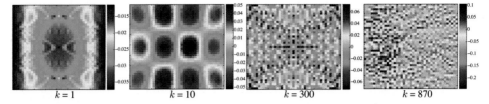

$k = 1$ $k = 10$ $k = 300$ $k = 870$

Figure 5.3-3   Samples of singular vectors (images) for the limited data X-ray tomography example.

The results of applying the pseudo-inverse to both noise-free data and data to which a small amount of noise is present are provided in Fig. 5.3-4. Evidently, when the data are noise-free, the pseudo-inverse yields a reconstruction that is more accurate than that provided by filtered back-projection [shown in Fig. 4.1-11(d)]. In the presence of even a small amount of noise, though, the problems with the pseudo-inverse become readily apparent. Indeed, the results in Fig. 5.3-4(c) bear no resemblance to the true object. The amplification by the noise of singular vectors like $\mathbf{v}_{870}$ is evident both in the random structure of this image and the amplitude of the pixels, which is far from that of truth.

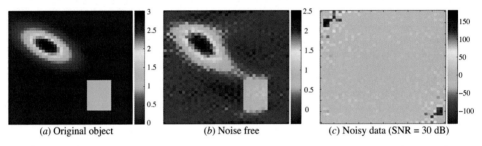

(a) Original object   (b) Noise free   (c) Noisy data (SNR = 30 dB)

Figure 5.3-4   Pseudo-inverse reconstruction for the limited-data ray tomography example.

EXAMPLE 5.3-2.   *Wave Tomography.*   Here we consider the use of the pseudo-inverse for solving a limited-data linearized inverse scattering problem in connection with wave tomography. The results are demonstrated for probe waves at two frequencies. The object, shown in Fig. 5.3-5(a), is assumed to reside in a square region with sides of length 1 m. Along the left side of the region we place 10 transmitters, while 10 receivers are arrayed along the right side [Fig. 5.3-5(b)] in a cross-well radar (CWR) configuration. Thus, we have 100 transmitter–receiver pairs. Since wave tomography is based on measurement of the complex amplitudes, a total of 200 pieces of data (the real and imaginary parts of each measurement) are provided to the inversion algorithms. Assuming no loss, the wavenumber k in (5.1-28) is simply $k = \omega/c = 2\pi\nu/c$. We consider two reconstructions: one at $\nu = 300$ MHz (corresponding to a free-space wavelength of 1 m) and the other at $\nu = 10$ GHz (corresponding to a free-space wavelength of 3 cm), called hereafter the low- and high-frequency reconstructions, respectively.

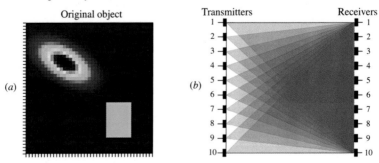

Figure 5.3-5   (a) Original 1 m × 1 m object. (b) Imaging by use of 10 transmitters and 10 receivers.

In Fig. 5.3-6, we plot the singular values for the low- and high-frequency matrices based on the Born approximation. Unlike the ray tomography case, we see that there is no clear break between *large* and *small* singular values. Indeed, for both cases here, we see a slow and continuous decrease in the singular values. One notable distinction between the high and low-frequency problems is the rate of decay. Qualitatively at least, the singular values for the high-frequency problem appear to fall off a bit more slowly than they do for the low-frequency matrix.

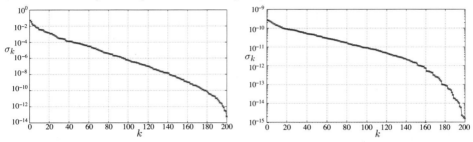

Figure 5.3-6   Singular-value spectrum for the wave tomography examples: (*a*) low frequency; (*b*) high frequency.

The impact of this decay is all the more important when examining the singular-vector "images" for the two cases in Figs. 5.3-7 and 5.3-8. As with the X-ray case in Example 5.3-1, large singular values tend to be associated with less oscillatory singular vectors. In contrasting the high- and low-frequency problems, though, we notice (again qualitatively), for the same index, the singular vectors for the high-frequency example are more oscillatory than the low-frequency case. Coupled with the fact that the associated singular values are relatively larger for the high frequency problem, we therefore expect that we will be able to more stably recover high spatial frequency structure using the high frequency sensing system. In other words, this analysis of the singular value and singular vector structure for the two sensing problems supports the idea that high-frequency probing leads to improved ability to recover high-frequency (i.e., fine scale) detail.

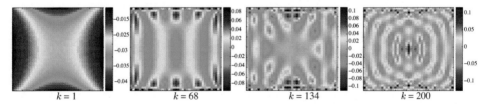

Figure 5.3-7   Samples of singular-vector "images" for the low-frequency wave tomography example.

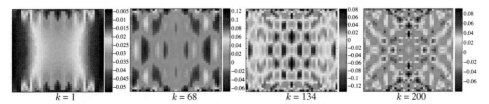

Figure 5.3-8   Samples of singular-vector "images" for the high-frequency wave tomography example.

This intuition is in fact borne out by the pseudo-inverse results shown in Figs. 5.3-9 and 5.3-10. In both cases, the smooth structure in the upper left corner of the image is pretty well captured; however, the high-frequency reconstruction does a significantly better job in recovering the edges of the block in the lower right portion of the image. As edges are inherently high spatial frequency structures, the advantage of using high temporal frequency probes is readily apparent. Finally, observe that, as was the case with the ray tomography problem, the pseudo-inverse performs quite poorly when presented with noise in the data. Again, the noise only serves to amplify the spatial structure from the singular vectors associated with small singular values. Indeed, comparing Figs. 5.3-9(b) and 5.3-10(b) with the singular-vector plots in Fig. 5.3-7(d) and 5.3-8(d) we can easily see the presence of $\mathbf{v}_{200}$ in both noisy-data pseudo-inverse reconstructions.

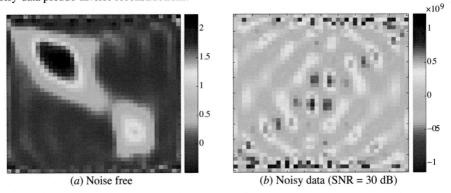

(a) Noise free   (b) Noisy data (SNR = 30 dB)

Figure 5.3-9   Pseudo-inverse reconstruction for the low-frequency wave tomography example: (a) Noise free; (b) Noisy data (SNR = 30 dB).

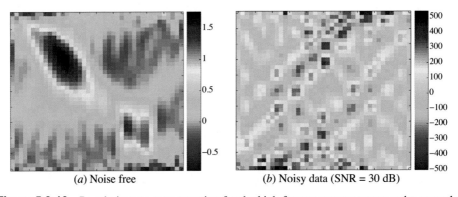

(a) Noise free   (b) Noisy data (SNR = 30 dB)

Figure 5.3-10   Pseudo-inverse reconstruction for the high-frequency wave tomography example: (a) Noise free; (b) Noisy data (SNR = 30 dB).

▶ Problems 5.3-4–5.3-6

5.4   Regularization

As indicated by the examples in the last section, although the pseudo-inverse works quite well when noise is absent, it can lead to severely degraded reconstructions in the presence of noise. This lack of robustness is directly related to the manner in which the pseudo-inverse treats the singular values. No matter how small a singular value is, as long as it is not zero, its associated mode is included in the reconstruction. This introduces large noise amplification that makes the reconstruction highly susceptible to small noise. This suggests one obvious modification to the pseudo-inverse: eliminate the contribution of singular values whose size is less than some predetermined threshold. The resulting approach opens the door to a sequence of **regularization** approaches for adding more robustness to inversion than is available from the conventional pseudo-inverse.

A. Truncated Singular-Value Decomposition

As we just indicated, perhaps the most obvious way of moving past the strict definition of the pseudo-inverse is to ignore the contribution from singular values that can safely be regarded as small. That is we define the truncated singular-value decomposition (TSVD) reconstruction as

$$\hat{\mathbf{f}} = \sum_{k=1}^{k_0} \frac{1}{\sigma_k} \left(\mathbf{u}_k^{\mathrm{T}} \mathbf{g} \right) \mathbf{v}_k,$$

(5.4-1)
TSVD Reconstruction

where k_0 is known as a *regularization parameter*. Its presence here represents a fairly major philosophical departure in inversion schemes from what we have so far been discussing. Exact inverse methods and the pseudo-inverse all derive their structures entirely from the physics of the sensing modality. With the introduction of k_0 here we now have a means of controlling the inverse procedure that is independent of the physics, i.e., is entirely user defined. While a number of somewhat rigorous techniques for algorithmically selecting regularization parameters have been developed in the literature on inverse problems, none is perfect, and in most practical cases some level of user intervention is really required to choose the *best* parameter.

The advantages of the TSVD are its ease of implementation and its strong performance for problems where the choice of k_0 is not difficult. Specifically, we would expect that the TSVD would perform best when a clear distinction can be made between significant and negligible singular values. For problems whose singular values decay gradually, as in Fig. 5.3-6, no obvious threshold exists. Hence, choosing k_0 becomes a more delicate, perhaps subjective, exercise. Such problems highlight the primary shortcoming of the TSVD: much like the pseudo-inverse, the contributions of the subspaces of $\mathbf{U}$ and $\mathbf{V}$ associated with the truncated singular values are completely absent from $\hat{\mathbf{f}}$. Thus, any important information contained in these subspaces is also lost. To address this issue requires a procedure in which these subspaces are allowed to play a limited role in the structure of $\hat{\mathbf{f}}$. However, their impact must be controlled to avoid the noise amplification issue seen with the pseudo-inverse.

B. Spectral Filtering

A first step in this process is again a somewhat natural approach to extending the pseudo-inverse and indeed the TSVD. We can view the TSVD as a windowing of the singular values of $\mathbf{H}$ where the window is either 1 for $1 \leq k \leq k_0$ and 0 for $k > k_0$. To moderate the impact of this sharp cutoff, we can construct inversion schemes using more general window functions:

$$\hat{\mathbf{f}} = \sum_{k=1}^{\min(M,N)} \frac{w_k}{\sigma_k} \left(\mathbf{u}_k^{\mathrm{T}} \mathbf{g} \right) \mathbf{v}_k,$$

(5.4-2)
Weighted TSVD

where w_k defines the weight given to each singular value. Thus, by appropriately designing w_k, we now have a mechanism for including in a controlled manner information from all components of $\mathbf{U}$ and $\mathbf{V}$.

A few examples of window functions are:

Flat top window:

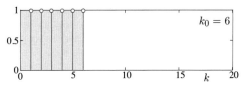

$$w_k = \begin{cases} 1 & k \le k_0 \\ 0 & k > k_0 \end{cases}, \qquad (5.4\text{-}3)$$

This window is identical to the TSVD.

Triangular window:

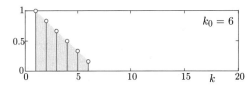

$$w_k = \begin{cases} 1 - \frac{k-1}{k_0} & k \le k_0 \\ 0 & k > k_0, \end{cases}, \qquad (5.4\text{-}4)$$

Exponential window:

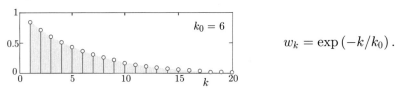

$$w_k = \exp\left(-k/k_0\right). \qquad (5.4\text{-}5)$$

It can be shown that, in all cases, as $k_0 \to \infty$ $w_k \to 1$ for all k.

Singular-value-dependent window.   Perhaps the most important window function we will encounter is fundamentally different from the above three in that its structure is dependent on the singular values in the following manner:

$$w_k = \frac{\sigma_k^2}{\sigma_k^2 + \lambda}, \qquad (5.4\text{-}6)$$

where λ is a regularization parameter playing the role of $1/k_0$. If σ_k is a monotonic decreasing function of k, then the weight w_k is a monotonic decreasing function of k, which reaches the value $1/2$ when $\sigma_k^2 = \lambda$.

The impact on the reconstruction is most clearly seen by substituting (5.4-6) into (5.4-2) to arrive at

$$\hat{\mathbf{f}} = \sum_k \frac{\sigma_k}{\sigma_k^2 + \lambda} \left(\mathbf{u}_k^{\mathsf{T}} \mathbf{g}\right) \mathbf{v}_k. \qquad (5.4\text{-}7)$$

From (5.4-7) we see that, as $\sigma_k \to 0$, the weight provided that mode in the reconstruction also goes to zero, as it should. By the same token, when σ_k is large relative to the regularization parameter λ,

$$\frac{\sigma_k}{\sigma_k^2 + \lambda} \to \frac{1}{\sigma_k},$$

indicating that such contributions to $\hat{\mathbf{f}}$ are treated in the same manner here as in the pseudo-inverse.

C. Tikhonov Inversion

The TSVD and spectral filtering methods both approach the problem of improved robustness to noise in terms of modifications to the matrix $\mathbf{H}$; specifically, its singular-value structure. An alternate idea (and one which we shall see is more closely related to windowing than one might first think) comes from thinking about the problem in terms of properties of $\mathbf{f}$. Looking at the inversion results in Figs. 5.3-9 and 5.3-10, we see that the artifacts produced by the pseudo-inverse come in the form of large-amplitude, high-frequency corruption in $\hat{\mathbf{f}}$. In most applications, however, we have prior expectations or even hard constraints on the behavior of the unknown object. In the case of X-ray tomography, for example, $\mathbf{f}$ is the density of the material being scanned and hence cannot assume negative values. In geophysics problems and certain classes of nondestructive evaluation problems, one model for the subsurface is a collection of layers with more or less constant properties (sound speed, electrical conductivity, etc.). In cases where properties do vary spatially in addition to non-negativity, one would expect gradual variations in some range of bounded amplitudes. In other words, even if we did not know the true distributions of $\mathbf{f}$, the results in Figs. 5.3-9 and 5.3-10 would still be rejected for being not natural, not in line with our prior expectations concerning how $\mathbf{f}$ should behave.

The issue we face, then, is how to incorporate this prior information into the inversion process in some quantitative way. While there are many mathematical methods for achieving this objective, we concentrate here on the most widely used. Specifically, one way to quantify the notion that the amplitude of $\mathbf{f}$ should not be large is to say that $\|\mathbf{f}\|_2^2 = \mathbf{f}^T\mathbf{f}$ should be small. Similarly, the highly oscillatory artifacts are manifest in the size not of $\mathbf{f}$, but of its derivative, or gradient, in multiple dimensions. To make this clearer, recall that the derivative of $\sin(\omega x)$ is $\omega \cos(\omega x)$. So, the higher the frequency ω is, the larger is the derivative. Constraining these oscillations amounts to a restriction on the $\|\mathbf{Df}\|_2^2$, where $\mathbf{D}$ is a matrix approximation to the gradient. Overall, the general form of regularization we consider here is $\|\mathbf{Lf}\|_2^2$. If we take $\mathbf{L} = \mathbf{I}$ we recover amplitude regularization, while the choice $\mathbf{L} = \mathbf{D}$ gives us a regularizer designed to create smooth reconstructions.

The question now is how to incorporate this mathematical prior information into an inversion scheme. We note that we really have two pieces of *information* now for the inverse problem. First, we have the data from the sensor $\mathbf{g}$ as well as the matrix $\mathbf{H}$, which represents the linear system, and we expect for good estimates that $\mathbf{g} \approx \mathbf{H\hat{f}}$. That is, owing to noise in the data and other inaccuracies, $\mathbf{H\hat{f}}$ will not be *exactly* equal to $\mathbf{g}$, but only an approximation. Another way of stating this is that $\mathbf{g} - \mathbf{H\hat{f}}$ is to be small in some suitable sense. The most common measure of smallness is that $\|\mathbf{g} - \mathbf{H\hat{f}}\|_2^2$ should be small. Second, we know that our prior expectations have been captured mathematically by the idea that $\|\mathbf{L\hat{f}}\|_2^2$ should also be small. To bring these two objectives together, we define $\hat{\mathbf{f}}$ as the solution of an optimization problem involving both sources of information:

$$\hat{\mathbf{f}} = \underset{\mathbf{f}}{\arg\min} \ \|\mathbf{g} - \mathbf{Hf}\|_2^2 + \lambda\|\mathbf{Lf}\|_2^2, \qquad (5.4\text{-}8)$$

where λ is again a regularization parameter. Choosing λ to be close to zero implies that the data play a much larger role than the prior information in defining $\hat{\mathbf{f}}$. As $\lambda \to \infty$, the prior dominates and the impact the data is diminished. In the case where $\mathbf{L} = \mathbf{I}$, this approach for determining $\hat{\mathbf{f}}$ is known as *Tikhonov regularization*. For $\mathbf{L}$ different from the identity, we refer to the method as generalized Tikhonov.

To solve (5.4-8) we note that we can write this equation equivalently as

$$\hat{\mathbf{f}} = \underset{\mathbf{f}}{\arg\min} \; \|\tilde{\mathbf{g}} - \tilde{\mathbf{H}}\mathbf{f}\|_2^2, \tag{5.4-9}$$

where

$$\tilde{\mathbf{g}} = \begin{bmatrix} \mathbf{g} \\ \mathbf{0} \end{bmatrix} \qquad \tilde{\mathbf{H}} = \begin{bmatrix} \mathbf{H} \\ \sqrt{\lambda}\mathbf{L} \end{bmatrix}. \tag{5.4-10}$$

Equation (5.4-9), though, is of the same form as the linear least-squares problem in (5.3-4), where the data vector and system matrix have been augmented to include the regularizer. We know the solution of this problem to be

$$\hat{\mathbf{f}} = \left(\tilde{\mathbf{H}}^{\mathrm{T}}\tilde{\mathbf{H}}\right)^{-1}\tilde{\mathbf{H}}^{\mathrm{T}}\tilde{\mathbf{g}} = \left(\mathbf{H}^{\mathrm{T}}\mathbf{H} + \lambda \mathbf{L}^{\mathrm{T}}\mathbf{L}\right)^{-1}\mathbf{H}^{\mathrm{T}}\mathbf{g}. \tag{5.4-11}$$

The analysis of Tikhonov regularization, $\mathbf{L} = \mathbf{I}$, is both straightforward (using the SVD of $\mathbf{H}$) and interesting. For simplicity, let us assume that $\mathbf{H}$ is of full rank with more rows than columns. We then have

$$\mathbf{H}^{\mathrm{T}}\mathbf{H} = \mathbf{V}\boldsymbol{\Sigma}_1^2\mathbf{V}^{\mathrm{T}} \quad \text{and} \quad \mathbf{I} = \mathbf{V}\mathbf{V}^{\mathrm{T}}.$$

Substitution into (5.4-11) gives

$$\hat{\mathbf{f}} = \left[\mathbf{V}\boldsymbol{\Sigma}_1^2\mathbf{V}^{\mathrm{T}} + \lambda\mathbf{V}\mathbf{V}^{\mathrm{T}}\right]^{-1}\mathbf{V}\boldsymbol{\Sigma}\mathbf{U}^{\mathrm{T}}\mathbf{g}$$

$$= \left[\mathbf{V}\left(\boldsymbol{\Sigma}_1^2 + \lambda\mathbf{I}\right)\mathbf{V}^{\mathrm{T}}\right]^{-1}\mathbf{V}\boldsymbol{\Sigma}\mathbf{U}^{\mathrm{T}}\mathbf{g}$$

$$= \mathbf{V}\left(\boldsymbol{\Sigma}_1^2 + \lambda\mathbf{I}\right)^{-1}\boldsymbol{\Sigma}_1\mathbf{U}\mathbf{g}. \tag{5.4-12}$$

Expanding (5.4-12) and taking advantage of the diagonal structure of $\boldsymbol{\Sigma}_1$ and $\mathbf{I}$ gives

$$\hat{\mathbf{f}} = \sum_k \frac{\sigma_k}{\sigma_k^2 + \lambda}(\mathbf{u}_k^{\mathrm{T}}\mathbf{g})\mathbf{v}_k, \tag{5.4-13}$$

Tikhanov-regularized
SVD Reconstruction

which is precisely the result we obtained using the singular-value-dependent window function in (5.4-7). Thus, we conclude that while Tikhonov regularization with an identity matrix was motivated by a desire to constrain the amplitude of the reconstruction, mathematically, this approach to inversion is identical to a specific instance of spectral windowing.

D. Examples and Applications

We now revisit the ray and wave tomography examples of Sec. 5.3D, looking this time at the utility of TSVD and Tikhonov regularization methods. In the case of Tikhonov, we choose as $\mathbf{L}$ the identity matrix. As we discussed in the previous section, when considering regularization methods, there is always the need to choose the value of the regularization parameter. In the case of TSVD, the parameter is the number of singular values to retain in the reconstruction, while λ must be selected for Tikhonov inversion. As we are considering purely synthetic examples where we know the true

$\mathbf{f}$, here we look at the error $\|\mathbf{f} - \hat{\mathbf{f}}\|_2$ as a function of the regularization parameter and display the reconstruction that provides the smallest error for all values of the parameter considered. In practice, where the true $\mathbf{f}$ is not known, one must resort to another method for selecting the "best" parameter.[1] Finally, because the primary failing of the pseudo-inverse was seen to be the processing of noisy data, here we concentrate specifically on this case. Specifically, the noise, $\mathbf{w}$ in (5.2-1), is taken to be a vector of independent, zero mean Gaussian random variables with identical variance, σ_w^2. The variance is selected such that the signal-to-noise ratio for each data set is 30 dB.

As described in the following ray tomography and wave tomography examples, both the TSVD and Tikhonov methods yield reconstructions under noisy conditions that are vastly superior to those that were obtained using the pseudo-inverse.

EXAMPLE 5.4-1.   *Limited-View Ray Tomography.*   The regularization results for the limited-view ray tomography Example 5.3-1 are shown in Fig. 5.4-1.

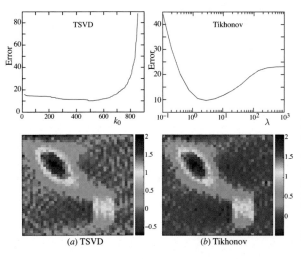

(a) TSVD   (b) Tikhonov

Figure 5.4-1 Regularized reconstruction applied to the limited-view ray tomography example. (*a*) TSVD method. Error dependence on the number of retained singular vectors k_0 (up) and minimum-error reconstruction (down). (*b*) Tikhonov method. Dependence of error on the Tikhonov regularization parameter λ (up) and minimum-error reconstruction (down).

Comparing Fig. 5.4-1 with the results of using filtered backprojection on noisy data in Fig. 5.3-4, we notice that the shapes of the objects are much better preserved, although the amplitudes for both the TSVD and Tikhonov cases are underestimated. For example, the maximum amplitude of the smooth structure in the top right portion of the image is about two as compared with the true value of three. This is typical of regularized reconstructions. We also note that the number of singular vectors used in the minimum-error TSVD reconstruction is about 510. The 510th singular value is about 0.16. This is within a factor of two or so of the noise standard deviation, $\sigma_w = 0.07$, for this example. Again, this is typical of Tikhonov inverse problems. As a rule of thumb, for problems where the noise is additive and Gaussian with zero mean the same variance for all elements of $\mathbf{w}$, the "best" regularization parameter tends to be close to the noise standard deviation.

EXAMPLE 5.4-2.   *Wave Tomography.*   In examining both the results of the low- and high-frequency wave tomography examples shown in Fig. 5.4-2 and Fig. 5.4-3, most all of the observations noted in the previous paragraph hold here as well. In line with the discussion of these problems in Sec. 5.3D, we also note that the low-frequency problem provides lower resolution reconstructions. The two recovered objects are more blurred for the low-frequency example than the high-frequency case. As was noted previously, the singular structure for the high-frequency matrix tended to be more

---

[1]C. R. Vogel, *Computational Methods for Inverse Problems*, Vol. FR23, SIAM, 2002.

oscillatory than that of the low-frequency matrix. This is reflected most strongly in the high-frequency TSVD reconstruction in which the lowest error estimate possessed more of the high spatial frequency artifacts that so corrupted the pseudo-inverse results.

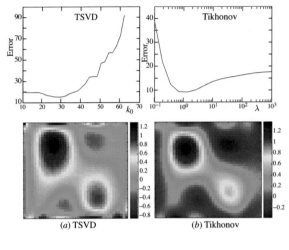

Figure 5.4-2 Regularized reconstruction applied to the low-frequency wave tomography example. (a) TSVD method. Error dependence on the number of retained singular vectors k_0 (up) and minimum-error reconstruction (down). (b) Tikhonov method. Dependence of error on the Tikhonov regularization parameter λ (up) and minimum-error reconstruction (down).

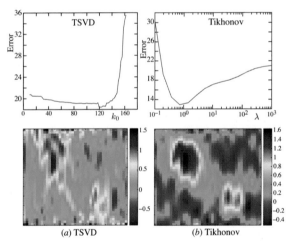

Figure 5.4-3 Regularized reconstruction applied to the high-frequency wave tomography example. (a) TSVD method. Error dependence on number of retained singular vectors k_0 (up) and minimum-error reconstruction (down). (b) Tikhonov method. Dependence of error on the Tikhonov regularization parameters λ (up) and minimum-error reconstruction (down).

EXAMPLE 5.4-3.   *Diffuse Optical Tomography.* In Fig. 5.4-4, inversion results are plotted for a diffuse optical tomography (DOT) problem using the same f as in the previous two examples. Here we are considering a linearized DOT problem with 10 optical sources equally spaced across the top of a 4 cm × 4 cm region and 10 detectors across the bottom. Two modulation frequencies are employed: $\Omega_1 = 0$ Hz and $\Omega_2 = 70$ MHz. The background medium is homogeneous with a nominal optical absorption of 0.05 cm^{-1} and a reduced scattering coefficient of 10 cm^{-1}. Both the geometry of the sensors and the properties of the medium are representative of a breast cancer imaging application. For this problem, the best results of both the TSVD and Tikhonov inversion methods are comparable. They resemble the smooth images produced in the low-frequency electromagnetic (EM) case as opposed to the more detailed reconstructions provided by the high-frequency EM and X-ray examples. Indeed, such results are typical of DOT reconstructions even when more sophisticated nonlinear inversion methods are employed. The diffusive nature of the physics underlying DOT makes this an extremely ill-posed problem. In a sense, the physics here, more than in the other examples, acts as a severe spatial low-pass filter. Thus, DOT is inherently a low-resolution imaging modality. Its utility is derived from the functional nature of the information it can convey which is not available from higher resolution modalities such as X-ray, which provide primarily structural information. Thus, since the middle 2000s there has been considerable effort in combining (or fusing) DOT with CT, magnetic resonance imaging (MRI), or other high-resolution modalities.

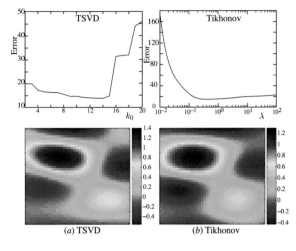

Figure 5.4-4 Regularized reconstruction applied to the DOT example. (*a*) TSVD method. Error dependence on number of retained singular vectors k_0 (up) and minimum-error reconstruction (down). (*b*) Tikhonov method. Dependence of error on the Tikhonov regularization parameter λ (up) and minimum-error reconstruction (down).

▶ Problems 5.4-1–5.4-4

5.5   Iterative Inversion

There are two main reasons for considering iterative techniques in the solution of inverse problems. The first, and perhaps most important, reason is computational. Large problems are often encountered in subsurface imaging and direct solutions of these problems require prohibitively large memory and computational resources. The second reason for considering iterative solution techniques is that iterative methods of solving the *unregularized* problem typically have a regularizing effect when terminated long *before convergence*. Thus, iterative solution methods can provide an efficient regularization method in their own right. We discuss each of these points below.

A. Iterative Methods

The first interest in iterative methods is computational. For problems of large size, as encountered in applications such as 3D X-ray tomography or geophysical inversion, the size of the matrices $\mathbf{H}$ and $\mathbf{L}$ in the discretized problems [see (5.4-11)] can be extremely large. For example, it is not unusual in a 3D medical tomography problem to have $512^3 \approx 10^8$ variables, and a corresponding matrix $\mathbf{H}$ of size $10^8 \times 10^8$. A gigabyte of memory is required just to store the unknown $\mathbf{f}$, while 10^8 gigabytes would be needed if one needed to store all the numbers in $\mathbf{H}$. In addition to storage, direct approaches of inversion, based on methods such as the SVD, would be prohibitively expensive to compute. Such direct solution methods generally have computational cost that scales as $O(N^3)$, where N is the size of $\mathbf{f}$ ($N \approx 10^8$ in our tomography example).

By contrast, iterative methods have a variety of attractive characteristics. First, reasonable approximate solutions can often be obtained with very few iterations, and thus with far less computation than required for the exact solution. Second, iterative approaches avoid the memory-intensive factorizations or explicit inverses required of direct methods, which is critical for large problems. Finally, many iterative schemes are naturally parallelizable, and thus can be easily implemented on parallel hardware for additional speed. Such parallel hardware is becoming a commodity, being found, for example, in general purpose graphical processing units (GP-GPUs) made by graphics card manufacturers.

Gradient Descent

Perhaps the simplest iterative approach can be obtained by using gradient descent to perform the minimization of the cost $J(\mathbf{f}) = \|\mathbf{g} - \mathbf{Hf}\|_2^2 + \lambda \|\mathbf{Lf}\|_2^2$ in (5.4-8). This approach, which is based on taking steps proportional to the negative of the gradient of J at the current point, yields the iteration:

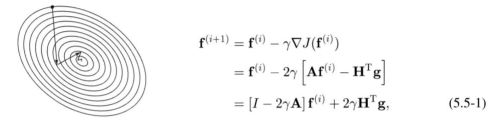

$$\mathbf{f}^{(i+1)} = \mathbf{f}^{(i)} - \gamma \nabla J(\mathbf{f}^{(i)})$$
$$= \mathbf{f}^{(i)} - 2\gamma \left[\mathbf{Af}^{(i)} - \mathbf{H}^{\mathsf{T}}\mathbf{g} \right]$$
$$= [I - 2\gamma \mathbf{A}] \, \mathbf{f}^{(i)} + 2\gamma \mathbf{H}^{\mathsf{T}}\mathbf{g}, \qquad (5.5\text{-}1)$$

where $\mathbf{A} = \mathbf{H}^{\mathsf{T}}\mathbf{H} + \lambda \mathbf{L}^{\mathsf{T}}\mathbf{L}$, $i = 1, 2, \ldots$, and γ is a relaxation parameter used for adjusting the step size in the gradient direction.

Computational Cost.   Let us consider the structure of the iteration in (5.5-1) and the associated computation involved in obtaining an iterative solution. This overall computation is given by $N_{\text{iter}} \times$ (Computations per iteration).

For most subsurface sensing systems the operator $h(\mathbf{r}, \mathbf{r}')$, and hence the associated matrix $\mathbf{H}$, possesses a highly sparse structure. That is, any particular measurement element in $\mathbf{g}$ only *sees* a small subset of the elements in $\mathbf{f}$, implying that the corresponding row of $\mathbf{H}$ has only a comparatively few nonzero elements. Often the number of such nonzero elements in $\mathbf{H}$ is on the same order as the *linear dimension* N_{linear} of the field $\mathbf{f}$. For example, for a 2D problem where $\mathbf{f}$ has N elements, the linear dimension would be $N_{\text{linear}} = \sqrt{N}$. The same sparsity properties usually hold (or are exceeded) for common choices of the matrix $\mathbf{L}$, representing a discrete derivative operator. Examining the iteration in (5.5-1), this implies that the number of nonzero computations needed for one iteration is also $O(N_{\text{linear}})$.[2] In addition, since only the sparse matrices $\mathbf{H}$ and $\mathbf{L}$ need to be stored, the storage requirements are significantly less than for the direct methods.

Overall, then, the amount of computation required of the iterative solution is typically $O(N_{\text{linear}} N_{\text{iter}})$. Consider the 3D tomography problem discussed earlier. In this case, direct solution of the regularized problem was $O(N^3)$. In contrast, the iterative solution would be $O(\sqrt{N} N_{\text{iter}})$. Further, the number of iterations N_{iter} is usually much less than N. Thus, the iterative solution requires much less computation than the direct methods.

---

[2] The big O notation describes the growth rate of a function when the argument tends towards infinity.

Conjugate Gradient Method

While the basic gradient descent approach in (5.5-1) is simple to understand and illustrates the advantages of iterative methods in a straightforward way, we can do much better. Reviewing our computational analysis, we can see that the overall computational cost of an iterative method depends directly on the number of iterations required until convergence (or until a satisfactory answer is obtained). The problem with the gradient descent approach is that it converges very slowly, so is rarely used in practice. The good news is that superior iterative methods have been devised which, while possessing similar costs per iteration, have significantly faster convergence rates. One such method is the conjugate gradient (CG) method. The CG method is one of the most powerful and widely used methods for the solution of symmetric, sparse linear systems of equations of the form $\mathbf{Af} = \mathbf{b}$. In our case we could apply it to the normal equations obtained from (5.4-11):

$$\mathbf{Af} = \mathbf{b}, \quad \mathbf{A} = \left(\mathbf{H}^{\mathrm{T}}\mathbf{H} + \lambda \mathbf{L}^{\mathrm{T}}\mathbf{L}\right), \quad \mathbf{b} = \mathbf{H}^{\mathrm{T}}\mathbf{g}. \tag{5.5-2}$$

The solution $\mathbf{f}$ is written as an expansion $\mathbf{f} = \sum_k \alpha_k \mathbf{p}_k$ in terms of a basis of vectors $\mathbf{p}_k$ that are conjugate to one another with respect to the matrix $\mathbf{A}$, i.e., the inner product $(\mathbf{p}_k, \mathbf{Ap}_{k'}) = 0$ for $k \neq k'$. If $\mathbf{p}_k$ are known, the expansion coefficients can be computed by use of the formula $\alpha_k = \mathbf{p}_k^{\mathrm{T}}/(\mathbf{p}_k^{\mathrm{T}}\mathbf{Ap}_k)$. An iterative procedure for the determination of $\mathbf{p}_k$ begins with an initial guess $\mathbf{f}_0$, from which the first vector $\mathbf{p}_1$ is computed by minimizing the quadratic function $J(\mathbf{f}) = \frac{1}{2}\mathbf{f}^{\mathrm{T}}\mathbf{Af} - \mathbf{b}^{\mathrm{T}}\mathbf{f}$, of which the solution $\mathbf{f}$ is a minimizer. Thus $\mathbf{p}_1$ is the gradient of $J(\mathbf{f})$ at $\mathbf{f} = \mathbf{f}_0$, and the other vectors are conjugates to the gradient; hence the CG name. Subsequent values of $\mathbf{p}_k$ are determined iteratively in terms of the residue vector $\mathbf{r}^{(i)} = \mathbf{b} - \mathbf{Af}^{(i)}$ at the ith iteration, and the solution $\mathbf{f}^{(i)}$ is updated, in accordance with the following algorithm.

Conjugate gradient algorithm:

$r^{(0)} = b - Af^{(0)}$ for some initial guess f_0

$p_1 = r^{(0)}$

for $i = 1, 2, \ldots$

    $\rho^{(i-1)} = r^{(i-1)\mathrm{T}} r^{(i-1)}$

    $r^{(i)} = \rho^{(i-1)} / \left[p_i^{\mathrm{T}} Ap_i\right]$

    $f^{(i)} = f^{(i-1)} + r^{(i)} p_i$

    $r^{(i)} = r^{(i-1)} - r^{(i)} Ap_i$

    Check convergence; continue if necessary

    $\beta^{(i)} = \left[r^{(i)\mathrm{T}} r^{(i)}\right] / \rho^{(i-1)}$

    $p_{i+1} = r^{(i)} + \beta_i p_i$

end

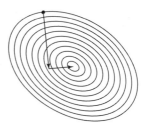

EXAMPLE 5.5-1.   Limited-View Ray Tomography: Iterative Inversion.   In this example, the gradient descent and the CG iterative inversion methods are applied to the limited-view ray tomography geometry described in Example 5.3-1. As illustrated in Fig. 5.5-1, the CG method converges more rapidly to an error comparable to the direct method (see Fig. 5.4-1).

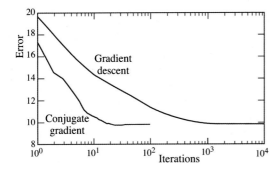

Figure 5.5-1 Dependence of the error on the number of iterations for the gradient descent and the CG methods for the ray tomography example.

B. Regularization

In addition to their computational advantages, when iterative methods are applied to the unregularized problem, they can provide a smoothing effect on the solution if terminated before convergence. We briefly examine this effect in this section. To gain insight into the regularizing behavior of iterative methods, consider the gradient descent iterative solution given in (5.5-1), but applied to the case when there is no regularization present so that $\lambda = 0$:

$$\mathbf{f}^{(i+1)} = \mathbf{f}^{(i)} - 2\gamma \mathbf{H}^{\mathrm{T}} \left(\mathbf{H} \mathbf{f}^{(i)} - \mathbf{g} \right). \tag{5.5-3}$$

If the iteration is started with $\mathbf{f}^{(0)} = 0$, then the estimate after i steps can be shown to be given by:

$$\mathbf{f}^{(i)} = \sum_{k=1}^{p} \left[1 - \left(1 - 2\gamma\sigma_k^2 \right)^i \right] \frac{1}{\sigma_k} (\mathbf{u}_k^{\mathrm{T}} \mathbf{g}) \mathbf{v}_k, \tag{5.5-4}$$

where $\{\sigma_k, \mathbf{u}_k, \mathbf{v}_k\}$ are the singular values and vectors of $\mathbf{H}$. Comparing this expression with (5.4-2), the effect of the iterative scheme is again to weight or filter the coefficients of the unregularized generalized solution, where the corresponding weight or filter function is now given by

$$w_k^{(i)} = 1 - \left(1 - 2\gamma\sigma_k^2 \right)^i. \tag{5.5-5}$$

Figure 5.5-2 is a plot of $w_k^{(i)}$ as a function of σ_k for several values of the iteration count i and for $\gamma = 1/2$. As can be seen, these weights have step-like behavior as a function of the size of σ_k, where the transition depends on the number of iterations. Thus, the iteration count of the iterative method does indeed play the role of the (inverse of the) regularization parameter. As the iterations are continued, the weighting function approaches unity, and the unregularized generalized solution is obtained. As discussed in Sec. 5.4, in general, such unregularized solutions are undesirable. Thus, to be effective as a regularizer the iteration must be stopped significantly *before* convergence is reached. This phenomenon is known as semi-convergence.

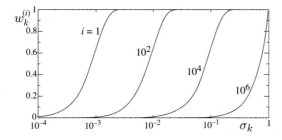

Figure 5.5-2   The Landweber weight function $w_k^{(i)}$ of (5.5-5) versus the singular value σ_k for various numbers of iterations i and for $\gamma = 1/2$.

EXAMPLE 5.5-2.   *Limited-View Ray Tomography: Effect of Iteration on Regularization.*   Consider again the limited-view ray tomography Example 5.3-1. In Fig. 5.5-3, we show iterative solutions corresponding to various numbers of iterations. When too few iterations are used the solution is overregularized and blurred. Conversely, when too many iterations are used the solution is underregularized and noisy, like the generalized solution.

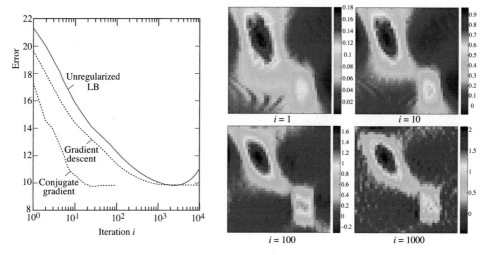

Figure 5.5-3   Graph shows reconstruction error as a function of number of iterations in the unregularized case (solid curve); the errors for the regularized case using gradient descent and conjugate gradient methods are also shown for comparison. Four reconstructed images are shown for $i = 1, 10, 100, 1000$ iterations.

While the analysis becomes more complicated for other iterative methods, such as the CG method, the general conclusions still hold. In particular, when CG is applied to the unregularized normal equations, intermediate iterates exhibit a smoothing effect, where this smoothing effect is inversely proportional to the number of iterations used. Since CG converges more quickly, the effect is accelerated and fewer iterations are needed to achieve semi-convergence.

Finally, there is a potential practical pitfall the practitioner needs to be aware of. The smoothing effect of iterative methods will hold whether the iterative method is applied to the unregularized equations or the regularized equations. If an iterative method is used to solve the regularized problem, then there will be two smoothing forces at work: one due to the explicit inclusion of regularization and one due to the implicit smoothing effects of the iterative method. If one is not careful and terminates the iterations prematurely, the final solution may be dominated by the iterative smoothing rather than the explicit regularization! When this happens, the solution may appear to be insensitive to the regularization parameter, for example resulting in seemingly confusing behavior.

Further Reading

P. C. Hansen, Regularization tools version 4.0 for Matlab 7.3, *Numerical Algorithms*, Vol. 46, pp. 189–194, 2007.

J. P. Kaipio and E. Somersalo, *Statistical and Computational Inverse Problems*, Springer, 2005.

A. R. Aster, B. Borchers, and C.Thurber, *Parameter Estimation and Inverse Problems*, 2nd ed., Academic Press, 2005.

Y. Saad, *Iterative Methods for Sparse Linear Systems*, 2nd ed., SIAM, 2003.

A. P. Dhawan, *Medical Image Analysis*, Wiley, 2003.

C. L. Epstein, *Introduction to the Mathematics of Medical Imaging*, Prentice-Hall, 2003.

C. R. Vogel, *Computational Methods for Inverse Problems*, SIAM, 2002.

E. N. Bruce, *Biomedical Signal Processing and Signal Modeling*, Wiley, 2001.

F. Natterer and F. Wubbeling, *Mathematical Methods in Image Reconstruction*, SIAM, 2001.

A. Wirgin, *Wavefield Inversion*, Springer, 2000.

P. C. Hansen, *Rank-Deficient and Discrete Ill-Posed Problems: Numerical Aspects of Linear Inversion*, SIAM, 1998.

R. Parker, *Geophysical Inverse Theory*, Princeton University Press, 1994.

P. C. Hansen, Analysis of discrete ill-posed problems by means of the *L*-curve. *SIAM Review*, Vol. 34, pp. 561–580, 1992.

M. Bertero, C. De Mol, and E. R. Pike, Linear inverse problems with discrete data, II: stability and regularisation, *Inverse Problems*, Vol. 4, pp. 573–594, 1988.

M. Bertero, C. De Mol, and E. R. Pike. Linear inverse problems with discrete data, I: general formulation and singular system analysis, *Inverse Problems*, Vol. 1, pp. 301–330, 1985.

C.C. Paige and M. A. Saunders, LSQR: an algorithm for sparse linear equations and sparse least squares, *ACM Transactions on Mathematical Software*, Vol. 8, pp. 43–71, 1982.

Problems

5.1-1   **Lexicographic Ordering.** As described in Sec. 5.1, the pixels of image $f(n_x, n_y)$ of dimensions $N_x \times N_y$ may be uniquely ordered to form a vector $f(n)$ of dimension $N_x N_y$ using the lexicographic ordering $n = \text{Lex}(n_x, n_y)$, as illustrated in Fig. 5.1-3.

   (a) Write a pair of functions that translate between (n_x, n_y) and n. The first function should take as input n_x, n_y, N_x, and N_y and return the corresponding value of n. The second function should take n, N_x, and N_y and return the corresponding n_x and n_y. You may do so by writing a pair of nested `for` statements that loop over rows and columns or by writing a single `for` loop that iterates over the index n.

   (b) MATLAB performs this lexicographic operation by the colon function `f1D = f(:)`, where f is a 2D array and f1D is the corresponding vector. Verify that your functions produces the same results by using, as an example, the 2D MATLAB array `f = reshape(1:10,2,5)`.

   (c) Verify the lexicographic operation and its inverse by "vectorizing" and "un-vectorizing" the image of the modified Shepp–Logan phantom generated by the MATLAB function `phantom ('Modified Shepp-Logan', 32)`.

   (d) The Matlab function `f1D = f(:)` is also applicable to 3D images, i.e., it generates a stacked form of the values in the 3D array $f(n_x, n_y, n_z)$. Write your own MATLAB program for this operation using triply nested loops. Verify your work by applying it to the function f = rand(3,2,4), which represents a 3D image of size $3 \times 2 \times 4$ filled with random numbers.

5.1-2 **Imaging Matrix for 1D Convolution.** A 1D imaging system is described by the convolution relation $g(x) = h(x) \otimes f(x)$, where $g(x)$ is the measured data, $f(x)$ is the object distribution, and $h(x)$ is the PSF describing the blur introduced by the imaging system. For the remainder of this problem, let $h(x) = \exp(-|x|)$.

(a) Assume that the detector measures M equally spaced samples of $g(x)$ at points in the interval starting at $x = -a$ and ending at $x = a$. Suppose that $f(x)$ is represented by its samples $x_n = -a + (2a/(N-1))n$ with $n = 0, 1, 2, ..., N - 1$. In this problem, therefore, both the object and the detector sampling functions, $\sigma(x)$ and $D(x)$, are delta functions. Write a program to construct the imaging matrix $\mathbf{H}$ given the inputs a, N and M. Compute $\mathbf{H}$ for $a = 5$, $M = 100$ and $N = 100$.

(b) Compute the imaging matrix $\mathbf{H}$ for $a = 5$, $M = 100$ and $N = 50$.

(c) Display the imaging matrices $\mathbf{H}$ from parts (a) and (b) using the MATLAB function imagesc to see their structure. Looking at the dimensions of the matrices, what can you say about the imaging systems?

5.1-3 **Imaging Matrix for 2D Defocused Imaging.** The PSF of a defocused imaging system is a circ function (uniform within a circle and zero outside; see Fig. A.2-2. Use a pixel basis to determine the array $h_{\mathbf{m},\mathbf{n}}$, where $\mathbf{n} = (n_x, n_y)$ and $\mathbf{m} = (m_x, m_y)$, for an object sampled with 31×31 pixels. With all convolution problems, there is an issue as to how to treat "boundary values." The simplest approach, and the one you are encouraged to use here, is to assume periodicity, meaning that in the relation $h_{\mathbf{m},\mathbf{n}} = h(m_x - n_x, m_y - n_y)$ the arguments $m_x - n_x$ and $m_y - n_y$ are replaced with $(m_x - n_x) \bmod N_x$ and $(m_y - n_y) \bmod N_y$, respectively, where $(a \bmod b)$ is the remainder of the division of a by b, and in this case $N_x = N_y = 31$. Assume that the PSF has a radius of 5 pixels. You may find it useful to use the results of Problem 5.1-1 with $n = 1, 2, \cdots 1024$ to determine the imaging matrix $\mathbf{H}$.

5.1-4 **Imaging Matrix for Ray Tomography.** One approach to building the imaging matrix for ray tomography is to make use of the MATLAB radon function. Although radon allows the user to specify the angles (in degrees) for the transform, the location of the samples along the axis of each projection are automatically determined by the function.

(a) Let $f_n(n_x, n_y)$ be the image that is all zero except for the n-th pixel, which is one. Explain how we can use the result of applying radon to $f_n(n_x, n_y)$ to construct the n-th column of the ray tomography matrix $\mathbf{H}$.

(b) Using the radon approach, implement a program to compute the $\mathbf{H}$ matrix for a *limited view* problem in which data are only collected for a limited range of angles, $\theta = -\theta_o$ to $\theta = +\theta_o$. The user should provide values for θ_o, the number of projections, and the dimensions of the input image. Generate the $\mathbf{H}$ matrix for the case where $\theta_0 = 30°$, 31 projections are used, and the image is of size 51×51.

(c) Using the radon approach, implement a program to compute the $\mathbf{H}$ matrix for a *sparse angle* problem in which data are only collected for a small number of projections over the full range of θ. The user should provide values for the number of projections, and the dimensions of the input image. You may assume that the projections are equally spaced between $0°$ to $180°$. Generate the matrix for the case where the image is of size 51×51 and 30 projections are measured.

5.1-5 **Imaging Matrix for 1D Wave Tomography.** Here we consider the class of wave tomography problems depicted in Fig. 5.1-5. While such problems are generally multidimensional, there are important instances where the properties of the medium can be approximated as only a function of depth, in this case y. For such problems, we are typically constrained to place sensors only along the x axis at $y = 0$ and perhaps a second set at $y = d$.

(a) Write a program to compute the imaging matrix $\mathbf{H}$ for a 1D wave tomography configuration with a single transmitter located at $(x, y) = (0, 0)$ and an array of L equally spaced receivers located along the line $y = 0$ between $x = -a_x$ and $x = +a_x$. The number L should be even so that one of the receivers does not lie on top of the transmitter. This is known as the *reflection* geometry. The object function f is represented using a piecewise constant basis whose pixels are δ functions in the y direction and rect functions in the x direction

$$f(x, y) = \sum_{n_y=0}^{N} f_{n_y} \delta(y - y_{n_y}) b(x),$$

where $y_{n_y} = (n_y/N)d$ for $n_y = 0, 1, 2, \ldots, N$ and $b(x)$ is equal to one for $|x| < 2a_x$ and zero otherwise. This representation of f will simplify one of the integrals in equation (5.1-28). The other will have to be evaluated numerically using, e.g., the MATLAB quad function or even a simple Riemann sum. Your function should take as input the (x, y) coordinates of the sources (in this case, only the one) and receivers, the array of y_{n_y} values, a_x, and the value of k needed in the exponential of (5.1-28). The matrix will generally be complex valued. Because we can measure both the real and imaginary parts of the data, the final $\mathbf{H}$ matrix should "stack up" the real and imaginary parts of the complex matrix.

(b) The use of a single transmitter for this problem is different from the configurations discussed for problems of this type in the text. Consider the problem where the object of interest extends from $-o_x$ to o_x with $o_x \gg a_x$ and there is an array of transmitters that are spaced halfway between each pair of receiver. Explain why there is little value provided by these "extra" transmitters for such a problem.

(c) Construct the $\mathbf{H}$ matrix for the case where $d = 0.5$, $N = 51$, $a_x = 0.5$, $L = 20$. To specify the value of the wave number k, assume that the system employs microwave radiation of angular frequency ω and the medium has permittivity ϵ, permeability μ, and conductivity σ so that k is a complex number $k = \omega\sqrt{\mu\epsilon}\,[1 - j(\sigma/\omega\epsilon)]^{1/2}$. You should construct a composite $\mathbf{H}$ matrix for twenty equally spaced values of ω between 10^7 and 10^9 rad/s. Take $\mu = 4\pi \times 10^{-7}$ H/m, $\epsilon = 8.85 \times 10^{-12}$ F/m, and experiment with σ between 0 and 0.5 S/m. Explain how frequency in this propblem basically provides multiple "views." How does the choice of and σ impact the imaging matrix?

(d) Repeat the computation for the case where the set of receivers is located along the line $y = 1.1d$. This is known as the *transmission* geometry.

5.1-6 **Imaging Matrix for 2D Wave Tomography.** Here we consider the wave tomography problem where $f(x, y)$ can vary in both dimensions. To start, assume that there are L equally spaced transmitters located along the line $y = 0$ between $x = -a_x$ and $x = +a_x$, and $L - 1$ receivers located at either $y = 0$ (reflection) or $y = 1.1d$ (transmission) with each receiver's x coordinate placing it half way between pairs of transmitters. For this problem the function $f(x, y)$ takes the form

$$f(x, y) = \sum_{n_x=0}^{N_x} \sum_{n_y=0}^{N_y} f_{n_x, n_y} \delta(x - x_{n_x}) \delta(y - y_{n_y}),$$

where $x_{n_x} = -a_x + 2a_x n_x/N_x$ for $n_x = 0, 1, \ldots N_x$; and $y_{n_y} = dn_y/N_y$ for $n_y = 0, 1, \ldots N_y$. Generate the $\mathbf{H}$ matrices for the reflection and transmission geometries for the case where $a_x = 0.5$, $L = 20$, $N_x = 31$ $N_y = 35$, $d = 0.5$, k is computed as in the previous problem with $\omega = 10^8$ and $\sigma = 0.01$.

5.2-1 **Rank and SVD of a Matrix.** Determine the rank and the SVD of the matrices $\mathbf{H}$ in (5.2-3) and (5.2-4) using the MATLAB functions rank(H) and svd(H). Comment on the number of non-zero singular values of these matrices and their ranks.

5.3-1 **Pseudo-Inverse.** Compute the pseudo-inverse of the matrices $\mathbf{H}$ in (5.2-3) and (5.2-4) using the MATLAB function pinv(H).

5.3-2 **Derivation of Minimization Problem for Pseudo-Inverse.** Derive (5.3-5) from (5.3-4).

5.3-3 **Derivation of the SVD Reconstruction.** Derive (5.3-11) for the SVD estimate in the under-determined case.

5.3-4 **1D Deconvolution.** Consider undoing (or deblurring) the blur introduced by the system defined in Problem $5.1 - 2$. This system is defined by a matrix $\mathbf{H}$ that was computed for two different special cases. We consider here the case defined in part (b) with $a = 5, M = 100$ and $N = 50$. We use, as an example, an object function $f(x)$ comprised of a single triangular pulse centered at the origin:

$$f(x) = \begin{cases} x+1 & -1 \le x \le 0 \\ 1-x & 0 \le x \le 1 \\ 0 & \text{otherwise.} \end{cases}$$

(a) Using the matrix equation $\mathbf{g} = \mathbf{Hf}$, determine the image $\mathbf{g}$ and plot it. Now, given the image $\mathbf{g}$ and the imaging matrix $\mathbf{H}$, reconstruct the original object $\mathbf{f}$ by use of the pseudo-inverse and an appropriate formula from Sec. 5.3.

(b) In the presence of additive noise blurred and noisy image is given by $\mathbf{g} = \mathbf{Hf} + \mathbf{w}$, where $\mathbf{w}$ is a vector of independent Gaussian noise with variance σ_w^2. Find the value of σ_w^2 that yields an SNR of 20 dB and create the corresponding noisy image $\mathbf{g}$. The signal-to-noise ratio (SNR) in decibel is given by (5.2-2).

(c) Repeat part (a) for the noisy image and determine the SNR of the reconstructed object.

5.3-5   **Ray Tomography Inversion.** A 51×51 pixels object with block distribution

$$f(n_x, n_y) = \begin{cases} 1 & (10 \le n_x, n_y \le 20) \text{ or } (20 \le n_x \le 40 \text{ and } 30 \le n_y \le 40) \\ 0 & \text{otherwise} \end{cases}$$

is measured by ray tomography using the limited-view configuration (60 projections between $-30°$ and $+30°$) or the sparse angle configuration (60 projections over the full range of possible angles) described by Problem 5.1-4(c) and (d). Construct the object of vector $\mathbf{f}$ and use the system matrix $\mathbf{H}$, which was constructed earlier in Problem 5.1-4, to determine the noise-free data $\mathbf{g} = \mathbf{Hf}$ in each case.

(a) Given $\mathbf{g}$, construct an estimate $\widehat{\mathbf{f}}$ using the pseudo-inverse of $\mathbf{H}$. Convert $\mathbf{f}$ into an image $\widehat{f}(n_x, n_y)$ using lexicographical conversion. Compare the result to the original object $f(n_x, n_y)$ and comment on the quality of this method of reconstruction for the two cases.

(b) Add white Gaussian noise to obtain observations with 20 dB SNR and repeat part (a).

5.3-6   **2D Wave Tomography Inversion.** In this problem we perform inversion for a variant of the 2D wave tomography Problem 5.1-6. For each of the two configurations considered in that problem:

(a) Determine the matrix $\mathbf{H}$, and both the noise-free and noisy observations corresponding to an SNR of 20 dB with

$$f(n_x, n_y) = \begin{cases} 1 & (10 \le n_x \le 15 \text{ and } 5 \le n_y \le 15) \\ & \text{or } (15 \le n_x \le 25 \text{ and } 20 \le n_y \le 30) \\ 0 & \text{else.} \end{cases}$$

(b) Produce the pseudo-inverse solutions corresponding to both the noise-free and noisy data and comment on your results. You can either construct your own pseudo-inverse or use the `pinv` function in Matlab in which case you will need to be careful in choosing a threshold for cutting off small singular values.

5.4-1   **Smoothness Regularization.** As described in Sec. 5.4C, the generalized Tikhonov inversion involves the computation of a smoothness measure $\|\mathbf{Lf}\|_2^2$, where $\mathbf{L}$ may be the identity matrix $\mathbf{I}$ or a matrix $\mathbf{D}$ representing a discrete form of the derivative (in the 1D case) or the gradient (in the multidimensional case).

(a) In the 1D case, the function $f(x)$ is approximated by a vector $\mathbf{f}$ of elements f_n. The derivative is approximated by the finite difference, so that $\mathbf{Df}$ is a vector of the adjacent differences:

$$\begin{bmatrix} f_2 - f_1 \\ f_3 - f_2 \\ \vdots \\ f_N - f_{N-1} \end{bmatrix}.$$

Determine the matrix $\mathbf{D}$. Since $\mathbf{D}$ has fewer rows than columns, does this cause a problem when this matrix is used as a regularizer for an inverse problem? Explain. Because the matrix has more columns than rows, it has a nullspace; describe precisely the class of vectors that lie in this nullspace and interpret the results. Hint: what kind of functions have zero first derivatives?

(b) In the 2D case, the image $f(x,y)$ is approximated by the array f_{n_x,n_y}, which is lexicographically converted into the vector $\mathbf{f}$. The gradient has components $\partial f/\partial x$ and $\partial f/\partial y$ so that the norm $\|\nabla f(x,y)\|_2^2$ is the integral of the sum of the squared derivatives $(\partial f/\partial x)^2 + (\partial f/\partial y)^2$. This norm is approximated by the norm of a vector $\begin{bmatrix} \mathbf{D}_x \\ \mathbf{D}_y \end{bmatrix} \mathbf{f}$, where $\mathbf{D}_x$ and $\mathbf{D}_y$ are approximations to the x and y derivatives, implemented by vertical (along the column) and horizontal (along the rows) differences, respectively. The x component of the gradient is a vector comprised of the differences $f(n_x+1,n_y) - f(n_x,n_y)$, while the y component is a vector of the differences $f(n_x,n_y+1) - f(n_x,n_y)$. As with the 1D case, some care must be taken with pixels at the edge of the image. Construct the matrices $\mathbf{D}_x$ and $\mathbf{D}_y$. Each row of these matrices should have only two nonzero elements. As a check, if the image had five rows and three columns, $\mathbf{D}_x$ should have 12 rows and 15 columns while $\mathbf{D}_y$ should be 10×15.

5.4-2 **1D Deconvolution with Regularization.** In this problem, we reconsider the inversion in Problem 5.3-4 by applying regularization to stabilize the inversion against noise.

(a) Find the truncated SVD based solution corresponding to the noisy data from part (b). What is a good choice for the truncation level? Explain.

(b) Now perform spectral filtering on the noisy data from part (b). Choose what you think is a good filter function and a suitable truncation level. Compare your results to part (a).

(c) Find the Tikhonov regularized solution to the problem with noisy data for the case where L is a discrete approximation of a derivative operator, as described in Problem 5.4-1. What is a good choice for the regularization parameter λ in this case? Compare and contrast the various solutions.

5.4-3 **Ray Tomography Inversion with Regularization.** To enhance the ray tomography inversion technique used in Problem 5.3-5(b), perform truncated SVD and Tikhonov regularization with L a discrete approximation of a derivative operator, as described in Problem 5.4-1 for the limited view and the sparse angle problems. Identify a good regularization parameter and compare the results. Which problem is easier to solve? Which regularization method leads to better results?

5.4-4 **Wave Tomography Inversion with Regularization.** This problem is a continuation of Problem 5.3-6.

(a) Generate the Tikhonov regularized solutions for $\mathbf{L} = \mathbf{I}$ and for L a discrete approximation of a derivative operator, as studied in Problem 5.4-1. Comment on the best regularization parameters for the methods and compare the resulting solutions.

(b) Apply the conjugate gradient method to the unregularized problem $\mathbf{g} = \mathbf{Hf}$ with noisy data. Initialize the iteration with all zeros. Show the results at iterations 1, 5, 10, 50, 100, and 200. Comment on how the quality varies with iteration.

Spectral Imaging

It was pointed out in Chapter 2 that the interaction of fields and waves with matter can be strongly dependent on the wavelength (or the frequency, or the photon energy for electromagnetic waves). Examples of wavelength-dependent physical parameters observed in subsurface imaging (the *alpha* parameters) are: velocity and refractive index (Sec. 2.2A), reflectance at boundaries between different media (Sec. 2.2B), absorption coefficient of atomic and molecular systems (Sec. 2.2A), scattering coefficient (Sec. 2.2C), fluorescence rate (Sec. 2.3A), and optical diffusion coefficient for turbid media (Sec. 2.2D). Wavelength dependence may obey a simple law (such as the λ^{-4} dependence of Rayleigh scattering) and may exhibit a complex pattern that uniquely identifies substances and chemicals (e.g., in the case of optical absorption). The concentration, or *abundance*, of certain substances, such as algae in water, oxygen in blood (see Fig. 2.2-4), or a specific molecular agent tagging some site in a cell, are important *beta* parameters whose spectral features can be used as identifiers of substances or conditions for functional imaging.

The penetration depth, which is crucial to subsurface imaging, is usually wavelength dependent, as exemplified in Fig. 6.0-1 for the propagation of electromagnetic waves in water and human skin. Waves at different wavelengths penetrate to different depths and therefore acquire images of different layers. Therefore, when a subsurface target is measured at multiple wavelengths, the wavelength dependence of the transmittance of the covering medium must be accounted for. For example, in remote sensing of earth or underwater objects, corrections for the atmospheric and/or water transmittance must be made.

Another important factor in subsurface imaging is the spatial resolution (both lateral and axial). As demonstrated in Chapters 3 and 4, the resolution is wavelength dependent, so that probes of different wavelengths *see* the object with different spatial scales. For example, in the millimeter-wave systems used for body scanners as the frequency increases, the spatial resolution improves, but clothing becomes more opaque.

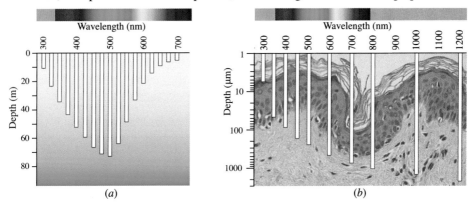

Figure 6.0-1 Wavelength dependence of the penetration depth of electromagnetic waves in (*a*) clear water (see Sec. 6.4B) and (*b*) skin (see Sec. 6.4A).

Certain spectral effects are more conveniently described in the time domain. For example, the finite lifetime of fluorescence, which is measured by use of pulsed excitation (see Fig. 2.3-1), is also a spectral effect that can be equivalently described in the Fourier domain and measured by use of sinusoidally modulated excitation. Another example is the temporal profile of the radiowaves emitted in MRI following excitation by radiowave pulses (see Sec. 2.3C). Also, interferometers that measure range by introducing a variable time delay between two paths can be equivalently and perhaps more conveniently replaced by spectral-domain interferometers using a source with a swept frequency or a broad spectral distribution (see Sec. 4.4). Some of these techniques have already been discussed in previous chapters.

This chapter describes subsurface imaging systems that probe and detect at multiple wavelengths/frequencies. Such spectral imaging systems acquire spectral data at various points of the object and make use of spectral and spatial information to map, detect, or classify objects. We begin with an introduction to spectral imaging and an overview of the various configurations for acquisition of the spectral image (Sec. 6.1). Mathematical models for spectral imaging systems in various configurations are formulated in Sec. 6.2. These models are generalizations of linear-systems models that are presented in Sec. 3.1B. Information extraction from measured spectral images is the subject of Sec. 6.3. This covers parameter estimation problems, including estimation of the spatial distribution of substances with distinct spectral characteristics, and classification of targets based on their spectral signatures. Two specific applications are then covered in Sec. 6.4: under-skin and underwater spectral imaging.

6.1   Spectral Imaging

A. The Spectral Image

In Chapter 3, an *image* was defined as a spatial function of position $f(\mathbf{r})$. We considered two-dimensional (2D) images of planar objects $f(x, y)$, three-dimensional (3D) images of thick objects $f(x, y, z)$, and one-dimensional (1D) images, such as the axial distribution $f(z)$ of a 3D object along a single line. In this chapter, we add a new dimension – the wavelength dependence or the spectrum.

A spectral image is a spatial–spectral distribution described by a function of position and wavelength $f(\mathbf{r}, \lambda)$. Again, $\mathbf{r}$ may be 1D, 2D, or 3D. For example, a 2D spectral image of the form $f(x, y, \lambda)$ may describe the reflectance of a flat object as a function of position and wavelength (e.g., a color photo). This is a 3D function with two spatial coordinates and one spectral coordinate, portrayed as a stack of 2D images, one for each wavelength – called a lambda stack or a spectral cube. At a fixed

Spectral image
$f(x, y, \lambda)$

position (x, y), the distribution of $f(x, y, \lambda)$ as a function of λ is a vertical line representing the spectral distribution. Such a spectral image may represent, for example, reflectance, transmittance, absorption, scattering, or fluorescence of a planar surface.

In certain cases, the dependence of the spectral image $f(\mathbf{r}, \lambda)$ on the position and the wavelength may take special forms, as follows.

Single-Spectum Model.   In the first special case, all points of an object have the same spectral distribution, but different intensities, so that

$$f(\mathbf{r}, \lambda) = f_0(\mathbf{r})s_0(\lambda) \qquad\qquad (6.1\text{-}1)$$

is a separable function, i.e., a product of a function of wavelength and a function of position, so that all points have the same spectral distribution. In this case, the processes of spatial imaging and spectral analysis are independent. The spectral dependence can be measured at a single position, and the spatial distribution can be measured at a single wavelength or by use of a panchromatic system that integrates over a broad range of wavelengths.

Double-Spectrum Model.   Another special case occurs when the object has two kinds of substances with spectral distributions $s_1(\lambda)$ and $s_2(\lambda)$. If the relative densities or concentrations of the two substances have the spatial distributions $f_1(\mathbf{r})$ and $f_2(\mathbf{r})$, normalized such that $f_1(\mathbf{r}) + f_2(\mathbf{r}) = 1$, then the composite result is the spectral image

$$f(\mathbf{r}, \lambda) = f_1(\mathbf{r})s_1(\lambda) + f_2(\mathbf{r})s_2(\lambda). \tag{6.1-2}$$

In remote sensing, for example, the two substances may be two types of vegetation with different spectral reflectances. The spectra of the two substances are called the **endmembers**, and their fractions $f_1(\mathbf{r})$ and $f_2(\mathbf{r})$ are called the **abundances**. They represent the geographic distributions of the two vegetation types. In microscopy, the two substances (endmembers) may be two types of dye with different fluorescence spectra, for example green fluorescent protein (GFP) and yellow fluorescent protein (YFP), attached to different sites of a cellular structure. The following image is an example of a mixture of green and yellow substances (endmembers) with increasing proportions in the x direction. The image is a color rendition of the abundance map:

$f_1 = 1, f_2 = 0$ ... $f_1 = 0, f_2 = 1$
x

The data acquisition and the information extraction systems can benefit significantly from the knowledge that the spectral image is expressed in the form in (6.1-2), particularly if the spectral distributions $s_1(\lambda)$ and $s_2(\lambda)$ are known. For example, if $s_1(\lambda)$ and $s_2(\lambda)$ do not overlap, as illustrated in Fig. 6.1-1(a), then $f_1(\mathbf{r})$ and $f_2(\mathbf{r})$ may be measured by use of appropriate filters. If they do overlap, as in Fig. 6.1-1(b), then the estimation of the abundance functions $f_1(\mathbf{r})$ and $f_2(\mathbf{r})$, i.e., the *unmixing* of the distributions of the two substances, requires the use of algebraic techniques, as will be discussed in Sec. 6.3A.

Figure 6.1-1   (a) Two nonoverlapping spectra. (b) Two overlapping spectra.

Multiple-Spectrum Model.   The double-spectrum model may be readily generalized to P types of substance (endmembers). In this case, (6.1-2) takes the form

$$f(\mathbf{r}, \lambda) = \sum_{i=1}^{P} f_i(\mathbf{r})s_i(\lambda), \tag{6.1-3}$$

where the fractions $f_i(\mathbf{r})$ add up to unity at each position. This model is also called a **mixed-spectrum** model. A simple illustrative example of this type of **linearly mixed spectra** is a color image composed of red, green, and blue endmembers mixed with different ratios within an image, as shown in Fig. 6.1-2. See also Sec. D.1 in Appendix D.

Figure 6.1-2   2D color images composed of red (R), green (G), and blue (B) endmembers. (a) Mixed R and G in equal proportions has the appearance of yellow; G and B yield cyan; B and R yield magenta. The region in the center has an equal mix of R, G, and B; it appears white. (b) Color mixing triangle. R, G, and B are mixed in varying amounts at various points of a triangle. Each vertex has a single color with an amount decreasing gradually away from the vertex and toward the center.

▶ Problems 6.1-1, 6.1-2

B. Spectral Imaging

Spectroscopy. The wavelength dependence of a physical parameter is referred to as the **spectrum**; the measurement process is called **spectroscopy**, and the instrument is called a **spectrometer**. Various types of spectroscopy are applicable to different types of wave–matter interaction. Examples are: absorption spectroscopy, emission spectroscopy, fluorescence spectroscopy, scattering spectroscopy, Raman spectroscopy, NMR spectroscopy, and so on. Likewise, spectroscopy may be labeled by the type of wave used; for example, X-ray spectroscopy, UV spectroscopy, and infrared spectroscopy. Many of these effects were described in Chapter 2.

Spectral Imaging. (Also called *Imaging Spectroscopy* or *Imaging Spectrometry*.) This is the acquisition of spectral images by means of an imaging system combined with a spectrally sensitive device — a spectrometer. Spectral imaging can provide valuable information that may be useful in identifying and mapping materials (e.g., molecules may be identified by the spectral signature of their emission). The spectral information can also help in delineating objects from the surrounding medium or fro clutter. Airborne and satellite spectral imaging is the foundation of many types of remote-sensing applications, including land use, forestry, exploration of mineral and water resources, assessment of natural hazards such as environmental contamination, management of ecosystems, and evaluation of biomass and productivity. Spectral imaging has also historically been a principal tool of astronomy and astrophysics.

Spectral Microscopy. Spectral imaging at a microscopic level, called spectral microscopy, has many valuable chemical, biological, and medical applications. Biological applications include observation of metabolic activity of cells and organs, estimation of hemoglobin concentration, visualization of tissue chemistry at the cellular level, and screening of biopsy samples for tumor detection. Other biological applications are based on the ability to determine the distribution of molecular species within observed cellular structures by observing fluorescence spectra of attached tags. Examples are: detection and automated sequencing of DNA, fluorescent-activated cell sorting (FACS), and imaging of calcium flow in cells.

Spectral Bands. Ideally, the spectral image $f(\mathbf{r}, \lambda)$ is measured at all wavelengths. In practice, it is sampled by use of a finite set of filters centered about different wavelengths and extending over finite spectral widths. Based on the number of these filters, their widths, and the relative location of their centers, spectral imaging systems are categorized as **panchromatic, multispectral,** or **hyperspectral,** as depicted in Fig. 6.1-3.

- A **panchromatic** image is a single-band image collected under broadband illumination and rendered in gray scale, as in black-and-white photography. A panchromatic imager yields a single integrated band containing no wavelength-specific information, but usually has high spatial resolution. Object discrimination is achieved solely by use of spatial features.
- In **multispectral** imaging, the electromagnetic spectrum is sampled at a number of bands of generally different widths and spacings, which may be overlapping. Visible as well as nonvisible regions, such as infrared or longer wavelengths, and X-rays and shorter wavelengths, can be included. Object discrimination is achieved by strategically selecting the spectral bands that best delineate selected object categories.
- In **hyperspectral** imaging, numerous contiguous regions of the electromagnetic spectrum are sampled at high spectral resolution (1–10 nm). This almost continuous measurement of the spectrum allows collection of detailed spectral information for applications in which the spectral characteristics change rapidly. Object

discrimination may be based on fine spectral details representing absorption lines of specific materials or on differences in overall spectral shape.

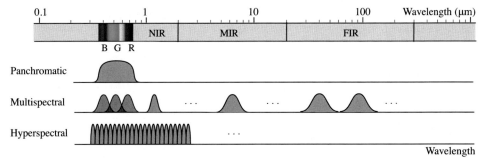

Figure 6.1-3 Types of spectral sampling. In panchromatic sensing, a single wideband image is measured; in multispectral sensing, multiple samples of the spectrum are measured at selected wavelength ranges spaced at different intervals; in hyperspectral imagery, the spectrum is sampled uniformly at narrowly spaced wavelengths.

Spectral Bands in Remote Sensing.   Airborne and satellite remote-sensing systems use panchromatic, multispectral, and hyperspectral sampling. Selection of the spectral bands in these systems is dictated by the applications:

- Blue light is used for atmospheric and underwater imaging (down to 45 m in clear water).
- Green light is used primarily for imaging vegetation and underwater features (down to 27 m in clear water).
- Red light is used for imaging of manmade objects, soil, and vegetation.
- Near-infrared (NIR) is used primarily for imaging vegetation.
- Mid-infrared (MIR) is used for imaging vegetation, soil, moisture, forest fires, and geological features.
- Far-infrared (FIR) thermal radiation, directly emitted by objects, is used for night studies, fires, and oceanic temperature distributions.

An example of a multispectral sensor is the Enhanced Thematic Mapper (ETM), which is carried onboard the LANDSAT 7 satellite. Examples of hyperspectral remote-sensing systems are the 224-band Airborne Visible/Infrared Imaging Spectrometer (AVIRIS) developed by the NASA Jet Propulsion Laboratory, the 210-band Hyperspectral Digital Imagery Collection Experiments (HYDICE) developed by the Naval Research Laboratory, and the HYPERION satellite sensor onboard NASA's EO-1 satellite.

EO-1 Satellite. (Artist rendition after NASA.)

Spectral Bands in Microscopy and Molecular Imaging.   Spectral bands used in microscopy depend on the application and the availability of sources and detectors. Microscopic chemical imaging (MCI) systems use the 3–20 μm region of the MIR, where most molecules show characteristic absorption spectra. In biology applications of fluorescence microscopy, the entire optical spectrum, from UV to far infrared may be used. Various fluorophores, such as dyes or proteins, are injected into the material and attached preferentially to different sites, where each selectively excited fluorescence species produces an emission with known spectral distribution. For example, green, yellow, and red fluorescent proteins (GFP, YFP, RFP) have excitation peaks at 395, 525, and 557 nm, respectively, and emission distributions with peaks at 509, 538, and 585 nm, respectively. For each excitation, the fluorescent spectral image is measured using a set of filters centered at appropriate wavelengths. Figure 6.1-4 shows the emission spectra of selected fluorescence proteins.

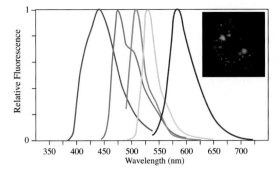

Figure 6.1-4 Emission spectra of blue, cyan, green, yellow, and red fluorescence proteins (EBFP, ECFP, EGFP, EYFP, and Ds-Red). An image of a distributed mixture of these proteins is shown in the inset. Adapted from G. Patterson, R. N. Day, and D. Piston, Fluorescent protein spectra, *Journal of Cell Science*, 114, pp. 837–838, 2001.

Spectral Bands in Astronomy. Although early astronomical observations have been made in the visible band, modern observations extend from radio frequencies, to X-rays and beyond. For example, the Arecibo Radio Telescope uses radio frequencies to calculate the mass and density of distant galaxies, NASA's CRISM instrument uses ultraviolet to mid-infrared wavelengths to examine surface properties of Mars, and the NASA Astrobiology Institute uses visible to near-infrared wavelengths to assess the potential for life on other Earth-like planets.

C. Spectral Image Acquisition

Acquisition of the spatial–spectral distribution of an object may be accomplished by observing multiple spatially co-registered images at each of the desired spectral bands. Two configurations are illustrated schematically in Fig. 6.1-5:

(a) The probe wave is broadband, or the object itself is self-luminous and its emission is broadband, or the object emits broadband fluorescence upon excitation by a laser, for example. The detector employs a bank of spectral filters centered at a set of wavelengths, or a **spectrometer** that separates different wavelengths. For optical and X-ray imaging, the spectral components are separated by means of a dispersive (i.e., wavelength-sensitive) device such as a prism, a diffraction grating, or an interferometer. We call this the **multisensor configuration**.

(b) A set of narrowband probe waves centered at different wavelengths are used, one at a time, and the reflected or scattered wave is detected by a broadband detector, i.e., a detector responsive to all wavelengths. The probe waves may be generated by different sources, a tunable single-wavelength source, or by filtering broadband radiation by means of a set of filters centered at different wavelengths. We call this the **multiprobe configuration**.

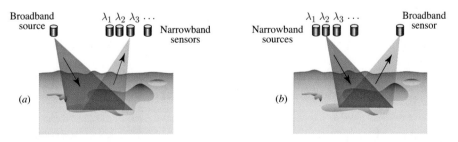

Figure 6.1-5 Spectral imaging. (*a*) Multisensor configuration: the image is collected by a bank of narrowband wavelength-selective sensors (a spectrometer); the object is either illuminated by a broadband probe, as shown, or emits its own broadband radiation. (*b*) Multiprobe configuration: the image is collected by a broadband sensor; the object is illuminated by multiple probes at different wavelengths.

There are several approaches for acquisition of a spectral image, depending on the order of acquiring spatial and spectral data, and whether the measurement is performed sequentially (in a scanning mode) or in parallel (in a gazing mode). Some of these approaches are illustrated below for a 2D object, such as a planar surface or a 2D slice of a 3D object, imaged by a localized imaging system (e.g., the systems described in Chapter 3). Figure 6.1-6 illustrates three common approaches to constructing the spectral cube: spatial scanning, gazing, and hybrid spatial scanning in one dimension and gazing in the other.

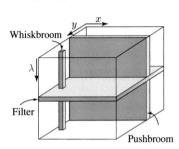

Figure 6.1-6   Three approaches to constructing the spectral cube. (*a*) The **filter method** uses a gazing system together with a spectrometer to build up the cube as a stack of horizontal slices, one for each wavelength (lambda stack). (*b*) The **whiskbroom method** uses a scanning system and a spectrometer to construct the cube as a set of vertical lines, one for each pixel. (*c*) The **pushbroom method** uses a hybrid system, gazing in the x direction combined with scanning in the y direction, so that the cube is constructed as a set of vertical slices, each containing spectral and 1D spatial measurements.

Gazing System: Filter Method

The filter method is simply a camera with a tunable filter. The spatial distribution of the entire 2D object is acquired at all points simultaneously using a gazing imaging system (e.g., by means of a lens) and the spectral image is measured, one wavelength at a time, using a spectrometer (e.g., a tunable filter such as a liquid-crystal tunable filter (LCTF) or an acousto-optic tunable filter), as illustrated in Fig. 6.1-7(*a*) and (*b*). Instead of a single tunable filter that scans the wavelength, we may use a set of fixed filters distributed around each point of the spatial sampling grid, as shown in Fig. 6.1-7(*c*), so that the spectral image is sampled in (x, y) and λ simultaneously. Since each filter is attached to its own detector, the number of detectors becomes quite large. This configuration, which provides a snapshot spectral image, is feasible only for a few spectral channels. An example is the color digital camera, which is a spectral imager using three spectral channels (red, green, and blue) for each spatial point.

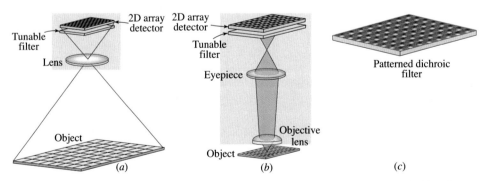

Figure 6.1-7   Schematic of an imaging system with a spectrometer using a tunable filter for (*a*) remote-sensing spectral imaging and (*b*) wide-field spectral microscopy. (*c*) Replacing the tunable filter with a fixed patterned filter, which is a set of spatially distributed dichroic filters.

Scanning System: Whiskbroom Method

The whiskbroom scanner, also referred to as an across-track scanner, scans the 2D object, point by point and measures the spectral distribution at each point (pixel), as illustrated in Fig. 6.1-8. Thus, the spectral cube is constructed as a set of spectra (vertical lines), one for each pixel.

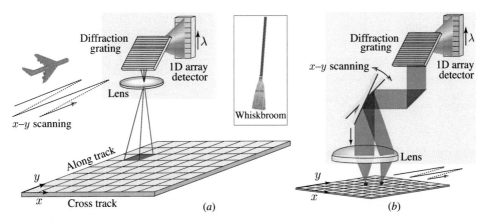

Figure 6.1-8   A whiskbroom scanner builds the spectral cube by collecting the spectral distribution one pixel at the time. (*a*) In remote sensing one spatial dimension is scanned by movement of the platform along track and the other spatial dimension is collected by scanning in the direction perpendicular to the platform movement (cross-track). (*b*) A scanning microscope in the multisensor configuration; mirrors are used to scan in both x and y directions. A scanning microscope in the multiprobe configuration is shown in Fig. 6.2-2(*b*).

The scanner may use rotating mirrors to scan the landscape from side to side (like a whiskbroom) in the direction orthogonal to the direction of sensor motion to obtain the first spatial dimension x (cross-track). The second spatial dimension y is obtained as the sensor moves along the scene (along track). At each pixel, the spectrometer (a prism or a diffraction grating) directs the spectral components of light to a linear array detector responsive within the spectral range. Since the sensor acquires the spectral distribution of each pixel with the same detector array, this approach simplifies the spectral calibration. The spatial resolution using this modality is a function of the forward motion of the sensor (y direction), the speed of the cross-track scanner (x direction), and the measurement speed of the spectrometer (x and y directions). In remote sensing, whiskbroom spectral imagers are used in AVIRIS and LANDSAT, among others.

Hybrid System: Pushbroom Method

The pushbroom spectral imager uses a hybrid scanning–gazing system in which the pixels of each row are (cross-track) simultaneously measured using a lens system and their spectral distributions simultaneously determined using a bank of spectrometers. The rows are scanned sequentially in the other spatial dimension (along track) by either moving the sensor platform or by moving the object itself. Thus, the spectral cube is constructed as a set of vertical planes.

A 2D array detector placed in the focal plane simultaneously records the spectral distribution of all pixels within each line, as illustrated in Fig. 6.1-9. Hyperion, Ikonos, and QuickBird are examples of pushbroom scanners used in remote sensing.

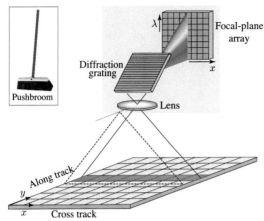

Figure 6.1-9 The pushbroom spectral imager builds the spectral cube by collecting the spectral distributions of all the pixels of each cross-track line (x direction) simultaneously. The other spatial dimension y is built by along-track movement of the platform.

Computed-Tomography Spectral Imaging

Another approach for the acquisition of a spectral image is based on tomography. A dispersive device (diffraction grating) is used to simultaneously spread the spectrum at each position to neighboring positions, and a spectrally insensitive detector records the intensity of the resultant image, as illustrated in Fig. 6.1-10(a). This converts the spectral image into an intensity image – a projection. The process is repeated with dispersive devices pointing along different orientations so that multiple projections are obtained, from which the spectral image is reconstructed using tomographic methods similar to those described in Sec. 4.1.

A diffraction grating oriented at an angle θ, for example, shifts the spectral component of wavelength λ by distances $s\lambda \cos\theta$ and $s\lambda \sin\theta$ in the x and y directions, respectively, where s is a coefficient of proportionality between the displacement and the wavelength. The spectral image $f(x, y, \lambda)$ at a single wavelength λ is therefore converted into an image $f(x - s\lambda \cos\theta, y - s\lambda \sin\theta, \lambda)$. If measured by a spectrally insensitive detector (a conventional camera or array detector), the result is an intensity:

$$g_{\theta,s}(x, y) = \int f(x - s\lambda \cos\theta, y - s\lambda \sin\theta, \lambda)\, d\lambda. \qquad (6.1\text{-}4)$$

This image is a 2D projection of the 3D function $f(x, y, \lambda)$ in a direction determined by the parameters θ and s. For example, for $\theta = 0$ and $s = 1$,

$$g_{0,s}(x, y) = \int f(x - \lambda, y, \lambda)\, d\lambda, \qquad (6.1\text{-}5)$$

which is a projection of the spectral cube $f(x, y, \lambda)$ in the x–λ plane at 45°, as shown in Fig. 6.1-10(b). By measuring these projections at different values of θ and s, $f(x, y, \lambda)$ can be reconstructed. Dispersive devices of different orientations θ and scales s may be implemented simultaneously by use of a single dispersive device – a hologram that generates dispersion at multiple θ and s, as illustrated in Fig. 6.1-10(c). The multiple projections are then measured in a single shot.[1]

---

[1]M. Descour and E. Dereniak, Computed-tomography imaging spectrometer: experimental calibration and reconstruction results, *Applied Optics*, Vol. 34, pp. 4817–4826, 1995; W. R. Johnson, D. W. Wilson, W. Fink, M. Humayun, and G. Bearman, Snapshot hyperspectral imaging in ophthalmology, *Journal of Biomedical Optics*, Vol. 12, p. 014036, 2007.

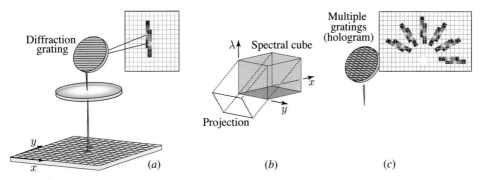

Figure 6.1-10 (*a*) A diffraction grating spreads the spectrum at each position over a neighboring area. (*b*) Projection of the spectral cube. (*c*) Computed-tomography spectral imaging.

6.2 Models of Spectral Imaging

The linear models described in Chapters 3 and 4 for subsurface imaging may be readily generalized to subsurface spectral imaging. We may think of the spectral dependence as an added dimension, so that the spectral imaging of a 2D object is analogous to 3D imaging. If the object is not spectrally dependent, but the image is acquired at different wavelengths or in different spectral bands, then this may be regarded as a form of multiview imaging, with the spectral bands playing the role of the views. We first consider models for measurement of the spectrum at a single position and subsequently extend the model to include spatial distributions in addition to the spectral.

A. Models of Spectroscopy

Spectroscopy is the measurement of a wavelength-dependent physical quantity $f(\lambda)$, such as the absorption coefficient, the scattering cross-section, the reflectance, or the radiance, as a function of the wavelength (or the frequency, or the photon energy). There are two configurations, as previously depicted in Fig. 6.1-5. The first employs a probe with broad spectral distribution and a bank of narrow-band sensors tuned to a set of sampling wavelengths. The second employs a set of narrow-band probes, with narrow spectral distributions centered about the sampling wavelengths, and a broadband sensor. We now show that these two configurations may be represented by the same mathematical model. We take as an example an object with spectrally dependent reflectance $f(\lambda)$, but the results are usable in other applications.

Multisensor Configuration

In this configuration, illustrated in Fig. 6.2-1 in the context of remote sensing, a broad-band probe $P(\lambda)$ illuminates the object. The reflected wave reaching the sensors is $g(\lambda) = P(\lambda)H_\mathrm{p}(\lambda)f(\lambda)H_\mathrm{o}(\lambda)$, where $H_\mathrm{p}(\lambda)$ is the transmittance of the medium between the illumination source and the object, and $H_\mathrm{o}(\lambda)$ is the transmittance of the medium between the object and the sensors. Therefore,

$$g(\lambda) = H(\lambda)f(\lambda), \tag{6.2-1}$$

where

$$H(\lambda) = P(\lambda)H_\mathrm{p}(\lambda)H_\mathrm{o}(\lambda). \tag{6.2-2}$$

The spectral function $g(\lambda)$ is measured by L sensors of response functions, $R^{(1)}(\lambda)$, $R^{(2)}(\lambda), \ldots, R^{(L)}(\lambda)$ (also called sampling functions), centered at wavelengths λ_1, λ_2, $\ldots, \lambda_L$, and covering an extended spectral range, as shown in Fig. 6.2-1. The reading of the ℓth sensor is the projection

$$g^{(\ell)} = \int R^{(\ell)}(\lambda)g(\lambda)\,d\lambda = \int R^{(\ell)}(\lambda)H(\lambda)f(\lambda)\,d\lambda, \quad \ell = 1, 2 \ldots, L. \quad (6.2\text{-}3)$$

The result is a representation of the continuous function $g(\lambda)$ with L samples, $g^{(1)}, g^{(2)}$, $\ldots, g^{(L)}$, via the sampling functions $\{R^{(\ell)}(\lambda)\}$. A similar representation was introduced in Sec. 5.1A for the sampling of spatial functions. In remote-sensing applications, the sampling functions are usually called **bands** and the number of bands L can range from a few to hundreds (as in hyperspectral imaging). In microscopy, the sampling functions are called **channels** and the number of channels is usually small. In summary, the spectral measurement is modeled mathematically by (6.2-3) and (6.2-2), as illustrated by the block diagram in Fig. 6.2-1. This model also applies to other situations. For example, if $f(\lambda)$ represents the emission spectrum of a self-luminous object, then $H(\lambda) = H_o(\lambda)$.

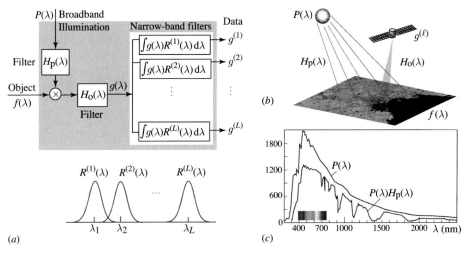

Figure 6.2-1   (a) Mathematical model for measurement of the spectral reflectance $f(\lambda)$ using an L-band spectrometer. The illumination source is transmitted through a filter $H_p(\lambda)$ and the reflected wave is transmitted through a filter $H_o(\lambda)$ before measurement. (b) Remote-sensing example of measurement of the spectral reflectance at a point or small ground area. A broadband source (sunlight) illuminates the object via the atmosphere. The reflected/backscattered radiation collected from a small area is measured after traveling once more through the atmosphere. (c) Wavelength dependence of the sun spectral irradiance $P(\lambda)$ [W/(m^2 μm)] outside the atmosphere and the direct spectral irradiance at sea level, which is the product of $P(\lambda)$ and the atmospheric transmitance $H_p(\lambda)$.

Multiprobe Configuration

This configuration, shown in Fig. 6.2-2 in the context of microscopy, employs a bank of probes with spectral distributions $P^{(1)}(\lambda), P^{(2)}(\lambda), \ldots, P^{(L)}(\lambda)$, centered at a set of sampling wavelengths, $\lambda_1, \lambda_2, \ldots, \lambda_L$, and a broadband sensor of responsivity $R_s(\lambda)$. When the reflectance $f(\lambda)$ of an object is measured, the ℓth probe produces a signal $I^{(\ell)}(\lambda) = P^{(\ell)}(\lambda)H_p(\lambda)f(\lambda)H_o(\lambda)$ at the input of the sensor, where $H_p(\lambda)$ and $H_o(\lambda)$

are filters representing the path between the source and the object, and between the object and the sensor, respectively. The sensor generates a signal

$$g^{(\ell)} = \int I^{(\ell)}(\lambda) R_{\rm s}(\lambda)\, d\lambda = \int I^{(\ell)}(\lambda) H(\lambda) f(\lambda)\, d\lambda, \quad \ell = 1, 2 \ldots, L, \quad (6.2\text{-}4)$$

where

$$H(\lambda) = H_{\rm p}(\lambda) H_{\rm o}(\lambda) R_{\rm s}(\lambda). \quad (6.2\text{-}5)$$

Comparing (6.2-4) and (6.2-3), we see that the multiprobe configuration is mathematically equivalent to the multisensor configuration, with the L probe distributions $P^{(\ell)}(\lambda)$ playing the role of the L sensor functions $R^{(\ell)}(\lambda)$, and the sensor responsivity $R_{\rm s}(\lambda)$ playing the role of the illumination function $P(\lambda)$. As illustrated in Fig. 6.2-2(b), the multiprobe configuration is used in laser scanning fluorescence microscopy to measure the spectral distribution of the absorption cross-section. Multiple lasers in the visible and UV spectral ranges are used.

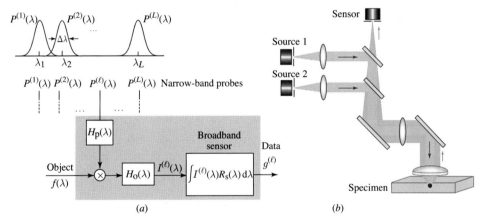

(a) (b)

Figure 6.2-2 (a) Model for measurement of a spectral function $f(\lambda)$ using a multiprobe configuration. The spectral distributions of the probes are centered at wavelengths $\lambda_1, \lambda_2, \ldots, \lambda_L$ and the sensor is broadband. The medium between the source and the object has transmittance $H_{\rm p}(\lambda)$ and the medium between the object and the sensor has transmittance $H_{\rm o}(\lambda)$. (b) An example: laser scanning microscope using multiple lasers.

Special Case: Measurement of a Linearly Mixed Spectrum

As a special case, consider the spectral function

$$f(\lambda) = \sum_{i=1}^{P} f_i\, s_i(\lambda), \quad (6.2\text{-}6)$$

which is a weighted sum of P known spectra $\{s_i(\lambda)\}$ representing certain components (endmembers). The weights $\{f_i\}$ represent the abundances of the endmembers so that $\sum_{i=1}^{P} f_i = 1$, as discussed in Sec. 6.1.

Multisensor Configuration.   If the spectrum is measured with an L-channel multi-sensor spectrometer, then the output of the ℓth band is

$$g^{(\ell)} = \int R^{(\ell)}(\lambda) f(\lambda) \, d\lambda, \tag{6.2-7}$$

where $R^{(\ell)}(\lambda)$ is the spectrometer responsivity at the ℓth channel. The functions $s_i(\lambda)$, $f(\lambda)$, and $R^{(\ell)}(\lambda)$ are illustrated in Fig. 6.2-3.

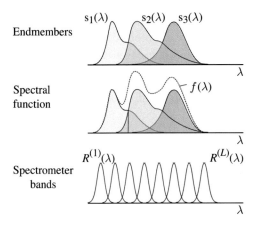

Endmembers $s_1(\lambda)$ $s_2(\lambda)$ $s_3(\lambda)$

λ

Spectral function $f(\lambda)$

λ

Spectrometer bands $R^{(1)}(\lambda)$ $R^{(L)}(\lambda)$

λ

Figure 6.2-3   A composite spectral function $f(\lambda)$ expressed as a weighted superposition of three endmembers, observed by an eight-band spectrometer. The shape of $f(\lambda)$ depends on the mixing ratios f_1, f_2, and f_3.

It follows from (6.2-7) and (6.2-6) that

$$g^{(\ell)} = \sum_{i=1}^{P} H_i^{(\ell)} f_i, \quad \ell = 1, 2, \ldots, L, \tag{6.2-8}$$

where

$$H_i^{(\ell)} = \int R^{(\ell)}(\lambda) s_i(\lambda) \, d\lambda \tag{6.2-9}$$

represents the relative contribution of the ith endmember to the ℓth spectrometer band. Equation (6.2-8), which relates the L readings of the spectrometer to the P values of the abundance, may be written in the matrix form

$$\mathbf{g} = \mathbf{Hf}, \tag{6.2-10}$$

where $\mathbf{f}$ is a vector of size P representing the abundance weights f_i, $\mathbf{g}$ is a vector of size L representing the outputs of the spectrometer $g^{(\ell)}$, and $\mathbf{H}$ is an $L \times P$ matrix with elements $H_i^{(\ell)}$ representing the spectral signatures of the endmembers in relation to the spectrometer bands. For a small number of endmembers P and a small number of spectrometer channels, the matrix $\mathbf{H}$ is relatively small and the spectral measurement process is not computationally demanding. In any case, the number of channels L must be greater than, or equal to, the number of endmembers P so that the problem of determining $\mathbf{f}$ from $\mathbf{g}$ has a solution (see Sec. 5.2).

Multiprobe Configuration. For a multiprobe configuration with probes $\{P^{(\ell)}(\lambda)\}$, we substitute (6.2-6) into (6.2-4) to reproduce (6.2-8) and (6.2-10) with the matrix elements

$$H_i^{(\ell)} = \int P^{(\ell)}(\lambda) s_i(\lambda) \, d\lambda. \tag{6.2-11}$$

▶ Problems 6.2-1, 6.2-2

B. Models of Spectral Imaging

When an L-band spectral imager measures a spectral image $f(\mathbf{r}, \lambda)$ it generates L images $g^{(\ell)}(\mathbf{r})$, $\ell = 1, 2, \ldots, L$, representing slices of the spectral cube. We now develop models for this operation for the multisensor and the multiprobe configurations, with the spatial effects now included.

Multisensor Configuration

Here, the object is illuminated with a probe $P(\mathbf{r}, \lambda)$, filtered by a filter $H_p(\lambda)$, and the transmitted, reflected or backscattered distribution $P(\mathbf{r}, \lambda) H_p(\lambda) f(\mathbf{r}, \lambda) H_o(\lambda)$ is imaged by a camera modeled as a linear system of impulse response function (point spread function) $h_o(\mathbf{r}, \mathbf{r}', \lambda)$, which is usually wavelength dependent. The captured spectral image

$$g(\mathbf{r}, \lambda) \propto \int h_o(\mathbf{r}, \mathbf{r}', \lambda) P(\mathbf{r}', \lambda) H_p(\lambda) H_o(\lambda) f(\mathbf{r}', \lambda) \, d\mathbf{r}' \tag{6.2-12}$$

is measured by the sensors (the spectrometer). The output for the ℓth band is an image

$$g^{(\ell)}(\mathbf{r}) = \int g(\mathbf{r}, \lambda) R^{(\ell)}(\lambda) \, d\lambda, \tag{6.2-13}$$

where $R^{(\ell)}(\lambda)$ is the spectral responsivity of the ℓth band. These operations are shown schematically in Fig. 6.2-4.

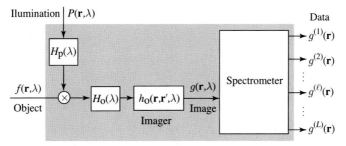

Figure 6.2-4 Linear model of a spectral imaging system in the multisensor configuration. The spectral responsivities of the spectrometer bands are centered at wavelengths $\lambda_1, \lambda_2, \ldots, \lambda_L$.

The following are some special cases.

Point-by-Point Spectrometer.   If the imager introduces no spatial blur, i.e., $h_o(\mathbf{r}, \mathbf{r}', \lambda) = \delta(\mathbf{r} - \mathbf{r}')H_o(\lambda)$, then

$$g(\mathbf{r}, \lambda) = P(\lambda)H_p(\lambda)H_o(\lambda)f(\mathbf{r}, \lambda), \tag{6.2-14}$$

so that we recover (6.2-1) and (6.2-2), which describe a spectrometer that measures the object spectral distribution at each point, independently of other points.

Area-by-Area Spectrometer.   Suppose now that the imager introducing a linear shift-invariant blur for which $h_o(\mathbf{r}, \mathbf{r}', \lambda) = h_o(\mathbf{r} - \mathbf{r}')H_o(\lambda)$, where $h_o(\mathbf{r})$ is a point spread function of finite extent (finite area in the 2D case). The imaging equation then has the simple form

$$g(\mathbf{r}, \lambda) = P(\lambda)H_p(\lambda)H_o(\lambda)\,[h_o(\mathbf{r}) \otimes f(\mathbf{r}, \lambda)]. \tag{6.2-15}$$

In this case, a spatially filtered version of the object $h_o(\mathbf{r}) \otimes f(\mathbf{r}, \lambda)$ is measured by the spectrometer. If $h_o(\mathbf{r})$ represents a low-pass filter that averages the object spatial distribution over some area, then the measured data at each position provides the average spectrum over that area. The spectral imager is then an area-by-area spectrometer.

Multiprobe Configuration

For L probes with spectral distributions $P^\ell(\lambda)$ and uniform spatial distributions, the input to the imager is the product $P^{(\ell)}(\lambda)H_p(\lambda)f(\mathbf{r}, \lambda)H_o(\lambda)$, where $H_p(\lambda)$ and $H_o(\lambda)$ are the transmittance of the illumination and sensing systems, so that its output is

$$I^{(\ell)}(\mathbf{r}, \lambda) = \int h_o(\mathbf{r}, \mathbf{r}', \lambda)P^{(\ell)}(\lambda)H_p(\lambda)H_o(\lambda)f(\mathbf{r}', \lambda)\,d\mathbf{r}'. \tag{6.2-16}$$

A broadband sensor of responsivity $R_s(\lambda)$ generates the data

$$I^{(\ell)}(\mathbf{r}) = \int R_s(\lambda)I^{(\ell)}(\mathbf{r}, \lambda)\,d\lambda. \tag{6.2-17}$$

These operations are illustrated schematically in Fig. 6.2-5.

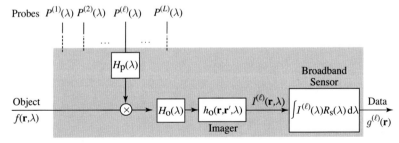

Figure 6.2-5   Linear model of a multispectral imaging system in the multiprobe configuration. The spectral distributions of the probes are centered at wavelengths $\lambda_1, \lambda_2, \ldots, \lambda_L$.

Upon substitution from (6.2-16) into (6.2-17), we obtain

$$I^{(\ell)}(\mathbf{r}) = \int P^{(\ell)}(\lambda)g(\mathbf{r}, \lambda)\,d\lambda, \tag{6.2-18}$$

where

$$g(\mathbf{r}, \lambda) = R_{\mathrm{s}}(\lambda) H_{\mathrm{p}}(\lambda) H_{\mathrm{o}}(\lambda) \int h_{\mathrm{o}}(\mathbf{r}, \mathbf{r}', \lambda) f(\mathbf{r}, \lambda) \, d\mathbf{r}'. \tag{6.2-19}$$

Equations (6.2-18) and (6.2-19) for the multiprobe configuration are equivalent to (6.2-13) and (6.2-12), which describe the multisensor configuration, where the role of the spectrometer functions $R^{(\ell)}(\lambda)$ is played here by the probe functions $P^{(\ell)}(\lambda)$.

▶ Problem 6.2-3

C. Digital Models of Spectral Imaging

Discretization.   Adopting a sampling approach similar to that described in Sec. 5.1A, we may represent the continuous spectral image $f(\mathbf{r}, \lambda)$, which represents the object, by a digital spectral image. For example, the sampled version of the 2D spectral image $f(x, y, \lambda)$ is the digital function $f(n_x, n_y, n_\lambda)$ defined on a 3D grid of dimensions $N_x \times N_y \times N_\lambda$. Similarly, the L output images of the spectral imager $g^{(\ell)}(x, y)$ may be described by a set of L digital images $g^{(\ell)}(m_x, m_y)$, each of dimensions $M_x \times M_y$, where L is the number of spectrometer bands. Thus, the continuous spectral cube (Fig. 6.2-6) takes a discrete form of dimensions $M_x \times M_y \times L$.

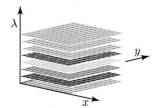

Figure 6.2-6   The discrete spectral cube as a λ-stack.

Matrix Description.   The discrete functions $f(n_x, n_y, n_\lambda)$ and $g^{(\ell)}(m_x, m_y)$ may also be converted into vectors (column matrices) $\mathbf{f}$ and $\mathbf{g}^{(\ell)}$ of dimensions $N = N_x N_y N_\lambda$ and $M = M_x M_y$, respectively. Since each of the measured images $g^{(\ell)}$ can be related to the object function f by a linear transformation, the relation between each of the vectors $\mathbf{g}^{(\ell)}$ and the vector $\mathbf{f}$ may be expressed as a matrix relation

$$\mathbf{g}^{(\ell)} = \mathbf{H}^{(\ell)} \mathbf{f}, \qquad \ell = 1, 2, \ldots, L. \tag{6.2-20}$$

The vectors $\mathbf{g}^{(\ell)}$, for $\ell = 1, 2, \ldots, L$, may also be stacked to form a single vector $\mathbf{g}$ so that (6.2-20) may be alternatively written as a single matrix equation

$$\mathbf{g} = \mathbf{H}\mathbf{f}, \tag{6.2-21}$$

where $\mathbf{H}$ is an $M \times N$ matrix representing the overall spectral imager.

For a typical hyperspectral imager, the dimensions of the measured spectral image are quite large. For example, for a small image of 100×100 pixels and 100 spectral bands, the dimensions of the spectral cube are $100 \times 100 \times 100 = 10^6$. If $\mathbf{f}$ has the same dimension, then (6.2-21) represents a set of a million equations with a million unknowns, which is quite astounding.

The spectral imaging system may also be modeled as a relation between the measured images $\mathbf{g}^{(\ell)}$ at the outputs of the spectrometer bands and the input spectral image

f, as filtered by the same spectrometer bands, labeled $\mathbf{f}^{(\ell)}$. The linear relation between $\mathbf{g}^{(\ell)}$ and $\mathbf{f}^{(\ell)}$ is then described by a matrix relation:

$$
\begin{bmatrix} g_1 \\ g_2 \\ \vdots \\ g_L \end{bmatrix} = \begin{bmatrix} \mathbf{H}_{11} & \mathbf{H}_{12} & \cdots & \mathbf{H}_{1L} \\ \mathbf{H}_{21} & \mathbf{H}_{22} & \cdots & \mathbf{H}_{2L} \\ \vdots & \vdots & \ddots & \vdots \\ \mathbf{H}_{L1} & \mathbf{H}_{L2} & \cdots & \mathbf{H}_{LL} \end{bmatrix} \begin{bmatrix} f_1 \\ f_2 \\ \vdots \\ f_L \end{bmatrix}. \tag{6.2-22}
$$

The diagonal entries $\mathbf{H}_{\ell\ell}$ represent the spatial transformation within the ℓth spectral band, while the off-diagonal entries $\mathbf{H}_{\ell\ell'}$ represent the cross-talk between band ℓ and band ℓ', which occurs when the spectral distributions of neighboring bands overlap.

Nonlinear Models.   The models of spectral imaging presented in this section are based on the assumption of linearity of the imaging process. These linear models are, of course, not applicable when nonlinear effects are present, as can happen, e.g., in radiative transfer in underskin imaging (see Sec. 6.4A) or underwater imaging (see Sec. 6.4B).

6.3   Information Extraction

The information to be extracted from a measured spectral image may be a full **mapping** of the object spectral cube, or simply an **estimation** of a few parameters characterizing the object, such as its location, size, shape, or spectral features (e.g., the strength of spectral components within a given band). In other applications, the goal is to detect the presence or absence of a target, or a feature of a target, based on the measured spectral image. This task is called **detection**. In yet other situations, the measured spectral image may be used to classify the target as belonging to one of a set of classes of objects with known spatial–spectral characteristics. This task is called **classification**. An introduction to the basic methods of detection and classification is provided in Appendix C. In any of these applications, the estimation or decision is based on the measured spectral image $g(\mathbf{r}, \lambda)$, which is related to the actual spectral image $f(\mathbf{r}, \lambda)$ that contains the relevant object information. This relation depends on the imaging configuration and the quality of the spatial and spectral imaging system, including the illumination source and the filtering effects introduced by the intervening media, as described by the models in Sec. 6.2.

Estimation of the Spectral Image.   Consider first the simpler problem of spectral imaging with a spectral imager that does not introduce spatial blur, e.g., a point-by-point spectrometer that measures the spectrum at each position $\mathbf{r}$. In this case, at any position, the measured spectrum is related to the true spectrum by

$$
g(\lambda) = H(\lambda)f(\lambda) + w(\lambda), \tag{6.3-1}
$$

where the filter $H(\lambda) = P(\lambda)H_\mathrm{p}(\lambda)H_\mathrm{o}(\lambda)$ includes the spectral distributions of the illumination and the spectral transmittance of the illumination and imaging systems, as in (6.2-1). This equation also includes an additive background term $w(\lambda)$ (e.g., resulting from reflection at intervening boundary layers of the medium before reaching the subsurface object) as well as noise. While the background term may be subtracted out, the accompanying noise or uncertainty cannot. To estimate $f(\lambda)$ from $g(\lambda)$, (6.3-1) may be inverted, so that $\hat{f}(\lambda) = H^{-1}(\lambda)[g(\lambda) - \bar{w}(\lambda)]$, where $\bar{w}(\lambda)$ is the mean value of $w(\lambda)$. However, regularized inverse filters may also be used, as described in

Sec. 3.3. Suppose now that a spectral imager introduces linear shift-invariant spatial blur. In this case, at any wavelength λ, the imaging is described by a convolution

$$g(\mathbf{r}, \lambda) = h(\mathbf{r}, \lambda) \otimes f(\mathbf{r}, \lambda) + w(\lambda), \tag{6.3-2}$$

where $\otimes$ represents the operation of convolution with respect to the spatial variable $\mathbf{r}$. At each wavelength λ, the inverse problem is a spatial deconvolution problem, which may be implemented by use of the techniques in (Sec. 3.3).

Discrete Formulation of the Estimation Problem. If $g(\mathbf{r}, \lambda)$ is measured by an L-band spectrometer producing a set of L images $g^{(\ell)}(\mathbf{r})$, which are digitized as a set of vectors $\mathbf{g}^{(\ell)}$ and stacked as a single vector $\mathbf{g}$, then the relation between the measured spectral image $g(\mathbf{r}, \lambda)$ and the actual spectral image $f(\mathbf{r}, \lambda)$ is converted into the matrix imaging equation

$$\mathbf{g} = \mathbf{H}\mathbf{f} + \mathbf{w}, \tag{6.3-3}$$

where $\mathbf{w}$ is a random vector representing additive noise. The inverse problem of re-constructing $\mathbf{f}$ from $\mathbf{g}$ may be solved by use of any of the inverse techniques described in Chapter 5. However, since the dimensions of the spectral image are typically very large, this problem can be challenging except under special simplifying conditions.

In this section, we consider two information extraction problems in the context of spectral imaging. The first (Sec. 6.3A) is a restoration problem involving a spectral image of an object composed of a finite number of constituents (endmembers), each of known spectral distribution, such as that described in Sec. 6.1A. The problem is to estimate the spatial distributions (abundances) of each of these constituents from the overall spectral image. This special *estimation* problem is called **unmixing**. The second (Sec. 6.3B) is a classification problem based on the measurement of a spectral image.

A. Unmixing of Linearly Mixed Spectra

An important estimation problem associated with point-by-point spectroscopy is the unmixing (or separation) of linearly mixed spectra. As described in Sec. 6.1A, in many applications the spectral function $f(\lambda)$ of the object is a weighted superposition of a few constitutents (endmembers or substances) of known spectral distributions $s_i(\lambda), i = 1, 2, \ldots, P$,

$$f(\lambda) = \sum_{i=1}^{P} f_i \, s_i(\lambda), \tag{6.3-4}$$

and the unknown mixing weights f_i are to be estimated. For brevity, the dependence of f_i on $\mathbf{r}$ has been suppressed, but the ultimate goal is to obtain the maps $f_i(\mathbf{r})$, since these represent the spatial distribution of the *concentration* or the *abundance* of the various substances. This type of estimation problem is called **spectrometry**.

For example, for an object made of two substances ($P = 2$), $f(\lambda) = f_1 \, s_1(\lambda) + f_2 \, s_2(\lambda)$. If the spectral image is measured at only two wavelengths, λ_1 and λ_2, we obtain two equations:

$$f(\lambda_1) = f_1 \, s_1(\lambda_1) + f_2 \, s_2(\lambda_1)$$
$$f(\lambda_2) = f_1 \, s_1(\lambda_2) + f_2 \, s_2(\lambda_2).$$

If the two substances have distinct spectra, these equations may be solved for the two unknown concentrations f_1 and f_2.

In most real systems, the spectral measurement is made by use of spectrometers with channels (bands) of finite spectral width or probes of finite spectral width. In any case, as shown in Sec. 6.2, if an L-band spectrometer is used to measure the spectral function, then the outcome is a vector $\mathbf{g} = [g_1 \ g_2 \ \ldots \ g_L]^\mathrm{T}$ related to the vector of unknown concentrations (or abundances) $\mathbf{f} = [f_1 \ f_2 \ \ldots \ f_P]^\mathrm{T}$ by the usual matrix relation

$$\mathbf{g} = \mathbf{Hf}, \tag{6.3-5}$$

where $\mathbf{H}$ is an $L \times P$ matrix with elements containing the spectra of the endmembers and the responsivities of the spectrometer bands in the multisensor case [as in (6.2-9)], or the spectral distributions of the probes in the multiprobe case [as in (6.2-11)]. In the presence of additive noise,

$$\mathbf{g} = \mathbf{Hf} + \mathbf{w}, \tag{6.3-6}$$

where $\mathbf{w}$ is a vector of random variables representing the noise.

Abundance Estimation

If the spectra of the endmembers are known, i.e., the matrix $\mathbf{H}$ is known, the problem is to estimate the abundance weights $\mathbf{f}$ from (6.3-6), given the measurement $\mathbf{g}$ under the conditions that elements of $\mathbf{f}$ are non-negative (since they represent fractional values). Also, since the fractional values must add up to unity,

$$\sum_{i=1}^{P} f_i = 1, \quad \text{or} \quad \mathbf{1}^\mathrm{T}\mathbf{f} = 1,$$

where $\mathbf{1}$ is a vector of length P with unity elements. This condition is called the sum-to-one (STO) constraint. Typically $L > P$, so (6.3-6) is an overconstrained linear set of algebraic equations. An estimation strategy is to minimize the square error, i.e., find an abundance vector estimate $\hat{\mathbf{f}}$ that minimizes the square error $\|\mathbf{g} - \mathbf{Hf}\|_2^2$ under the constraints $\mathbf{1}^\mathrm{T}\mathbf{f} = 1$ and $f_i \geq 0$, or

$$\hat{\mathbf{f}} = \arg \min_{f_i \geq 0, \ \mathbf{1}^\mathrm{T}\mathbf{f}=1} \|\mathbf{g} - \mathbf{Hf}\|_2^2. \tag{6.3-7}$$

Many algorithms exist for solving this constrained optimization problem, as discussed next.

Unconstrained Linear Least-Squares (ULS) Solution.   The simplest solution of the abundance estimation problem is obtained by completely ignoring the constraints. The unconstrained least-squares (ULS) problem has an explicit solution in terms of the pseudo inverse matrix (see Sec. 5.3):

$$\boxed{\hat{\mathbf{f}}_{\mathrm{ULS}} = (\mathbf{H}^\mathrm{T}\mathbf{H})^{-1}\mathbf{H}^\mathrm{T}\mathbf{g}.} \tag{6.3-8}$$

This solution is also obtained if the noise components of $\mathbf{w}$ in (6.3-6) are assumed to be independent, identically distributed Gaussian random variables. Although this solution is simple to implement, it has the disadvantage that the estimated fractional abundances could be negative and their sum could differ from unity. This would be a solution without physical meaning.

Solution Satisfying the Sum-To-One (STO) Constraint.   An explicit solution that enforces the STO constraint, but not the positivity constraint, is[2]

$$\hat{\mathbf{f}}_{\mathrm{STO}} = \hat{\mathbf{f}}_{\mathrm{ULS}} + (1 - \mathbf{1}^{\mathrm{T}}\hat{\mathbf{f}}_{\mathrm{ULS}}) \frac{(\mathbf{H}^{\mathrm{T}}\mathbf{H})^{-1}\mathbf{1}}{\mathbf{1}^{\mathrm{T}}(\mathbf{H}^{\mathrm{T}}\mathbf{H})^{-1}\mathbf{g}\mathbf{1}}. \qquad (6.3\text{-}9)$$

This solution is also easily implemented, but does not guarantee non-negativity of the fractional abundances.

Nonnegative Linear Least-Squares (NNLS) Solution.   The linear least-squares problem with only the non-negativity constraints is referred to in the linear algebra literature as the NNLS problem. The Lawson and Hansons algorithm[3] is the most commonly used solution, and is available in MATLAB. Other iterative algorithms can also be used, including the multiplicative iterative algorithms.[4]

Fully Constrained Problem.   No explicit solution exists when both the STO and the non-negativity constraints are enforced. Algorithms to solve this problem have been proposed. One algorithm is based on transforming the unmixing problem to a least-distance least-squares problem.[5] The advantage of this approach is that the resulting dual problem is an NNLS problem for which several solution algorithms exist, as described previously.

**EXAMPLE 6.3-1.   *Fluorescence Microscopy.*   As mentioned in Sec. 6.1A, fluorescence microscopy is an important technique for biological imaging that relies on fluorophores (fluorescent dyes or fluorescent proteins) that are injected into the cells. Different fluorophores have different excitation spectra, different emission spectra, and attach to different cellular sites. They are therefore excellent agents for imaging. A single fluorophore can be selectively excited, or its emission selectively detected, so that an image of the spatial distribution of its concentration, and hence the concentration of its host molecule, can be acquired by use of the appropriate excitation source or the appropriate detection spectrometer.

Emission-Based Unmixing.   When several fluorophores (endmembers) with overlapping spectra are used, the spectral image measured by a fluorescence scanning microscope contains mixed contributions from different fluorophores and unmixing is necessary to separate the relative contributions (abundances). If $s_i(\lambda)$ is the emission spectrum of the ith fluorophore and f_i is its relative concentration at that position, then the total fluorescence spectral image is $f(\lambda) = \sum_{i=1}^{P} f_i s_i(\lambda)$, where P is the number of fluorophores. When detected by a spectrometer with L channels (bands), the result is a set of L numbers forming a vector $\mathbf{g} = \mathbf{H}\mathbf{f}$, where $\mathbf{f}$ is the vector of the unknown fluorophore concentrations f_i and $\mathbf{H}$ is a matrix whose elements are determined by the contributions of each of the fluorophores to each of the spectrometer channels, in accordance with (6.2-9). Unmixing techniques can be readily used to determine $\mathbf{f}$ from $\mathbf{g}$ at each position, resulting in an unmixed image $f_i(\mathbf{r})$ for

---

[2]C. L. Lawson and R. J. Hanson, *Solving Least Square Problems*, Prentice-Hall, 1974.

[3]ibid.

[4]M. Vélez-Reyes, S. Rosario, A. Puetz, R. B. Lockwood, Iterative algorithms for unmixing of hyperspectral imagery, in *Algorithms and Technologies for Multispectral, Hyperspectral, and Ultraspectral Imagery IX, Proceedings of SPIE*, Vol. 5093, pp. 418–429, 2003.

[5]S. Rosario-Torres and M. Vélez-Reyes, An algorithm for fully constrained abundance estimation in hyperspectral unmixing, in *Algorithms and Technologies for Multispectral, Hyperspectral, and Ultraspectral Imagery XI, Proceedings of SPIE*, Vol. 5806, pp. 711–719, 2005.

each fluorophore. Figure 6.3-1 illustrates an example of two fluorescent proteins with overlapping spectra, excited by a single excitation source, and detected with a two-channel spectrometer (using two filters in the same CDD camera), i.e., in this example $P = L = 2$.

Excitation-Based Unmixing.   The same concept applies for fluorophores with different excitation spectra. Here, L probes with spectral distributions $P^{(\ell)}(\lambda)$ excite P fluorophores with absorption spectra $s_i(\lambda)$, and the total fluorescence is detected with a single broadband detector. The total absorption is $f(\lambda) = \sum_{i=1}^{P} f_i\, s_i(\lambda)$, where f_i is the relative concentration of the ith fluorophore. When the ℓth excitation is applied, the total fluorescence is proportional to the integral of $P^{(\ell)}(\lambda)f(\lambda)$. This results in the vector relation $\mathbf{g} = \mathbf{Hf}$, where $\mathbf{H}$ is a matrix whose elements are determined by the excitation spectra in accordance with (6.2-11). This is the same mathematical model as in the emission-based case, with the excitation spectra $P^{(\ell)}(\lambda)$ playing the role of the spectrometer functions $R^{(\ell)}(\lambda)$.

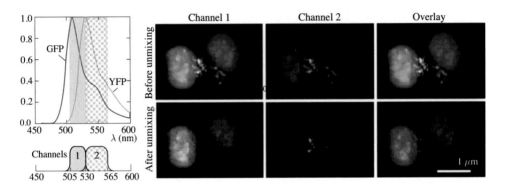

Figure 6.3-1   Cellular spectral imaging with two fluorophores (EGFP and YFP fusion proteins) of overlapping fluorescence spectra and a two-channel spectrometer (channel 1 in the 505–530 nm band and channel 2 in the 530–565 nm band). The nuclei are labeled with histone-EGPF and the Golgi complex with a Golgi-targeted YFP. Upper and lower images are before and after unmixing, respectively. Left images are acquired by detection channel 1, middle images are acquired by detection channel 2, and right images are overlays of the two channels. All images are projections of a 3D stack. Unmixing clearly separates the GFP and YFP distributions, as indicated by the bottom left and middle images. Adapted from T. Zimmermann, J. Rietdorf, and R. Pepperkok, *FEBS Letters*, Vol. 546, pp. 87–92, 2003.

EXAMPLE 6.3-2.   *Oximetry and Diffuse Optical Tomography of Brain Activity.*   As described in Sec. 2.2A (see Fig. 2.2-4), biological tissue has a transparent window in the electromagnetic spectrum in a near-infrared band nestled between absorption bands of water in the mid-infrared and hemoglobin absorption in the visible region. At wavelengths within this window, light penetrates significantly through the tissue and can be used for sensing and imaging. For example, since the spectral dependence of the absorption coefficients of light by oxygenated (HbO_2) and deoxygenated (Hb) hemoglobin is different, as shown in Fig. 6.3-2, their concentrations (abundances) may be readily estimated by measuring the overall absorption coefficient at multiple wavelengths and using an unmixing procedure. Measurement of blood oxygenation is called **oximetry.**

As described in Sec. 4.5A, diffuse optical tomography (DOT) may be used for brain imaging, i.e., interrogating blood beneath the skull using multiple wavelengths of infrared light. Applications include mapping task-related changes in neural activity, which is correlated with venous changes in the concentration of oxyhemoglobin and deoxyhemoglobin in the brain. In this application, $s_1(\lambda)$ and $s_2(\lambda)$ are the absorption coefficients of oxygenated and deoxygenated hemoglobin, respectively, and $f_1(\mathbf{r})$ and $f_2(\mathbf{r})$ are their concentrations. The images $f_1(\mathbf{r})$ and $f_2(\mathbf{r})$, which provide measures of brain activity, are usually obtained as a function of time following, e.g., some motor task.

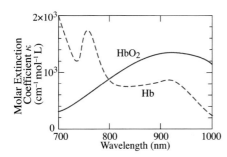

Figure 6.3-2 Wavelength dependence of the molar extinction coefficients κ [cm^{-1} mol^{-1} L] of oxygenated hemoglobin (HbO$_2$) and deoxygenated hemoglobin (Hb). The absorption coefficient μ_a [cm^{-1}] $=$ ln(10)κC_m, where C_m is the molar concentration (moles/liter). The typical concentration of hemoglobin in whole blood is 150 g/L corresponding to C_m = 2.326 × 10^{-3} mol/L, so that for κ = 10^3, μ_a = 5.36 cm^{-1}. Lower concentrations in tissue correspond to proportionally smaller absorption coefficients.

EXAMPLE 6.3-3. *Dual-Energy X-Ray Imaging.* Two X-ray radiographs recorded at two levels of X-ray energy can provide information on the material composition of the object. Consider an object composed of two materials with different absorption coefficients $\alpha_1(\lambda)$ and $\alpha_2(\lambda)$, which are known function of the wavelength λ, or the photon energy $E = hc/\lambda$, e.g., as exemplified in Fig. 6.3-3. If the fractions of these materials in the object are f_1 and f_2, then the total attenuation coefficient is $\alpha(\lambda) = f_1\alpha_1(\lambda) + f_2\alpha_2(\lambda)$, so that the X-ray transmittance through a layer of thickness d is $\mathcal{T}(\lambda) = \exp[-\alpha(\lambda)d]$. Therefore, the signal $g(\lambda) = -\ln[\mathcal{T}(\lambda)]$ is related to the concentrations f_1 and f_2 by the linear relation

$$g(\lambda) = f_1 s_1(\lambda) + f_2 s_2(\lambda), \tag{6.3-10}$$

where $s_1(\lambda) = \alpha_1(\lambda)d$ and $s_2(\lambda) = \alpha_2(\lambda)d$ are known functions. If the signal $g(\lambda)$ is measured at two or more wavelengths, then the fractions f_1 and f_2 can be estimated using the unmixing techniques described earlier. These results may be readily generalized to more than two materials.

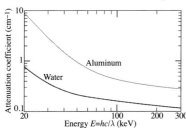

Figure 6.3-3 Dependence of the absorption coefficient of aluminum and water on the X-ray photon energy $E = hc/\lambda$. If λ is in units of nm and E in units of keV, then $E \approx 1.24/\lambda$.

Dual-energy X-ray scanners are routinely used for inspection of carry-on bags in airports. Two X-ray sources, high energy and low energy, are used and the transmitted X-rays are filtered and detected to generate two images. An unmixing algorithm is used to generate a color-coded image (e.g., the image on the right; after Wikipedia) showing different types of materials, e.g., metals, organic materials, and narcotics and explosives in liquids and powders. Other applications include **dual-energy X-ray absorptiometry (DXA)**, which is used to measure bone mineral density for the diagnosis of osteoporosis.

Note that (6.3-10) oversimplifies the unmixing problem, since it assumes that monochromatic sources and/or detectors responsive to a single wavelength are used. In reality, X-ray sources and detectors have finite spectral widths, say $P_\ell(\lambda)$ and $R_\ell(\lambda)$, respectively, where $\ell = 1, 2$ denotes the low- and high-energy measurements. Therefore, the measured signal g_ℓ is an integral over the wavelength

$$g_\ell = \int P_\ell(\lambda)R_\ell(\lambda)\exp[-\alpha(\lambda)d]\,d\lambda = \int P_\ell(\lambda)R_\ell(\lambda)\exp[-f_1 s_1(\lambda) - f_2 s_2(\lambda)]\,d\lambda.$$

Clearly, the relation between the measurements g_1 and g_2 is *not* linearly related to the unknown quantities, f_1 and f_2 and taking the logarithm would not linearize the problem in this case. To solve this nonlinear unmixing problem, sophisticated mathematical techniques, beyond the scope of this book, are necessary.

▶ Problems 6.3-1–6.3-4

B. Classification

Basic Principle.   Pattern classification is the process of identifying a pattern as a member of one of a set of categories, or classes, of known properties. A pattern class can have singular unique characteristics or may consist of *similar* but not identical objects. The objects within each class are samples, examples, or prototypes of that particular class, ideally representing the full intra-class variability. The classification decision may utilize the full data in the measured pattern (e.g., the measured spectral image), but it is usually based on a few key features derived from the measured data by use of linear or nonlinear transformations. The process of feature extraction may be regarded as a form of data compression aimed at reducing data dimensionality while still preserving the ability to discriminate between the classes.

For any particular object, the features defining that object form a point in the feature space. Because of natural variability within each class, features measured from many objects in the same class will form a cluster in the feature space, which is described statistically by some probability distribution. When an unknown object is measured, the computed features are also represented by a single point in the feature space. The object is assigned to the class whose cluster best encompasses this point. In effect, the feature space is divided into disjoint regions, each assigned to a class. Classification is therefore reduced to identifying the features and determining in which region, or cluster, the unknown feature point lies.

Appendix C is a brief introduction to the basic methods of statistical pattern classification. In this section we apply these general methods to classification of objects based on their spectral images.

Point-by-Point Spectral Classification

Classification based on a measured spectral image $f(\mathbf{r}, \lambda)$ may use spectral, spatial, or combinations of spatial and spectral features. However, since the coupling between spatial and spectral characteristics of targets can be complex, in many applications the spatial characteristics are often ignored altogether, and the classification is performed at each point separately, based only on the spectral function $f(\lambda)$ at that point. In practice, a single pixel of finite area is used, so that the classification is actually based on the integrated spectral response over that discrete finite area. The problem is then known as point-by-point spectroscopy, i.e., identifying targets based solely on their spectra. For instance, features extracted from the spectral function $f(\lambda)$ can be a subset of N selected bands (channels) extracted from the full spectra measured by the spectrometer.

EXAMPLE 6.3-4.   *Environmental Remote Sensing.*   Figure 6.3-4(a) shows an example of three spectral functions, $f^{(1)}(\lambda)$, $f^{(2)}(\lambda)$, $f^{(3)}(\lambda)$, for three classes of substances. Figure 6.3-4(b) shows an associated feature space of dimension $M = 2$, where each spectral function is represented by two numbers, the readings of the two selected spectrometer bands. Each substance is therefore represented by a point in the 2D feature space. In this example, appropriate selection of the wavelengths used for the two spectrometer bands easily separates the three substances in the feature space, thus enabling good discrimination using only two features. In other situations, as the number of bands used as features increases, the dimensionality of the problem becomes quite large. Thus, feature extraction and selection can be used to reduce the dimensionality of classification while maintaining class separability. However, in complex environments where objects have similar or overlapping features, the full dimensionality is often necessary to adequately resolve differences in classes.

EXAMPLE 6.3-5.   *Remote Sensing of Enrique Reef.*   To illustrate the application of classification methods to a subsurface image, we use a remote-sensing example of Enrique Reef, which consists of five general classes: deep water, sand, reef crest, mangrove, and sea grass. The purpose of the classification exercise is to create a **classification map** (called a **thematic map** in the remote-sensing literature) using the spectral measurements at each point to classify the point into one of the five classes.

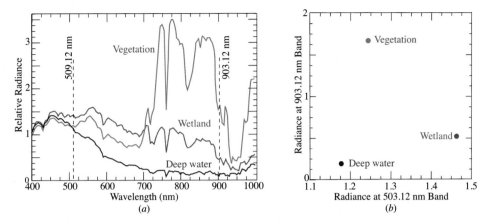

Figure 6.3-4 Spectral versus feature-space representation for the measured spectral signature: (*a*) spectral space; (*b*) feature space.

The five classes have different average spectral signatures, as illustrated in Fig. 6.3-5. However, the similarity between most of the signatures confounds our ability to discriminate between the subsurface classes and therefore makes the classification challenging. This similarity in reflectance spectra at the water surface is attributed to the attenuation introduced by the water column, as well as a similarity in the spectral characteristics of the features on the bottom. A more explicit model of the water column can better address this problem, as discussed in Sec. 6.4B.

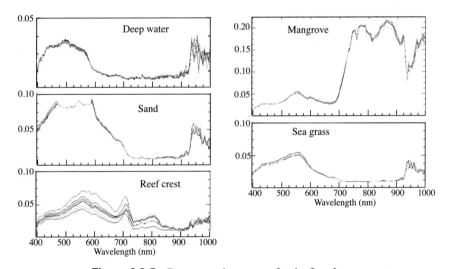

Figure 6.3-5 Representative spectra for the five classes.

For this example, the decision rule in supervised classification is obtained following several steps (as discussed in Appendix C):

(1) **Training.** In this step, samples with known class labels, called the ground truth, are collected for classifier training. In typical remote-sensing applications, ground truth data is collected using in situ measurements, field observations, or by using a priori information of the area under observation (e.g., maps and other image products). The areas shown in Fig. 6.3-6 were labeled based on knowledge of the reef area and subsequently divided into separate sets of testing and training samples.

(2) **Decision Rule.** Training data is used to compute the parameters of the classifier. In this example a minimum distance assignment (MDA) rule, based on the class means, is used. Thus, each class is represented by the mean of all spectra in its training area, and classification is achieved by assigning each pixel to whichever class mean is closest in feature space. As used in this example, the decision rule uses a feature-space dimension of $M = 25$ spectral bands.

(3) **Testing.** Once the decision rule is determined, testing data is used to evaluate the performance of the classifier. Accuracy is traditionally reported in terms of the producer's accuracy (error of omission – ratio of correctly classified test pixels in a class test area to the total number of pixels in that class test area) and the user's accuracy (error of commission – ratio of correctly classified test pixels in a class test area to the total number of pixels assigned to that class across all training areas).

Results. The classification map (thematic map) that results from applying the decision rule to the entire Enrique Reef image is shown in Fig. 6.3-7. The accuracy of this classification was very reasonable considering the simplifying assumptions used for this analysis. It is typical to assign a different color to each class as the class label. This visual depiction of the thematic map is very useful to users of remote-sensing products, since it provides information on the spatial distributions of the different classes, which in the current example helps improve the monitoring and management of coral reef ecosystems.

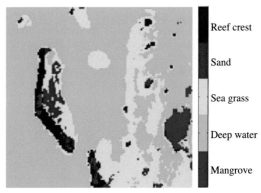

Figure 6.3-6 Training and testing areas used for classification of the Enrique Reef image (solid lines are training samples and dashed lines are testing samples): deep water (green), sea grass (cyan), reef crest (magenta), sand (blue), and mangrove (yellow).

Figure 6.3-7 Classification map for Enrique Reef obtained using a minimum distance classifier applied in a feature space of 25 spectral dimensions.

Spatial–Spectral Classification

Optimal classification should also take full advantage of information in the spatial and the spectral domains. Spatial features can be used to spatially segment images before spectral classification, to spatially filter and segment the results of spectral classifications, or to contribute additional dimensions in feature space for use in the classification.

For instance, spatial features, such as texture properties, may be used together with spectral features to classify images. An example method for incorporating spatial information into spectral classification is the extraction and classification for homogenous objects (ECHO) method. As implemented here for post-processing, once pixels are classified, they are compared with their neighbors; if the pixel class is different from its neighbors but the neighborhood is sufficiently spectrally uniform, then the class of the pixel in question is changed to the class of its neighbors. This type of spatial–spectral integration reduces the classification error.

EXAMPLE 6.3-6.   *Remote Sensing Enrique Reef Revisited.* Figure 6.3-8 shows the resulting thematic map for the Enrique Reef example after applying the ECHO as a post-processing method. Note how ECHO produces more uniform regions than when using just point-by-point spectral classification.

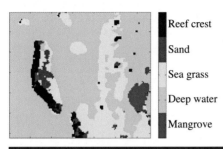

Reef crest

Sand

Sea grass

Deep water   **Figure 6.3-8** Classification map for Enrique Reef obtained using MDA classifier and ECHO post-processing.

Mangrove

▶ Problems 6.3-5, 6.3-6

6.4   Applications of Spectral Subsurface Imaging

Spectral subsurface imaging techniques are used in many applications, including remote sensing (under atmosphere, under snow, and under water) and biological applications (e.g., cellular imaging by use of fluorescent dyes and proteins). In this section, we describe two such applications: under-skin and underwater imaging.

A. Spectral Imaging of Skin

Optical imaging of the skin surface is routinely implemented by means of a **dermatoscope**, which is simply a magnifier or a microscope. The use of immersion oil between the objective lens and the skin makes the upper layers of the skin translucent and allows the deeper layers to be observed with minimal reflected light. Optical microscopes are used for examination of capillaries under normal and pathological conditions, common skin disorders, and melanocytic lesions, including melanoma. The field is known as **dermatoscopy** or **dermoscopy**. Confocal microscopy is another modality that is being increasingly used to image skin, where optical sectioning at 1–5 µm depth and with 0.2–1.0 µm lateral resolution is comparable to that obtained by examining physically cut sections in conventional pathology. Nuclear, cellular, and organelle structure can be imaged in thin optical sections with high resolution and high contrast, allowing *in vivo* noninvasive differentiation of disorders and cancers from normal skin. While these recent techniques provide rich detail about subcellular structures, there is also a need for imaging with a larger field of view. For such applications, hyperspectral imaging is attractive, as demonstrated in this section.

Optics of Human Skin

Morphology.   The human skin consists of three primary layers of tissue (Fig. 6.4-1):
- The **stratum corneum** is the outermost skin surface. It is composed mainly of dead cells, which are continuously replaced.
- The **epidermis** provides waterproofing and serves as a barrier to infections. It contains no blood vessels and is nourished by diffusion from the dermis.
- The **dermis** lies beneath the epidermis and consists of connective tissue. It cushions the body from stress and strain, and contains nerve endings that provide the sense of touch and heat, hair follicles, sweat glands, and blood vessels. The dermis

is structurally divided into two areas: a superficial area adjacent to the epidermis, called the papillary region because of its finger-like projections extending toward the epidermis, and a deep, thicker area known as the reticular region, which consists of collagen fibers and bundles.

Below the dermis is a subcutaneous (i.e., under-skin) layer of fat and muscle. Different layers of skin have varying amounts of keratin (protein), melanin (pigment), water, and other components and microstructures that give each layer its own bulk optical properties.

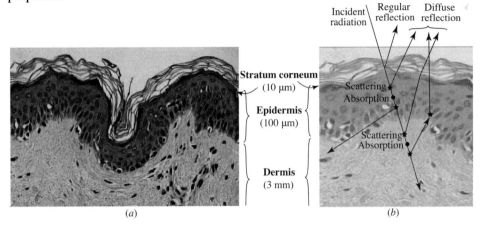

(a)   (b)

Figure 6.4-1   (*a*) Human skin morphology. This histological section of tissue is orthogonal to the skin surface, which is at the top of the picture. (*b*) Optical processes in skin.

Reflection and Refraction.   The average refractive indexes of the principal skin layers are:

Stratum corneum	$n_{sc} = 1.55$
Epidermis	$n_{epi} = 1.33$
Dermis	$n_{derm} = 1.50$

If these layers were smooth and planar, there would be small regular reflection at each of the layer boundaries, with the largest reflection occurring at the boundary between air ($n = 1$) and the stratum corneum (about 4.7% at normal incidence). Since the surface of the stratum corneum is not smooth, however, the refracted light entering the epidermis will be diffused. As it travels through the epidermis and the dermis it will undergo absorption and scattering and a portion of it will be re-emitted into air, as illustrated in Fig. 6.4-1(*b*), and may be measured with a spectral imager and used to extract useful information.

Scattering Microstructures.   Fine and coarse inhomogeneities within each layer contribute to Rayleigh and Mie scattering (see Sec. 2.2C). The sizes of individual microstructures or organelles range between 0.1 and 1.0 µm and their refractive indexes vary between 1.34 and 1.70. For example, mitochondria are of size ≈ 1 µm and refractive index 1.40. The pigment melanin, which exists in the form of melanosomes, is of size ≈ 0.6 to 1.2 µm and refractive index 1.70.

Absorbing Chromophores.   Absorption in the skin layers is determined by chromophores, primarily hemoglobin (Hb) and water. The hemoglobin molecule has the function of carrying oxygen from the lungs to the organs where it is needed. Each hemoglobin molecule can bind up to four molecules of oxygen, and when it does, its spectrum is modified. In whole blood, the concentration of hemoglobin is approximately 2.3 mM (millimolar), and for skin is approximately 0.12 mM. Figure 6.4-2 shows the wavelength dependence of the absorption coefficient for these two concentrations of hemoglobin, and also for water.

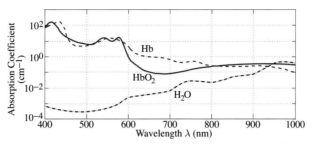

Figure 6.4-2   Absorption coefficients of primary chromophores in skin. Upper curves are for oxygenated and deoxygenated hemoglobin at a concentration of 0.12 mM/L, typical for skin. (plotted using tabulated data for molar extinction coefficient of hemoglobin in a webpage by Scott Prahl http://omlc.ogi.edu/spectra/hemoglobin/; see also O. W. Van Assendelft, *Spectrophotometry of Haemoglobin Derivatives*, Thomas, 1970). Lowest curve is the absorption coefficient of water (plotted using data in Table I of G. M. Hale and M. R. Querry, Optical constants of water in the 200 nm to 200 μm wavelength region, *Applied Optics*, Vol.12, pp. 555–563, 1973).

Absorption and Scattering in the Epidermis and the Dermis.   Reported values of the absorption and scattering coefficients of the epidermis and the dermis in the 400–800 nm wavelength range are displayed graphically in Fig. 6.4-3. These may be fitted to rational functions of the wavelength λ with only a few coefficients. In this range, the coefficient of scattering anisotropy g (which relates the reduced scattering coefficient $\mu_s' = (1 - g)\mu_s$ to the scattering coefficient μ_s, as described in see Sec. 2.2D) in the dermis is approximately constant ($g_{\mathrm{derm}} \approx 0.81$) and that in the epidermis may be fitted by the linear relation

$$g_{\mathrm{epi}} \approx 0.29 \times 10^{-3}\lambda + 0.62 \qquad (\lambda \text{ in units of nm}),$$

so that its value ranges from 0.736 at 400 nm to 0.852 at 800 nm.

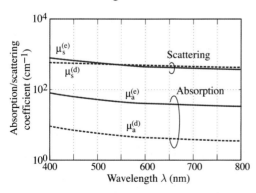

Figure 6.4-3   Absorption and scattering coefficients of the epidermis, $\mu_a^{(e)}$ and $\mu_s^{(e)}$, and dermis, $\mu_a^{(d)}$ and $\mu_s^{(d)}$.

For the upper part of the dermis, it is often useful to assume a homogeneous medium with approximately 5% blood, or 0.12 mM hemoglobin. This assumption is valid if the part of the skin being measured consists of small, closely spaced blood vessels. The two hemoglobin spectra are plotted at this concentration in Fig. 6.4-2. If the blood vessels are larger, then the homogeneous-layer model of the dermis fails because of the strong contrast in absorption between vessels and surrounding tissue.[6] If a vessel is sufficiently large, then almost no light penetrates to its center, thus reaching an effective maximum threshold for absorption. In this case, the total amount of light absorbed is almost the same as it would be in a smaller vessel, and the reflectance measurements would incorrectly suggest that the hemoglobin concentration is correspondingly smaller. A correction can be applied to the homogeneous-layer model to account for vessel size. Unfortunately, the correction is dependent on the absorption coefficient, and thus on the wavelength, so neglecting these complications will lead to erroneous inversion algorithms.

Radiative Transport Models.   Since propagation through the skin layers is dominated by multiple scattering it is best described by use of radiative transport models such as the Kubelka–Munk model, the photon diffusion model, or numerical techniques (e.g., Monte Carlo simulation), as described in Sec. 2.2D. For simplicity, it is frequently assumed that the boundaries between the skin layers are flat. It is also common to use a two-layer model including only the epidermis and the dermis, where the most pronounced differences occur.

Two-Layer Model.   The diffuse reflectance $\mathcal{R}$ from the epidermis–dermis combination may be expressed in terms of the reflectance of these two layers $\mathcal{R}_e$ and $\mathcal{R}_d$ and the transmittance of the epidermis $\mathcal{T}_e$. In accordance with the Kubelka–Munk model (2.2-47),

$$\mathcal{R} = \mathcal{R}_e + \mathcal{T}_e^2 \mathcal{R}_d \frac{1}{1 - \mathcal{R}_e \mathcal{R}_d}. \tag{6.4-1}$$

A simpler model[7] ignores multiple reflections within the dermis [the term $(1 - \mathcal{R}_e \mathcal{R}_d)^{-1}$] and assumes that the reflectance of the dermis $\mathcal{R}_d$ is simply equal to the albedo $\mathcal{A}_d$ (see Sec. 2.2D), so that

$$\mathcal{R} = \mathcal{R}_e + \mathcal{T}_e^2 \mathcal{A}_d, \qquad \mathcal{A}_d = \frac{\mu_s^{(d)}}{\mu_s^{(d)} + \mu_a^{(d)}}. \tag{6.4-2}$$

The parameters $\mathcal{R}_e$ and $\mathcal{T}_e$ depend on the absorption and scattering coefficients of the epidermis and the reflectance at the epidermis–dermis boundary.

Information Extraction

Since the wavelength dependence of the spectral reflectance $\mathcal{R}(\lambda)$ of the skin is sensitive to skin conditions, a classification system may be trained to use such experimental data to establish the existence or nonexistence of an anomaly, or the viability or nonviability of tissue, by use of standard classification or detection methods (see Appendix C).

Measurement of the skin spectral reflectance may also be used in combination with a model of the skin to determine the concentrations of the various chromophores

---

[6]T. Shi and C. A. DiMarzio, Multispectral method for skin imaging: development and validation, *Applied Optics*, Vol. 46, pp. 8619–8626, 2007.

[7]P. J. Dwyer and C. A. DiMarzio, Hyperspectral imaging for dermal hemoglobin spectroscopy, *Proceedings of SPIE*, Vol. 3752, pp. 72–82, 1999; P. J. Dwyer, R. R. Anderson, and C. A. DiMarzio, Mapping blood oxygen saturation using a multi-spectral imaging system, *Proceedings of SPIE*, Vol. 2976, pp. 270–280, 1997.

and estimate physiologically related effects as functions of position (i.e., as images). Specifically, the two most commonly desired quantities are the total hemoglobin concentration and the oxygen saturation. The level of hydration may also be of interest in some cases. These are the *beta* parameters for this subsurface imaging problem (see Sec. 1.2). However, because of the complexity of the model, it is often difficult or impossible to obtain all the desired information from a given set of measurements. The first step in this process is inversion, i.e., using the measured reflectance $\mathcal{R}(\lambda)$ to estimate the absorption coefficient $\mu_a(\lambda)$, which is the *alpha* parameter in this subsurface imaging problem.

Inversion. The principal difficulty in solving the inversion problem is coming up with an adequate forward model relating the reflectance $\mathcal{R}(\lambda)$ to the absorption coefficients $\mu_a(\lambda)$ in the different layers. This effort will of course be thwarted by the lack of knowledge of the other parameters, such as the specific scattering coefficients of the different layers. As an example of a simple approach to this problem, we take the simplified model described by (6.4-2) and assume that only the dermal reflectance is a function of wavelength, i.e., the parameters $\mu_s^{(d)}$, $\mathcal{R}_e$, and $\mathcal{T}_e$ are wavelength independent in the wavelength region of interest (see Fig. 6.4-3). Therefore,

$$\mathcal{R}(\lambda) = \mathcal{R}_e + \frac{\mathcal{T}_e^2}{1 + \mu_a^{(d)}(\lambda)/\mu_s^{(d)}}. \tag{6.4-3}$$

This relation between the wavelength-dependent measurement $\mathcal{R}(\lambda)$ and the wavelength-dependent dermis absorption coefficient $\mu_a^{(d)}(\lambda)$, which contains the desired fluorophore information, is nonlinear with some unknown wavelength-independent coefficients. Since $\mu_a^{(d)}(\lambda)$ appears solely as a ratio $\mu_a^{(d)}(\lambda)/\mu_s^{(d)}$, it is not possible to separate its value from the constant, but unknown, scattering coefficient $\mu_s^{(d)}$.

Unmixing of Chromophore Concentrations. The spectral dependence of the absorption coefficient may be expressed in terms of the unknown concentrations of the chromophores and their known absorption spectra as a linearly mixed spectrum. For example, if we consider only oxygenated and deoxygenated hemoglobin (Hb), then

$$\mu_a^{(d)}(\lambda) = sc\kappa_{\text{oxy}}(\lambda) + (1 - s)c\kappa_{\text{deoxy}}(\lambda) + \mu_{a0}, \tag{6.4-4}$$

where sc, $(1 - s)c$, and c are the concentrations of oxygenated, deoxygenated, and total Hb, respectively, s is the oxygen saturation factor, $\kappa_{\text{oxy}}(\lambda)$ and $\kappa_{\text{deoxy}}(\lambda)$ are the molar absorptivities of oxygenated and deoxygenated Hb, respectively (assumed to be known), and μ_{a0} is the absorption coefficient of other chromophores besides Hb (assumed to have negligible dependence on the wavelength within the spectral range of interest).

The nonlinear inversion problem in (6.4-3) and the linear unmixing problem in (6.4-4) are best addressed as a single inversion problem by substituting (6.4-4) into (6.4-3) to obtain

$$\mathcal{R}(\lambda) = \mathcal{R}_e + \frac{1}{A + B\left[s\kappa_{\text{oxy}}(\lambda) + (1 - s)\kappa_{\text{deoxy}}(\lambda)\right]}, \tag{6.4-5}$$

where $A = (\mu_s^{(d)} + \mu_{a0})/\mathcal{T}_e^2\mu_s^{(d)}$ and $B = c/\mathcal{T}_e^2\mu_s^{(d)}$. The problem is then one of estimating four unknown parameters: $\mathcal{R}_e$, A, B, and s. Therefore, if $\mathcal{R}(\lambda)$ is measured at four wavelengths, the oxygen saturation factor s and the relative Hb concentration

$B = c/\mathcal{T}_e^2 \mu_s^{(d)}$ may be readily determined. Thus, from these measurements and based on this model, one can obtain the relative hemoglobin concentration and the absolute oxygen saturation.

A more comprehensive model of $\mu_a^{(d)}(\lambda)$ including other chromophores may also be developed. In this case, with measurements at additional wavelengths, the relative chromophore concentrations (e.g., the ratio of hemoglobin concentration to water concentration) may be estimated.

▶ Problem 6.4-1

Skin Imaging Systems

Hyperspectral skin imagers commonly use broadband illumination sources and tunable filters (liquid crystal or acousto-optic) in the multisensor configuration depicted in Fig. 6.1-5(b) and Fig. 6.1-7(b). The wavelengths are selected depending on the application. Longer wavelengths in the near infrared penetrate deeper into the skin, as is evident from Fig. 6.4-2 and Fig. 6.4-3. Also, by including the longer wavelengths, the system is sensitive to hydration. A few wavelengths or a dozen wavelengths may be used, depending on the application.

It is also common to operate in the cross-polarized mode, i.e., transmit the illumination through a polarizer and the scattered light through an orthogonal polarizer (an analyzer), as illustrated in Fig. 6.4-4. This suppresses specular (Fresnel) reflection, which may enter the camera and produce strong glints (with almost no spectral information). Since specular reflection (and also singly backscattered light from the superficial layers) retains polarization much better than light scattered from the tissue, it is rejected by the analyzer. This mode of operation is sometimes called **polarized dermoscopy**.

Different instruments are distinguished by their specific applications and the algorithms used to obtain the desired information. Actual instruments were developed for measurement of **oxygen saturation**, relative **hemoglobin concentration, tissue viability**, and **tissue perfusion**. Algorithms depend on whether the application requires mapping (concentration, for example) or classification (viability, for example). See references in the reading list.

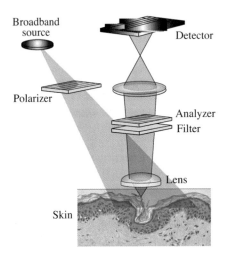

Figure 6.4-4 Hyperspectral skin imager. A broadband light source reflects from the area to be imaged. A filter selects a wavelength band for each image. Crossed polarizers are used to minimize specular reflections.

B. Spectral Imaging of Underwater Benthic Habitat

Benthic habitats vary as a function of geographic location, environmental characteristics and water depth, and are typically characterized according to their dominant structural features and biological communities. The relatively shallow estuarine and nearshore benthic habitats, portions of which can be monitored using satellite remote sensing, can be divided into categories such as submerged mudflats, sandflats, rocky hard-bottom, seagrass beds, kelp forests, shellfish beds, and coral reefs. These habitats support a wide diversity of marine life by providing spawning, nursery, refuge, and foraging grounds. They also provide important functions in nutrient cycling, as well as contributing to the removal of contaminants from the water. Benthic organisms within these habitats are important members of the lower food web, consuming organic matter and phytoplankton and serving as food sources for higher level consumers. Benthic habitats also serve as shelter, and provide storm protection by buffering wave action along coastlines.

Benthic Habitat Mapping. Knowledge of seafloor habitats is necessary for the development and implementation of resource management policies. For instance, benthic habitat mapping provides a means to both identify essential fish habitat and characterize it in the context of the larger seafloor for determining the most effective means for preservation. Furthermore, important habitats, such as coral reefs, can be monitored over time using benthic mapping techniques, which facilitates more effective management and preservation of these ecosystems. Benthic habitat mapping is also a useful tool for determining the effects of habitat change due to natural or human impacts.

Photograph by James Goodman

Spectral remote sensing is an important imaging tool for evaluating the complex dynamics associated with estuarine and nearshore benthic habitats. Benthic habitat mapping is an aquatic subsurface sensing problem in which the spectral signature of interest from the sea bottom is distorted by the water column above it, which has spatially variant optical properties and depth, by interactions at the air–water interface, and by atmospheric influences between the sensor and water surface. Furthermore, light penetration of water depends on the optical properties of the water column. As was shown in Fig. 6.0-1(a), light penetration in clear water can reach 60 m for some wavelengths. However, in other situations, light penetration in turbid water can be limited to less than a meter, depending on turbidity. In cases when bottom features are visible in the measured spectral image of optically shallow waters, hyperspectral imagers, with their high spectral resolution, provide sufficient spectral information to retrieve bottom and water column contributions to the measured spectral signature, as we will see in this section.

Example of Spectral Imaging at Multiple Bands.   Figure 6.4-5 shows images obtained at different bands, from blue to near infrared, collected with the NASA AVIRIS hyperspectral imager over a reef area in southwestern Puerto Rico. Features with different spectral characteristics located at different depths are evident in different bands. Note that features are evident in all bands, but only for the portions of the image that are above water or are relatively shallow (here shallower than 10 m water depth). This is due to the strong scattering and absorption properties of water and its constituents, which limits the effective penetration depth of light.

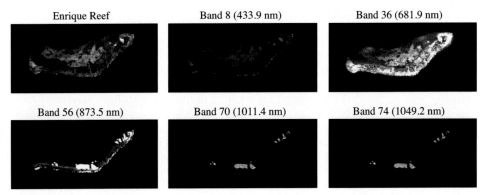

Figure 6.4-5 Sample bands of a hyperspectral image taken with the AVIRIS sensor over Enrique Reef in southwestern Puerto Rico . Different underwater and above-surface features are highlighted at different bands (work supported by NASA award NNH06ZDA001N-IDS).

Band 8 shows the strongest response from submerged sand areas, which have higher reflectance than other features, and to a lesser extent areas of coral, algae, and seagrass. Band 36 is located near a wavelength region of strong chlorophyll absorption. Because chlorophyll is common in marine benthic features, including algae, seagrass, coral, and sand, this band exhibits a response for all features across the entire shallow reef area, but sand still has the strongest response due to its relative overall brightness. As the images move into the near infrared, water absorption plays a stronger role and the underwater features are reduced and ultimately eliminated at these longer wavelengths. Band 56 still exhibits some response in the shallow regions, but the most prevalent response is from the mangrove features, which are located above water. Bands 70 and 74 then show only the mangroves and all subsurface reef features are no longer evident. As we shall see in this section, combining this spectral information with bio-optical models enables delineation of the different reef features and hence the assessment of benthic habitats.

Remote-Sensing Model of Underwater Imaging

Underwater remote sensing of coastal environments by use of satellite or airborne spectral sensors is illustrated schematically in Fig. 6.4-6. Five paths of solar radiation received at the sensor via atmospheric and underwater radiative processes are identified:

- **Path Radiance**. Sun radiation scattered by the atmosphere in the field of view of the sensor.
- **Sky Radiance**. Sky radiation scattered by the atmosphere in the field of view of the sensor after interacting with the ground or water surface (via reflection or emission).
- **Sunglint**. Sun radiation reflected at the water surface, which is significant when viewed from angles at or approaching the specular direction.
- **Scattering from Water Column**. Sun radiation scattered by the water column in the field of view of the sensor.
- **Reflection from Sea Bottom**. Sun radiation reflected from the sea bottom. This contribution carries the desired information on the spectral characteristics of the sea bottom.

The first three contributions require preprocessing procedures, but may be regarded as a background that is independent of underwater effects. The last two are underwater effects that must be modeled jointly in order to determine the water-leaving radiation. Other effects, such as water emission and fluorescence, and emission by the sea bottom, are not included since they are negligible within the wavelength range used in underwater remote sensing.

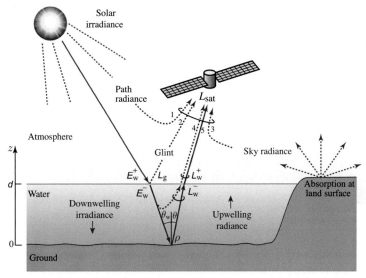

Figure 6.4-6   Satellite imaging of shallow water bottom using sun radiation as the probing source. Radiation from the sun reaches the satellite via multiple paths: (1) direct atmospheric scattering (path radiance), (2) atmospheric scattering of radiation reflected from the water or ground surface, (3) reflection from air–water surface, (4) scattering from the water column, and (5) reflection from the underwater ground surface. Information on the ground reflectance ρ is carried by incoming radiation that reaches the ground surface and travels back through the water and the atmosphere to the satellite (marked by the solid rays and the number 5).

The fundamental quantity measured with remote sensing instruments is the **spectral radiance** L_λ (power per unit area, per unit solid angle, per unit wavelength). The incoming solar radiation is described in terms of the **spectral irradiance** E_λ (power per unit area, per unit wavelength). For notational simplicity, the subscript λ will be suppressed, but it should be understood that both the spectral radiance and irradiance are wavelength dependent.

The spectral radiance measured by the sensor is given by (see Fig. 6.4-6)

$$L_{\text{sat}} = L_{\text{path}} + L_{\text{sky}} + \left(L_{\text{g}} + L_{\text{w}}^+ \right) H_{\text{atm}}.$$

The first two terms result from atmospheric scattering of path radiance and sky radiance, respectively. The last two represent the spectral radiance from the water surface L_{g} and the water-generated spectral radiance L_{w}^+, measured just above the water surface, both multiplied by the atmospheric transmittance H_{atm}, which is also dependent on wavelength. The spectral radiance L_{w}^+ includes both the radiation scattered by the water column and the radiation reflected from the sea bottom.

Preprocessing.   Since information about the sea bottom is only contained in the term L_{w}^+ we need to remove the contributions from L_{path}, L_{sky}, and L_{g}. This process is not trivial, since L_{w}^+ is usually less than 10% of the total measured signal at the sensor. Although atmospheric influences are interrelated with surface reflectance (L_{sky} and $L_{\text{g}} H_{\text{atm}}$), suggesting the need for an integrated correction, retrieval of L_{w}^+ is commonly achieved using a separated two-step process. For example, an atmospheric correction code is used to first estimate and subtract contributions from $L_{\mathrm{path}} + L_{\mathrm{sky}}$ and to remove the atmospheric effect H_{atm}. If needed, sunglint is then subtracted using an additional correction algorithm, several of which are described in the literature. Rather than working with radiance for image analysis, however, it is more common in remote sensing to work with reflectance. Knowing the upwelling water-leaving radiance L_{w}^{+} and estimating the downwelling solar irradiance E_{w}^{+}, just above the surface of the water, the **remote-sensing reflectance**

$$\mathcal{R}_{\mathrm{rs}} = L_{\mathrm{w}}^{+} / E_{\mathrm{w}}^{+} \qquad (6.4\text{-}6)$$

may be determined. The remaining, and more difficult, task is to estimate the underwater ground reflectance ρ from $\mathcal{R}_{\mathrm{rs}}$. This requires separating the scattering and absorption from the water column and accounting for transmission through water and through the water–air interface, an operation that is best achieved using a physical model for radiative transfer in water, as described next.

Radiative Transfer in Water

Propagation of light in water containing particles such as sediment and phytoplankton (microscopic algae that impart a green contribution to water color), color dissolved organic matter (CDOM), and gelbstoff (organic compounds that impart a yellow color) can be described in terms of radiative transfer models characterized by absorption and scattering coefficients (see Sec. 2.2D). The simplest model describes the process in terms of a downwelling flux characterized by the spectral irradiance $E_{\mathrm{d}}(z)$, and an upwelling flux characterized by the spectral radiance $L_{\mathrm{u}}(z)$, as illustrated in Fig. 6.4-7. The upwelling flux is generated by scattering of the downwelling flux as well as reflection at the bottom. Likewise, the downwelling flux is supplemented by scattering of the upwelling flux. This two-flux model is described by coupled differential equations, as in the Kubelka–Munk model (see Sec. 2.2D).

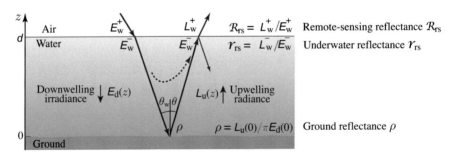

Figure 6.4-7   Downwelling and upwelling model of radiation transfer.

Underwater Reflectance.   If the contribution of the upwelling flux to the downwelling flux is negligible, the two-flux model leads to a simple approximate expression (2.2-40) for the reflectance of the medium in terms of the absorption and scattering coefficients, the bottom reflectance, and the depth d. When applied to our problem, (2.2-40) provides the following expression for the **underwater reflectance** $r_{\mathrm{rs}} = L_{\mathrm{w}}^{-} / E_{\mathrm{w}}^{-} = L_{\mathrm{u}}(d) / E_{\mathrm{d}}(d)$, just below the surface of water:

$$r_{\mathrm{rs}} = \frac{\mu_{\mathrm{se}}}{2\mu_{\mathrm{e}}} \left[1 - \exp(-2\mu_{\mathrm{e}}d) \right] + \frac{\rho}{\pi} \exp(-2\mu_{\mathrm{e}}d), \qquad (6.4\text{-}7)$$

where ρ is the bottom reflectance and

$$\mu_e = \frac{1}{2}\left(\frac{\mu_{ad} + \mu_{sd}}{\cos\theta_w} + \frac{\mu_{au} + \mu_{su}}{\cos\theta}\right) \tag{6.4-8}$$

is an effective extinction coefficient and $\mu_{se} = \mu_{su}/\cos\theta$ is an effective scattering coefficient. Here, μ_a and μ_s denote absorption and scattering coefficients, with the additional subscripts d and u referring to downwelling and upwelling fluxes, respectively. The angles θ_w and θ are the in-water solar zenith angle and the viewing angle, respectively. The effective attenuation coefficients are increased by the factors $1/\cos\theta_w$ and $1/\cos\theta$ to account for the longer propagation distances at these inclinations.

The first term of (6.4-7) represents the contribution of the sun radiation in the water column and the second represents reflection from the ground surface. The second term, which is the important term in sea-bottom remote sensing, becomes negligible if $\mu_e d \gg 1$, i.e., if the water is too deep or too optically dense; we are then left with an underwater reflectance $r_{rs} \approx \mu_{se}/2\mu_e$ proportional to the albedo of water.

Bottom Spectral Reflectance. The sea-bottom spectral reflectance $\rho = \pi L_u(0)/E_d(0) = L_u(0)/L_d(0)$ is a wavelength-dependent function $\rho = \rho(\lambda)$ that carries the desired information on the benthic habitat. It has a different spectral signature for different substances, as illustrated in Fig. 6.4-8 for sand, coral, and algae, but more realistically represents a heterogeneous mix of different substances.

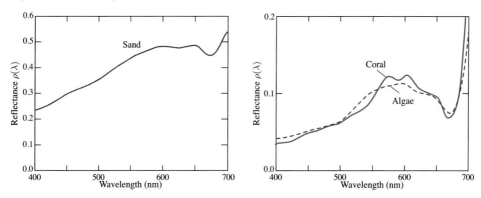

Figure 6.4-8 Reflectance spectra $\rho(\lambda)$ of sand, coral, and algae from the Kaneohe Bay, Hawaii. Adapted from J. A. Goodman and S. L. Ustin, Classification of benthic composition in a coral reef environment using spectral unmixing, *Journal of Applied Remote Sensing*, Vol. 1, 011501, 2007.

Remote-Sensing Reflectance. The ratio $\mathcal{R}_{rs} = L_w^+/E_w^+$ of the incoming irradiance E_w^+ and the outgoing radiance L_w^+ immediately above the surface of water may be related to the underwater reflectance $r_{rs} = L_w^-/E_w^-$ by accounting for the air-to-water irradiance transmittance $\mathcal{T}_+$ and the water-to-air radiance transmittance $\mathcal{T}_-$. However, the process is more complex, since the upwelling radiation that is reflected from the surface back into the water may itself be scattered in the upward direction, and may thus undergo multiple reflections and transmissions. This phenomenon is described by the expression (6.4-1) for the diffuse reflectance at the boundary of a two-layer medium in terms of the transmittance and reflectance of each of the layers. In our case, this leads to

$$\mathcal{R}_{rs} = \frac{\mathcal{T}_-\mathcal{T}_+}{n^2}\frac{r_{rs}}{1 - Q\gamma r_{rs}}, \tag{6.4-9}$$

where γ is the water-to-air internal reflection coefficient, Q is the ratio of upwelling irradiance to upwelling radiance at the water-to-air interface, and $n = 1.33$ is the refractive index of water. This nonlinear relation between $\mathcal{R}_{rs}$ and r_{rs} is symptomatic of the multiple reflection and scattering process (see Sec. 3.2A). Evidently, if r_{rs} is small, the term $Q\gamma r_{rs}$ in the denominator is negligible and $\mathcal{R}_{rs}$ is approximately proportional to r_{rs}, so that the relation is approximately linear.

Summary of the Model.   Equations (6.4-7)–(6.4-9) provide an approximate model for the remote-sensing reflectance $\mathcal{R}_{rs}$ in terms of the underwater reflectance r_{rs}, which is related to the ground reflectance ρ. While the relation between r_{rs} and ρ is linear, that between $\mathcal{R}_{rs}$ and r_{rs} is nonlinear.

$$\rho \rightarrow \boxed{\diagup} \xrightarrow{r_{rs}} \boxed{\diagup} \xrightarrow{\mathcal{R}_{rs}}$$

The following parameters appear in this model:
- Underwater depth d (bathymetry), sun zenith angle θ_w, viewing angle θ in water.
- Absorption and scattering coefficients μ_a and μ_s. These parameters are functions of the wavelength λ that depend on the constituents in the water column.
- Air–water transmittance and reflectance parameters, $\mathcal{T}_+$ and $\mathcal{T}_-$, and γ, which depend on the atmospheric conditions and the angles θ and θ_w. For example, typical values of $\mathcal{T}_+$ range between 0.97–0.98 for clear sky conditions and solar zenith angles below 45° and 0.05–0.07 for overcast skies, and $\mathcal{T}_-$ is in the range 0.43 to 0.50.

EXAMPLE 6.4-1.   *Remote Sensing of Kaneohe Bay: Dependence of Reflectance on Bathymetry.* An example of measurements demonstrating the dependence of the remote-sensing reflectance $R_{rs}(\lambda)$ on the bathymetry (depth d) is illustrated in Fig. 6.4-9 for sand, coral, and algae, whose reflectance $\rho(\lambda)$ is shown in Fig. 6.4-8. Clearly, both the magnitude and shape of $\mathcal{R}_{rs}(\lambda)$ are significantly different at different water depths, even though the bottom reflectance is fixed.

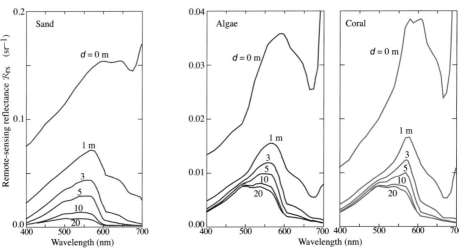

Figure 6.4-9   Remote-sensing reflectance spectra $\mathcal{R}_{rs}(\lambda)$ of sand, coral, and algae from Kaneohe Bay, Hawaii, at different water depths d. Adapted from J. A. Goodman and S. L. Ustin, Classification of benthic composition in a coral reef environment using spectral unmixing, *Journal of Applied Remote Sensing*, Vol. 1, 011501, 2007.

▶ Problems 6.4-2, 6.4-3

Other Models.   Phenomenological models with equations similar to (6.4-7)–(6.4-9), including parameterized formulas for the wavelength dependence of the absorption and scattering coefficients, have been advanced in the literature. For example, the Lee model[8] describes the remote-sensing reflectance $\mathcal{R}_{rs}(\lambda)$ in terms of an assumed bottom reflectance $\rho(\lambda)$ and five parameters describing the optical properties of the water, the magnitude of the bottom reflectance, and the water depth d.

Model-Based Information Extraction

Model-Based Parameter Estimation.   If the remote-sensing reflectance $\mathcal{R}_{rs}(\lambda)$ at the water surface is determined from hyperspectral remote-sensing measurements, could the spectral distribution of the bottom reflectance $\rho(\lambda)$ be estimated? Clearly, if the five parameters describing the water optical properties, the water depth, and the imaging geometry are known, then $\rho(\lambda)$ may be readily computed by inverting the basic equations of the model at each wavelength. However, since the depth and water properties vary from one location to another and are typically not known, particularly the water properties, these parameters must be estimated from the measured remote-sensing reflectance $\mathcal{R}_{rs}(\lambda)$. This makes direct estimation of the full spectral distribution $\rho(\lambda)$ not possible, without significant prior information, further generalizing the problem, or utilizing additional simplifying assumptions. Approaches commonly include preselecting a range of water properties and/or representative bottom-reflectance spectra, and utilizing forward modeling to optimize the fit between measured and modeled $\mathcal{R}_{rs}(\lambda)$. These approaches may be further augmented by lidar bathymetry data (an active imaging modality) or other source of bathymetry data, which reduces the complexity of the problem by providing measured values of water depth at each location. In this case, the measured remote-sensing reflectance may be used to estimate a reduced set of parameters (e.g., just four parameters for the Lee model). The problem is then posed as a nonlinear least-squares estimation (nonlinear regression) aimed at finding the model parameters that provide the best fit between modeled $\mathcal{R}_{rs}(\lambda)$ and measured $\mathcal{R}_{rs}(\lambda)$.

Parameter Estimation.   Using the Lee model as an example, the set of parameters of the model, which describe the water optical properties, the bathymetry (depth), and the magnitude of the bottom reflectance, are denoted by a vector $\boldsymbol{\gamma} = [\gamma_1 \ \gamma_2 \ \cdots \ \gamma_5]^{\mathrm{T}}$. If these five parameters are known, the reflectance $\mathcal{R}_{rs}(\lambda)$ may be computed at any wavelength. We denote the set of such reflectances at the spectrometer wavelengths $\lambda_1, \lambda_2, \ldots, \lambda_L$ by the vector $\mathbf{R}_{rs}(\boldsymbol{\gamma}) = [R_{rs}(\lambda_1) \ R_{rs}(\lambda_2) \ \cdots \ R_{rs}(\lambda_L)]^{\mathrm{T}}$. If $\mathbf{g}_{rs} = [g_{rs}(\lambda_1) \ g_{rs}(\lambda_2) \ \cdots \ g_{rs}(\lambda_L)]^{\mathrm{T}}$ is the vector of values of $\mathcal{R}_{rs}(\lambda)$ that are actually measured by the spectrometer at $\lambda_1, \lambda_2, \ldots, \lambda_L$, following atmospheric and sunglint corrections, then the least-squares estimate of $\boldsymbol{\gamma}$ is given by

$$\hat{\boldsymbol{\gamma}} = \arg \min_{\boldsymbol{\gamma}} \ \|\mathbf{g}_{rs} - \mathbf{R}_{rs}(\boldsymbol{\gamma})\|_2^2, \tag{6.4-10}$$

where $\| \cdot \|_2^2$ is the Euclidean norm (see Appendix B). This nonlinear regression approach to parameter estimation has been widely used for studies of water properties in coastal regions. It also provides some information on bottom composition as a function of the assumed bottom reflectance and the derived parameter indicating changes in magnitude from one location to the next.

---

[8]Z. Lee, K. Carder, C. D. Mobley, R. Steward, and J. Patch, Hyperspectral remote sensing for shallow waters. 1. A semianalytical model, *Applied Optics*, Vol., 37, pp. 6329–6338, 1998; Z. Lee, K. Carder, C. D. Mobley, R. Steward, and J. Patch, Hyperspectral remote sensing for shallow waters: 2. Deriving bottom depths and water properties by optimization, *Applied Optics*, Vol. 38, pp. 3831–3843, 1999.

Combined Parameter Estimation and Unmixing.   Linear unmixing can be used for benthic habitat mapping in shallow waters by applying standard unmixing methodologies (see Sec. 6.3A) to the measured remote-sensing reflectance $\mathcal{R}_{rs}(\lambda)$ to obtain abundance distributions of the principal constituents (endmembers) of the underwater bottom surface (e.g., sand, coral, and algae). However, a key assumption of most surface unmixing approaches is that the endmembers are the same for all pixels in the image. This condition is not met in subsurface unmixing over coastal environments because of the variability of water optical properties and bathymetry, which interact to distort the subsurface bottom signature. For example, as was shown in Fig. 6.4-9, both the magnitude and shape of $\mathcal{R}_{rs}(\lambda)$ for each of the endmembers change significantly with bathymetry even though the bottom reflectance is fixed.

Under these conditions, the problem of unmixing must be solved in conjunction with the parameter estimation problem, by posing it as an expanded parameter estimation problem with a larger number of parameters. The bottom reflectance $\rho(\lambda)$ at each pixel is expressed as a sum of n endmembers,

$$\rho(\lambda) = \sum_{i=1}^{n} f_i \, \rho_i(\lambda), \tag{6.4-11}$$

where $\rho_i(\lambda)$ are known spectral distributions of the endmembers and f_i are the unknown abundances. With this parametric model of the bottom reflectance, the parameters $f_1, f_2, \ldots, f_n$ may be added to the set of four parameters describing the bathymetry and water optical properties (the fifth parameter describing magnitude of bottom reflectance is no longer necessary), resulting in a larger parameter estimation problem, which may be solved by use of the nonlinear regression equation (6.4-10) with a parameter vector of size $4 + n$ instead of 5.[9]

Hybrid Parameter Estimation and Linear Unmixing.   A hybrid approach[10] exploits existing fast algorithms for linear unmixing to avoid the high computational penalty associated with nonlinear regression methods. Here, the parameter estimation problem is adressed in two steps:

- First, using the Lee model as a foundation, an estimate $\hat{\gamma}$ of the water properties and bathymetry parameters is calculated using a generic bottom reflectance $\bar{\rho}$:

$$\hat{\gamma} = \arg \min_{\gamma} \ \|\mathbf{g}_{rs} - \mathbf{R}_{rs}(\gamma, \bar{\rho})\|_2^2. \tag{6.4-12}$$

- Second, a linear mixing problem is formulated in terms of the remote-sensing reflectance $\sum_{i=1}^{n} f_i \, \mathbf{R}_{rs}(\hat{\gamma}, \rho_i)$, where $\mathbf{R}_{rs}(\hat{\gamma}, \rho_i)$ is the remote-sensing reflectance at each pixel for the ith endmember bottom reflectance ρ_i generated using the model parameters $\hat{\gamma}$ that were estimated in the first step as input to the forward model. The abundance estimates are then determined by using the standard linear unmixing optimization equation:

$$\hat{\mathbf{f}} = \arg \min_{f_i \geq 0, \, \mathbf{1}^T \mathbf{f} = 1} \left\| \mathbf{g}_{rs} - \sum_{i=1}^{n} f_i \, \mathbf{R}_{rs}(\hat{\gamma}, \rho_i) \right\|_2^2, \tag{6.4-13}$$

which may be solved by use of the methods described in Sec. 6.3A.

[9]M. C. Torres-Madronero, M. Vélez-Reyes, and J. A. Goodman, Underwater unmixing and water optical properties retrieval using HyCIAT, in *Imaging Spectrometry XIV, Proceedings of SPIE*, Vol. 7457, pp. 74570I–74570I, 2009.

[10]J. A. Goodman and S. L. Ustin, Classification of benthic composition in a coral reef environment using spectral unmixing, *Journal of Applied Remote Sensing*, Vol. 1, p. 011501, 2007.

EXAMPLE 6.4-2.   *Remote Sensing of Enrique Reef.* Figure 6.4-10 shows an example of remote-sensing reflectance computed from hyperspectral data collected by AVIRIS, as well as abundance images estimated by use of this hybrid method.

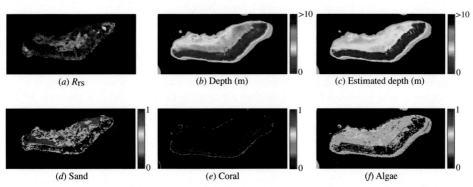

Figure 6.4-10   Example of hyperspectral imaging of underwater benthic habitat for Enrique Reef, Puerto Rico, using AVIRIS data (work supported by NASA award NNH06ZDA001N-IDS). The raw data collected from a 550×250 pixel image (approximately 2.2 km^2) were first preprocessed using atmospheric and sunglint corrections to determine the remote-sensing reflectance $\mathcal{R}_{rs}(\lambda)$ in 38 bands in the ranges 400–800 nm. An RGB composite of the remote-sensing reflectance $\mathcal{R}_{rs}(\lambda)$ is shown in panel (*a*) and the measured bathymetry (depth) maps are shown in panel (*b*). Bathymetry estimated from the model, shown in panel (*c*), agrees with the lidar measured bathymetry shown. Data on the three endmembers (sand, coral and algae) were measured in situ (see Fig. 6.4-8). Abundance maps of (*d*) sand, (*e*) coral, and (*f*) algae, estimated from $\mathcal{R}_{rs}$ by use of the hybrid parameter estimation and linear unmixing method are shown.

Further Reading

Spectroscopy and Imaging Spectroscopy

D. J. Brady, *Optical Imaging and Spectroscopy*, Wiley, 2009.

R. Salzer and H. W. Siesler, *Infrared and Raman Spectroscopic Imaging*, Wiley–VCH, 2009.

J. Hill and J. Mégie (eds.), *Imaging Spectrometry—a Tool for Environmental Observations*, Springer, 2007.

B. Hapke, *Theory of Reflectance and Emittance Spectroscopy*, Cambridge University Press, 2005.

F. D. van der Meer and S. M. de Jong, *Imaging Spectrometry: Basic Principles and Prospective Applications*, Kluwer, 2003.

A. Richards, *Alien Vision: Exploring the Electromagnetic Spectrum with Imaging Technology*, SPIE, 2001.

D. W. Ball, *The Basics of Spectroscopy*, Tutorial Texts in Optical Engineering, Vol. TT 49, SPIE, 2001.

W. L. Wolfe, *Introduction to Imaging Spectrometers*, Tutorial Texts in Optical Engineering, Vol. TT 25, SPIE, 1997.

X. F. Wang and B. Herman, *Fluorescence Imaging Spectroscopy and Microscopy*, Wiley, 1996.

Multispectral and Hyperspectral Remote Sensing

N. Short, Remote Sensing Tutorial, NASA Reference Publication 1078, 2009. *http://rst.gsfc.nasa.gov/*

M. Borengasser, W. S. Hungate, R. Watkins, *Hyperspectral Remote Sensing: Principal and Applications*, CRC, 2008.

H. F. Grahn and P. Geladi, *Techniques and Applications of Hyperspectral Image Analysis*, Wiley, 2007.

C. H. Chen, *Signal and Image Processing for Remote Sensing*, CRC, 2007.

J. B. Adams and A.R. Gillespie, *Remote Sensing of Landscapes with Spectral Images: A Physical Modeling Approach*, Cambridge University Press, 2006.

R. A. Schowengerdt, *Remote Sensing: Models and Methods for Image Processing*, 3rd ed., Elsevier, 2006.

J. A. Richards and X. Jia, *Remote Sensing Digital Image Analysis*, 4th ed., Springer, 2005.

P. K. Varshney and M. K. Arora, *Advanced Image Processing Techniques for Remotely Sensed Hyperspectral Data*, Springer, 2004.

C.-I. Chang, *Hyperspectral Imaging Techniques for Spectral Detection and Classification*, Kluwer Academic/Plenum, 2003.

D. A. Landgrebe, *Signal Theory Methods in Multispectral Remote Sensing*, Wiley–IEEE, 2003.

Spectral Unmixing

N. Keshava and J. F. Mustrad, A survey of spectral unmixing algorithms, *Lincoln Laboratory Journal*, Vol. 14 (1), pp. 55–78, 2003.

N. Keshava and J. F. Mustard, Spectral unmixing, *IEEE Signal Processing Magazine*, pp. 44–57, 2002.

Algorithms and Technologies for Multispectral, Hyperspectral, and Ultraspectral Imagery XI, Proceedings of SPIE, Vol. 5806, 2005.

M. Vélez-Reyes and S. Rosario, Solving abundance estimation in hyperspectral unmixing as a least distance problem, in *Proceedings of the IEEE International Geosciences and Remote Sensing Symposium*, Alaska, 2004.

C. L. Lawson and R. J. Hanson, *Solving Least Square Problems*, Prentice-Hall, 1974.

Coastal Remote Sensing

L. Miller, C. E. Del Castillo, and B. A. McKee, *Remote Sensing of Coastal Aquatic Environments: Technologies, Techniques and Applications*, Springer, 2007.

L. L. Richardson, and E. LeDrew, *Remote Sensing of Aquatic Coastal Ecosystem Processes: Science and Management Applications*, Springer, 2006.

A. Castrodad-Carrau, M. Vélez-Reyes, and J. A. Goodman, An algorithm to retrieve coastal water optical properties, bathymetry, and bottom albedo from hyperspectral imagery, *Photonics for Port and Harbor Security II, Proceedings of SPIE*, Vol. 6204, p. 62040H, 2006.

S. M. Adler-Golden, P. K. Acharya, A. Berk, M. W. Matthew, and D. Gorodetsky, Remote bathymetry of the littoral zone from AVIRIS, LASH, and QuickBird imagery, *IEEE Transactions on Geoscience and Remote Sensing*, Vol. 43(2), pp. 337–347, 2005.

H. Arst, *Optical Properties and Remote Sensing of Multicomponental Water Bodies*, Springer, 2003.

V. E. Brando and A. G. Dekker, Satellite hyperspectral remote sensing for estimating estuarine and coastal water quality, *IEEE Transactions on Geoscience and Remote Sensing*, Vol. 41, pp. 1378–1387, 2003.

R. P. Bukata, J. H. Jerome, and K. Y. Kondratyev, *Optical Properties and Remote Sensing of Inland and Coastal Waters*, CRC, 1995.

C. D. Mobley, *Light and Water: Radiative Transfer in Natural Waters*, Academic, 1994.

Spectral Imaging of Skin

T. Shi and C. A. DiMarzio, Multispectral method for skin imaging: development and validation, *Applied Optics*, Vol. 46, pp. 8619–8626, 2007.

K. J. Zuzak, M. D. Schaeberle, M. T. Gladwin, R. O. Cannon, and I. W. Levin, Noninvasive determination of spatially resolved and time-resolved tissue perfusion in humans during nitric oxide inhibition and inhalation by use of a visible-reflectance hyperspectral imaging technique, *Circulation*, Vol. 104, pp. 2905–2910, 2001.

P. J. Dwyer and C. A. DiMarzio, Hyperspectral imaging for dermal hemoglobin spectroscopy, *Proceedings of SPIE*, Vol. 3752, pp. 72–82, 1999.

P. J. Dwyer, R. R. Anderson, and C. A. DiMarzio, Mapping blood oxygen saturation using a multispectral imaging system, *Proceedings of SPIE*, Vol. 2976, pp. 270–280, 1997.

J. R. Mansfield, M. G. Sowa, J. R. Payette, B. Abdulrauf, M. F. Stranc, and H. H. Mantsch, Tissue viability by multispectral near infrared imaging: a fuzzy C-means clustering analysis, *IEEE Transactions on Medical Imaging*, Vol. 17, pp. 1011–1018, 1998.

R. D. Shonat, E. S. Wachman, W. Niu, A. P. Koretsky, and D. L. Farkas, Near-simultaneous hemoglobin saturation and oxygen tension maps in mouse brain using an AOTF microscope, *Biophysical Journal*, Vol. 73, pp. 1223–1231, 1997.

S. L. Jacques, J. C. Ramella-Roman, and K. Lee, Imaging skin pathology with polarized light, *Journal of Biomedical Optics*, Vol. 7, pp. 329–340, 2002.

R. R. Anderson and J. A. Parrish, The optics of human skin, *Journal of Investigative Dermatology*, Vol. 77, pp. 13–19, 1981.

Problems

6.1-1   **Linearly Mixed Spectrum.** The spectral function $f(\lambda)$ is a linear superposition $f(\lambda) = \alpha s_1(\lambda) + (1 - \alpha)s_2(\lambda)$ of the spectra of two endmembers representing generic vegetation and generic soil with spectra

$$s_1(\lambda) = \frac{0.7\,(\lambda/800)^{10}}{[1 + (\lambda/800)^{10}][1 + (\lambda/2000)^{10}]} + 0.15 \exp\left[-\frac{(\lambda - 500)^2}{2(100)^2}\right],$$

$$s_2(\lambda) = (\lambda/10000) + 0.03,$$

respectively, where $\alpha \in [0, 1]$ and λ is the wavelength in nanometers. Plot $f(\lambda)$ for $\alpha = 0, 0.25, 0.5, 0.75, 1$ and compare it with the spectra of the individual endmembers.

6.1-2   **Phantom Spectral Image.** Generate a phantom spectral image of three overlapping spots with different spectral distributions:

$$f(x, y, \lambda) = f_1(x, y)s_1(\lambda) + f_2(x, y)s_2(\lambda) + f_3(x, y)s_3(\lambda),$$

where

$$f_i(x, y) = f_0 \exp\left[-\frac{(x - x_i)^2 + (y - y_i)^2}{2\sigma_s^2}\right], \qquad s_i(\lambda) = \frac{1}{\sqrt{2\pi}\sigma_\lambda} \exp\left[-\frac{(\lambda - \lambda_i)^2}{2\sigma_\lambda^2}\right],$$

and $i = 1, 2, 3$. Here, $f_i(x, y)$ are Gaussian spots of width σ_s centered at the positions (x_i, y_i), and $s_i(\lambda)$ are Gaussian spectral distributions of width σ_λ centered at the wavelengths λ_i. This spectral image is discretized using $32 \times 32 \times 32$ pixels. The coordinates of the spot centers (x_i, y_i) are (10,10), (16,16), and (22,22) pixels, as measured from the top left corner of the image, and the central wavelengths λ_i are at the pixels 10, 16, and 22. Take $\sigma_s = \sigma_\lambda = 8$ pixels and the value of the parameter f_0 is such that at the central position $(x_0, y_0) = (16, 16)$, $f_1 + f_2 + f_3 = 1$. Use MATLAB to perform the following operations:

(a) Print the three images $f_i(x, y)$, $i = 1, 2, 3$, as intensity images.

(b) Plot the three spectral distributions $s_i(\lambda)$, $i = 1, 2, 3$.

(c) Plot the spectral distribution of the spectral image $f(x, y, \lambda)$ at the central point $(x_0, y_0) = (16, 16)$.

(d) Print the spectral image $f(x, y, \lambda)$ as an RGB color image with the functions $f_i(x, y)$, $i = 1, 2, 3$, playing the role of the red, green, and blue components (see Appendix D, Sec. D.1).

6.2-1   **Spectral Sampling.** The phantom spectral image $f(x, y, \lambda)$ in Problem 6.1-2 is filtered by a spectral filter $H(\lambda)$ that is a Gaussian function of width $\sigma_H = 10$ pixels centered at the central wavelength $\lambda_0 = 16$. The spectrum at the central pixel $(x_0, y_0) = (16, 16)$ is measured using an eight-channel spectrometer with response functions $R^{(\ell)}(\lambda)$ that are also Gaussian functions of width $\sigma_R = 4$ pixels centered at wavelengths $2, 6, 10, \ldots, 30$. Determine the elements $H_i^{(\ell)}$ of the matrix that relates the spectrometer readings $\{g^{(\ell)}\}$ to the parameters $\{f_i\}, i = 1, 2, 3$ [see (6.2-9)]. Compute the readings of the spectrometer channels $g^{(\ell)}, \ell = 1, 2, \ldots, 8$.

6.2-2   **Spectrometer Resolution.** The reflectance spectrum of a generic mineral is

$$s(\lambda) = \frac{0.5}{1 + (\lambda/2000)^{10}} - 0.4 \exp\left[-\frac{(\lambda - 250)^2}{2(500)^2}\right] - 0.25 \exp\left[-\frac{(\lambda - 1500)^2}{2(158)^2}\right].$$

(a) Mineral identification and composition is often done by examining absorption features near $\lambda = 1500$ nm. What should be the spectral resolution of a spectrometer capable of capturing such features? Explain your reasoning.

(b) The reflectance spectrum is measured by use of an L-channel spectrometer with sampling functions $\mathcal{R}^{(\ell)}(\lambda)$ that are Gaussian functions centered at wavelengths $\lambda_\ell, \ell = 1, 2, \ldots, L$, and having a standard deviation $\sigma_{\mathcal{R}}$ corresponding to a full-width-at-half-maximum (FWHM) spectral resolution of $2\sqrt{2 \ln 2}\sigma_{\mathcal{R}} = 2.35\sigma_{\mathcal{R}}$. For spectral resolutions of 50, 100, 200, and 400 nm, determine the spectrometer parameters, $\sigma_{\mathcal{R}}$, L, and λ_ℓ, assuming uniform spacing of the spectrometer channels. If the spectrometer measures a spectral function $g(\lambda)$ proportional to the spectral reflectance $s(\lambda)$, compute and plot the spectrometer outputs $g^{(\ell)}$ for each of the values of the spectral resolution. For comparison, also plot the original spectrum $s(\lambda)$ on the same graph. Describe how well the spectrometer reproduces the absorption features of the mineral signature.

6.2-3   **Spatial Filtering of a Spectral Image.** The phantom spectral image in Problem 6.1-2 is imaged by a camera with a point spread function equal to a circularly symmetric Gaussian function of width $\sigma_r = 4$ pixels at all wavelengths.

(a) Plot and print the same functions as in Problem 6.1-2 for the filtered spectral image. Compare and comment on the effect of spatial filtering.

(b) If the spectrum of the spatially filtered phantom is measured at the central pixel using the spectrometer in Problem 6.2-1, determine the readings of the eight spectrometer channels $g^{(\ell)}$.

6.3-1   **Unmixing.** Let $s_1(\lambda)$, $s_2(\lambda)$, and $s_3(\lambda)$ be the spectral reflectances of vegetation, soil, and mineral, used in Problems 6.1-1 and 6.2-2. A mixed pixel composed of these three endmembers is measured by use of a spectrometer covering the 400–2500 nm range with 10 nm resolution and wavelength spacing equal to the resolution. The measured signals generate vectors $\mathbf{s}_1$, $\mathbf{s}_2$, and $\mathbf{s}_3$. A mixed pixel is generated by the operation $\mathbf{g} = \mathbf{Sf}$, where $\mathbf{S} = [\mathbf{s}_1\ \mathbf{s}_2\ \mathbf{s}_3]$ and $\mathbf{f} = [0.3\ 0.5\ 0.2]^{\mathrm{T}}$ is the abundance vector. Compute the vector $\mathbf{g}$ and use it to solve the inverse problem, i.e., determine estimates of the abundance vector $\mathbf{f}$ as follows:

(a) Use the unconstrained least-squares equation (6.3-8).

(b) Use the STO constrained least-squares equation (6.3-9).

(c) Use the NNLS MATLAB function `lsqnonneg`.

(d) Use the constrained linear least-squares MATLAB function `lsqlin` (both nonnegativity and STO constraints can be incorporated in this function).

How do these estimates compare?

6.3-2   **Unmixing with Noise.** A more realistic situation in unmixing involves noise in the measured spectral signature, i.e., $\mathbf{g} = \mathbf{Sf} + \mathbf{w}$, where $\mathbf{w}$ is a vector of independent Gaussian random variables. Repeat Problem 6.3-1 for signal-to-noise ratios SNR = 100, 10, and 1 dB. How do the estimated abundances compare with the actual abundances for each case?

6.3-3   **Unmixing with Wrong Number of Endmembers.** In practical applications, the number of endmembers present in a spectral image is often unknown. Suppose that the unmixing tasks in Problem 6.3-1(a)–(d) are undertaken under the incorrect assumption that only two endmembers, instead of three, are present. Use the same $\mathbf{g}$ vector generated in Problem 6.3-1 and estimate the abundance values under the following assumptions:

(a) Vegetation and soil are the only endmembers present (i.e., $\mathbf{S} = [\mathbf{s}_1\ \mathbf{s}_2]$).

(b) Vegetation and mineral are the only endmembers present (i.e., $\mathbf{S} = [\mathbf{s}_1\ \mathbf{s}_3]$)).

(c) Soil and mineral are the only endmembers present (i.e., $\mathbf{S} = [\mathbf{s}_2\ \mathbf{s}_3]$)).

In each of these cases, compare the estimates to the actual abundance values.

6.3-4   **Thematic Map.** Consider the spectral distribution $f(x_0, y_0, \lambda)$ at the central pixel $(x_0, y_0) = (16, 16)$ of the phantom spectral image in Problem 6.1-2. Assuming that you know this distribution and also the spectral functions $s_i(\lambda)$, $i = 1, 2, 3$, use an unmixing procedure to estimate the values $f_i(x_0, y_0)$, $i = 1, 2, 3$, at the central pixel. Repeat this unmixing procedure at each of the pixels of the spectral image $f(x, y, \lambda)$ in order to estimate the spatial distribution of the endmembers $f_i(x, y)$, $i = 1, 2, 3$, and generate a thematic map. Compare with the true endmember images.

6.3-5 **Band Selection for Classification.** Consider the data in Fig. 6.3-4 of Example 6.3-4, which characterize the spectral reflectance signatures of various materials.

(a) In what region of the spectrum is water differentiable from wetland?

(b) What wavelength region has the largest degree of change in reflectance for vegetation?

(c) If a two-band sensor with bands at 400 nm and 950 nm is used, which signatures cannot be discriminated?

(d) If a narrowband sensor centered at 800 nm is used to image regions with these three classes, how will the measured intensities of the three regions compare?

6.3-6 **MDA Classification.** This problem deals with classification of three classes by use of measurement of the spectral reflectance in two bands, as listed in the following table. For each class, randomly choose five points for training and five points for testing.

(a) Using the training data, determine the mean for each class.

(b) Draw spectral- and feature-space diagrams similar to Fig. 6.3-4 of Example 6.3-4.

(c) Determine the discriminant functions for the minimum distance to mean assignment rule (MDA) (see Sec. C.2 of Appendix C).

(d) Classify each training and testing pixel using the MDA rule.

(e) Determine the user's accuracy of the classifier (percentage of the number of correctly classified pixels to the total number of pixels) for each of the classes. Use the testing data first and then use the training data, and discuss the reason for the differences (if any).

Pixel #		1	2	3	4	5	6	7	8	4	10
Class 1	Band 1	16	18	20	11	17	8	14	10	4	7
	Band 2	13	13	13	12	12	11	11	10	9	9
Class 2	Band 1	8	9	6	8	5	7	4	6	4	3
	Band 2	8	7	7	6	5	5	4	3	2	2
Class 3	Band 1	19	19	17	17	16	14	13	13	11	11
	Band 2	6	3	8	1	4	5	8	1	6	3

6.4-1 **Turbid Medium with Two Absorbers.** A light beam is emitted from a source located inside a deep turbid medium with a scattering coefficient $\mu_s = 10$ cm^{-1}. The reflected (back-scattered) beam is measured by a sensor at the same location. The medium itself is non-absorbing, but it has two absorbing materials of molar concentrations c_1 and c_2 and molar absorption coefficients $\kappa_1(\lambda)$ and $\kappa_2(\lambda)$ that are modeled as Gaussian functions with peak values centered at the wavelengths $\lambda_1 = 500$ nm and $\lambda_2 = 600$ nm and widths $\sigma_\lambda = 50$ nm.

(a) Assuming that $c_1 = 2c_2 = 2$ mol/L and that $\kappa(\lambda_2) = 2\kappa(\lambda_1) = 4$ cm^{-1} mol^{-1} L, compute and plot the reflectance $\mathcal{R}(\lambda)$ as a function of the wavelength in the 400–700 nm band.

(b) Assuming that all you know is the reflectance $\mathcal{R}(\lambda)$ that you computed in (a) and the molar absorption coefficients, demonstrate how you can estimate the ratio c_1/c_2 of the concentrations of the absorbing materials.

6.4-2 **Effect of Bathymetry on Remote-Sensing Reflectance.** Figure 6.4-9 shows the dependence of the remote-sensing reflectance spectra of water on the bathymetry (depth) for various classes of the bottom (sand, algae, and coral).

(a) At what depth for each of the spectral classes is the remote-sensing reflectance no longer sensitive to the bottom type. How does the resulting depth compare across the three signatures. What do you think causes the differences, if any?

(b) How do you think the depth to which the remote-sensing reflectance is sensitive to the bottom type changes for fixed depth but increasing water turbidity.

6.4-3 **Bathymetry by Multispectral Lidar.** Lidar systems are used to measure bathymetry (depth) in coastal areas. The idea is to use two lidars, one in the green region and one in the red region of the electromagnetic spectrum. Using the data in Fig. 6.0-1(a), describe how the return signals from the red and the green lidars can be combined to extract bathymetry information (see V. I. Feygels, C. W. Wright, Y. I. Kopilevich, and A. I. Surkov, Narrow-field-of-view bathymetrical lidar: theory and field test, *Proceedings of SPIE*, Vol. 5155, p. 1, 2003).

Mosaicing, Change Detection, and Multisensor Imaging

It is sometimes desired to capture a high-resolution image of a large object by use of an imaging system with adequate resolution but insufficient number of pixels/voxels. This can be accomplished by taking multiple images of smaller segments of the object and subsequently collating them into a single image. In other applications, multiple images of a single object are obtained by use of different imaging modalities or technologies. The extraction of meaningful information on the object from such multiple images can be challenging. In yet other applications, an object is imaged with the same instrument before and after some change has occurred and the two images are to be compared to assess the change. Dealing with multiple images is an important task that requires precise alignment often under uncertain conditions.

This chapter describes a set of related techniques that involve multiple images. First, **mosaicing** is the stitching together of multiple partial views of a region that is much larger than the field of view of the imaging instrument, into a single large synthetic image of the entire region. Second, **multisensor fusion** is the combination of images of the same region acquired by two or more imaging modalities, e.g., optical and ultrasonic. Third, **change detection** is the identification of changes occurring in a sequence of images of the same region. Underlying these three important applications is the need for **image registration** – a method for accurately aligning multiple images, and transforming them into a common coordinate frame. Mosaicing, change detection, and multisensor fusion can then be performed in this common coordinate space.

In Sec. 7.1, we introduce these three basic problems of interest briefly, and illustrate the common need to solve the image registration problem. We delve into the details of image registration methods in Sec. 7.2. In Sec. 7.3–Sec. 7.5, we revisit mosaicing, change detection, and multisensor fusion in more detail using the image registration methods. An overview of software tools for registration is provided in Sec. D.4 of Appendix D.

7.1 Introduction

A. Mosaicing

Mosaicing (or mosaic synthesis) is the process by which two or more partial images [two-dimensional (2D) or three-dimensional (3D)] of a region are aligned and joined together to synthesize (compose) a single complete image of the entire region. The partial views are commonly called **tiles** and the synthetic complete view is called the **mosaic**. A closely related term is *montaging*. Some authors use the term *mosaicing* when the tiles do not overlap, as shown in Fig. 7.1-1(*a*), and *montaging* when the tiles overlap, as shown in Fig. 7.1-1(*b*). In this chapter, we choose not to make a distinction between these two terms and simply use the term mosaicing throughout.

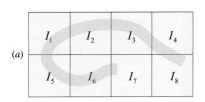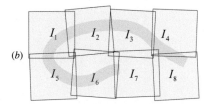

Figure 7.1-1 Synthesis of a *wide-area* image by joining multiple partial views (tiles). (*a*) Non-overlapping tiles with known relative geometric relationships. (*b*) Overlapping tiles whose geometric relationships are inferred from the images themselves.

The most common reason for mosaicing is to produce an image of a region that is much larger than the field of view of the imaging instrument. With most imaging instruments, one must sacrifice the field of view in order to capture finer details. In other words, higher resolution imaging entails a corresponding reduction in the spatial extent. Mosaicing enables us to image large regions of space at high spatial resolution.

In order to join the tiles correctly, one must know their geometric relationships with each other. In some cases, these relationships are known from the imaging instrument. For instance, many microscopes come equipped with an accurate computer-controlled stage that makes it easy to acquire a series of images with known offsets. In some other cases, it is not nearly as convenient. The following are two examples.

EXAMPLE 7.1-1.   *Imaging the Human Retina.*   In this example from ophthalmology, 11 partial views of a healthy human retina (the light-sensitive tissue in the posterior region of the eye) were captured by a clinical instrument known as a fundus camera. The camera illuminates the retina in a ring-shaped pattern and records a digital image capturing a 30° view of the retina at a time. A mosaic computed from the partial views provides a more complete 70° view of the retina, as illustrated in Fig. 7.1-2.

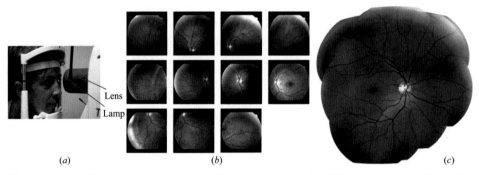

(a)   (b)   (c)

Figure 7.1-2   Mosaicing in the context of retinal imaging. (*a*) Clinical instrument for retinal imaging. (*b*) A series of 30° images (tiles) captured by asking the patient to point her eye in a variety of directions, aided by a small blinking lamp positioned at different locations. (*c*) A 70° mosaic computed from the 11 images in (*b*).

EXAMPLE 7.1-2.   *Brain Imaging.*   Figure 7.1-3 shows an example from neurobiology where there is a need to map all of the cells in a mammalian brain (commonly, a rat/mouse brain). A laser-scanning confocal microscope (LSCM) can create large 3D images with lateral sizes of 1024×1024 voxels or more, and with a spatial resolution approaching 0.25 µm/voxel. Even these large images only cover 256 µm of lateral extent – much less than the regions of interest in many studies. A natural method to image a much greater extent of tissue without sacrificing spatial resolution is to record an overlapping series of tiles and stitch them together to create a mosaic image of the region of interest in the brain.

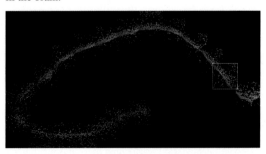

Figure 7.1-3   Mosaicing in the context of microscopic brain imaging. An LSCM can only image the cell nuclei in a tiny portion of the rat brain region known as the hippocampus (256 µm wide, shown as a box). To create an image of the entire hippocampus, an overlapping series of images must be collected and "stitched" together to form a mosaic.

Constructing Mosaics

This section introduces the main steps involved in constructing mosaics. A more detailed description of mosaicing is provided in Sec. 7.3. We begin with a simple example of an original object shown schematically in Fig. 7.1-4(*a*), from which two *overlapping* partial images (tiles) are captured by an ideal imaging system. The tiles, shown in Fig. 7.1-4(*b*), are denoted $I_1(\mathbf{x})$ and $I_2(\mathbf{x})$, where $\mathbf{x}$ denotes the spatial coordinates of a point in the images, which may be 2D, i.e., $\mathbf{x}=(x, y)$, or 3D, i.e., $\mathbf{x}=(x, y, z)$. We want to compute a mosaic image, denoted $I_M(\mathbf{x})$, by joining these two tiles. A good mosaic presents an accurate and seamless view of the combined region covered by the two tiles. The mosaic is constructed in two steps. First, the tiles are aligned geometrically so that they can be mapped into a common coordinate frame. This step is called *registration*. The second step is to use these aligned tiles to form a single image $I_M(\mathbf{x})$, as illustrated in Fig. 7.1-4(*c*).

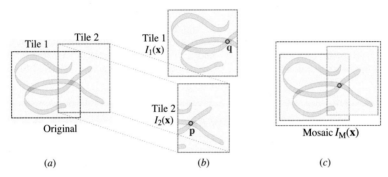

Figure 7.1-4 Mosaicing of two tiles imaged by an ideal camera displaced parallel to itself. (*a*) Original image with the boundaries of the two tiles marked. (*b*) Two tiles with a common landmark point q and p used for alignment. (*c*) Mosaic obtained by displacing tile 2 relative to tile 1 such that corresponding landmarks coincide.

Registration of Displaced Tiles.   If the imaging instrument is merely displaced parallel to itself by a precisely known displacement vector, as it moves from the first tile to the second, then accurate registration is straightforward. Simply displace the second tile relative to the first by the same displacement vector. However, if the displacement between the two tiles is unknown, then it must be figured out by matching the content of the measured tiles in the overlapping area. This is often facilitated by using common distinctive points in the two tiles as landmarks. For example, the points marked q and p in the tiles in Fig. 7.1-4(*b*) are actually the same point in the original object. Such a matching of landmark points is called a **correspondence**. If tile 2 is displaced until the corresponding points coincide, the registration task is complete.

Registration of Displaced and Geometrically Distorted Tiles.   Tile registration is not easy in real image-acquisition systems since the imaging conditions can be different from one tile to the next, in uncontrollable ways. In addition to the displacements that are not precisely known, unknown geometric distortions, such as slight changes in magnification, rotation, and shearing, are introduced, as exemplified in Fig. 7.1-5(*b*). This makes the process of registration nontrivial. Again, these unknown geometric transformations can only be figured out by matching the content of the measured tiles in the overlapping area using mathematical tools described in this section. This results in the identification and correction of the geometric distortion and spatial transformation of the tiles into a common coordinate frame, as shown in Fig. 7.1-5. In this figure, the spatially transformed version of tile 2 is denoted $I_2^T(\mathbf{x})$. This enables the subsequent step of combining the two tiles to create the mosaic.

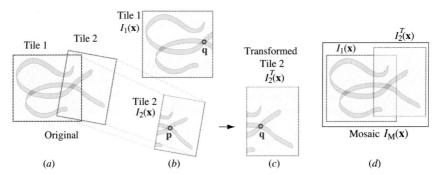

(a)   (b)   (c)   (d)

Figure 7.1-5   Mosaicing of two tiles. (*a*) Original image with the boundaries of the two tiles marked. (*b*) Two tiles with geometric distortion (rotation + minification) introduced in tile 2. Points q and p are common landmarks in tiles 1 and 2, used for alignment. (*c*) Geometric distortion is eliminated by the registration process. (*d*) Mosaic obtained by displacing registered tile 2 relative to tile 1.

EXAMPLE 7.1-3.   **Mosaicing a Pair of Retinal Images.**   As a real-life example, Fig. 7.1-6 illustrates the mosaicing of two retinal images of the same eye taken by a fundus camera from different angles. The registration algorithm for this application relies on branch points of blood vessels as landmarks in the overlapping region, and accounts for the known distortions introduced by the curvature of the retina.

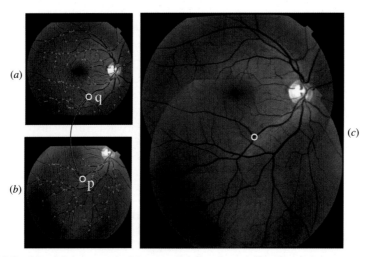

Figure 7.1-6   Mosaicing two retinal images. (*a*) Two image tiles showing a common landmark representing a vessel branch point. An automatic vessel-tracing algorithm was used to locate branch points. Vessel traces are shown in red and branch points are shown in green. (*b*) Mosaic computed from the two image tiles using a transformation that is capable of accommodating the curvature of the retina. The common landmark branch point is circled.

Signal Corrections and Combining.   Once the tiles $I_1(\mathbf{x})$ and $I_2^T(\mathbf{y})$ are registered, they must be corrected to remove degradations introduced during the image acquisition process. This process is called **signal correction**. The last step in the mosaic reconstruction process is the combining of the corrected intensities of the tiles to construct the mosaic image $I_M(\mathbf{x})$. A fundamental problem arises. In the overlapping region, the two images may have different intensity values. This can happen for two reasons. The first has to do with illumination variations and/or imaging noise. If you examine closely the image tiles in Fig. 7.1-2, you will notice that the illumination in the individual tiles is not uniform, e.g., some of the image tiles suffer from glare. The second reason has to do with actual changes in the imaged scene between the times that the two images were recorded. Overall, we must pay careful attention to the manner in which the image intensity values are combined together in computing a seamless mosaic. The signal correction and the combining process are discussed in Sec. 7.3.

B. Change Detection

Change detection is the process of identifying points (pixels) in a given region that have undergone appreciable change. Specifically, given two images, $I(\mathbf{x}, t_1)$ and $I(\mathbf{x}, t_2)$ describing a changing physical property of a region at two different times t_1 and t_2, respectively, it is of interest to determine the pixels that have changed in the interim. The result of change detection is a binary-valued image

$$B(\mathbf{x}) = \begin{cases} 1, & \text{if pixel } \mathbf{x} \text{ has changed} \\ 0, & \text{otherwise,} \end{cases} \tag{7.1-1}$$

known as the **change map**. At first glance, the change detection problem appears trivial – examine corresponding pixels in the two images and check if any of them are different, i.e.,

$$B(\mathbf{x}) = \begin{cases} 1, & \text{if } I(\mathbf{x}, t_1) = I(\mathbf{x}, t_2) \\ 0, & \text{otherwise.} \end{cases} \tag{7.1-2}$$

In practice, however, the problem is a bit more challenging. First, the two images have to be aligned precisely, since image registration errors produce false indications of change. Second, signal degradations such as imaging noise and variations in illumination can affect pixel values even though the object of interest itself is actually unchanged. Finally, some detectable changes may be important for a practical application while others may be totally uninteresting.

Change detection, therefore, is concerned with principal ways for identifying real changes that are of interest and rejecting false changes and/or incidental changes that are not of interest from the standpoint of a practical application.

To perform change detection, we follow the following steps:

- **Image Registration.** We start by performing image registration, i.e., transform $I(\mathbf{x}, t_2)$ into an image $I^T(\mathbf{x}, t_2)$ in the coordinate frame of $I(\mathbf{x}, t_1)$.

- **Signal Corrections.** Next, we perform signal corrections to compute the aligned and corrected images $\hat{I}(\mathbf{x}, t_1)$ and $\hat{I}^T(\mathbf{x}, t_2)$.

- **Decision.** At this point, we compare corresponding pixels in a statistical manner to test whether they are significantly different. One approach is to test if the magnitude of the difference in intensities $|\hat{I}(\mathbf{x}, t_1) - \hat{I}^T(\mathbf{x}, t_2)|$ is greater than a prescribed threshold ϑ, known as the *decision threshold*.

The problem of change detection can then be expressed as

$$B(\mathbf{x}) = \begin{cases} 1, & \left|\hat{I}(\mathbf{x}, t_1), - \hat{I}^T(\mathbf{x}, t_2)\right| > \vartheta \\ 0, & \text{otherwise.} \end{cases} \tag{7.1-3}$$

Other measures of the change can also be used, as described in Sec. 7.4. This decision rule has some limitations. For instance, it treats each pixel independently of others. In practice, more sophisticated rules that take into account dependencies among pixels in an image are needed, and some will be considered in Sec. 7.4.

Change detection is a valuable capability, but it has its limitations, as demonstrated in the following example.

EXAMPLE 7.1-4.   *Changes in Retinal Images.*   In this example, two retinal images of a patient, shown in Panels (*a*) and (*b*) of Fig. 7.1-7, are taken 6 months apart. Some changes are immediately apparent. Also apparent is the differences in lighting. Panel (*c*) is the result of change detection. The region labeled A is due to a stick-like pointer placed by the photographer in front of the camera in panel (*a*); it does not represent a real retinal change. This pointer can be discerned in panel (*a*) upon careful examination. Region B is an artifact of glare on the upper right-hand corner of the second image in panel (*b*) and not a real retinal change. Region C is the fovea (the center of the retina responsible for sharp vision). The change-detection algorithm treats this region the same way as any other part of the image, notwithstanding its greater importance from a medical standpoint. The ultimate limitation of change masks is highlighted by region D, which can be discerned as a slight discoloration in panels (*a*) and (*b*) upon closer examination. This condition is known as *geographic atrophy*, a condition of most concern to the physician. The change mask fails to capture the most diagnostically important change.

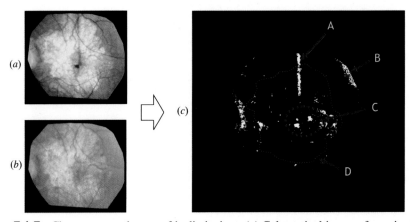

Figure 7.1-7 Change map and some of its limitations. (*a*) Color retinal image of a patient taken with a fundus camera. (*b*) Color retinal image of the same eye taken 6 months later, showing changes. (*c*) The change map, with white indicating changed pixels and black indicating unchanged pixels. The four labeled regions are discussed in the text.

So, what can be done to overcome the limitations described in Example 7.1-4? The general idea is to develop algorithms that exploit additional information and constraints that are applicable to the application of interest. For instance, specialized pattern analysis algorithms are available to identify retinal structures (e.g., blood vessels, optic disk, background) and various retinal regions of interest (e.g., fovea). These algorithms, in effect, provide "labels" for each pixel indicating the retinal structure represented by that pixel. These labels can be used to vary change-detection criteria (e.g., the test statistic and/or threshold) across the image.

C. Multisensor Imaging

In *multisensor imaging* (also called *multimodality imaging*), different sensors are used to acquire images of the same object. Such images capture either the same distribution with different resolution and/or contrast, or capture different types of information about the object, as illustrated by Examples 7.1-5–7.1-7. Other examples are presented in Sec. 7.5, in which this topic is revisited.

In multisensor imaging, there is often a need to align (register) the recorded images in order to construct a single image or to make the images more useful to the user. The registration methods discussed thus far in this chapter, which are intended for aligning two images recorded by the same imaging instrument, must then be adapted to meet the needs of multisensor imaging.

EXAMPLE 7.1-5.   *Combined CT, MRI, and PET Medical Imaging.*   Figure 7.1-8 shows an example from medical imaging. The left half of panel (*a*) is one transverse slice of a 3D image of a human head as imaged by an X-ray computed tomography (CT) scanner. This instrument mainly reveals bone and skin. The right half of this panel shows part of the same patient's head as imaged by magnetic resonance imaging (MRI). This instrument mainly "sees" soft tissues (the bony regions appear dark), and provides much more contrast between different types of soft tissue compared with the CT scanner. Similarly, the left half of panel (*b*) was acquired using a positron emission tomography (PET) scanner, which images the distribution of a radioactive tracer that is mostly indicative of regions with high blood flow (high activity). PET data is very noisy compared with MRI/CT data. The right half of this panel shows the same patient's head as imaged by an MRI scanner. The MRI instrument captures structure but not the activity, and vice versa. Clearly, different imaging modalities sense different aspects of the tissue, but they do exhibit consistency that can be exploited for registration if a single image is to be generated.

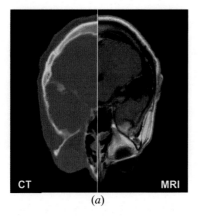 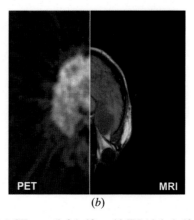

(*a*)   (*b*)

Figure 7.1-8   Examples of multisensor imaging. (*a*) CT scan (left half) and MRI (right half) of the head of the same patient. (*b*) PET scan (left half) and MRI (right half) of the head of the same patient. (Courtesy of Asad Abu-Tarif.)

EXAMPLE 7.1-6.   *Multisensor Retinal Imaging.*   This example of two-sensor retinal imaging is illustrated in Fig. 7.1-9. The first image is captured by injecting the patient with a fluorescent dye (indocyanine green) and imaging the dye to show the early phase of blood flow through the subsurface (choroidal) vessel network. The second is acquired without the dye. This provides the physician with two different and complementary pieces of diagnostic information.

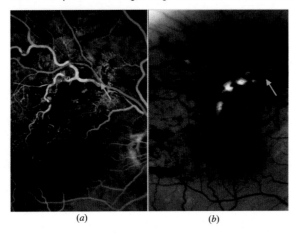

Figure 7.1-9   Two registered retinal images. (a) An image captured by injecting the patient with a fluorescent dye (indocyanine green), and imaging the dye. (b) An image of the same retina recorded without the dye. The arrows in the two images indicate corresponding points. This is another way to display the results of image registration, which allows the physician to detect and confirm vessel blockages by examining both views together.

(a)   (b)

EXAMPLE 7.1-7.   *Multisensor Undersea Imaging.* In this example, an autonomous remote-controlled underwater vehicle equipped with a pair of stereoscopic cameras and an acoustic (sonar) depth sensor was used to survey an underwater archaeological site of an ancient Roman shipwreck using two types of imagery of the seafloor – acoustic and visual, as illustrated in Fig. 7.1-10. The acoustic (sonar) sensor produces a depth map. The stereoscopic cameras provide two brightness images from which a second depth map is also estimated. Results of sensor integration combining the brightness information from the cameras and depth information from the sonar device, aided by depth cues from the stereoscopic depth estimation algorithm, are used to compute a realistic 3D virtual view of the shipwreck. One can interactively move this view around on a computer screen to view the scene from any desired angle.

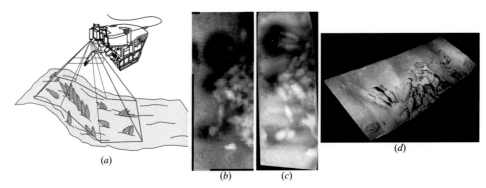

(a)

(b)   (c)

(d)

Figure 7.1-10   Multisensor undersea imaging. (a) An autonomous remote-controlled underwater vehicle equipped with a pair of stereoscopic cameras and an acoustic (sonar) depth sensor surveys an underwater archaeological site of an ancient Roman shipwreck using two types of imagery of the seafloor — acoustic and visual. The bottle-shaped objects lying on the sea floor are amphorae used by ancient Romans to store household materials. (b) Data from the acoustic (sonar) depth sensor. (c) A second depth image estimated from the stereoscopic cameras. (d) Results of sensor integration combining the brightness information from the cameras and depth information from the sonar device, aided by depth cues from the stereoscopic depth estimation algorithm. Sensor integration has served to provide a realistic 3D virtual view of the shipwreck.

The cameras also record the image intensity. In this case, the mosaic data can be represented as 3D surface whose points are assigned a height (elevation) obtained from some combination of acoustic and/or stereoscopic sensing, and whose brightness is obtained from the imaging cameras. In the language of computer graphics, the image intensities represent a texture that is mapped to a 3D surface defined by the depth map. The surface is represented as a triangular mesh. Once this mapping is done, standard computer graphics rendering tools (available on most graphics cards of computers) can be used to visualize the amphorae in a much more realistic 3D manner.

Multisensor integration is the process by which signals from different sensors (usually sensing different physical properties $\alpha_1, \alpha_2, \ldots$) are used synergistically for some purpose, such as mapping a single underlying property β. Often, the signals are actually combined using an appropriate mathematical function to produce a composite signal, which serves as an estimate of β. This process is known as multisensor integration or *multisensor fusion*. The goal of this process is to produce a combined representation that is more *informative* than any one of the sensors alone (since it provides complementary information, e.g., one sensor mapping structure and the other mapping activity), more *reliable* (since it can exploit redundancy in the multiple images, all related to a single underlying physical property), more *timely*, more *accurate*, or *less expensive*. Multisensor imaging therefore enables detection of targets with better sensitivity or specificity, and allows better classification of objects since it has access to more features. The subject of multisensor imaging and multisensor integration will be revisited in Sec. 7.5.

D. Image Registration

Image registration is the process of aligning two images of a common/overlapping region by establishing a geometric transformation that casts them into a common coordinate frame. This allows us to combine and/or compare pixels in the two images. Accurate image registration is a necessary and enabling step for diverse imaging problems, including mosaic synthesis, multisensor integration, and change detection. The accuracy of registration is very important for mosaicing. Seemingly modest registration errors of the order of a pixel can cause distortion of image details. Furthermore, when we attempt to construct large mosaics with hundreds or thousands of tiles, small registration errors can add up. Indeed, sub-pixel registration accuracy (i.e., average registration errors of less than 1 pixel) is highly desirable for mosaicing.

Consider two images, $I_1(\mathbf{x})$ and $I_2(\mathbf{x})$, originating from two overlapping regions of an object/scene and captured by an image acquisition system that introduces some unknown, or partially known, geometric transformation denoted T. The purpose of registration is to estimate the relative geometric transformation between the two images so that they may be brought into alignment. There are three steps to registration:

(i) Establish correspondences between landmarks in the two images.
(ii) Estimate the geometric transformation that relates the two images.
(iii) Apply a counter transformation to realign the two images.

(i) Establishing the Correspondences

The first step in registration is to establish points of correspondence between the two images within their overlap region. Let $\mathbf{p}$ denote the coordinates of a point in the first image $I_1(\mathbf{x})$ and let $\mathbf{q}$ denote the coordinates of the same physical point (i.e., the homologous point) in the overlapping region of the second image $I_2(\mathbf{x})$. The ordered pair $(\mathbf{p}, \mathbf{q})$ is called a **correspondence**. There are many such correspondences forming a set denoted $\mathcal{C}$, so that $(\mathbf{p}, \mathbf{q}) \in \mathcal{C}$, as shown in Fig. 7.1-11. Knowing the set of all correspondences, the next step is to determine a single geometric transformation denoted T that consistently generates from each point $\mathbf{p}$ the correct corresponding point $\mathbf{p}$. The inverse transformation, denoted T^{-1} transforms $\mathbf{q}$ into $\mathbf{p}$.

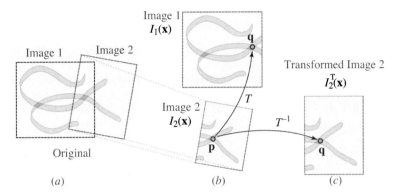

Figure 7.1-11   Forward and inverse geometric transformations linking corresponding points. (*a*) Original image. (*b*) Estimation of the geometric transformation T that brings image 2 into alignment with image 1 by use of correspondences such as $(\mathbf{p}, \mathbf{q})$. (*c*) Bringing image 2 into alignment with image 1 by applying the inverse geometric transformation T^{-1} on all points of image 2.

(ii) Estimating the Geometric Transformation

Several geometric transformations relating images were described in Sec. 3.1B. Here, we express a geometric transformation as a function $\mathbf{q} = T(\mathbf{p}, \Theta)$ that relates the coordinates of points $\mathbf{p}$ and $\mathbf{q}$. Specifying the transformation function requires one or more transformation parameters, forming a vector Θ. These parameters describe the amount of translation, rotation, magnification, and other adjustments required to map $\mathbf{p} = (x, y)$ into $\mathbf{q} = (x', y')$, as the following examples illustrate.

- The **rigid/similarity transformation** is described by the similarity transformation $\mathbf{q} = s\mathbf{R}(\theta)\mathbf{p} + \mathbf{t}$, where $\mathbf{R}(\theta)$ is the 2×2 orthonormal rotation matrix, $\mathbf{t} = (t_1, t_2)$ is the translation vector, and s is the scale factor. Using **homogeneous coordinates**, this may be written as a single matrix multiplication

$$\begin{bmatrix} \mathbf{q} \\ 1 \end{bmatrix} = \begin{bmatrix} s\mathbf{R}(\theta) & \mathbf{t} \\ 0 & 1 \end{bmatrix} \begin{bmatrix} \mathbf{p} \\ 1 \end{bmatrix}. \tag{7.1-4}$$

  Two correspondences are minimally sufficient to estimate the four transformation parameters $\Theta = [t_1, t_2, \theta, s]$.
- As noted earlier, many imaging scenarios are not adequately described in rigid terms. The **affine transformation** defined below is a nonrigid transformation that extends the similarity transformation by also adding the ability to also nonuniformly scale (i.e., skew) images:

$$\begin{bmatrix} \mathbf{q} \\ 1 \end{bmatrix} = \begin{bmatrix} \mathbf{A} & \mathbf{t} \\ 0 & 1 \end{bmatrix} \begin{bmatrix} \mathbf{p} \\ 1 \end{bmatrix}, \tag{7.1-5}$$

  where $\mathbf{A}$ is a 2×2 invertible submatrix with four parameters. The additional flexibility comes at the expense of additional transformation parameters or *degrees of freedom* from four to six.

■ An extension of the affine transformation is **quadratic transformation**

$$\begin{bmatrix} \mathbf{q} \\ 1 \end{bmatrix} = \begin{bmatrix} \mathbf{B} & \mathbf{A} & \mathbf{t} \\ 0 & 0 & 1 \end{bmatrix} \mathbf{X}(\mathbf{p}), \tag{7.1-6}$$

where $\mathbf{X}(\mathbf{p}) = [\ x^2\ \ xy\ \ y^2\ \ x\ \ y\ \ 1\ ]^T$ and $\mathbf{p} = (x, y)$, $\mathbf{B}$ is a 2×3 submatrix containing the *quadratic parameters*, and $\mathbf{A}$ is a 2×2 submatrix implementing an affine transformation. Altogether, the quadratic transformation has 12 parameters. Equation (7.1-6) may also be written in the form

$$\mathbf{q} = \mathbf{\Theta}\mathbf{X}(\mathbf{p}), \tag{7.1-7}$$

where $\mathbf{\Theta} = [\mathbf{B}\ \ \mathbf{A}\ \ \mathbf{t}]$ is a matrix representing the transformation parameters. Since the affine transformations and the similarity transformations are special cases of the quadratic transformation, (7.1-7) provides a general description for all three transformations. Describing a transformation simply as a matrix product makes it convenient to describe registration algorithms, as will be subsequently shown.

Estimating the Transformation Parameters.   If the selected geometric transformation $T(\mathbf{p}; \mathbf{\Theta})$ model describes the actual geometric distortion, then the error between the actual coordinates of $\mathbf{q}$ and the value indicated by $T(\mathbf{p}; \mathbf{\Theta})$ would be zero for all correspondences in the set $\mathcal{C}$. In reality, the transformation function only produces an estimate of $\mathbf{q}$,

$$\hat{\mathbf{q}} = T(\mathbf{p}; \mathbf{\Theta}), \tag{7.1-8}$$

where the "hat" symbol is used to indicate estimated quantities. The error is the "distance" between the estimated location $\hat{\mathbf{q}}$ and the actual location $\mathbf{q}$

$$d(\mathbf{p}, \mathbf{q}) = \|\hat{\mathbf{q}} - \mathbf{q}\| = \|T(\mathbf{p}; \mathbf{\Theta}) - \mathbf{q}\|, \tag{7.1-9}$$

where $\|.\|$ represents the norm of the vector (see Appendix B). Assuming that the correspondences are known, the registration problem can be described as a search for the transformation parameters $\widehat{\mathbf{\Theta}}$ that minimize the total squared error. This is expressed mathematically as

$$\widehat{\mathbf{\Theta}} = \underset{\mathbf{\Theta}}{\arg\min} \sum_{(\mathbf{p},\mathbf{q})\in\mathcal{C}} \|T(\mathbf{p}; \mathbf{\Theta}) - \mathbf{q}\|^2. \tag{7.1-10}$$

This is a minimum mean-square error (MMSE) estimation problem in which the Euclidean distance between $T(\mathbf{p}; \mathbf{\Theta})$ and $\mathbf{q}$ is minimized.

MMSE Solution.   If the transformation is known to be quadratic (or similarity or affine), then it can be expressed as in (7.1-7), i.e., $T(\mathbf{p}_n; \mathbf{\Theta}) = \mathbf{\Theta}\mathbf{X}(\mathbf{p}_n)$. With this, (7.1-10) becomes

$$\widehat{\mathbf{\Theta}} = \underset{\mathbf{\Theta}}{\arg\min} \sum_{n} \|\mathbf{\Theta}\mathbf{X}(\mathbf{p}_n) - \mathbf{q}_n\|^2. \tag{7.1-11}$$

This minimization problem may be solved by expanding the squared function in (7.1-11) using matrix algebra and setting the derivative with respect to $\mathbf{\Theta}$ to zero. The result is

$$\widehat{\Theta} = \left[\sum_n \mathbf{X}^\mathrm{T}(\mathbf{p}_n)\mathbf{X}(\mathbf{p}_n)\right]^{-1}\left[\sum_n \mathbf{X}(\mathbf{p}_n)\mathbf{q}_n\right]. \tag{7.1-12}$$

Equation (7.1-12) provides the desired solution: an expression for the transformation parameters Θ in terms of the known correspondences $\{\mathbf{p}_n, \mathbf{q}_n\}$.

Joint Estimation of the Transformation and the Correspondences. The registration problem becomes more difficult if the correspondences $\mathcal{C}$ are not known, since we will have to search for the transformation parameters $\widehat{\Theta}$ *and* the correspondence set $\widehat{\mathcal{C}}$ that together minimize the total squared error. This is expressed mathematically as:

$$[\widehat{\Theta}, \widehat{\mathcal{C}}] = \underset{\{\Theta, \mathcal{C}\}}{\arg\min} \sum_{(\mathbf{p}, \mathbf{q}) \in \mathcal{C}} \|T(\mathbf{p}; \Theta) - \mathbf{q}\|^2. \tag{7.1-13}$$

This equation is minimally sufficient for introducing the basic concept of registration, but does not convey many of the practical details. We still need to learn how to actually perform the optimization. We also need to learn many subtleties and extensions, e.g., how to make it robust to erroneous correspondences. This topic and other related topics will be discussed in greater detail in Sec. 7.2.

(iii) Realigning Images

Once the geometric transformation $T(\mathbf{p}; \widehat{\Theta})$ has been determined, the last step in the registration process is to apply it to one image to align it with the other. For example, we can apply the inverse geometric transformation $T^{-1}(\mathbf{y}; \widehat{\Theta})$ to each point in $I_2(\mathbf{x})$ to compute a new image, denoted $I_2^\mathrm{T}(\mathbf{y})$ that is in the coordinate frame of $I_1(\mathbf{x})$. We can also do the reverse – transform each point in $I_1(\mathbf{x})$ using the geometric transformation $T(\mathbf{y}; \widehat{\Theta})$ to compute a new image, denoted $I_1^\mathrm{T}(\mathbf{x})$ in the coordinate frame of $I_2(\mathbf{x})$. Either operation brings the two images into a common coordinate frame.

The backward operation carried out by the inverse transformation $\mathbf{p} = T^{-1}(\mathbf{q}; \Theta)$ is often preferable to the forward operation. In many applications, one of the images to be registered represents a *sensed image*, or the *moving image*, whereas the other image represents a *reference image*, or the *fixed image*. For example, the fixed image may represent a preconstructed mosaic or a wide-area view, and the sensed image may represent a partial view. When the application requires the sensed image to be aligned with the fixed image, we can run into a practical problem – the transformed point $T(\mathbf{p}; \Theta)$ may not correspond to a pixel in the fixed image due to discretization and rounding, so we can get holes (unmapped pixels) and/or overlaps (pixels with multiple mappings). In such cases, the backward transformation is preferable. The inverse transformation can often be estimated even if the function $T(\cdot)$ is not directly invertible. We simply swap images I_1 and I_2 and conduct a registration. This works as long as the transform accurately reflects the spatial relationships between the images.

Sampling Issues. An image, after all, represents a sampling of a continuous physical region using a discrete grid. When we geometrically transform a pixel $\mathbf{p}$ to its transformed location $\mathbf{q}$, the result may be a set of real-numbered coordinates. One question that arises is how best to reconcile the transformed location to the rectangular coordinate space of the target image. The simplest method is to use interpolation. Specifically, we identify the four nearest pixels and use a bilinear interpolation to compute the new pixel value. Indeed, image interpolation algorithms are a necessary component of registration methods, especially intensity-based methods described in the next section. *Image resampling* is a related operation in which we change the grid over which the underlying physical region is sampled.

Registration of 3D Images.   Although, the preceding description of registration was presented in terms of 2D images, registration, mosaicing, and change-detection methods for 3D images are analogous. The main issue to consider for 3D images is the necessarily higher dimensionality of the spatial transformations, entailing a greater amount of computation and the need to use more correspondences. For example, the 3D affine transformation has 12 parameters.

▶ Problems 7.1-1, 7.1-2

7.2   Image Registration Algorithms

The previous sections highlighted the fact that image registration is a common building block for mosaic synthesis, change detection, and multisensor imaging. The basic method of image registration using correspondences between landmarks was also introduced. In this section, we present a more comprehensive overview and a deeper understanding of registration methods, and describe techniques that make the registration algorithms as automated as possible. We begin with an overview of three approaches to image registration.

- **Feature-based registration** refers to a class of registration methods that estimate the correspondences and the spatial transformation from features (landmarks) alone, ignoring all other pixels in the images. This class was introduced in Sec. 7.1D and will be described in more detail in this section. One motivation for considering features is computational efficiency – most images contain large numbers of pixels, so it is much more efficient to work with a sparse set of, say 10–100, landmarks, rather than millions of pixels. Another motivation is reliability – we can be very selective about landmarks by only choosing points that are sufficiently prominent, distinctive, unique, stable, and invariant to distortions introduced by the imaging process. Finally, it could be argued that the non-landmark pixels add little to the registration performance anyway, so should properly be ignored.

- **Intensity-Based Registration.** For many images, reliable landmarks are simply not available. In such cases, we resort to intensity-based registration algorithms that operate directly on all pixel values. Intensity-based registration may be regarded as a special case of feature-based registration in which *all pixels* are included, rather than just the set of sparse landmarks. Although this description is conceptually correct, it does not convey the fact that alternative strategies are needed to minimize the amount of computation required.

- **Mutual-Information-Based Registration.** These are a class of registration algorithms that are specifically designed to align images acquired using different modalities. These methods are in some ways similar to intensity-based registration, but differ in terms of how the image intensity information is handled. Specifically, they utilize image-matching measures inspired by the concept of mutual information from the field of information theory.

We now describe each of these registration methods in some detail.

A. Feature-Based Registration

Feature-based registration algorithms operate by identifying a distinctive set of **land-mark points** in the images and then relying only on these points for conducting the registration. Indeed, that is how the registration problem was introduced in Sec. 7.1D. Some authors refer to landmarks as **features**. Another term (used in the MATLAB image processing toolbox) is **control points**. The terms **interest points** and **keypoints** are also used. We use these terms interchangeably in this chapter. A good landmark has a rich amount of structure in its neighborhood (flat regions are uninteresting). It must be distinctive and unique, and must have a well-defined location that can be computed reproducibly. Landmarks must also be invariant to spatial transformations, such as changes in the viewing angle or the scale, and degradations, such as changes in illumination.

Feature Selection

Manual Feature Identification.   One straightforward method for identifying land-marks is to do it manually. For example, the MATLAB image processing toolbox provides an interactive graphical control point selection tool (cpselect) to view the two images side by side, and specify corresponding landmarks by pointing and clicking. Since manual pointing is not particularly accurate, MATLAB also provides a function (cpcorr) to refine the locations of the landmarks by use of the cross-correlation function. This is a practical method for registering a small number of images. However, when a large number of images must be registered, and/or when the registration must be performed rapidly (e.g., within milliseconds), automated landmark extraction algorithms are necessary.

Application-Specific Features.   In some applications, landmarks are obvious or nat-ural. For example, the locations of branching and crossover points of blood vessels in retinal images have long been used by physicians to visually relate pairs of retinal images. This suggests the idea of developing automatic algorithms to trace the vessels and find their branching/crossover points. Similarly, roads and rivers are often used as landmarks in satellite imagery. As another example, if the image consists of distinct blobs (such as cell nuclei), the centroids of these blobs can be used as good landmarks.

Fiducial Points.   In some applications, it is practical to place man-made objects in the scene to serve as landmarks. These are known as fiducial points. Ideal fiducials are designed to be easily and accurately located. Fiducials are commonly used in complex environments, such as image-guided surgery, where high reliability and/or real-time registration is needed.

Corner Points.   When obvious or natural landmarks are not available, it is common to use *generic* features, such as sharp corners. Formally, a point in an image is considered a corner if there are two dominant and different edge directions in a local neighborhood of the point. Because of its invariance to affine transformations and illumination vari-ation, the *Harris corner detector* is widely used to find corners. This detector is based on computing from an image $I(x, y)$ a map $S(x, y)$ representing the local variations in the x and y directions. Consider a small window $W(x, y)$ of pixels centered around a point (x, y) and determine the average difference of the image intensities at points separated by a fixed displacement $(\Delta x, \Delta y)$, i.e., the sum of the squared differences between $I(u, v)$ and $I(u + \Delta x, v + \Delta y)$ for all (u, v) within the window:

$$S(x, y) = \sum_{(u,v) \in W(x,y)} [I(u + \Delta x, v + \Delta y) - I(u, v)]^2. \qquad (7.2\text{-}1)$$

Note that (x, y) and (u, v) are discrete points on the sampling grid. If Δx and Δy are sufficiently small, then, using a Taylor series approximation,

$$I(u + \Delta x, v + \Delta y) - I(u, v) \approx I_x(u, v)\Delta x + I_y(u, v)\Delta y = [\; I_x \quad I_y \;] \begin{bmatrix} \Delta x \\ \Delta y \end{bmatrix},$$
$$(7.2\text{-}2)$$

where I_x and I_y are partial derivatives with respect to x and y, respectively. By substituting (7.2-2) into (7.2-1) we obtain

$$S(x, y) \approx [\; \Delta x \quad \Delta y \;] \mathbf{A}(x, y) \begin{bmatrix} \Delta x \\ \Delta y \end{bmatrix}, \qquad (7.2\text{-}3)$$

where the matrix

$$\mathbf{A}(x, y) = \begin{bmatrix} \displaystyle\sum_W I_x^2 & \displaystyle\sum_W I_x I_y \\ \displaystyle\sum_W I_x I_y & \displaystyle\sum_W I_y^2 \end{bmatrix}, \qquad (7.2\text{-}4)$$

sometimes called the **structure tensor**, characterizes the intensity variations in the x and y directions in the neighborhood of the point (x, y). Since we are interested in variation in *any* direction, not just the x and y directions, we compute the matrix eigenvalues λ_1 and λ_2 at each point. These represent variations along the principal directions. If both eigenvalues are small, we infer that the region within the window area is of approximately flat intensity – this is uninteresting. If one eigenvalue is low and the other is a high positive value, then we infer that the region contains an edge. If both eigenvalues are high positive numbers, we infer that a corner (or a region with large variation in two directions) exists. One single measure that may be used as an indicator of the presence of corners is therefore $\mathcal{M} = \min(\lambda_1, \lambda_2)$. This is the basis for the Harris corner detector.

Since direct computation of eigenvalues at each pixel is computationally expensive, another measure[1] that does not require such computation is

$$\mathcal{M} = \lambda_1 \lambda_2 - \kappa(\lambda_1 + \lambda_2)^2 = \det(\mathbf{A}) - \kappa \operatorname{trace}^2(\mathbf{A}), \qquad (7.2\text{-}5)$$

where κ is an experimentally determined sensitivity parameter (typically ≈ 0.1). This measure can be computed rapidly from the determinant and the trace of the matrix $\mathbf{A}$ at each point (x, y).

The computation of the derivatives in $\mathbf{A}$ must be approached with care, since a direct pixel differencing approximation would be overly sensitive to image noise. A standard strategy to compute derivatives involves pre-smoothing the image by a Gaussian kernel of some width σ. Since the choice of σ can affect the results, several variations of a

---

[1]C. Harris and M. Stephens, A combined corner and edge detector, *Proceedings of the 4th Alvey Vision Conference*, pp. 147–151, 1988.

multi-scale Harris operator have been suggested in which the optimal scale value is selected by the algorithm. One simple idea is to compute $\mathcal{M}$ for different scale values and choose the scale value for which it is highest (at each pixel).

EXAMPLE 7.2-1.   *Detection of Corner Points in Images of a Fluorescently Labeled Neuron.*   Figure 7.2-1(a) shows two images of a fluorescently labeled neuron, one being a scaled and rotated version of the other. The Harris corner detector was used to determine corner points in each, and the results are shown in Fig. 7.2-1(b) as circles.

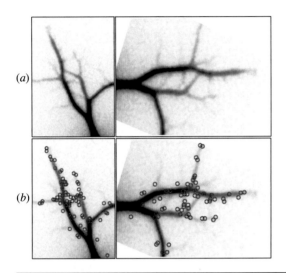

Figure 7.2-1   Corner points in the images in (a) determined by use of the Harris corner detector and displayed as circles in (b).

Lowe's Keypoints.   One particularly well-behaved class of interest points, named *Lowe's keypoints*, is widely used for image registration. To compute keypoints, the image $I(x, y)$ is blurred by a bank of filters of impulse response functions equal to the difference of two Gaussian functions of different widths,

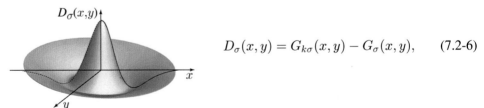

$$D_\sigma(x, y) = G_{k\sigma}(x, y) - G_\sigma(x, y), \qquad (7.2\text{-}6)$$

where $G_\sigma(x, y) = (1/2\pi\sigma^2) \exp[-(x^2 + y^2)/2\sigma^2]$ is the 2D Gaussian function of width σ, and k is a positive constant, usually a power of 2. As σ is increased by multiples of 2, a hierarchy of images,

$$I_\sigma(x, y) = D_\sigma(x, y) \otimes I(x, y), \qquad (7.2\text{-}7)$$

is generated, each of which provides a view at a different scale. Since the difference of Gaussians (DOG) filter is an isotropic bandpass filter sensitive to variations such as edges of any orientation, the bank of filtered images displays variation at different scales. This type of representation of a single image $I(x, y)$ by a set of filtered images $I_\sigma(x, y)$ at different scales σ is called a **scale-space representation**.

The keypoints may be extracted from the scale-space representation $I_\sigma(x, y)$ by looking for local minima/maxima of $I_\sigma(x, y)$ in space (x, y) and scale σ. Specifically, each pixel in $I_\sigma(x, y)$ is compared with its nine neighbors at the same scale, and nine corresponding pixel neighbors in adjacent scales. If the value is maximum or minimum, it is selected as a candidate keypoint. Usually, this operation results in numerous candidate keypoints, and it makes sense to exclude keypoints in image regions that have too little contrast, high edge response, too much noise, etc.

EXAMPLE 7.2-2.   *Lowe's Keypoints of Images of a Fluorescently Labeled Neuron.*
We consider again the two images of a fluorescently labeled neuron shown in Fig. 7.2-1(a) of Example 7.2-1. The Lowe's keypoints of these images were determined and are marked in Fig. 7.2-2 by circles of sizes proportional to the spatial scale of the interest points.

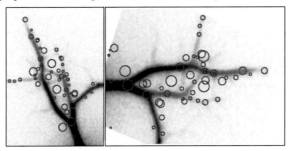

Figure 7.2-2   Lowe's keypoints of images of a fluorescently labeled neuron.

Features with Descriptors

The region surrounding an interest point contains significant additional information that can be exploited to distinguish interest points. For example, consider a retinal image in which a point **p** in the first image corresponds to a vessel bifurcation point with a bifurcation angle of $30°$. Suppose that there are two points $\mathbf{q}_1, \mathbf{q}_2$ in the second image that are potential correspondences with similar distance errors (so they cannot be distinguished based on distance error alone). If $\mathbf{q}_1$ has a bifurcation angle of $31°$ and $\mathbf{q}_2$ has an angle of $42°$, then clearly $\mathbf{q}_1$ is a better match to **p**. This is an example of an application-specific *descriptor* or *signature* of a landmark point. In general, *descriptors* of an interest point are numbers that quantify one or more aspects of the point's local surroundings, such as local intensity structure, color or spectral profile, scale value, orientation, and local texture. Clearly, the most useful descriptors are those that are invariant to expected geometric transformations, illumination variations, and imaging noise.

Orientations as Descriptors.   The orientations associated with an interest point may be computed by first filtering the original image with filters approximating the partial derivatives in the x and y directions:

$$I_x(x, y) = [G_\sigma(x + \Delta x, y) - G_\sigma(x - \Delta x, y)] \otimes I(x, y), \qquad (7.2\text{-}8)$$

$$I_y(x, y) = [G_\sigma(x, \Delta y + h) - G_\sigma(x, y - \Delta y)] \otimes I(x, y), \qquad (7.2\text{-}9)$$

where Δx and Δy are pixel sizes. A filter with impulse response function equal to the difference between two displaced Gaussian functions provides an approximation to the partial derivative. The magnitude and orientation are given approximately by

$$m(x, y) = \sqrt{I_x^2 + I_y^2}, \quad \theta(x, y) = \arctan{(I_y/I_x)}, \quad (7.2\text{-}10)$$

respectively. In practice, this calculation is done over a neighborhood of the keypoint to make it robust. A histogram of orientations $\theta(x, y)$ weighted by the magnitudes $m(x, y)$ is computed over the neighborhood. The peaks of this histogram (of which there may be more than one) provide the dominant local orientation(s) around the keypoint.

Descriptors Based on the Scale-Invariant Feature Tansform (SIFT).   Descriptors for Lowe's keypoints based on the scale-invariant feature transform (SIFT) are widely used. The SIFT vector consists of 128 numbers computed as a set of orientation histograms on a 4×4 neighborhood of the keypoint. Usually, each histogram has four bins, yielding a set of $4 \times 4 \times 8 = 128$ numbers, collectively known as the SIFT vector. To make these numbers invariant to rotation, all the angles are relative to the dominant orientation. To make it invariant to illumination variations, the SIFT vector is normalized to unit magnitude. Overall, SIFT vectors have proven to be extremely distinctive and robust to substantial affine transformations and illumination variations. They therefore provide an effective basis for establishing correspondences.

EXAMPLE 7.2-3.   *SIFT Vectors for Two Images of a Fluorescently Labeled Neuron.*
As in the two previous examples, we consider again two images of a fluorescently labeled neuron, one being a scaled and rotated version of the other (images 1 and 2 in Fig. 7.2-3). Keypoints were determined for the two images using SIFT vectors. The correspondences were established based on the SIFT vectors. For example, given a pair of keypoints **p** and **q**, with SIFT vectors $\Sigma(\mathbf{p})$ and $\Sigma(\mathbf{q})$, respectively, we can simply use the Euclidean distance between $\Sigma(\mathbf{p})$ and $\Sigma(\mathbf{p})$ as a measure of dissimilarity. Highly dissimilar points will have a large distance, and vice versa.

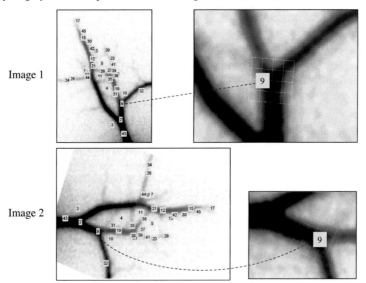

Figure 7.2-3   Matching keypoints using SIFT vectors for the images of a fluorescently labeled neuron used in previous examples [see Fig. 7.2-1(*a*)]. The left panels show numbered keypoints that form the correspondence set. The right panels show an enlarged view of keypoint 9. The descriptor grid is shown rotated and scaled according to the scale and orientation of the corresponding keypoint.

Feature-Based Registration Algorithm

A feature-based registration algorithm is a computational procedure that accepts two (or more) images, each having a set of features (landmarks), and simultaneously estimates correspondences $\mathcal{C}$ between the landmarks and a geometric transformation $T(\mathbf{p}; \Theta)$ relating the two images. These estimates are obtained by minimizing some measure of error so that the transformed landmarks of image 2 are "closest" to the corresponding landmarks in image 1. Many measures of error and many algorithms for solving the minimization problem are described in the literature. An ideal algorithm produces accurate estimates, is robust to imaging artifacts and noise, is capable of recognizing failure, and is computationally efficient. The ultimate goal is to design a *universal* or generalized registration algorithm capable of handling all types of images.

Optimization Models

The following are some commonly used optimization models:

(1) Minimum mean distance. A measure of error is the "distance" $d(T(\mathbf{p}; \Theta), \mathbf{q})$ between the landmark position $\mathbf{q}$ in image 1 and the transformed position $T(\mathbf{p}; \Theta)$ of the corresponding landmark $\mathbf{p}$ in image 2, averaged over all landmarks. This leads to the optimization problem

$$[\widehat{\Theta}, \widehat{\mathcal{C}}] = \underset{\{\Theta, \mathcal{C}\}}{\arg\min} \sum_{(\mathbf{p}, \mathbf{q}) \in \mathcal{C}} d(T(\mathbf{p}; \Theta), \mathbf{q}). \tag{7.2-11}$$

(2) Minimum mean-square error (MMSE). If $d(\cdot)$ is the squared Euclidean distance $\| \cdot \|^2$, then the optimization in (7.2-11) becomes

$$[\widehat{\Theta}, \widehat{\mathcal{C}}] = \underset{\{\Theta, \mathcal{C}\}}{\arg\min} \sum_{(\mathbf{p}, \mathbf{q}) \in \mathcal{C}} \|T(\mathbf{p}; \Theta) - \mathbf{q}\|^2, \tag{7.2-12}$$

which reproduces (7.1-13). This model is the simplest and most commonly used.

(3) Least median of squares (LMS). The MMSE model lacks an upper bound. In the summation over all correspondences, a single *bad* correspondence can upset the sum. For example, if 999 out of 1000 correspondences have distance values in the range of 0.9–1.1 pixels, but a single erroneous correspondence has a value of 1000, this bad correspondence can significantly affect the mean-square error. In statistics, such bad points are called *outliers*. Recognizing and eliminating outliers enhances the robustness of the model. This problem can be addressed by use of the median instead of the mean (the sum) in (7.2-12). The result is the least median of squares (LMS) model:

$$[\widehat{\Theta}, \widehat{\mathcal{C}}] = \underset{\{\Theta, \mathcal{C}\}}{\arg\min} \underset{(\mathbf{p}, \mathbf{q}) \in \mathcal{C}}{\text{median}} \|T(\mathbf{p}; \Theta) - \mathbf{q}\|^2. \tag{7.2-13}$$

The median automatically rejects the "extreme" correspondences, especially those with distances that are much too large. In effect, this approach forces the registration to be driven by a conforming majority of correspondences (the *inliers*) without the influence of a nonconforming minority (the *outliers*). This method is remarkably robust (up to 50% of the correspondences can be outliers, and yet the median remains unchanged). However, it is computationally expensive, in part because computation of the median requires repeated sorting of the data.

(4) Minimum mean-square weighted error. M-estimator.   A robust alternative to the LMS model is to use a minimum mean distance model with a distance $d(\cdot) = \rho(\|\cdot\|)$, where $\rho(.)$ is a nonquadratic continuous function, called the loss function, designed to de-emphasize outliers. This leads to the optimization

$$[\widehat{\Theta}, \widehat{\mathcal{C}}] = \underset{\{\Theta, \mathcal{C}\}}{\arg\min} \sum_{(\mathbf{p},\mathbf{q})\in\mathcal{C}} \rho\left(\|T(\mathbf{p}; \Theta) - \mathbf{q}\|^2 / \sigma\right). \qquad (7.2\text{-}14)$$

A commonly used loss function, known as the **Beaton–Tukey loss function**, is

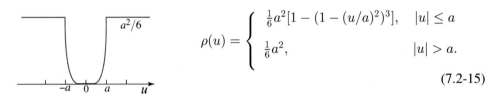

$$\rho(u) = \begin{cases} \frac{1}{6}a^2[1 - (1 - (u/a)^2)^3], & |u| \le a \\[2mm] \frac{1}{6}a^2, & |u| > a. \end{cases}$$

$$(7.2\text{-}15)$$

This function grows monotonically (but less slowly than the quadratic function u^2) until u reaches a value a whereupon it levels off to a fixed value of $a^2/6$ so that errors greater than a are given equal weight. Typically, $a \approx 4$–5. With this loss function, outliers have a limited impact no matter how "far" out they are. The parameter σ in (7.2-14) is known as the **robust scale**. In the robust statistics literature, (7.2-14) is known as an **M-estimator**. Theoretically, the M-estimator lacks the ultimate robustness of the LMS, but has been found to be extremely effective in practice and easier to work with.

Solution of the Minimization Problem

Once the error model is selected, the next step is to develop an algorithm to solve the minimization problem to determine the correspondences $\mathcal{C}$ and the transformation parameters Θ. We first consider two easier special cases: (a) solving for Θ if $\mathcal{C}$ is known, and (b) solving for $\mathcal{C}$ if Θ is known. We will subsequently present an algorithm for solving the optimization problem when both $\mathcal{C}$ and Θ are unknown.

(a) Known Correspondences.   If we already know a set of N correspondences $\mathcal{C} = \{(\mathbf{p}_1, \mathbf{q}_1), (\mathbf{p}_2, \mathbf{q}_2), \dots (\mathbf{p}_N, \mathbf{q}_N)\}$, then (7.2-11) reduces to the simpler minimization

$$\widehat{\Theta} = \underset{\{\Theta\}}{\arg\min} \sum_n d(T(\mathbf{p}_n; \Theta), \mathbf{q}_n), \qquad (7.2\text{-}16)$$

which provides an estimate $\widehat{\Theta}$ of Θ. The solution is simplified when T is expressed in the matrix form $T(\mathbf{p}_n; \Theta) = \Theta \mathbf{X}(\mathbf{p}_n)$.

For the MMSE model, for which $d(\cdot) = \|\cdot\|^2$, (7.2-16) yields the minimization problem (7.1-11) whose solution (7.1-12) is reproduced here for convenience:

$$\widehat{\Theta} = \left[\sum_n \mathbf{X}^{\mathrm{T}}(\mathbf{p}_n)\mathbf{X}(\mathbf{p}_n)\right]^{-1} \left[\sum_n \mathbf{X}(\mathbf{p}_n)\mathbf{q}_n\right]. \qquad (7.2\text{-}17)$$

For the M-estimator model, for which $d(\cdot) = \rho(\|\cdot\|)$, the minimization problem in

(7.2-14), with known $\mathcal{C}$, has the solution

$$\Theta = \left[\sum_n \mathbf{X}(\mathbf{p}_n) w \left([\Theta \mathbf{X}(p_n) - \mathbf{q}_n]/\sigma \right) \right]^{-1} \left[\sum_n \mathbf{q}_n w \left([\Theta \mathbf{X}(p_n) - \mathbf{q}_n]/\sigma \right) \right],$$

(7.2-18)

where σ is the scaling factor and $w(u) = \rho'(u)/u$ is known as the robust weight term ($\rho'(u)$ is the derivative of the loss function $\rho(u)$). Since (7.2-18) contains Θ on both sides it can only be solved numerically; for example, by use of an iterative approach for which a guessed value of Θ is substituted in the right-hand side to compute an updated value of Θ, which is substituted again in the right-hand side to obtain a better value, and so on.

(b) Known Transformation Parameters. If the transformation parameters Θ are known, then it is possible to estimate the correspondences. Specifically, suppose that we have two sets of landmark points $\mathbf{P} = \{\mathbf{p}_1, \mathbf{p}_2, ... \mathbf{p}_N\}$ and $\mathbf{Q} = \{\mathbf{q}_1, \mathbf{q}_2, ... \mathbf{q}_M\}$, respectively, extracted from the two images (note that the number of landmarks in the two images can differ). A simple way to establish correspondences between landmark sets $\mathbf{P}$ and $\mathbf{Q}$ is to transform each landmark $\mathbf{p}_n$ to yield the estimated location $\hat{q}_n = T(\mathbf{p}_n; \widehat{\Theta})$ and find the nearest landmark in $\mathbf{Q}$ (assuming that the closest landmark is the correct one), i.e.,

$$\hat{\mathbf{q}}_n = \underset{\mathbf{q} \in \mathbf{Q}}{\arg\min} \left\{ d(T(\mathbf{p}_n; \widehat{\Theta}), \mathbf{q}) \right\}.$$

(7.2-19)

The overall estimated correspondence set is

$$\widehat{\mathcal{C}} = \left\{ (\mathbf{p}_n, \mathbf{q}_n) | \mathbf{p}_n \in \mathbf{P}, \quad \hat{\mathbf{q}}_n = \underset{\mathbf{q} \in \mathbf{Q}}{\arg\min} \left\{ d(T(\mathbf{p_n}; \widehat{\Theta}), \mathbf{q}) \right\} \right\}.$$

(7.2-20)

The optimization problem in (7.2-19) may be solved by means of an exhaustive search over all landmarks in the entire set $\mathbf{Q}$. This can be computationally expensive when the set is large.

The Iterative Closest Point (ICP) Algorithm

The iterative closest point (ICP) algorithm is based on iterating between the two cases (a) and (b). This algorithm is widely used, effective, and easy to understand. Starting from an initial guess of correspondences $\widehat{\mathcal{C}}^{(0)}$, the ICP algorithm estimates the transformation parameters $\widehat{\Theta}^{(1)}$. Then, using these estimated parameters, it generates an improved estimate of the feature correspondences, denoted $\widehat{\mathcal{C}}^{(1)}$. In iteration two, these correspondences are used to re-estimate the transformation

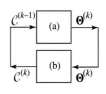

parameters $\widehat{\Theta}^{(2)}$, and so on. This procedure is carried out iteratively until some stopping criterion is met, e.g., the estimated parameters and correspondences change negligibly from one iteration to the next, indicating convergence. We could also start with an initial guess of the transformation parameters Θ.

Several practical details about how the ICP algorithm works are now discussed.

(1) Sensitivity to Initial Guess.   To get the ICP algorithm started, we must identify a good initial guess of $\mathcal{C}$ or Θ. This step is important, since a bad initialization of the ICP algorithm can make it diverge. An obvious and simple strategy is to specify some initial correspondences manually. In doing so, we must specify a sufficient number of correspondences to estimate the transformation parameters. For instance, if the transformation is a simple 2D translation (t_x, t_y), then just one correspondence is minimally sufficient. Higher order transformations require proportionately more correspondences. Automatic methods for identifying correspondences mostly rely on feature descriptors (landmark signatures). If descriptors $\Sigma(\mathbf{q}_n)$ and $\Sigma(\mathbf{p}_n)$ are available for the features $\mathbf{q}_n$ and $\mathbf{q}_n$, we can make sure that they are sufficiently close, i.e., $\|\Sigma(\mathbf{q}_n) - \Sigma(\mathbf{p}_n)\| \le \eta$, where η is some threshold. If the threshold is exceeded, we choose not to form a correspondence. The optimization problem can also be modified to include the descriptors. For example, an initial guess of the correspondences may be

$$\widehat{\mathcal{C}}^{(0)} = \left\{ (\mathbf{p}_n, \mathbf{q}_n) | \mathbf{p}_n \in \mathbf{P}, \quad \mathbf{q}_n = \arg\min_{\mathbf{q} \in \mathbf{Q}} \|\Sigma(\mathbf{q}_n) - \Sigma(\mathbf{p}_n)\|^2 \right\}. \qquad (7.2\text{-}21)$$

Although this idea is adequate for initializing the ICP algorithm in many applications, it has its limitations. One limitation is the fact that a landmark in one image $\mathbf{q}_n$ may be mapped to multiple landmarks in the other image. This can happen especially when the descriptors are not unique.

(2) Speeding Up the Computation of Correspondences.   Since an exhaustive search for the correspondences (given the transformation) can be time consuming when the set is large, and also because this search must be conducted repeatedly in the iterative algorithm, a number of methods have been developed to speed up the search. The following are some commonly used methods for speeding up the search:

- Organize the landmarks into rectangular bins and localize each search to a bin, rather than the entire set.
- Organize the landmarks using a k-dimensional tree (kD-tree) data structure that can be searched hierarchically instead of sequentially.
- Limit the search to the most promising pairs, while rejecting unpromising pairs (those that are too far apart) early on.
- Compute a map that stores the distance of each point in the image to the nearest landmark. Interestingly, this seemingly exhaustive computation can be performed rapidly. Once this distance map is available, it can be looked up to identify the nearest landmark without a search.
- Rank order all the pairs based on their distance and limit the ICP computation to a fraction of the pairs whose distances are the least.

(3) Improving Convergence.   Unfortunately, there is no guarantee that the ICP algorithm will converge. When a landmark $\mathbf{p}_n$ in image 2 is transformed, the estimated location $\hat{\mathbf{q}}_n$ may not be close to any landmark in image 2; or worse, it may be close to a wrong landmark, in which case the algorithm can actually diverge from the correct answer and converge to a wrong answer. This may be due to a missed landmark, a falsely detected landmark in one of the images, the presence of ambiguous landmarks such as nearly parallel lines instead of corners, or an actual change in the scene. Because of this potential for nonconvergence it is prudent to optimize the initialization step as much as possible and set a limit on the number of iterations in this algorithm. Now, the robust ICP is guaranteed to converge to at least a locally optimal solution. However, when it does converge, there is no guarantee that the estimated parameters are indeed the correct ones, so it is prudent to add some additional application-specific steps to detect a valid convergence, when possible. Notwithstanding all of these caveats, we can usually take reasonable steps to improve the likelihood of achieving correct convergence, and detecting divergence and/or erroneous convergence.

(4) Hierarchical Initialization.   The need for a good initial guess is especially important for transformations of high dimensions. This fact has motivated the development of hierarchical registration algorithms. Given a set of landmarks, we first use a low-dimensional transformation model (e.g., similarity) and the ICP algorithm to estimate correspondences and transformation parameters. These are then used to initialize the ICP algorithm using a higher order transformation model (e.g., affine). The results are then used to initialize yet another ICP algorithm using an even higher order transformation model (e.g., quadratic). This approach is remarkably successful and has been used widely. The effect of the order of the transformation on registration quality is demonstrated in Example 7.2-4.

EXAMPLE 7.2-4.   *Registration of Retinal Images with Transformations of Different Order.*   Figure 7.2-4 demonstrates the value of using higher order transformations for registering retinal images, which are flat images of the curved human retina. For these types of image, the similarity transformation yields a registration error of about 5 pixels, the affine transformation yields an error of about 4.5 pixels, while the quadratic transformation yields an error of 0.64 pixels.

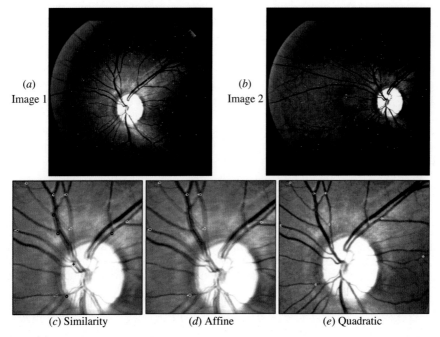

(a)
Image 1

(b)
Image 2

(c) Similarity   (d) Affine   (e) Quadratic

Figure 7.2-4   Illustration of the value of higher order transformations. Panels (a) and (b) show a pair of retinal images overlaid with white dots indicating landmark points. (c) When the images are registered using a similarity transformation, significant error is observed. In this illustration, the landmarks from the two images are shown using two different symbols (circles and crosses). (d) The affine transformation is more accurate. (e) A quadratic transformation is the most accurate, correctly accounting for the retinal curvature.

A natural question that arises in designing a hierarchical ICP algorithm is how and when to switch from one transformation to another. One simple approach is to use all the possible transformation models (e.g., similarity, affine, and quadratic) at each iteration and choose the model that yields the lowest error. This is known as *automated model selection*. Another idea is to limit the model selection to an appropriately small region (sometimes referred to as a *keyhole* or an *aperture*) surrounding landmarks rather than the entire image, keeping in mind the limited validity of a model. For example, a similarity model may work over a small region, but a quadratic model may be applicable over a larger region. The size of the keyhole can often be set automatically, based on the degree of uncertainty as measured by estimating the covariance matrix. The combination of these ideas can be remarkably effective; it forms the basis for the *dual-bootstrap ICP algorithm* and its generalizations (see references in the Reading List).

B. Intensity-Based Registration

When landmarks are either unavailable or unreliable registration may still be possible by using all of the intensity values in the image rather than a selected few landmarks. Intensity-based registration methods are sometimes referred to as *area-based methods* or *correlation-based methods*, since they usually perform a correlation operation over one or more (usually rectangular) area(s) of the image. One major concern with intensity-based registration is the amount of computation required. Unlike feature-based algorithms that operate on a concise set of coordinate locations, intensity-based methods must process every pixel in the images. Several approaches have been described in the literature to improve computational efficiency. We describe a few common approaches here.

Registration of Displaced Images.   For simplicity, consider two 2D images $I_1(x, y)$ and $I_2(x, y)$ that are shifted relative to each other by an unknown translation vector $[t_x, t_y]$ but are otherwise identical, so that $I_2(x, y) = I_1(x - t_x, y - t_y)$. One popular method for aligning the images is to translate $I_1(x, y)$ by a variable translation vector $[\tau_x, \tau_y]$ and compute the mean-squared error between $I_1(x - \tau_x, y - \tau_y)$ and $I_2(x, y)$ in the region of overlap A

$$e(\tau_x, \tau_y) = \iint_A [I_1(x - \tau_x, y - \tau_y) - I_2(x, y)]^2 \, dx \, dy, \qquad (7.2\text{-}22)$$

and find the values of $[\tau_x, \tau_y]$ that minimize this error. Clearly, under ideal conditions, i.e., the two images are exact displaced replicas of one another, the error vanishes when $(\tau_x, \tau_y) = (t_x, t_y)$. Since the right-hand side of (7.2-22) may be expanded as a sum,

$$\iint_A [I_1^2(x - \tau_x, y - \tau_y) + I_2^2(x, y)] \, dxdy - 2 \iint_A I_1(x - \tau_x, y - \tau_y)I_2(x, y)dxdy,$$

$$(7.2\text{-}23)$$

in which the first two terms do not depend upon τ_x and τ_y, minimizing the mean-square error is equivalent to maximizing the third term, or the cross-correlation function [see (A.2-7)]

$$R(\tau_x, \tau_y) = \iint_A I_2(x, y)I_1(x - \tau_x, y - \tau_y) \, dx \, dy. \qquad (7.2\text{-}24)$$

The registration problem therefore amounts to finding the transformation parameters that maximize the cross-correlation between the two images, as illustrated in Fig. 7.2-5. This method is actually optimal when the two images are contaminated by additive Gaussian noise, and is known as *matched filtering*.

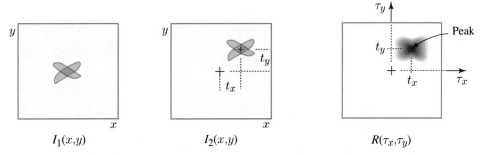

$$I_1(x,y) \qquad\qquad I_2(x,y) \qquad\qquad R(\tau_x,\tau_y)$$

Figure 7.2-5 Estimation of the displacement (t_x, t_y) between two images $I_1(x, y)$ and $I_2(x, y)$ by locating the peak of their cross-correlation function $R(\tau_x, \tau_y)$.

The cross-correlation function may be computed more efficiently in the Fourier domain by use of the fast Fourier transform (FFT). In accordance with (A.1-9) in Appendix A, the Fourier transform of the cross-correlation function $R(\tau_x, \tau_y)$ in (7.2-24) equals the product of the Fourier transforms of the two images (with one conjugated), i.e., $R(k_x, k_y) = I_1^*(k_x, k_y)I_2(k_x, k_y)$. A normalized version

$$r(k_x, k_y) = \frac{I_1^*(k_x, k_y)I_2(k_x, k_y)}{|I_1^*(k_x, k_y)I_2(k_x, k_y)|} \tag{7.2-25}$$

is a unimodular phase function that can be easily computed and used for registration. If $I_2(x, y)$ is an identical version of $I_1(x, y)$ translated by a vector (t_x, t_y), then $I_2(k_x, k_y) = I_1(k_x, k_y) \exp[j(k_x t_x + k_y t_y)]$ so that

$$r(k_x, k_y) = \exp\left[j(k_x t_x + k_y t_y)\right]. \tag{7.2-26}$$

The inverse Fourier transform $r(k_x, k_y)$ is then an impulse function $r(x, y) = \delta(x - t_x, y - t_y)$ located at the position (t_x, t_y). In practice, we can expect $r(x, y)$ to have a strong peak at this location. With this in mind, we simply find the coordinates (t_x, t_y) with the highest magnitude and use them to align the images.

Registration of Rotated Images. The use of the cross-correlation function to estimate the translation between two images may be extended to handle image rotation. As illustrated in Fig. 7.2-6(a) a Cartesian-to-polar coordinate transformation converts rotation into translation so that if $I_2(x, y)$ is equal to $I_1(x, y)$ rotated by an angle φ, then in polar coordinates centered at the origin $(x = y = 0)$, $I_2(r, \theta) = I_1(r, \theta - \varphi)$. We can therefore use the cross-correlation method described above to estimate the rotation φ after the images have been resampled in polar coordinates.

Registration of Scaled Images. If $I_2(x, y)$ is scaled by a factor s relative to $I_1(x, y)$, i.e., $I_2(x, y) = (1/s^2)I_1(sx, sy)$, then we use a logarithmic scale, which converts scaling into translation, i.e.,

$$I_2(\log x, \log y) = (1/s^2)I_1(\log(sx), \log(sy)) = (1/s^2)I_1(\log x + \log s, \log y + \log s),$$

as illustrated in Fig. 7.2-6(*b*). The cross-correlation technique may then be used to estimate the translation parameter $\log s$, from which the scaling parameter s can be determined.

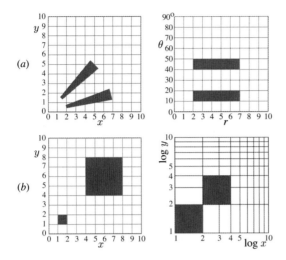

Figure 7.2-6 (*a*) Rotation is converted into translation by use of a polar coordinate system. (*b*) Scaling is converted into translation by use of a logarithmic coordinate system.

Registration of Translated, Scaled, and Rotated Images. Since scaling does not cause rotation, we can use a coordinate transformation $(x, y) \rightarrow (\log r, \theta)$ to convert each of these operations into translation. Also since the Fourier transform maintains rotation and converts scaling by a factor s into scaling by a factor $1/s$ (see properties of the Fourier transform in Sec. A.1 of Appendix A), we can now describe a complete methodology to register a pair of images $I_1(x, y)$ and $I_2(x, y)$ that are scaled and rotated relative to each other by a factor s and an angle ϕ, and translated by a vector (t_x, t_y) as follows:

- We first compute the Fourier transforms $I_1(k_x, k_y)$ and $I_2(k_x, k_y)$ and transform the rectangular coordinates (k_x, k_y) to log-polar coordinates $(\log k_r, k_\theta)$, which represent rotation and scaling as translation.
- We then compute the inverse Fourier transform of the ratio $r(k_x, k_y)$ defined in (7.2-25). The point with the highest magnitude corresponds to the estimated scale $\hat{s}$ and rotation $\hat{\phi}$.
- Using these estimated values, we transform $I_1(x, y)$ by a scaling factor $1/\hat{s}$ and rotation $\hat{\phi}$ to compute a new image denoted $I_1^T(x, y)$. Next, we compute the inverse Fourier transform of the ratio $r(k_x, k_y)$ for $I_1^T(x, y)$ and $I_2(x, y)$. The peak of $r(x, y)$ yields the estimated shift value $(\hat{t}_x, \hat{t}_y)$. At this point, we have the complete set of transformation parameters.

A few practical notes are in order.

- The transformation from rectangular to polar coordinates requires the use of fill-in zero values where the two coordinate spaces do not overlap, as shown in the illustration to the right.
- Since this intensity-based registration algorithm is sensitive to image brightness and variations in illumination, it is helpful to preprocess the images to normalize the intensity levels of the two images, and equalize the image

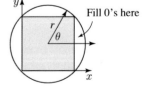

histograms to improve performance. It is also a good idea to perform high-pass filtering to enhance the helpful fine details (high spatial frequencies) and suppress the unhelpful low-frequency information in the image.

- All of the Fourier transform calculations can be conducted efficiently using the FFT. When using the FFT, one must keep in mind the circular nature of the discrete Fourier transform and provide sufficient *padding* to the images.
- One idea for reducing the computations and the sensitivity to nonuniform illumination is to apply the method on a small number of regions that are rich in spatial cues (non-flat regions with high gradient values in multiple directions), rather than the entire image.

Correlation-based registration algorithms, as described above, are good at handling correlated noise and, with proper pre-processing, nonuniform illumination. On the other hand, the are difficult to adapt to more complex spatial transformations (e.g., affine and quadratic).

C. Mutual-Information-Based Registration

The registration methods discussed thus far are intended for aligning two images recorded by the same imaging modality (instrument). In multisensor imaging, there is a need to align images that are recorded by two different instruments. Perhaps the most commonly used registration method in this case is based on the *mutual information* between the pair of images. Before we describe this measure, let us build up a little intuition using medical imaging as an example. Usually, image regions representing characteristic types of tissue (e.g., brain, muscle, fat, etc.) exhibit characteristic distributions of intensity values for a given imaging modality. This distribution can be captured by a histogram, and associated measures such as the mean and standard deviation of intensity values. Importantly, these intensity values also behave in a consistent manner as we compare one imaging modality against another for the same region. For example, bone tissue will consistently appear bright in the CT images and appear consistently dark in the magnetic resonance images. Mutual information is a measure from the field of information theory that quantifies this intuition.

Entropy. Let i_1 and i_2 denote intensity values in images $I_1(\mathbf{x})$, and $I_2(\mathbf{x})$, respectively. Let $p(i_1)$ and $p(i_2)$, respectively, denote the probability distributions of i_1 and i_2. These distributions can be computed from the images, e.g., by using the normalized image histogram as an estimate of the probability distribution. The entropy of intensity values for the first image is defined as

$$H(I_1) = -\sum_{i_1} p(i_1) \log p(i_1) \tag{7.2-27}$$

and $H(I_2)$ is similarly defined. The entropy is highest when the intensity values are uniformly distributed. We can also compute the joint distribution of intensity values at corresponding (homologous) locations – this is denoted $p(i_1, i_2)$. The **joint entropy** between the two distributions is defined as:

$$H(I_1, I_2) = -\sum_{i_1} \sum_{i_2} p(i_1, i_2) \log p(i_1, i_2). \tag{7.2-28}$$

Mutual Information.   The mutual information (MI) between the two images

$$\mathrm{MI}(I_1, I_2) = H(I_1) + H(I_2) - H(I_1, I_2) = \sum_{i_1} \sum_{i_2} p(i_1, i_2) \log \frac{p(i_1, i_2)}{p(i_1)p(i_2)} \quad (7.2\text{-}29)$$

is a measure of dependence between the two images. If the pixel values in the two images are statistically independent, then $p(i_1, i_2) = p(i_1)p(i_2)$ and $H(I_1, I_2) = 0$. In this case, no knowledge is gained about one image when the other is given. Conversely, the mutual information can be expected to be high when the corresponding pixels in the images are strongly related. The following are some basic properties:

- The mutual information between a pair of images is symmetric, i.e., $\mathrm{MI}(I_1, I_2) = \mathrm{MI}(I_2, I_1)$.
- It is nonnegative, i.e., $\mathrm{MI}(I_1, I_2) \geq 0$, so that the uncertainty about one image (entropy) cannot be increased by learning about the other image.
- The mutual information of an image with itself is equal to the entropy of the image, i.e., $\mathrm{MI}(I_1, I_1) = H(I_1)$.
- The information contained by one image about the other can never exceed the entropy of either image, so that $\mathrm{MI}(I_1, I_2) \leq H(I_1)$ and $\mathrm{MI}(I_1, I_2) \leq H(I_2)$.

MI-Based Registration.   The idea can be expressed simply as a search for the transformation parameters Θ that maximize the mutual information $\mathrm{MI}(I_1, I_2)$. Mathematically,

$$\widehat{\Theta} = \underset{\{\Theta\}}{\arg\max} \ \mathrm{MI}\left(T(I_1; \Theta), I_2\right). \quad (7.2\text{-}30)$$

The idea of using mutual information to register images is conceptually elegant, but does not work well when the region of overlap between the images is small. The *normalized mutual information* measure

$$\mathrm{NMI}(T(I_1; \Theta), I_2) = \frac{\mathrm{MI}\left(T(I_1; \Theta), I_2\right)}{\frac{1}{2}\left[H(T(I_1; \Theta)) + H(I_2)\right]} \quad (7.2\text{-}31)$$

is known to work much better in such cases.

Optimization.   The main challenge in carrying out the optimization in (7.2-30) is that the mutual information expression is not differentiable. There are two basic approaches. One approach is to estimate the probability densities $p(i_1)$, $p(i_2)$, and $p(i_1, i_2)$ in a differentiable form from the image data instead of using the normalized histogram, and use gradient descent optimization methods. Another approach is to use optimization methods that do not require the derivatives. Hybrid methods that combine the above two approaches have also been used. The discussion below describes the second approach.

Direction Set Method for Optimization without Derivatives.   Also known as Powell's method, this is a widely used algorithm for maximizing (or minimizing) a function of multiple variables when its derivatives with respect to the optimized parameters are not available. Starting with an initial guess $\widehat{\Theta}^{(0)}$ of the N-dimensional vector of transformation parameters Θ, this method repeatedly searches the parameter space along a set of directions (hence the name *direction set method*).

Suppose that $e_1, e_2, \ldots, e_N$ are linearly independent unit vectors representing the coordinate axes of the N-dimensional parameter space. Let $u_1, u_2, \ldots, u_N$ denote a set of *search directions* for locating the optimal parameters. At the outset, the search directions are chosen as the directions along the coordinate axes, i.e.,

$$[\mathbf{u}_1, \mathbf{u}_2, \dots, \mathbf{u}_N] = [\mathbf{e}_1, \mathbf{e}_2, \dots, \mathbf{e}_N]. \qquad (7.2\text{-}32)$$

Starting from the initial guess $\widehat{\boldsymbol{\Theta}}^{(0)}$, this method conducts a series of steps, together known as the *basic procedure* to arrive at the next estimate $\widehat{\boldsymbol{\Theta}}^{(1)}$. Another execution of the basic procedure yields the next estimate $\widehat{\boldsymbol{\Theta}}^{(2)}$. This iterative procedure is repeated for $\widehat{\boldsymbol{\Theta}}^{(k)}, k = 1, 2, 3, \dots$ until the values of parameters stop changing, i.e., $\left\| \widehat{\boldsymbol{\Theta}}^{(k+1)} - \widehat{\boldsymbol{\Theta}}^{(k)} \right\| < \varepsilon$, where ε is a small number.

We next describe the *basic procedure*. Starting with an estimate from the previous iteration $\widehat{\boldsymbol{\Theta}}^{(k-1)}$, we conduct a line search along direction $\mathbf{u}_1$ to find the point $\boldsymbol{\Theta}_1^{(0)}$ in parameter space for which the objective function is a maximum. Then, we search direction $\mathbf{u}_2$ to find the point $\boldsymbol{\Theta}_2^{(k-1)}$ in parameter space for which the objective function is a maximum. In this manner, we conduct successive line searches, culminating in a search along direction $\mathbf{u}_N$ to arrive at the optimal point $\boldsymbol{\Theta}_N^{(k-1)}$, which becomes the new vector $\boldsymbol{\Theta}^{(k)}$. At this point, we choose a new set of direction vectors given by $[\mathbf{u}_2, \mathbf{u}_3, \dots, \mathbf{u}_N, (\boldsymbol{\Theta}^{(k)} - \boldsymbol{\Theta}^{(k-1)})]$ and repeat the basic procedure. The initial steps of this procedure are illustrated in Fig. 7.2-7.

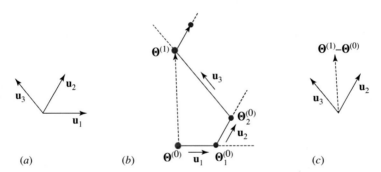

Figure 7.2-7 Initial steps of optimization using the direction set method. (*a*) Initial directions of optimization $(\mathbf{u}_1, \mathbf{u}_2, \mathbf{u}_3)$. (*b*) Basic procedure begining from the initial vector $\boldsymbol{\Theta}^{(0)}$ and ending with the first iteration $\boldsymbol{\Theta}^{(1)}$ by successive optimization along $\mathbf{u}_1$, $\mathbf{u}_2$, and $\mathbf{u}_3$. (*c*) New directions for subsequent application of the basic procedure to obtain $\boldsymbol{\Theta}^{(2)}$.

Powell showed that if the objective function was a quadratic form, then K iterations of the *basic procedure* produces a set of directions $\mathbf{u}_i$ that are mutually conjugate. This fact makes the search a lot more efficient compared with naively searching along one direction at a time. The proof of this fact is beyond the scope of this book, but the interested reader is referred to the references at the end of this chapter. One practical detail is worth mentioning, though. After N iterations of the *basic procedure*, the conjugate property fails, and the directions $\mathbf{u}_i$ must again be reset to the coordinate directions $\mathbf{e}_i$ as was done at the outset. Finally, we skipped lightly over the idea of searching a multi-dimensional space along a line.[2]

▶ Problems 7.2-1–7.2-3

[2]W. H. Press, S. A. Teukolsky, W. T. Vetterling, and B. P. Flannery, *Numerical Recipes, The Art of Scientific Computing*, 3rd ed., Cambridge University Press, 2007.

7.3   Mosaicing

As described in Sec. 7.1A, mosaicing is carried out in three steps: registration for alignment of the tiles, signal correction, and signal combining. The alignment of tiles was introduced in Sec. 7.1A and registration methods were described in greater detail in Sec. 7.1D. This section covers signal correction and combining, and introduces methods for large-scale mosaicing.

A. Signal Correction

Signal correction is the term we use to describe the process by which the image data are corrected for signal degradations, such as nonuniform illumination and noise. Whereas registration is a geometric operation, signal correction is concerned with the strength of the image signal (intensity) at each pixel, but may also include deblurring operations. This subject was described in Sec. 3.3 under the general topic of image restoration. An application for which signal correction plays an important role is described next in Example 7.3-1.

EXAMPLE 7.3-1.   *Underwater Imaging.*   This example highlights the importance of signal corrections in mosaicing. The two images of panel (*a*) in Fig. 7.3-1 were recorded by a digital camera mounted on a deep-submergence underwater craft surveying the sea floor. The sea floor was illuminated by an on-board light source (the sea water is very dark at great depths). Observe the spatial nonuniformity of the illumination – points in the middle of the image appear much brighter than points on the periphery. The greenish color of these image tiles is very different from the true color of the sandy sea floor, as confirmed by actual soil samples that were brought to the surface. This is due to a combination of factors, including the spectrum of the light source, its spatial radiation pattern, reflection from the sea floor, and spectrally nonuniform attenuation of light as it passes through the murky water to the sea floor and back again to the camera. All of these effects can be modeled mathematically and used to reconstruct the reflectance of the sea floor. When these reconstructed images are mosaiced, as shown in panel (*b*), one obtains a seamless mosaic. Indeed, this technique has been scaled up significantly. A spectacular example of this can be seen in the December 2005 issue of the *National Geographic Magazine* featuring a large mosaic of the famous sunken ship R.M.S. Titanic.

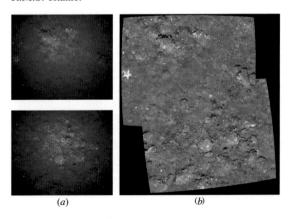

(*a*)   (*b*)

Figure 7.3-1 Signal correction for mosaicing of images of the sea floor as recorded by a deep-submergence craft. (*a*) Actual tiles. (*b*) Mosaic formed after correcting the actual tiles for spatially nonuniform illumination, as well as spectrally nonuniform attenuation of the signal as it passes through the murky water.

B. Signal Combining

Once the image tiles are aligned and signal correction is applied to each tile individually, the final step is to construct the mosaic. However, when signal correction is applied individually to each tile, there is no guarantee that pixels in adjacent tiles will end up with the same intensity values. This is because the process of reconstructing one tile is uninformed about the results of reconstructing adjacent tile(s). The net result of this practical limitation is a mosaic in which the boundaries (seams) of the tiles are visible as false edges. To achieve a seamless mosaic, it is important to smoothly blend intensity values from adjacent tiles. This is accomplished by use of a **signal combining function**, denoted $\mathsf{C}(\cdot)$, that accepts two or more images and blends the intensity values in the spatially overlapping region in a manner than minimizes the appearance of seams, and corrects signal defects that can be recognized only when multiple readings are available for the same pixel.

Two corrected images $\hat{I}_1(\mathbf{x})$ and $\hat{I}_2^{\mathrm{T}}(\mathbf{x})$ that overlap in some region are combined (blended) to produce a single image $I_{\mathrm{M}}(\mathbf{x})$ by designing an appropriate combining function $\mathsf{C}(\cdot)$ whose output

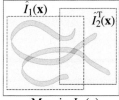

$$I_{\mathrm{M}}(\mathbf{x}) = \mathsf{C}\left(\hat{I}_1(\mathbf{x}), \hat{I}_2^{\mathrm{T}}(\mathbf{x})\right). \qquad (7.3\text{-}1)$$

Mosaic $I_{\mathrm{M}}(\mathbf{x})$

is the mosaic. A well-chosen combining function can also achieve some form of signal correction in a simple manner that cannot be performed on individual tiles.

Averaging. In the region of overlap, there are two *readings* for the same point. One simple use of these readings is to average them for the purpose of reducing the noise variance, and/or increasing the dynamic range of the image intensity values. Indeed, one form of the mosaicing problem has precisely this intention – highly overlapped images of a scene are captured and combined for the purpose of obtaining a *better* image rather than a larger image.

Selecting One of the Two Values. Suppose that one of these readings is significantly greater than the other. If we expect instances of *glare*, as in the retinal imaging example of Fig. 7.1-2, over-exposure, and/or saturation, then we can choose to simply drop the high value and accept the lower value, i.e., use the combining function $I_{\mathrm{M}}(\mathbf{x}) = \min\{I_1^{\mathrm{T}}(\mathbf{x}), I_2^{\mathrm{T}}(\mathbf{x})\}$. Conversely, if there is reason to believe that the image signal may occasionally be faded or blanked for some reason (e.g., sensor defects), then we can choose to keep the higher value instead, i.e., use the combining function $I_{\mathrm{M}}(\mathbf{x}) = \max\{I_1^{\mathrm{T}}(\mathbf{x}), I_2^{\mathrm{T}}(\mathbf{x})\}$.

Weighted Averaging. Another approach is to compute a weighted sum of the pixels from the respective tiles. For instance, suppose we consider the aligned pair of images $I_1(\mathbf{x})$ and $I_2^{\mathrm{T}}(\mathbf{x})$ in the common coordinate frame of the mosaic image $I_{\mathrm{M}}(\mathbf{x})$, then each image can have as associated weight map denoted $w_1^{\mathrm{T}}(\mathbf{x})$ and $w_2(\mathbf{x})$, respectively. We require the weights to be non-negative numbers in the range zero to one, and that they sum to one. When the weights are equal (0.5 each), then we get a simple average.

Feathering.   The problem with simple averaging is the possibility of a seam – an abrupt change in intensity at the image boundary. One approach to avoiding a seam is to vary the weights in a smooth/gradual manner with respect to the boundary. This is known as *feathering*. For example, a bi-quadratic weighting function for an image with width d and height h is

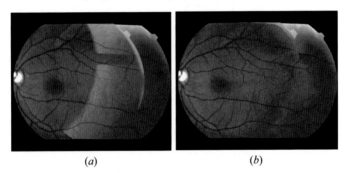

$$w(x, y) = \left[1 - \left(x - \tfrac{1}{2}d\right)^2\right]\left[1 - \left(y - \tfrac{1}{2}h\right)^2\right]. \qquad (7.3\text{-}2)$$

Nearest Image Center Method.   Another method, known as the nearest image center method, works as follows. At each location in the overlapping region, one computes the distance to the image center for each tile and uses the intensity value from the tile for which the point is closest to the center. One might ordinarily think that computing distance values at each point in an image is a computationally expensive procedure. However, this is not so. The advent of fast and readily available algorithms for computing Euclidean distance maps makes this computation affordable. Example 7.3-2 demonstrates blending in the context of retinal imaging.

EXAMPLE 7.3-2.   *Blending of Two Retinal Images.*   Figure 7.3-2 demonstrates the blending of two tiles of a retinal image by use of averaging and feathering in the presence of glare.

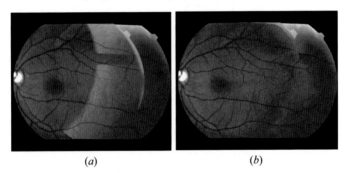

(a)   (b)

Figure 7.3-2   Effect of image blending for a two-tile mosaic in which one of the tiles exhibits a glare artifact. Image (a) was computed by simple averaging of intensities. Image (b) used feathered blending and the minimum intensity value in the overlapped region.

Resampling.   Image resampling is a necessary tool for constructing a mosaic. Specifically, each point x in the mosaic image $I_M(x)$ is specified by integer coordinates, but when this point is transformed back to the corresponding image tile, it will most likely not result in a set of integer coordinates. In this case, one must seek out a set of the nearest integer-valued coordinates (usually four nearest neighbors) and perform an interpolation calculation. A simple bilinear interpolation is often used.

C. Large-Scale Mosaicing

The previous sections largely focused on the problem of aligning a pair of tiles. To synthesize a full mosaic, we commonly need to align more than two tiles, and some mosaics consist of hundreds of tiles. Even if we consider just three tiles, some rather frustrating consistency issues can easily arise. If three overlapping tiles A, B, and C of an image are registered in pairs, for example, A with B and A with C, then there is no reason to expect tiles B and C to be well aligned, since we have left them unconstrained. This observation is demonstrated in Example 7.3-3. More generally, in large-scale mosaicing, even small registration errors between pairs of tiles can accumulate from one of the mosaics to the other, and this accumulated error can be large. The inadequacy of pairwise registration has motivated the development of *joint registration* algorithms (also termed *bundle adjustment*), which have become essential to the successful mosaicing of a large number of tiles without losing accuracy due to factors such as accumulation error and error drifts.

Joint Mosaicing.   The joint registration algorithm is based on two ideas:
1. The transformations linking the tiles are estimated simultaneously by formulating a single optimization rather than a set of independent pairwise registrations.
2. The objective function for the joint registration incorporates terms that enforce appropriate consistency constraints.

Since each tile can potentially define a different coordinate system for the mosaic, it is necessary to choose one of the tiles to define the desired coordinate system, and call it the **anchor**. Usually, the anchor is chosen so as to provide the most convenient view, e.g., a central tile in the mosaic. It is helpful to use a network (graph) representation in which the tiles are the nodes and links indicate special connections between pairs of tiles, as illustrated in Example 7.3-3. The idea of joint registration is to register all tiles to the anchor tile, but include in the optimization metric a measure of consistency in the spatial relations between the non-anchor tiles.

Joint Registration to an Anchor Tile.   If I_0 is the anchor tile, and $I_1, I_2, \cdots, I_N$ are N non-anchor tiles, then we need to estimate the transformations

$$\Theta = \{\Theta_{1,0}, \Theta_{2,0}....\Theta_{N,0}\} \qquad (7.3\text{-}3)$$

that register each of the non-anchor tiles to the anchor tile. Transformations between non-anchor tile pairs can be determined in terms of Θ by referring both tiles to the anchor. If

$$e_{(k,0)} = \sum_{(i,j)\in\mathcal{C}(k,0)} d(T(\mathbf{p_i}; \Theta_{k,0}), \mathbf{p}_j) \qquad (7.3\text{-}4)$$

is the error in registering tile k to the anchor tile, where $\mathcal{C}(k,0)$ is the set of correspondences between tile k and the anchor tile 0, then the average error in registering all tiles to the anchor tile, called the direct error, is

$$e_D(\Theta) = \sum_{k=1}^{N} e_{(k,0)}. \qquad (7.3\text{-}5)$$

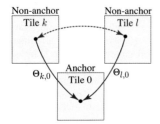

Figure 7.3-3   Anchor and non-anchor tiles used in joint registration.

Consistency Between Non-Anchor Tiles.   A measure of inconsistency in the way points in two non-anchor tiles l and k map to a common point in the coordinate space of the anchor image, is the error

$$e_{(k,l)} = \sum_{(i,j)\in\mathcal{C}(k,l)} d(T(\mathbf{p}_i; \mathbf{\Theta}_{k,0}), T(\mathbf{p}_j; \mathbf{\Theta}_{l,0})), \tag{7.3-6}$$

where $\mathcal{C}(k, l)$ is the set of correspondences between tiles k and l. Note how both tiles are transformed to the anchor tile 0 before being compared. The average error defines an "indirect" cost function:

$$e_I(\mathbf{\Theta}) = \sum_{k,l=1}^{N} e_{(k,l)}. \tag{7.3-7}$$

Joint Optimization.   The sum of the direct and indirect errors may be used as an overall cost function, so that the joint registration problem becomes

$$\widehat{\mathbf{\Theta}} = \arg\min_{\mathbf{\Theta}} \{e_D(\mathbf{\Theta}) + e_I(\mathbf{\Theta})\}. \tag{7.3-8}$$

The optimization may be carried out by use of the Euclidean distance $d(.) = \|\cdot\|^2$ or a robust measure $d(.) = \rho(\|\cdot\|)$, as described in Sec. 7.2A. If the transformation is expressed in the linear form $T(\mathbf{p}; \mathbf{\Theta}) = \mathbf{\Theta}\mathbf{X}(\mathbf{p})$, then the overall minimization problem is linear. Computing the gradient of the argument with respect to each of the parameters and setting it to zero yields a set of simultaneous linear equations that can be solved using standard linear algebraic methods.

EXAMPLE 7.3-3.   *Multi-Tile Mosaicing in Retinal Imaging.*   The retinal images illustrated in Fig. 7.3-4 demonstrate the improvement in quality of the mosaic obtained by joint registration as compared with separate pairwise registrations. The figure also illustrates a network of linked tiles with an anchor tile in the middle. Registering all tiles jointly to the anchor and enforcing some measure of consistency between non-anchor tiles can improve the overall quality of large-scale mosaics.

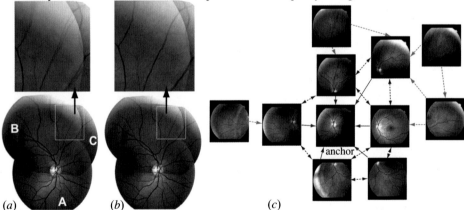

Figure 7.3-4 Multi-tile registration of a retinal image. (*a*) The result of mosaicing three overlapping tiles (A, B, C) by registering separately A with B and A with C. Note the poor alignment of the vessels in the region of overlap between B and C ((boxed and enlarged region), although the pairwise registrations themselves are accurate. (*b*) Joint registration of the same three images aligns the vessels in the overlapped region more accurately. The tile in which the bright optic disk is centrally located was chosen as the anchor. (*c*) Eleven tiles represented as a network. The solid red links connect non-anchor tiles to the anchor tile. The dashed links connect non-anchor tiles that overlap (blue) or do not overlap (green); these links are used as constraints in the joint registration optimization problem.

▶ Problem 7.3-1

7.4 Change Detection

As described earlier in Sec. 7.1B, to perform change detection we start by perform-ing image registration, i.e., transforming the second image $I(\mathbf{x}, t_2)$ into the coor-dinate frame of the first image $I(\mathbf{x}, t_1)$. We denote the resultant image $I^{\mathrm{T}}(\mathbf{x}, t_2)$. Next, we perform signal corrections to compute the aligned and corrected images $\hat{I}(\mathbf{x}, t_1)$ and $\hat{I}^{\mathrm{T}}(\mathbf{x}, t_2)$. These images are then compared using a suitable test statistic $S\left(\hat{I}(\mathbf{x}, t_1), \hat{I}^{\mathrm{T}}(\mathbf{x}, t_2)\right)$, such as the magnitude of the difference $|\hat{I}(\mathbf{x}, t_1) - \hat{I}^{\mathrm{T}}(\mathbf{x}, t_2)|$, designed to identify pixels representing a real and interesting change, to the extent possible. The result is a binary-valued *change mask*:

$$B(\mathbf{x}) = \begin{cases} 1, & \text{if } S(\hat{I}(\mathbf{x}, t_1), \hat{I}^{\mathrm{T}}(\mathbf{x}, t_2)) > \vartheta \\ 0, & \text{otherwise,} \end{cases} \qquad (7.4\text{-}1)$$

where ϑ is an appropriate threshold. These steps are illustrated in Fig. 7.4-1. The main sources of error in change-detection algorithms can be tied to each of these steps:

(i) **Registration.** Registration or alignment errors lead to detection of false changes. As a rule of thumb, sub-pixel registration accuracy (average alignment error less than 1 pixel) are necessary for change detection.

(ii) **Signal Correction.** Image-formation-related phenomena that introduce changes to pixel values, even when the intrinsic properties of the objects of interest are unchanged, are an important source of error. For example, nonuniform illumina-tion and changes in the illumination profile lead to detection of false changes or masking of real changes.

(iii) **Decision Rule.** A suboptimal decision rule produces greater change-detection errors. Specifically, it is important that the probabilistic nature of random per-turbations such as imaging noise be modeled as accurately as possible and that these models are incorporated into carefully chosen statistical decision rules.

(iv) **Post-Processing.** Well-chosen post-processing algorithms can effectively "clean up" the results of initial change detection and produce a better change mask $\hat{B}(\mathbf{x})$. This step must correctly reflect known aspects of the change mask. For instance, if it is known that the smallest connected regions in $\hat{B}(\mathbf{x})$ are of a given size, then any smaller regions must necessarily be erroneous and should be eliminated.

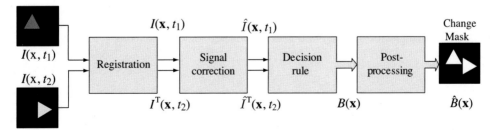

Figure 7.4-1 The main steps used for change detection.

We now consider the steps following image registration in greater detail.

A. Signal Correction

Ideally, the signal correction step is formulated as an image reconstruction problem in which we use physics-based models of the image formation process to estimate the physical property whose changes we are interested in detecting. In some applications, one can adopt a pragmatic strategy designed to enhance the change-detection results without necessarily being true to the imaging physics.

Image Normalization.   The most common form of signal correction is intensity normalization, in which the pixel intensity values in one image are normalized to have the same mean and variance as in the other image, i.e., $[\hat{I}^{\mathrm{T}}(\mathbf{x}, t_2) - \mu_1]/\sigma_1 = [I^{\mathrm{T}}(\mathbf{x}, t_2) - \mu_2]/\sigma_2$ or

$$\hat{I}^{\mathrm{T}}(\mathbf{x}, t_2) = \mu_1 + \frac{\sigma_1}{\sigma_2}\{I^{\mathrm{T}}(\mathbf{x}, t_2) - \mu_2\}, \tag{7.4-2}$$

where (μ_1, μ_2) are the mean intensities of $I(\mathbf{x}, t_1)$ and $I^{\mathrm{T}}(\mathbf{x}, t_2)$, respectively, and (σ_1, σ_2) are the corresponding standard deviations.

Homomorphic Filtering.   Another common signal correction method models the image $I(\mathbf{x})$ as the product of an illumination component denoted $I_{\mathrm{I}}(\mathbf{x})$, and a reflectance/response component $I_{\mathrm{R}}(\mathbf{x})$, also known as the *Lambertian model*. In most applications, the illumination field is nearly uniform, or at least slowly varying across the field. This observation provides the basis for the simple and widely used **homomorphic-filter**-based correction. Taking the logarithms of both sides, the image formation model can be written in the additive form

$$\log I(\mathbf{x}) = \log I_{\mathrm{I}}(\mathbf{x}) + \log I_{\mathrm{R}}(\mathbf{x}).$$

A high-pass filter can now be used to filter out the largely low-frequency components in the illumination term $\log I_{\mathrm{I}}(\mathbf{x})$. An estimate of the reflectance component alone is

$$\hat{I}_{\mathrm{R}}(\mathbf{x}) = \exp\{h(x) \otimes \log I(\mathbf{x}))\},$$

where $h(x)$ is the impulse response function of the high-pass filter. The signal correction step can be as simple as replacing an image with its reflectance estimate. The intuition behind this idea is that changes in the reflectance component are indicative of intrinsic/real changes in the objects/scene, independent of illumination changes.

Variations of the Homomorphic Filter.   Many variations of the homomorphic filter have been described in the literature. One common idea is to model the illumination component using low-dimensional polynomials, or piecewise smooth functions. More complex applications require specialized illumination models. For example, when processing hyperspectral images, a principal components analysis is helpful in separating bands that exhibit changes from others. As another example, when processing time-lapse image series (movies), one can model changes in illumination over time. Most of these changes are gradual and can be modeled accurately using linear models; for example:

$$\hat{I}(\mathbf{x}, t) = \sum_{k=1}^{K} a_k I(\mathbf{x}, t - k).$$

The model parameters a_k are chosen to minimize the discrepancy between the average predicted intensity $\hat{I}(\mathbf{x}, t)$ and the actual intensity $I(\mathbf{x}, t)$. Large prediction errors also indicate changes. Interestingly, some illumination can be abrupt (e.g., turning an illumination source on/off). These can be accounted for by using a criterion (e.g., more than 70% of the pixels have changed) to detect a sudden change and re-initializing the above-mentioned linear illumination variation model.

B. Decision Rule and Post Processing

Decision Rule

As noted earlier, the simplest decision rule is based on pixel differencing. If the signal-corrected pixels differ by more than a set amount, one declares a change. There are several limitations of this simple idea. Importantly, it does not provide us with an adequately precise method to specify what changes are *statistically significant*, and what changes are not. It does not provide us with a mechanism to specify what types of error are tolerable for a specific application and what types are not. In other words, how conservative do we want the change detector to be? A *statistical hypothesis testing* approach (see Appendix C) addresses these limitations. Change detection corresponds to choosing one of two competing hypotheses: the change has occurred (H_1), or it has not (H_0). There are two possible decisions: the change has occurred (D_1) or it has not (D_0). There are therefore four scenarios:

- H_0 is true and the decision is D_0, correctly.
- H_0 is true, but the decision is D_1. This type of error, known as a false positive, corresponds to a falsely detected change.
- H_1 is true, but the decision is D_0. This type of error, known as a miss or a false negative, corresponds to a missed change.
- H_1 is true and the decision is D_1, correctly.

As described in Appendix C, given the observation $s = \{\hat{I}(\mathbf{x}, t_1), \hat{I}^{\mathrm{T}}(\mathbf{x}, t_2)\}$, several statistical decision rules exist. In the maximum likelihood rule, the probabilities $p(s|H_1)$ and $p(s|H_0)$ are compared and the hypothesis with the greater probability of generating the observation is selected. A Bayesian decision rule is based on assigning numerical "costs" $\{C_{00}, C_{10}, C_{11}, C_{01}\}$, respectively, to the possible four scenarios above, and assigning prior probabilities P_0 and P_1 to the hypotheses H_0 and H_1, respectively. The Bayesian decision rule, which minimizes the average cost, is based on a comparison of the likelihood ratio $L(\mathbf{x}) = p(s|H_1)/p(s|H_0)$ to a threshold value

$$\vartheta = \frac{P_0(C_{10} - C_{00})}{P_1(C_{01} - C_{11})},$$

which depends on the costs and the prior probabilities. When the likelihood ratio exceeds the threshold, we declare that a change has occurred at the pixel $\mathbf{x}$, and vice versa.

Typically, it makes sense to assign lower costs for correct decisions and higher costs for incorrect decisions, i.e., $C_{10} > C_{00}$ and $C_{01} > C_{11}$. Also, in most applications, the consequences of false positives and false negatives are not the same. For example, in medical change detection, for which change indicates disease onset, a false negative (miss) may have grave consequences for the patient. A false positive error is relatively benign because it can often be overridden by the physician based on additional medical examinations/tests.

In the above discussion, we have treated each pixel independently, implying that the decision at a given pixel is oblivious of what is happening in the local neighborhood of this pixel. One can improve upon this strategy by realizing that interesting changes are often associated with groups of neighboring pixels, rather than isolated pixels. One common way to addressing this issue is to formulate the likelihood ratio over a block of pixels centered at $\mathbf{x}$ instead. This improves the performance of the detector by providing many more data points to the decision making.

Post-Processing

In this step we clean up the results of pixel-wise or block-wise change detection. The most common type of post-processing is to treat all pixels representing isolated *islands* or *holes* in the change mask as errors, and so invert them. A more sophisticated form of post-processing incorporates smoothness constraints into the previous step (decision rule).

▶ Problem 7.4-1

7.5   Multisensor Imaging

As noted in Sec. 7.1C, a multisensor imager combines two or more imaging modalities in a synergistic manner to observe a single object. The need for multisensor imaging arises when a single imaging modality has inherent limitations (e.g., inadequate contrast or insufficient resolution) preventing it from meeting the needs of the application by itself. One modality may offer good resolution with weak contrast (e.g., X-ray CT), while the other exhibits good contrast with poor resolution (e.g., PET). Multisensor imagers may also be used to extract different information about the object, e.g., one modality acquiring morphological information while the other capturing functional information, such as metabolic information.

We assume in this section that the multiple images are captured independently, i.e., the probe waves do not interact physically during the measurement process. Imaging systems employing two (or more) interacting waves (e.g., one altering the physical properties of the medium and thereby generating or modulating another wave, which is measured) can also be effective; these are described briefly in Sec. 1.5 under the title **multiwave imaging** and an example [photoacoustic tomography (PAT)] is described in Sec. 4.2C.

Mechanically Attached Multisensor Imaging Systems.   The preferred method to build a multisensor system is for the two sensors to be mechanically attached so that they are linked by a fixed geometric transformation, which is known in advance and verified by means of calibration. As described in Examples 7.5-1 and 7.5-2, the two imaging sensors may be mounted on a common platform. Such systems can be difficult to design and are often expensive. When it is impractical or impossible to attach the systems mechanically, computational cross-modality registration is required – a procedure that is particularly difficult when the object is deformable, as in the case of imaging of mammary soft tissue.

EXAMPLE 7.5-1.   *Combined X-ray and Ultrasound Breast Imaging.*   In this example of multisensor imaging, an X-ray mamography system and a 3D ultrasonic imaging system are mounted on a common platform so that they are physically aligned.[3,4] The measured images, shown in Fig. 7.5-1, demonstrate how the two images may be jointly used to determine if a suspicious tumor is an actual tumor.

---

[3] A. Kapur, P. L. Carson, J. Eberhard, M. M. Goodsitt, K. Thomenius, M. Lokhandwalla, D. Buckley, R. Hoctor, M. A. Roubidoux, M. A. Helvie, R. C. Booi, G. L. LeCarpentier, R. Q. Erkamp, H. P. Chan, J. B. Fowlkes, A. Dattamajumdar, A. Hall, J. A. Thomas, and C. E. Landberg, Combination of digital mammography with semi-automated 3D breast ultrasound, *Technology in Cancer Research and Treatment*, Vol. 3(4), pp. 325–334, 2004.

[4] S. P. Sinha, M. A. Roubidoux, M. A. Helvie, A. V. Nees, M. M. Goodsitt, G. L. LeCarpentier, J. B. Fowlkes, C. L. Chaleck, and P. L. Carson, Multi-modality 3D breast imaging with X-ray tomosynthesis and automated ultrasound, *Procs. 29th Ann. Internat. Conf.*, IEEE Engineering in Medicine and Biology Society, pp. 1335–1338, Lyon, France, August 23–26, 2007.

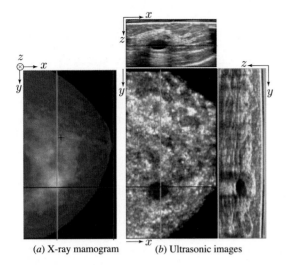

(a) X-ray mamogram   (b) Ultrasonic images

Figure 7.5-1 Ultrasound and X-ray mammography as an example of multisensor imaging (courtesy of the University of Michigan, Department of Radiology). (a) X-ray mammogram of a human breast. The physician noticed a suspicious region at the intersection of the green and blue cursor lines. (b) Image is acquired by 3D ultrasound, and presented as a set of x–y, y–z, and x–z projections. The round region in this case was found to be a simple cyst, rather than a tumor.

EXAMPLE 7.5-2. *Mapping Activity to Anatomy by Combined CT and PET.* A conceptually similar example is combined X-ray CT and PET medical imaging. These two modalities are quite synergistic. X-ray CT is effective in generating a strong contrast between the hard bony tissues and soft tissues; it provides excellent spatial resolution but little differentiation among the soft tissues and no indication of biological activities. On the other hand, PET imaging provides poor spatial resolution, i.e., poor delineation of anatomy, but provides an excellent indication of activity, depending upon the radiotracer used. With FDG (fluorine 18 fluorodeoxyglucose) as the contrast agent, PET highlights regions that are actively metabolizing glucose, which happens in tumors. Combining the two images into a single color-coded representation, as illustrated in Fig. 7.5-2, allows the physician to relate the region of activity to the anatomic region of the patient. In this example, accurate alignment is vital since the high-activity region in the PET image is close to the border of the organ. Alignment errors can lead to an incorrect diagnosis. In the case of CT and PET fusion, mutual-information-based registration was in widespread use until recently, when a single imaging instrument with attached CT and PET scanners was developed. Similar progress in combining SPECT and CT scanners has been reported.

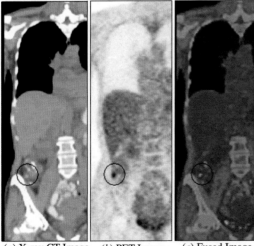

(a) X-ray CT Image   (b) PET Image   (c) Fused Image

Figure 7.5-2 Fusion of X-ray CT and PET images. (a) Section through a 3D X-ray CT image. (b) PET image has poor spatial resolution but provides an excellent indication of glucose consumption (dark spot in the circled region) indicating a colorectal tumor. (c) Fused image helps localize the activity indication from the PET image precisely to anatomic regions delineated by the CT image.

Strategies for Using Multisensor Images

An N-sensor imager generates images $I_1(\mathbf{x}), I_2(\mathbf{x}), \ldots, I_N(\mathbf{x})$ mapping physical properties $\alpha_1(\mathbf{x}), \alpha_2(\mathbf{x}), \ldots, \alpha_N(\mathbf{x})$. The combined imaging system is superior in some sense to any of the individual modalities. For example, the combined system may aim at mapping a single underlying physical property $\beta(\mathbf{x})$ on which each of the measured distributions $\alpha_1(\mathbf{x}), \alpha_2(\mathbf{x}), \ldots, \alpha_N(\mathbf{x})$ depends. The measured images may be used collectively for mapping $\beta(\mathbf{x})$, for the detection of a target with better sensitivity or specificity, or for the classification of objects based on features contained in the various modalities. Strategies for what to do with the measured images therefore vary depending on the application, be it mapping, target detection, or object classification. Some of these strategies are discussed next.

Direct Presentation of Multisensor Images.   One obvious strategy is not to combine the measured images at all, and to merely present them to the human observer in a suitable form for visual interpretation. In this case, some effort is made to develop software tools that allow the user to examine corresponding points in the multiple images. For example, dual cursors may be used for viewing two images, as in Fig. 7.5-1. Another approach is to build a *vector mosaic* in which a vector of all quantities is stored at each pixel. These quantities are simply displayed on a screen in a color-coded manner for a user to interpret, as was done in Fig. 7.5-2.

A more sophisticated form of direct presentation using techniques from 3D computer graphics was illustrated in Example 7.1-7 in Sec. 7.1C, which described sonar and optical underwater imaging using an autonomous remote-controlled underwater vehicle. In that example, sensor integration served to provide a realistic 3D virtual view of a shipwreck. Sensor integration has served to provide a realistic 3D virtual view of a shipwreck with an ability to interactively move this view around on a computer screen to view the data from any desired angle.

Fusion of Multisensor Images.   Multisensor fusion refers to a process by which the measurements of the different sensors are combined to generate a single image that is more informative and/or useful. For example, for a two-sensor imager, the two images $I_1(\mathbf{x})$ and $I_2(\mathbf{x})$ are combined to compute a single image $I(\mathbf{x})$ using an appropriate **sensor fusion function**

$$I_f(\mathbf{x}) = \Phi(I_1(\mathbf{x}), I_2(\mathbf{x})).$$

The exact form of this function depends heavily upon the particular application of interest. One consideration for designing this function is whether the two sensors are estimating the same physical property (perhaps with different techniques of different capabilities), or altogether different properties (e.g., acoustic sensing versus electromagnetic sensing). These cases are termed **homogeneous sensor fusion** and **heterogeneous sensor fusion**, respectively.

Homogeneous Sensor Fusion.   The simplest form of homogeneous sensor fusion is to have redundant sensors observing a single property $\alpha(\mathbf{x})$. If N imagers are used, a set of images

$$I_i(\mathbf{x}) = \mathcal{O}_i\{\alpha(\mathbf{x})\}, \quad i = 1, 2, \ldots, N$$

are obtained, where $\mathcal{O}_i\{\cdot)\}$ represents some mathematical operation describing the ith imaging system. The goal is to estimate $\alpha(\mathbf{x})$, given $I_i(\mathbf{x})$ and $\mathcal{O}_i\{\cdot\}$ for $i = 1, 2, \ldots, N$.

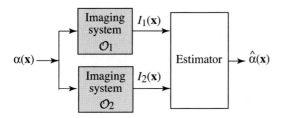

Figure 7.5-3   Two-sensor imaging.

For example, if the imagers are linear, then each imaging equation may be represented by a linear transformation such as a convolution or a projection. In this case, the inverse problem may be formulated as a single linear inverse problem (much like the multiview tomography formulation in Sec.5.1B) and solved using the inverse methods developed in Chapter 5. The homogeneous fusion problem may also be addressed using ad hoc approaches. For example, if the imaging systems are identical, then the measurements may simply be averaged to produce a single image with reduced uncertainty. Nonlinear operations may also be useful. For example, the deficiencies of a single sensor may be compensated for. Often, a sensor has a defined domain over which it works well. One way to quantify the performance of a sensor is to compute a confidence value. Suppose that property $\alpha_i(\mathbf{x})$ is accompanied by a confidence value $c_i(\mathbf{x})$, with $i = 1, 2$, then one way to structure the fusion function is to select the value measured by the sensor of the greater confidence value:

$$\hat{\alpha}(\mathbf{x}) = \begin{cases} \alpha_1(\mathbf{x}), & \text{if } c_1(\mathbf{x}) \geq c_2(\mathbf{x}) \\ \alpha_2(\mathbf{x}), & \text{else,} \end{cases} \qquad (7.5\text{-}1)$$

or use a weighted average of the sensor values when the confidence values are similar. Another approach is to look for discrepancies between the two sensor values in the overlapping domain. A high discrepancy could indicate a faulty sensor requiring corrective action.

Heterogeneous Sensor Fusion.   Methods for fusing data from heterogeneous sensors providing complementary measurements are more complex and varied and they depend upon the degree of interdependence among the sensor measurements. One measurement may provide data that can be used directly to improve the processing of another measurement. For example, most ultrasound imaging systems use the assumption that the speed of sound is uniform within the medium (see Sec. 3.2C). This assumption makes practical sense in the absence of any other measurement. However, if it becomes possible to add a second sensor that provides information on the distribution of sound velocity, then this new measurement can be exploited by developing a more sophisticated reconstruction algorithm to produce a more accurate ultrasonic image.

The fusion problem may be formulated in the following generic form, assuming only two sensors, for simplicity, as depicted in Fig. 7.5-4. Let the two sensors measure the physical properties $\alpha_1(\mathbf{x})$ and $\alpha_2(\mathbf{x})$ and produce the images

$$I_1(\mathbf{x}) = \mathcal{O}_1\{\alpha_1(\mathbf{x})\}, \quad I_2(\mathbf{x}) = \mathcal{O}_2\{\alpha_2(\mathbf{x})\},$$

respectively, where $\mathcal{O}_1\{\cdot\}$ and $\mathcal{O}_2\{\cdot\}$ represent a mathematical operation describing the imaging systems. Let $\beta(\mathbf{x})$ be an underlying property that we wish to estimate. Both $\alpha_1(\mathbf{x})$ and $\alpha_2(\mathbf{x})$ depend on $\beta(\mathbf{x})$ in accordance with the relations

$$\alpha_1(\mathbf{x}) = \mathcal{Q}_1\{\beta(\mathbf{x})\}, \quad \alpha_2(\mathbf{x}) = \mathcal{Q}_2\{\beta(\mathbf{x})\},$$

where $\mathcal{Q}_1\{\cdot\}$ and $\mathcal{Q}_2\{\cdot\}$ are mathematical operations governed by the physical relation between the *alphas* and *beta*. The fusion problem is then to find an estimate of $\beta(\mathbf{x})$ given the two measured images and assuming that the mathematical operations $\mathcal{O}_1\{\cdot\}$, $\mathcal{O}_2\{\cdot\}$, $\mathcal{Q}_1\{\cdot\}$, and $\mathcal{Q}_2\{\cdot\}$ are all known. If all these relations are linear, then the problem may be formulated as a linear relation between the measurements $I_1(\mathbf{x})$ and $I_2(\mathbf{x})$ and the unknown distribution $\beta(\mathbf{x})$, and solved using matrix inversion methods (Chapter 5).

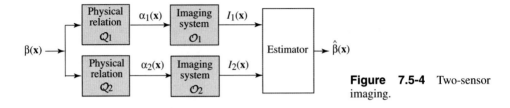

Figure   7.5-4   Two-sensor imaging.

A statistical formulation of the inverse problem may also be formulated. For example, a maximum likelihood estimator may be expressed in the general form

$$\hat{\beta}(\mathbf{x}) = \underset{\beta(\mathbf{x})}{\arg\max}\ p\,[I_1(\mathbf{x}), I_2(\mathbf{x}) \mid \beta(\mathbf{x})],$$

where $p\,[I_1(\mathbf{x}), I_2(\mathbf{x}) \mid \beta(\mathbf{x})]$ is the conditional probability of measuring $I_1(\mathbf{x})$ and $I_2(\mathbf{x})$ given $\beta(\mathbf{x})$. This function may be obtained by use of a probabilistic model of the measurement noise together with the relations $I_i(\mathbf{x}) = \mathcal{O}_i\{\alpha_i(\mathbf{x})\} = \mathcal{O}_i\{\mathcal{Q}_i\{\beta(\mathbf{x})\}\}$, $i = 1, 2$, between the measurements $I_1(\mathbf{x})$ and $I_2(\mathbf{x})$ and the unknown distribution $\beta(\mathbf{x})$.

Multisensor Classification.   Classification theory provides another body of tools for sensor fusion. As noted earlier, registration of the data from two sensors results in a vector $[\alpha_1(\mathbf{x}), \alpha_2(\mathbf{x})]$ of physical properties at each image location $\mathbf{x}$, which can be thought of as two *features* and used in classification algorithms based on scatter plots, as described in Appendix C. Such vector data can also be thought of as *pixel labeling*, in which we compute a discrete-valued label for each pixel indicating its *type*. For example, the first sensor may measure the speed of movement of objects and the second sensor measures the depth. In a training session, we obtain a large number of readings of the vector $[\alpha_1(\mathbf{x}), \alpha_2(\mathbf{x})]$ at each position. The first step is to normalize these features. The most common procedure is to normalize the features to zero mean and unit variance by subtracting the mean value and dividing by the standard deviation to yield normalized feature values denoted $[\bar{\alpha}_1(\mathbf{x}), \bar{\alpha}_2(\mathbf{x})]$. These are plotted in a scatter diagram, as illustrated in Fig. 7.5-5. In this example, it is easy to see that there are two types of object in the scene being imaged: slow-moving objects in the shallow region (Group 1) and fast-moving objects in the deep region (Group 2). The dotted line in this figure is a *discriminant* that allows us to *label* or *classify* the pixels into one of two *types* based on their normalized feature values. This discrimination could not have been done with one sensor value alone.

Multisensor Target Detection.   Until now, we have considered fusion methods at the level of individual pixels. It is also possible to develop fusion algorithms that operate on groups of pixels representing objects in the scene, or parts thereof. These methods draw upon the field of image analysis and computer vision that describe methods for **image segmentation** and **object recognition**. Image segmentation is the process of

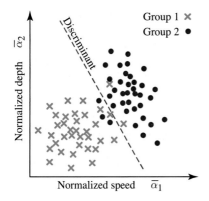

Figure 7.5-5 Scatter diagram showing normalized values of two features for two groups.

delineating objects in images by labeling pixels. A group of pixels representing an object are all assigned the same label. Object recognition is the process of labeling the segmented group of pixels at the next level of abstraction, identifying the type of object they represent. Both these subjects are beyond the scope of this book. However, there are several well-written books on these subjects, and the interested reader should refer to them for more in-depth information.

Summary.   An essential first step to multisensor integration and fusion is registration. Methods for fusing data from two or more sensors are drawn from traditional disciplines, including detection and estimation theory, signal processing, statistical and logical inference, image analysis, artificial intelligence, and pattern recognition. Sensor fusion remains an active area of research, and the interested reader is referred to several well-written reviews at the end of this chapter. There are several advanced topics that are beyond the scope of this book. For example, the interested reader should learn about Dempster–Schafer theory – a statistical inference method that enables fusion of homogeneous and heterogeneous forms of data, taking into account confidence values and the potential for conflict between sensor readings. Another topic of recent interest is multisensor object tracking and prediction using techniques such as Kalman filters.

▶ Problems 7.5-1, 7.5-2

Further Reading

Registration

D. Lowe, Distinctive image features from scale-invariant keypoints, *International Journal of Computer Vision*, Vol. 60, pp. 91–110, 2004.

K. Mikolajczyk and C. Schmid, Scale and affine invariant interest point detectors, *International Journal of Computer Vision*, Vol. 60, pp. 63–86, 2004.

B. Zitova and J. Flusser, Image registration methods: a survey, *Image and Vision Computing*, Vol. 21, pp. 977–1000, 2003.

J. P. W. Pluim, J. B. A. Maintz, and M. A. Viergever, Mutual-information-based registration of medical images: a survey, *IEEE Transactions on Medical Imaging*, Vol. 22, pp. 986–1004, 2003.

O. Al-Kofahi, A. Can, S. Lasek, D. H. Szarowski, J. N. Turner, and B. Roysam, Hierarchical algorithms for affine 3-D registration of neuronal images acquired by confocal laser scanning microscopy, *Journal of Microscopy*, Vol. 211, pp. 8–18, 2003.

A. Can, C. V. Stewart, B. Roysam, and H. L. Tanenbaum, A feature-based robust hierarchical algorithm for registration pairs of images of the curved human retina, *IEEE Transactions on Pattern*

Analysis and Machine Intelligence, Vol. 24, pp. 347–364, 2002.

A. Can, C. V. Stewart, B. Roysam, and H. L. Tanenbaum, A feature-based robust hierarchical algorithm for joint, linear estimation of high-order image-to-mosaic transformations: mosaicing the curved human retina, *IEEE Transactions on Pattern Analysis and Machine Intelligence*, Vol. 24, pp. 412–419, 2002.

J. V. Hajnal, D. L.G. Hill, and D. J. Hawkes (eds.), *Medical Image Registration*, CRC, 2001.

B. S. Reddy and B. N. Chatterji, An FFT-based technique for translation, rotation, and scale-invariant image registration, *IEEE Transactions on Image Processing*, Vol. 5, pp.1266–1271, 1996.

P. J. Besl and N. D. McKay, A method for registration of 3D shapes, *IEEE Transactions on Pattern Analysis and Machine Intelligence*, Vol. 14, pp. 239–256, 1992.

Change Detection

H. Narasimha-Iyer, A. Can, B. Roysam, C. V. Stewart, H. L. Tanenbaum, A. Majerovics, and H. Singh, Robust detection and classification of longitudinal changes in color retinal fundus images for monitoring diabetic retinopathy, *IEEE Transactions on Biomedical Engineering*, Vol. 53, pp. 1084–1098, 2006.

R. J. Radke, S. Andra, O. Al-Kofahi, and B. Roysam, Image change detection algorithms: a systematic survey, *IEEE Trans. on Image Processing*, Vol. 14, pp. 294–307, 2004.

Multisensor Fusion

D. L. Hall and J. Llinas, An introduction to multisensor data fusion, *Proceedings of the IEEE*, Vol. 85, pp. 6–23, 1997.

Numerical Methods

W. H. Press, S. A. Teukolsky, W. T. Vetterling, and B. P. Flannery, *Numerical Recipes: The Art of Scientific Computing*, 3rd ed., Cambridge University Press, 2007.

Toolboxes and Websites

Numerical Recipes: The Art of Scientific Computing. An on-line book with codes: *http://www.nr.com/*

Registration toolboxes are described in Appendix D.

A summary of feature detectors, region detectors, descriptors, and associated software is available at:

http://www.robots.ox.ac.uk/ vgg/research/affine/index.html

Problems

7.1-1   **Registration.** This exercise introduces the fundamentals of image registration by applying tools in the MATLAB Image Processing Toolbox (*www.mathworks.com/products/image/*, Chapter 7) to images of a healthy red-free human eye available in the folder Imageset/retina-images-grayscale in the book website.

(a) Use the function `imread` to read the images IMG0027.pgm, IMG0028.pgm, and IMG0031.pgm. Use the function `imtool` to view these images on your computer screen. The first two images are just slightly displaced relative to each other. The third is displaced more substantially. Get to know the image coordinate system by viewing the coordinates of various points on the image. Use the `cpselect` tool to locate 20 corresponding vessel bifurcation points between IMG0027.pgm and IMG0028.pgm. Spread these 20 points evenly across the image. One of these images can be regarded as the *base* image and the other as the *input* image, following the terminology of the manual. These 20 points will serve as control points. Pan and zoom the images as needed. Export the control points to the MATLAB workspace.

(b) Compute the mean-squared displacement between the 20 corresponding points recorded in part a). Also compute the median of absolute differences between these points. The latter should be robust to occasional errors in control points (try to make a few deliberate errors and see if this is really true!).

(c) Use the `cpcorr` function to adjust the control points using image correlation, following the manual instructions on using this function. Recompute the mean-squared and median of absolute differences between the adjusted control points.

(d) Use the `cp2tform` function to compute a similarity transformation linking the control points. Use the resulting `TFORM` structure to transform the input control points to the space of the base control points, and vice versa. Recompute the mean-squared and median of absolute differences between the transformed control points. You should see a significant reduction in these numbers compared with the untransformed control points. Register the images by using the `imtransform` function to transform one image into the coordinates of the other. Visually confirm the result of the registration process.

e) To learn about the limitations of the similarity transformation when dealing with images that are significantly displaced, repeat the registration process for the image pair IMG0028.pgm and IMG0031.pgm. Now, replace the similarity transformation with the affine transformation and note the improvement.

7.1-2   **Registration (advanced).** This exercise requires advanced C++ language skills and familiarity with software building tools such as CMake. Download and compile the RGRL (Rensselaer Generalized Registration Library) from the website *www.vxl.sourceforge.net* (See Sec. D.4 of Appendix D for an overview). Use this library to align the retinal images in Problem 7.1-1 by means of a quadratic spatial transformation. Compare the results with the affine registration results obtained in Problem 7.1-1.

7.2-1   **Interest Points and Landmark Matching.** The goal of this exercise is to familiarize you with the most widely used interest point operator: Lowe's scale-invariant keypoints (SIFT).

(a) Start by downloading the SIFT demo program from the author's website *http://people.cs.ubc.ca/ lowe/keypoints/* and running it on the images provided by the author (basmati.pgm, book.pgm, scene.pgm, and box.pgm). This demo does not provide the complete source code, so, if you prefer, you may obtain source codes from alternate websites (e.g., *http://www.vlfeat.org/ vedaldi/code/sift.html*).

(b) Once you have successfully run the author-provided demonstrations, compute SIFT features for the retinal images in the folder Imageset/retina-images-grayscale, which is available in the book website. Then, using the matching algorithm provided by Lowe, or otherwise, compute matches for pairs of landmarks (vessel bifurcations) that you select manually. Compare these results against invalid pairs of landmarks. Study the differences. Develop a method to quantitatively compare automatic matching with your manual matching, for a set of 10 randomly selected landmarks.

7.2-2   **Registration using ICP.** Implement the ICP image registration on your own and use the pairs of landmarks from the previous exercise as a starting point. Initially use the affine transformation and select a pair of images that are shifted by a small amount (e.g., two nearly frontal views of the retina). Add outliers manually and examine their impact on the registration.

7.2-3   **Registration using ICP (Advanced).** Reregister the landmarks from the previous exercise using a robust ICP algorithm and quantify the improvement in terms of mean-squared error between corresponding points.

7.3-1   **Mosaicing.** The folder Imageset/confocal-microscopy-mosaicing in the book website contains a set of four 3D images of brain tissue collected using a CLSM with multispectral capability. You may view these images by use of the free NIH viewer ImageJ viewer (*http://rsbweb.nih.gov/ij/*) or the free Zeiss LSM Image Browser (*http://www.zeiss.com/*). The multispectral image data was unmixed computationally to yield five image channels showing cell nuclei (cyan), microglia (yellow), astrocytes (red), neurotrace (purple), and blood vessels (green). Start off by creating maximum-intensity projections of these images (you may choose just one channel initially) and see if you can align them visually. Next, use the MATLAB Image Processing Toolbox to mosaic pairs of these projected images.

7.4-1   **Change Detection.** The retinal images Retina_Original_01.png and Retina_original_02.png in the folder Imageset/retina-retina-changes in the book website are images of the same human eye taken several months apart. Start off by visually identifying changes in these two images. In the same folder you will find the registered and spatially transformed pair of these same images, named Retina_Registereed_01.png and Retina_Registereed_02.png, respectively. Write a program to detect pixel-level changes between these images. First do this without any correction for nonuniform illumination. You may also want to start off with grayscale versions of these color images before attempting change detection with the color images. Next, experiment with signal correction methods (e.g., homomorphic filtering, described in Sec. 7.4). The folder contains two images that show the expected results. Compare your results with these provide ones.

7.5-1   **Fusion and Change Detection.** The folder Imageset/feeder-vessel in the book website contains three retinal images named Whole-eye-color.png, Indocyanine-Early.png, and Indocyanine-Late.png. The latter two images were captured by injecting the patient with a fluorescent dye (indocyanine green) and imaging the dye to show the two phases of blood flow through the subsurface (choroidal) vessel network. They are also cropped to reveal a small portion of interest (the discolored region in Whole-eye-color.png).

(a) Align the indocyanine images to the color image and carefully study the characteristics of these three images.

(b) Create fused images that show the information from multiple images simultaneously for visual inspection. (An example of a fused image is the image fused.tif in the same folder.) Do these fused images help you see the differences better?

(c) Use a change-detection algorithm to identify pixels at which these two images differ significantly. How do your results compare with your visual observations from the original images and the fused images?

7.5-2   **Registration of 3D Images (Advanced).** This exercise will require significant programming skills and effort. The objective here is to study the application of mutual information (MI)-based registration methods to 3D medical images. Several sources of such images exist. The OSIRIX site *http://pubimage.hcuge.ch/* hosted by the Radiology Department at the Geneva University Hospital contains a rich collection of medical images from diverse modalities. The file CEREBRIX.zip was downloaded from this site and contains brain images (MRI, PET, X-ray CT) of a human subject with a tumor. You will need a DICOM image viewer (supported by MATLAB) to read and view these images. Another source of images is from the BrainWeb collection, a part of which is accessible via *http://public.kitware.com/pub/itk/Data/BrainWeb/*. These latter images can be viewed using the free Paraview viewer *http://www.paraview.org/*. The source code for MI registration is available as part of the free and open source Insight Toolkit *www.itk.org*. Search for *InsightApplications/LandmarkInitializedMutualInformationRegistration* and *InsightApplications/LandmarkInitializedMutualInformationRegistration/imageRegTool* on this site. You may also download the pre-compiled executable for this tool. For instance, the Windows executable is found at:

http://public.kitware.com/pub/itk/InsightApplicationsBin/ImageRegistrationTool.exe.

Numerical Simulation

In real-world subsurface imaging it is essential to consider the details of the geometry and properties of the object and the surrounding background. Often, it is sharp edges, small indentations, misalignments, randomly changing features, rough interfaces, volumetric inhomogeneities, or random shape variations that give the scattered waves their particular form, which in turn may provide the features necessary to identify the subsurface target. Examples of realistic subsurface imaging geometries that require numerical modeling to accurately predict the sensed responses (Fig. 8.0-1) include: small distinctly shaped buried objects, such as land mines; objects with fins or cavities, such as an open can; objects with multiple material types, such as rocks underwater with attached coral; background media with distributed inclusions, such as blood vessels in tissue; or large irregularly shaped background regions, such as a layered rock formation; or media with significant frequency-dependent material properties, such as biological tissue.

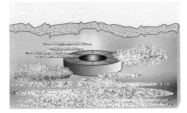

Figure 8.0-1 Example of a subsurface imaging problem requiring numerical simulation: a target in a continuously varying background with volumetric inhomogeneities and a rough interface.

Real-world problems are therefore difficult to analyze, and exact solutions to the differential equations describing wave propagation in such inhomogeneous environments often do not exist. Numerical methods, the subject of this chapter, are therefore indispensable.

8.1   Overview of Numerical Methods

A. Exact, Approximate, and Numerical Solutions

Before embarking on a solution by numerical simulation, exact analytical solutions and analytical solutions based on appropriate approximations must first be considered. We will develop a progression of decisions to determine the most appropriate method to use for a given subsurface imaging problem: (1) an exact analytical solution, (2) an analytical solution based on some appropriate approximation, or (3) a numerical solution.

First, assuming that the geometry of the problem is not one of the few simple ones that afford a direct analytical solution, such as a spherical scatterer in an infinite homogeneous medium, the decision is to apply techniques specifically suited to half-space or layered media. While all of the subsurface numerical modeling methods apply to problems without strong layered geometry, special considerations are needed if a significant portion of the space has a distinctly different background.

Next, various types of approximations must be considered. For waves of sufficiently short wavelength (high frequency), a **ray model** may be used. With rays following lines or curves, the problem is considerably simplified. A low-frequency approximation may also simplify the problem. For the intermediate domain in which the scattering objects or their sub-components (or elements of the background) are of the order of the probing wavelength, a full-wave solution is required. For a medium with random inhomogeneities causing strong multiple scattering, a **photon diffusion** or **radiative transfer** model may be adopted (see Sec. 2.2D).

For small scatterers with low contrast relative to the background, the simplest approximation within a full-wave model is the **Born approximation**, discussed in Sec. 2.2C and used in Chapters 3–5. Since it is based on the Helmholtz equation, it includes many of the details of wave scattering. However, it is hard to use in layered media, as instantiated in Fig. 8.1-1(*b*), because it requires specially derived Green functions that apply to the specific geometry, and these are nontrivial. In addition, the Born approximation does not consider multiple scattering in media with multiple objects, as illustrated in Fig. 8.1-1(*c*), and hence cannot model resonant behavior of objects, nor coupling between objects.

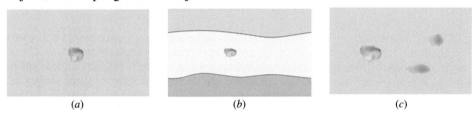

(*a*)	(*b*)	(*c*)

Figure 8.1-1   (*a*) Single scatterer in a homogeneous medium. (*b*) Single scatterer in a layered medium. (*c*) Multiple scatterers in a homogeneous medium.

A flow chart for selection of a suitable approximation method or numerical model is depicted in Fig. 8.1-2.

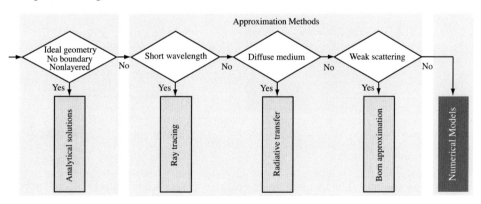

Figure 8.1-2   Flow chart for selection of a suitable approximation method or numerical model.

When none of the known approximations is appropriate, the only recourse is to use one of several numerical models to simulate the accurate physical model. These make up the bulk of this chapter.

At times, however, it is necessary to use numerical simulation techniques for computations based on an approximate model. For example, in Chapter 5, the Born approximation was used to express the imaging equation in integral form and numerical techniques were used to express this equation as a summation and write it in matrix form. Another example of applying numerical methods to an approximate model is the use of Monte Carlo techniques to simulate the process of photon diffusion (see Sec. 2.2D).

B. Differential, Integral, and Modal Methods

There are three basic approaches to modeling the propagation of fields and waves in complex media – differential, integral, and modal – as depicted pictorially in Fig. 8.1-3.

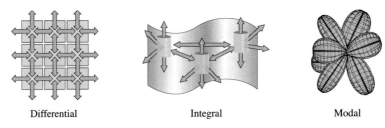

Differential   Integral   Modal

Figure 8.1-3   Pictorial illustration of differential, integral, and modal methods.

Differential methods.   The field values at a large set of sampling points are related by algebraic equations that are solved under appropriate boundary conditions. In the **finite difference** (FD) method, the sampling grid is uniform in each dimension [as in Fig. 8.5-5(a)] and the algebraic equations are derived directly from the partial differential equations, which the fields must obey, by simply replacing derivatives with differences. In the **finite element method** (FEM), the sampling grid is not necessarily uniform [as in Fig. 8.5-5(b)] and the fields are fitted to linear or quadratic functions at points within each sampling element. The fitting coefficients are determined by use of the variational principle, in lieu of the differential equation. It is essential to terminate the computational space with effective absorbing boundary conditions that simulate limitless space.

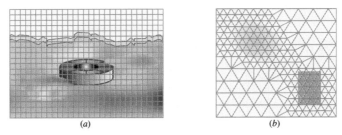

(a)   (b)

Figure 8.1-4   Sampling grid for discretization of space. (a) Uniform sampling. (b) Nonuniform sampling.

Integral methods.   The incident fields give rise to secondary sources located at scattering objects, which in turn radiate secondary fields, as illustrated in Fig. 8.1-3(b). These are described by integral equations that are approximated numerically. The idea is to solve for the distribution of secondary sources that are not only self-consistent, but which also radiate fields throughout all of space, even outside the computational region. While such methods can be effective, accounting for all of the possible interactions of the radiated fields in complicated geometries is often challenging.

Modal methods are based on expressing the field as superpositions of a finite number of modes, i.e., simple solutions of the differential equations that satisfy the boundary conditions [Fig. 8.1-3(c)]. Modal methods tend to be the fastest modeling approach, building up a complete field from solutions that already obey the equations. The issue for modal methods is to match the fields at every boundary when there is limited flexibility of field dependence for each mode. As with Fourier series analysis, getting a particular field value at an interface might require combining many modes, some of which have large values that must cancel each other. Perfect agreement is possible in the limit of infinitely many modes so that terminating the series of modes appropriately requires some insight.

A flow chart for selection of a suitable numerical model is depicted in Fig. 8.1-5.

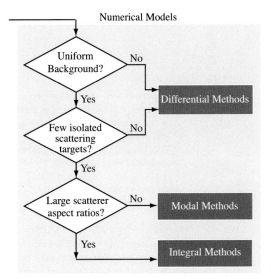

Figure 8.1-5   Flow chart for selection of a suitable numerical model.

C. Frequency Domain versus Time Domain

Numerical models are also divided broadly into frequency-domain and time-domain models. While this division is basic in engineering analysis, when considering numerical models the distinction leads specifically to different solution methods. Time-domain methods involve iterative, time-marching solutions, while frequency-domain methods usually involve solving simultaneous equations.

Time-domain methods are usually easier to code, and have the advantage of showing the progression of waves as they propagate, scatter, and interfere, while frequency-domain methods need only to be solved once for any given excitation to give the field response at all points of interest. Time-domain methods must consider stability to prevent unintended explosive growth, and must incorporate special formulations for frequency-dependent media. They may also require many iterations to ensure that transients have died out (especially in resonant structures with narrow-band excitation).

Frequency-domain methods are best for analyzing resonant structures and continuous wave excitation, while time-domain methods are best for time-delay analyses and with impulsive and short pulse excitations.

> **Summary.** The three-way classification – differential (finite difference and finite element), integral, and modal – and the two-way classification – frequency domain and time domain – cover many types of models, as illustrated in Fig. 8.1-6 and described in this chapter.

Popular Frequency-Domain Methods.   The most popular frequency-domain methods used in subsurface sensing and imaging are:

1. The FDFD methods, which are described in Sec. 8-1.
2. The FEM, which is described in Sec. 8-2.
3. The MoM, which is an integral model described in Sec. 8-3, with acceleration approaches such as the FMM.

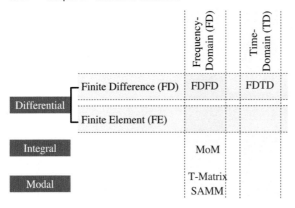

Figure 8.1-6 Summary of classes of numerical methods. The method of moments (MoM) is an integral method described in Sec. 8.3. The T-matrix method and the semi-analytical mode matching (SAMM) method are modal methods described in Sec. 8.4.

Figure 8.1-7 shows schematically the relative accuracy and computational complexity of various frequency-domain methods. Full three-dimensional (3D) models are more realistic than two-dimensional (2D) models, but obviously require more computer memory, storage, and computation time. For simple idealized geometries of infinite planar layers or perfect spherical scatterers, analytic methods are fast and accurate, but for realistic shapes and imperfect boundaries, they can only vaguely approximate most of the important scattering features.

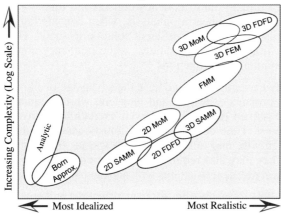

Figure 8.1-7 Summary of popular frequency-domain numerical methods, indicating the trade-off between accuracy and computational expense. FDFD = finite-difference frequency-domain; FEM = finite element method; FMM = fast multiple multilevel; MoM = method of moments; SAMM = semi-analytical mode matching.

Computational Resources.   The first step in numerical modeling is the development of a scheme for sampling the object space and the time (for time-dependent problems). As discussed in Sec. 5.1, it is important to choose the sampling carefully to approximate the spatial and temporal dependence with good accuracy, without demanding too much computing resources. Too coarse a grid spacing will lead to excessive discretization error; too fine calculations made at points so close to others would result in values that are practically the same, and would waste resources. A good rule of thumb is that there should be 10 space points per wavelength or 10 time points per period. For aperiodic functions, the sampling should be taken at similar resolution. For example, a 3D scattering geometry of dimensions $10 \times 20 \times 30$ wavelengths, with time records over 40 periods, sampled at 10 samples per wavelength and period would require an array of $100 \times 200 \times 300 \times 400 = 24 \times 10^6$ elements. Clearly, numerical models usually require significant computer resources. Improving the modeling resolution by, say, doubling the sampling in space, can lead to eight times as much required computational resource. The sampling may be uniform or nonuniform as illustrated in Fig. 8.5-5.

8.2 Differential Methods

A. Finite Difference (FD) Methods

The FD method is a method of discretization of ordinary and partial differential equations by approximating derivatives in terms of finite differences using a uniform sampling grid. When applied to subsurface image problems, FD methods are very effective in modeling small-scale variations of both an object of interest and its surrounding environment. Specific nonideal target shapes, rough surface boundaries, and volumetric inhomogeneities can all be discretized and numerically analyzed.

Discretization of Functions and Derivatives.   Consider a continuous function $f(x)$ approximated by the discrete function $f_m = f(mh)$, where $m = 1, 2, \ldots$ and h is a sampling interval. The **central FD** is defined by

$$\Delta^{(1)} f_m = f_{m+1} - f_{m-1}. \tag{8.2-1}$$
FD

The derivative of the original continuous function $f(x)$ at $x = mh$ is approximated by

$$\frac{df}{dx} \approx \frac{1}{2h} \Delta^{(1)} f_m = \frac{1}{2h}(f_{m+1} - f_{m-1}).$$

The error in this approximation is proportional to h^2, as can be shown by use of a Taylor series expansion of $f(x)$ and neglecting terms of order h^2 and higher [assuming that $f(x)$ is twice continuously differentiable].

Similarly, the second difference (the FD of the FD) is $\Delta^{(2)} f_m = (f_{m+2} - f_m) - (f_m - f_{m-2})$, so that

$$\Delta^{(2)} f_m = (f_{m+2} - 2f_m + f_{m-2}), \tag{8.2-2}$$
Second FD

and the second derivative is approximated by

$$\frac{d^2 f}{dx^2} \approx \frac{1}{(2h)^2} \Delta^{(2)} f_m = \frac{1}{(2h)^2}(f_{m+2} - 2f_m + f_{m-2}).$$

These approximations may be used to model an ordinary differential equation by a difference equation, simply by replacing the function and its derivatives with a discrete function and its FD, respectively.

Example: The FD Helmholtz equation.   The FD approximation to the 1D Helmholtz equation $d^2 U/dx^2 + k^2 U = 0$, is

$$\left[\Delta^{(2)} + (2hk)^2\right] U_m = 0, \tag{8.2-3}$$
FD Helmholtz Equation

where $\Delta^{(2)} U_m = U_{m+2} - 2U_m + U_{m-2}$ is the second FD of U_m. Since the wavenumber $k = 2\pi/\lambda$, the coefficient $hk = 2\pi h/\lambda$ in the FD Helmholtz equation is proportional to the ratio of the sampling interval h to the wavelength λ. Clearly, in order for the FD equation to be a good approximation of the continuous equation, this ratio must be small. Since the harmonic function $U(x) = \exp(-jkx)$ is an exact solution of the Helmholtz equation, one may wonder if the discrete function $U_m = \exp(-jmhk)$, which approximates the continuous function $U(x) = \exp(-jkx)$, is an exact solution of the FD Helmholtz equation (8.2-3). The answer is negative. However, $U_m = \exp(-jmhk)$ is an *approximate* solution, and the error is of the order of $\frac{4}{3}(hk)^4 =$

$\frac{32}{3}\pi^4(h/\lambda)^4$, which is small when $hk = 2\pi h/\lambda$ is small (e.g., for $h = \lambda/10$, the error is ≈ 0.1, and for $h = \lambda/20$, the error ≈ 0.006). This may be shown by writing $U_{m\pm 2} = \exp[-\mathrm{j}(m\pm 2)hk] = \exp(\mp\mathrm{j}2hk)U_m$ and using a Taylor series expansion

$$\exp(\mp\mathrm{j}2hk) = \left[1 + (\mp\mathrm{j}2hk) + \tfrac{1}{2!}(\mp\mathrm{j}2hk)^2 + \tfrac{1}{3!}(\mp\mathrm{j}2hk)^3 + \tfrac{1}{4!}(\mp\mathrm{j}2hk)^4 + \cdots\right].$$

Neglecting terms of order higher than $(hk)^3$, we write $U_{m\pm 2} \approx [1 \mp \mathrm{j}2hk - 2(hk)^2 + (\mp\mathrm{j}2hk)^3/3!]U_m$. This approximate expression satisfies the FD Helmholtz equation (8.2-3) exactly, but the next term in the expansion, $(2hk)^4/4!$, results in an error $2(2hk)^4/4! = \frac{4}{3}(hk)^4$.

Inhomogeneous Media.   In an inhomogeneous medium, the coefficient k is position dependent, i.e., $k = k(x)$, so that the one-dimensional (1D) FD Helmholtz equation is the same as (8.2-3) with a variable $k = k_m$,

$$\left[\Delta^{(2)} + (2hk_m)^2\right]U_m = 0. \tag{8.2-4}$$

If k_m is known, then (8.2-4) can be solved numerically for U_m.

Reflection and Transmission at a Boundary.   At the boundary between two homogeneous media, an incident wave creates a reflected and a transmitted wave. The reflection and transmission coefficients may be obtained by applying appropriate boundary conditions (see Sec. 2.2B). In the discrete formulation of the problem, it is not necessary to impose any conditions at the boundary since the FD Helmholtz equation ensures that these conditions are met. To demonstrate this important point, consider two media with $k = k_i$ for $x < 0$ and $k = k_t$ for $x > 0$. The FD Helmholtz equation is then

$$\left[\Delta^{(2)} + (2hk_i)^2\right]U_m = 0, \quad m \leq 0, \tag{8.2-5}$$

$$\left[\Delta^{(2)} + (2hk_t)^2\right]U_m = 0, \quad m > 0. \tag{8.2-6}$$

A solution takes the form of a transmitted wave in the right medium and the sum of incident and reflected waves in the left medium, i.e.,

$$U_m = \exp(-\mathrm{j}mhk_i) + \mathrm{r}\exp(+\mathrm{j}mhk_i), \quad m \leq 0, \tag{8.2-7}$$

$$U_m = \mathrm{t}\exp(-\mathrm{j}mhk_t), \quad m > 0, \tag{8.2-8}$$

where t and r are transmission and reflection coefficients. Clearly, (8.2-7) satisfies (8.2-5) with an error of order $\frac{4}{3}(hk_i)^4$ and (8.2-8) satisfies (8.2-6) with an error of order $\frac{4}{3}(hk_t)^4$. What happens at the boundary ($m = 0$) is dictated by the FD Helmholtz equation at $m = 0$,

$$U_2 - 2U_0 + U_{-2} + (2hk_i)^2 U_0 = 0. \tag{8.2-9}$$

Substituting the values

$$U_{-2} = \exp(+\mathrm{j}2hk_i) + \mathrm{r}\exp(-\mathrm{j}2hk_i), \quad U_0 = 1 + \mathrm{r}, \quad U_{+2} = \mathrm{t}\exp(-\mathrm{j}2hk_t)$$

obtained from (8.2-7) and (8.2-8) into (8.2-9) and using the approximation $\exp(\pm\mathrm{j}2hk) \approx 1 + (\pm\mathrm{j}2hk)$ for both $k = k_i$ and $k = k_t$, we find that (8.2-9) is satisfied if $1 + \mathrm{r} = \mathrm{t}$ and $(1 - \mathrm{r})k_i = \mathrm{t}k_t$. This yields the law of reflection $\mathrm{r} = (k_i - k_t)/(k_i + k_t) = (n_i - n_t)/(n_i + n_t)$, where $n_i = \sqrt{\epsilon_{ri}} = k_i/k$ and $n_t = \sqrt{\epsilon_{rt}} = k_t/k$ are the refractive indices, and ϵ_{ri} and ϵ_{rt} are the dielectric constants. The approximation error is of the order of $8\mathrm{r}(\bar{k}h)^2$, where $\bar{k} = \frac{1}{2}(k_i + k_t)$. Therefore, as long as the sampling interval h is sufficiently small, the laws of reflection and transmission are built into the FD Helmholtz equation.

Discretization of Partial Differential Equations. A function of several variables $f(x, y, z)$ may be sampled at points of a Cartesian grid and represented by the discrete function $f_{i,j,k} = f(ih_x, jh_y, kh_z)$, where (i, j, k) are integers and h_x, h_y, and h_z are sampling intervals for each coordinate direction.

The first and second partial FDs with respect to x are

$$\Delta_x^{(1)} f_{i,j,k} = f_{i+1,j,k} - f_{i-1,j,k}$$

and

$$\Delta_x^{(2)} f_{i,j,k} = f_{i+2,j,k} - 2f_{i,j,k} + f_{i-2,j,k},$$

respectively. Partial finite differences with respect to y and z may be similarly defined.

FD 3D Helmholtz Equation. For example, the FD version of the 3D Helmholtz equation $[\nabla^2 + k^2]U = 0$ is

$$\left[\Delta_x^{(2)} + \Delta_y^{(2)} + \Delta_z^{(2)} + (2hk)^2\right] U_{i,j,k} = 0, \qquad (8.2\text{-}10)$$

$$\text{FD Helmholtz Equation}$$

where $h = h_x = h_y = h_z$ is the sampling interval, assumed to be the same in all directions. For an inhomogeneous medium with slowly varying wave velocity and attenuation coefficient, $k = k(x, y, z)$ is a position-dependent complex function represented by the discrete function $k_{i,j,k} = k(ih_x, jh_y, kh_z)$.

The FD Helmholtz equation is an example of an FD description of wave propagation in the frequency domain (i.e., when the wave is assumed to be harmonic with a fixed frequency). This type of modeling is known as finite-difference frequency domain (**FDFD**).

FD Wave Equation. The wave function $u(x, y, z, t)$ a four-dimensional (4D) function satisfying the wave equation $\nabla^2 u - (1/v^2)\partial^2 u/\partial t^2 = 0$. Its discrete representation in space and time $u_{i,j,k}^n = u(ih_x, jh_y, kh_z, nh_t)$ satisfies approximately the FD wave equation

$$\left[\Delta_x^{(2)} + \Delta_y^{(2)} + \Delta_z^{(2)} - \frac{1}{r^2}\Delta_t^{(2)}\right] u_{i,j,k}^n = 0, \qquad (8.2\text{-}11)$$

$$\text{FD Wave Equation}$$

where $r = vh_t/h_s$, $h_s = h_x = h_y = h_z$ is the spatial sampling interval, and h_t is the temporal sampling interval. For an inhomogeneous medium with slowly varying properties, the wave velocity $v = v_{i,j,k}$ is position dependent. This type of modeling is known as finite difference time domain (**FDTD**). FDTD is a fast iterative method in which values of the wave function are updated at each time step, so that it shows how waves progressively propagate and scatter in time.

FDFD Electromagnetic Fields

For vector waves, it is essential to work with the equations that relate the vector fields and use FD methods (FDTD or FDFD) for their discretization. For electromagnetic waves, these vector relations are Maxwell's equations.

FDFD Maxwell's Equations. Take, for example, Maxwell's equations for a harmonic electromagnetic wave in a 2D transverse electric (TE) configuration where the electric field points in the x direction and the magnetic field has components in the y and z directions and the fields do not depend on x. In this case, Maxwell's equations

(2.3-7)–(2.3-10), with ϵ replaced by $\epsilon' = \epsilon + \sigma/j\omega$, have the continuous and discrete forms:

$$\frac{\partial E_x}{\partial z} = -j\omega\mu H_y$$

$$\frac{\partial E_x}{\partial y} = +j\omega\mu H_z \qquad\Rightarrow$$

$$\frac{\partial H_z}{\partial y} - \frac{\partial H_y}{\partial z} = (\sigma + j\omega\epsilon)E_x,$$

$$\boxed{\begin{aligned}\Delta_z^{(1)} E_x &= -j2h\omega\mu H_y \\ \Delta_y^{(1)} E_x &= +j2h\omega\mu H_z \\ \Delta_y^{(1)} H_z - \Delta_z^{(1)} H_y &= 2h(\sigma + j\omega\epsilon)E_x.\end{aligned}}$$

$$(8.2\text{-}12)$$

The discrete field functions $E_{x:i,j,k}$, $H_{y:i,j,k}$, $H_{z:i,j,k}$ are therefore related by

$$E_{x:i,\,j,k+1} - E_{x:i,j,k-1} = -j2h\omega\mu H_{y:i,j,k}$$

$$E_{x:i,j+1,k} - E_{x:i,j-1,k} = +j2h\omega\mu H_{z:i,j,k} \qquad (8.2\text{-}13)$$

$$H_{z:i,j+1,k} - H_{z:i,j-1,k} - H_{y:i,j,k+1} + H_{y:i,j,k-1} = 2h(\sigma + j\omega\epsilon)E_{x:i,j,k},$$

where μ, ϵ, and σ are generally position dependent, e.g., $\epsilon = \epsilon_{i,j,k}$.

Yee Cube. It is efficient to discretize the electric and magnetic field components on complementary interlocking cubical grids. As shown in Fig. 8.2-1, the corner of one cube lies at the center of the other. This grid is referred to as the Yee cube. In the first cube, the electric field components are specified at the midpoints of the edges with each component parallel to its edge. Likewise, the magnetic field components are specified at the midpoints of the edges of the second cube, so that they are located at the centers of the faces of the first cube. Since the electric and magnetic fields are staggered, the Yee cube is usually indexed in terms of step size $2h$.

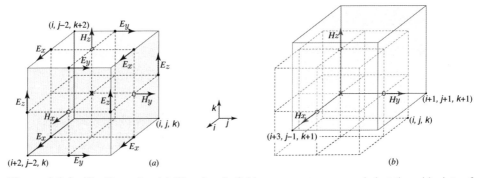

Figure 8.2-1 The Yee cube. (*a*) The electric field components are sampled at the midpoints of edges of cubes of dimensions $2 \times 2 \times 2$ in a Cartesian grid. The magnetic field components are sampled at centers of the cube faces, which are also midpoints of edges of a complementary cubical grid (*b*) displaced by one step in all three directions.

For example, for the electromagnetic wave described in (8.2-14), using the Yee cube with unit sides we obtain

$$E_{x:i+1,j,k+2} - E_{x:i+1,j,k} = -j2h\omega\mu H_{y:i+1,j,k+1}$$

$$E_{x:i+1,j,k} - E_{x:i+1,j-2,k} = +j2h\omega\mu H_{z:i+1,j-1,k}$$

$$H_{z:i+1,j+1,k} - H_{z:i+1,j-1,k} - H_{y:i+1,j,k+1} + H_{y:i+1,j,k-1} = 2h(\sigma + j\omega\epsilon)E_{x:i+1,j,k}.$$

$$(8.2\text{-}14)$$

FDTD Electromagnetic Fields

In the time domain, for a wave with an electric field pointing in the x direction, Maxwell's equations are

$$\frac{\partial E_x}{\partial z} = -\mu \frac{\partial H_y}{\partial t}$$

$$\frac{\partial E_x}{\partial y} = +\mu \frac{\partial H_z}{\partial t} \tag{8.2-15}$$

$$\frac{\partial H_z}{\partial y} - \frac{\partial H_y}{\partial z} = \epsilon \frac{\partial E_x}{\partial t} + \sigma E_x.$$

Using sampling intervals $h_x = h_y = h_z = h_s$ and time step h_t, their FDTD approximation is:

$$E^n_{x:\,i+1,j,k+2} - E^n_{x:\,i+1,j,k} = -\mu(h_s/h_t)(H^{n+1}_{y:\,i+1,j,k+1} - H^{n-1}_{y:\,i+1,j,k+1})$$

$$E^n_{x:\,i+1,j,k} - E^n_{x:\,i+1,j-2,k} = +\mu(h_s/h_t)(H^{n+1}_{z:\,i+1,j-1,k} + H^{n-1}_{z:\,i+1,j-1,k}) \tag{8.2-16}$$

$$H^{n+1}_{z:\,i+1,j+1,k} - H^{n+1}_{z:\,i+1,j-1,k} - (H^{n+1}_{y:\,i+1,j,k+1} - H^{n+1}_{y:\,i+1,j,k-1})$$

$$= \epsilon(h_s/h_t)(E^{n+2}_{x:\,i+1,j,k} - E^n_{x:\,i+1,j,k}) + \sigma(2h_s)E^n_{x:\,i+1,j,k}.$$

The updated form of the FDTD equations express the magnetic field components at time $n+1$ and the electric field components at time $n+2$ in terms of components at prior times:

$$H^{n+1}_{y:\,i+1,j,k+1} = H^{n-1}_{y:\,i+1,j,k+1} - (r/\eta)\left[E^n_{x:\,i+1,j,k+2} - E^n_{x:\,i+1,j,k}\right]$$

$$H^{n+1}_{z:\,i+1,j-1,k} = H^{n-1}_{z:\,i+1,j-1,k} + (r/\eta)\left[E^n_{x:\,i+1,j,k} - E^n_{x:\,i+1,j-2,k}\right] \tag{8.2-17}$$

$$E^{n+2}_{x:\,i+1,j,k} = \zeta E^n_{x:\,i+1,j,k} + r\eta\left[H^{n+1}_{z:\,i+1,j+1,k} - H^{n+1}_{z:\,i+1,j-1,k}\right.$$

$$\left. - H^{n+1}_{y:\,i+1,j,k+1} + H^{n+1}_{y:\,i+1,j,k-1}\right],$$

where $r = vh_t/h_s$, $\eta = \sqrt{\mu/\epsilon}$, and $\zeta = (1 - 2\sigma h_t/\epsilon)$. Note that the electric field is only computed on even time steps, and the magnetic field is computed only on odd time steps. In fact, no point in space or time has more than one field component calculated. The full polarization and temporal characteristics of the field must be determined by interpolating between the separate disjointed components. For an inhomogeneous medium, the parameters ϵ, σ, and μ (and therefore v, η, and r) are generally position dependent and must be appropriately indexed, e.g., $\epsilon = \epsilon_{i,j,k}$.

Solving the FD Equations

With Maxwell's equations written in the FD form as a set of linear algebraic equations [e.g., (8.2-14)], all that is left is to solve these equations simultaneously for the unknown field components $E_{x:\,i,j,k}$, $H_{y:\,i,j,k}$, and $H_{z:\,i,j,k}$, at all points i, j, k of the computational grid. This is done by casting these equations in a matrix form

$$\mathbf{Ax} = \mathbf{0}, \tag{8.2-18}$$

where the column vector $\mathbf{x}$ is a stacked version of the lexicographically ordered field components (see Fig. 5.1-3) and the matrix $\mathbf{A}$ has known elements determined by the parameters ϵ, σ, and μ of the medium at all grid points i, j, k. The structure of the matrix $\mathbf{A}$ represents the physical laws (Maxwell's equations) that govern the relations between the field components at each set of adjacent points of the grid. Note that there is no need for boundary conditions at material interfaces, since these are already included in the different values of the medium parameters.

A trivial solution of (8.2-18) is, of course, $\mathbf{x} = 0$, and this is to be expected, since information on the applied probe wave is not yet incorporated. One approach for including this information is to divide the computational space into two regions, as illustrated schematically in Fig. 8.2-2: a forward region containing the transmitted (forward scattered) field and a backward region containing the incident probe and the reflected (backscattered) wave. If $\mathbf{x}_p$ is the vector of components of the probe wave and $\mathbf{x}_s$ is the vector of components of the wave generated by the scattering process (in both the forward and backward directions), then it can be shown that

$$\mathbf{A}\mathbf{x}_s = \mathbf{S}, \qquad \mathbf{S} = (\mathbf{Q}\mathbf{A} - \mathbf{A}\mathbf{Q})\,\mathbf{x}_p, \qquad (8.2\text{-}19)$$

where $\mathbf{Q}$ is a diagonal matrix, called the **masking matrix**, whose elements are set to 1 where they correspond to points in the backward region and 0 elsewhere. Given the probe vector $\mathbf{x}_p$, the source $\mathbf{S}$ may be readily computed and the linear vector equation $\mathbf{A}\mathbf{x}_s = \mathbf{S}$ inverted numerically to solve for the unknown scattered field components $\mathbf{x}_s$ using the techniques described in Chapter 5. This approach is the basis of available software for numerical simulation of electromagnetic propagation and scattering problems (see Appendix D).

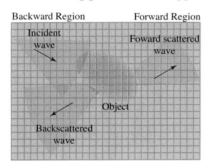

Backward Region   Forward Region

Incident wave

Foward scattered wave

Object

Backscattered wave

Figure 8.2-2   Various regions in a scattering configurations.

Boundary Conditions

For modeling scattering problems with open geometries, it is essential to replace the boundary of the finite-size computational space with an artificial boundary condition that makes it appear transparent to the scattered or radiated field. Without such a boundary, the grid edges generate reflection artifacts that can completely dominate the field distribution. For example, simply by ending the computation of the electric field at the grid edge would be equivalent to setting the electric fields to zero right outside the computational space, which would result in field distributions within a perfectly conducting box. Any desired scattering response of objects in the space would be overwhelmed by the modal resonance pattern of the box.

Absorbing Boundary Conditions (ABCs).   A class of boundary conditions that achieve this goal are called absorbing boundary conditions (ABCs). The simplest ABCs are based on using an asymptotic far-zone solution for one-way (outgoing) waves to derive first-order wave equations that approximate the exact second-order wave equation. Such equations, which admit only forward waves and no backward (reflected) waves, are used at the boundary in lieu of the exact equation. These ABCs are very effective for waves with incident angles close to normal, but tend to be less effective as the wave approaches grazing incidence. Since ABCs must prevent grid termination reflections for waves with all incident angles and frequencies simultaneously, they must be robust and all-encompassing.

Perfectly Matched Layer (PML).   Maxwell's equations can only admit solutions with zero reflection at an interface for all incident angles and frequencies when the material characteristics on both sides of the interface are the same (i.e., when there is no actual interface!). Thus, there is no possible manipulation of the equations or the media to reduce the grid termination reflection with an ABC to zero. However, a modified set of equations, similar to Maxwell's, has been developed to maintain all of the propagation, uniqueness, and reciprocity conditions, yet permit no reflected field.[1] The derivations are beyond the scope of this text. However, in the frequency domain, the idea can be summarized by imagining the field dependence in the perfectly matched layer (PML) along the direction normal to an edge (say the x-direction) be given by $\exp[-jk_x(1-jS)x]$, where k_x is the wavenumber in the x-direction and $S = \sigma^{\mathrm{PML}}/\omega\epsilon$ is the loss tangent in the PML medium. The dependence in the transverse direction $\exp(-jk_y y)$ is not changed in the PML. This can be accomplished by mapping the real x coordinate in the PML to the complex coordinate $x_{\mathrm{PML}} = x(1 - jS)$.[2] If Maxwell's equations are now written with x replaced by x_{PML}, the solutions will have the necessary attenuation normal to and away from the boundary, and because the transverse dependence is unaffected, the transverse impedance will be the same as in the rest of the grid, and there will be no reflection at the grid edge.

Simulation of Waves in Dispersive Media

As mentioned in Sec. 2.2A, most real media have frequency-dependent properties. The frequency dependence of the velocity of propagation and the attenuation coefficient causes a pulsed wave to undergo temporal dispersion: spreading and distortion of the pulse temporal profile, shifting of the zero crossings, and possibly ringing at the pulse tail. This in turn makes focusing difficult or impossible, and contributes to uncertainty in signal timing.

Dispersion is modeled differently in the frequency and time domains. For example, for an electromagnetic wave traveling in a dielectric medium, the relation between the electric flux density $D(\omega)$ and the electric field $E(\omega)$ for a harmonic wave at frequency ω is given by the products $D(\omega) = \epsilon(\omega)E(\omega)$. In the time domain, this product relation is a convolution (see Appendix A). In numerical modeling, convolution requires the storage of the current and all the past values of the E-field for all points in the grid, which is computationally expensive. To avoid the operation of convolution, several methods have been suggested, including: recursive convolution, which takes advantage of the special forms of standard frequency-dependent Debye and Lorentz models;[3] or use of a supplemental equation that models the frequency dependence by means of a differential equation in time. Although using another equation increases the complexity, FD readily handle the already discretized field variables, requiring only a few additional stored field values. For example, the Nth-order Debye model for the complex permittivity in (2.2-3):

$$\epsilon' = \epsilon_0\epsilon'_\infty + \epsilon_0 \sum_{n=1}^{N} \frac{A_n}{1 + j\omega\tau_n} \tag{8.2-20}$$

can be combined into a ratio of polynomials in powers of $j\omega$. Since $D = \epsilon E$, the equation consisting of the denominator times D minus the numerator times E can be readily converted into the time domain, with the understanding that $j\omega$ factors

---

[1] J. Berenger, A perfectly matched layer for the absorption of electromagnetic waves, *Journal of Mathematical Physics*, Vol. 114, pp.185–200, 1994.

[2] C. Rappaport, Perfectly matched absorbing boundary conditions based on anisotropic lossy mapping of space, *IEEE Microwave and Guided Wave Letters*, Vol. 5, pp. 90–92, 1995.

[3] R. Luebbers and F. Hansberger, FDTD for Nth-order dispersive media, *IEEE Transactions on Antennas Propagation*, Vol. 40, pp. 1297–1301, 1992.

transform into time derivatives, and into FDs. It is also possible to model the material frequency dependence in terms of a rational function of the Z-transform variable $Z = \exp(j\omega h_t)$, which transforms immediately into unit time delays.[4]

EXAMPLE 8.2-1.   *FDFD Simulation of Full-Wave Scattering.*   As an example of the full-wave FDFD computation, we reconsider the 2D scattering problem described in Example 5.3-2 in the context of wave tomography. There are two dielectric objects: a rectangular homogeneous object and an elliptical object with graded dielectric constant, as illustrated in Fig. 8.2-3, which is a reproduction of Fig. 5.3-5. The overall dimension of the medium is 1 m×1 m. The objects are illuminated with a 10 GHz plane wave from the left, and the scattered field is to be calculated. The wavelength in the background medium is 3 cm and is 2.1 cm in the rectangular object and varies from 1.5 cm to 3 cm in the elliptical scatterer. Since the wavelength is comparable to the length scale of the geometric variation, high- and low-frequency approximations are not feasible. The FDFD is one method that can capture the fine geometric variation of the dielectric constant. We model the geometry with 16 sample points per wavelength and use the PML absorbing boundary condition along each of the four edges of the computational lattice.

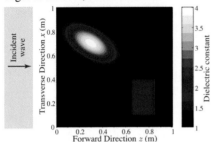

Figure 8.2-3   Dielectric constant distribution of a 1 m × 1 m medium with two embedded dielectric objects, a uniform rectangle and an ellipse with a continuously varying dielectric distribution.

The results of the FDFD simulation are shown in Fig. 8.2-4(a), as a brightness image of the spatial distribution of the magnitude of the scattered field (not including the incident field). Also shown are the reflected and transmitted fields at the front and back edges of the medium. In particular, one observes: (1) a modal pattern of 3 × 7 maxima within the rectangular object, (2) concentric elliptical rings within the elliptical object, and (3) a number of peaks distributed between the two objects, representing coupling between the two objects. Also, it can be observed that there is more forward scattering than backscattering. This forward scattering combines with opposite phase with the incident wave to create shadows in the total field on the far side of the objects. The backscattering (reflection back toward the source) is non-negligible.

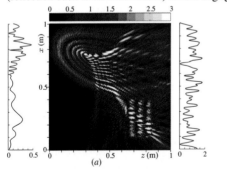

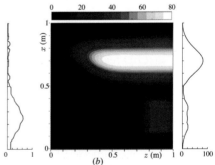

Figure 8.2-4   Spatial distribution of the magnitude of the scattered field, shown as a brightness image, and normalized spatial profiles of the field at the front and back sides of the medium. (a) FDFD model. (b) Born approximation.

To compare the scattered field calculated using FDFD with that modeled by use of the Born approximation discussed in Example 5.3-2, the same geometry is analyzed at 10 GHz using the latter

---

[4]W. Weedon and C. Rappaport, A general method for FDTD modeling of wave propagation in arbitrary frequency-dispersive media, *IEEE Transactions on Antennas and Propagation*, Vol. 45, pp. 401–410, 1997.

method. In this model, each point of the two objects radiates a cylindrical wave (since the object is assumed to be 2D) with an amplitude proportional to the difference between its dielectric constant and that of the nominal uniform background; all waves are added up (as complex numbers). The result is shown in Fig. 8.2-4(*b*). Unlike the FDFD method, the Born approximation ignores the interactions between these scattering points, and hence cannot predict the internal resonances and modes, nor can it model the coupling between the scattering objects. For electromagnetically large scatterers, and for finite objects with large dielectric contrasts, more sophisticated full-wave computational models, like FDFD, are essential.

To test the degree of coupling between scattering points, the scattering from the same geometry – but with progressively reduced relative dielectric constant – is modeled with FDFD. Figure 8.2-5 shows the scattered field magnitudes with the objects, dielectric constant differences from the background scaled to 1/10th, 1/20th, and 1/50th of their original values in Fig. 8.2-3(*a*) (i.e., the rectangle dielectric constant would scale to 1.1, 1.05, and 1.02). The modal field patterns become gradually less prominent with lower dielectric contrast, and the coupling between the scattering objects diminishes. For the 1/50th scaled case, Fig. 8.2-5(*c*), the scattered pattern converges to the expected configuration predicted by the Born approximation, shown in Fig. 8.2-4(*b*) (but with 50 times lower scattering intensity).

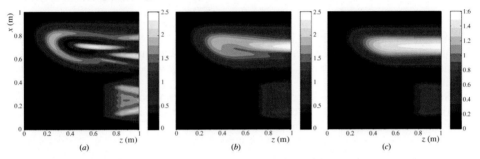

Figure 8.2-5   Magnitude of the scattered field (shown as a brightness image) computed by FDFD for objects with dielectric constant contrast reduced to (*a*) 1/10th, (*b*) 1/20th, and (*c*) 1/50th.

Figure 8.2-6 shows the fields computed on the front and back edges of each of the computational grids of Fig. 8.2-4 and Fig. 8.2-5(*c*). Note the quantitative similarity of the curves for the 1/50th scale contrast and that of the Born approximation, and how the larger contrast scatterer produces much more spatial variation.

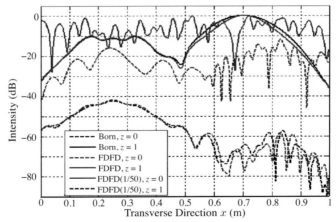

Figure 8.2-6   Log magnitudes of scattered fields on left side ($z = 0$, dashed curves) and right side ($z = 1$, solid curves) of the computational lattice, normalized to maximum scattered field value for each case: Born approximation, FDFD model, and FDFD model applied to dielectric constant contrast reduced to 1/50th of original values.

▶ Problems 8.2-1–8.2-4

B. Finite Element Method (FEM)

Like the FD method, the FEM is based on dividing the coordinate space into an array of small cells. However, in the FEM, the cells (elements) need not be of identical size or shape. In the 2D geometry, nonuniform triangular or general quadrilateral cells may be used, and in the 3D geometry, tetrahedral or hexahedral (bricks without parallel faces) cells may be used. Figure 8.2-7 illustrates the kind of nonuniform triangular sampling that is used in the FEM.

Figure 8.2-7   Nonuniform elements of the FEM.

   Another feature of the FEM is that the field $U(x, y)$ (in the 2D case) or $U(x, y, z)$ (in the 3D case) within each element is approximated by simple functions of the coordinates, such as linear functions, and represented by a few coefficients to be determined as the problem is solved.

   Since the sampling is not necessarily uniform it is not possible to replace the field partial differential equations with their discrete versions, as is done in the FD method. Instead, the differential equation is formulated in terms of a functional, whose minimum provides the solution under the boundary condition. This type of formulation, known as the **variational principle**, is a third feature of the FEM. For example, the solution of the Helmholtz equation $[\nabla^2 + k^2]U = 0$ is obtained by minimization of the functional

$$F(U) = \frac{1}{2} \iint \left[|\nabla U|^2 - (kU)^2 \right] \mathrm{d}S \qquad (8.2\text{-}21)$$

over the area of each cell. Implemented at each element, this minimization provides the unknown coefficients describing the field, but since the elements share boundaries, we end up with a set of coupled linear algebraic equations that are solved for the entire set of coefficients by use of matrix methods. This provides the final approximate solution.

   The major advantage of the FEM over FD is better fitting of triangular or free-form quadrilateral cells to complex geometries, compared with squares or rectangles. Diagonal and curved contours are easily and accurately broken into FEM cell shapes without staircase effects. Also, the regions within the computational domain that have relatively slowly spatially varying fields could have larger elements, as indicated at the upper right and lower left portions of Fig. 8.2-7. As a result, the FEM cells can often be chosen to be larger than FD grid cells, which in turn reduces the required number of cells for the entire region. In addition, since the functional dependence of the field within the elements can be specified as being linear or of higher order, the accuracy of the discretized approximation in the FEM can be chosen to be higher than for the FD method. Exterior boundary conditions can be handled by use of ABC, including PML methods as in the FD method.

Specification of the elements.   The most challenging aspect of the FEM is the specification of the elements and how they connect to one another. In Fig. 8.2-8, we consider, as an example, a 2D geometry with triangular elements. The object space is first sampled with N points: $(x_i, y_i), i = 1, \ldots, N$, that are joined with line segments in such a manner to avoid obtuse triangles. The triangles are labeled by the Roman numerals

I, II, III. Each triangle is associated with three points, for example the three corners of triangle I have coordinates $(x_a^I, y_a^I), (x_b^I, y_b^I), (x_c^I, y_c^I)$, with appropriate bookkeeping between the local (e.g., a, b, c, and I, II, III) and global coordinates (e.g., $i = 1, 2, 3$), as indicated in Fig. 8.2-8.

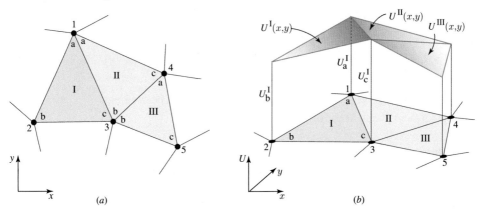

Figure 8.2-8 (a) Number convention for a simple triangular mesh. (b) Approximation of the solution by a linear function of x and y within each mesh.

Approximation of the field within each element.   The field within the area of each triangle is approximated, for example, by the linear function

$$U^I(x, y) = p^I + q^I x + r^I y,$$

where the coefficients p^I, q^I, r^I depend on the field values at the nodes $U_i = U(x_i, y_i)$ and the position of the nodes (x_i, y_i). It can be verified by inspection that in terms of the three local field values U_a^I, U_b^I, U_c^I, and the coordinates of the vertices of that triangle, the field at any point within the triangle is given by:

$$U^I(x, y) = p_a U_a^I + p_b U_b^I + p_c U_b^I, \tag{8.2-22}$$

where

$$p_a = \frac{1}{2A} [(x_b y_c - x_c y_b) + (y_b - y_c)x + (x_c - x_b)y]$$

$$p_b = \frac{1}{2A} [(x_c y_a - x_a y_c) + (y_c - y_a)x + (x_a - x_c)y] \tag{8.2-23}$$

$$p_c = \frac{1}{2A} [(x_a y_b - x_b y_a) + (y_a - y_b)x + (x_b - x_a)y],$$

and

$$A = \frac{1}{2} [(x_b - x_a)(y_c - y_a) + (x_a - x_c)(y_b - y_a)] \tag{8.2-24}$$

is the area of the triangle. For convenience, the triangle index I has been suppressed from the coordinates in (8.2-23) and (8.2-24). As an example, when $(x, y) = (x_a, y_a)$, p_b and p_c become zero, and $p_a = 1$.

Equations (8.2-22) and (8.2-23) therefore approximate the field $U^I(x, y)$ within the cell as a linear function of x and y with three unknown coefficients U_a^I, U_b^I, and U_c^I, usually expressed as a vector $\mathbf{U}^I$ with elements $\{U_a^I, \; U_b^I, \; U_c^I\}$. Differential and integral operations can now be performed on the field, and because of the linear dependence, these operations are relatively simple.

The Functional.   Substituting (8.2-22) and (8.2-23) in the expression (8.2-21) for the Helmholtz functional and evaluating the integral, we obtain

$$F(\mathbf{U}) = \tfrac{1}{2}\,\mathbf{U}^{\mathrm{I^T}}\left(\mathbf{C}^{\mathrm{I}} - k^2 \mathbf{P}^{\mathrm{I}}\right)\mathbf{U}^{\mathrm{I}}, \qquad (8.2\text{-}25)$$

where $\mathbf{C}^{\mathrm{I}}$ and P^{I} are 3×3 symmetric matrices of known elements:

$$C_{\alpha\beta}^{\mathrm{I}} = \iint \nabla p_\alpha \cdot \nabla p_\beta \, \mathrm{d}S, \quad P_{\alpha\beta}^{\mathrm{I}} = \iint p_\alpha p_\beta \, \mathrm{d}S, \quad (\alpha, \beta) = \mathrm{a, b, c}.$$

For example, $C_{\mathrm{aa}}^{\mathrm{I}} = \left[(y_{\mathrm{b}} - y_{\mathrm{c}})^2 + (x_{\mathrm{c}} - x_{\mathrm{b}})^2\right]/4A$. The elements $P_{\alpha\beta}^{\mathrm{I}}$ are equal to $A/12$ for $\alpha \neq \beta$ and $A/6$ for $\alpha = \beta$.

Combining elements.   The one remaining difficult aspect of the FEM is to combine the contributions of the operations performed across each element (triangle) with those of all other elements. The field value at a given node must satisfy the equations for every triangle that shares a vertex at that node. For example, for the geometry of Fig. 8.2-8, $U_{\mathrm{a}}^{\mathrm{I}} = U_{\mathrm{a}}^{\mathrm{II}}, U_{\mathrm{c}}^{\mathrm{I}} = U_{\mathrm{b}}^{\mathrm{II}} = U_{\mathrm{b}}^{\mathrm{III}}$, and $U_{\mathrm{c}}^{\mathrm{II}} = U_{\mathrm{a}}^{\mathrm{III}}$, so that there are five unique unknown field values, which can be assembled as a new vector $\mathbf{U}'$ of elements $\{U_{\mathrm{a}}^{\mathrm{I}},\ U_{\mathrm{b}}^{\mathrm{I}},\ U_{\mathrm{c}}^{\mathrm{I}},\ U_{\mathrm{c}}^{\mathrm{II}},\ U_{\mathrm{c}}^{\mathrm{III}}\}$. When the three equations (8.2-23), one for each triangle, are combined and the common field values are collected, the functional becomes

$$F(\mathbf{U}') = \tfrac{1}{2}\,\mathbf{U}'^{\mathrm{T}}(\mathbf{C}' - k^2 \mathbf{P}')\mathbf{U}'. \qquad (8.2\text{-}26)$$

The extended coefficient matrix $\mathbf{C}'$ is determined by considering the association between each pair of nodes in terms of the coefficient matrix elements local to each triangle, with two local coefficients added when a triangle edge is shared by two triangles, or with three coefficients added for the case of node 3, which is a vertex for three triangles. This gives

$$\mathbf{C}' = \begin{bmatrix} C_{\mathrm{aa}}^{\mathrm{I}} + C_{\mathrm{aa}}^{\mathrm{II}} & C_{\mathrm{ab}}^{\mathrm{I}} & C_{\mathrm{ac}}^{\mathrm{I}} + C_{\mathrm{ab}}^{\mathrm{II}} & C_{\mathrm{ac}}^{\mathrm{II}} & 0 \\ C_{\mathrm{ab}}^{\mathrm{I}} & C_{\mathrm{bb}}^{\mathrm{I}} & C_{\mathrm{bc}}^{\mathrm{I}} & 0 & 0 \\ C_{\mathrm{ac}}^{\mathrm{I}} + C_{\mathrm{ab}}^{\mathrm{II}} & C_{\mathrm{bc}}^{\mathrm{I}} & C_{\mathrm{cc}}^{\mathrm{I}} + C_{\mathrm{bb}}^{\mathrm{II}} + C_{\mathrm{bb}}^{\mathrm{III}} & C_{\mathrm{bc}}^{\mathrm{II}} + C_{\mathrm{ab}}^{\mathrm{III}} & C_{\mathrm{bc}}^{\mathrm{III}} \\ C_{\mathrm{ac}}^{\mathrm{II}} & 0 & C_{\mathrm{bc}}^{\mathrm{II}} + C_{\mathrm{ab}}^{\mathrm{III}} & C_{\mathrm{cc}}^{\mathrm{II}} + C_{\mathrm{aa}}^{\mathrm{III}} & C_{\mathrm{ac}}^{\mathrm{III}} \\ 0 & 0 & C_{\mathrm{bc}}^{\mathrm{III}} & C_{\mathrm{ac}}^{\mathrm{III}} & C_{\mathrm{cc}}^{\mathrm{III}} \end{bmatrix}$$

and similarly for $\mathbf{P}'$. Both 5×5 matrices are symmetric and the 25 elements contain only 12 unique nonzero elements on and above the principal diagonal, seven (of different indices) of which are from the seven segments making up the triangles of Fig. 8.2-8, and five along the principal diagonal (with repeated indices) from the vertices. The 25 elements comprise a total of 27 local coefficients: nine for each triangle.

Minimization and solution.   The final step in the FEM procedure requires minimizing the function $F(\mathbf{U}')$. This is done by setting each derivative $\partial F/\partial U_i' = 0$, for each $i = 1, \ldots, N$. The resulting matrix equation,

$$(\mathbf{C}' - k^2 \mathbf{P}')\mathbf{U}' = 0,$$

involves a dense but square $N \times N$ matrix, which is readily solvable for the unknown field values U_i'.

8.3 Integral Methods

When objects buried in layered media with extended homogeneous regions are imaged, it is often not efficient to work with the differential field equations throughout the entire space. One can instead use analytical solutions that are applicable for each of the homogeneous regions and relate the solutions by use of appropriate boundary conditions. Since these analytical solutions are expressed in integral form, such approaches to computational simulation are called *integral methods*. For scattering problems involving piecewise homogeneous dielectric or acoustic media, where the scattering surfaces take up a small percentage of the problem space, integral methods are often superior to differential methods.

We have already seen a simple example of computational simulation using an integral approach. In the Born approximation described in Sec. 2.2C, the object is regarded as a small perturbation in material properties of the homogeneous background. Excited by the incident wave, these perturbations generate virtual sources that radiate secondary spherical waves at each point encompassing a scatterer. The scattered field $U(\mathbf{r})$ is therefore related to the source distribution $s(\mathbf{r})$ by the familiar linear integral relation [see (2.2-33)],

$$U(\mathbf{r}) = \int s(\mathbf{r}') \frac{e^{-jk|\mathbf{r}-\mathbf{r}'|}}{4\pi |\mathbf{r} - \mathbf{r}'|} \, d\mathbf{r}'. \tag{8.3-1}$$

The source $s(\mathbf{r})$ is approximated as being proportional to the incident wave $U_0(\mathbf{r})$ and to the perturbation $k_s^2(\mathbf{r}) - k^2$, where $k_s(\mathbf{r})$ and k are the wavenumbers of the object and the background, respectively. Discretization of linear integral equations of this type was described in Sec. 5.1. In this section, we describe a similar approach appropriate for piecewise homogeneous media with multiple boundaries. The assumption of weak scattering, which is necessary for the Born approximation is not necessary here.

A. Equivalence Theorem Formulation of Scattering

For a medium made of two or more homogeneous regions, scattering occurs at the boundaries and is mediated by sources created on these surfaces. Each point source radiates a spherical wave (or a cylindrical wave in the 2D case) and these secondary waves are added together to produce the scattered field. The sources are distributed in such a way as to maintain all the boundary conditions. We rely on the equivalence theorem (see Sec. 2.1A), whereby the field on one side of a boundary (*inside*) is replaced with sources at the boundary that radiate into the other side of the boundary (*outside*) in a manner such that all boundary conditions are met. For simplicity, the description in this section is limited to an introductory scalar formulation of the problem; a full vector formulation is necessary for electromagnetic problems. Here, the scalar wavefunction denotes the electric or magnetic fields and the surface sources denote electric and/or magnetic surface currents.[5]

A full formulation of the equivalence theorem must ensure that the field inside the boundary is nulled. This is accomplished by using a second surface source $p_{eq}(\mathbf{r})$. The result is a second equivalence theorem whereby the field is expressed generically by

---

[5]For more general details, see W. C. Chew, *Waves and Fields in Inhomogeneous Media*, IEEE, 1995. For applications to subsurface imaging, see M. El-Shenawee, C. Rappaport, E. Miller, and M. Silevitch, 3-D subsurface analysis of electromagnetic scattering from penetrable/PEC objects buried under rough surfaces: Application of the steepest descent fast multipole multilevel (SDFMM), *IEEE Transactions on Geoscience and Remote Sensing*, Vol. 39, pp. 1174–1182, 2001.

the surface integrals

$$U(\mathbf{r}) = \int_{S} s_{eq}(\mathbf{r}') \frac{e^{-jk|\mathbf{r}-\mathbf{r}'|}}{4\pi|\mathbf{r}-\mathbf{r}'|} d\mathbf{r}' + \int_{S} p_{eq}(\mathbf{r}') \nabla\left(\frac{e^{-jk|\mathbf{r}-\mathbf{r}'|}}{4\pi|\mathbf{r}-\mathbf{r}'|}\right) \cdot \hat{\mathbf{n}}' \, d\mathbf{r}', \qquad (8.3\text{-}2)$$

where $\hat{\mathbf{n}}'$ is a unit vector along the outward normal to the boundary surface S. The equivalent sources p_{eq} and s_{eq} are related to the field $U(\mathbf{r}')$ at the surface by

$$p_{eq}(\mathbf{r}') = U(\mathbf{r}'), \qquad s_{eq}(\mathbf{r}') = \nabla U(\mathbf{r}') \cdot \hat{\mathbf{n}}', \qquad \mathbf{r}' \in S, \qquad (8.3\text{-}3)$$

where $\nabla U \cdot \hat{\mathbf{n}}'$ is the normal component of the gradient of the field U at the surface S. The gradient in equation (8.3-2) can be computed by the formula

$$\nabla\left(\frac{e^{-jk|\mathbf{r}-\mathbf{r}'|}}{4\pi|\mathbf{r}-\mathbf{r}'|}\right) = -\frac{\mathbf{r}-\mathbf{r}'}{|\mathbf{r}-\mathbf{r}'|}\left(jk + \frac{1}{|\mathbf{r}-\mathbf{r}'|}\right)\frac{e^{-jk|\mathbf{r}-\mathbf{r}'|}}{4\pi|\mathbf{r}-\mathbf{r}'|}. \qquad (8.3\text{-}4)$$

Scattering from a Single Boundary.   Consider first a medium with two homogeneous regions $\mathcal{R}_1$ and $\mathcal{R}_2$, characterized by wavenumbers k_1 and k_2, and separated by a boundary surface $\mathcal{B}$, as illustrated in Fig. 8.3-1. An incident field U_0, produced by a known source in region $\mathcal{R}_1$, generates scattered fields in both regions so that the total fields are U_1 and U_2 in regions $\mathcal{R}_1$ and $\mathcal{R}_2$, respectively. This scattering process is mediated by secondary sources distributed on the $\mathcal{B}$ boundary in accordance with the equivalence theorem: sources s and p radiating into the $\mathcal{R}_1$ region, and sources $\tilde{s}$ and $\tilde{p}$ radiating into the $\mathcal{R}_2$ region. The field U_1 is the sum of the incident field U_0 and the field radiated by the secondary sources s and p, while U_2 is the field radiated solely by the secondary sources $\tilde{s}$ and $\tilde{p}$, so that

$$U_1(\mathbf{r}) = U_0(\mathbf{r}) + \int_{\mathcal{B}} s(\mathbf{r}') \frac{e^{-jk_1|\mathbf{r}-\mathbf{r}'|}}{4\pi|\mathbf{r}-\mathbf{r}'|} d\mathbf{r}' + \int_{\mathcal{B}} p(\mathbf{r}') \nabla\left(\frac{e^{-jk_1|\mathbf{r}-\mathbf{r}'|}}{4\pi|\mathbf{r}-\mathbf{r}'|}\right) \cdot \hat{\mathbf{n}}_1' \, d\mathbf{r}', \qquad \mathbf{r} \in \mathcal{R}_1$$

$$(8.3\text{-}5)$$

$$U_2(\mathbf{r}) = \int_{\mathcal{B}} \tilde{s}(\mathbf{r}') \frac{e^{-jk_2|\mathbf{r}-\mathbf{r}'|}}{4\pi|\mathbf{r}-\mathbf{r}'|} d\mathbf{r}' + \int_{\mathcal{B}} \tilde{p}(\mathbf{r}') \nabla\left(\frac{e^{-jk_2|\mathbf{r}-\mathbf{r}'|}}{4\pi|\mathbf{r}-\mathbf{r}'|}\right) \cdot \hat{\mathbf{n}}_2' \, d\mathbf{r}', \quad \mathbf{r} \in \mathcal{R}_2. \quad (8.3\text{-}6)$$

The sources are related to the total fields at the boundary by

$$p(\mathbf{r}') = U_1(\mathbf{r}'), \quad s = \nabla' U_1(\mathbf{r}') \cdot \hat{\mathbf{n}}_1'; \qquad \tilde{p} = U_2(\mathbf{r}'), \quad \tilde{s} = \nabla' U_2(\mathbf{r}') \cdot \hat{\mathbf{n}}_2',$$

where $\hat{\mathbf{n}}_1'$ and $\hat{\mathbf{n}}_2' = -\hat{\mathbf{n}}_1'$ are the unit normal vectors pointing to the region $\mathcal{R}_1$ and $\mathcal{R}_2$, respectively.

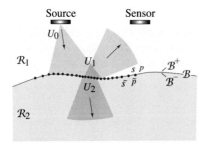

Figure 8.3-1   Scattering from a single boundary.

Equations (8.3-5) and (8.3-6) may be written in the compact form:

$$U_1(\mathbf{r}) = U_0(\mathbf{r}) + s(\mathbf{r}) \otimes h_{s1}(\mathbf{r}) + p(\mathbf{r}) \otimes h_{p1}(\mathbf{r}), \quad \mathbf{r} \in R_1 \qquad (8.3\text{-}7)$$

$$U_2(\mathbf{r}) = \qquad\quad -\tilde{s}(\mathbf{r}) \otimes h_{s2}(\mathbf{r}) - \tilde{p}(\mathbf{r}) \otimes h_{p2}(\mathbf{r}), \quad \mathbf{r} \in R_2, \qquad (8.3\text{-}8)$$

where

$$h_{s1}(r) = \exp(-jk_1 r)/4\pi r, \quad h_{p1}(r) = \nabla h_{s1}(r) \cdot \hat{\mathbf{n}}_1',$$

$$h_{s2}(r) = \exp(-jk_2 r)/4\pi r, \quad h_{p2}(r) = \nabla h_{s2}(r) \cdot \hat{\mathbf{n}}_1'.$$

We now impose the boundary conditions for points on the two sides of the surface B and the condition $U_1(\mathbf{r}) = U_2(\mathbf{r})$ leads to $p(\mathbf{r}) = \tilde{p}(\mathbf{r})$. The condition $c_1 \nabla' U_1(r') \cdot \hat{\mathbf{n}}_1' = c_2 \nabla' U_2(r') \cdot \hat{\mathbf{n}}_1'$ leads to $c_1 s(\mathbf{r}) = c_2 \tilde{s}(\mathbf{r})$, where $c_1 = \epsilon_1$, $c_2 = \epsilon_2$ for transverse magnetic (TM) waves, and $c_1 = \mu_1$, $c_2 = \mu_2$ for TE waves. The nulling condition requires that the field $U_1(\mathbf{r}) = 0$ for $\mathbf{r} \in R_2$ and $U_2(\mathbf{r}) = 0$ for $\mathbf{r} \in R_1$, so that (8.3-7) and (8.3-8) lead to:

$$U_0(\mathbf{r}) = \qquad -s(\mathbf{r}) \otimes h_{s1}(\mathbf{r}) - p(\mathbf{r}) \otimes h_{p1}(\mathbf{r}), \quad \mathbf{r} \in B^+ \qquad (8.3\text{-}9)$$

$$0 = -c_{12}\, s(\mathbf{r}) \otimes h_{s2}(\mathbf{r}) - p(\mathbf{r}) \otimes h_{p2}(\mathbf{r}), \quad \mathbf{r} \in B^-, \qquad (8.3\text{-}10)$$

where $c_{12} = c_1/c_2$, and where B^+ and B^- are surfaces infinitesimally close to the boundary B in the regions R_1 and R_2, respectively.

The final step is to solve (8.3-9) and (8.3-10) to determine the virtual sources s and p on the boundary B. Once this inverse problem is solved, the field U_1 at the sensor may be readily computed by use of (8.3-7) and the field U_2 below the surface may be computed by direct use of (8.3-8).

Scattering from Two Boundaries. A similar approach may be applied to a subsurface imaging configuration with a single object under a surface, as shown in Fig. 8.3-2. Here, there are three homogeneous regions R_1 (e.g., air), R_2 (e.g., ground), and R_3 (e.g., an object buried underground). The media are characterized by wavenumbers k_1, k_2 and k_3. An incident field U_0 is generated by a source in region R_1 and measured by a sensor also in R_1 (e.g., transmitting and receiving antennas in air).

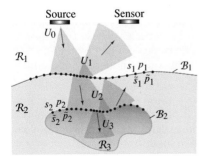

Figure 8.3-2 Scattering from two boundaries.

The fields in the three regions are related to the virtual secondary sources distributed at the surface boundaries B_1 and B_2 by

$$U_1(\mathbf{r}) = U_0(\mathbf{r}) + s_1(\mathbf{r}) \otimes h_{s1}(\mathbf{r}) + p_1(\mathbf{r}) \otimes h_{p1}(\mathbf{r}), \quad \mathbf{r} \in \mathcal{R}_1 \quad (8.3\text{-}11)$$

$$U_2(\mathbf{r}) = \quad -c_{12}s_1(\mathbf{r}) \otimes h_{s2}(\mathbf{r}) - p_1(\mathbf{r}) \otimes h_{p2}(\mathbf{r})$$

$$+ s_2(\mathbf{r}) \otimes h_{s2}(\mathbf{r}) + p_2(\mathbf{r}) \otimes h_{p2}(\mathbf{r}), \quad \mathbf{r} \in \mathcal{R}_2 \quad (8.3\text{-}12)$$

$$U_3(\mathbf{r}) = \quad -c_{23}s_2(\mathbf{r}) \otimes h_{s3}(\mathbf{r}) - p_2(\mathbf{r}) \otimes h_{p3}(\mathbf{r}), \quad \mathbf{r} \in \mathcal{R}_3. \quad (8.3\text{-}13)$$

Each of these fields vanishes outside its own region, e.g., $U_1 = 0$ outside the $\mathcal{R}_1$ region, where we have used the boundary conditions $p_1(\mathbf{r}) = \tilde{p}_1(\mathbf{r})$ and $c_1 s_1(\mathbf{r}) = c_2 \tilde{s}_1(\mathbf{r})$ for points on $\mathcal{B}_1$, and $p_2(\mathbf{r}) = \tilde{p}_2(\mathbf{r})$ and $c_2 s_2(\mathbf{r}) = c_3 \tilde{s}_2(\mathbf{r})$ for points on $\mathcal{B}_2$. Also, $c_{12} = c_1/c_2$ and $c_{23} = c_2/c_3$. Requiring that each of the three fields vanishes outside its own region, e.g., $U_1 = 0$ outside the $\mathcal{R}_1$ region, we obtain the four conditions

$$U_0(\mathbf{r}) = \quad -s_1(\mathbf{r}) \otimes h_{s1}(\mathbf{r}) - p_1(\mathbf{r}) \otimes h_{p1}(\mathbf{r}), \quad \mathbf{r} \in \mathcal{B}_1^- \quad (8.3\text{-}14)$$

$$0 = -c_{12}s_1(\mathbf{r}) \otimes h_{s2}(\mathbf{r}) - p_1(\mathbf{r}) \otimes h_{p2}(\mathbf{r})$$

$$+ s_2(\mathbf{r}) \otimes h_{s2}(\mathbf{r}) + p_2(\mathbf{r}) \otimes h_{p2}(\mathbf{r}), \quad \mathbf{r} \in \mathcal{B}_1^+ \quad (8.3\text{-}15)$$

$$0 = -c_{12}s_1(\mathbf{r}) \otimes h_{s2}(\mathbf{r}) - p_1(\mathbf{r}) \otimes h_{p2}(\mathbf{r})$$

$$+ s_2(\mathbf{r}) \otimes h_{s2}(\mathbf{r}) + p_2(\mathbf{r}) \otimes h_{p2}(\mathbf{r}), \quad \mathbf{r} \in \mathcal{B}_2^- \quad (8.3\text{-}16)$$

$$0 = -c_{23}s_2(\mathbf{r}) \otimes h_{s3}(\mathbf{r}) - p_2(\mathbf{r}) \otimes h_{p3}(\mathbf{r}), \quad \mathbf{r} \in \mathcal{B}_2^+. \quad (8.3\text{-}17)$$

Equations (8.3-14)–(8.3-17) must now be solved to determine the sources s_1, s_2, p_1, and p_2. Once this difficult inverse problem is solved, the field $U_1(r)$ at the sensor may be computed by use of (8.3-11), and the fields at any point in regions R_2 and R_3 may be determined by direct use of (8.3-12) and (8.3-13), respectively.

B. Method of Moments (MoM)

Once the scattering problem is formulated in terms of secondary sources distributed on the boundaries, the remaining barrier is the solution of the boundary-condition integral equation(s) [(8.3-9) and (8.3-10) for the single boundary case or (8.3-14)–(8.3-17) for the double boundary case] to determine these distributions. This may be accomplished by using discretization methods similar to those adopted in Sec. 5.1. A mathematical procedure called the MoM, is based on expanding all continuous functions in terms of bases of orthogonal functions defined on each of the surfaces. These functions are usually nonoverlapping functions centered at sampling points defined by a grid on the surface. To demonstrate this procedure we consider the single-boundary and double-boundary scattering problems in turn.

Single-Boundary Scattering.   To solve (8.3-9) and (8.3-10) we use an orthonormal basis $\phi_n(\mathbf{r})$ defined on the surface boundary $\mathcal{B}$ and expand the unknown secondary distribution $s(\mathbf{r})$ and the known incident field $U_0(\mathbf{r})$ in the form

$$s(\mathbf{r}) = \sum_{n=1}^{N} f_n \phi_n(\mathbf{r}), \qquad p(\mathbf{r}) = \sum_{n=1}^{N} e_n \phi_n(\mathbf{r}), \qquad U_0(\mathbf{r}) = \sum_{n=1}^{N} g_n \phi_n(\mathbf{r}). \quad (8.3\text{-}18)$$

The expansion has been truncated to N terms, where N is sufficiently large. By substitution into (8.3-9) and (8.3-10), and using the fact that $\phi_n(\mathbf{r})$ are orthonormal, we express the boundary conditions (8.3-9) and (8.3-10) in the discrete form:

$$g_m = \sum_{n=1}^{N} A_{mn} f_n + \sum_{n=1}^{N} B_{mn} e_n, \quad m = 1, \ldots N, \tag{8.3-19}$$

$$0 = \sum_{n=1}^{N} C_{mn} f_n + \sum_{n=1}^{N} D_{mn} e_n, \quad m = 1, \ldots N, \tag{8.3-20}$$

where A_{mn}, B_{mn}, C_{mn}, and D_{mn} are the inner products

$$A_{mn} = -\int_{\mathcal{B}} \phi_m(\mathbf{r})[\phi_n(\mathbf{r}) \otimes h_{s1}(\mathbf{r})]d\mathbf{r}, \quad B_{mn} = -\int_{\mathcal{B}} \phi_m(\mathbf{r})[\phi_n(\mathbf{r}) \otimes h_{p1}(\mathbf{r})]d\mathbf{r},$$

$$C_{mn} = -c_{12}\int_{\mathcal{B}} \phi_m(\mathbf{r})[\phi_n(\mathbf{r}) \otimes h_{s2}(\mathbf{r})]d\mathbf{r}, \quad D_{mn} = -\int_{\mathcal{B}} \phi_m(\mathbf{r})[\phi_n(\mathbf{r}) \otimes h_{p2}(\mathbf{r})]d\mathbf{r}.$$

$$\tag{8.3-21}$$

The problem is now represented as a set of linear algebraic equations relating the coefficients f_n and e_n, which represent the unknown source distribution s and p, to the coefficients g_m, which represent the known incident field at the boundary, and the matrix coefficients: A_{mn}, B_{mn}, C_{mn}, and D_{mn}, which represent known parameters of the physical system and the basis functions. Equations (8.3-19) and (8.3-20) may now be expressed in the familiar matrix form

$$\mathbf{Af} + \mathbf{Be} = \mathbf{g}, \tag{8.3-22}$$

$$\mathbf{Cf} + \mathbf{De} = 0. \tag{8.3-23}$$

Finally, the two equations (8.3-22) and (8.3-23) may be cast in terms of a single matrix equation that may be solved for the unknown vector $\mathbf{f}$ by use of the techniques described in Chapter 5.

Double-Boundary Scattering. In this case, a similar discretization procedure may be used to represent the integral equations (8.3-14)–(8.3-17) in matrix form. Using bases functions $\phi_n^{(1)}(\mathbf{r})$ and $\phi_n^{(2)}(\mathbf{r})$, we represent the source distributions $s_1(\mathbf{r})$, $p_1(\mathbf{r})$, $s_2(\mathbf{r})$, and $p_2(\mathbf{r})$ in terms of coefficients $f_n^{(1)}$, $e_n^{(1)}$, $f_n^{(2)}$, and $e_n^{(2)}$, respectively. Likewise, we represent the incident field $U_0(\mathbf{r})$ in the basis $\phi_n^{(1)}(\mathbf{r})$ by the coefficients g_n. The boundary-condition integral equations, derived from equations (8.3-14)–(8.3-17), take the matrix form

$$\mathbf{A}_{11}\mathbf{f}^{(1)} + \mathbf{B}_{11}\mathbf{e}^{(1)} \qquad\qquad\qquad = \mathbf{g} \tag{8.3-24}$$

$$\mathbf{C}_{11}\mathbf{f}^{(1)} + \mathbf{D}_{11}\mathbf{e}^{(1)} + \mathbf{A}_{12}\mathbf{f}^{(2)} + \mathbf{B}_{12}\mathbf{e}^{(2)} = 0 \tag{8.3-25}$$

$$\mathbf{C}_{21}\mathbf{f}^{(1)} + \mathbf{D}_{21}\mathbf{e}^{(1)} + \mathbf{A}_{22}\mathbf{f}^{(2)} + \mathbf{B}_{22}\mathbf{e}^{(2)} = 0 \tag{8.3-26}$$

$$\mathbf{C}_{22}\mathbf{f}^{(2)} + \mathbf{D}_{22}\mathbf{e}^{(2)} = 0, \tag{8.3-27}$$

where $\mathbf{A}$, $\mathbf{B}$, $\mathbf{C}$, and $\mathbf{D}$ are matrices with elements derived from the integral equations, as was done in the single-boundary case. The matrix $\mathbf{A}_{11}$ ($\mathbf{B}_{11}$, $\mathbf{C}_{11}$, $\mathbf{D}_{11}$) represents interactions between source elements on the B_1 surface, and similarly for

A_{22} (B_{22},C_{22},D_{22}), while A_{12} (B_{12},C_{21},D_{21}) represents cross-talk between source elements on the B_1 and B_2 surfaces. Finally, the four equations (8.3-24)–(8.3-27) may be cast in terms of a single matrix equation, a discrete version of the four boundary-condition integral equations that must now be solved for $f^{(1)}$, $e^{(1)}$, $f^{(2)}$, and $e^{(2)}$ by use of matrix inversion techniques, as described in Chapter 5.

EXAMPLE 8.3-1.   *MoM Simulation of Scattering from Multiple Objects.*   Since the MoM computes the scattered fields due to currents induced on interfaces, it cannot be used to model the scattering from the geometry of Fig. 8.2-3. Instead, the continuously varying dielectric ellipse is approximated by an ellipse with uniform dielectric constant (Fig. 8.3-3).

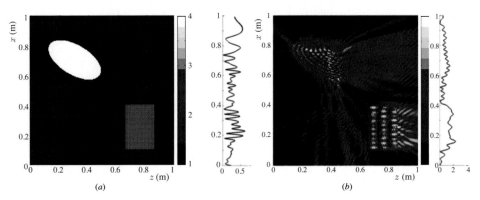

(a)   (b)

Figure 8.3-3   (*a*) Dielectric constant distribution approximating that of Fig. 8.2-3. (*b*) Spatial distribution and normalized left- and right-edge spatial profiles of the magnitude of the field scattered by the uniform elliptical and rectangular dielectric objects, as computed by the MoM.

8.4   Modal Methods

The third major type of numerical methods makes use of combinations of simple exact *solutions* to the partial differential equations of interest (the wave equation, Helmholtz equation, or Maxwell's equations, for example), rather than discrete approximations of the differential or integral equations. For example, a solution of the Helmholtz equation may by expressed as an expansion

$$U(\mathbf{r}) = \sum_{n=-\infty}^{\infty} c_n \phi_n(\mathbf{r}),$$

where $\phi_n(\mathbf{r})$ are known solutions of the Helmholtz equation, called **modes**, and c_n are coefficients. Thus, the continuous function $U(\mathbf{r})$ is represented by an infinite number of discrete coefficients c_n.

In practice, the expansion is truncated to a finite number $2N + 1$ of coefficients so that

$$U(\mathbf{r}) \approx \sum_{n=-N}^{N} c_n \phi_n(\mathbf{r}).$$

Since the modes already satisfy the partial differential equation, their sum also does. The coefficients c_n are determined such that the boundary conditions are matched sufficiently well across every boundary. The greater the number of modes, the better the boundary conditions are satisfied, and the better the numerical model.

The conventional modal method specifies the fields in all space as truncated series of harmonic modes, each series centered at the source or primary scatterer of the problem geometry. For simple, nonlayered problems, this expansion is not too cumbersome. For geometries with multiple layers or other types of regions with piecewise constant dielectric properties, however, the expansion of fields into the modal functions centered outside one region might require unreasonably many terms, each of which may be large, but must be highly accurate to ensure that their small differences are sufficiently precise. Modal methods fail when the geometry contains many scattering objects.

Special Case: Electromagnetic Fields in 2D Cylindrical Geometry. For 2D cylindrical geometry with no variation in the z direction, it is convenient to express the fields in terms of TM modes with components (H_x, H_y, E_z) and TE modes with components (E_x, E_y, H_z). An incident TM field will give rise only to TM scattering components, even if the surface is rough and the object has a noncylindrical cross-section. The TM field components can be expanded in terms of the cylindrical modes $\phi_n(\mathbf{r}) = F_n(k\rho)\exp(jn\phi)$, where (ρ, ϕ) are the cylindrical coordinates and $F_n(k\rho) = J_n(k\rho)$ (cylindrical Bessel function) for interior regions where $\rho \to 0$, or $H_n^{(2)}(k\rho)$ (Hankel function of the second kind) for exterior regions, so that

$$E_z = \lim_{N \to \infty} \sum_{n=-N}^{N} c_n^{\mathrm{TM}} F_n(k\rho)\, \mathrm{e}^{jn\phi} \tag{8.4-1}$$

$$H_x = \lim_{N \to \infty} \frac{1}{2\eta} \sum_{n=-N}^{N} (c_{n-1}^{\mathrm{TM}} + c_{n+1}^{\mathrm{TM}}) F_n(k\rho)\, \mathrm{e}^{jn\phi} \tag{8.4-2}$$

$$H_y = \lim_{N \to \infty} \frac{1}{2j\eta} \sum_{n=-N}^{N} (c_{n-1}^{\mathrm{TM}} - c_{n+1}^{\mathrm{TM}}) F_n(k\rho)\, \mathrm{e}^{jn\phi}. \tag{8.4-3}$$

The TE field components may be similarly written and can be expressed by simple use of duality: $\mathbf{E} \to \mathbf{H}$, $\mathbf{H} \to -\mathbf{E}$, and modal coefficients $c_n^{\mathrm{TM}} \to c_n^{\mathrm{TE}}$, $c_n^{\mathrm{TE}} \to -c_n^{\mathrm{TM}}$, and $\epsilon \leftrightarrow \mu$ (here, c_n^{TM} and c_n^{TE} have units of electric and magnetic field, respectively).

T-Matrix Method. In a multi-region configuration, a modal expansion in terms of a basis in one region may be expressed in terms of another basis function centered within the second region. The coefficients are related by use of matrix methods and the technique is known as the T-matrix method. This popular technique works best for multiple isolated nearly circular or spherical scatterers, especially if they are not too close to one another. It becomes less suitable when scattering objects are separated by many wavelengths, since representing a second remote basis expansion in terms of the globally centered basis requires increasingly many terms.

Semi-Analytic Mode Matching (SAMM) Algorithm. One new approach that overcomes the globally centered approach is the SAMM algorithm, which uses moderately low-order superpositions of cylindrical (2D) or spherical (3D) modes centered at multiple coordinate scattering centers (CSCs), and then optimally matching all boundary conditions numerically on discrete sample points along relevant interfaces in a least-squares sense. Figure 8.4-1 illustrates this approach.

For noncircular scattering objects and rough interfaces, multiple CSCs are placed within the object or along the rough boundary layer. In the most robust version of the

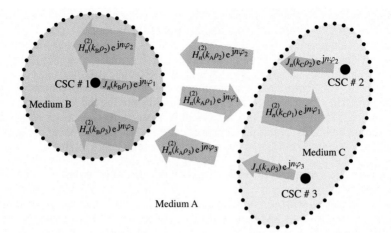

Figure 8.4-1   Application of the SAMM method for two scatterers in a 2D geometry. The circle has a single CSC from which emanate modes as functions of the position vector (ρ_1, ϕ_1). Within the circle (medium B), these modes are Bessel functions with wavenumber k_B, while outside, the modes are Hankel functions with wavenumber k_A in the intervening space (medium A). In the second scatterer (medium C), the modes are also Hankel functions, but with wavenumber k_C. Similarly, the ellipse has two CSCs, each generating modes as a function of (ρ_2, ϕ_2) or (ρ_3, ϕ_3), which are Bessel functions with wavenumber k_C within the ellipse and Hankel functions exterior to it. These modes are matched at points on boundaries of the circle and the ellipse.

SAMM algorithm, increasingly large subsets of the large nonsquare matrix linking the unknown mode coefficients to the boundary conditions are inverted in a fast iterative procedure, efficiently directing the least-squares solution toward its global minimum; matrix coefficients need only be calculated once per frequency.[6]

The SAMM algorithm is a useful near-field algorithm, substantially faster than FDFD and requiring less computational overhead. The SAMM algorithm is most successful with smooth or moderately rough surfaces without sharp discontinuities; sharp metallic target corners, for which fields can become singular, are poorly modeled by SAMM. Smooth surface scattering is particularly well described by SAMM, with accuracy levels exceeding practical FDFD calculations. Rough surface scattering is currently accurate to about 1%, and improving the algorithm is still an area of active research. The ability to quickly find a moderately accurate solution to a realistic scattering problem makes the SAMM algorithm particularly well suited for generating good initial scattering solutions, which may then be refined by other iterative modeling methods. In addition, SAMM can provide low-order scattering behavior that can be used as a fast robust forward model for inversion algorithms, providing estimates of position, size, and contrast of scattering objects in layered media.

EXAMPLE 8.4-1.   *SAMM Simulation of Scattering from Multiple Objects.* The characteristics of the scattering geometry in Fig. 8.2-3 of Example 8.2-1 is particularly challenging to model because of the distributed dielectric constant smoothly varying from 1 to 4 in the elliptical scatterer. Modal methods (and also the MoM) make use of boundary conditions at discrete interfaces to address scattering. Since the continual dielectric variation does not have an interface to compute boundary conditions, this type of scattering problem is better modeled by FDs. In this example, the

---

[6]A. Morgenthaler and C. Rappaport, Scattering from lossy dielectric objects buried beneath randomly rough ground: validating the semi-analytic mode matching algorithm with two-dimensional FDFD, *IEEE Transactions on Geoscience and Remote Sensing*, Vol. 39, pp. 2421–2428, 2001.

SAMM modal method is applied to a two-layer elliptical scatterer shown in Fig. 8.4-2(*a*), which approximates the distributed dielectric geometry in Example 8.2-1. Also shown are the coordinate scattering centers which lead to efficient low-order modal expansions across the region defined by the two scatterers.

The field generated by SAMM with 19 CSCs, 49 modes per CSC, and a total of 900 surface matching points at the boundaries of the rectangle, the outer ellipse, and the inner ellipse is given in Fig. 8.4-2(*b*). This scattered field plot compares with that of Fig. 8.2-3 of Example 8.2-1. Clearly, the smooth dielectric variation produces less scattering by the outer layers of the ellipse, as well as a channeling of field within the ellipse. Also, there appears to be more coupling between the two scatterers and less forward scattering of the rectangle for the smoothly varying ellipse case. One very prominent difference between the two results is the scattering space border fields shown by the line plots on each side. Aside from the frequency of field variation and average amplitude, there is very little correspondence between these two model results.

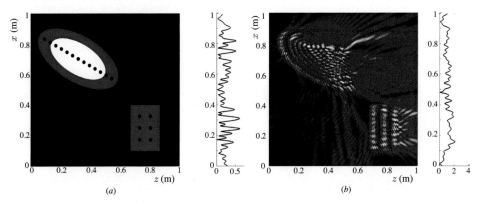

(*a*)   (*b*)

Figure 8.4-2   (*a*) Phantom geometry with two distinct dielectric regions making up the elliptical scatterer. This geometry is a simplified version of the phantom in Example 8.2-1 (Fig. 8.2-3). (*b*) Magnitude of the scattered field generated by SAMM (shown as a brightness image) and normalized spatial profiles of the magnitude of the field at the left and right edges.

▶ Problems 8.4-2, 8.4-3

8.5   Comparison, Limitations, and Validation

Computational modeling tools can be challenging to implement, but they are a necessary aspect in understanding the subtle behavior of wave-based probes interacting with realistic objects that are comparable in size to the probe wavelength. These tools vary in complexity, accuracy, and applicability, but each method requires high-performance computing and significant memory resources. The knowledge of how best to apply and validate them and assess their limitations is important for conducting subsurface sensing and imaging.

A. Comparison

Each of the numerical methods described in earlier sections of this chapter has its advantage and its limitations. It is important to understand the particular costs these limitations present. The trade-offs are usually between accuracy and processing speed and memory. Finer sampling of the computational space requires more points, each of which requires additional manipulation. This section describes some of the important limitations for the principal numerical methods. But first we begin with an example in which various methods are compared.

EXAMPLE 8.5-1. *Comparison of Major Methods.*   To illustrate the difference and similarities of the three principal types of computational models (differential, integral, modal), we apply
the FDFD, MoM, and SAMM methods to the same phantom. We use the phantom with a uniform
elliptical scatterer of dielectric constant 4 and a uniform rectangular scatterer with dielectric constant
2, as shown in Fig. 8.3-3(a). In the FDFD run, the grid has 24 points per wavelength (altogether
800×800 points). In the MoM run, we discretize the surfaces of the scatterers at 1/16th of a
wavelength (1600 current elements). In the SAMM run, 11 CSCs , 21 modes per CSC, and 400
matching points are used. The computed fields are shown in Fig. 8.5-1 with the outer elliptical layer
set to 1.0. Only slight differences are visible among the three plots. The relative computational times
are 20 min, 10 min, and 1.5 min, respectively on a 2GB desktop computer. However, for the SAMM
and MoM computations, most of the CPU time was spent on generating the fields throughout the
space. If instead, the fields are required only on the edges of the computational domain, SAMM and
MoM run more than an order of magnitude faster, taking 20 s and 30 s, respectively.

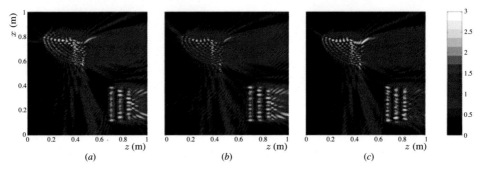

Figure 8.5-1 Scattered field generated by (a) SAMM, (b) MoM, and (c) FDFD for a single
elliptical scatterer with dielectric constant 4 and rectangle with dielectric constant 2.

   For a more visible assessment of the agreement, the field values along the left and right edges for
the three models are compared in Fig. 8.5-2. The curves show the general agreement between the
three methods. While there are some differences, the major peaks and nulls tend to be at the same
locations, and the relative field intensities are rather close.

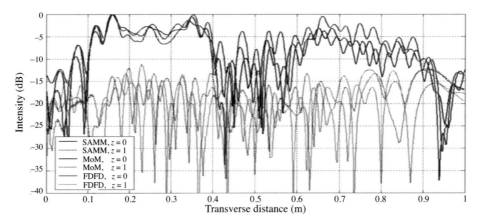

Figure 8.5-2 Scattered field on the left (solid curves) and right (dashed curves) edges of the
computational lattice in Fig. 8.5-1 generated by SAMM (black), MoM (blue), and FDFD (red).

Inadequacy of the Born Approximation.   As demonstrated in the previous examples, the Born approximation can generate scattered field patterns with significant errors for high-contrast scatterers. Many methods have been suggested for the improvement of the Born approximation. Although the Born approximation can be performed iteratively, using better estimates for the total field interacting with the scatterers or numerically improving the Green function based on the previously reconstructed scatterer geometry, this technique fails unless the first iteration is substantively correct.

Comparison of Methods.   Choosing the most suitable computational model depends on the where fields need to be calculated. For example, the field received at a single point that is distant from a scatterer might be best computed using the MoM, while searching for the optimal locations to place sensors to measure scattering features would be best analyzed with an FD method. Modal methods are best for obtaining overall field behavior with the fewest number of discrete modes, and the FEM is best for showing field distributions in the immediate vicinity of a scatterer with complex shape. For instance, detecting the mere presence of an anomaly rather than predicting its extent, or determining position and size of a target rather than imaging its exact shape, might be performed with modal methods requiring significantly less computational resources.

Computational Accuracy.   For subsurface sensing applications, it is often most important to calculate the fields on or near an interface (such as ground or skin surface). As was shown in this chapter, the shapes of the computed scattered field distributions throughout the surrounding space are quite similar for the various methods, but the field profiles on the edges may present large quantitative differences. Fortunately, reconstruction problems generally use many field observation points exterior to the subsurface region, and it is the overall behavior of the fields that establishes the basis for reconstruction. The computational requirements are much more stringent if it is necessary to determine unique spatial features at only a few exterior points. For instance, if one is interested in observing a null in the field pattern, or the ratio of fields at two specific points, much greater care must be used in the numerical algorithms to ensure sufficient modeling accuracy.

▶ Problem 8.5-1

B. Limitations

Sampling Points per Feature

To accurately capture the field configuration in and around fine geometric details, the spatial grid must be fine enough to describe the important details. In particular, wide but thin layers can produce reflections that must not be neglected. Angled and curved surfaces can require significantly greater sampling than rectangular boundaries. Metal and other highly scattering objects must be faithfully rendered to model their strong effects on incident waves.

However, if a thick layer interface has irregularities with a length scale that is small compared with the illuminating wavelength, it can be down-sampled without introducing significant error. Similarly, thin metallic scatterers can be made infinitely thin without having much scattering difference. The former follows from the fact that the phase change of a wave in a small extension (much less than a wavelength) of material is also small: less than the order of the discretization.

For FDTD, it is important to understand that the finite number of points per wavelength also limits the sharpness of waveforms such as transients and impulses. For example, the standard abrupt step turn-on temporal excitation ideally has infinite frequency content, and would lead to artifacts as a wave propagates. To avoid this error, impulses and step waveforms must be softened with smooth transitions. Impulses are often approximated with Gaussian functions and steps with half Gaussians, as shown in Fig. 8.5-3

Figure 8.5-3 Approximations used to avoid high-frequency artifacts (*a*) Gaussian waveform approximating a short rectangular pulse. (*b*) Half-Gaussian waveform at the beginning of a sinusoid as an approximation of a sinusoidal function with a step-function envelope.

Sampling Points per Wavelength

It is important to sample both the computational geometry and the scattering wave finely enough to capture the important scattering features adequately. For each of the methods discussed in this chapter, the field must be discretized in space with enough resolution so that, when the sample points are connected by interpolating functions, the difference between the interpolated and true field values is insignificant. In addition to sampling the field, the geometry variations must be discretized or pixelated so that the interaction with the sampled geometry is sufficiently close to the true geometry. This is of particular concern for the FD methods, which specify points on a rectangular Cartesian grid which may not fit slanted or curved boundaries well. The tradeoff between resolution and computation is an important consideration, since doubling the sampling rate increases the number of computation points by a factor of four (or eight) for 2D (or 3D) geometries, and even greater increases in computations for iterations in time or matrix inversion.

The general rule of thumb is to discretize finite difference, finite element, and moment method signals at 10 or more points per smallest wavelength. The FD error varies as $(kh)^2$, which is inversely proportional to the square of the number of points per wavelength (ppw). The modeling accuracy, therefore, improves dramatically with increased sampling. Figure 8.5-4 shows this improvement and convergence as a function of ppw by displaying the magnitude of the field scattered from a 500 wavelength object, computed by FDFD. Although the general field behavior is predicted well by 10 ppw sampling, 24 ppw sampling is necessary to indicate every pattern null, while one must use 30 ppw for field accuracy to within a few percent of the convergent values generated with 70 ppw. The second figure shows the convergence rate by comparing the normalized sum over all field points of the magnitudes of the differences between n and $n + 1$ ppw, as a function of n.

The variations in scatterer shape do not have to be discretized more finely than the variations in the probing wave unless the scatterer has small, discrete parts or layers, such as fins on slots. In these cases, the small parts must be at least one cell wide. The precision in specifying the part width is less important than modeling the material discontinuity represented by the part. Thus, in modeling microwave interaction with the human body for example, the skin must be modeled with at least one cell width, but unless the wavelength is shorter than 10 skin thicknesses, matching the exact skin thickness is less important.

Matrix Size

The most effective numerical models reduce the governing equations to a system of linear equations, which can be simply represented as a matrix equation. It is clear that

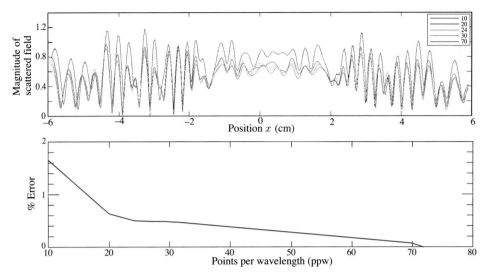

Figure 8.5-4 Simulated scattered field E_z from a large scatterer using an increasing number of sampling points per wavelength (ppw). Top: field distribution for ppw= 10, 20 24, 30, and 70. Bottom: Normalized relative difference (error) between successive values of ppw.

bigger matrices require more computational resources than smaller ones. However, the type of matrix and the way the matrix equation is solved often make more difference in CPU time than its size.

Iterative methods, such as the time-stepping FDTD algorithm, are explicit methods, meaning that the fields determined at a given time result from a simple matrix multiplication of the fields with the transformation matrix. This matrix is the discrete version of the differential equation explicitly describing the time behavior of the fields. Since explicit methods do not require solving simultaneous equations, no matrix inversion is needed. For N field values in a problem, at most N multiplications and N additions would be required to compute each new field value. If the method only considers nearest neighbors, like FDTD, only a handful of operations (three for 2D, five for 3D) are needed for each new field value. This makes the explicit method operation count of order N per time step, or $O(NM)$ for M total time steps.

Explicit methods are computationally inexpensive, but are often limited by issues of stability, which will be discussed subsequently in this section. Implicit methods require solving N simultaneous equations for N field values. Frequency-domain models that specify the fields everywhere in the computational grid simultaneously and self-consistently are implicit. Solving matrix equations of the form $\mathbf{Ax} = \mathbf{b}$ for an unknown array of field values $\mathbf{x}$ can be very computationally expensive. If the matrix $\mathbf{A}$ is dense, with mostly nonzero entries as with MoM, it may take as many as $O(N^3)$ operations to solve for $\mathbf{x}$. Even sparse matrices, such as those appearing in FDFD models with as few as five (or seven for 3D) nonzero values in any row of $\mathbf{A}$, require $O(N^2 \log N)$ operations. Explicit methods do not have stability limitations, but may be prohibitively slow and memory intensive.

Computational Overhead of Boundary Conditions.   The numerical finite difference or finite element implementation of the PML introduces unavoidable errors. These are due to the alternate sampling of electric and magnetic fields on staggered finite grid spacings. Whereas the continuous PML presents no reflection (as long as the PML layer is thick enough to attenuate the waves to insignificance) the PML layer conductivity σ^{PML} in the layer adjacent to the computational space cannot be modeled perfectly smoothly with discrete sampling. To avoid reflection artifacts from the abrupt loss change in the PML, the PML is specified as having multiple layers, with progressively increasing loss. The standard choice is eight one-cell thick layers (or 16 half-cell layers) with an exponential increase in PML conductivity away from the edge given by[7] $\sigma_n^{\text{PML}} = 0.02\,(n/8)^{3.7}/\Delta$, which results in about -100 dB reflection for waves incident at 0 to 60°. For an N^3-point grid, this eight layer PML ABC adds $8\times6N^2+64\times12N+512\times8$ extra computation points. This constitutes a considerable, but necessary, amount of extra computational overhead.

Summary. Computational modeling has benefited greatly from the rapidly advancing performance of computers. The FD methods, in particular, have become practical as gigabyte memory has become commonplace. Further improvements in computing capability will make large-scale, highly accurate models sufficient to replace many physical experiments. The primary limitations to computational experiments will shift from computer resources to faithfully representing the physical characteristics of the sensing problems.

Stability

In passive media (i.e., media without gain), iterative time-domain computations must generate field values that stay finite as time goes to infinity. Unfortunately, in some computational methods, improper specification of parameters can lead to unstable or explosive behavior in finite time, rendering these methods unusable.

The most common stability test was developed by von Neumann. Its fundamental idea is to substitute in the FD equations a field with harmonic spatial dependence and exponential time dependence, $A^{nh_t}e^{-j(k_x ih_x + k_y jh_y + k_z kh_z)}$. The result is a polynomial equation in the amplitude A. Solving for A provides a sense of whether the FD equation will grow uncontrollably with time. If $|A| \leq 1$, the field will remain finite as $n \to \infty$, and the model will be stable. If not, there will be excitations that will lead to field values that amplify numerical noise explosively.

Alternatively, one can write the time dependence of the field in the form z^n, where $z = e^{j\omega h_t}$ is the z-transform variable (where z^{-1} corresponds to a unit time delay). Substituting in the FD equations yields a polynomial equation in powers of z. As before, stability requires that the roots of this polynomial all be within the unit circle.

For nondispersive, loss-free FDTD models, stability is ensured if the ratio $r = (h_t/h_x)v$, called the **Courant number**, is less than the reciprocal of the square root of the number of dimensions of the model, i.e.,

$$r = vh_t/h_x \leq 1/\sqrt{2}, \quad \text{for a 2D square grid}$$

$$r = vh_t/h_x \leq 1/\sqrt{3}, \quad \text{for a 3D cubic grid.}$$

Therefore, the stability condition limits the minimum sample spacing h_x for a time step h_t, and hence sets the smallest features that can be modeled. Also, given a required spatial sampling size, the stability condition establishes a maximum time step h_t. If it is desired to run a simulation for a particular length of time for a fine geometry, this may lead to computations requiring many iterations without much change in each iteration.

For lossy or dispersive media typical of subsurface sensing problems with frequency-dependent relative permittivity $\epsilon'(z)$ and conductivity $\sigma(z)$, the same stability analysis

---

[7]S. Winton and C. Rappaport, Specifying the PML conductivities by considering numerical reflection dependencies, *IEEE Transactions on Antennas and Propagation*, Vol. 48, pp. 1055–1063, 2000.

is used, but the Courant number becomes only part of the condition. For FDTD, the z-transform of the FD wave equation is

$$P(z) = (z-1)\left[(1-z^{-1})\epsilon'(z) + (h_t/\epsilon_0)\sigma(z)\right] + 12r^2 = 0. \qquad (8.5\text{-}1)$$

If $\epsilon'(z)$ and $\sigma(z)$ are rational functions of z, the numerator of $P(z)$ will be a polynomial. Its roots will be either real or in complex conjugate pairs that must lie within the unit circle for stable models. This establishes constraints on the spatial spacings h_x and the time step h_t.

▶ Problems 8.5-2, 8.5-3

C. Validation

The models described in this chapter can be applied to many types of geometries, media, and excitations, but each method has its limitations and domain of validity. Users often accept the results of a simulation as correct, without carefully checking the limitations of the method used. It is unreasonable, of course, to question the basis of each and every result, but validation is possible by use of simple intuitive tests that can identify common problems. Validation can be made by comparison with analytical formulas (if they exist), with other established simulation methods (if available), or with actual measurements, although this is often difficult or impossible since the measurement probes perturb the fields and the media that they sample. It is therefore necessary to assess the domains of validity and the expected errors for each method.

Higher Resolution Tolerance Analysis.   One of the major sources of error for computational methods is improper spatial or temporal resolution. Since one always strives to minimize the number of grid cells to reduce memory and CPU time, one often approaches the limits of model accuracy with too few ppw or geometric feature. This can be tested by running a test with an identical geometry and excitation with higher spatial and/or temporal resolution. For example, observe the results when the space between samples is halved. Do results remain essentially the same? If not, then the original spacing of grid points is too coarse. This test should be repeated until the results stabilize, and then the lower acceptable resolution case can be used with confidence.

The trade-off with higher resolution analysis is that often one starts with the highest spatial sampling and largest problem geometry that can be specified on the available computing platform. For these cases, it is not possible to double the number of points, as this would exceed the maximum problem size. An acceptable alternative is to test a smaller region of the computational space. This does not validate the entire geometry, but does serve to test scattering from particular geometric features of interest.

Oversized Grid Boundary.   The fields reflecting from a terminating boundary can lead to artifacts within the computational grid in scattering problems. Although absorbing boundaries are quite effective in simulating the grid extending to infinity, their effectiveness degrades as the scatterer grows to occupy more of the computational space. Since the fields in the empty space surrounding the scatterer are not important to the scattering analysis, they are often reduced to decrease the number of grid points and conserve memory. The acceptable amount of reduction is hard to determine a priori, but it can be simply tested. As with the higher resolution tolerance, the ABC test is based on increasing the problem size by extending the outer geometry, and comparing the computed fields with the original case. Since the ABC must make outward-going waves appear to continue propagating outward, the waves computed for the extended test space should appear to be the same in the common region, as illustrated in Fig. 8.5-5.

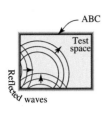

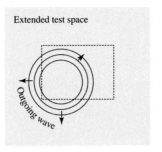

Figure 8.5-5 Absorbing boundary conditions (ABCs).

Fourier Transformation Analysis.   The behavior of time-domain simulations of frequency-dependent (dispersive) media can be validated by Fourier transforming the signal at two points separated by a known distance *d*. As long as the propagation between the two points is directly through a uniform medium and is unaffected by reflections from scatterers, the ratio of the Fourier-transformed signals will correspond to the frequency response of the medium between the two points, which is the propagation factor $\exp(-jkd)$, where k is the propagation constant. For example, for an electromagnetic wave traveling in a medium with frequency-dependent permittivity $\epsilon(\omega)$ and conductivity $\sigma(\omega)$, $k = \omega\sqrt{\mu[\epsilon(\omega) + \sigma(\omega)/j\omega]}$ [see (2.2-2)]. The accuracy of the time-domain model can thus be verified.

Similarly, a frequency-domain simulation can be tested by running a time-domain computation of the given geometry with a single-frequency continuous-wave signal sufficiently long for transients to die out. The result at each point is a cosine function whose maximum value and argument determine the magnitude and phase of the frequency-domain phasor. Consistency of the frequency-domain and time-domain analysis can therefore be established.

8.6   Simulation for Sensing and Imaging

All of the computational methods presented in this chapter model the scattering of a probe wave from a *known* object distribution, i.e., known alpha parameters $\alpha(\mathbf{r})$, e.g., $\epsilon(\mathbf{r})$ and $\sigma(\mathbf{r})$ for an electromagnetic probe. In subsurface sensing and imaging, however, the object distribution is not known, or is generally not completely specified, so that the simulation cannot be implemented, i.e., in these applications the forward model is not known. The problem is actually one of estimating the unknown object distribution from the measured scattered field, under possibly some prior information such as knowledge of a target's shape but not its size or position, or knowledge of the presence of a number of targets but not their relative positions or configuration, etc. How, then, can numerical simulation be used to solve the inversion problem associated with subsurface sensing or imaging?

Numerical Simulation for Detection and Classification.   One obvious approach is to use numerical simulation to compute the scattered field under each and every possible configuration of the target(s), i.e., each forward model, and compare the results with the actual measurement (Fig. 8.6-1). If the purpose of the sensing problem is to detect the presence or absence of an anomaly, then numerical simulation may be used to compute the scattered field distributions in the absence and presence of various configurations of the anomaly. The computed fields under these hypotheses are then compared with the actual measurement in order to reach a decision on the presence or absence of the anomaly. A similar approach can be followed for problems of target classification (see Appendix C for a brief review of principles of detection and classification). This approach is not practical if the object distribution is totally unknown, since the number of possibilities for the forward model are too many to compute. Iterative techniques can then be helpful.

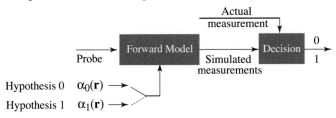

Figure 8.6-1 Numerical simulation for detection.

Iterative Inversion. The inversion problem may be solved iteratively by use of numerical simulation to compute the scattered field for each iteration. An initial guess of the object distribution is used as the forward model and an accurate computational method is used to compute the scattered field, which is compared with the measured scattered field. The error is recorded. The object distribution is then adjusted (subject to any constraints set by the prior information) such that the new computed scattered field is closer to the measured scattered field, i.e., the error is reduced. The process is repeated iteratively, until the error is minimal. The system is illustrated schematically in Fig. 8.6-2.

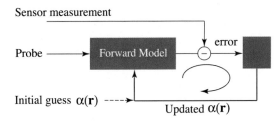

Figure 8.6-2 Iterative approach to inversion.

Further Reading

General

N. A. Kampanis, J. A. Ekaterinaris, and V. Dougalis, *Effective Computational Methods for Wave Propagation*, CRC, 2008.

A. Bondeson, T. Rylander, and P. Ingelström, *Computational Electromagnetics*, Springer, 2005.

L. Sevgi, *Complex Electromagnetic Problems and Numerical Simulation Approaches*, Wiley, 2003.

W. C. Chew, J. Jin, E. Michielssen, and J. Song, *Fast and Efficient Algorithms in Computational Electromagnetics*, Artech, 2000.

M. N. O. Sadiku, *Numerical Techniques in Electromagnetics*, 2nd ed., CRC, 2000.

R. Booton, *Computational Methods for Electromagnetic and Microwaves*, Wiley, 1992.

Finite Difference Methods

A. Taflove and S. C. Hagness, *Computational Electrodynamics: The Finite-Difference Time-Domain Method*, 3rd ed., Artech, 2005.

K. Kunz and R. Luebbers, *The Finite Difference Time Domain Method for Electromagnetics*, CRC, 1993.

A. Taflove and M. Brodwin, Numerical solution of steady state electromagnetic scattering problems using the time-dependent Maxwell's equations, *IEEE Transactions on Microwave Theory and Techniques*, Vol. 23, pp. 623–630, 1975.

K. Yee, Numerical solution of initial boundary value problems involving Maxwell's equations in isotropic media, *IEEE Transactions on Antennas and Propagation* Vol. AP-14, pp. 302–307, 1966.

Finite Element Methods

P. I. Kattan, *MATLAB Guide to Finite Elements: An Interactive Approach*, Springer, 2007.

J. N. Reddy, *An Introduction to the Finite Element Method*, 2nd ed., McGraw-Hill, 2005.

J. Jin, *The Finite Element Method in Electromagnetics*, 2nd ed., Wiley–IEEE, 2002.

G. Pelosi, R. Coccioli, and S. Selleri, *Quick Finite Elements for Electromagnetic Waves*, Artech, 1998.

Integral Methods

K. F. Warnick and W. C. Chew, *Numerical Analysis for Electromagnetic Integral Equations*, Artech, 2008.

Absorbing Boundary Conditions

E. Marengo, C. Rappaport, and E. Miller, Optimum PML ABC conductivity profile in FDFD, *IEEE Transactions on Magnetics*, Vol. 35, pp. 1506–1509, 1999.

S. Gedney, An anisotropic perfectly matched layer-absorbing medium for the truncation of FDTD lattices, *IEEE Transactions on Antennas and Propagation*, Vol. 44, pp. 1630–1639, 1996.

C. Rappaport, Interpreting and improving the PML absorbing boundary condition using anisotropic lossy mapping of space, *IEEE Transactions on Magnetics*, Vol. 32, pp. 968–974, 1996.

G. Mur, Absorbing boundary conditions for the finite-difference approximation of the time-domain electromagnetic field equations, *IEEE Transactions on Electromagnetic Compatibility*, Vol. EMC-23, pp. 377–382, 1981.

B. Engquist and A. Majda, Absorbing boundary conditions for the numerical simulation of waves, *Mathematical Computation*, Vol. 31, pp. 629–651, 1977.

Dispersive Media

T. Kashiwa and I. Fukai, A treatment by the FD-TD method for the dispersive characteristics associated with electronic polarization, *Microwave and Guided Wave Letters*, Vol. 16, pp. 203–205, 1990.

O. Ghandi, A frequency-dependent finite difference time domain formulation for general dispersive media, *IEEE Transactions on Microwave Theory and Techniques*, Vol. 41, pp. 658–665, 1993.

C. Rappaport, S. Wu, and S. Winton, FDTD wave propagation modeling in dispersive soil using a single pole conductivity model, *IEEE Transactions on Magnetics*, Vol. 35, pp. 1542–1545, 1999.

Problems

8.2-1   **FDFD Simulation of Reflection/Transmission at a Single Planar Boundary.** Consider a homogeneous dielectric medium with dielectric constant $\epsilon_r = 4$ in the half space $z > 0$, with the other half ($z < 0$) being free space. For an incident harmonic electromagnetic plane wave traveling in the z direction toward the boundary $z = 0$, the solution is known to be a reflected plane wave with wavenumber k_0 in the region $z < 0$, and a transmitted wave with wavenumber $k_1 = 2k_0$ in the region $z > 0$. The reflection coefficient is $\mathsf{r} = (1 - \sqrt{4})/(1 + \sqrt{4}) = -1/3$ [see (2.2-12)]. Write the 1D FD Maxwell equations for TEM waves with components E_x and H_y and develop an FDFD code for simulating this scattering problem using a 1D geometry of 64 free-space wavelengths, and a sampling rate of 16 points per free-space wavelength. Compare the results obtained by simulation with the known solution.

8.2-2   **FDFD Simulation of Reflection/Transmission at a Planar Slab.** Write an FDFD code for simulating Maxwell's equations in a 1D medium made of a single homogeneous dielectric planar layer with dielectric constant $\epsilon_r = 4$ and width d in free space. The incident electromagnetic wave is a harmonic transverse electromagnetic plane wave traveling in the z

direction, which is orthogonal to the boundaries of the dielectric layer. Take d to be equal to four free-space wavelengths and use a geometry of 64 free-space wavelengths with a sampling rate of 16 points per free-space wavelength.

8.2-3 **FDFD Simulation of 2D Scattering.** The scattering of an electromagnetic wave from a metallic object in air is to be simulated in a 2D configuration. For an FDFD calculation using a geometry of 50×30 wavelengths:

(a) If the geometry is sampled at 20 points per wavelength, how many simultaneous equation need to be solved?

(b) How many nonzero entries are there in each row of the matrix representing these equations?

(c) For the same geometry, if the scatterer were a dielectric with dielectric constant 9, what would the size be of the matrix that maintains a uniform 20 point per wavelength grid spacing? How many more nonzero entries would there be compared with (b)?

8.2-4 **FDTD Simulation of Acoustic Wave.** Write the FD equations corresponding to (2.1-52) and (2.1-52), which describe the dynamics of a pulsed acoustic wave.

8.3-1 **Method of Moments: Single Opaque Boundary.** In this problem the integral methods described in Sec. 8.3 are applied to a wave incident on a single boundary with a medium in which the field must vanish (i.e., the medium is non-penetrable). This property may be mathematically modeled by setting the functions $h_{s2}(\mathbf{r})$ and $h_{p2}(\mathbf{r})$ in (8.3-7)–(8.3-10) to zero.

(a) Write the integral equations (8.3-7) and (8.3-8) and the boundary equations (8.3-9) and (8.3-10) when medium 2 is non-penetrable. Also write the algebraic equations (8.3-19) and (8.3-20), which are discretized version of these equations.

(b) Assuming that the basis functions used to expand the incident wave $U_0(x, y)$ and the source function $s(x, y)$ at the boundary $(y = 0)$ are delta functions located at N points $x_1, \ldots, x_N$. As a simple demonstration, take $N = 4$ and $x_1 = -3\Delta/2$, $x_2 = -\Delta/2$, $x_3 = \Delta/2$, $x_4 = 3\Delta/2$, where $\Delta = \lambda/20$ and λ is the wavelength in the upper medium. Show that the coefficients A_{mn} in (8.3-19) are given by $A_{mn} = \exp(-j2\pi|x_m - x_n|)/(4\pi|x_m - x_n|)$. Since A_{mn} is infinite when $m = n$, in order to avoid this singular behavior use the approximation $A_{mn} = \exp(-j\Delta/2)/(4\pi\Delta/2)$.

(c) Solve the matrix equation $\mathbf{A}\mathbf{f} = \mathbf{g}$ for the vector $\mathbf{f}$ of the source coefficients (use the Matlab function `inv(A)`) and compute the magnitude and phase of the scattered field $U_1(x, y)$ at the points $(x, y) = (0, 1)$ and $(x, y) = (1, 1)$. Comment on your results.

8.4-1 **SAMM Simulation.** In the 2D SAMM algorithm, any field $E(\rho, \phi)$ is expressed in terms of a modal expansion (8.4-1) in terms of functions $F_n(k\rho)$, which may be one of the four special functions $J_n(k\rho)$, $Y_n(k\rho)$, $H_n^{(1)}(k\rho)$, and $H_n^{(2)}(k\rho)$, corresponding to Bessel, Neumann, Hankel functions of the first kind and Hankel functions of the second kind. These functions may be thought of as cylindrical analogs of the harmonic functions $\cos(n\theta)$, $\sin(n\theta)$, $\exp(jn\theta)$, and $\exp(-jn\theta)$.

(a) Which are the functions that are physically appropriate for different regions of the two-boundaries scattering configuration? How many from the set are sufficient to construct any field?

(b) In a realistic simulation, the infinite expansion in (8.4-1) must be truncated such that $|n| \leq N$, where N is the truncation limit. How many modes are needed if $N = 9$?

8.4-2 **SAMM Simulation.** A problem easily solved by the SAMM algorithm is the case of a dielectric object placed within a half space of a different dielectric. It turns out to be very useful to put CSCs at both the center of the object and at an image location as much above the ground plane as the object is buried below, as in Fig. 8.4-1. Describe what modes could be used in each of the three regions of Fig. 8.4-1 originating at CSC-1 and CSC-2.

8.4-3 **3D Modal Expansion and SAMM Algorithm.** The modal expansions described in Sec. 8.4 for the 2D case may be generalized to the 3D configuration. Here, the modes are more complicated but the general ideas still apply. Using a spherical coordinates (r, θ, ϕ), spherical Bessel functions $F_n(kr)$ and Legendre polynomials $P_n^m(\cos \theta)$ make up the modal expansions such that each field component is given by

$$E(\rho, \phi) = \lim_{N \to \infty} \sum_{n=1}^{N} \sum_{m=-n}^{n} c_{nm} F_n(k\rho) P_n^m(\cos\theta) e^{jm\phi},$$

where now two mode indices (n, m) are used. If the truncation limit is $N = 4$, what is the maximum number of modes needed for one "mode family," where a mode family is defined as the set of modes originating from a single CSC and located within a specific dielectric region?

8.5-1   **Selection of Computational Model.** For the following sensing problems determine the most suitable computational model to analyze wave propagation and scattering and justify your choice:

(a) A single uniform dielectric elliptical void of air in a uniform dielectric background.

(b) A metal object within the body surrounded by large organs with relatively smooth boundaries.

(c) A nonmetallic land mine buried in soil with a rough surface and with many rocks.

(d) An annular shaped uniform dielectric object 200 wavelengths from an antenna.

(e) A container of material with a continuously varying moisture content.

8.5-2   **Stability of FDTD Simulation.** It is necessary to sample a particular geometry in material with dielectric constant 25 at 1 mm steps.

(a) Will a wave with wavelength 15 mm in air be suitably represented at this scale of sampling?

(b) If the spectral distribution of the probe pulse extends from 1 GHz to 10 GHz, what is the best time step h_t to use to ensure stablity for all frequencies?

8.5-3   **Resolution and Stability of FDTD Simulation.** A ground-penetrating radar is used to probe a pair of targets buried in soil with complex dielectric constant $6.25(1 - j0.03)$. The probe is a Gaussian pulse modulated at 3 GHz and the scattered wave is measured.

(a) How far apart must the targets be in order to be resolved (one-half a wavelength in soil)?

(b) If the field is sampled at 10 points per wavelength in soil, what is the maximum time step possible for an FDTD model of this wave propagation to be stable?

(c) For grid spacing of part (b), what would the step size be as a fraction of a wavelength in air? Would the FDTD computation still be stable in air?

(d) If instead the time step is 10 ps, what is the closest distance between the targets (i.e., smallest space step) for which a stable FDTD model can indicate separate targets, but for which it would not be able to resolve them?

Design of Subsurface Imaging Systems

The basic concepts and methods of subsurface imaging were introduced in previous chapters, starting with the acquisition of information by use of localized or tomographic probes (Chapters 3 and 4) of single or multiple wavelengths (Chapter 6), and including inversion methods for estimating (mapping) the spatial distribution of the sensed parameter(s) (Chapter 5). Applications other than mapping included image classification (Chapter 6), and change detection (Chapter 7).

In this chapter, we revisit these topics with the goal of developing a set of guidelines for systematically designing subsurface imaging systems suitable for any new application. The optimization involved in the design process naturally depends on the ultimate goal, be it imagery, target detection, or object classification. Some common attributes are, of course, applicable to all of these different tasks. For example, the ability to resolve details of an object's shape and structure, which is necessary for good imagery, may also be useful for target detection, since it helps discriminate the target from the surrounding clutter. In other situations, however, high spatial resolution may be unnecessary, or even undesirable, for target detection if the target is recognized totally on the basis of a spectral signature that is distinguishable from the clutter's. The end result of this process is a working system for the task at hand.

Two case studies of subsurface detection problems are presented in some detail as examples of the use of these general guidelines: **humanitarian demining** and **breast cancer detection**. Both of these deal with target detection problems that are important unsolved global problems with the potential of a huge payoff in the improvement of human health and safety. Although both of these problems are presently the subject of intense research, no comprehensive solutions exist. There is no "right answer" to either, and tradeoffs of various detection techniques must be adopted. These examples offer good lessons that may be applied to other unsolved problems.

9.1   The Design Process

The wide variety of subsurface imaging and sensing systems that exist today have been historically developed to meet the specific demands of the various applications, often without considering the underlying similarities. The principles developed in this chapter provide a systematic approach to dealing with new problems and guidelines for the design process. These guidelines begin with definition of the problem and its specifications, including identification of the imaging or detection/classification task, and proceed to selections of the probe, the imaging configuration, the forward model, and the inversion method. As illustrated schematically in the following diagram, this is followed by an end-to-end system design process through which the various selections are adjusted to enhance the performance measure for the task at hand.

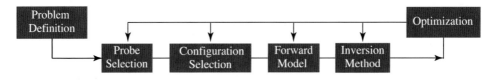

A. Problem Definition

The first step in the design process is to define the sensing and imaging task and gather all of the known information about the problem:

(a) Identify the target and the medium geometries and the materials and their main physical properties, including the relevant *(beta)* (β) parameter(s). Examples of such data are the approximate dimensions and depth of the target below the surface, the expected scale of the spatial details of the target structure, and the expected contrast between the target and the medium.

(b) Identify the specific task to be accomplished. For example:

- Estimate the spatial distribution of a physical parameter β of the object.
- Estimate the target shape or location.
- Detect the presence of a specific target, an anomaly, or a change.
- Classify the target among a library of known classes of objects.

Examples of β parameters of interest to the user:

- Density, pressure, temperature
- Young's modulus of elasticity, bulk modulus and fluid elasticity, viscosity
- Humidity, porosity, pH number, thermal resistivity
- Molecular concentration, ion concentration, chemical composition
- Biological and physiological properties such as blood flow, tissue oxygenation, concentration of hemoglobin, metabolic rates, membrane integrity
- Concentration of extrinsic markers such as dyes, chemical tags, chromophores and fluorophores, and fluorescence protein markers
- Gene expression, cellular differentiation, morphogenesis.

These physical parameters will be measured and analyzed to extract information of interest about the object.

B. Probe Selection

The first consideration in designing the subsurface imaging system is the choice of the probe. This process begins by checking all possible probes that may be used for the task at hand. Table 9.1-1 provides a list of the most popular probes. However, possibilities for passive imaging by detecting emissions from self-luminous objects (e.g., thermal imaging), objects injected by emitting particles or contrast agents, or objects illuminated by natural sources, such as the sun, must also be examined.

Sensitivity to Relevant Physical Parameters. The parameter α, which is to be measured by the selected probe, must be sensitive to the relevant physical parameter β, which is to be mapped or used as the basis for detection or classification. For example, an electrical probe can be used to map the *concentration of water* in a medium since it measures the *electric conductivity*, which is sensitive to the water concentration. If the target is a wet region and the medium is a dry region, then this sensitivity means that the target-to-medium water-content contrast $\Delta\beta$ must translate to conductivity contrast $\Delta\alpha$ that is sufficiently large to be sensed by the detector. If the task is to detect the target, then high contrast between the target and the background is a prerequisite for adequate detection probability.

Adequate Penetration Depth. The next condition is that the probe must be able to penetrate through the medium and reach the target. Additionally, the reflected, scattered, or transmitted wave must retain sufficient power after it travels to the sensor so that it is detectable with sufficient accuracy (i.e., discriminated from noise or from signals generated by clutter objects at the same distance or closer to the surface). Since

Table 9.1-1   Physical parameters *alpha* (α) sensed by probes used in various subsurface imaging technologies

Probe	α Parameters	Imaging System
Mechanical Acoustic	Density, compressibility	Seismic imaging Ultrasonic imaging
Elastic	Stiffness	Elastography
Electrical	Conductivity and permittivity	Electrial impedance tomography (EIT)
Magnetic	Permeability	Electromagnetic induction (EMI)
Radiowave	Permittivity conductivity Density of nuclear spins	Ground penetrating radar (GPR) Magnetic resonance imaging (MRI)
Microwave		Microwave imaging
mm wave		Millimeter wave imaging
THz		Terahertz imaging
Optical	Thermal emittance	Infrared (thermal) imaging
	Absorption coefficient and refractive index	Optical imaging
	Fluorescence rate	Fluorescence scanning microscopy
	Fluorescence lifetime	Fluorescence lifetime imaging
	Diffusion and absorption coefficient	Diffuse optical tomography (DOT)
X-rays	Absorption coefficient Scattering coefficient	Computed tomography (CT) X-ray backscattering
γ-rays	Density of radio nucleides	Nuclear medicine
Particles	Flux of chemical emissions	Chemical sensing
	Flux of nuclear emissions Scattering cross-section	Nuclear medical imaging
	Rate of secondary emissions	Scanning electron microscopy (SEM)

the penetration depth is often sensitive to the wavelength (usually smaller at shorter wavelengths, except near absorption lines), the selection of the appropriate probe must also include selection of the appropriate wavelength or wavelength range. Sources and detectors must also be readily available (at an acceptable cost) at the selected wavelength(s).

Adequate Spatial Resolution.   Probes that satisfy the sensitivity and penetration tests must now be put to the resolution test. The transverse and axial resolution required to resolve the target dimensions, location, or scale of detail must be deliverable by the selected probe. Exact localization can be very important if the target is a tumor to be removed by some surgical remediation. It is essential to the correct mapping of fine structures such as three-dimensional (3D) networks of brain cells. In target detection, acquisition of fine spatial details can be useful in distinguishing the target from the surrounding clutter by shape or texture. Since the maximum spatial resolution is limited by the wavelength in far-field imaging, this sets a condition on acceptable wavelengths. Greater spatial resolution requires shorter wavelength, which often means smaller penetration depth, so that the penetration requirement can come in conflict with the resolution requirement. In these cases, near-field imaging may be able to capture details considerably smaller than the wavelength if the probe can be scanned across the target at standoff distances considerably less than the wavelength. An example of the trade-off between penetration and resolution is illustrated in Fig. 9.1-1. In certain applications, however, spatial resolution may not be necessary. For example, for target

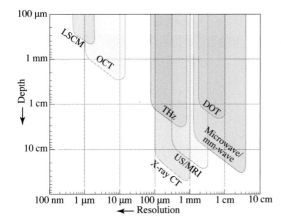

Figure 9.1-1 Example of tradeoff between depth and resolution in tissue imaging: laser scanning confocal microscopy (LSCM), optical coherence tomography (OCT), diffuse optical tomography (DOT), ultrasonic imaging (US), and magnetic resonance imaging (MRI). The shaded areas cover the applicable wavelength ranges and depths.

detection, if the target can be distinguished solely by its spectroscopic signature, all that is needed is adequate *spectral* resolution, which may be provided by hyperspectral imagery (Chapter 6).

Clutter Discrimination.   In applications of target detection, many systems fail not because the probe is insensitive to the target or because the penetration depth is insufficient, but because the subsurface environment contains other objects ("clutter") that cannot be discriminated from a target. Spurious detections of other objects (clutter) in the environment are referred to as *false alarms*. Clutter discrimination is thus an important criterion for probe selection. For example, if the spectral properties of the target and the clutter are different, the wavelength of the probe should be selected to maximize their discrimination.

C. Imaging Configuration

As described in Chapters 3 and 4, two principal configurations may be used for acquisition of the 3D spatial distribution of a subsurface object: localized and tomographic. The use of either of these configurations is dictated primarily by the nature of the probe, particularly the wavelength, and by its interaction with the medium (absorption, reflection, elastic or inelastic scattering, etc.). Various applications of localized and tomographic imaging are listed in Table 9.1-2. Once an imaging configuration is selected, the spatial resolution (both transverse and axial) must be assessed to ensure that the requirements and expectations are met.

Localized Imaging.   Localization is possible if the probe beam and/or the sensed beam can be localized in the transverse and axial directions. As described in Sec. 3.2, this is usually accomplished by use of focused beams or by adopting a gazing apparatus such as an image-forming lens with short depth of focus. Examples are found in optical imaging and microscopy. Axial localization may also be implemented by use of pulsed beams along with detectors that measure the times of arrival of reflections from various locations along the beam, as in radar, sonar, and lidar imaging (Sec. 3.2C). Interferometric techniques may also be used for axial localization (Sec. 3.2D), as in optical reflectometry.

Tomographic Imaging.   As described in Chapter 4, a tomographic system employs multiple beams or waves in a configuration for which each measurement is sensitive to the sum of contributions from points on a line passing through the object, or a surface or volume within the object. The lines, surfaces, or volumes intersect or overlap so that

Table 9.1-2   Localized and tomographic imaging

	Localized Imaging	Tomographic Imaging
Ultrasonic	Sonar	Ultrasonic diffraction tomography (UDT) Photoacoustic tomography (PAT)
Electrical		Electrial resistance tomography (ERT) Electrial impedance tomography (EIT)
Radiowaves Microwaves	Radar	Ground penetrating radar (GPR) Cross-well radar (CWR) Magnetic resonance imaging (MRI)
Optical	Z-scan microscopy Laser scanning confocal microscopy (LSCM) Two-photon confocal microscopy Optial coherence "tomography" (OCT)	Optical diffraction tomography (ODT) Diffuse optical tomography (DOT)
X-rays		Computed tomography (CT)
γ-rays		Single-photon emission CT (SPECT)
Particles	Scanning electron microscopy (SEM)	Positron emission tomography (PET)

each point contributes to multiple measurements. The spatial distribution of the object is reconstructed by computational methods. Measurements from multiple angles of view can be implemented with transmitters and receivers that fully or partially surround the object so that regions that may be occluded in one view can be fully visible in the reconstructed image. Tomography can be especially effective at mapping regions where the value of the measured parameter varies gradually. Such variation is difficult to image in localized imaging systems since reflection or scattering therefrom may be too weak.

The following is a brief summary of principal tomographic configurations:

(i) **Ray Tomography**. If the probe can be shaped into rays whose paths are not altered by the medium, then each ray probes the medium by integrating a local physical property, such as the absorption coefficient or the phase shift (refractive index), along its path. The data at various points of each ray are separated by use of a set of crossing rays. In X-ray CT (Sec. 4.1C), for example, parallel rays pointing along multiple angles within each plane (slice) are used to compute a full two-dimensional (2D) distribution of the absorption coefficient within the plane (slice). The process is repeated for parallel slices to generate the full 3D distribution. Another example is the imaging of *phase-only* targets, i.e., objects that alter only the phase of the wave via a position-dependent refractive index. Phase-imaging tomographic techniques have been demonstrated in optical and acoustic modalities using phase-sensitive detection schemes. Ray tomography can be an effective technique when there are no sizable reflections that can be used for localization by observing time of arrival (as done in ultrasonic and radar imaging).

(ii) **Range Tomography**. Here, a pulsed probe is launched from a transmitter at one point and the strength of the signal received by a receiver at another (or the same) point is measured as a function of the time of arrival, which is proportional to the distance from the transmitter to the scatterer plus the distance from the scatterer to the receiver. For each time of arrival, there are multiple possible paths from the transmitter to the receiver via different scattering points lying on a specific surface. Points of the received temporal profile correspond to contributions from a set of surfaces. Measurements with transmitters and receivers at multiple locations generate data from multiple sets of surfaces and complete the tomographic paradigm. This technique is the basis of GPR (Sec. 4.2).

(iii) **Wave Tomography and Generalized Tomography**. Probes with long wavelength cannot be focused in the form of rays, thin beams, or thin planar slices, so
that only fully distributed tomographic methods can used. Here, multiple sensors
are used to detect the wave generated by each of a set of multiple probes. An
example is the spread of electric currents and fields in conductive media. In EIT
(Sec. 4.5B), 3D images of conductivity and permittivity distributions are acquired
by use of multiple sources of electric current and multiple sensors of electric potential. Another example is optical waves in turbid media. These waves diffuse via
multiple scattering and cannot be localized. Imaging is then accomplished by use
of multiple optical sources and sensors, as in DOT (Sec. 4.5A). A third example
is cross-well radar (CWR), in which radiowaves spread in inhomogeneous media
underground. Sets of antennas placed in ground holes are used as the sources and
sensors.

Placement of Sources and Detectors.   In each of these tomographic methods, the
geometry of the problem dictates the positioning of the sources and detectors, as illustrated by the examples in Fig. 9.1-2. The placement of sources and detectors must
also take account of the position of the target in relation to any obscuring objects. For
example, sources (transmitters) and detectors (receivers) are placed above the surface
in GPR and DOT imaging. A full 360° view is generated in X-ray CT of the torso,
and only a limited angular view, as low as 15°, is used in breast imaging by X-ray
tomosynthesis. Transmitters and receivers may also be placed on opposite sides of the
object, as in cross-well radar.

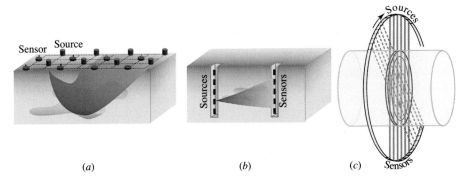

(a)   (b)   (c)   Sensors

Figure 9.1-2 Placement of sources (transmitters) and detectors (receivers) in tomographic
imaging. (a) Above the surface in GPR and DOT imaging. (b) Inside holes on opposite sides, as
in CWR. (c) In a full 360° configuration, as in X-ray CT of the torso.

D. Forward Models

Once the probe and the imaging configurations are selected, the next step is to test the
operation of the system for sample targets and media that capture the important characteristics expected in the real environment. However, before such tests are conducted in
actual experiments using real targets or physical phantoms, it is important to undertake
an analysis and characterization of the system using simulation. This is accomplished
by means of forward modeling – mathematical or numerical simulation of the signals
to be sensed by the detectors for sample targets/media. Forward modeling can be based
on exact or approximate analytical models, or on numerical models (see introduction
to Chapter 8, especially the flow chart in Fig. 8.1-2).

Analytical Models. An exact mathematical model usually takes the form of a set of partial differential equations for the field(s) U expressed in the generic form $\mathcal{O}\{U, \alpha\} = 0$, where $\alpha = \alpha(\mathbf{r})$, the physical parameter of interest, is a position-dependent coefficient also denoted by the symbol f

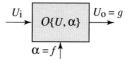

(see Sec. 1.1 and also Sec. 2.3D, which describes propagation in inhomogeneous media). This equation (or equations) is solved with the boundary conditions established by the incident field U_i to determined the field U_o that is detected by the sensors to generate the signal g. The forward model is used to compute g for any given distribution f. Since this relation is nonlinear, an exact analytical solution relating g to f is available only for special simple geometries and under idealized conditions (e.g., planar layered media or homogeneous spherical targets in homogenous media, etc.).

Linearized Approximate Models. Linearizing approxima-tions, such as the Born approximation (Sec 2.2C), lead to analytical solutions in which the sensed signal g is linearly related to $\alpha(\mathbf{r})$, the physical parameter of interest, also denoted by the symbol f. In this case, the imaging process is

completely characterized as a linear system relating g to f. For localized imaging, the system is usually shift invariant and can be characterized by a convolution operation $g = h \otimes f$, where h is a point spread function (see Sec. 3.2A). For tomographic imaging, the linearized model is characterized by a shift-variant linear transformation. For example, in ray tomography (Sec. 4.1) it is represented by the Radon transform $g = \mathcal{R}\{f\}$, and in wave tomography (Sec. 4.3) it is characterized by another linear transformation.

Matrix Models. Whether shift invariant or shift variant, the linearized system can be discretized and modeled as a matrix multiplication $\mathbf{g} = \mathbf{Hf}$, where $\mathbf{H}$ is a matrix whose dimensions, rank, and principal values characterize the imaging system (Sec. 5.1).

Numerical Models. When analytical solutions are not available and linearizing ap-proximations are not appropriate, the only recourse is to use one of the numerical meth-ods described in Chapter 8 to approximate the equations $\mathcal{O}\{U, \alpha\} = 0$, for example by replacing differential equations with finite difference equations. This allows us to compute the fields sensed by the detector, given the incident probe field for any known distribution α. Numerical methods can readily provide a tool for forward modeling of realistic situations, including media with high-contrast inhomogeneities, target/clutter details, and surface roughness.

E. Inversion Method

Inversion is the determination of the position-dependent medium parameter **f** from the measured values of the field **g**. The inversion method depends on whether the forward model is exact, linearized, or numerical.

Exact Models. Inversion of the exact field equations $\mathcal{O}\{U, \alpha\} = 0$ is difficult. Since these equations are nonlinear, exact analytical solutions exist only in a few special cases, and rely on sophisticated mathematical tools (e.g., the D-bar method in EIT).

Linearized Models. For localized imaging systems described by the convolution op-eration, deconvolution techniques can be used for inversion (Sec. 3.3). For tomographic imaging, the measurement is related to the unknown $f(\mathbf{r}) = \alpha(\mathbf{r})$ by a linear integral transformation. In some cases, an analytical expression for the inverse transformation may be available. For example, in ray tomography the forward model is the Radon transform and the inverse system is filtered backprojection (Sec. 4.1B). A similar situation is applicable in wave tomography (Sec. 4.3) and in MRI (Sec. 4.4D).

Matrix Models.   If no exact inverse is available, the problem may be discretized and described in the matrix form $g = Hf$, where $f = \alpha$. As described in Chapter 5, the dimensions and rank of the matrix H determine the level of difficulty of the inversion process – existence, uniqueness, and stability. Inversion techniques based on singular value decomposition (SVD) and other matrix methods are described in Sec. 5.2B. Iterative solutions are also possible, as described in Sec. 5.5.

Numerical Models.   Numerical models can be used to compute the field sensed by the detector, given the field created by the probe, for any known object/medium parameter $\alpha(\mathbf{r})$. Since $\alpha(\mathbf{r})$ is not known, an **iterative inversion** approach can be used, as illustrated in Fig. 9.1-3. Iterative methods using numerical forward models such as finite difference or finite element require enormous computational resources. Nevertheless, with the rapid increases in processing speed and memory size, such approaches are becoming conceivable.

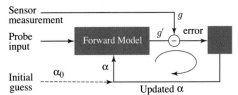

Figure 9.1-3   Iterative inversion: The forward model is used with an initial guess α_0 to compute the signal g', which is compared with the measured signal g to determine the error. An appropriate change in α is made such that the error is reduced. The process is repeated iteratively until the error reaches a minimum.

F. End-to-End System Design and Optimization

The previous elements of the design process – selection of the probe and the imaging configuration, establishment of a forward model, and selection of the inversion method – must now be followed by an assessment and optimization of the overall performance of the system in accomplishing the required task. The optimization process includes changes of the layout geometry, e.g., locations of the sources and sensors, changes of the wavelength(s), or adjustments of the parameters used in the inversion process.

Performance Measures

Imaging.   The performance of an imaging system is measured by the fidelity between the measured image and the true distribution of the object. Many measures of fidelity are described in the literature, the simplest of which is the mean-square error. Two factors are responsible for this error: blur and noise.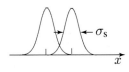

(*a*) **Blur** is determined by the finite width σ_s of the point spread function (PSF). As described in Sec. 3.1B, σ_s sets the **spatial resolution** of the imaging system; two objects separated by a distance smaller than σ_s cannot be distinguished. The Fourier transform of the PSF is the transfer function; its width, which is inversely proportional to σ_s, is indicative of the highest spatial frequency that can be imaged. The shape and width of the PSF is determined by the quality of the components of the imaging system, and is limited by the wavelength. Shorter wavelengths lead to a narrower PSF (higher cutoff frequency of the transfer function), all other things being equal.

(b) **Noise** also limits the image fidelity. The principal source of noise comes from the detector (receiver). A measure of the significance of noise in the measurement process is the **signal-to-noise ratio** (SNR). The noise floor of the detector determines the smallest distinguishable signal and therefore the system's **dynamic range**, which is the ratio of the largest signal that can be measured to the smallest signal that can be detected. Inadequate dynamic range prevents distinguishing an object from one of similar brightness, much the same as inadequate resolution prevents distinguishing an object from another that is too close in space.

Spectral Imaging. A measure of the performance of a spectral imager is the fidelity with which the spectral image is acquired. As described in Sec. 6.2, a spectrometer is used to acquire the spectral distribution at each position of the image. 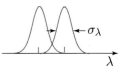 The spectrometer is characterized by the number of channels (bands) L, the wavelength range, and the **spectral resolution** σ_λ, which limits the ability to discriminate two close wavelengths (or frequencies) in order to capture fine spectral features. Two configurations for acquiring the spectral distribution are described in Sec. 6.2. In the multisensor configuration, a broadband probe is used together with multiple narrowband sensors tuned to the various wavelengths. In the multiprobe configuration, a set of probes tuned to multiple wavelengths is used in combination with a broadband sensor. In optical systems operating in the multisensor configuration, the spectral distribution is often converted to a spatial distribution by dispersing the wavelengths with a prism or diffraction grating. The performance of the spectrometer is then determined by the size, density, and sensitivity of the sensor array. In the multiprobe configuration, tunable lasers are used and the performance is limited by the laser spectral width and the wavelength range. The choice of the most appropriate spectrometer depends on the selected probe and the application.

Target Detection. Performance measures of target detection include the **sensitivity** (rate of correct detection P_D) and the **specificity** or selectivity ($1 - P_F$, where P_F is the rate of false alarm) [see Appendix C for an introduction to detection theory]. A high-sensitivity subsurface imaging system must be able to distinguish the target from the surrounding medium almost all the time. This requires a probe that penetrates the medium far enough to reach the target, and generates a response with sufficient contrast to distinguish the target from 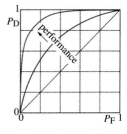 the medium. A high-specificity system must distinguish the target from other objects that may be misconstrued as the target. A term for such irrelevant objects is *clutter*. The inability of a system to distinguish a target from the surrounding clutter is what leads to false alarms. Subsurface detection systems are often unsatisfactory because of excessive false alarm rates, which can be costly in terms of the time and expense of confirmation measurements. Detection systems are characterized by their **receiver operating characteristics (ROC)**. These are plots of the rate of correct detection P_D versus the rate of false alarm P_F, as the detection threshold is varied. If the detection threshold of the system is raised (sensitivity reduced) to reduce the false alarm rate, real target objects go undetected. If the sensitivity is increased to avoid missing any targets, the false alarm rate can increase rapidly until essentially all detections are false alarms. Performance is measured by how closely the system can approximate the ideal of $P_D = 1$ and $P_F = 0$, i.e., operating in the upper left-hand corner of the ROC curve space. If clutter is strong enough that the probability that a target is detected is the same as the probability that a detection event is a false alarm, i.e., $P_D = P_F$ (the 45° diagonal line of the ROC curve), one could do just as well by flipping a coin at each detection opportunity, and the detection system is useless. A superior ROC is achieved by increasing the contrast between the target and the background (to raise P_D) and enhancing discrimination against clutter (to lower P_D). These themes of contrast and clutter discrimination will pervade any discussion of subsurface target detection systems, as we will see in the case studies.

Classification.   For classification tasks, the system design aims at reducing the average classification error, or enhancing the **average probability of correct classification** (see Sec. C.2 of Appendix C). This is accomplished by use of classification features that highlight the distinctions among the classification categories. Classification accuracy will degrade as the class features become more similar (or overlap in the feature space). Here too, rejecting clutter that mimics one of the objects to be classified is one of the prime design considerations.

Other Design Alternatives

If the performance of the overall system, as initially designed and optimized, does not meet the basic requirements or expectations, then major changes, such as use of an alternative configuration or inversion method, or an altogether different probe, must be considered. In this case, the previous design steps must be repeated until a satisfactory result is ultimately obtained.

Multisensor Imaging.   When the performance of a single modality is poor or inadequate for the required task, the use of two or more types of probes should be considered. In detection or classification tasks, an additional modality provides new features that can be used to implement the classification paradigm. For example, in a three-way classification task, one modality may discriminate between classes A and B and between A and C, but not between B and C. Another modality can distinguish between B and C. The two modalities together complete the classification task. If that task is to distinguish A and B in the presence of clutter C, then one modality could be used to distinguish against clutter and the other to separate A from B. Thus, the additional sensing modality can enhance the detectability of the targets and reduce the false alarm rate. Imaging systems may also benefit from the introduction of an additional modality. As described in Sec. 7.5, the measurement of two distributions α_1 and α_2 with two different probes, may help provide an estimate of a desired underlying distribution β with better performance. The application of multimodality in subsurface imaging systems is just beginning, and there are no simple rules for fusion or concurrent optimization of each of the modalities. Nevertheless, it is becoming clear that multimodal imaging will be an important tool for imaging, classification, and target detection since it provides greater clutter rejection (false positive reduction) in many applications.

Simulation and Testing

The final step in end-to-end design and development is assembly and hardware testing. Rigorous simulation of the system, however, can yield performance predictions and establish sensitivity of performance to design parameters, before anything is committed to costly hardware prototyping and testing. The importance of simulation results in performance projections is one of the reasons that modeling is a critical part of the design process. End-to-end system optimization is a goal, not a reality, for almost all current subsurface imaging systems. But to the extent that systems are modified in design and adjusted for optimum performance, the impetus for these design modifications is likely to arise from system simulation.

▶ Problems 9.1-1–9.1-9

9.2   Case Study I: Humanitarian Demining

Landmines are inexpensive and effective weapons used by regular armed forces as well as irregular and insurgent forces. The problem of cleaning up emplaced landmines after a conflict ends is known as humanitarian demining. The scale of this problem is huge. There are more than 200 million undetected landmines, which cause on the order of 8000 civilian casualties annually and render over 1 million acres of arable land unusable. Humanitarian demining has particularly demanding requirements and constraints. Essentially 100% detection and clearance is necessary before an area can be declared safe for civilian resettlement. Demining techniques need to be cost effective, since they are often used in countries with limited resources. However, the problem is not particularly time sensitive, and low-tech methods employing large numbers of lightly trained personnel can be appropriate.

Landmines are made in two types: antivehicle and antipersonnel. Antivehicle mines are larger ($\approx$20 cm in diameter) and heavier (>5 kg), and are typically emplaced deeper underground. They require a larger force to detonate. Anti-personnel mines are designed to be detonated by the weight of a single person or by filamental trip wires. They are smaller ($\approx$5–15 cm in diameter) and lighter (<1 kg) and are emplaced within 5 cm of soil on top, or concealed in grass or foliage.

Problem Definition

The goal of this case study is to develop a subsurface sensing system that detects antipersonnel landmines buried in soil in the presence of clutter, such as small battlefield metal fragments, with the highest probability of detection and the lowest probability of false alarm. The mines are assumed to have circular or square shape of 5–15 cm dimensions and are located at depths of 5–10 cm. They are made of plastic, with some metallic ring pins or fuse caps, and filled with common explosive material.

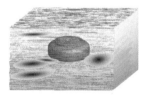

The system may use an external probe to detect the metal pieces of the mine and distinguish them from metallic clutter, such as shell casings and shrapnel, by resolving their shape, size, or emplacement patterns. It may also use passive detection such as "sniffing" vapors from the landmine's explosive filler or detecting emitted infrared radiation exhibiting a temperature distribution different from the surrounding medium.

The sensitivity of the system (the rate of correct detection) must be very high, but the false alarm rate must not be too high since this would make the mine-clearing operation useless. For wide-area screening, the speed at which an area is covered can also be an important performance factor.

The crux of the demining problem is distinguishing the landmine from battlefield and other underground clutter.

Probes

Electromagnetic induction (EMI) metal detectors. Metal landmines can be easily detected by use of metal detectors, which are based on the principle of EMI. An alternating electric current at frequencies of the order of 10–100 kHz (or a pulsed current) generated in a transmitter coil positioned parallel to the ground creates a magnetic field that induces eddy currents in the buried metal. This, in turn, creates its own magnetic field that is detected by a second receiver coil (or the same coil) in the form of an electric potential or electromotive force. If the strength of

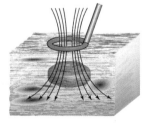

the detected signal exceeds a prespecified threshold, the metal is declared to be present; otherwise, it is assumed to be absent. If appropriately calibrated for the conductivity and magnetic properties of the soil and used by a skilled operator, state-of-the-art EMI metal detectors can successfully detect all metal landmines as well as most plastic landmines with a small amounts of metal in their firing pins or fuse caps. However, EMI metal detectors lack the imaging capability necessary to distinguish mines with low metal content from other metallic battlefield clutter by size or shape. For the required high sensitivity, the rate of false alarm is, therefore, often as high or higher than 99%, particularly in areas covered with metal fragments. Under such conditions, EMI detection may become impractical and other detection techniques with enhanced target/clutter discrimination are necessary. The spectral characteristics of the EMI signal have been proposed as a method of distinguishing landmines from metallic clutter, but the viability of this approach has not been firmly established.

Radiowaves. The penetration depth of radiowaves through soil can be tens of meters (see Fig. 2.2-1), with the actual value depending on the moisture content. However, since the wavelength is much greater than the dimensions of the mine and the clutter, radiowaves do not have the spatial resolution necessary to distinguish mines from clutter.

Microwaves. The penetration depth of microwaves in soil depends on the soil type and conditions (water content, porousness, magnetic impurities, etc.), and is of the order of a meter (see Fig. 2.2-1). Because of their shorter wavelength, microwave probes offer the potential for imaging spatial structures. For example, at 3 GHz, the free-space wavelength is about 10 cm and the wavelength in soil is about 5 cm, i.e., is comparable to the size of the mine. Higher frequencies are strongly attenuated by soil, so that there is an inherent depth–resolution tradeoff. Also, at higher frequencies (>5 GHz), in addition to the severe attenuation by soil there is strong surface scattering that obscures scattering from underground objects. The contrast between soil and metal is strong, but plastic mines have a dielectric permittivity very close to some soils. Plastic and common explosive fillers have a dielectric constant of 2.9, which is close to the permittivity of silica sand, for example.

Millimeter waves are strongly absorbed within fractions of a centimeter and are not viable for the problem at hand.

Infrared. Passive detection based on observation of temperature differences on the ground surface above emplaced mines, due to the heating and cooling diurnal cycle, have been used with some limited success in landmine detection. Because it is sensitive to natural soil moisture and density variations, as well as cloud and vegetation shading, this is not a reliable technique.

Optical waves are clearly not appropriate, since the penetration depth is a micrometer or less.

X-ray and γ-ray photons are transmitted well through soil and are localized in the form of rays, but since the other side of the mine cannot be accessed, some mechanism of backscattering must be used for detection. Compton scattering (incoherent collision with the atomic electrons) offers such a possibility. The scattering cross-section depends on the electron density (and therefore the mass density of the medium) as well as the atomic number. A combination of density and atomic number can be used to characterize the presence of explosives or other anomalies in the soil.

Acoustic Waves.   The attenuation of sound in soil increases with frequency at a rate from 0.1 to 1 dB/(cm kHz) and the sound speed varies between 100 and 300 m/s.[1] At seismic frequencies (<50 Hz), acoustic waves penetrate deeply in soil, but ground-contact seismic sources (thumpers) are undesirable in a mine field for obvious reasons. At frequencies above 20 KHz the attenuation is substantial (20 dB/cm, corresponding to a penetration depth of approximately 2.2 millimeter) and, therefore, targets buried deeper than a few centimeters cannot be detected. With the much lower wave velocity, the acoustic wavelength is smaller and the resolution higher than electromagnetic waves at the same frequency, but the range–resolution tradeoff remains a principal barrier. At 10 kHz, the wavelength is 1–3 cm and the attenuation is 1–10 dB/cm. Since there is a relatively strong contrast in the acoustic velocity and the acoustic impedance between the porous soil and the solid plastic case of the landmine (and also the explosive filler therein), acoustic waves are viable probes for landmine detection. However, clutter such as rocks may also have similar contrast, so that discrimination can be a challenge.

Chemical Sensing.   Remote sensing of bulk chemical characteristics of emitted vapors from the explosive filler in the landmine may be detected by using spectroscopic chemical sensors. For example, the specific spectral signatures of nitrogen in TNT or RDX may be detected by using **nuclear quadrupole resonance (NQR) spectroscopy**, which relies on measuring radio-frequency (RF) resonances due to the interaction of the nitrogen-14 nuclear electric quadrapole moment with the electric field gradient associated with the chemical environment of the nitrogen atom. NQR spectroscopy has been used as a confirmation sensor for suspected landmines that have been located by other means. However, the signal-to-noise ratio is very low and the detection process is time consuming ($\approx$20 min per detection). Also, the equipment is too bulky to be carried in a hand-held package. These limitations have thus far prevented the technique from being effective for demining.

Summary.   Electromagnetic induction metal detectors, electromagnetic waves at microwave frequencies, and acoustic waves are the principal probes for detection of landmines. However, it appears that no single probe is fully satisfactory by itself and combinations of probes might be necessary.

Configurations and Data Processing

The configuration of the sensing system depends on the selected probe. The data processing necessary for optimal detection depends on whether a single measurement is made, as in the case of the EMI metal detector, or a full image is acquired in order to distinguish the mine from the clutter.

Microwave Sensing by GPR.   As mentioned earlier, for microwaves at 3 GHz, the wavelength in soil is approximately 5 cm, so that these waves may be used to form a blurred image of the mine and the clutter. Higher microwave frequencies have shorter wavelength and greater resolution, but the penetration depths are too short to reach the mine. The image may be formed by use of ground-penetrating radar (GPR) and range tomography, but the resolution is limited. As described in Sec. 4.4D, GPR works by transmitting into the ground a short microwave pulse and recording the amplitude(s) and the return time(s) of the pulses reflected from edges and boundaries. Using an estimate of the wave speed in soil, the return times are converted into distances or ranges.

---

[1]M. L. Oelze, W. D. O'Brien, Jr., and R. G. Darmody, Measurement of attenuation and speed of sound in soils, *Soil Science Society America Journal*, Vol. 66, p. 788, 2002.

The amplitudes are measures of the size of the scattering target and its dielectric-constant contrast relative to that of the soil background. With a probe beam of adequate angular width, backscattering from multiple directions reaches the detector. Multiple scans observing views from different positions are used, as illustrated in Fig. 9.2-1, and the data are processed tomographically to construct the image. The range resolution is governed by the pulse width. A one-nanosecond pulse extends over a length of 30 cm in free space and 15 cm in soil. Pulses of sub-nanosecond widths offer better range resolution, but since such pulses have broad spectral distributions, their profiles are altered as they propagate through the soil (because high frequencies are more severely attenuated than low frequencies). In any case, range resolution can be as small as 5 cm. Transverse resolution is determined by the angular width of the antenna and the number of views taken during the scanning process. Values similar to the range resolution can be obtained. Although this is adequate to detect a mine of 5–15 cm dimensions at a depth of 5–10 cm, the image will be blurred and its fine details will be washed out, so that it not easy to distinguish the mine from clutter of similar dimensions. Likewise, a shallow (<2 cm) buried target will not be distinguishable from the strong surface reflection. Clearly, the application of GPR to landmine detection has its limitations.

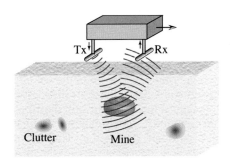

Figure 9.2-1 Sensing of a mine by ground-penetrating radar (GPR). A transmitting antenna Tx launches microwave pulses into the soil and a receiving antenna Rx detects the recording the amplitude(s) and the return time(s) of the pulses in the scattered wave. The apparatus collects data as it is moved parallel to the surface.

Acoustic sensing by ground-penetrating sonar (GPS). GPS is similar to GPR and has similar limitations. An additional challenge is the difficulty of coupling sound from air into and out of the soil since the impedance mismatch is close to 1000:1, which corresponds to reflectance exceeding 99%, at normal incidence. Even greater reflectance is encountered at oblique incidence, which is desirable for look-ahead detection. There is, therefore, a need to place sources and detectors on or within the soil, and this offers possibilities for acoustic near-field imaging. One approach for generating acoustic waves within the soil is **photoacoustics**. A short CO_2 laser pulse (100 ps) is used to create a localized acoustic "snap" on the surface of the soil. With a wavelength of 10.6 μm, CO_2 laser radiation is absorbed in the first few micrometers of soil. The rapid heating and expansion of the surface produces a short acoustic pulse with frequency centered at about 20 kHz. The sound scattered by the buried mine travels back to the soil surface and is partially transmitted and detected by a microphone suspended in the air.

An approach for detecting an acoustic wave at the surface of the soil directly above the emplaced mine is **laser Doppler vibrometry (LDV)**. A laser illuminates a small section (a few square millimeters) of the surface that is subjected to the sound wave. The scattered light is proportional to the amplitude of the sound wave at the surface and is Doppler shifted by a frequency equal to that of the sound wave. LDV can measure moderate to large acoustic amplitudes. Experimental LDV scans over the acoustically excited area revealed nearly circular regions of large acoustic amplitudes over each emplaced mine. Probability of detection above 90% was reported with essentially zero false alarms. However, the technique is very slow and less effective in the look-ahead mode. Figure 9.2-2 illustrates a system using combined photoacoustic sound generation and LDV sound detection.

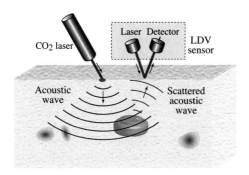

Figure 9.2-2 Photoacoustic generation of sound, and sound detection by laser Doppler vibrometry (LVD).

Nonlinear Acoustics.   Another acoustical technique exploits the nonlinear acoustic properties of the air bladder associated with the triggering mechanism in the landmine to create an acoustic signal with unique spectral signature. Since these air bladders are more compliant in compression than in extension against the covering soil, they create a diode-like stress–strain behavior, or elastic discontinuity, which exhibits nonlinear acoustic phenomena such as signal mixing and harmonic generation. The acoustic excitation is at two acoustic frequencies and the detected acoustic wave is at the difference frequency generated by the nonlinear acoustic response. Preliminary experiments suggest that such acoustic wave mixing could be observed, which would provide a unique signature for the presence of the buried landmine. Since the nonlinear elastic properties of each mine type is unique, this technique can possibly identify not only the presence but the type of mine.

Multisensor EMI and GPR.   Since each of the viable methods of mine detection has limitations in target/clutter discrimination, it is natural to consider hybrid multi-sensor methods. EMI metal detectors and GPR imaging systems combined in a single instrument have been developed. The hybrid system discriminates a plastic landmine with metal in the triggering mechanism from a neighboring large nonmetallic object, such as a stone, by use of the EMI metal detector. It can also discriminate the landmine from a metal fragment in close physical proximity by use of the GPR signal which is sensitive to the large GPR target. However, the hybrid system fails to discriminate against compound clutter, such as a small piece of metal near a stone. The result is false alarms. Nevertheless, the addition GPR to the EMI detector reduces its false alarm rate by a large factor, which enormously improves its usefulness. While some success has been demonstrated by combining EMI and GPR sensors in a single system, true sensor fusion, in which the modalities guide each other's decision, has not been implemented in actual systems.

Forward Modeling

GPR.   Modeling of electromagnetic scattering from emplaced landmines has been carried out by a variety of techniques.[2] Since soil surface roughness and irregularities on the order of mine details is a feature of realistic mine detection scenarios, computationally intensive finite-difference techniques are required for the best modeling of ground-surface reflections. These computations[3] indicate that while GPR can often detect the presence of an underground mass, the signals detected are not very sensitive to the detailed shape, i.e., cannot distinguish square objects from round objects, or sharp corners from rounded corners, for example. Modeling also indicates that distinguishing the GPR signal of an underground target from the return from the soil surface is a challenging task, especially for shallowly buried antipersonnel mines.

GPS.   Acoustic modeling of objects in soil is not nearly as mature as electromagnetic modeling. Since acoustic wavelengths (≈ 1–100 cm) can be on the order of soil inhomogeneities, acoustic propagation is very complex. The propagating modes in porous media are dependent on a bewildering number of parameters that are difficult to determine, such as the connectivity of the matrix and the relative volume density of the frame and the fluid. Multiple propagating modes (in-phase and out-of-phase Biot modes,[4] surface waves, and shear waves) may be created by a single excitation. No realistic models of acoustic landmine detection have been tested and data interpretation has been based on simplistic models.

End-to-End System Design and Optimization

EMI.   Relatively little end-to-end system optimization has been applied to the problem of detection of landmines with low metallic content. Commercial EMI systems are manufactured with variable-frequency radio-frequency transmitters. Generally, the frequency and pulse shape are adjusted by the operator based on test objects in the field, and are not changed thereafter. The return signal is coded into an audio signal which an experienced operator can use to identify real targets, but no systematic processing of the signal is provided to discriminate targets from clutter objects. A high level of operator expertise can improve the probability of detection and reduce the false-alarm rate, but these operator experience/intuition methods have not been successfully implemented in an automatic expert system.

GPR.   GPR systems have been constructed based on forward modeling to optimize the return signal from underground objects. Specially shaped antennas directing plane waves onto the soil at the Brewster angle to minimize the signal reflected from the ground surface and receiver antennas are positioned at the position of the maximum expected signal from underground objects. Prototype GPR systems were demonstrated to have better performance, but the difficulty of resolving rough-surface scatter and underground clutter objects from real landmines limits the performance.

---

[2]D. Daniels (ed.) *Ground-Penetrating Radar*, IEE Press, UK, 2004.

[3]C. Rappaport, S. Wu, M. Kilmer, and E. Miller, Distinguishing shape details of buried nonmetallic mine-like objects with GPR, *SPIE Aerosense Conference*, Orlando, FL, pp. 1419–1428, 1999.

[4]M. A. Biot, Generalized theory of acoustic propagation in porous dissipative media, *Journal of the Acoustical Society of America*, Vol. 34, pp. 179–191, 1962.

9.3   Case Study II: Breast Cancer Detection

Breast cancer is a major health concern worldwide. Despite advances in screening, breast cancer continues to pose a significant health risk to the female population: one in eight women will suffer this disease, and ≈40000 women died from it in the USA in 2009.[5] The chance of successful treatment of breast cancer is increased if the tumor is detected while it is still localized in the breast and the cancer has not spread (metastasized) to the adjacent lymph nodes or elsewhere in the body.

Many breast tumors are detected through feeling (**palpating**) the tumor during self-examination or a routine physical examination, but palpation is more likely to detect a tumor when it is larger and more likely to have already metastasized. The early detection and treatment of breast tumors while they are still small (≈1 cm in diameter) and confined to a local area is a goal of public health measures.

The primary screening technique for breast cancer is **X-ray mammography**. Annual screening mammography is recommended for all women over 40 years of age in the USA. About 8% of screening mammograms result in a callback for additional imaging, which can be X-ray imaging, ultrasound imaging or MRI. Additional imaging results in dismissal of 75% of the callbacks (6% of the total screens) with a balance of 25% (2% of the total screens) going on to some form of biopsy to remove and test a tissue sample by standard pathology methods of tissue preparation and staining. A pathologist makes a diagnosis, which is usually reported back to the patient's physician about a week later. Of 1000 women undergoing routine mammogram screening, approximately 80 will be called back for further examination. Of these, about 20 will receive a biopsy, and three to five will be diagnosed with cancer. The cost of this screening process – about $100 for a screening mammogram, $200 for the callback X-ray examination, $500 for an ultrasound, $2500 for an MRI exam, and an additional $800–3000 for the biopsy – is a significant healthcare expense, in addition to the discomfort and psychological distress of the biopsy procedure.

A more effective subsurface detection system that reduces the number of false alarms would provide a major cost and convenience benefit to the health system. In addition, 10–30% of "detectable" tumors are missed in mammogram screening. These tumors are detected in a subsequent screening examination or by palpation, often after the cancer has spread and become more difficult to treat. Studies have shown that as many as 70% of breast cancers that are detected at screening could have been detected one or more years before. The need for a more sensitive and specific sensing technique for breast cancer is widely recognized, and many alternative sensing technologies are now being investigated.

Problem Definition

The objective of this case study is to explore various technologies for breast cancer detection using subsurface sensing and imaging techniques. The difficulty in this case lies in the lack of a well-defined physical description of the tumor. The final diagnosis is ultimately made either by surgical biopsy or image-guided needle biopsy. Nevertheless, tumors are distinguishable from normal tissue in their rapid growth and consequent vascularization, which are observable by various probes. The following are some of the main structural and functional characteristics of tumors:

1. **Densities.** Tumors form regions of greater density, called *densities*, characterized by their size, heterogeneity, and the presence of spiculation (threadlike patterns radiating radially from the main mass).
2. **Microcalcifications.** Some tumors are identified by small flecks of calcium, called microcalcifications, deposited as precipitated calcium by dying tumor

---
[5] *American Cancer Society, Facts and Figures*, 2009.

cells, usually within the milk ducts of the breast tissue. These present as clusters in a characteristic set of patterns that are associated with both ductal carcinoma in situ (DCIS) and malignant masses. DCIS describes a colony of tumor cells that has not yet breached the epithelial lining of the milk ducts. Once a cell or a cell colony breaks through this barrier and enters the glandular tissue, the tumor is called "invasive." Microcalcifications also occur in normal breast tissue, giving false positive readings.

3. **Anomalies in tissue elasticity**. The elastic constant of tumor tissue can vary by up to 100:1 from normal tissue. This contrast in tissue stiffness is the reason that many tumors are initially detected by discovery of a "lump" through self-examination palpation.

4. **Anomalies in tissue blood oxygenation and flow.** Rapidly growing tumor tissue is characterized by two to three times increased blood flow and tissue deoxygenation, while tissue in the interior of large tumors is often characterized by relatively low or no blood flow and low oxygenation levels, called *necrotic* (dead and dying) tissue. Tumor aggressiveness can be assessed from reduced tissue oxygenation relative to normal tissue and benign breast lesions.

5. **Vascularization.** Disorganized and erratically structured blood vessels, which grow to support the growth of the tumor, are common characteristics. There is considerable evidence that tumor growth is dependent on *angiogenesis* (growth of new blood vessels from pre-existing vessels). Tumor microvessel density (an index of angiogenesis) has been shown to increase in association with metastatic cancer and to possibly serve as a prognostic indicator to assist in selecting patients for aggressive therapy.

6. **Dysfunctional membrane properties** of tissue structure due to crowding at the site and immediately surrounding invading tumors.

7. **Increased glucose consumption.** Among the metabolic changes associated with breast cancer is increased glucose consumption. Such metabolic changes in a tumor occur before the tumor produces the structural changes described in the previous items.

These physical attributes constitute beta parameters β of the imaging process, which must be matched to alpha parameters α for each of the probes to be considered for tumor detection.

Another challenge in breast cancer detection is that human tissue is a complex absorbing and scattering medium for both electromagnetic and acoustic waves. It is highly inhomogeneous both on a large scale on the order of organs, muscles, and tendons (fractions of a centimeter to many centimeters), and on a small scale characteristic of cells (on the order of micrometers). In such an environment, it is difficult to observe small anomalies. Contrast and clutter are thus key issues in breast cancer detection (as they are in humanitarian demining).

Since numerous alternative sensing technologies have been investigated for breast cancer detection, and some are now in actual use, this case study is basically a review of these technologies and a discussion of their tradeoffs.

Probes

Low-Frequency Electric Currents/Fields.   Low-frequency (kilohertz) electric currents can be used as probes of the electrical conductivity, which can be a factor of seven higher for tumor tissue than for fatty breast tissue (as measured on excised tissue). This is primarily due to the disorganization of the structured blood vessels and the dysfunctional membrane properties of tumor tissues. Studies of excised tissue suggest that the frequency dependence of the electrical resistance versus reactance could permit direct identification of tumors, even without structural information. The difficulty is that electric currents/fields spread through the medium and cannot be sufficiently localized for conventional imaging.

Radiowaves, Microwaves, and Millimeter Waves.   Because of its electrical conductivity, the absorption of electromagnetic waves in tissue increases with the frequency, from long-wavelength radiowaves all the way to millimeter waves. At long wavelengths, however, the waves cannot be localized sufficiently for effective imaging of tumor details, unless some other localization mechanism is adopted, such as a magnetic field gradient in MRI (Sec.4.4D). Millimeter waves can provide adequate resolution, but the penetration depth is small. In the submillimeter to the mid-infrared spectral region, molecular absorptions reduce the penetration depth to millimeters or micrometers, making such waves unsuitable as probes.

Optical Waves.   Tissue has a transparent window in a near-infrared band nestled between absorption bands of water in the mid-infrared and hemoglobin in the visible, as shown in Fig. 2.2-4. At wavelengths within this window, light penetrates significantly through the tissue but is subjected to strong scattering and travels as a diffuse wave (see Sec. 2.2D). By measuring the absorption and diffusion coefficients, various structures in the tissue can be delineated. For example, since the absorption coefficients of oxygenated and deoxygenated hemoglobin have distinct dependence on the wavelength, as shown in Example 6.3-2, this probe can provide spectroscopic information about blood volume and flow, and blood oxygenation levels could be used to identify vascularization in rapidly growing malignant tumors as well as oxygen-starved tissue in the center of a tumor. Unfortunately, the strong scattering reduces the spatial resolution significantly.

X-rays are highly penetrating through human tissue and provide excellent contrast between bone and tissue, but contrast between tumors and normal breast tissue is weaker (on the order of 10%). This relatively low contrast, along with the overlap and blending of tumors with normal glandular and fibrous breast tissue, limits the performance of X-ray mammography. On average, 25% of mammography false-positives are determined to be superimposed tissue. The use of contrast agents injected into the blood can improve the conspicuity of lesions in dense tissue. Contrast-enhanced mammography exploits the fact that tumor growth is directly linked to angiogenesis.

γ-Rays.   Like X-rays, γ-rays propagate through tissue along linear trajectories. They are emitted in pairs moving in exactly opposite directions when a positron, emitted by a short-lived radioactive tracer isotope, mutually annihilates with an electron. The isotope may be chemically incorporated in metabolically active molecules injected in the body. This is the basis of PET (Sec. 4.1D), which measures the distribution of metabolic activity. In PET, deoxyglucose molecules are radio-labeled with flourine-18, a positron-emitting isotope incorporated in the metabolic pathway of cancer cells. Increased glucose consumption is characteristic of breast cancer; thus, high concentrations of radio-labeled glucose molecules are indicative of the disease.

Ultrasonic Waves.   The attenuation coefficient of acoustic waves in tissue increases with frequency from the audible through the ultrasonic region. Through ultrasonic frequencies, the attenuation is about 1 dB/(cm MHz). At 10 MHz, for example, attenuation is on the order of 10 dB/cm. Since 40–60 dB loss is the limit of acceptable ultrasound imaging, a depth of about 2–3 cm can be imaged at 10 MHz. The acoustic wavelength at 10 MHz is 0.15 mm. Greater penetration can be obtained at 1 MHz but the wavelength is 1.5 mm, which is not adequate for imaging fine structures smaller than a millimeter. Contrast in acoustic attenuation, reflection, or velocity are three possibilities for differentiation of tumors from the surrounding tissue. The reflectance of ultrasound can be used to differentiate fluid-filled cysts from solid cysts, but it has limited capability for differentiating benign lesions from malignant lesions. Normal breast parenchyma and fat have easily visualized boundaries. Tumors have identifiable features but often appear with irregular boundaries that may not have high contrast with surrounding tissues by reflective ultrasound imaging. The principal means of differentiation is the contrast in the speckle pattern on the image: benign cysts tend to appear dark because they have little acoustic scatter, while tumors tend to have lots of internal structure. Proposals for differentiation based on identifying regions of anomalous acoustic velocity or absorption by measuring travel-time differences or by tomographic methods have been recently advanced. Differences in tissue stiffness (elasticity) at tumor boundaries and other interfaces between tissues and within tissues lead to sharp acoustic velocity changes, but primarily in the shear wave ultrasonic propagation, not in the longitudinal acoustic waves used in normal ultrasonic imaging.

Elastic Fields.   The large contrast in the stiffness of tumor tissue from normal tissue suggests direct measurement of the elastic modulus by application of local stress and measurement of strain. Elastography could be a useful technique for local mapping of the elastic modulus on the scale of the small tumors.

Configurations

X-Ray Mammography.   Although X-rays are transmitted through the breast without spreading, full 3D images of the absorption coefficient can only be obtained by use of tomographic imaging. This has been recognized since the inception of CT in the early 1970s, when linear array detectors became available. Nevertheless, because of technical complexities of the tomographic apparatus, conventional mammography has continued to consist of only two exposures of each breast, one in the cranio-caudal (CC) view and another in the medial-lateral oblique (MLO) view. Each view provides a projection of the density along the direction of the rays. The two X-ray exposures of each breast are examined by a radiologist for suspiciously shaped areas of X-ray density greater than the background's. Examples of X-ray mammography images are shown in Fig. 9.3-1.

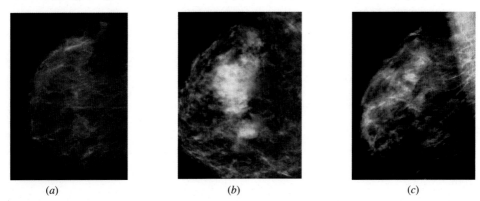

(a)   (b)   (c)

Figure 9.3-1   X-ray mammography images of (a) normal breast, (b) breast with fibroadenoma, (c) breast with invasive ductal carcinoma. (Courtesy of Richard H. Moore.)

Digital Breast Tomosynthesis (DBT).   In X-ray mammography, which is a form of projection radiometry, overlapping structures can obscure a small tumor. Conventional CT cannot be used for breast screening due to unnecessary irradiation of the thoracic cavity. However, X-ray tomography restricted to the breast tissue with a limited angular range ($\pm 20°$ from the central view axis) can avoid unwanted exposure of the chest and still provide 3D rendition with adequate resolution. This system, called digital breast tomosynthesis (DBT) (see Sec. 4.1C and Fig. 4.1-15), is being clinically applied in screening trials in an effort to reduce call-backs and missed tumors. Commercial multiview radiographic instrumentations have become available and tomosynthesis is considered one of the most promising advances in mammography.

Ultrasonic Imaging.   A standard reflective ultrasonic imaging system employs a handheld probe that images a fan-shaped slab of tissue by measuring the times of arrival of reflected pulses (Sec. 3.2C). The probe must be meticulously moved and monitored by a highly trained individual, and a radiologist will check the scans if there is an issue. Screening using ultrasound is extremely operator dependent, time consuming, and has a high false positive rate (as high as four times that of mammography). Nevertheless, ultrasonic imaging can detect tumors in dense breast tissue, which are difficult to detect by conventional mammography. Ultrasound tomography has been tested in acoustic phantoms, demonstrating that a 3D spatial map of the acoustic properties could be obtained. Quantitative mapping of ultrasound velocity and absorption could enable the identification of regions of anomalous elastic constants associated with tumor vascularization, and this possibility has been pursued clinically.

MRI.   Breast MRI offers a full 3D image of the breast. It uses a nonradioactive contrast agent, gadolinium, which concentrates in abnormal breast issue. MRI monitors blood flow and vascular permeability and is consequently able to identify some tumors before they are otherwise detectable. However, MRI is unlikely to become a routine test for most women because it is an extremely expensive and time-consuming technique, and also because it requires the intravenous injection of a contrast agent.

DOT.   Imaging with infrared diffuse optical waves can only be implemented by means of tomographic techniques (see Sec. 4.5A). In DOT, red or near-infrared light is injected at a number of spatially distributed points on the skin and the emerging light is detected at other interspersed points. Solution of the optical diffusion equation can be used to spatially map the optical characteristics of the tissue at several wavelength so that spectral characteristics are measured. DOT has been tested with tissue-mimicking phantoms and is beginning clinical trials for breast tumor detection.

EIT.   Localized probing of tissue conductivity requires the insertion of electrodes under the skin, which is undesirable for any screening procedure. This may be circumvented by use of a tomographic configuration. In EIT (Sec. 4.5B), electrodes are distributed uniformly on the skin. Current is injected through each electrode using a constant current source and the voltages between the electrodes are measured. From these measurements, the 3D distribution of the conductivity and permittivity can be inferred. Resolution is a function of the number of electrodes. A radiolucent 64×64 probe array designed to be mounted on standard mammography compressive paddles has been built and is now undergoing clinical trials to look for anomalies in the complex impedance (resistance and reactance). Resolution is predicted to be of the order of 5 mm.

Forward Modeling

Electromagnetic propagation in breast tissue has been extensively modeled. Microwave and millimeter wave propagation has been modeled by finite-difference calculations with the hope that the high conductivity contrast of the tumor can be easily imaged by standard radar imaging techniques. At millimeter-wave frequencies, where the wavelengths are sufficiently small to image tumors, initial calculations for objects with a conductivity characteristic of tumors in a background of fatty breast tissue suggest that imaging would be possible. When the higher permittivity–conductivity properties of the inhomogeneously distributed glandular and fibrous breast tissues are added to the model, however, the scattered field becomes so complex that the perturbations added by a tumor are undetectable.

Ultrasonic modeling using finite-element time-domain methods has been used to confirm that tumors can be detected in transmissive ultrasound geometries, based on the greater ultrasound velocities resulting from the increased tissue stiffness. Whether tumors can be distinguished from the clutter due to the large number of breast tissue structures on the scale of ultrasound wavelengths awaits a realistic acoustic model of a normal breast.

Inversion Methods

Although most breast tumor screening is still done by visual examination of X-ray images, tomographic inversion is included in MRI systems and is necessary in DBT, DOT, EIT, and ultrasonic tomography. Other mathematical inverse-scattering techniques are also beginning to be deployed in these systems.

DBT.   Techniques of ray tomography may be applied to configurations of multiple views over a limited angular range, as described in Sec.4.1C. The reconstruction produces a 3D image with overlying and underlying breast tissue signal (clutter) removed from the plane of interest, allowing the radiologist to computationally section a suspected lesion. Reconstruction consisting of a stack of 1 mm spaced slices has been reported. An example of a DBT image is shown in Fig. 9.3-2. Widespread application of tomosynthesis has been inhibited by the intense computational burden of the limited-view tomographic reconstruction necessary. Computational speedup through code optimization and transition to multiprocessor graphics processor units has largely alleviated this problem.

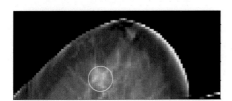

Figure 9.3-2   X-ray DBT image. The circle indicates a 2 cm invasive carcinoma with DCIS. (Courtesy of Qianqian Fang.)

DOT.   DOT requires the inversion of the diffusion equation for the photon density wave. Inversion using shape parameterization has succeeded in identifying regions of increased absorption in model cases, and these solutions have been shown to agree reasonably well with experiments on tissue phantoms. Extensive simulations indicate that localized optical properties can be extracted at a sub-centimeter resolution by use of a large array ($\approx 64 \times 64$) of optical fiber transmitters and receivers. An example of a DOT image is shown in Fig. 9.3-3.

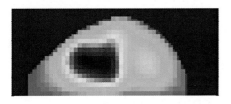

Figure 9.3-3   DOT reconstructed image showing total hemoglobin concentration. (Courtesy of Qianqian Fang.)

EIT. Inversion of the EIT data is a challenging nonlinear and ill-posed inverse problem involving a solution to the generalized Laplace equation given a (possibly incomplete) map of mixed Neumann and Dirichlet boundary conditions on the voltages and currents at the surface of the breast. The most sophisticated solution of this problem is referred to as the D-bar method for the complex partial derivative operators employed. Clinical EIT trials are in progress now with a 64×64 probe array that is expected to yield position resolution on the order of 5 mm.

Ultrasonic Diffraction Tomography has been considered extensively through modeling, and the distinctions between ray tomography, which is used in X-ray tomography, and wave tomography, which is required when the wavelength is comparable to the size of object details, have been demonstrated.[6] Ultrasonic wave tomography, however, has not been extensively applied in actual clinical studies, and the limitations due to the complex internal structure of the breast are unknown.

Elastography. Elastography depends on measuring the local tissue strain fields induced by a specified external applied stress. This has been done by observing the motion of small inhomogeneities imaged by ultrasound. This has been observed in tissue-mimicking phantoms, but regions of minimum strain in the higher elastic constant target region are accompanied by artifacts at other positions in the sample caused by the interactions with the pressure-applying apparatus and other rigid boundaries. Inverting the data to clearly locate small-tumor-scale regions of increased stiffness is a subject of current research.

End-to-End System Optimization

The goal of breast cancer screening is to detect tumors at an early stage of development before the carcinoma cells have spread to the nearby lymph nodes or throughout the body. Palpation, X-ray mammography, and ultrasound detect *structural* changes in the breast induced by the growth of tumors. MRI and PET, on the other hand, measure *functional* (metabolic) processes that ultimately lead to those changes. EIT and DOT also provide functional information. Measurement of functional anomalies can be highly informative, since they are capable of identifying the tumor before it produces structural changes. The high examination cost and the need for intravenous injections for MRI and PET, however, have prevented their widespread deployment in breast screening and diagnosis.

Combined Structural and Functional Imaging. An optimized breast cancer screening system would utilize both structural and functional information. Different technologies must therefore be used concurrently and must also be co-registered (see Sec. 7.2). The coincidence of a structural lesion with a metabolic anomaly in the same location would improve both sensitivity and specificity for cancer screening, i.e., reduces both missed tumors and false positives. A barrier to adoption of any new technology in a cost-sensitive and risk-adverse environment is convincing practicing physicians to abandon a technology that is familiar and effective. If the functional imaging scan could be made simultaneously with normal X-ray mammography screening at little extra expense, the transition to multi-sensor screening would be most likely to be accepted and utilized by radiologists.

Multi-Sensor Screening. Metabolic sensing modalities that are compatible with normal X-ray screening procedures include EIT and DOT. A configuration for combined X-ray mammography and EIT, currently employed in clinical trials, uses radiolucent

---
[6]R. G. Pratt, L. Huang, N. Duric, and P. J. Littrup, Sound-speed and attenuation imaging of breast tissue using waveform tomography of transmission ultrasound data, *Proceedings of SPIE*, Vol. 6513, pp. 6510–174, 2007.

electrodes mounted on mammography compression paddles. X-ray markers on the electrode array provide common points for registration. DOT can also be included in the same configuration by mounting sources and sensors on the compression paddles and connecting them to optical fibers, which are electrically insulating and nearly transparent to X-rays, i.e., are compatible with both EIT and X-ray systems. Advances in quantitative ultrasonic imaging in transmission or tomographic configurations are promising. Likewise, elastography in conjunction with ultrasonic imaging may also mature into yet another combination. The availability of multiple sensor modalities will enable a variety of strategies. Present practice suggests that standard mammography would be the primary sensing modality, at least at first, with EIT and/or DOT as a second confirming modality to trigger a call-back evaluation. In this scenario, the multiple sensors would be used primarily to lower the rate of false positives and reduce the number of call-backs. If the functional sensing techniques are demonstrated to provide higher contrast for tumors, the EIT and/or DOT reading could be utilized to provide an immediate trigger for closer examination of radiological data, reducing the number of missed tumors and possibly enabling confirmatory evaluation. In either case, the result would be an improvement in both sensitivity and selectivity.

Cost Factors.   Applications other than screening include diagnosis confirmation, treatment planning, and treatment monitoring. In these applications, where tumors are present or at least strongly suspected, the cost of the imaging procedure is not as critical an issue. MRI or PET imaging will be increasingly important for these applications. Since the beginning of the public health campaign to screen post-menopausal women annually for breast tumors, breast cancer detection has evolved as a system that must be carefully optimized for maximum outcome and minimum cost. An analysis similar to that that led to the ROC in Appendix C quantifies the tradeoff between outcomes and cost. For example, while it is possible that MRI could catch some tumors that are presently missed, routine MRI screening for breast cancer is not considered a reasonable use of healthcare resources. It is clear that, with many emerging new imaging techniques, overall system optimization of breast tumor detection will be an area that will attract more attention in the future. With the intense public interest in reducing breast cancer deaths as well as the persisting pressure on limiting health care costs, the evolution of breast cancer screening with additional imaging technologies is likely to become a model of end-to-end system optimization employing multi-sensor fusion. The ultimate public health solution may resemble an extension of the present annual mammography screening with a wide variety of confirmation sensing technologies, or it may evolve to some entirely different set of screening and confirmation imaging. An overall end-to-end optimization of breast cancer detection is a goal, but cost will continue to be an important driver.

Further Reading

Landmine Detection

U.S. Department of State, *To Walk the Earth in Safety*. 7th ed., Report on international demining efforts undertaken by U.S. Government, 2008. *http://www.state.gov/t/pm/rls/rpt/walkearth/*

H. M. Jol (ed.), *Ground Penetrating Radar Theory and Applications*, Elsevier, 2009.

D. Daniels (ed.), *Ground-Penetrating Radar*, 2nd ed., IEE, UK, 2004.

J. MacDonald and J. R. Lockwood, *Alternatives for Landmine Detection*, Rand Corporation, 2003. *http://www.rand.org/pubs/monograph_reports/MR1608/*

A. C. Dubey, J. F. Harvey, J. T. Broach, and V. George (eds.), *Detection and Remediation Technologies for Mines and Minelike Targets VI*, Proceedings of SPIE, Vol. 4394, 2001.

Breast Cancer Detection

M. Tartar, C. E. Comstock, and M. S. Kipper, *Breast Cancer Imaging: A Multidisciplinary, Multi-modality Approach*, Mosby, 2008.

D. B. Kopans, *Breast Imaging*, Lippincott Williams & Wilkins, 2006

J. S. Suri and R. M. Rangayyan, eds., *Recent Advances in Breast Imaging, Mammography, and Computer-Aided Diagnosis of Breast Cancer,* Proceedings of SPIE, Vol. PM155, 2006.

J. Law, The development of mammography, *Physics in Medicine and Biology*, Vol. 51, pp. R155–67, 2006.

K. C. Young, Recent developments in digital mammography, *Imaging*, Vol. 18, pp. 68–74, 2006.

E. D. Pisano and M. J. Yaffe, Digital mammography, *Radiology*, Vol. 234, pp. 353–362, 2005.

T. Wu, A. Stewart, M. Stanton, T. McCauley, W. Phillips, D. B. Kopans, R. H. Moore, J. W. Eberhard, and B. Opsahl-Ong, Tomographic mammography using a limited number of low-dose cone-beam projection images, *Medical Physics*, Vol. 30, pp. 365–380, 2003.

J. A. Rowlands, The physics of computed radiography, *Physics in Medicine and Biology*, Vol. 47, pp. R123–65, 2002.

L. T. Niklason, L. E. Niklason, and D. B. Kopans, United States Patent #5872828: Tomosynthesis system for breast imaging, 1997.

L. T. Niklason, B. T. Christian, L. E. Niklason, D. B. Kopans, *et al.*, Digital tomosynthesis in breast imaging, *Radiology*, Vol. 205, pp. 399–406, 1997.

L. W. Bassett and R. H. Gold, *Breast Cancer Detection: Mammography and Other Methods in Breast Imaging*, 2nd ed., Grune & Stratton, 1987.

Problems

9.1-1 **Cracks in Marble.** In quarrying operations it would be useful to know if the marble at some location is free of cracks before cutting the stone. Suppose that a block of marble of 3×2.5 m^2 area and 1.25 m depth to be used for a sculpture is required to be crack free. Suggest possible subsurface probes that could be useful in this process. After the block is cut out and before the sculptor begins work, it would be desirable to re-examine the marble. Suggest other methods of crack detection.

9.1-2 **Skiers in Snow Avalanche.** Every year outdoor enthusiasts are buried alive in snow avalanches. A rescue team of skiers with test poles is thrust into the snow to "detect" the buried victim(s). Using passive or active acoustic or electromagnetic tools, design a *person finder* and determine the maximum depth at which it may operate.

9.1-3 **Railbed Maintenance.** Railbed problems, such as gravel-bed hydration, rotting ties, and ground voids, are a long-term maintenance problem. What approaches to sensing such problems are available? Consider the both acoustic and electromagnetic probes.

9.1-4 **Submarine Shipwreck.** When submarines lose control they can end up on the seafloor with trapped crew. Given the uniformity of seawater and the likely responses of survivors (e.g., banging on the hull) in response to acoustic probes, discuss possible systems for scanning the seafloor and then amplifying signals from survivors.

9.1-5 **Miners in Collapsed Mine.** Every few years, mines or portions of mines collapse where miners are later determined to have lived for hours to days. The location of the miners and getting air/water to them are the lifesaving measures that are undeliverable and therefore result in death. What approaches are available for locating miners in semi-uniform rockbeds underground?

9.1-6 **Composite Material in Airplane Structures.** Airplane fuselages and wings are periodically examined for fatigue cracks that might lead to catastrophic failure. Point-contact electrical conductivity measurements are useful in detecting concealed micro-cracks in metal wings, but with the growing use of weakly or nonconducting composite materials in airplane structures, the problem is more difficult. Consider the application of other imaging probes for finding micro-cracks in airplane metallic and composite structures and describe the advantages and limitations of each.

9.1-7 **Pigments in Oil Paint.** Forgeries of old master paintings can sometimes be detected by the presence of modern pigments in the painting or by different brush-stroke or overpainting techniques. Imagine that you were asked to determine if a painting claimed to be by Vincent Van Gogh was authentic. You have access to established paintings by Van Gogh, but, of course, none of the techniques that you use should damage the paintings in any way. Consider ways that you might use to determine the painting's authenticity including 3D laser scanning, Raman spectroscopy, CARS, OCT, and THz imaging.

9.1-8 **Lead Detection.** Lead-based paint is recognized as a harmful environmental pollutant. What would be required for a system to detect lead-based paint, possibly buried under more recent non-lead-containing coats of paint? One technique that has been suggested is X-ray backscattering. How does this technique work and what characteristics of the paint is it sensitive to? Is this something that a prudent buyer of a house might consider using before closing on the house?

9.1-9 **Security Screening.** Protecting airline passengers from possible weapons or explosive materials smuggled aboard an airplane is a challenging subsurface problem. Consider the detection of a metal weapon or hazardous liquid concealed under heavy clothing of a passenger at a standoff distance of 3 meters. Which of the following technologies is viable and what are the advantages and drawbacks of viable technologies in each case?
- Magnetometer array for ferric metal weapon detection
- Passive infrared thermal detection
- Passive millimeter wave temperature detection
- Active radiowave, millimeter-wave, terrahertz, or microwave radar
- MRI
- Laser radar
- X-ray backscattering
- Ultrasonic scanner.

What if the same objects are instead hidden in luggage?

Multi-Dimensional Signals and Systems

This appendix is a brief overview of the basic principles of signals and linear systems. It begins with one-dimensional (1D) functions and follows with generalizations to two- and multi-dimensional functions.

A.1 One-Dimensional Signals and Systems

A. One-Dimensional Fourier Transform

The harmonic function $F \exp(j\omega t)$ plays an important role in science and engineering. It has an angular frequency ω and complex amplitude F. Its real part $|F| \cos(\omega t + \arg\{F\})$ is a cosine function with amplitude $|F|$ and phase $\arg\{F\}$. The variable t usually represents time, in which case the angular frequency ω has units of radians/s and the frequency $\nu = \omega/2\pi$ has units of cycles/s or Hz. The harmonic function is regarded as a building block from which other functions may be obtained by a simple superposition.

In accordance with the Fourier theorem, a complex-valued function $f(t)$, satisfying some rather unrestrictive conditions, may be decomposed as a superposition integral of harmonic functions of different frequencies and complex amplitudes,

$$f(t) = \frac{1}{2\pi} \int_{-\infty}^{\infty} F(\omega) \exp(j\omega t)\, d\omega. \qquad \text{(A.1-1)}$$

Inverse Fourier Transform

The component with angular frequency ω has a complex amplitude $(2\pi)^{-1} F(\omega)$, where

$$F(\omega) = \int_{-\infty}^{\infty} f(t) \exp(-j\omega t)\, dt, \qquad \text{(A.1-2)}$$

Fourier Transform

is termed the **Fourier transform** of $f(t)$ and where $f(t)$ is the **inverse Fourier transform** of $F(\omega)$. The functions $f(t)$ and $F(\omega)$ form a Fourier transform pair; if one is known, the other may be determined.

The squared-absolute value $|f(t)|^2$ is called the **power**, and $|F(\omega)|^2$ is the energy spectral density. The frequency range over which the function $|F(\omega)|^2$ extends is called the **bandwidth**.

The physical meaning of the mathematical function $f(t)$ and its Fourier transform $F(\omega)$ depend on the application. In communication systems, $f(t)$ represents a time-dependent signal. In imaging systems, $f(t)$ may represent the temporal profile of the amplitude of a pulsed wave used to probe a remote object or the radiowave emitted in a magnetic resonance imaging system. In other imaging applications, a 1D function of position $f(z)$, represents the spatial distribution of a wave as a function of distance z. In this case, the Fourier transform $F(k)$ represents a spatial spectrum, where k is the spatial frequency in rad/mm. The Fourier transform relations (A.1-1) and (A.1-2) are then written in terms of the variables z and k as

$$f(z) = \frac{1}{2\pi} \int_{-\infty}^{\infty} F(k) \exp(-\mathrm{j}kz)\,\mathrm{d}k, \quad F(k) = \int_{-\infty}^{\infty} f(z) \exp(\mathrm{j}kz)\,\mathrm{d}z. \quad \text{(A.1-3)}$$

The careful reader will note a difference in the signs of the exponents in (A.1-3) compared with those in (A.1-1) and (A.1-2). Both conventions for the definition of the Fourier transform and its inverse are valid. In (A.1-1) and (A.1-2), we adopt the convention that $\exp(\mathrm{j}\omega t)$ is a harmonic function of time with positive angular frequency ω. In (A.1-3), we say that the spatial harmonic function $\exp(-\mathrm{j}kz)$ has positive spatial frequency k. In this book, when we deal with temporal functions we will use the definition in (A.1-1) and (A.1-2); when we deal with spatial functions we will use the definition in (A.1-3). The rationale for this switch between conventions is that the temporal and spatial dependence of the function $\exp[\mathrm{j}(\omega t - kz)]$, which represents a traveling wave, differ by a minus sign (see Chapter 2).

Properties of the Fourier Transform

The following properties can be proved by direct application of the definitions (A.1-1) and (A.1-2) (see any of the books in the reading list).

- **Linearity.** The Fourier transform of the sum of two functions is the sum of their Fourier transforms.

- **Scaling.** If $f(t)$ has a Fourier transform $F(\omega)$, and τ is a real scaling factor, then $f(t/\tau)$ has a Fourier transform $|\tau|F(\tau\omega)$. This means that if $f(t)$ is scaled by a factor τ, its Fourier transform is scaled by a factor $1/\tau$. For example, if $\tau > 1$, then $f(t/\tau)$ is a stretched version of $f(t)$, whereas $F(\tau\omega)$ is a compressed version of $F(\omega)$. The Fourier transform of $f(-t)$ is $F(-\omega)$.

- **Time Translation.** If $f(t)$ has a Fourier transform $F(\omega)$, the Fourier transform of $f(t-\tau)$ is $\exp(-\mathrm{j}\omega\tau)F(\omega)$. Thus, delay by time τ is equivalent to multiplication of the Fourier transform by a phase factor $\exp(-\mathrm{j}\omega\tau)$.

- **Frequency Translation.** If $F(\omega)$ is the Fourier transform of $f(t)$, the Fourier transform of $f(t)\exp(\mathrm{j}\omega_0 t)$ is $F(\omega - \omega_0)$. Thus, multiplication by a harmonic function of frequency ω_0 is equivalent to shifting the Fourier transform to a higher frequency ω_0.

- **Area.** The area under a function $f(t)$ equals the Fourier transform $F(\omega)$ at $\omega = 0$,

$$\int_{-\infty}^{\infty} f(t)\,\mathrm{d}t = F(0). \quad \text{(A.1-4)}$$

- **Power.** The signal energy, which is the integral of the signal power $|f(t)|^2$, equals the integral of the energy spectral density $|F(\omega)|^2$, so that

$$\int_{-\infty}^{\infty} |f(t)|^2\,\mathrm{d}t = \frac{1}{2\pi} \int_{-\infty}^{\infty} |F(\omega)|^2\,\mathrm{d}\omega. \quad \text{(A.1-5)}$$

Parseval's Theorem

■ **Convolution.** If the Fourier transforms of $f_1(t)$ and $f_2(t)$ are $F_1(\omega)$ and $F_2(\omega)$, respectively, then the inverse Fourier transform of the product

$$F(\omega) = F_1(\omega)F_2(\omega) \tag{A.1-6}$$

is

$$f(t) = \int_{-\infty}^{\infty} f_1(\tau)f_2(t-\tau)\,d\tau. \tag{A.1-7}$$

Convolution

The operation defined in (A.1-7) is called the convolution of $f_1(t)$ with $f_2(t)$. Convolution in the time domain is therefore equivalent to multiplication in the Fourier domain.

■ **Cross-correlation function.** The cross-correlation of $f_1(t)$ and $f_2(t)$ is the function

$$f(t) = \int_{-\infty}^{\infty} f_1^*(\tau)f_2(\tau+t)\,d\tau. \tag{A.1-8}$$

Correlation

The Fourier transforms of $f_1(t)$, $f_2(t)$, and $f(t)$ are related by

$$F(\omega) = F_1^*(\omega)F_2(\omega). \tag{A.1-9}$$

When $f_2(t) = f_1(t)$, (A.1-8) is called the *auto-correlation function* or simply the correlation function, and in this case $F(\omega) = |F_1(\omega)|^2$.

Special Functions

The Fourier transforms of some important functions used in this book are listed in Table A.1-1. By use of the properties of linearity, scaling, delay, and frequency translation, the Fourier transforms of other related functions may be readily obtained. In this table:

■ **rect function**: $\text{rect}(t) = 1$ for $|t| \leq \frac{1}{2}$ and is zero elsewhere, i.e., it is a pulse of unit height and unit width centered about $t = 0$.
■ **delta function**: $\delta(t)$ is the impulse function (Dirac delta function), defined as $\delta(t) = \lim_{\alpha \to \infty} \alpha \, \text{rect}(\alpha t)$. It is the limit of a rectangular pulse of unit area as its width approaches zero (so that its height approaches infinity).
■ **sinc function**: $\text{sinc}(t) = \sin(\pi t)/(\pi t)$ is a symmetric function with a peak value of 1.0 at $t = 0$ and zeros at $t = \pm 1, \pm 2, \ldots$

Table A.1-1   Selected functions and their Fourier transforms

Function		$f(t)$	$F(\omega)$	
Uniform		1	$2\pi\delta(\omega)$	
Impulse		$\delta(t)$	1	
Rectangular		$\text{rect}(t)$	$\text{sinc}(\omega/2\pi)$	
Gaussian		$\exp(-\pi t^2)$	$\exp(-\omega^2/4\pi)$	

Discrete Fourier Transform (DFT)

The principles of Fourier transform and linear systems, which were defined for continuous functions, have their counterparts for discrete functions. For example, the counterpart of the continuous function $f(t)$ is the discrete function $f[n]$, $n = 0, 2, \ldots, N - 1$, where N is the signal length.

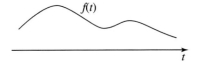

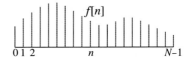

DFT and Inverse DFT. The DFT of $f[n]$ is

$$F[k] = \sum_{n=0}^{N-1} f[n] \exp\left(-j\frac{2\pi kn}{N}\right), \quad k = 0, 1, \ldots, N - 1 \qquad \text{(A.1-10)}$$

DFT

and the corresponding inverse Fourier transform is

$$f[n] = \frac{1}{N} \sum_{k=0}^{N-1} F[k] \exp\left(j\frac{2\pi kn}{N}\right), \quad n = 0, 1, \ldots, N - 1. \qquad \text{(A.1-11)}$$

Inverse DFT

The discrete variables n, k, and $2\pi k$ are analogous to the continuous variables t, ν, and $\omega = 2\pi\nu$, respectively. The DFT and the inverse DFT operations are usually computed by a fast algorithm called the **fast Fourier transform** (FFT).

■ MATLAB functions F=fft(f) and f=ifft(F) implement the DFT and the inverse DFT, respectively, where f and F are vectors of elements $f[n]$ and $F[k]$, respecively.

Convolution. The discrete version of the convolution $f(t) = f_1(t) \otimes f_2(t)$ is $f[n] = f_1[n] \otimes f_2[n]$. This is defined by the sum

$$f[m] = \sum_{n=0}^{N-1} f_1[n]f_2[m - n]. \qquad \text{(A.1-12)}$$

Discrete Convolution

■ MATLAB function f=conv(f1,f2) implements discrete convolution.

The discrete version of the convolution theorem is

$$F[k] = F_1[k]F_2[k], \qquad \text{(A.1-13)}$$

where $F_1[k]$, $F_2[k]$, and $F[k]$ are the DFT of $f_1[n]$, $f_2[n]$, and $f[n]$, respectively.

Sampling

In many applications, a continuous function $f(t)$ is converted into a discrete function $f[n]$ by uniform sampling at sampling points $t_n = n\Delta_t$, i.e.,

$$f[n] = f(n\Delta_t), \quad n = \ldots, -1, 0, 1, \ldots, \tag{A.1-14}$$

where Δ_t is the sampling period.

Sampling Theorem.   The sampling theorem provides a formula for reconstructing a continuous function $f(t)$ from its samples $f[n]$ under certain conditions. If $f(t)$ is band-limited, i.e., the magnitude of its Fourier transform $F(\omega)$ vanishes at frequencies greater than a frequency $\Omega = B/2\pi$, called the bandwidth, then $f(t)$ can be recovered exactly from its samples $f[n]$, provided that the sampling period Δ_t is equal to, or smaller than, $\pi/\Omega = 1/2B$. If $\Delta_t = 1/2B$, then the reconstruction formula is

$$f(t) = \sum_{n=-\infty}^{\infty} f[n]\sigma(t - t_n), \tag{A.1-15}$$

Sampling Theorem

where $\sigma(t) = \mathrm{sinc}(t/\Delta_t)$ and $t_n = n\Delta_t$, as illustrated in Fig. A.1-1.

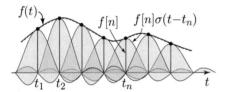

Figure A.1-1   Reconstruction of a bandlimited function from its samples at $t_n = n\Delta_t$.

Sampling in Frequency.   If the discrete function $f[n]$ is generated by uniform sampling of a continuous function $f(t)$ at $t_n = n\Delta_t$, where Δ_t is the sampling interval, then the DFT $F[k]$ is a sample of the Fourier transform $F(\omega)$ at $\omega_k = k\Delta_\omega$, where Δ_ω is the frequency sampling interval. The sampling intervals are related by

$$\Delta_\omega \Delta_t = 2\pi, \tag{A.1-16}$$

so that the kernel $2\pi kn/N$ in the DFT formula equals $\omega_n t_n$, which reproduces the kernel ωt in the continuous Fourier transform formula. In view of (A.1-16), a small Δ_t (i.e., fine sampling of t) corresponds to large $\Delta_t = 2\pi/\Delta_\omega$ (i.e., coarse sampling of ω), and vice versa.

B. One-Dimensional Linear Systems

Consider a system whose input and output are the functions $f(t)$ and $g(t)$, respectively. An example is a pulse $f(t)$ whose shape is modified upon traveling through and reflecting from an object, leading to an echo, or a sequence of echos $g(t)$. The system is characterized by a rule or a mathematical operation that relates the output to the input. This may take the form of a differential equation, an integral transform, or a simple mathematical operation such as $g(t) = \log f(t)$.

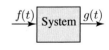

A system is said to be *linear* if it satisfies the principle of superposition, i.e., if its response to the sum of any two inputs is the sum of its responses to each of the inputs separately. In this case, the output at time t is, in general, a weighted superposition of the input contributions at different times τ,

$$g(t) = \int_{-\infty}^{\infty} h(t;\tau)f(\tau)\,d\tau, \qquad (A.1\text{-}17)$$

where $h(t;\tau)$ is a weighting function representing the contribution of the input at time τ to the output at time t. If the input is an impulse at τ, so that $f(t) = \delta(t-\tau)$, then (A.1-17) gives $g(t) = h(t;\tau)$. Thus $h(t;\tau)$ is the **impulse-response function** of the system [also known as **point spread function (PSF)** or **Green's function**].

Linear Shift-Invariant Systems

A linear system is said to be **time invariant** or **shift invariant** if, when its input is shifted in time, its output is shifted by an equal time, but otherwise remains the same. In this case, the impulse-response function is a function of the time difference $h(t;\tau) = h(t-\tau)$ and (A.1-17) becomes

$$g(t) = h(t) \otimes f(t) = \int_{-\infty}^{\infty} h(t-\tau)f(\tau)\,d\tau. \qquad (A.1\text{-}18)$$

Thus, the output $g(t)$ is the convolution of the input $f(t)$ with the impulse-response function $h(t)$ [see (A.1-7)]. If $f(t) = \delta(t)$, then $g(t) = h(t)$; and if $f(t) = \delta(t-\tau)$, then $g(t) = h(t-\tau)$, as illustrated in Fig. A.1-2.

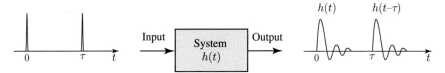

Figure A.1-2   Response of a linear shift-invariant system to impulses.

Transfer Function

In accordance with the convolution theorem, the Fourier transforms $F(\omega)$, $G(\omega)$, and $H(\omega)$, of $f(t)$, $g(t)$, and $h(t)$, respectively, are related by

$$G(\omega) = H(\omega)F(\omega). \qquad (A.1\text{-}19)$$

If the input $f(t)$ is a harmonic function $F(\omega)\exp(j\omega t)$, then the output $g(t) = H(\omega)F(\omega)\exp(j\omega t)$ is also a harmonic function of the same frequency but with a modified complex amplitude $G(\omega) = F(\omega)H(\omega)$, as illustrated in Fig. A.1-3. The multiplicative factor $H(\omega)$ is known as the system's **transfer function**. The transfer function is the Fourier transform of the impulse-response function. Equation (A.1-19) is the key to the usefulness of Fourier methods in the analysis of linear shift-invariant systems. To determine the output of a system for an arbitrary input, we simply decompose the input into its harmonic components, multiply the complex amplitude of each harmonic function by the transfer function at the appropriate frequency, and add up the resultant harmonic functions.

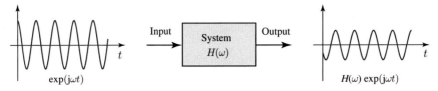

Figure A.1-3   Response of a linear shift-invariant system to a harmonic function.

Examples

- *Ideal system:* $H(\omega) = 1$ and $h(t) = \delta(t)$; the output is a replica of the input.

- *Ideal system with delay:* $H(\omega) = \exp(-j\omega\tau)$ and $h(t) = \delta(t - \tau)$; the output is a replica of the input delayed by time τ.

- *System with exponential response:* $H(\omega) = \tau/(1 + j\omega\tau)$ and $h(t) = \exp(-t/\tau)$ for $t \geq 0$, and $h(t) = 0$ otherwise; this represents the response of a system described by a first-order linear differential equation with time constant τ. An impulse at the input results in an exponentially decaying response.

Discrete Linear Systems.

As in the continuous case, a discrete linear system is characterized by its impulse response function $h[n]$ and its DFT $H[k]$. The input and output functions $f[n]$ and $g[n]$ of such a system are related by

$$g[n] = h[n] \otimes f[n] \tag{A.1-20}$$

$$G[k] = H[k]F[k], \tag{A.1-21}$$

where $F[n]$, $H[n]$, and $G[n]$ are the DFTs of $f[n]$, $h[n]$, and $g[n]$, respectively.

A.2   Two-Dimensional Signals and Systems

A. Two-Dimensional Fourier Transform

We now consider a function of two variables $f(x, y)$. If x and y represent the co-ordinates of a point in a two-dimensional (2D) space, then $f(x, y)$ represents a spatial pattern (e.g., the amplitude of a wave in a given plane). The harmonic function $F \exp[-j(k_x x + k_y y)]$ is regarded as a building block from which other functions may be composed by superposition. The variables $k_x/2\pi$ and $k_y/2\pi$ represent spatial frequencies in the x and y directions, respectively. Since x and y have units of length (mm), $k_x/2\pi$ and $k_y/2\pi$ have units of cycles/mm, or lines/mm. Examples of 2D harmonic functions are illustrated in Fig. A.2-1.

The Fourier theorem may be generalized to functions of two variables. A function $f(x, y)$ may be decomposed as a superposition (integral) of harmonic functions of x and y,

$$f(x, y) = \frac{1}{4\pi^2} \int\limits_{-\infty}^{\infty}\!\!\int F(k_x, k_y) \exp\left[-j(k_x x + k_y y)\right] \, dk_x \, dk_y, \tag{A.2-1}$$

Inverse Fourier Transform

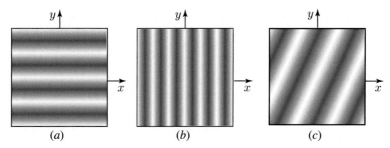

Figure A.2-1 Brightness image of the real part $|F| \cos[k_x x + k_y y + \arg\{F\}]$ of a 2D harmonic function with white and dark points representing positive and negative values, respectively. (*a*) $k_x = 0$; (*b*) $k_y = 0$; (*c*) arbitrary case.

where the coefficients $F(k_x, k_y)$ are determined by use of the 2D Fourier transform

$$F(k_x, k_y) = \iint\limits_{-\infty}^{\infty} f(x, y) \exp\left[j(k_x x + k_y y)\right] dx\, dy. \qquad \text{(A.2-2)}$$
Fourier
Transform

Properties

The 2D Fourier transform has some properties that are obvious generalizations of those of the 1D Fourier transform, and others that are unique to the 2D case.

- **Rotation Invariance.** If $F(k_x, k_y)$ is the 2D Fourier transform of $f(x, y)$, then the Fourier transform of $f(x, y)$ rotated by some angle is the function $F(k_x, k_y)$ rotated by the same angle.

- **Projection-Slice (P–S) Theorem.** For a fixed y, if the 2D function $f(x, y)$ is integrated with respect to x at a fixed value of y and the result is plotted as a 1D function of y,

$$p(y) = \int_{-\infty}^{\infty} f(x, y)\, dx, \qquad \text{(A.2-3)}$$
Projection

is called the projection along the x direction. The P–S theorem states that

$$P(k_y) = F(0, k_y), \qquad \text{(A.2-4)}$$
Projection-Slice
Theorem

where $P(k_x)$ is the 1D Fourier transform of the projection $p(x)$. Thus, the 1D Fourier transform of the projection is a slice of the 2D Fourier transform of the original function along the line $k_y = 0$. Because of rotational invariance, the P–S theorem is applicable to projections along other directions. The slice is always orthogonal to the direction of projection. This theorem is a basic tool in ray tomography (Chapter 4).

- **Convolution and cross-correlation.** If $f(x, y)$ is the 2D convolution of two functions $f_1(x, y)$ and $f_2(x, y)$ with Fourier transforms $F_1(k_x, k_y)$ and $F_2(k_x, k_y)$, respectively, i.e.,

$$f(x, y) = \iint_{-\infty}^{\infty} f_1(x', y') f_2(x - x', y - y') \, dx' \, dy', \qquad (A.2\text{-}5)$$

then the Fourier transform of $f(x, y)$ is

$$F(k_x, k_y) = F_1(k_x, k_y) F_2(k_x, k_y). \qquad (A.2\text{-}6)$$

Thus, as in the 1D case, convolution in the space domain is equivalent to multiplication in the Fourier domain. Likewise, the cross-correlation function is a generalization of (A.1-8),

$$f(x, y) = \iint_{-\infty}^{\infty} f_1^*(x', y') f_2(x' + x, y' + y) \, dx' \, dy', \qquad (A.2\text{-}7)$$

and $F(k_x, k_y) = F_1^*(k_x, k_y) F_2(k_x, k_y)$.

Special Functions

- **Separable Functions.** If $f(x, y) = f_x(x) f_y(y)$ is the product of one function of x and another of y, then its 2D Fourier transform is the product of the 1D Fourier transforms of $f_x(x)$ and $f_y(y)$, i.e., $F(k_x, k_y) = F_x(k_x) F_y(k_y)$. The following are two examples:

    - The Fourier transform of $\delta(x - x_0)\delta(y - y_0)$, which represents an impulse located at (x_0, y_0), is the harmonic function $\exp[j(k_x x_0 + k_y y_0)]$.
    - The Fourier transform of the Gaussian function $\exp[-\pi(x^2 + y^2)] = \exp(-\pi x^2)\exp(-\pi y^2)$ is the Gaussian function $\exp[-(k_x^2 + k_y^2)/4\pi] = \exp(-k_x^2/4\pi)\exp(-k_y^2/4\pi)$.

- **Circularly Symmetric Functions.** The Fourier transform of a circularly symmetric function is also circularly symmetric. Three examples are illustrated in Fig. A.2-2. Another example is the 2D function

$$f(x, y) = \frac{\exp(-jkr)}{r}, \quad r = \sqrt{\rho^2 + d^2}, \quad \rho = \sqrt{x^2 + y^2}, \qquad (A.2\text{-}8)$$

which represents a spherical wave of wave number k centered at the origin and measured in the plane $z = d$. Its 2D Fourier transform is

$$F(k_x, k_y) = 2\pi \frac{\exp(-jk_z d)}{jk_z}, \quad k_z = +\sqrt{k^2 - k_\rho^2}, \quad k_\rho = \sqrt{k_x^2 + k_y^2}. \qquad (A.2\text{-}9)$$

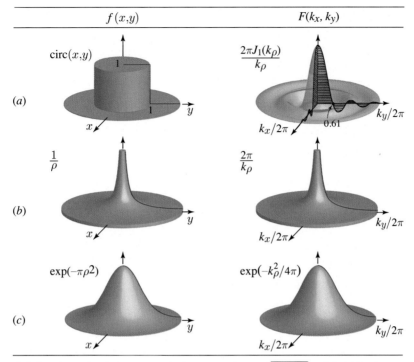

Figure A.2-2 Three circularly symmetric functions of $\rho = \sqrt{x^2 + y^2}$ and their Fourier transforms, which are functions of $k_\rho = \sqrt{k_x^2 + k_y^2}$. (a) The function circ$(x, y)$ equals unity for $\rho \leq 1$ and zero otherwise. Here, the function $J_1(.)$ is the Bessel function of order 1. (b) The function $1/\rho$. (c) The Gaussian function $\exp(-\pi\rho^2)$.

Two-Dimensional Discrete Fourier Transform (DFT)

Generalization of the 1D DFT to the 2D case is straightforward. In 2D, the signal is an array $f[n_x, n_y]$ of dimensions $N_x \times N_y$.

DFT and Inverse DFT.   The DFT of $f[n_x, n_y]$ is

$$F[k_x, k_y] = \sum_{n_y=0}^{N_y-1} \sum_{n_x=0}^{N_x-1} f[n_x, n_y] \exp\left[j2\pi\left(\frac{k_x n_x}{N_x} + \frac{k_y n_y}{N_y}\right)\right], \qquad \text{(A.2-10)}$$

DFT

for $k_x = 0, 1, \ldots, N_x - 1$ and $k_y = 0, 1, \ldots, N_y - 1$, and the corresponding inverse Fourier transform is

$$f[n_x, n_y] = \frac{1}{N_x N_y} \sum_{k_x=0}^{N_x-1} \sum_{k_y=0}^{N_y-1} F[k_x, k_y] \exp\left[-j2\pi\left(\frac{k_x n_x}{N_x} + \frac{k_y n_y}{N_y}\right)\right]. \qquad \text{(A.2-11)}$$

Inverse DFT

■ MATLAB functions F=fft2(f) and f=ifft2(F) implement the 2D DFT and the 2D inverse DFT, respectively, where f and F are matrices of elements $f[n_x, n_y]$ and $F[k_x, k_y]$, respectively.

2D Convolution.   The discrete version of the convolution

$$f(x, y) = f_1(x, y) \otimes f_2(x, y)$$

is denoted as

$$f[n_x, n_y] = f_1[n_x, n_y] \otimes f_2[n_x, n_y]$$

and is defined by

$$f[m_x, m_y] = \sum_{n_y=0}^{N_y-1} \sum_{n_x=0}^{N_x-1} f_1[n_x, n_y] f_2[m_x - n_x, m_y - n_y]. \qquad (A.2\text{-}12)$$

2D Convolution

■ MATLAB function f=conv(f1,f2) implements discrete convolution.

B. Two-Dimensional Linear Systems

A 2D system relates two 2D functions $f(x, y)$ and $g(x, y)$, called the input and output functions, respectively; or the object and image, respectively. These functions may, for example, represent fields at two parallel planes, with (x, y) representing the position variables; the system comprises the media that lie between the two planes.

The concepts of linearity and shift invariance defined for 1D systems are easily generalized to 2D (imaging) systems. The output $g(x, y)$ of the *linear* system is generally related to its input $f(x, y)$ by a superposition integral

$$g(x, y) = \iint_{-\infty}^{\infty} h(x, y; x', y') f(x', y') \, dx' \, dy', \qquad (A.2\text{-}13)$$

where $h(x, y; x', y')$ is a weighting function that represents the effect of the object at the point (x', y') on the image at the point (x, y). The function $h(x, y; x', y')$ is called the **impulse response function** or the **point spread function (PSF)**.

The system is said to be **shift invariant** (or isoplanatic) if shifting the object in some direction leads to a shift of the image by the same distance and in the same direction, without any other change (see Fig. A.2-3). The PSF is then a function of position differences so that $h(x, y; x', y') = h(x - x', y - y')$. Equation (A.2-13) then becomes the 2D convolution of $f(x, y)$ and $h(x, y)$:

$$g(x, y) = h(x, y) \otimes f(x, y) = \iint_{-\infty}^{\infty} h(x - x', y - y') f(x', y') \, dx' \, dy'. \qquad (A.2\text{-}14)$$

2D Convolution

This operation may be visualized as a set of four operations: invert–shift–multiply–add, i.e., invert the function $h(x', y')$ to a mirror image $h(-x', -y')$, shift it to the position (x, y), multiply it with the input function $f(x', y')$ and integrate. The process is repeated for all shifts (x, y) to generate the output function $g(x, y)$.

■ MATLAB function g = conv2(h,f) computes the discrete 2D convolution.

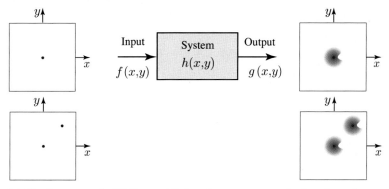

Figure A.2-3 Response of a 2D linear shift-invariant system to a single point and to two points.

Receptive Function

As mentioned earlier, the image of a fixed single point located at (x', y') in the object plane is $g(x, y) = h(x, y; x', y')$, where $h(x, y; x', y')$ is the PSF. An equivalent way of visualizing the imaging process is to focus our attention on a fixed single point in the image plane located at (x, y). Such a point receives a contribution from a point (x', y') in the object plane equal to $f(x', y') = h(x, y; x', y')$. This function of (x', y'), called the **receptive function**, is commonly used in vision science where it is called the *receptive field*. Here, a single sensor (electrode) placed at single point (x, y) records the signal received as a point stimulus is moved at a variable position (x', y') in the object plane. In summary:

- The **PSF** at a fixed position (x', y') in the object plane is the function $h(x, y; x', y')$ plotted as a function of (x, y).

- The **receptive function** at a fixed position (x, y) in the image plane is the function $h(x, y; x', y')$ plotted as a function of (x', y').

If the imaging system is shift invariant, then $h(x, y; x', y') = h(x - x', y - y')$. For a point at the origin of the object plane, $(x', y') = (0, 0)$, the PSF is $h(x, y)$. Likewise, for a point at the origin of the image plane, $(x, y) = (0, 0)$, the receptive function is $h(-x, -y)$. Therefore, the receptive function, denoted $\eta(x, y)$, is nothing but a transposed version of the PSF $h(x, y)$, as illustrated in Fig. A.2-4.

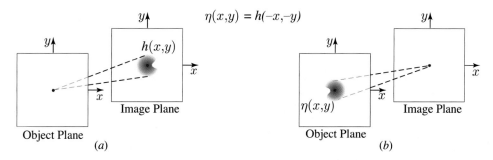

Figure A.2-4 (*a*) PSF. (*b*) Receptive function.

The convolution relation in (A.2-14) may be expressed in terms of the receptive function as

$$g(x, y) = \iint\limits_{-\infty}^{\infty} \eta(x' - x, y' - y)f(x', y')\, dx'\, dy'. \tag{A.2-15}$$

This operation may be implemented in terms of three operations: shift–multiply–add.

Transfer Function

As in the 1D case, the convolution relation in (A.2-14) corresponds to multiplication in the Fourier domain, i.e.,

$$G(k_x, k_y) = H(k_x, k_y)F(k_x, k_y), \tag{A.2-16}$$

where $G(k_x, k_y)$, $H(k_x, k_y)$, and $F(k_x, k_y)$ are the 2D Fourier transforms of $g(x, y)$, $h(x, y)$, and $f(x, y)$, respectively.

A harmonic input of complex amplitude $F(k_x, k_y)$ therefore produces a harmonic output of the same spatial frequency but with complex amplitude $G(k_x, k_y) = H(k_x, k_y)F(k_x, k_y)$, as illustrated in Fig. A.2-5. The multiplicative factor $H(k_x, k_y)$ is the system's **transfer function**.

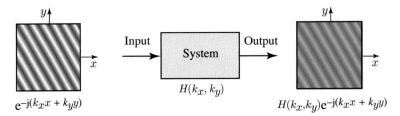

Figure A.2-5   Response of a 2D linear shift-invariant system to harmonic functions.

The transfer function is the Fourier transform of the impulse response function. Either of these functions characterizes the system completely and enables us to determine the output corresponding to an arbitrary input. Examples of transfer functions are shown in Fig. A.2-6.

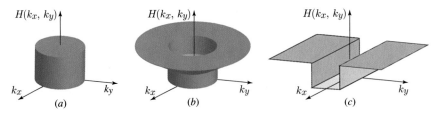

Figure A.2-6   Transfer functions of (a) a low-pass filter, (b) a high-pass filter, (c) a filter that transmits horizontal (x-direction) spatial frequencies and blocks high vertical (y-direction) spatial frequencies.

EXAMPLE A.2-1.   *System Whose PSF is a circ Function.* A system with an impulse response function in the form of a uniform circular patch of radius ρ_s, i.e.,

$$h(x,y) = \frac{1}{\pi \rho_s^2} \operatorname{circ}\left(\frac{x}{\rho_s}, \frac{y}{\rho_s}\right),$$

has a transfer function

$$H(k_x, k_y) = \frac{2J_1(\rho_s k_\rho)}{\rho_s k_\rho}, \quad k_\rho = \sqrt{k_x^2 + k_y^2},$$

as illustrated in Fig. A.2-7. The system severely attenuates spatial frequencies higher than $0.61/\rho_s$ lines/mm.

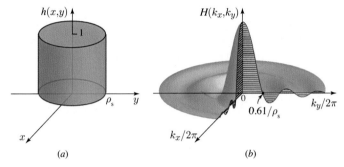

(a)   (b)

Figure A.2-7   (*a*) PSF is a circ function with radius ρ_s. (*b*) Transfer function has its first zero at a spatial frequency $k_\rho/2\pi = 0.61/\rho_s$ cycles/mm.

2D Discrete Linear Systems.   As in the continuous case, a discrete linear system is characterized by its impulse response function $h[n_x, n_y]$ and its DFT $H[k_x, k_y]$. The input and output functions $f[n_x, n_y]$ and $g[n_x, n_y]$ of such a system are related by

$$g[n_x, n_y] = h[n_x, n_y] \otimes f[n_x, n_y] \tag{A.2-17}$$

$$G[k_x, k_y] = H[k_x, k_y] F[k_x, k_y], \tag{A.2-18}$$

where $F[k_x, k_y]$, $H[k_x, k_y]$, and $G[k_x, k_y]$ are the DFTs of $f[n_x, n_y]$, $h[n_x, n_y]$, and $g[n_x, n_y]$, respectively.

Two-Dimensional Sampling

As in the 1D case, the sampling of a continuous 2D function $f(x, y)$ at regular spacings Δ_x and Δ_y in the x and y directions, respectively, will yield a discrete function

$$f[n_x, n_y] = f(n_x \Delta_x, n_y \Delta_y), \quad n_x, n_y = \dots, -1, 0, 1, \dots \tag{A.2-19}$$

The sampling theorem for 1D signals can be extended to 2D signals in a straightforward manner and provides conditions whereby the continuous signal $f(x, y)$ can be reconstructed exactly from its samples $f[n_x, n_y]$. Suppose that the continuous function $f(x, y)$ is band-limited, i.e., its Fourier transform $F(k_x, k_y)$ is nonzero only for frequencies satisfying the conditions $|k_x|/2\pi \le B_x, |k_y|/2\pi \le B_y$. Then, as long as the sampling interval Δ_x is smaller than $1/2B_x$ and the sampling interval Δ_y is smaller than $1/2B_y$, the function $f(x, y)$ can be recovered without error from its samples $f[n_x, n_y]$ using the reconstruction formula

$$f(x, y) = \sum_{n_x=-\infty}^{\infty} \sum_{n_y=-\infty}^{\infty} f[n_x, n_y]\, \sigma_x\,(x - n_x\Delta_x)\, \sigma_y\,(y - n_y\Delta_y), \qquad \text{(A.2-20)}$$

where $\sigma_x(x) = \operatorname{sinc}(x/\Delta_x)$ and $\sigma_y(y) = \operatorname{sinc}(y/\Delta_y)$ are sampling functions.

A.3 Multi-Dimensional Signals and Systems

The ideas of Fourier transforms and linear systems can easily be generalized to the three-dimensional (3D) case, as well as to higher dimensions. It is convenient to present these ideas by use of concise vector notations. For example, in the 3D case, the image $f(x, y, z)$ is written as $f(\mathbf{r})$, where $\mathbf{r}$ is a vector with components (x, y, z). Likewise, its Fourier transform is written as $F(\mathbf{k})$, where $\mathbf{k} = (k_x, k_y, k_z)$. In these notations, the Fourier transform relations are

$$F(\mathbf{k}) = \int f(\mathbf{r}) \exp\,(\mathrm{j}\mathbf{k} \cdot \mathbf{r})\, d\mathbf{r} \qquad\qquad \text{(A.3-1)}$$
$$\text{Fourier Transform}$$

$$f(\mathbf{r}) = \frac{1}{(2\pi)^3} \int F(\mathbf{k}) \exp\,(-\mathrm{j}\mathbf{k} \cdot \mathbf{r})\, d\mathbf{k} \qquad\qquad \text{(A.3-2)}$$
$$\text{Inverse Fourier Transform}$$

where $\mathbf{k} \cdot \mathbf{r} = k_x x + k_y y + k_z z$.

Projection-Slice (P–S) Theorem.   The P–S theorem in (A.2-3) may be generalized to higher dimensions. For example, if $p(x, y)$ is the projection of $f(x, y, z)$ along the z direction, i.e.,

$$p(x, y) = \int_{-\infty}^{\infty} f(x, y, z)\, dz,$$

then

$$P(k_x, k_y) = F(k_x, k_y, 0). \qquad\qquad \text{(A.3-3)}$$
$$\text{Projection-Slice}$$
$$\text{Theorem}$$

Thus, the 2D Fourier transform of the projection is a planar slice of the 3D Fourier transform of the original function. The slice plane is orthogonal to the direction of projection. This property, which applies generally to projections along any direction, is useful in applications of wave tomography (Chapter 4).

Linear Systems.   In the multi-dimensional case, the output of a linear system is related to the input by the multi-dimensional integral

$$g(\mathbf{r}) = \int h(\mathbf{r}; \mathbf{r}') f(\mathbf{r}')\, d\mathbf{r}'. \qquad\qquad \text{(A.3-4)}$$
$$\text{Linear Transformation}$$

In the shift-invariant case, (A.3-4) becomes the multi-dimensional convolution

$$g(\mathbf{r}) = h(\mathbf{r}) \otimes f(\mathbf{r}) = \int h(\mathbf{r} - \mathbf{r}')f(\mathbf{r}')\,\mathrm{d}\mathbf{r}'.$$

(A.3-5)
Convolution

The function h is the PSF of the system. For example, for a 3D system, $h(x, y, z)$ represents the spatial spread introduced when a 3D object is imaged by an imperfect imaging system.

Further Reading

P. D. Cha and J. I. Molinder, *Fundamentals of Signals and Systems: A Building Block Approach*, Cambridge University Press, 2006.

E. W. Kamen and B. S. Heck, *Fundamentals of Signals and Systems Using the Web and Matlab*, 3rd ed., Prentice Hall, 2006.

B. P. Lathi, *Linear Systems and Signals*, 2nd ed., Oxford University Press, 2005.

R. N. Bracewell, *Fourier Analysis and Imaging*, Kluwer, 2003.

R. N. Bracewell, *The Fourier Transform and Its Applications*, 3rd ed., McGraw–Hill, 2000.

A. V. Oppenheim, A. S. Willsky, and S. H. Nawab, *Signals and Systems*, 2nd ed., Prentice Hall, 1997.

B

Linear Algebra

Presented in this appendix is a brief review of some principles of linear algebra that are useful in image processing and inverse problems. A discrete signal or an image is described by a set of real or complex numbers $(f_1, f_2, \cdots, f_N)$ forming a vector in an N-dimensional Euclidean space $\mathbb{R}^N$ or its complex version $\mathbb{C}^N$. Such vectors will be denoted by the bold face lower case Roman letter, e.g., $\mathbf{f}$, and represented by a column matrix, e.g.,

$$\mathbf{f} = \begin{bmatrix} f_1 \\ f_2 \\ \vdots \\ f_N \end{bmatrix}, \tag{B.0-1}$$

where f_n is the nth component of the vector $\mathbf{f}$. Note that the components of a vector are denoted by lower case italic letters, e.g., f_n.

As describe in Chapter 5, linear imaging systems are described by linear transformations represented by matrices. Acting on $\mathbf{f} \in \mathbb{R}^N$ (or $\in \mathbb{C}^N$) is a matrix $\mathbf{H}$ that produces a vector $\mathbf{g} \in \mathbb{R}^M$ (or $\in \mathbb{C}^M$). The vectors $\mathbf{f}$ and $\mathbf{g}$ are called the *input* and *output* vectors, or the *object* and *image*, respectively. The components of $\mathbf{g}$ are related to those of $\mathbf{f}$ by superpositions defined via the standard matrix-vector product

$$g_m = \sum_{n=1}^{N} h_{m,n} f_n, \qquad m = 1, 2, \ldots, M. \tag{B.0-2}$$

Here, $h_{m,n}$ is the element of the matrix $\mathbf{H}$ on row m and column n. The matrix has M rows and N columns and is said to be an $M \times N$ matrix. With this, (B.0-2) can be written more concisely as the matrix-vector product

$$\mathbf{g} = \mathbf{Hf}. \tag{B.0-3}$$

In the context of this book, this matrix relation plays the role of the imaging equation and a principal goal is to invert it, i.e., compute $\mathbf{f}$, given $\mathbf{g}$ and $\mathbf{H}$.

This appendix covers: (1) some properties of linear vector spaces, particularly the Euclidean space $\mathbb{R}^N$ and its complex extension $\mathbb{C}^N$, and (2) some basic properties of matrices, particularly singular value decomposition (SVD).

B.1   Linear Vector Spaces

The vectors in this text are assumed to reside in the Euclidean space $\mathbb{R}^N$ or its complex version $\mathbb{C}^N$, which are linear vector spaces in which every vector is assigned a length, called the *norm*, and every pair of vectors are assigned an *inner product*, which defines their *angle*. These concepts are defined in this appendix.

Linear Vector Space and $\mathbb{R}^N$ and $\mathbb{C}^N$

Definition.   The linear vector space (or just vector space) $\mathbb{X} = \mathbb{R}^M$ is a set of N real numbers $f_1, f_2, \ldots, f_n \in \mathbb{R}$ arranged in the form of a column matrix that is closed under the operations of vector addition and scalar multiplication, i.e.,

1. for $\mathbf{f} \in \mathbb{X}$ and $\mathbf{g} \in \mathbb{X}$, $\mathbf{f} + \mathbf{g} \in \mathbb{X}$.
2. for α a real number (denoted as $\alpha \in \mathbb{R}$) and $\mathbf{f} \in \mathbb{X}$, $\alpha\mathbf{f} \in \mathbb{X}$.

The linear vector space $\mathbb{X} = \mathbb{C}^N$ is defined similarly, where the numbers f_i are complex and the scalar α is also complex (denoted as $\alpha \in \mathbb{C}$).

Addition in both $\mathbb{R}^N$ and $\mathbb{C}^N$ is described as element-by-element addition, so that the nth element of the vector $\mathbf{f} + \mathbf{g}$ is $f_n + g_n$. Scalar multiplication is defined similarly, so that the nth element of the vector $\alpha\mathbf{f}$ is αf_n.

It follows that a *linear combination* of the vectors $\mathbf{f}_1, \mathbf{f}_2 \ldots, \mathbf{f}_N$, i.e., a sum of the form $\mathbf{f} = \alpha_1\mathbf{f}_1 + \alpha_2\mathbf{f}_2 + \ldots + \alpha_N\mathbf{f}_N$ for scalars α_n, is also $\in \mathbb{X}$.

A special example is the familiar 3D space $\mathbb{R}^3$ space with the familiar three unit vectors:

$$\widehat{\mathbf{x}} = \begin{bmatrix} 1 \\ 0 \\ 0 \end{bmatrix} \quad \widehat{\mathbf{y}} = \begin{bmatrix} 0 \\ 1 \\ 0 \end{bmatrix} \quad \widehat{\mathbf{z}} = \begin{bmatrix} 0 \\ 0 \\ 1 \end{bmatrix},$$

which are used to define an arbitrary vector as a linear combination

$$\mathbf{r} = x\widehat{\mathbf{x}} + y\widehat{\mathbf{y}} + z\widehat{\mathbf{z}}.$$

Direct Sum.   A vector space $\mathbb{X}$ is the direct sum of two other spaces $\mathbb{X}_1$ and $\mathbb{X}_2$ if all vectors $\mathbf{f} \in \mathbb{X}$ have a unique representation

$$\mathbf{f} = \mathbf{f}_1 + \mathbf{f}_2$$

with $\mathbf{f}_1 \in \mathbb{X}_1$ and $\mathbf{f}_2 \in \mathbb{X}_2$. In this case we write

$$\mathbb{X} = \mathbb{X}_1 \oplus \mathbb{X}_2.$$

Subspaces.   The set S is a *subspace* of a linear vector space $\mathbb{R}^N$ ($\mathbb{C}^N$) if for all $\mathbf{f}, \mathbf{g} \in S$ and $\alpha, \beta \in \mathbb{R}(\mathbb{C})$, it is the case that $\alpha\mathbf{f} + \beta\mathbf{g} \in S$ as well.

If S_1 and S_2 are subspaces of a linear vector space $\mathbb{X}$, then $S_1 + S_2$ is a subspace of $\mathbb{X}$ as well. The sum $S_1 + S_2$ of two subsets, S_1 and S_2, of $\mathbb{X}$ is defined as the collection of all vectors of the form $\mathbf{s}_1 + \mathbf{s}_2$, where $\mathbf{s}_1 \in S_1$ and $\mathbf{s}_2 \in S_2$.

For $\mathbb{R}^3$, the three Cartesian unit vectors $\widehat{\mathbf{x}}$, $\widehat{\mathbf{y}}$, and $\widehat{\mathbf{z}}$ may be used to define subspaces. The collection of vectors that can be written as $\alpha\mathbf{x}$, where α is any real number, is just the "x" axis. Similarly, the y–z plane is a subspace comprised of all those vectors in $\mathbb{R}^3$ that can be written as $\alpha\mathbf{y} + \beta\mathbf{z}$, where α and β are both arbitrary real numbers.

Linear Dependence and Independence.   A vector $\mathbf{f}$ is said to be *linearly dependent* on a set of vectors S if $\mathbf{f}$ can be written as a linear combination of vectors from S. Otherwise, $\mathbf{f}$ is said to be *linearly independent* of the elements of S. A set of vectors is said to be linearly independent if each is linearly independent from the others. It follows that $\mathbf{f}_1, \mathbf{f}_2, \ldots, \mathbf{f}_n$ are linearly independent if and only if

$$\sum_{n=1}^{N} \alpha_n \mathbf{f}_n = 0 \quad \text{holds only for all } \alpha_n = 0.$$

For $\mathbb{R}^2$, examples of linearly independent and linearly dependent vectors are easy to visualize by examining vectors in the plane. For the case of linear dependence, choosing the three coefficients α_n identically equal to unity will yield the zero vector.

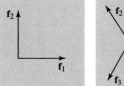

Linearly Independent   Linearly Dependent

For $\mathbb{R}^3$, the single vector $\hat{\mathbf{x}}$ forms a basis for the x axis subspace. The pair $\hat{\mathbf{y}}$ and $\hat{\mathbf{z}}$ form a basis for the y–z plane subspace.

Norms and Inner Products

Normed Linear Vector Space.   A normed linear vector space is a vector space $\mathbb{X}$ equipped with a real-valued function called a *norm* satisfying the following three properties for $\mathbf{f}, \mathbf{g} \in \mathbb{X}$ and α a scalar ($\in \mathbb{R}$ or $\mathbb{C}$ for $\mathbb{X} = \mathbb{R}^N$ or $\mathbb{C}^N$):

1. Non-negativity: $\|\mathbf{f}\| \geq 0$ with equality if and only if $\mathbf{f} = 0$.
2. Triangle inequality: $\|\mathbf{f} + \mathbf{g}\| \leq \|\mathbf{f}\| + \|\mathbf{g}\|$.
3. Scalar multiplication: $\|\alpha \mathbf{f}\| = |\alpha|\|\mathbf{f}\|$.

For $\mathbb{R}^N$, one widely used set of norms are the p-norms defined as

$$\|\mathbf{f}\|_p = \left[\sum_{n=1}^{N} |f_n|^p \right]^{1/p}. \tag{B.1-1}$$

The case of $p = 2$, which will be used throughout the text, corresponds to

$$\|\mathbf{f}\|_2^2 = \sum_{n=1}^{N} |f_n|^2. \tag{B.1-2}$$

For $\mathbb{R}^3$, the $\|\mathbf{f}\|_2$ norm of a vector $\mathbf{r} = (x, y, z)$ is the familiar Euclidean length $r = \sqrt{x^2 + y^2 + z^2}$.

Inner Product   An *inner product* in $\mathbb{C}^N$ is a scalar $(\mathbf{f}, \mathbf{g}) \in \mathbb{C}$ associated with any pair of vectors $\mathbf{f}$ and $\mathbf{g}$ such that the following properties are satisfied:

1. $(\mathbf{f}, \mathbf{g}) = (\mathbf{g}, \mathbf{f})^*$
2. $(\mathbf{f} + \mathbf{g}, \mathbf{z}) = (\mathbf{f}, \mathbf{g}) + (\mathbf{f}, \mathbf{z})$
3. $(\alpha \mathbf{f}, \mathbf{g}) = \alpha(\mathbf{f}, \mathbf{g})$
4. $(\mathbf{f}, \mathbf{f}) \geq 0$ with equality if and only if $\mathbf{f} = 0$,

where α^* is the complex conjugate of α. An inner product on $\mathbb{R}^N$ is defined similarly, except that $(\mathbf{f}, \mathbf{g}) \in \mathbb{R}$. Two vectors, $\mathbf{f}$ and $\mathbf{g}$ are said to be **orthogonal** if $(\mathbf{f}, \mathbf{g}) = 0$, in which case we write $\mathbf{f} \perp \mathbf{g}$.

The following properties relate the norms of vectors to their inner products:
1. $\|\mathbf{f}\|_2 = \sqrt{(\mathbf{f}, \mathbf{f})}$.
2. $|(\mathbf{f}, \mathbf{g})| \le \|\mathbf{f}\|_2 \|\mathbf{g}\|_2$ with equality if and only if $\mathbf{g} = 0$ or $\mathbf{g}$ is a scalar multiple of $\mathbf{g}$.
3. $\|\mathbf{f} + \mathbf{g}\|_2^2 + \|\mathbf{f} - \mathbf{g}\|_2^2 = 2 \left(\|\mathbf{f}\|_2^2 + \|\mathbf{g}\|_2^2 \right)$.
4. If $\mathbf{f} \perp \mathbf{g}$ then $\|\mathbf{f} + \mathbf{g}\|_2^2 = \|\mathbf{f}\|_2^2 + \|\mathbf{g}\|_2^2$.

For $\mathbb{C}^N$, the *inner product* of two vectors $\mathbf{f}$ and $\mathbf{g}$ with components $(f_1, f_2, \ldots, f_N)$ and $(g_1, g_2, \ldots, g_N)$ is

$$(\mathbf{f}, \mathbf{g}) = \sum_{n=1}^{N} f_n g_n^*. \tag{B.1-3}$$

For $\mathbb{R}^3$, the vectors $\hat{\mathbf{x}}$, $\hat{\mathbf{y}}$, and $\hat{\mathbf{z}}$ are all orthogonal to one another. Moreover, for any scalars a, b, and c, $a\hat{\mathbf{x}} + b\hat{\mathbf{y}}$ is orthogonal to $c\hat{\mathbf{z}}$ since

$$a\hat{\mathbf{x}} + b\hat{\mathbf{y}} = \begin{bmatrix} a \\ b \\ 0 \end{bmatrix}$$

so that

$$(a\hat{\mathbf{x}} + b\hat{\mathbf{y}}, c\hat{\mathbf{z}}) = \sum_{n=1}^{3} (a\hat{\mathbf{x}} + b\hat{\mathbf{y}})_n (c\hat{\mathbf{x}}_n) = a \times 0 + b \times 0 + 0 \times c = 0.$$

Bases.   A finite set of linearly independent vectors $\mathbf{f}_1, \mathbf{f}_2, \ldots \mathbf{f}_N$ is said to form a *basis* for the vector space $\mathbb{X}$ if any vector $\mathbf{f} \in \mathbb{X}$ can be written as a linear combination of the $\mathbf{f}_n$. *Finite* dimensional spaces are those whose bases are comprised of a finite number N of vectors. Otherwise, the space is termed *infinite dimensional*. The vectors of the basis may always be selected such that they are mutually orthonormal, i.e.,

$$(\mathbf{\Phi}_n, \mathbf{\Phi}_m) = \begin{cases} 1 & n = m, \\ 0 & \text{else.} \end{cases}$$

It can be shown that an arbitrary vector $\mathbf{f}$ may be expanded in such a basis as

$$\mathbf{f} = \sum_{n=1}^{N} a_n \mathbf{\Phi}_n, \qquad a_n = (\mathbf{f}, \mathbf{\Phi}_n). \tag{B.1-4}$$

Orthogonal Projection.   Let S be a subset of $\mathbb{X}$. The set of all vectors in $\mathbb{X}$ that are orthogonal to S is called the *orthogonal complement* of S in $\mathbb{X}$ and is denoted $S^\perp$. That is

$$S^\perp = \{ \mathbf{f} \in \mathbb{X} \,|\, (\mathbf{f}, \mathbf{s}) = 0 \text{ for all } \mathbf{s} \in S \}$$

Two properties hold: $\mathbb{X} = S \oplus S^\perp$ and $S^{\perp\perp} = S$. For $\mathbf{f} \in \mathbb{X}$, we define any $\mathbf{s} \in S$ for which $\mathbf{f} - \mathbf{s} \in S^\perp$ as the *orthogonal projection* of $\mathbf{f}$ into S.

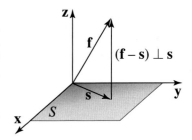

For $\mathbb{X} = \mathbb{R}^3$, and if S is the subspace spanned by the vectors $\mathbf{x}$ and $\mathbf{y}$, then the orthogonal projection of $\mathbf{f}$ into S is the vector $\mathbf{f} - \mathbf{s}$, where $\mathbf{s}$ is part of S. In this simple picture $S^\perp$ is spanned by $\mathbf{z}$.

For $\mathbb{X} = \mathbb{R}^N$, there is only one orthogonal projection of a vector $\mathbf{f}$ onto a subspace S.

For $\mathbb{X} \in \mathbb{R}^N$, there is a unique way of decomposing an arbitrary vector $\mathbf{f} \in \mathbb{R}^N$ into a component that is in an M-dimensional subspace S (with $M < N$) and a component that is in $S^\perp$. This decomposition may be found by use of an orthonormal basis of vectors $\boldsymbol{\phi}_m, m = 1, 2, \ldots M$. It can be shown that the projection of $\mathbf{f}$ onto S is given by

$$\mathbf{f}_s = \sum_{m=1}^M (\mathbf{f}, \boldsymbol{\phi}_m) \boldsymbol{\phi}_m. \tag{B.1-5}$$

B.2   Linear Transformations: Matrices

Linear imaging systems are described by linear transformations represented by the matrix operation $\mathbf{g} = \mathbf{A}\mathbf{f}$. An $M \times N$ real-valued matrix $\mathbf{A}$ maps vectors in $\mathbb{R}^N$ into vectors in $\mathbb{R}^M$, as defined by (B.0-2). A few of the basic properties of matrices are reviewed in this section.

Transpose and Hermitian Transpose.   Closely associated with a matrix $\mathbf{A}$ is its Hermitian transpose matrix $\mathbf{A}^H$ (also called conjugate transpose or adjoint), defined by the relation $A_{m,n}^H = A_{n,m}^*$ and obtained by *swapping* the rows and columns of $\mathbf{A}$ and taking the complex conjugate of each entry. When a matrix $\mathbf{A}$ is known to be real-valued, the complex conjugation is irrelevant and the Hermitian transpose is merely the transpose, denoted $\mathbf{A}^T$. If $\mathbf{A}$ is an $M \times N$ matrix, then $\mathbf{A}^H$ is an $N \times M$ matrix. For example, the Hermitian transpose of a vector $\mathbf{f} \in \mathbb{R}^N$, which is an $N \times 1$ column matrix, is a $1 \times N$ row matrix $\mathbf{f}^H$.

The Hermitian transpose operation provides flexibility in conducting matrix operations as illustrated by the following examples:

- The **inner product** of two vectors $\mathbf{f}$ and $\mathbf{g}$ in (B.1-3) may be written in the matrix form $(\mathbf{f}, \mathbf{g}) = \mathbf{g}^H \mathbf{f}$.

- The **norm** of a vector $\mathbf{f}$ is expressed as $\|\mathbf{f}\|_2 = (\mathbf{f}^H \mathbf{f})^{1/2}$.

- The **projection** operation defined by the expansion in (B.1-5) may be expressed in terms of a product of a matrix and its Hermitian transpose:

$$\mathbf{f}_s = \sum_{m=1}^M (\mathbf{f}, \boldsymbol{\phi}_m) \boldsymbol{\phi}_m = [\,\boldsymbol{\phi}_1 \mid \boldsymbol{\phi}_2 \mid \cdots \mid \boldsymbol{\phi}_M\,] \begin{bmatrix} \boldsymbol{\phi}_1^H \\ \boldsymbol{\phi}_2^H \\ \vdots \\ \boldsymbol{\phi}_M^H \end{bmatrix} \mathbf{f} = \boldsymbol{\Phi}\boldsymbol{\Phi}^H \mathbf{f},$$

where the M matrices $\boldsymbol{\phi}_m$ have been arranged into a single matrix $\boldsymbol{\Phi}$ whose mth column is just $\boldsymbol{\phi}_m$. It follows that the orthogonal projector is represented by $\boldsymbol{\Phi}\boldsymbol{\Phi}^{\mathrm{H}}$.

■ In MATLAB the Hermitian transpose $\mathbf{A}^{\mathrm{H}}$ of a matrix $\mathbf{A}$ is simply $\mathbf{A}'$ (the matrix followed by $'$). The transpose $\mathbf{A}^{\mathrm{T}}$ is implemented by $\mathbf{A}.'$ (the matrix followed by $.'$). The inner product between vectors $\mathbf{f}$ and $\mathbf{g}$ is $\mathbf{g}'\mathbf{f}$. The outer product between two square matrices is $\boldsymbol{\Phi}\boldsymbol{\Phi}'$.

Hermitian Operators.   A square matrix $\mathbf{A}$ ($N \times N$) is said to be **Hermitian** if and only if $\mathbf{A} = \mathbf{A}^{\mathrm{H}}$.

Rank.   The rank of a matrix is the maximum number of linearly independent rows (or, equivalently, the maximum number of linearly independent columns). For an $M \times N$ matrix, the rank K is smaller than or equal to the smaller dimension. A matrix with the largest possible rank (i.e., $K = \min(N, M)$) is said to have full rank; otherwise, the matrix is rank deficient.

■ MATLAB function `rank(A)` provides the rank of the matrix $\mathbf{A}$.

Inverse.   The inverse of a square matrix $\mathbf{A}$, denoted $\mathbf{A}^{-1}$, satisfies the property $\mathbf{A}^{-1}\mathbf{A} = \mathbf{I}$, where $\mathbf{I}$ is the identity matrix. An $N \times N$ matrix is invertible if it is full rank, i.e., $K = N$; otherwise, the marix $\mathbf{A}$ is referred to as singular.

■ MATLAB function `inv(A)` provides the inverse of the matrix $\mathbf{A}$.

A. Eigenvalues and Eigenvectors

Definition.   For an $N \times N$ square matrix, the special vectors $\mathbf{f}$ and scalars λ that satisfy the linear equation

$$\boxed{\mathbf{A}\mathbf{f} = \lambda\mathbf{f}}$$

(B.2-1)
Eigenvalue Equation

are known as the *eigenvectors* and *eigenvalues* of the matrix $\mathbf{A}$ and are denoted $\mathbf{f}_n$ and λ_n. These special vectors maintain their direction upon operation of the matrix $\mathbf{A}$; they only change their norm by the scalar λ. In general, an $N \times N$ matrix may have several eigenvalues with the same value, and may not have N distinct eigenvectors. Each distinct eigenvalue has at least one eigenvector.

Hermitian Matrices.   Many of the square matrices $\mathbf{A}$ in this book are Hermitian. Hermitian matrices have the special property that they have N linearly independent and orthogonal eigenvectors, and all of the corresponding eigenvalues are real-valued and nonnegative.

Computation.   The eigenvectors and eigenvalues may be computed by considering the set of algebraic equations resulting from the matrix equation

$$(\mathbf{A} - \lambda\mathbf{I})\mathbf{f} = 0,$$

where $\mathbf{I}$ is the identity matrix. A nontrivial solution exists if, and only if, the matrix $(\mathbf{A} - \lambda\mathbf{I})$ is singular. This condition provides an equation in λ, known as the *characteristic equation*, whose roots are the set of eigenvalues.

The eigenvalues and eigenvectors of an $N \times N$ matrix $\mathbf{A}$ are often presented in the form of two $N \times N$ matrices. The matrix $\mathbf{\Lambda}$ is a diagonal matrix of the eigenvalues and the matrix $\mathbf{F}$ contains the eigenvectors, with the nth column being the nth eigenvector $\mathbf{f}_n$, so that

$$\mathbf{\Lambda} = \mathrm{diag}(\lambda_1, \lambda_2, \cdots, \lambda_N), \qquad \mathbf{F} = \begin{bmatrix} \mathbf{f}_1 & \mathbf{f}_2 & \mathbf{f}_3 & \cdots & \mathbf{f}_N \end{bmatrix}.$$

■ MATLAB equation $[\mathbf{F}, \mathbf{\Lambda}] = \mathrm{eig}(\mathbf{A})$ provides the eigenvalue and eigenvector matrices $\mathbf{\Lambda}$ and $\mathbf{F}$ for a matrix $\mathbf{A}$.

Decomposition of a Matrix in terms of its eigenvectors and eigenvalues. If a matrix has N linearly independent eigenvectors, then the matrix $\mathbf{A}$ can be expanded in terms of its own eigenvectors and eigenvalues as

$$\mathbf{A} = \sum_{n=1}^{N} \lambda_n \mathbf{f}_n^{\mathrm{T}} \mathbf{f}_n = \mathbf{F}^{\mathrm{T}} \mathbf{\Lambda} \mathbf{F}. \tag{B.2-2}$$

Decomposition of a Matrix Equation in a Basis of Eigenvectors. For square matrices that possess a complete set of N linearly independent eigenvectors with N associated eigenvalues, the eigenvectors form a basis, which may be used to decompose arbitrary vectors. For example,

$$\mathbf{f} = \sum_{n=1}^{N} a_n \mathbf{f}_n, \qquad \mathbf{g} = \sum_{n=1}^{N} b_n \mathbf{f}_n.$$

Since $A\mathbf{f}_n = \lambda_n \mathbf{f}_n$, it can be readily shown that:

$$\text{If} \quad \mathbf{g} = \mathbf{Af}, \quad \text{then} \quad b_n = \lambda_n a_n. \tag{B.2-3}$$

It follows that, in this eigenvector basis, the linear transformation represented by the matrix multiplication $\mathbf{g} = \mathbf{Af}$ is equivalent to multiplication of the expansion coefficients, each by the corresponding eigenvalue. Expansion in an eigenvector basis is therefore similar to the Fourier transform discussed in the previous appendix, which translates convolution in the time domain to multiplication by the transfer function in the frequency domain. The eigenvector expansion is a form of spectral expansion, with the eigenvalues playing the role of the transfer function.

B. Singular Value Decomposition (SVD)

The nature of the matrix equation $\mathbf{g} = \mathbf{Af}$ becomes more subtle when the matrix $\mathbf{A}$ is not square, i.e., $M \neq N$. A central linear algebra tool required for the study of inverse problems is the SVD.

The SVD may be thought of as an extension of the eigenvector expansion of a square matrix for problems where $\mathbf{A}$ might not possess a full set of eigenvectors and eigenvalues or where $\mathbf{A}$ is not square. The SVD is like an eigen-decomposition for the *square* of $\mathbf{A}$.

There are two natural ways of obtaining a square of an $M \times N$ matrix $\mathbf{A}$, namely an $M \times M$ matrix $\mathbf{A}\mathbf{A}^{\mathrm{H}}$ and an $N \times N$ matrix $\mathbf{A}^{\mathrm{H}}\mathbf{A}$. For the sake of exposition, assume $M \geq N$. In general, these two matrices are not the same, and have different dimension, but they are both Hermitian, so they have full eigen-decompositions:

$$(\mathbf{A}\mathbf{A}^{\mathrm{H}})\,\mathbf{u}_k = \sigma_k^2 \mathbf{u}_k, \quad k = 1, \ldots, M$$

$$(\mathbf{A}^{\mathrm{H}}\mathbf{A})\,\mathbf{v}_n = \sigma_n^2 \mathbf{v}_n, \quad n = 1, \ldots, N.$$

Thus, there are *two* sets of singular vectors in an SVD, **left singular vectors** $\mathbf{u}_n$ and **right singular vectors** $\mathbf{v}_n$, but remarkably a *single* set of nonnegative real-valued eigenvalues $\sigma_n^2, n = 1, \ldots, N$ plus $M - N$ additional values $\sigma_k, k = N+1, \ldots, M$ that are equal to zero. The nonnegative values σ_n are called the **singular values**.

The singular values and singular vectors are arranged in the form of three matrices:

- A singular value matrix $\boldsymbol{\Sigma}$ of size $M \times N$ that is all zeros except along the main diagonal, where $\Sigma_{nn} = \sigma_n \geq 0$.

- An $M \times M$ matrix $\mathbf{U} = [\mathbf{u}_1\ \mathbf{u}_2\ \ldots \mathbf{u}_M]$ whose columns are the left singular vectors.

- An $N \times N$ matrix $\mathbf{V} = [\mathbf{v}_1\ \mathbf{v}_2\ \ldots \mathbf{v}_N]$ whose columns are the left singular vectors.

The matrices $\mathbf{U}$ and $\mathbf{V}$ are orthonormal, which means that $\mathbf{U}\mathbf{U}^{\mathrm{H}} = \mathbf{U}^{\mathrm{H}}\mathbf{U} = \mathbf{I}$ and $\mathbf{V}\mathbf{V}^{\mathrm{H}} = \mathbf{V}^{\mathrm{H}}\mathbf{V} = \mathbf{I}$, where $\mathbf{I}$ is the identity matrix.

The matrix $\mathbf{A}$ can be written in terms of its own singular values and singular vectors as

$$\mathbf{A} = \sum_n \sigma_n \mathbf{U}_n \mathbf{V}_n^{\mathrm{T}} = \mathbf{U}\boldsymbol{\Sigma}\mathbf{V}^{\mathrm{T}}. \tag{B.2-4}$$

Reduced-Rank SVD. While all matrices possess an SVD, it is not always the case that there are a full assortment of nonzero singular values. When some of the singular values are zero, the matrix $\mathbf{A}$ does not have full rank. Take, for example, a matrix for which $M > N$ with $K < N$ nonzero singular values. All elements of the matrix $\boldsymbol{\Sigma}$ are zero, except for a $K \times K$ diagonal submatrix $\boldsymbol{\Sigma}_1 = \mathrm{diagonal}(\sigma_1, \sigma_2, \ldots, \sigma_K)$ with the K nonzero eigenvalues. We can therefore decompose the singular matrix $\mathbf{U}$ into submatrices, $\mathbf{U}_1$ and $\mathbf{U}_0$, associated with the nonzero and the zero singular values, respectively, and similarly for $\mathbf{V}$, as shown in the following illustration.

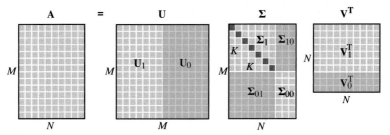

The SVD of **A** may then be written as

$$\mathbf{A} = \mathbf{U}\boldsymbol{\Sigma}\mathbf{V}^{\mathrm{T}} = [\mathbf{U}_1 \mid \mathbf{U}_0\ ] \begin{bmatrix} \boldsymbol{\Sigma}_1 & \mathbf{0}_{10} \\ \mathbf{0}_{01} & \mathbf{0}_{00} \end{bmatrix} \begin{bmatrix} \mathbf{V}_1^{\mathrm{T}} \\ \mathbf{V}_0^{\mathrm{T}} \end{bmatrix}, \tag{B.2-5}$$

where $\mathbf{0}_{10}, \mathbf{0}_{01}$, and $\mathbf{0}_{00}$ are matrices of zeros with dimensions $K \times (N - K), (M - K) \times K$, and $(M - K) \times (N - K)$, respectively. The matrices $\mathbf{U}_1, \mathbf{V}_1$, and $\boldsymbol{\Sigma}_1$ form the reduced SVD decomposition.

■ MATLAB equation $[\mathbf{U}, \boldsymbol{\Sigma}, \mathbf{V}] = \mathrm{svd}(\mathbf{A}, 0)$ provides the singular values and singular vectors of the matrix $\mathbf{A}$. The equation $[\mathbf{U}_1, \boldsymbol{\Sigma}_1, \mathbf{V}_1] = \mathrm{svd}(\mathbf{A})$ computes the *reduced* SVD.

C. Domain, Range, and Nullspace

The notions of domain, range, and nullspace of a matrix **A**, illustrated schematically in Fig. B.2-1, are helpful in characterizing the nature of the transformation $\mathbf{g} = \mathbf{A}\mathbf{f}$. We restrict the discussion to real-valued $N \times M$ matrices; extension to complex-valued matrices is straightforward.

- The **domain** of **A** is that subset $\mathbb{X} \subset \mathbb{R}^M$ in which the input vector $\mathbf{f} \in \mathbb{R}^M$ exists, and over which the transformation $\mathbf{g} = \mathbf{A}\mathbf{f}$ is considered.

- The **range** of **A** is the set of $\mathbf{g} \in \mathbb{R}^N$ such that there exists an $\mathbf{f} \in \mathbb{X}$ for which $\mathbf{A}\mathbf{f} = \mathbf{g}$. It turns out that since we are concerned here with matrix operators, the range is more than just a set if the domain is all of $\mathbb{R}^M$. It is in fact a subspace of $\mathbb{R}^N$ and is denoted as R(**A**).

- The **nullspace** of a matrix **A** is defined as the set N(**A**) of all $\mathbf{f} \in \mathbb{R}^M$ for which $\mathbf{A}\mathbf{f} = \mathbf{0}$.

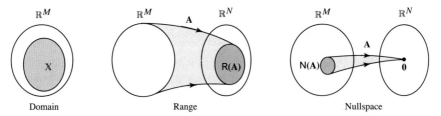

Figure B.2-1   Domain, range, and nullspace of an $N \times M$ matrix **A**.

EXAMPLE B.2-1.   *Range of An Overdetermined Matrix.*   Linear systems for which there are more rows in **A** than columns, termed overdetermined systems, provide classic examples of cases where solutions may not exist. In this example, we determine the range of the 3×2 overdetermined matrix $\mathbf{A}$ and a system equation $\mathbf{g} = \mathbf{Af}$ given by

$$\mathbf{A} = \begin{bmatrix} 1 & 2 \\ 3 & -4 \\ 4 & 3 \end{bmatrix}, \qquad \begin{bmatrix} g_1 \\ g_2 \\ g_3 \end{bmatrix} = \begin{bmatrix} 1 & 2 \\ 3 & -4 \\ 4 & 3 \end{bmatrix} \begin{bmatrix} f_1 \\ f_2 \end{bmatrix}. \tag{B.2-6}$$

This is accomplished by varying f_1 and f_2 in $\mathbb{R}^2$ and determining the corresponding vectors in $\mathbf{g} \in \mathbb{R}^3$. For $f_2 = 0$, we obtain a straight line defined by the parametric equations

$$g_1 = f_1, \qquad g_2 = 3f_1, \qquad g_3 = 4f_1.$$

This is the linear span of the first column of $\mathbf{A}$, denoted $\mathbf{A}(:,1)$. Similarly, for $f_1 = 0$, another straight line defined by the linear span of the second column $\mathbf{A}(:,2)$ is generated. These lines are the blue lines shown in Fig. B.2-2. The range $R(\mathbf{A})$ is the plane containing these two blue lines. A red line perpendicular to this plane is $R^{\perp}(\mathbf{A})$. Any vector in $\mathbb{R}^3$ that contains a component along the red line cannot be generated by any choice of $\mathbf{f}$.

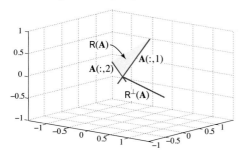

Figure B.2-2   The plane defined by the blue lines is the range $R(\mathbf{A})$. The orthogonal red line represents $R^{\perp}(\mathbf{A})$.

EXAMPLE B.2-2.   *Range and Nullspace of an Underdetermined Matrix*   Here, we determine the nullspace of the 2×3 underdetermined matrix $\mathbf{A}$ specified in the equation

$$\begin{bmatrix} g_1 \\ g_2 \end{bmatrix} = \begin{bmatrix} -1.3 & -0.5 & 1.0 \\ -1.0 & 1.0 & 0.0 \end{bmatrix} \begin{bmatrix} f_1 \\ f_2 \\ f_3 \end{bmatrix}. \tag{B.2-7}$$

The range of this matrix is the entire $\mathbb{R}^2$ space, and it is not difficult to show that multiple choices of $\mathbf{f}$ may generate the same vector $\mathbf{g}$. The nullspace is determined by setting $g_1 = g_2 = 0$ and determining (f_1, f_2, f_3). The nullspace $N(\mathbf{A})$ is that spanned by the vector

$$\mathbf{f}_{\text{null}} = \begin{bmatrix} 0.4369 \\ 0.4369 \\ 0.7863 \end{bmatrix};$$

i.e., $N(\mathbf{A})$ is defined by all vectors parallel to $\mathbf{f}_{\text{null}}$.

The Range and Nullspace in Terms of the SVD.   The SVD in (B.2-5) is a convenient way of characterizing the nullspace, the range and their orthogonal complements. For example, the nullspace $N(\mathbf{A})$ is the space spanned by the columns of the matrix $\mathbf{V}_0$ associated with the zero singular values. This may be shown by noting that if $\mathbf{f}$ is in the linear span of the K vectors of $\mathbf{V}_1$, then, since $\sigma_n > 0$ for all n, $\mathbf{Af} \neq 0$. Hence the nullspace of $\mathbf{A}$ is spanned by columns of the complementary subspace $\mathbf{V}_0$. Because $\mathbf{V}$ is orthonormal, the columns of $\mathbf{V}_1$ must be a basis for $N^{\perp}(\mathbf{A})$. Similar statements can be made about $\mathbf{U}$ and the range space of $\mathbf{A}$.

Detection and Classification

Reasoning and decision based on observation is an important human activity with extensive applications in science and engineering. In the presence of uncertainty, a probabilistic description is necessary and the subject is known as *statistical inference*. This appendix is a brief introduction to the principles of detection and classification, which are important branches of statistical inference. These subjects are presented in the context of subsurface imaging examples.

C.1 Detection

Detection theory deals with decisions on the presence or absence of a target, a property or an effect, based on a measured signal or signals. In subsurface imaging applications, for example, the observer may wish to make a decision on the presence or absence of a subsurface target, such as a buried landmine or a tumor in an organ, based on a signal generated by a sensor or an image measured by an imaging system.

Hypotheses and Decisions.   A detection problem is cast as a binary choice between two hypotheses:

$$H_1: \text{ the target is present}$$
$$H_0: \text{ the target is absent.}$$

There are therefore two possible decisions:

$$D_1: \text{ the target is present}$$
$$D_0: \text{ the target is absent.}$$

The decision is based on some measurement, which may be a single scalar quantity represented by a one-dimensional (1-D) signal s, or several quantities (a multi-dimensional signal) represented by a vector s. It is also useful to have some prior knowledge of the expected outcome of the measurement under each of the hypotheses. We will consider first detection based on a 1D signal and subsequently generalize the results to multi-dimensional signals.

Detection Based on a One-Dimensional Signal

Example.   A metal detector is used to detect the presence or absence of an underground metal target, based on the strength of the signal s generated by the detector. The signal is expected to be high if the target is present, and low otherwise. A sensible decision rule is to declare the target present if s exceeds some threshold ϑ, and absent otherwise. The threshold is selected based on prior knowledge acquired by testing the detector under the two conditions during the instrument calibration (or training) process.

Decision Rule Based on a Single Training Measurement.   If the signal was measured once in the presence of metal and once in the absence of metal and the results were s_1 and s_0, respectively, then a reasonable decision rule may be to compare the signal s measured under the unknown condition with each of these two values and select the hypothesis corresponding to the closer value. This **minimum distance assignment (MDA) rule**

$$\text{D}_1 \text{ if } |s - s_1| < |s - s_0|$$
$$\text{D}_0 \text{ if } |s - s_1| > |s - s_0|$$

is equivalent to a **threshold decision rule**:

$$\text{D}_1 \text{ if } s > \vartheta$$
$$\text{D}_0 \text{ if } s < \vartheta,$$

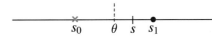

where the threshold $\vartheta = \frac{1}{2}(s_1 + s_0)$ is the average of the two training signals measured in the presence or absence of the target. This is a simple decision rule: the target is said to be present if the signal strength is above average and absent otherwise.

Decision Rule Based on Multiple Training Measurements.   Since all measurements are accompanied by uncertainties, variability, and errors, it is usually necessary to calibrate the detection system by taking multiple measurements with the target present and multiple measurements when it is absent, i.e., obtain multiple values of s_1 and s_0. If the measured values of s_1 and those of s_0 overlap, as illustrated below, then the decision rule is less certain and errors may be encountered. A decision rule may be based on computing the average $\bar{s}_1$ of the signals s_1 measured under H_1, and the average $\bar{s}_0$ of the signals s_0 measured under H_0, and using a threshold rule with a threshold $\vartheta = \frac{1}{2}(\bar{s}_1 + \bar{s}_0)$ determined from the averages $\bar{s}_1$ and $\bar{s}_0$.

Decision Based on Probability Distributions.   If a sufficiently large number of measurements of the signals s_1 and s_0 are made during the calibration or training process for each of the two hypotheses H_1 and H_0, then it is possible to construct a histogram of the measured values indicating their frequencies of occurrence in each case. Ultimately, probability density functions $p(s|H_1)$ and $p(s|H_0)$ can be constructed, describing the random variable s for each of the two hypotheses, with $\bar{s}_1$ and $\bar{s}_0$ representing the respective sample means. These functions can be used to determine the probabilities of various outcomes. For example, the probability that the target is present when s lies in the interval $a < s < b$ is the area under the function $p(s|H_1)$ within this interval. An important decision rule based on these probabilities is the **maximum likelihood (ML) decision rule**:

$$\text{D}_1 \text{ if } p(s|H_1) > p(s|H_0)$$
$$\text{D}_0 \text{ if } p(s|H_0) > p(s|H_1),$$

i.e., select the hypothesis for which the probability (likelihood) of the measured value s is higher. If the functions $p(s|H_1)$ and $p(s|H_0)$ intersect at a single point $s = \vartheta$, then the ML decision rule is equivalent to a threshold decision rule with a threshold ϑ at the intersection point.

Errors.   There are two types of errors possible in any detection problem:

Type I. Deciding that the target is present (D_1) when it is actually absent (H_0). This type of error is called **false alarm** or false positive.

Type II. Deciding that the target is absent (D_0) when it is actually present (H_1). This type of error is called **miss**.

	Decision	
	Present	Absent
Reality Present	Correct detection	Miss
Reality Absent	False alarm	Correct rejection

Sensitivity and Specificity.   A good detection system has a small rate of miss, i.e., a high rate of correct detection, a property called **sensitivity**. It must also have a small rate of false alarm, a property called selectivity or **specificity**. The cost of a miss can be enormous (e.g., in tumor or mine detection). Excessive false alarm rates make the system ineffective because of the cost involved in confirmation measurements. A decision strategy for enhancing the sensitivity (i.e., the rate of correct detection) uses a very low detection threshold, i.e., declares that the target is present if there is the slightest sign that it is present. Such a strategy would naturally result in a high rate of false alarm, i.e., low specificity. Conversely, a strategy for lowering the rate of false alarm uses a very high detection threshold, which naturally comes with a high miss rate, i.e., low rate of correct detection. Consequently, there is an inherent tradeoff between sensitivity and specificity.

Receiver Operating Characteristics (ROC).   Originally applied to the field of radar target-detection, the ROC is a quantitative expression of the tradeoff between sensitivity and specificity expressed as a plot of the probability of correct detection P_D versus the probability of false alarm P_F, where:

P_D = probability of declaring the target to be present, if it is present = $P(D_1|H_1)$
P_F = probability of declaring the target to be present, if it is absent = $P(D_1|H_0)$.

Here, P_D represents the sensitivity and $1 - P_F$ represents the specificity. The ROC curve is generated by changing the detection threshold. As the threshold increases, both P_D and P_F create an ROC as illustrated in Fig. C.1-1.

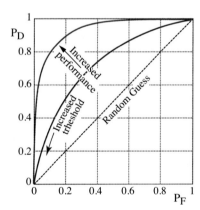

Figure C.1-1   ROC with two example curves. An ideal detection system would operate in the upper left corner with $P_D = 1$ and $P_F = 0$, but this is not possible. Realistically, an ROC hugging the lines $P_D = 1$ and $P_F = 0$ offers superior performance, and system optimization aims at pushing the curve toward the upper left corner of the diagram. A system operating on the $P_D = P_F$ line offers a worse performance since it does not do any better than a random flip of a coin, i.e., being just as likely to fail to detect a true target as to falsely detect an absent target.

Construction of the ROC.   The ROC may be readily constructed from the probability density functions $p(s|H_1)$ and $p(s|H_0)$ for the threshold decision rule by computing the probabilities of error for each value of the threshold ϑ. As illustrated in Fig. C.1-2(a), the probability of false alarm P_F is the probability that $s > \vartheta$ given that H_0 is true. This is the area under the function $p(s|H_0)$ to the right of the value $s = \vartheta$ [the blue shaded area in Fig. C.1-2(a)]. Similarly, the probability of miss P_M is the probability that $s < \vartheta$ given that H_1 is true. This is the area under the function $p(s|H_1)$ to the left of the value $s = \vartheta$ [the red shaded area in Fig. C.1-2(a)]. The probability of detection $P_D = 1 - P_M$. The ROC can be constructed by varying the threshold ϑ and plotting P_D versus P_F, as shown in Fig. C.1-2(b). Clearly the shape of the curve depends on the widths of the probability density functions $p(s|H_1)$ and $p(s|H_0)$ and their separation. For example, if the signal s is a normal (Gaussian) random variable with means $\bar{s}_1$ and $\bar{s}_0$ under hypotheses H_1 and H_0, respectively, and of the same variance σ_s^2 under both hypotheses, then the shape of the ROC depends on the ratio $\bar{s}/\sigma_s$ of the mean separation $\bar{s} = \bar{s}_1 - \bar{s}_0$ and the width σ_s.

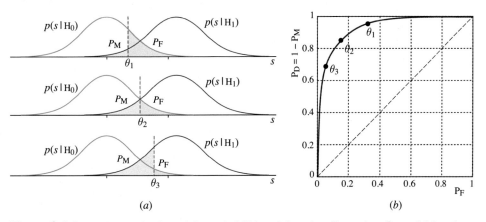

(a)   (b)

Figure C.1-2 (a) Determination of the probabilities of detection $P_D = 1 - P_M$ and false alarm P_F from the probability density functions of the signal s for the two hypotheses. (b) The ROC is constructed by varying the threshold ϑ. Three values of ϑ with their corresponding areas are shown as dots in the ROC.

Bayesian Decision Rules. If the hypotheses H_1 and H_0 have known prior probabilities p_1 and p_0 (i.e., probabilities before the observation is made), then such information can be accounted for in the decision rule. For example, the **maximum a posteriori probability (MAP)** decision rule is based on comparing the posterior conditional probabilities $p(H_1|s)$ and $p(H_0|s)$ and selecting the hypothesis with the greater probability, given the observation s, i.e.,

$$\begin{array}{l} D_1 \text{ if } p(H_1|s) > p(H_0|s) \\ D_0 \text{ if } p(H_1|s) < p(H_0|s). \end{array}$$

The conditional probability $p(H_1|s)$ can be determined from $p(s|H_1)$ by use of Bayes' theorem, $p(H_1|s)p(s) = p(s|H_1)p(H_1)$, where $p(H_1) = p_1$ and $p(s) = p(s|H_1)p(H_1) + p(s|H_0)p(H_0)$ is the total probability of s. Likewise, $p(H_0|s)$ can be determined in terms of $p(s|H_1)$ and the prior probability $p_0 = p(H_0)$. The MAP decision rule can be written in terms of the likelihood ratio $L(s) = p(s|H_1)/p(s|H_0)$ as

$$\begin{array}{l} D_1 \text{ if } L(s) > \vartheta \\ D_0 \text{ if } L(s) < \vartheta, \end{array} \qquad\qquad (C.1\text{-}1)$$

where the threshold $\vartheta = p_0/p_1$ is the ratio of the prior probabilities.

In most applications, the consequences of false positives and false negatives are not the same. For example, when detecting the onset of a disease, a false negative (miss) may have grave consequences for the patient. A false positive error is relatively benign because it can often be overridden by the physician based on additional tests.

One way to quantify this is to assign numerical "costs" to each of the possibilities of hypotheses and decisions, e.g., C_{10} is the cost of decision D_1 when hypothesis H_0 is true. Typically, it makes sense to assign lower costs for correct decisions and higher costs for incorrect decisions, i.e., $C_{10} > C_{00}$ and $C_{01} > C_{11}$. The average cost incurred is

Decision		
	Present	Absent
Reality — Present	Correct detection C_{11}	Miss C_{01}
Reality — Absent	False alarm C_{10}	Correct rejection C_{00}

$$C = C_{00}\, p(D_0|H_0) + C_{10}\, p(D_1|H_0) + C_{01}\, p(D_0|H_1) + C_{00}\, p(D_1|H_1).$$

The optimal decision rule that minimizes this cost results in the likelihood ratio test in (C.1-1), with a threshold

$$\vartheta = \frac{P_0(C_{10} - C_{00})}{P_1(C_{01} - C_{11})}.$$

Detection Based on a Multi-Dimensional Signal

Detection is often based on multiple signals measured by several sensors or computed from a single image $f(\mathbf{r})$, or spectral image $f(\mathbf{r}, \lambda)$. Such signals represent multiple properties that distinguish the target from the background or from other targets. Examples of signals extracted from an image are quantitative descriptors of size, shape, contrast, texture, color, or spectral content of the suspected target. A set of M such signals $s_1, s_2, \ldots, s_M$ forms a vector $\mathbf{s}$, or a point in an M-dimensional signal space. In this case, the decision rule amounts to dividing the signal space into two regions, corresponding to the two possible decisions, target presence or target absence. The basic detection principles described earlier will now be generalized to the M-dimensional case, with $M = 2$ as the working example. In this case, the signal space is two-dimensional (2D) and each measurement is represented by a 2D vector $\mathbf{s} = (s_1, s_2)$.

Decision Based on a Single Training Measurement.   If the instrument is calibrated by taking one measurement for each case, i.e., one with the target present (H_1) and another with the target absent (H_0), we have two points, $\mathbf{s}_1$ and $\mathbf{s}_0$. In this case, an MDA is based on comparing the signal vector $\mathbf{s}$ measured under the unknown condition with each of these two vectors and selecting the hypothesis corresponding to the minimum Euclidian distance (see Appendix B), i.e.,

$$\left| \begin{array}{l} \text{select } D_1 \text{ if } \|\mathbf{s} - \mathbf{s}_1\| < \|\mathbf{s} - \mathbf{s}_0\|, \\[2mm] \text{select } D_0 \text{ if } \|\mathbf{s} - \mathbf{s}_1\| > \|\mathbf{s} - \mathbf{s}_0\|. \end{array} \right.$$

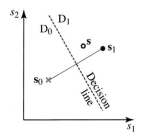

This decision rule divides the signal space into two regions, D_1 and D_2, using a straight decision line. If the measured signal $\mathbf{s}$ lies to the right of the decision line, the target is declared present. Otherwise, it is declared absent.

Another decision rule is the **minimum angle assignment (MAA)** rule. In accordance with this rule, the angles between $\mathbf{s}$ and each of the vectors $\mathbf{s}^{(1)}$ and $\mathbf{s}^{(0)}$ are determined. The hypothesis with the smaller angle is selected. The angle between two vectors is defined in Appendix B.

Decision Based on Multiple Training Measurements. Here, multiple measurements are obtained during the calibration process for each of the two hypotheses. This provides multiple points in the 2D space. A decision rule may be devised by computing the average vectors $\bar{s}_1$ and $\bar{s}_0$ under the two hypotheses and using these for an MDA rule. The result is a straight decision line.

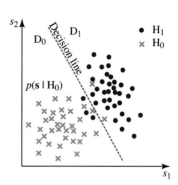

Other decision rules can lead to nonlinear decision curves, as shown in the figure on the right. An example is the **k nearest neighbor rule**, which is based on the training data in the neighborhood of the observed signal. The most common hypothesis amongst the k nearest neighbors is selected, where k is a small odd number (to avoid tied votes).

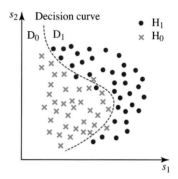

Decision Based on Probability Distributions. The probability density functions $p(s|H_1)$ and $p(s|H_0)$ in this case are multi-dimensional functions, which may be estimated from measurements during the training process or based on physical statistical models.

Knowing the probability density functions, the ML decision rule may be used: for a measured signal vector s, select the hypothesis with the higher probability, i.e.,

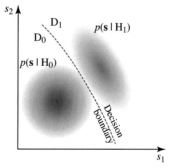

D_1 if $p(s|H_1) > p(s|H_0)$,
D_0 if $p(s|H_0) > p(s|H_1)$.

The decision line in this case is generated by the intersection of $p(s|H_1)$ and $p(s|H_0)$, and is not necessarily a straight line.

Linear Discriminant Analysis (LDA). Some of the decision rules defined earlier for 1D and 2D signals may be readily generalized to higher dimensions, while others become significantly more complex. A simple decision rule, which is applicable to signals with arbitrary dimension M, is a threshold rule using a single scalar parameter s computed from the components of the signal vector s by a linear superposition

$$s = \sum_{i=1}^{M} w_i s_i,$$

where w_i are appropriate weights. This rule is called **Fisher's linear discriminant**. For $M = 2$, this corresonds to a straight decision line $w_1 s_1 + w_2 s_2 = \vartheta$, where ϑ is the threshold. For $M = 3$, the decision rule is defined by the plane $w_1 s_1 + w_2 s_2 + w_3 s_3 = \vartheta$. For $M > 3$, the decision rule divides the signal space by a hyperplane separating the D_1 and D_0 decisions. The weights w_i and the corresponding decision threshold ϑ are selected to optimize the performance, e.g., maximize the probability of detection at a fixed probability of false alarm. In all cases, the computation of performance requires knowledge of the probability density functions under both hypotheses.

C.2   Classification

Classification is a generalization of the binary hypotheses testing problem to multiple hypotheses. Here, there are N classes to which unknown objects can be assigned, each identified by certain characteristics that are measured during a training process or extracted from an existing library. An object is observed and the goal is to determine its class, i.e., select one of the N hypotheses. The idea is to measure the characteristics of the observed object and select the class with the best matching characteristics.

Feature-Based Classification

A principal challenge in classification is the selection of quantitative measures of the class "characteristics." These are scalar quantities $(s_1, s_2, \ldots, s_M)$, called **features**, represented by a feature vector **s** of dimension M, which plays the role of the *signal vector* used for decision in the detection problem. For imaging applications, the measurement is an image $f(\mathbf{r})$ or a spectral image $f(\mathbf{r}, \lambda)$, which is discretized and represented by a vector **f**. The features obtained from an image may be parameters describing, e.g., target geometry, texture coarseness, strength and orientation of certain spatial frequencies, etc. For spectral images, features may include the strength of spectral components within certain wavelength bands, the curvature or slope at specific wavelength, and so on. Combinations of spatial and spectral features may also be used.

Features associated with each of the N library classes are described by a feature vector, so that we have N feature vectors $\mathbf{s}^{(1)}, \mathbf{s}^{(2)}, \ldots, \mathbf{s}^{(N)}$ representing the N classes. The idea of feature-based classification is to compare the feature vector **s** of the observed object with the feature vectors of the library classes and to look for the best match. This is facilitated by constructing a feature space in which each of the feature vectors is marked by a point, as was done in the binary hypothesis testing (detection) problem described in the previous section of this appendix.

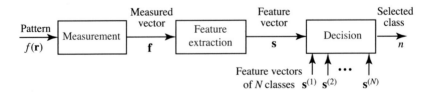

The number of features M is naturally much smaller than the dimension of the image itself (dimension of **f**). The decision task becomes significantly more difficult as the number of features increases (this is commonly known as the curse of dimensionality). For example, for hyperspectral classification with tens to hundreds of bands, if all bands are used as features, the dimensionality of the problem can be quite large. In essence, feature extraction and selection are used to reduce the dimensionality of classification while trying to maintain class separability.

Decision Rule

Consider classification of an object by measurement of a spectral signature cast in digital form as a vector $\mathbf{f}$. The spectral signature is used to generate a set of features represented by the vector $\mathbf{s}$.

The goal of classification is to make use of the measured feature vector $\mathbf{s}$ and assign it to one of N classes. The classes are taken to be disjoint, so that each input is assigned to one and only one class. The feature space is thereby divided into disjoint decision regions whose boundaries are called decision boundaries or decision surfaces, as was done in the binary hypothesis testing problem. Note that more advanced techniques exist that, for instance, allow partial membership in one or more classes (e.g., spectral unmixing). These are not discussed here, but left for the reader to explore in additional sources. Selection of an appropriate decision rule depends on the differentiating characteristics present in the selected classes. As in the detection case, the decision may be based on a single or multiple features for each class, or knowledge of the full probability distribution of class feature vectors $\mathbf{s}^{(1)}, \mathbf{s}^{(2)}, \dots, \mathbf{s}^{(N)}$, as shown next. Likewise, the decision boundaries may be planes or hyperplanes, in which case the classes are said to be linearly separable, or curved surfaces representing nonlinearly separable classes.

Decision Rules Based on a Single Training Measurement. When features are extracted from one measurement for each class during the training process, the result is a set of feature vectors $\mathbf{s}^{(1)}, \mathbf{s}^{(2)}, \dots, \mathbf{s}^{(N)}$. A simple rule for finding the best match between the observed feature vector $\mathbf{s}$ and each of these class vectors is the MDA rule, wherein class n is selected if the norm of the difference $\mathbf{s} - \mathbf{s}^{(n)}$ is smaller than that for all other classes, i.e.,

$$\|\mathbf{s} - \mathbf{s}^{(n)}\| = \text{minimum.}$$

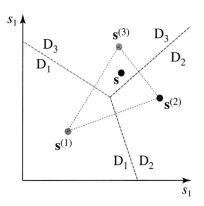

The figure on the right shows an MDA classification problem with $N = 3$ classes and $M = 2$ features. Each class is represented by a single feature vector obtained from training measurements, so that we have three vectors $\mathbf{s}^{(1)}, \mathbf{s}^{(2)}, \mathbf{s}^{(3)}$. The feature vector of the observed object is $\mathbf{s}$. The class with minimum distance to $\mathbf{s}$ is selected. In this example, class 3 has minimum distance. Another rule is the MAA rule, where the decision is based on the difference in angle between $\mathbf{s}$ and each of the feature vectors, $\mathbf{s}^{(1)}, \mathbf{s}^{(2)}, \mathbf{s}^{(3)}$.

Decision Rules Based on Multiple Training Measurements. Because of the natural variability typically present within each class, it is necessary to obtain multiple measurements of actual objects from each class during the training process. When the feature vectors are obtained, the result is a cluster of points for each class.

The figure on the right shows an example of these clusters in the case of three classes, H_1, H_2, and H_3, for classification using two features. In this case, $M = 2$ and $N = 3$. A simple rule for finding the best match between an observed feature vector s and each of these class clusters is again an MDA rule based on the means of each cluster $\bar{s}^{(1)}, \bar{s}^{(2)}, \bar{s}^{(3)}$. This results in the decision lines shown. If the classification is based on three features, instead of two, then the feature space is three-dimensional and the MDA decision boundaries are planar surfaces. For higher dimensions, the boundaries become hyperplanes.

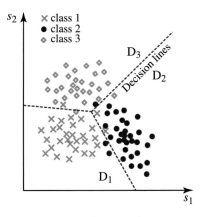

Other decision rules are also possible. For example, in the **k nearest neighbor rule**, the most common hypothesis amongst the k nearest neighbors is selected. Hence, the decision boundaries are then not necessarily straight lines but can be curved.

Decision Rules Based on Probability Distributions.   If the feature vectors of the classes are described by known probability density functions $p(s|H_1)$, $p(s|H_2)$, ..., $p(s|H_N)$, then statistical techniques may be used to determine the decision rule. For example, an ML classifier assigns class n to a measured feature vector s if the probability $p(s|H_n)$ is higher than that for all other classes.

The figure on the right shows an example of classification of three classes, H_1, H_2, and H_3, based on two features, s_1, and s_2, i.e., $N = 3$ and $M = 2$. For the ML classifier, each point s in the plane is assigned to the class for which the probability density function is the highest. This divides the feature space (here a 2D plane) into three regions bounded by decision lines that are generally curved lines, with each region assigned to a class. Classification is therefore reduced to measurement of the features and determining in which region the resulting feature point lies.

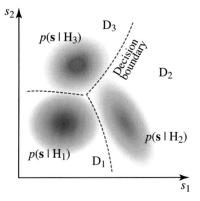

If the classification is based on three features, instead of two, then the feature space is three-dimensional and the decision boundaries become surfaces. For higher dimensions, surfaces in hyperspace separate the different classes.

Since the probability density functions are usually not known, certain statistical models are often assumed and their missing parameters are determined from the training data. For example, the probability density functions may be assumed to be normal (Gaussian) distributions and their means, variances, and covariances are estimated from the training data.

Performance Measures.   The quality of a classification system is assessed by the probability of correct classification, $P(D_n|H_n)$, i.e., the probability that class n is selected, if the target actually belongs to class n. Assuming that all classes have equal prior probabilities, the average of $P(D_n|H_n)$ for all n is a measure of the performance of the system. Clearly, the quality of the classification system is high if the features are selected such that the clusters of different classes in the feature space are well separated, i.e., different classes have distinct features, or if the features are selected to highlight the distinctions among the classes. Classification accuracy will degrade as the class features become more similar or overlap.

Summary: Classification System.   A statistical pattern classification system consists of two stages, training and classification, as illustrated by the block diagram in Fig. C.2-1.

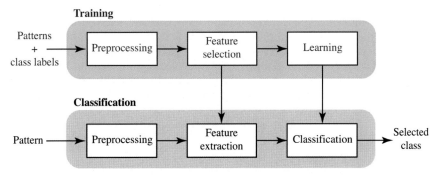

Figure C.2-1   Statistical pattern classification system.

- The training process involves preprocessing, feature selection, and learning. Preprocessing (e.g., calibration or normalization) depends on the types of pattern to be classified. In the feature selection process, features with the largest class separability or those that minimize intraclass variability and maximize interclass variability are selected. The learning step consists of iteratively testing a select number of samples with known labels from each class, so that the system learns to tell whether or not new patterns belong to a particular class. In most common statistical classifiers, this reduces to computing certain feature statistics such as the mean vector and covariance matrix for each class.

- In the classification process, a pattern with unknown label is assigned to a particular class depending on the classifier metric. In statistical pattern recognition, minimum distance classifiers are commonly used. First, features are extracted from the sample data and then the classifier assigns the label of the closest class to the pattern.

Further Reading

C. M. Bishop, *Pattern Recognition and Machine Learning*, Springer, 2006.

S. Theodoridis and K. Koutroumbas, *Pattern Recognition*, 3rd ed., Elsevier, 2006.

P. Bhagat, *Pattern Recognition in Industry*, Elsevier, 2005.

R. O. Duda, P. E. Hart, and D. G. Stork, *Pattern Classification*, 2nd ed., Wiley, 2001.

K. Fukunaga, *Statistical Pattern Recognition*, Morgan Kaufmann, 1990.

Software Tools

This appendix introduces selected software tools that are used in subsurface imaging. Many of the examples and problems in this text are MATLAB based. MATLAB (*www.mathworks.com*) is a widely used software package available on most academic campuses and corporations, and a low-cost student edition is also widely available. It is ideal for rapid prototyping of algorithm ideas using a rich library of built-in functions. MATLAB is accompanied by several toolboxes designed for specific disciplines, including the Image Processing Toolbox.

D.1   MATLAB Image Processing Toolbox

Perhaps the most widely used software for image processing is the MATLAB Image Processing Toolbox.[1] The following is a brief summary of some of the principal functions and commands that are necessary for importing and exporting images and converting them into matrices and vectors for further MATLAB algebraic processing. Familiarity with these tools is necessary for solving many of the problems in this book.

Representation of an Image by a Matrix

An image $I(x, y)$ is discretized into a digital image represented by the discrete function

$$I(n, m), \quad n = 1, 2, .., N, \quad m = 1, 2, .., M,$$

where N and M are the number of pixels in the horizontal (x) and the vertical (y) directions, respectively. The (n, m) pixel is the pixel located at a distance n pixels east and m pixels south, as illustrated in Fig. D.1-1(a) and (b).

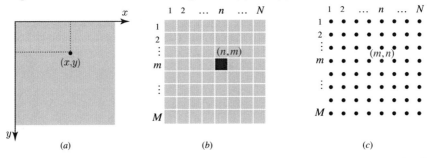

Figure D.1-1   Various representations of a two-dimensional (2D) image: (a) image $I(x, y)$; (b) digital image $I(n, m)$; (c) matrix $\mathbf{I}$ with elements $I(m, n)$;

---

[1]The complete manual for the MATLAB toolbox is available on the MathWorks website (*http://www.mathworks.com/products/image/*). See also C. M. Thompson, and L. Shure, *Image Processing Toolbox for Use with MATLAB*, Mathworks, Inc., 1995.

In MATLAB, the image I is represented by a matrix $\mathbf{I}$ with elements:

$$I(m, n), \quad m = 1, 2, .., M, \quad n = 1, 2, .., N,$$

where M and N are the number of rows and columns, respectively. The (m, n) element of the matrix is located at the mth row and the nth column of the matrix, as illustrated in Fig. D.1-1(c). Therefore:

the (n, m) pixel of the digital image has the value of the (m, n) element of the matrix.

Intensity images

An intensity image is a gray-scale image. Each pixel has a single number with value dependent on the brightness of the image at the pixel location. There are several classes of intensity images:

- The **double class** (or data type) uses floating numbers ("a number with decimals") between 0.0 and 1.0, with 0.0 for black and 1.0 for white.

- The **uint8 class** uses integers between 0 and $2^8 = 255$, with 0 assigned to black and 255 to white.

- **Binary images** use only two values: 0 for black or 1 for white (and nothing in between).

The image should be stored as a uint8 image, since this requires far less memory than double. When the image is processed it should be converted to the double class.

Conversion between classes

```
Id = im2double(I) converts an intensity image I to class double.
Iu = im2uint8(I)) converts an intensity image I to class uint8.
Ib = dither(I)) converts an intensity image I to the binary class
```

Conversion of a matrix into an intensity image

`I=mat2gray(A)` converts a matrix $\mathbf{A}$ to a double-class intensity image $\mathbf{I}$. This is done by scaling the values to the range 0.0 to 1.0.

Displaying an intensity image

`imshow(I)` displays an intensity image $\mathbf{I}$.
`imshow(I,L)` displays an intensity image $\mathbf{I}$ in L gray values.

Displaying a matrix as an image

`image(A)` displays a matrix $\mathbf{A}$.
`imagesc(A)` displays a matrix $\mathbf{A}$ after scaling the values to the entire range.

Color Images

RGB image.   An $M \times N$ color image is represented by three $M \times N$ arrays R, G, and B, representing the weights (R, G, B) of the red, green, and blue primary components at each pixel. These arrays may also be regarded as a single $M \times N \times 3$ array.

Indexed image.   An $M \times N$ color image may also be represented as a single $M \times N$ array of numbers, each being an index. An indexed image stores a color image as two matrices. The first matrix X has the same dimensions as the image with one number (an index) for each pixel, indicating the color at that pixel. The second matrix **map** provides a lookup table, called the colormap. The image is denoted as [X,map]. The colormap matrix lists the RGB values of the color for each index. Each row of the color map contains three numbers, each ranging from 0.0 to 1.0, which specify the red, green, and blue components of the color. The size of the colormap array is $L \times 3$ for an image containing L colors. For example, if the image matrix X contains the number 7 at some pixel, then the color for that pixel is the color stored in row 7 of the color map. If the numbers in row 7 are (0, 0.5, 0.5), then the color of the pixel is an equal mixture of green and blue, which is cyan. For example, the colormap

$$\text{map} = \begin{bmatrix} 1 & 0 & 0 \\ 0 & 1 & 0 \\ 0 & 0.5 & 0.5 \end{bmatrix}$$

means that color number 1 is red (1,0,0), color number 2 is green (0,1,0), and color number 3 is cyan (0,0.5,0.5). The statement

$$X = \begin{bmatrix} 2 & 3 \\ 1 & 2 \end{bmatrix}$$

defines a 2×2 image with green at the pixels (1,1) and (2,2), red at the pixel (2,1), and cyan at the pixel (1,2).

MATLAB supports a number of built-in colormaps. The command colormap(map) sets the colormap to the matrix map. The command colormap(gray) forces MATLAB to use a gray scale when displaying an image.

Conversions

Conversion between different color image formats
[X,map] = rgb2ind(R,G,B) converts an RGB image into an indexed image
[R,G,B] = ind2rgb(X,map) converts an indexed image into an RGB image

Conversion of a color image into an intensity image
I=rgb2gray(r,g,b) converts an RGB image (r,g,b) to the intensity format I.
I=ind2gray(X,map) converts an indexed image to an intensity image.

Displaying a color image
imshow(R,G,B) displays an RGB color image.
imshow(X,map) displays an indexed color image X.
imshow('Name') displays a color image in the graphics file Name.
imagesc(I);colorbar displays an intensity image **I** in false colors.

Importing Images
Image files in any of the common formats (BMP, GIF, HDF, PCX, TIFF, XWB) can be read into MATLAB. For example, a color image file image.gif in the Graphics Interchange Format (GIF) may be read into a MATLAB indexed image [X,map] using
[X,map] = gifread('image.gif');
Likewise, a color image file image.tiff in the Tagged Image File Format (TIFF) may be read into a MATLAB RGB file [r,g,b] using
[r,g,b] = tiffread('image.tiff');
A generic function imread returns the image data into a MATLAB matrix

A= imread('< filename>')

of an appropriate format based on the file content. If the file contains an intensity image, A is a 2D ($M \times N$) array. If the file contains a color image, A is a three-dimensional inner loo ($M \times N \times 3$) array.

Exporting Images

A MATLAB indexed image [X,map] may be written into a GIF file image.gif or a TIFF file image.tiff using

```
gifwrite(X,map,'image.gif');
```

and

```
tiffwrite(X,map,'image.tiff');
```

The generic function

```
imwrite(A,'<filename>.<fmt>')
```

is applicable to any format of the image A (intensity or color) and any file format. The function

```
imwrite(X,map,'<filename>.<fmt>')
```

writes an indexed color image into a file with arbitrary format.

EXAMPLE D.1-1.   The 41×41 ellipse–square image shown in Fig. D.1-2 is used in several sections of this book. This image is available in the book website as a vector **f** in the file f-ellipse-sq.mat in the folder Imageset. It may be loaded to the MATLAB workspace using load and converted to a matrix **I** by use of reshape. It is displayed as a gray image using imshow and as a color image with a color bar using imagesc. The following commands may be used. The vector **f** or the matrix **I** may of course be subjected to mathematical operations such as filtering, projection, or other transformations, before being displayed.

```
load f-ellipse-sq.mat
I=reshape(f-ellipse-sq,41,41);
imagesc(I); colorbar
```

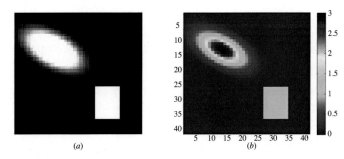

(a)   (b)

Figure D.1-2   Intensity image (a) displayed as a color image (b).

D.2   Field Simulation Software

There are numerous software packages for simulation of the waves/fields radiated by various sources (antennas or transducers) and the waves/fields scattered from objects of of various geometries upon excitation by various probing waves/fields. These packages are based on the simulation techniques described in Chapter 8 including: finite difference time domain (FDTD), finite element method (FEM), and the method of moments (MoM). The following is a list of selected commercial toolboxes that are applicable to problems in subsurface imaging:

- **Remcom** *www.remcom.com*

  Antenna analysis/design, radiowave propagation and scattering, and biomedical EM effects. Simulation methods used include FDTD.

- **Ansoft Maxwell** *www.ansoft.com/products/em/maxwell/*

  3D full-wave electromagnetic field simulation for design and analysis of 3D/2D electromechanical structures. Simulation methods used include FEM.

- **COMSOL** *www.comsol.com*

  Comprehensive software for applications including simulation of electro-acoustic and electromagnetic transducers and sensors, radio-frequency antennas, scattering field formulation for radar cross-section computation, and applications to oil exploration and seabed logging.

- **FEKO** *www.feko.info/*

  Simulation of radiation patterns from various excitations, including waveguide aperture, plane wave, magnetic and electric point sources, and other structures created from a large array of primitives. Radar cross-section computation. Synthetic aperture radar (SAR). Simulation methods used include FEM, MoM, FEM/MoM.

- **CST** *www.cst.com*

  A specialist tool for 3D simulation of high-frequency electromagnetic problems. A tool for the analysis and design of static and low-frequency structures.

- **Zeland** *www.zeland.com*

  Full-wave MoM-based electromagnetic simulator solving the current distribution on 3D and multilayer structures of general shape. Full-wave FDTD electromagnetic simulator for complicated 3D structures of arbitrary shape and materials.

- **Sonnet Software** *www.sonnetsoftware.com*

  Simulation of electromagnetic fields radiated by planar antennas and array radiators. Modeling high-frequency electromagnetic field interaction with biological material.

- **WIPL-D** *www.wipl-d.com*

  High-frequency electromagnetic modeling and simulation, including design of 3D antennas and antenna arrays for desired radiation patterns, scattering from large scatterers and metallic and/or dielectric scatterers of arbitrary shapes. Simulation methods used include MoM. A time-domain solver is also available.

- **Vector Fields** *www.vectorfields.com/*

  2D and 3D finite-element modeling of static and low-frequency electromagnetic fields, particle beams, and electric field analysis in conducting and dielectric media. FDTD modeling of radio-frequency and microwave electromagnetic fields.

- **Lucernhammer** *www.lucernhammer.tripointindustries.com*

  Calculation of high-frequency radar cross-section based on diffraction theory and 3D MoM. Also, an inverse SAR imaging and visualization tool.

- **Weidingler Associates**   *www.wai.com/emflex.aspx*

  FEM solver for Maxwell's equations for optical modeling, simulation of scattering, and particles in free space.

Ultrasonic Simulation: Field II

Developed by the Technical University of Denmark, Field II is a program for simulating the ultrasonic fields emitted by transducers of arbitrary spatial distribution for both pulsed and continuous waves. It also simulates linear imaging, including realistic images of human tissue. The computations are based on methods of linear systems theory, by regarding the emitted fields as superpositions of emissions from points (delta-functions) in time and space, i.e., superpositions of impulse response functions (see Appendix A). Field II runs under MATLAB and supports major operating systems (Windows, Linux, Mac OSX, HP-UX, SUN, SGI, IBM and Alpha). The toolbox software may be downloaded from *http://server.oersted.dtu.dk/personal/jaj/field/?downloading.html* and also has MATLAB m-files for various phantoms.

D.3   Hyperspectral Image Analysis Toolbox

There are several commercially available software tools for spatial and spectral classification based on spectral imaging, among many other functions. These include:

- **ENVI**   *http:www.ittvis.comProductServicesENVI.aspx*

  A software solution for processing and analyzing geospatial imagery.

- **Geomatica©**   *http:www.pcigeomatics.com*

  An integrated software system for remote sensing and image processing.

- **ERDAS IMAGINE**   *http:www.erdas.comtabid84currentid1050default.aspx*

  A software for geospatial data analysis and spatial modeling

MATLAB Hyperspectral Image Analysis Toolbox (HIAT).   Developed by the Laboratory of Applied Remote Sensing and Image Processing at the University of Puerto Rico at Mayagüez, HIAT is a collection of MATLAB and MATLAB Image Processing Toolbox functions that are useful for the analysis of multispectral and hyperspectral data. The following are examples.

- **Preprocessing algorithms.** Resolution enhancements and principal component analysis filters.
- **Feature extraction/selection algorithms.** Principal components analysis, discriminant analysis, singular value decomposition band subset selection, information divergence band, subset selection, information divergence projection pursuit.
- **Supervised and unsupervised classifiers.** Euclidean distance, Fisher's linear discriminant, Mahalanobis distance, maximum likelihood, angle detection, ECHO classifier.

The toolbox also offers online help documentation and a hyperspectral data set. It supports major computing platforms (UNIX/Linux, MS-Windows 2000 and XP, Mac OSX) and most popular image formats for loading and saving (.mat, .bsq, .bil, .bip, .jpg, with ENVI header info and .tiff). The toolbox is available for download at *http://www.censsis.neu.edu/software/hyperspectral/hyperspectral.html*.

D.4 Image Registration Software

Several open-source and commercial libraries of core registration routines are available. On the commercial side, perhaps the simplest registration tools are part of the MATLAB image processing toolkit. For users willing to do some programming, perhaps the most well-known open-source C++ software is the Insight Toolkit developed under the sponsorship of the National Library of Medicine. Another open-source toolkit that is suitable for more advanced users is the Rensselaer Generalized Registration Library (RGRL), which is part of the VXL package. A brief overview of each of these toolkits is provided in this section.

MATLAB Registration Tools

The MATLAB Image Processing Toolbox provides routines for feature-based image registration. One image is referred to as the base image or reference image, to which other images, termed input images, are aligned. The documentation refers to features as control points. The main MATLAB registration routines and their roles are illustrated in Fig. D.4-1.

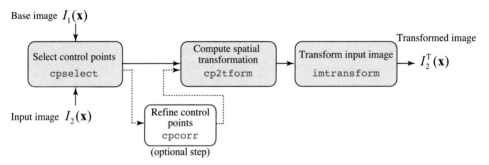

Figure D.4-1 Main steps to image registration using the MATLAB image processing toolkit.

The `cpselect` routine brings up a graphical tool (the control point selection tool) that allows the user to view the base and input images side by side, and use the computer mouse to indicate corresponding pairs of control points. The control points can be exported as MATLAB vectors, or as a data structure named `cpstruct` for subsequent use. Using this manual method, it is impractical to specify the control points precisely. Using a simple correlation-based routine named `cpcorr`, the control points entered by the user can be nudged by a small number of pixels (up to 4 pixels). This is an optional step. Using the (refined) control points, the spatial transform linking the two images is computed using the `cp2transform` routine. At this stage, the user can choose the type of transformation from a menu of choices that include linear conformal, affine, polynomial (order 2, 3, or 4), piecewise-linear and local-weighted mean transformations. The linear conformal transformation is the simplest and requires the fewest control points to estimate (just two), whereas the polynomial transformation of order 4 requires 15 control points. The resulting spatial transformation is returned to the user as a data structure named `TFORM`. Using this data structure, the input image can be transformed to the coordinate space of the base image using the routine `imtransform`.

NLM Insight Toolkit (ITK)

The MATLAB toolkit is simple to use but unsophisticated compared with the Insight toolkit (ITK) (*www.itk.org*), which was developed for the National Library of Medicine by a consortium of companies and academic laboratories. ITK contains a library of building blocks written in C++ for medical image processing, segmentation, and registration. Figure D.4-2 shows the architecture of intensity-based registration as implemented in ITK.

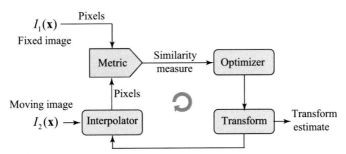

Figure D.4-2   Main modules in ITK for intensity-based registration. Note the central role of image interpolation in the core processing loop.

Intensity values of the fixed and moving images are taken at the sampled locations. The metric provides a means of choosing a similarity measure for intensity-based registration, such as normalized correlation or mutual information (Sec. 7.2) for cross-modality registration. The optimizer is the component that drives the registration process using the chosen metric. A common choice of optimizer is a fixed-step gradient-descent optimization algorithm that takes a step along the direction of the metric derivative and reduces the step length by half each time the direction of the derivative abruptly changes. To measure the fitness of the transformed moving image with the fixed image, the former is generated by performing the backward transformation of the grid locations of the fixed image and interpolating the intensities of the nongrid positions in the moving image using interpolators such as linear interpolation. Importantly, there are several variations for each component of the registration framework. Using the already-implemented algorithm classes provided by ITK, students can try out existing algorithms or prototype new ideas by mixing-and-matching components in the registration toolkit, within the general framework. Advanced users can also contribute novel components to the ITK system. The best way to explore ITK is to start with the ITK Software Guide, which is available both online and in hardcopy.

Rensselaer Generalized Registration Library (RGRL)

The RGRL (*www.vxl.sourceforge.net*) implements a general correspondence (feature)-based registration architecture, as shown schematically in Fig. D.4-3. Implemented as a C++ library of functions, RGRL consists of an inner flow loop (indicated by the circular arrow) that implements a basic but versatile correspondence framework and a set of outer loops controlled by a registration engine to allow the flexibility of multiple initial estimates, feature types, and resolutions.

The following are brief descriptions of the functionality of each core component of the inner loop:

- **Feature/feature set.** A feature set is a collection of features with suitable data structures for spatial queries, such as finding the nearest neighbors.

- **Initialization.** This component provides crude estimates of the starting position for the minimization process. A variety of initialization methods are implemented, including the method of invariant indexing, which uses the signatures of features for indexing.

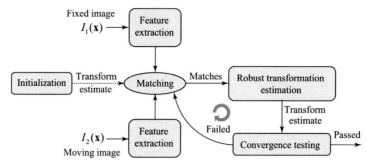

Figure D.4-3   Main components of RGRL and how they work together to perform the registration task.

- **Matching.** The matching process generates correspondences from the two image feature sets. The choices depend on the feature type as well as the type of matching, such as closest point.

- **Robust transformation estimation.** This process estimates the transformation that takes the moving image to the reference image by minimizing the alignment error of the two feature sets with robustness. Transformation models implemented are similarity, affine, quadratic, and homography.

- **Convergence testing.** The registration process terminates when the estimation has converged to a stable solution or reached a certain number of iterations.

Visualization.   A very practical issue when performing image registration experiments is to visualize the results. The most convenient method is to create a *flicker animation*. This is a movie file consisting of just two frames, $I_1(\mathbf{x})$ and $I_2^T(\mathbf{x})$. This movie is played in a loop, so that the two frames are displayed in succession at a speed of about one frame per second. When this is done, the overlapping region of the registration result can be examined. Any pixels that are misregistered appear to blink. A steady view indicates good registration. Another simple idea is to display the registered image using synchronized cursors. This approach can be helpful to an analyst (e.g., a physician) to interactively examine a set of registered images with greater precision than is possible with visual observation.

Index

Printed in the United States
by Baker & Taylor Publisher Services